SOCIAL WORK PRACTICE

FIFTH EDITION

SOCIAL WORK PRACTICE

A Generalist Approach

Louise C. Johnson

Professor Emeritus
The University of South Dakota

Allyn and Bacon
Boston • London • Toronto • Sydney • Tokyo • Singapore

Executive Editor: Karen Hanson
Vice President and Publisher: Susan Badger
Series Editorial Assistant: Sarah L. Dunbar
Cover Administrator: Linda Knowles
Composition Buyer: Linda Cox
Manufacturing Buyer: Louise Richardson
Cover Designer: Susan Paradise
Marketing Manager: Joyce Nilsen
Production Coordinator: Deborah Brown
Editorial-Production Service: P.M. Gordon Associates

This textbook is printed on
recycled, acid-free paper.

Library of Congress Cataloging-in-Publication Data

Johnson, Louise C.
    Social work practice : a generalist approach / Louise C. Johnson.
    —5th ed.
        p. cm.
    Includes bibliographical references and index.
    ISBN 0–205–15618–5
    1. Social service. 2. Social case work. I. Title.
HV40.J64   1994
361.3′2—dc20   94-7156
                                                                    CIP

Printed in the United States of America

10 9 8 7 6 5 4 3 2 1   99 98 97 96 95 94

BRIEF CONTENTS

CONTENTS

PREFACE

Written from a generalist perspective, *Social Work Practice: A Generalist Approach* synthesizes historical and current understandings into a logically developed sequence for learning about and teaching the practice of social work. As a textbook for beginning students, it should be particularly useful for undergraduates in introductory practice or methods courses. The material can be used on a one-semester basis but would be most effective in a two-semester sequence.

Generalist social work, as developed in this text, begins with the need of an individual or a social system. The social worker explores or assesses the situation in which the need exists with the client and significant others. Based on the findings of this exploration, a plan for work to alleviate the dysfunctional aspects of the situation is developed and a contract between the worker and the client is drawn up. The focus of the plan can be an individual, a small group, a family, an organization, or a community. Once the plan is developed, the worker and client, and perhaps other persons, work to carry out the plan. At some point, the worker and client decide whether to terminate their relationship or continue to work together on further plans.

Students should have certain prerequisites before using the material covered in this book. These include:

1. At least one introductory course covering the history and development of social welfare and an introduction to the profession.
2. A broad liberal arts base providing a wide variety of knowledge explaining the human situation, an appreciation of history, and some understanding about the nature of knowledge.
3. Courses providing an understanding of human behavior and the social environment such as those in psychology, sociology, anthropology, political science, and economics. Courses that include understandings of human development and human diversity, including racial and ethnic differences, are particularly important.

A course on human behavior in the social environment taken in a social work program is *not* a prerequisite or a corequisite. This book provides the content needed for integration of social science content into the social work practice frame of reference. Examples of concepts and how they are used in practice situations are given as one means to assist students in applying this knowledge to practice.

The book does not attempt to present any one model or approach to social work but rather synthesizes material from a number of sources into a coherent whole. Although at points it may seem that the major focus is on work with individuals, this is not the case. It is often easier, however, for students to grasp concepts when their application to work with individuals is presented, which can then be used as a base for considering their application to other systems (family, small group, organization, and community). Also, no attempt is made to consider practice with any particular population or social problem area. Rather, the assumption is made that the generalist approach can be used with a wide variety of situations, such as older people, those who have medical and mental health problems, those who are discriminated against because of lifestyle, and those who suffer because their social situation does not provide for their basic needs. This focus, then, includes service to discrete groups such as homosexuals, the homeless, and veterans.

PLAN FOR THE TEXT

Part One develops five perspectives on social work practice and a framework on which the other two parts are based. Parts Two and Three consider two processes essential to the social work endeavor: the interactional process and the service process—which is conceptualized as assessment, planning, action, evaluation, and termination.

Social work background material about minority groups and women has been emphasized in the text, which specifically addresses issues of working with these groups. The material on minority groups is not focused on working with a particular minority group but on providing the student with a framework from which to view all persons of minority status. It seeks to provide an understanding of what knowledge and attitudes are needed if a social worker is to work effectively with persons of minority status. It is expected that the learning environment will then provide specific materials for those minority groups that students are most apt to encounter in their practice of social work. Readings that are useful in the development of understanding about practice with minorities and women are suggested. In order to enhance readability, yet maintain a nonbiased gender content, the pronouns *he* and *she* are used alternately throughout the book.

The organization chosen for this text seems most appropriate to the author, based on twenty years of experience in teaching generalist social work practice. As the concepts are developed, attention is given to building on material presented in earlier sections of the book. Repetition is used to reinforce learning. The author assumes that the present cannot be understood apart from the past, so that historical as well as contemporary aspects of the material covered are noted.

Since this is a book for beginning students, it was written with their needs in mind and does not attempt to detail all aspects of the concepts introduced. It does develop concepts so that students will have more than a superficial introduction yet not be overwhelmed by material for which they have no experiential knowledge. An attempt has been made to minimize the use of jargon yet to introduce the student to professional language. Extensive use of charts and schemas is made as a means to help students organize considerable amounts of information into a coherent whole to maximize understanding.

The book contains many case examples. Most major sections of each chapter contain vignettes that depict the major concepts in action. In addition, from time to time, longer case examples are provided. In some chapters, a case may be provided in several parts, illustrating several major concepts. An attempt has also been made to use case examples from practice in a wide variety of settings. In choosing case material, dimensions of size and kind of community, client age and problem, and agency purpose and source of sanction have been considered. Although much can be learned from a textbook, thorough learning takes place only as the conceptualizations are applied in actual practice experiences. Each chapter contains a summary, a statement of learning expectations for that chapter, study questions, and suggested readings for use by student and teacher. An appendix with summaries of models of social work practice, as well as a glossary of key terms, are included at the end of the text.

ACKNOWLEDGMENTS

The formulation of social work practice presented in this book has developed from the author's teaching experiences. Encouragement and support of students and colleagues have been the major incentive for developing the formulations and for writing the book. It is to these persons, too numerous to name, that the book is dedicated.

I also wish to acknowledge the reviewers who critiqued this manuscript at various stages: Emma Quartaro, Seton Hall University; Art Preciado, California State University, Chico; Ralph Gilmore, Westfield State College; and Judy Norman, Brigham Young University.

L. C. J.

PART ONE

PERSPECTIVES ON SOCIAL WORK PRACTICE

Part one provides an overview of the nature of social work practice. The author contends that, until the reader has an understanding of the complexity of the practice situation and has developed a framework against which to place the details, study of the details of practice is premature. In other words, the reader must know how the details fit into an overall picture. Part One provides such an overview. It is expected that the reader will return to the concepts presented to develop a greater depth of understanding.

Social work is complex, with a wide variety of applications and no universally accepted definition. Because of the complexity of social work practice, there are a number of descriptions—termed *perspectives* here—of its nature. The writer has chosen five descriptions or perspectives by which to provide the overall framework of generalist social work practice. Those chosen are those most often referred to in social work literature and those that, when taken together, best explain the nature of contemporary generalist social work practice. No attempt has been made to identify a particular ideology or model as the approach of this book, although a specific approach has developed with each subsequent edition. The author refers to this as an *interactive-transactional* approach to generalist social work practice. Concepts, ideas, and understandings gained from a wide variety of practice literature and experiences are synthesized so as to describe the realities of generalist social work practice as perceived by the author.

A **generalist approach** requires that the social worker assess the situation with the client and decide which system is the appropriate **unit of attention,** or focus of the work, for the change effort. As the unit of attention may be an individual, a family, a small group, an agency or organization, or a community, the generalist approach emphasizes knowledge that can be applied to a variety

1

of systems. Each of the five perspectives discussed in Part One has application to all the units of attention noted above.

Each of the perspectives describes social work practice from contrasting but complementary views. Each may be seen as a different facet of a complex way of thinking, feeling, and doing, and each provides a way of understanding the activity which has come to be known as generalist social work practice. Together, they provide a description of the essential nature of generalist social work practice.

The first two perspectives address the "why" of social work practice. Perspective one, "Social Work as a Response to Concern/Need," discusses the basic reason for the social work endeavor. It focuses on the desirable outcome of the combined work of worker and client, and develops the concepts of need, common human needs, human diversity, social systems needs, and social functioning. The second perspective, "Social Work as a Developing Profession," examines practice historically in order to understand why practice exists in its current form. The author believes that contemporary practice has many vestiges from the past. Thus, some understanding of the development of practice theory as contrasted with social welfare history is important for understanding the major concepts which underlie the practice. Chapter 2 also introduces the concepts of profession, assessment, person in the situation, relationship, process, and intervention. These were chosen because of their common usage in many conceptualizations of social work practice.

The last three perspectives discuss the "how" of social work practice. Perspective three, "Social Work as a Creative Blending of Knowledge, Values, and Skills," discusses how knowledge, values, and skills are used in understanding and taking action in relation to social-functioning needs. The concepts developed are knowledge, values, skills, and creative blending. Perspective four, "Social Work as a Problem-Solving Process," presents a way of thinking about the process of social work or the steps used in responding to need. It develops the concepts of problem and process. Perspective five, "Social Work as Intervention into Human Transactions," discusses the way in which the social worker seeks to bring about change. It develops the concepts of intervention, transaction, and influence.

The assumption is made throughout the book that the reader is bringing a knowledge base developed through previous social work courses and experiences. Also, it is assumed the reader has some basic understanding of social science concepts, especially those from psychology and sociology. These will be developed in Part II, which considers the interactional processes present in the social work endeavor, and Part III, which describes the ongoing process undertaken by worker and client as they seek to respond to need and reach commonly set goals.

1

SOCIAL WORK AS A RESPONSE TO CONCERN/NEED

Learning Expectations

1. Understanding of the concept of need and the difference between concern and need.
2. Ability to identify common human needs.
3. Understanding of how concepts about human development are used in identifying need.
4. Some understanding of the relationship of powerlessness to human need.
5. Understanding of the concept of human diversity and its use in identifying human need.
6. Understanding of the concept of social systems and its use in identifying human need.
7. Understanding of social functioning as the focus of social work.

Social work seen as a response to concern and/or need primarily relates to the "why" of practice. This perspective helps to identify appropriate goals for service and considers the appropriate target for change and the context of the concern and/or need. It allows the thinking about social work practice to "start where the client is," at the point a concern is felt or a need is identified. And it begins to provide the means for integrating knowledge about human behavior and the social environment from a variety of sources into the social work practice approach to meeting human need.

This chapter explores some conceptualizations which clarify this facet of social work practice. These understandings are derived from classical and contemporary themes which have been useful in describing the nature of human need by social workers. They are themes that most students will have encountered in previous learning experiences, for example, a sociology course or a human behavior in the social environment course.

FROM CONCERN TO NEED

In order to begin to understand the complexity of a situation, it is helpful first to identify some of the possible ways concern may be felt in one situation. For example, a parent is concerned because his child is not learning in school; a teacher, because a student is disruptive in the classroom; a merchant, because an adolescent boy is taking merchandise without paying for it. A student is concerned because his family seems to be falling apart. He cannot concentrate in school, fights with his classmates, and takes a candy bar from a local store to help ease his pain. An agency is concerned because there are no resources to help families with communication problems. A community group is concerned that so many young people are in trouble with the law. Each of these concerns may exist around the same situation, and each indicates some difficulty in the relationship between individuals and social systems.

Human situations and, thus, human need are complex. Not only must the social worker have developed a frame of reference for understanding the reasons behind the behaviors of people, she must also understand the environmental factors that influence these behaviors. Each situation must be viewed as complex and unique.

Concern is a feeling that something is not right. It is interest in, regard for, and care about the well-being of self or other individuals. The feeling of concern is often the result of some behavior that affects the relationship of the individual to other individuals or to a social system. All behavior has meaning, and people express and fulfill need through behavior. Need also generates feelings. As a part of understanding what is causing a concern and why the concern is important, feelings relative to the concern should be identified and explored. The social work response to behaviors and related feelings of concern for self and others is to identify need and discover alternate ways of need fulfillment so that the need of each party in a situation may be met.

NEED

Need is that which is necessary for either a person or a social system to function within reasonable expectations, given the situation that exists. Need is not a want for something that would be nice to have but the lack of which does not inhibit the development or functioning of the person or the system. In a situation in which a boy is caught taking merchandise without paying for it, an unreasonable expectation would be that he be given the items he took because he "felt he needed them." A reasonable expectation would be that the reasons behind the desire for the items are identified and alternate ways of meeting the related need in a socially acceptable manner are found.

Need that is identified by others has often been a focus of social work. This sometimes results in people being told what they need. But the concept of **felt need**—a need identified by the client—is also relevant. Often the "they need" and the felt need are different or are expressed in different ways. Social workers often use their expert knowledge and professional value system in identifying need that does not seem relevant or realistic to clients or people in their immediate environment. The felt need of the client and concerned persons must always be considered. This practice is consistent with a basic social work principle, to "start where the client is." In using this principle, the social worker starts with the concern or felt need of clients and other concerned persons; uses his knowledge to identify various needs (felt needs or "they needs") in situations; and, with clients, determines goals based on both kinds of need. In the example discussed in this chapter, the debate would be whether services should be focused on John and his family or on conditions that interfere with family functioning. Conditions to be investigated might be: Are the father's working hours too long? Is there insufficient income to meet the family's needs? Is there a problem of alcoholism in the family?

CAUSE-FUNCTION DEBATE

A social worker needs to consider whether the response to need should be on a person-to-person basis or should address societal problems that cause the persons to have unmet needs. This issue has often been referred to as the **cause-function debate.** In 1929, Porter Lee, in a classic paper, defined a *cause* as "movement directed toward the elimination of an entrenched evil . . . [or] a new way of meeting human need."[1] He went on to say that once the evil was eliminated the new response to need became a "function of well-organized community life." He saw social work sixty years ago as moving from cause to function. At that time social work was concerned with the response to need and with whether one profession could respond to both societal problems and individual need. This issue has continued to be of concern to a profession that contains both clinical social workers and community organizers, with their different approaches to meeting need. There is still debate about whether the same profession can respond to human need on an individual, case-by-case level and also be involved in changing a society that is frequently the cause of individual problems.

The sociologist C. Wright Mills refers to these two kinds of need as **private troubles** and **public issues.** Private troubles have to do with "the individual and . . . the range of his immediate relations with others. . . . Issues have to do with matters that transcend these local environments."[2] William Schwartz saw this issue of the "social vs. the psychological . . . [as] responsibility for social reform on one hand and individual help to persons in trouble on the other" as the "granddaddy of dilemmas of social work." He believed that these two positions should not be polarized. Since personal troubles (needs) arise out of relationships with the larger society, the social worker must address this relationship. This view would seem to imply that the social worker must address the needs of both the individual and the larger systems that are a part of contemporary society.[3] It calls for recognition not only of the need of an individual client but also of the needs of others who may be significant in any situation. It may call for examination of significant systems (families, small groups) of which the individuals may be a part. It may call for consideration of community or societal institutions such as, for example, a school system or the economic system. It also calls for recognition of how situations sometimes prevent the meeting of individual needs.

COMMON HUMAN NEEDS

In *Common Human Needs,* a social work classic, Charlotte Towle discusses need in relation to the factors that affect human development. Towle contends that the following elements are essential if persons are to be motivated toward social goals:

1. Physical welfare: food, shelter, and health care;
2. Opportunity for emotional and intellectual growth;
3. Relationships with others; and
4. Provision for spiritual needs.[4]

She also points out that need is relative to a person's age and life situation. For instance, the infant must have physical care, an opportunity to learn, and a relationship with a loving adult. Adults must have survival opportunities in the form of food, shelter, and clothing, but ordinarily they do not need physical care. They do need human relationships, but these can be of varying nature.

Abraham Maslow developed a hierarchy of needs that supports Towle's thinking and expands the understanding of need. In his expanded list, needs are placed in ascending order; in order to meet each need one must have met the previous ones. With the most essential need at the top of the list, the list includes:

1. Physiological needs: food, water, air;
2. Safety needs: avoidance of pain and physical damage through external forces;
3. Need for belonging and love: feeling secure when in close, intimate contact with others;
4. Esteem needs: having status and acceptance in one's group;
5. Needs for self-actualization: expression of potentialities and capabilities;
6. Need for cognitive understanding, that is, understanding of self and the external world.[5]

According to Maslow's hierarchy, a person must first satisfy primary physiological needs such as the need for food before social needs can be considered. Yet it must be remembered that, particularly with the young child, the need for food cannot be satisfied without a relationship with another person.

Currently, social workers are becoming aware of the need for individuals and groups to feel that they have the power or the control necessary for them to meet their needs or to change situations which are affecting need fulfillment. The literature has been particularly focused on the need for *empowerment* of discriminated against groups (persons of color and women). While in no way negating the extreme importance of empowering these groups, it seems that contemporary American society has characteristics that lead many individuals and groups within the society to feel helpless and hopeless. Thus, the need for feelings of hope for the "good life" and control of resources and situations which can lead to need fulfillment is an important aspect of contemporary social work practice.[6] This is a theme which will be explored throughout this book.

To identify and understand the human need in any situation, three knowledge bases are helpful: human development, human diversity, and social systems theory.* Each considers human need from a different point of view; together they provide the base for a response that considers the complexity of human situations.

Human Development Perspective

Human need from a human development perspective indicates that people develop physically, cognitively, socially, emotionally, and spiritually over the life cycle.[7] There are benchmarks that can be used to measure growth in each area. Physically, there are such measures as the age of beginning to walk or the age of onset of puberty. Cognitively, the work of Jean Piaget is often used to examine how a person deals with concepts, or IQ tests are given to measure intelligence. In the social-emotional area, the work of Erik Erikson is often used as a reference point. His "eight stages of man,"[8] based on the mastery of psychosocial tasks relevant to each age, are useful in determining whether expected psychosocial growth has taken place.

From a developmental perspective, human need may be identified in two ways. First, at each stage of life individuals should be developing in certain age-specific ways and for this development to take place, certain conditions must be present. The infant needs love and physical care as well as sensory stimulation. The school-age child still needs physical care, though not to the same degree as the infant. This child needs protection but also the freedom and opportunity to learn skills and develop creativity. The adolescent needs opportunities to resolve the normal conflicts of growing up, to find out who she is, to deal with sexuality, to make vocational decisions. Adults need opportunities in which they can feel a

---

*It is assumed that readers will have knowledge of each of these areas from courses in the social sciences. The focus of this discussion is on the translation of that knowledge into action. No attempt will be made to list all possible needs to be considered or all the knowledge included in each area. The focus will be on the complexity of human need based on knowledge of the three areas.

sense of accomplishment, fulfill their nurturing needs, and participate in group life and the society in which they live. Older adults need economic security; provision for health needs; and the opportunity to deal with feelings arising from retirement, failing health, and impending death.

A second way to identify human need would be to note development that would be expected at a particular life stage but that has not taken place. This includes needs from the past that have not been met and are contributing to problems in present social functioning. It also includes identification of developmental lags or situations in which there is a danger that the expected development will not take place.

In working with John, the boy who stole merchandise, a social worker would be aware that John is entering the developmental stage of adolescence, a time of confusion for many boys. John is probably trying to discover who he is in relationship to others. He is experiencing new sexual feelings. He is probably testing out various value systems. All of this can threaten his sense of security. If he does not feel secure in his home situation, he may believe his needs for belonging are threatened. His need for self-esteem may also be threatened. If family problems are long-standing, John may have felt so insecure that he was not able to use his middle-childhood years to develop a sense of competency. He may be entering adolescence with a lower sense of self-esteem than is desirable.

The response to concern/need from a developmental point of view is to provide the necessary conditions that will allow development to progress and to eliminate those that block development. These conditions are heavily dependent on social interaction between individuals and their environment. Problems in social functioning often exist when necessary conditions are not present. In responding to these common human needs, the social worker should have a thorough understanding of human development in all its aspects throughout the life span.

Human Diversity

Though there are common human needs, people fulfill those needs in different ways. The way in which needs are fulfilled is greatly influenced by cultural factors, as well as by physical handicaps, socioeconomic factors, gender or sexual preference, and discriminatory practices against certain groups in our society. The human diversity perspective is useful in considering human need in a multicultural society.

The concept of **human diversity** has been introduced into the social work literature only recently. It brings together understandings about the nature of culture and its effect on the development and functioning of human beings and is also more specifically concerned with the effects of social institutions on human behavior and calls for a consideration of power factors.

The concept of human diversity is based on the premise that American society is composed of a wide variety of cultures. Some cultural groups have difficulties in functioning because they differ from the dominant cultures of U.S.

society. Some of these groups have experienced prejudice and discrimination; some have experienced institutional racism and poverty. These effects can be negative due to institutional racism, the built-in characteristics of societal institutions which have a negative effect on certain segments of a society. These segments of society are further impacted because they tend to be powerless or appear powerless to modify societal institutions such that these institutions can better provide culturally congruent means for meeting human need.

The human diversity approach considers human behavior from the stance of cultural relativity. It sees normal behavior as an irrelevant concept and behavior as functional or dysfunctional relative to the social situation in which a person is functioning. What may be functional in one situation may be dysfunctional in another. Deviations of developmental patterns found in different cultures should not be considered as necessarily abnormal. According to this approach, the response to need is not to measure norms but to determine the meaning of perceptions, experiences, and events as they affect the growth and functioning of individuals in their own cultural context.

Ronald Federico, in discussing the concept of human diversity, sees behavior as being influenced by three factors: 1) the genetic, 2) the cultural, and 3) the societal. The genetic influences include growth potential, both mental and physical; the ability to tolerate stress; and ways of responding to stress. The cultural influences include life goals, behavior patterns, resource utilization patterns, self-concepts and attitudes, and ways of perceiving events. The social influences include the social institutional structure, which comprises systems of socialization, social control, social gratification, and social change. These three sets of influences—genetic, cultural, and social—interact in a complex manner.[9] This conceptualization also enables consideration of handicapping conditions that are not cultural in source, such as developmental disability, blindness, or a chronic physical illness.

Dolores Norton, who has developed a similar concept, "the dual perspective," sees each person as part of two systems: 1) the nurturing system, which includes the family and immediate community environment (the culture of an individual); and 2) the sustaining system, which includes the organization of goods and services, political power, economic resources, educational system, and larger societal systems. If the perspective of the two systems is such that there are broad areas of incongruence between the two, then individuals are prone to difficulties in functioning.[10] Such individuals will have special needs. In our society this incongruence is particularly evident in the situation of racial-minority groups. The dual perspective provides another way of considering human development and functioning in a diverse society. The response to need is helping individuals and groups find ways of living together in such a way that the needs of all are met*

---

*Norton has further developed her thinking about the dual perspective. This revision will be considered in Chapter 7.

In order to understand human need, the social worker must also have significant knowledge about the role of environmental factors as they affect the development and functioning of individuals. Environmental factors include social, economic, and geographical and climactic conditions that are a part of the immediate surroundings of the individual. Discriminatory attitudes toward the person, extremes of climate, and sociocultural expectations all influence individual behavior. The worker should also understand the effect of handicapping conditions on individual functioning and development. This would include physical and mental handicaps as well as prejudice and discrimination. The causes and nature and effects of prejudice and discrimination should be understood, as should differences in lifestyle patterns among socioeconomic groups.

If, in the example presented earlier, John and his family are black and his father is absent from the home, issues of discrimination, culture, and the effects of growing up in a single-parent family must be considered. The community would tend to react to his stealing by involving the police. He might be arrested. The social worker would need understanding of black culture, of the particular black culture of John, his family, and his peer group. Also needing consideration would be the phenomenon of growing up in a female-headed, single-parent family. All of these factors would be important in determining need in the situation.

To understand these environmental factors, a social worker needs to have considerable knowledge of the culture of the ethnic and racial groups with which he is working. This involves knowledge of a cultural group's history, values, mores, family and community patterns, attitudes and thinking patterns, religious traditions, child-rearing practices, and ways of coping with change and stress. Also important are the group's experiences in relating to the dominant culture, which involves social and economic factors and acculturation experiences and their results. The worker also needs to be aware of the different subgroups that exist within any cultural group. This knowledge may be used to identify special needs of individuals and groups of individuals that arise in relation to their development and functioning because of human diversity.

Recently, some social workers have begun to substitute the term **special populations** for human diversity. The author believes this can result in stereotyping people according to population groups to which they may belong. The concept of human diversity encourages social workers to look at differences in an individual manner. It also recognizes that diversity is more than identification with specific population groups.

Social Systems Theory

Human need cannot be considered apart from the larger systems of which humans are a part. These larger systems include the family; the small group; the community; and various social institutions, such as the school, the church, and the social agency. All persons belong to several larger systems that often make conflicting demands on them. These systems are a part of each individual's environment. Some social workers call the demands of these systems **environ-mental demands.** Social systems theory provides a means of understanding these systems and identifying their needs.*

Much discussion has taken place about the usefulness of social systems theory in social work practice. Ann Hartman has pointed out a distinction between the use of a social systems approach and the use of social systems theory, with its distinctive terminology. Hartman describes the approach as a "means of ordering the . . . world in terms of its relatedness. . . . A system would be a whole composed of interrelated and interdependent parts. . . . It has boundaries."[11] The system of focus also has a relationship to individuals and systems outside its boundary. The relationships across the boundary are not as intense as those within it; they do not have the strength of influence that the parts (subsystems) have on one another. The environment nevertheless does affect the social system. A social systems approach calls for a kind of thinking that considers parts, wholes, and environments and the relationships that exist among them.[12]

Social systems theory, on the other hand, is useful to social workers for it gives a means for conceptualizing linkages and relationships among seemingly different entities: individuals, families, small groups, agencies, communities, and societies. It notes similarities and differences among different classifications of systems. It aids social workers in considering both private troubles and public issues within the nurturing system and the sustaining system of a situation they are assessing.

Social systems theory is conceptualized in a variety of ways. The conceptualization used in this book sees any system as having structural, functional, and developmental aspects.

When considering the structure of a **social system,** the relationships among parts and wholes are of prime interest. Usually a **focal system** or **holon** is identified. This system is itself made up of parts or subsystems, and it is also a part of other systems (or supersystems). All systems are more than the sum of their parts. The parts are interacting and interdependent. The relationship of parts and wholes is relatively stable. Sometimes the relationship between systems is referred to as a **network.** Systems theory focuses on communication patterns, on the transactions among the parts, and on the relationships among parts.

The boundary of any system is an important structural concept—an imaginary line drawn around the focal system. It may be relatively open or relatively closed. **Openness** and **closedness** refers to the ease with which ideas, energy, resources, people, or information can enter or leave the system. Closely related to the concept of boundary are environment, situation, and frame of reference. These all refer to the supersystems within which a focal system exists.

---

*Special understandings about each of these systems are also needed. It is assumed that this knowledge is available to the reader. Some of the specific knowledge will be considered later in this book.

Another structural consideration is encompassed in the terms **steady state, equilibrium,** and **homeostasis.** While each carries a slightly different meaning, they all refer to the balance that exists among the various parts of the system. This balance is not fixed or static but maintained within a range of change that allows the system to function and maintain itself.

The functioning aspects of the system are related to the use of energy, the manner in which a system carries out its purpose, and the way it maintains itself. Terms from communication theory such as *input, throughput, output,* and *feedback* are used. **Equifinality,** the capacity of two systems to achieve identical goals when starting from different conditions, and **multifinality,** beginning from similar conditions and achieving different end states, are also used.

System needs are fulfilled by means of communication among the parts or across the systems boundary; by means of a decision-making process; and by use of resources both within and without the system to carry out the tasks necessary to accomplish its functions. A means of task distribution (specialization) often develops. In order to be functional each system develops these processes over time, not only as a way of accomplishing the necessary tasks but also as a means of maintaining itself. Goals and norms for functioning are established, and roles and relationships are created. The system develops its unique way of functioning.

Developmental aspects of a system relate to the continuous process of change in any system. Each system progresses through identifiable stages of development. If this does not occur, the system becomes less capable of using its energy and carrying out its function. This latter situation is known as **entropy. Negative entropy**—or efficient use of energy and development of means for adding new energy from across the system boundary—results in greater specialization and complexity in the organization of a system. No system can maintain a status quo; the system either tends toward entropy or toward negative entropy. The process of development is continuous, and systems are in a constant process of change. Change in any part of a system brings about change in the system itself.

In the situation described earlier in this chapter, John could be the focal system or, if the dysfunctioning is believed to be in the family, the family could be the focal system. If the family is the focal system, John becomes a subsystem. The community, school, and merchant are outside the system boundary and are a part of the environment. A factor affecting John's behavior may be that his steady state has been upset due to the onset of adolescence. The family may not be carrying out one of its functions, the provision of security for children, because communication is not being managed effectively. Energy use may be inefficient and entropy may have set in. A social worker using social systems theory would consider these areas of John's and the family's functioning when identifying need in this situation.

For a social system to be able to maintain itself and fulfill its function, the subsystems or parts (individuals and groups of individuals) must make adjustments in their own functioning to meet the needs of the larger systems. When these adjustments are supportive of the need fulfillment of individuals, no problem exists, but this is often not the case. The task of the social worker is to focus on both the personal trouble (individual need) and the public issues (system need). The response identifies the needs of all persons and systems involved and seeks to enable each to function in such a manner that need fulfillment is complementary and the needs of all are fulfilled. This response calls for identification of all the component parts (systems) of a situation in which need exists. It then calls for consideration of the need of each system in relation to the situation under consideration. A social systems approach to human functioning leads to understanding of the great complexity of that functioning and thus to an understanding that any response to human need should take that complexity into consideration.

Response to need is complex because human functioning is complex. Knowledge of human development, human diversity, and social systems theory develops an understanding of the complexity of human functioning and provides the means for identifying the various components of the need: 1) common human need, 2) need because of human diversity, and 3) social system need. This knowledge base also gives direction to the response to need.

SOCIAL FUNCTIONING

Social workers become involved when individuals are having difficulty living in relationship with other people, in growing so as to maximize their potential, or in meeting the demands of the environment, or when there is a relatively high potential that developing needs will not be met. It is then that concern and need become apparent. Harriet Bartlett has described this situation as "people coping" and "environmental demands." The bringing together of these two aspects of living in society can be termed **social functioning**.[13] The core of the social work endeavor is the worker and the client interacting in relation to present or potential problems in social functioning; problems in social functioning are the reasons for the worker-client interaction. These problems arise from concern over unmet need. The response is one in which the worker and client *together* assess the need in all its complexity, develop a plan for responding to that need, carry out the plan, and evaluate the results of their work together. Both the worker and the client have a responsibility for the work. Since the roles are reciprocal, both must carry out their roles if the process is going to work.

This is, in essence, the meaning of **generalist practice**. In developing a plan, the focal system for change may be any system experiencing a lack of need fulfillment or contributing to the lack of need fulfillment. The change strategy is chosen from a repertoire or group of strategies that the generalist worker possesses. This repertoire contains strategies appropriate for work with a variety of systems (individuals, families, small groups, agencies, and communities).

The social work process usually begins with a **feeling** of concern about something. This concern arises because a need is not being met. After **thinking** about the situation in a particular way—a process called assessment—some **action** is taken. This response—feeling, thinking, acting—is cyclical in nature. As the worker and client think and act together, new feelings of concern arise and

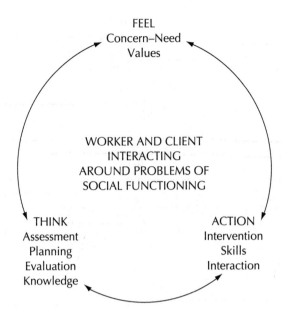

FIGURE 1–1   The Social Work Process: A Feeling, Thinking, Acting Endeavor

new needs become apparent. As they act, they think about what is happening and gain new insights into the situation. The worker's knowledge about human development, human diversity, and social systems theory is used in thinking about the situation. (See Figure 1–1.)

CASE EXAMPLE

Mrs. A comes to a mental health center. She tells the social worker that her thirteen-year-old son, John, is not getting along very well in school. His last report card had all D's and C's. Last year he had B's and two A's. She talked to the teacher and learned that John does not pay attention in class and disturbs the other students. Mrs. A thinks that the teacher is not very capable and that John is bored. After some time, she tells the worker her husband got a call from Mr. W at the local drugstore telling him John had stolen a candy bar. Mrs. A thinks that John "did that awful thing" because he is so upset about not learning. She says that everything is fine at home. Her husband works long hours in the store he manages and is not home very much. The worker senses some uneasiness on Mrs. A's part as she discusses things at home, but Mrs. A continues to say they are a "good family"; no one has ever been in trouble before.

The worker suggests that he talk with John, and Mrs. A agrees to this plan. John confirms that he is doing poorly in school; he says he just cannot do the work. He thinks the teacher expects too much and yells at him too often. He is just "fooling around." He says he doesn't want to talk about the candy bar incident. The worker asks about things at home. His reply is, "Okay, I guess." The worker notes a sad tone in his voice and so asks about what he does with Dad. From this they talk about Dad not being home, and eventually John talks about feeling that something is wrong at home; no one ever seems to talk to anyone about anything.

With these facts, the worker begins to speculate on the needs of John in this situation. He thinks about the developmental needs of a thirteen-year-old boy. Important is his lack of security, which could in part explain his behavior in school and his stealing from the drugstore. He knows the teacher cannot teach John, that is, carry out her assigned function, if John is so concerned about the situation at home that he is unable to pay attention at school. Also, if he is bothering others, their learning may be disrupted as well. The worker knows that the storekeeper cannot allow his goods to be stolen and that John's father needs to be well thought of by fellow merchants. The most important system is the family. There seems to be a need for improved communication, though there may be other needs also. This family is a third-generation Italian-American family. The worker needs to consider how cultural factors affect its functioning. He is not yet sure of all the needs involved. As a worker, he needs to know more about the situation.

In this simplified situation we see the worker converting the explicit concern of Mrs. A and John and the implicit concern of other systems into an identification of need. He is identifying systems and individuals within this situation who have need and the needs of each. While the worker is focusing on the needs of John and his family, the need to modify John's behavior in the school and in the community is also considered, for John's behavior is disruptive to these systems.

The components of this situation are the people involved—the child, each parent, the teacher, the merchant, and the child's classmates and peers—and the social systems of the family and the classroom group. It also involves the concerned agency, the school, and community groups. It reflects the culture and expectations of the community that is its context. As the need of each component in relation to the situation is identified, the interdependent and reciprocal nature of the need becomes apparent. This is the beginning of a social work endeavor.

SUMMARY

One perspective of social work sees social work practice as a response to concern and need. Concern derives from a feeling that all is not right. Social workers respond to concern by identifying any unmet needs in the situation. In doing this they use knowledge about human development, human diversity, and social systems. They identify not only the unmet need of a particular client but also the needs of significant individuals and systems in the situation. When people attempt to meet their needs (to cope) and when the environment makes demands on people in response to environmental needs, a process of social functioning exists. Social functioning is a major focus of social work practice.

The social work endeavor begins with the concern and translates it to need. The need to be identified in this approach is not only that of the client but of other individuals and social systems significant to the situation. The focus is on helping individuals to cope and the environmental factors impinging on social functioning. The decision on what the focus of service is to be relates to what is causing the difficulty—the barrier to need fulfillment and on what can be changed—client, situation, or both.

When identifying needs, a social worker uses understandings from human development theory and social systems theory as well as consideration for human diversity.

QUESTIONS

1. In what ways does concern express itself?

2. What do you consider to be the minimal need level for a person to function in contemporary American society? What would be the ideal need level?

3. If a social worker is to focus on both the private troubles and the public issues, what do you think will be some difficulties she will face in practice situations?

4. Discuss the relationship of the conceptualization of need as encompassing both private troubles and public issues and the nature of powerlessness in contemporary American society.

5. How can the developmental perspective and the human diversity perspective be integrated into social work practice? What are the differences between the two perspectives?

6. Illustrate the concepts discussed in this chapter with examples from a social system with which you are familiar.

7. Describe the coping behaviors and the environmental demands in a situation related to your present functioning.

SUGGESTED READINGS

Brennan, Eileen M., and Weick, Ann. "Theories of Adult Development: Creating a Context for Practice." *Social Casework* 62 (January 1981): 13–19.

Cook, Alicia S. "A Model for Working with the Elderly in Institutions." *Social Casework* 62 (September 1981): 420–425.

Cox, Enid O. "The Critical Role of Social Action in Empowerment Oriented Groups." *Social Work with Groups* 14 (1991): 77–90.

Dehoyos, Genevive, and Jensen, Claigh. "The Systems Approach in American Social Work." *Social Casework* 66 (October 1985): 490–497.

Federico, Ronald C. "Human Behavior and the Social Environment Within a Human Diversity Framework." In Betty L. Baer and Ronald C. Federico, *Educating the Baccalaureate Social Worker: A Curriculum Development*

Resource Guide, Vol. 2. Cambridge, MA: Ballinger, 1979 (pp. 181–208).

Gutierrez, Lorraine M. "Working with Women of Color: An Empowerment Perspective." *Social Work* 35 (March 1990): 149–153.

Hartman, Ann. "Homelessness: Public Issue and Private Trouble." *Social Work* 34 (November 1989): 483–484.

Minahan, Anne, Ed. *Encyclopedia of Social Work*, 18th ed. Silver Spring, MD; National Association of Social Workers, 1987 ("Generalist Perspective," pp. 660–669, "Human Development: Biological Perspective," "Human Development: Psychological Perspective," "Human Development: Sociocultural Perspective," pp. 835–866).

Norton, Dolores G., Ed. *The Dual Perspective*. New York: Council on Social Work Education, 1978 (Chapter 2).

Rhodes, Sonya L. "A Developmental Approach to the Life Cycle of the Family." *Social Casework* 58 (May 1977): 310–311.

Schwartz, William. "Private Troubles and Public Issues: One Social Work Job or Two?" *The Social Welfare Forum.* New York: Columbia University Press, 1969 (pp. 22–43).

Serzoff, Joan. "From Separation to Connections: Shifts in Understanding Women's Development." *Affilia: Journal of Women and Social Work* 4 (Spring 1989): 45–58.

Sotomayer, Marta. "Language, Culture, and Ethnicity in Developing Self-Concept." *Social Casework* 58 (April 1977): 195–203.

Streever, Kristyn L., and Wodarski, John S. "Life Span Developmental Approach: Implications for Practice." *Social Casework* 65 (May 1984): 267–278.

Towle, Charlotte. *Common Human Needs.* Washington, D.C.: National Association of Social Workers, 1945.

Weick, Ann. "Reframing the Person-in-Environment Perspective." *Social Work* 26 (March 1981): 140–143.

Williams, Sharon E., and Wright, Dolores G. "Empowerment: The Strengths of Black Families Revisited." *Journal of Multicultural Social Work* 2 (1992): 21–36.

Zacks, Hanna. "Self-Actualization: A Midlife Problem." *Social Casework* 61 (April 1980): 223–233.

NOTES

1. Porter R. Lee, "Cause and Function," *Proceedings of the National Conference of Social Work, 1929* (Chicago: University of Chicago Press, 1930), pp. 3–20.

2. C. Wright Mills, *The Sociological Imagination* (New York: Grove Press, 1959), p. 8.

3. William Schwartz, "Private Troubles and Public Issues: One Social Work Job or Two?," in *Social Welfare Forum 1969* (New York: Columbia University Press, 1969), p. 25.

4. Charlotte Towle, *Common Human Needs* (Washington, DC: National Association of Social Workers, 1945).

5. Adapted from Abraham H. Maslow, *Motivation and Personality* (New York: Harper & Row, 1954).

6. One of the best discussions of the empowerment perspective is Lorraine M. Gutierrez, "Working with Women of Color: An Empowerment Perspective," *Social Work* 35 (March 1990): 149–153.

7. Anne Minahan, Ed., *Encyclopedia of Social Work,* 18th ed. (Silver Spring, MD: National Association of Social Workers, 1987), "Human Development: Biological Perspective," "Human Development: Psychological Perspective," "Human Development: Sociocultural Perspective," pp. 835–866.

8. Erik H. Erikson, *Childhood and Society* (New York: W. W. Norton, 1950), chap. 7.

9. Ronald C. Federico, "Human Behavior and the Social Environment Within a Human Diversity Framework," in *Educating the Baccalaureate Social Worker: A Curriculum Resource Guide,* vol. 2, Betty L. Baer and Ronald C. Federico, Eds. (Cambridge, MA: Ballinger, 1979).

10. Dolores G. Norton, *The Dual Perspective* (New York: Council on Social Work Education, 1978).

11. Ann Hartman, "To Think About the Unthinkable," *Social Casework* 58 (October 1970): 467–474.

12. Genevive Dehoyos and Claigh Jensen, "The Systems Approach in American Social Work," *Social Casework* 66 (October 1985): 490–497.

13. Harriet M. Bartlett, *The Common Base of Social Work Practice* (New York: National Association of Social Workers, 1970), chap. 6.

2

SOCIAL WORK AS A DEVELOPING PROFESSION

Learning Expectations

1. Understanding of the nature of professions and of social work as a profession.
2. Some understanding of the following concepts and how they developed: assessment, person in the situation, relationship, process, and intervention.
3. Some understanding of how earlier conceptualizations of social work practice affect the nature of contemporary practice.

Social work as a developing profession is a second major theme of social work practice. In order to understand social work as it is conceptualized and practiced today, it is necessary to have some idea of how it developed. Contemporary social work practice is the product of a heritage of responses to need and concern in other times and situations. The response to need has always been influenced by the events of the times and by the current philosophical stance, knowledge base, and social welfare concerns and events.

While the development of the social work profession, including the development of its theory base, is related to the development of social welfare in the United States, the two are not the same.[1] Any understanding of contemporary generalist social work practice is enhanced by an understanding of the development of the profession, particularly the way in which practice theory developed. This understanding includes some attention to the earlier conceptualizations of practice.

Social work, which began in the life and thought of the late nineteenth and early twentieth centuries, is a fairly new profession, although its roots are firmly planted in the Judeo-Christian heritage. All professions must change to meet constantly changing times. Social work, as a young profession, has experienced growth not only relative to the concerns and climate of changing times but also relative to the process of developing its knowledge, value, and skill bases.

To gain an understanding of how the theory and practice of social work developed, it is necessary to examine the nature of professions generally and to be aware of some of the important milestones in social work. Because the development of a systematic knowledge base is one of the important aspects of a profession, an understanding of the development of the practice theory enhances one's understanding of contemporary social work practice and theory.

SOCIAL WORK AS A PROFESSION

There is no clear, consistent definition of the term **profession.**[2] Many attempts have been made to develop frameworks for describing the attributes of a profession. While some continue to question whether social work is a profession, by most definitions and criteria social work does seem to meet the requirements of a profession. Ernest Greenwood has stated that "all professions seem to possess: 1) systematic theory, 2) authority, 3) community sanction, 4) ethical codes, and 5) a culture."[3]

These are the attributes most often referred to in social work literature when discussing social work as a profession. Leslie Leighninger has referred to Greenwood's approach as a "trait-attribute" approach. She points out that a "process model" focuses on movement toward professional status, particularly the development of professional organizations and professional education.[4] Another approach might be a power/control approach that looks at the status of a profession. Authority and monopoly of service delivery are considered as indicators of professional status.[5] Elizabeth Howe has pointed out that some professions, such as medicine and law, operate from a "private practice model." She suggests that other professions, such as social work, in which the vast majority of practitioners are employed in agencies, probably should operate from what she identifies as a "public model." The difference between the two models relates to issues of autonomy. Public professions are subject to a greater degree of control by the public. Not only do professionals in the public professions have less autonomy but they are also responsible to clients, the agency, and those to whom the agency is responsible.[6]

When considering social work as a profession, it seems most appropriate to begin by considering Greenwood's attributes. First among these is the possession of a systematic theory. Social work has struggled long and hard to develop this attribute. Because of the complexity of the human situation and other factors, which will be discussed later in this chapter and in Chapter 3, this development is incomplete. It is then that thinking about the process of knowledge development by the social work profession (process model) becomes useful. This approach allows for considering social work as a still-developing profession and leads to consideration of the influence of the past on the present. (See the next section of this chapter, "Development of Social Work Knowledge.")

When thinking about the attributes of authority and community sanction, the power/control model becomes useful. The social work profession has not established a monopoly over the delivery of services relative to social functioning. It is only one of many professions (such as education, nursing, and alcoholism treatment) concerned with social functioning. In addition, it has been possible, especially in public social welfare agencies, for employees who carry out certain functions to carry the title of social worker even though they have not had professional social work education. Recently licensing laws have been most helpful in identifying who is a social worker. That identification is strongly tied to educational qualifications (BSW or MSW degrees). Through licensing and other types of regulations, at least now there is some authority, community sanction, and recognition of an area of expertise and its services.

An ethical code and a culture are provided through the National Association of Social Workers (NASW). The NASW *Code of Ethics* (see Table 3–1) is discussed in Chapter 3 as a part of the values system a social worker must consider when making practice decisions.

Through discussion of Greenwood's attributes of professions and through consideration of other models for describing the development of professions, it seems appropriate to label social work as a developing profession. This does not imply that social work does not possess the attributes of a profession, but rather that those attributes are still in a state of flux and will continue to change over time.

One important area in understanding the nature of social work practice is the appreciation for how its knowledge base has developed over time. Understanding how the profession's knowledge base has developed also helps to explain how contemporary practice, particularly generalist practice, is in part a continuous development of the practice of the past.

DEVELOPMENT OF SOCIAL WORK KNOWLEDGE

As social work developed, several concepts became important in expressing the nature of its practice. Five of these concepts are useful in developing an understanding of how the knowledge base developed, not in isolation but in the social climate of the day and in the contemporary social welfare scene. These five concepts are assessment, person in the situation, relationship, process, and intervention.

It is not possible to present here all the details either of social history and its effects on the development of social welfare institutions or of the history of the profession itself.[7] (See Appendix 2–1 at the end of this chapter for an overview of this historical material.) It is the development of the five concepts of social work practice theory during each particular historical era that will be examined. The sources for this study have generally been those books most often cited in the social work literature of the era. Because theory about the practice of social work has been strongly influenced by the development of the casework method, the major sources for the development of the material presented here have been from that area of social work. However, the development of both group work and community organization work will also be considered. These five concepts are still important for the explication of generalist practice and will be further developed in subsequent chapters of this book.

Pre-1920

The early practice of social work can generally be characterized as pretheoretical. Workers saw needs and responded. They were caught up in the pragmatic philosophy of the times; they were a part of the liberal movement. They had preconceived views of the causality of pauperism and poverty from individual defects such as laziness, mismanagement, or alcoholism. They felt that by using a "friendly visitor" approach they could help people overcome the causes of their difficulties.

The first major statement of social work practice theory was Mary Richmond's *Social Diagnosis*.[8] She developed the original framework for the **assessment** construct. However, rather than the term *assessment*, the term **diagnosis** was used, a borrowing of medical terminology and the source for what was to become known as the **medical model**.

Richmond's work reflects a period when social sciences, particularly sociology, were highly influential on social work practice. Psychology had not yet developed to the point at which personality could be explained in any but global, imprecise terms. Emphasis was on a broad study, as there was still a great deal of uncertainty about which factors were most important for diagnosis. It was assumed that a cause-effect relationship existed; in other words, the social worker was looking for the cause of the problem. The cause was generally assumed to be either moral inadequacy or lack of appropriate use of social resources. The process of careful, thorough, systematic investigation of the evidence surrounding those in need of service, and then putting that evidence together so that the worker gained an accurate picture of the situation, was the heart of the social work process. This was **scientific philanthropy,** a study of the social situation.

The description of the information to be gathered was comprehensive and meticulously specific. The sources to be used included not only the client but the family, other relatives, schools, medical sources, employers, neighbors, and pertinent documents. The guiding principles were sociological in nature. Richmond defined diagnosis as

> the attempt to make as exact a definition as possible of the situation and the personality, that is, in relation to other human beings upon whom he [the client] in any way depends or who depends on him, and in relation also to the social institutions of his community.[9]

There seems to have been an assumption that the painstaking gathering of information would lead to an understanding of the cause of the problem. Further, it was assumed that if the cause were known, the remedy would be simple to apply. This idea, which grew out of the Charity Organization Society, assumed that the problem lay primarily within the individual. It saw poverty as a result of immorality, misuse of money, and excessive drinking.

Settlement houses, the originators of the group work method, responded to the same social conditions with a different approach. This approach saw the source of problems as lying in the environment and in a lack of understanding about how to cope with one's surroundings. Workers at settlement houses used educational and enriching group activities and worked within the political system to bring about needed change.

The beginning of professional social work was a response to the social milieu of the early twentieth century, a time when new immigrants, with their different cultures and lifestyles, were of concern to the larger society. It was also a time when the progressives were working for reforms that they believed would eliminate poverty. This era saw the development of the social sciences, which were rooted in the belief that application of a scientific method could identify the causes of poverty and deviance. It was felt that if these causes could be identified, solutions would be apparent and social ills eliminated.

The early articulation of social work practice theory, that is, theory about the *practice* of social work (as opposed to theory regarding understanding of the person in the situation), reflected efforts to work with the new immigrants in ways that would enable them to live "moral lives" and thus avoid pauperism. As has been noted, it was strongly based on the new sociological understandings and called for meticulously searching for facts that would illuminate the causes of deviance. This early development of practice theory was a response to a concern that helping be scientific. Science was seen as based on facts; facts led to answers. Thus, the answers as to how to help lay in the collection of facts. Thus, a strong emphasis on diagnosis (assessment) developed and remains an important legacy in contemporary social work practice.

1921–1930

By 1930, changes had taken place in the understandings of diagnosis. Much has been written about the adoption of the Freudian psychoanalytic view of man by social workers during this period.[10] Though it has been shown that this adoption was not as complete or dramatic as often depicted,[11] the Freudian influence was nevertheless considerable and long lasting. The psychological aspects of social behavior became an influential aspect of the *social case history.*

The report of the Milford Conference (a group representing casework agencies that met to seek commonalities in different settings, for example, hospitals or schools) reflected the development of social casework theory during the 1920s. It identified the common elements of social study from the various fields of practice. It also noted that whereas a particularization specific to a field of practice existed, such as understanding medical terminology in medical social work, the social history component of each field demonstrated an essential unity.

This report also began to develop the concept of **intervention**, though it used the medical concept of **treatment**. At this time in history, treatment was aimed at assisting the client to "adjust" and assumed deviance from normal social standards. It noted three fundamental processes that were used: 1) use of resources, 2) assistance of the client in self-understanding, and 3) assistance for the client to develop the ability "to work out [his or her] own social program."[12]

Rather than focusing on the social situation, the worker was far more concerned about "value and meaning as individual experience."[13] The focus of attention was on the individual and included a detailed study of behavior, attitudes, and relationships. Particular emphasis was placed on early childhood experience. The emphasis on the source of information was also shifted. No longer was a wide variety of information sources used; rather, it was felt that the individual must be primarily depended on for information if the meaning of experiences to him was to be obtained. Through careful interviewing of the client a full picture necessary for understanding could be obtained. Assessment or diagnosis was better organized than in the past, when cause and effect were emphasized.

The concept of treatment (intervention) changed from "impulsive action on the client's behalf" to "respecting the client's individuality which leads to identification with the client's experience." Little knowledge about treatment existed at this time.

Considerable emphasis was placed on the relationship between client and worker. Meaningful interaction between worker and client was seen as a sharing experience vital for developing the worker's understanding of the client and for treatment to take place.[14] This understanding marked a movement away from attitudes of "doing for" or "doing to." This theoretical development of the 1920s reflected both the individualism of the times and a decreased emphasis on social problems. Psychology, particularly psychoanalysis, with a theory useful in explaining individual functioning in a manner not possible until this time, was becoming a viable tool. As society turned inward, so did social work. It sought a theory base; it sought to clarify itself as a profession by looking for the common knowledge base used in diverse settings; and it sought a function broader than working with poverty groups, no longer a popular cause. As the knowledge base began to develop, so did the need for means to teach that knowledge. Thus, attention was given to education and theory development.

During this era, group work placed more emphasis on people than it did on conditions. The growing informal education movement and the work of John Dewey were particularly influential. Youth service organizations and recreation developed, thus placing considerable emphasis on the use of activity and on group process as means to enhance growth, democratic functioning, and change. The heritage of this era for today's practice might be characterized as the movement from doing *to* or *for* to working *with* the client.

1931–1945

During this period, Gordon Hamilton, an important theorist of the diagnostic approach to practice, clarified the term *diagnosis*. In 1940, she described diagnosis as a "working hypothesis for understanding the person with the problem as well as the problem itself."[15] This concept of diagnosis included the client's subjective version of the situation. The diagnostic statement was seen as interpretative and always tentative.

This view of diagnosis led to the development of the concept **person in the situation**—an interpretation of the way a person meets the situation (as has been noted). Hamilton saw this interpretation as being evaluative rather than diagnostic. Evaluation considered the resources available to the client and recognized that problems are both individual and social.

The helping process was conceptualized as "study, diagnosis, and treatment." These three aspects of the helping process were not performed in logical, step-by-step sequence but wove in and out, often paralleling one another.[16]

The treatment relationship was seen as important in helping. Its nature and intensity depended upon both the client's need and the service being provided. Hamilton defined *treatment* as "furnishing a service" or "behaving toward someone."[17] It might involve meeting deficiencies with social resources, program modification, or resource adjustment as well as counseling or therapy.

Hamilton's statement of social casework theory in *The Theory and Practice of Social Casework,* in the 1940 edition already cited and in the 1951 edition to be noted later on, remained for many years an important statement of one approach to social work practice, known as the **diagnostic approach.** Hamilton's classic formulation greatly influenced subsequent practice, and it underlies much of the subsequent practice theory development. It was based on psychoanalytic thinking and thus was a factor in the continued use of that frame of reference in thinking about the personality.

Another approach to practice was developing during this era. The **functional approach** did not consider the client as sick or deviant but as a person requesting a specific service and was largely based on the work of Otto Rank. Jessie Taft and Herbert Aptekar are sources for early statements of this approach.[18]

The term *diagnosis* had a different meaning in the functional approach from its use in the diagnostic approach. It was seen as an attempt by the worker and the client to discover whether there was a common ground for working together. It led not to treatment but to working together, and this relationship was seen as professional when the worker was carrying out an agency function and was applying her professional knowledge to the work at hand. It recognized a process in the relationship that was expressed as beginnings, middles, and endings. As the relationship developed and individuals came to affect one another, the opportunity for change developed.

A third important theory development of the 1931–1945 era was the recognition of social group work and community organization work as methods of social work. Hamilton noted the importance of group process as a means of under-standing the family. The actual theoretical development of these new methods was, however, only in the preliminary stage.

The rich development of theory during the late 1930s and early 1940s was at least partly a result of the tremendous impact of the depression era on social work. No longer did older theories about personal deficiencies as the cause of poverty and deviance hold up. Rather, the influence of a person's situation was seen in terms of how it affected his well-being. Psychological knowledge, particularly that based on Freud's work, provided understandings of deviance that looked at cause for deviance in the intrapsychic part of the personality and provided a usable, organized theory for assessing the personality.

The interest in the psychological sphere was also furthered as government agencies took over much of the work of relief and social provision. The private agencies had freedom to focus on psychological factors as well as on new groups of clients. While the early 1930s found social workers far too busy with the realities of people in need to engage in much theory development, later on they had time to reflect on that experience, which resulted in rich theory development. One important outgrowth still present in contemporary practice is the notion that the individual must be seen in a situation (a context or an environment) and that assessment must include that dimension.

1946–1960

During the early part of this era, the diagnostic-functional controversy continued. Social workers either used Freud's psychoanalytic approach and were adherents of the diagnostic school of practice or the Rankian approach that underlay the functional school. Most of the theory development was in the form of statements of one position or the other, and these statements clarified the details of the two positions. In 1951, a revised edition of Hamilton's 1940 book was published.[19] This revision reflected new understandings developed in psychoanalysis and clarified differences between psychoanalysis and social work. Considerably more attention was given to the content of the diagnostic statement. The material on treatment was clarified, and much attention was paid to intrapsychic factors.

In his 1957 book, *The Casework Relationship*,[20] Felix Biestek defined the case-work relationship as "the dynamic interaction of attitudes and emotions between the caseworker and the client, with the purpose of helping the client achieve a better adjustment between himself and his environment." He also identified seven principles of that relationship:

1. Individualization
2. Purposeful expression of feeling
3. Controlled emotional environment
4. Acceptance
5. Nonjudgmental attitude

6. Client self-determination
7. Confidentiality[21]

Biestek's work is an example of the development or fleshing out of the social work theory that was taking place during this period.

Near the end of this era, a new statement of casework was presented by Helen Harris Perlman in *Social Casework: A Problem-Solving Process.*[22] In many ways this new statement was a blending of the diagnostic and functional approaches, and essentially it marked the end of the diagnostic-functional controversy. Perlman saw the casework endeavor as "a person with a problem comes to a place where a professional representative helps him by a given process."[23]

Perlman continued the use of the term *diagnosis,* but her meaning seems closer to the term *assessment* used in the contemporary social work literature. She saw diagnosis as dynamic, as "a cross-sectional view of the forces interacting in the client's problem situation."[24] Diagnosis was seen as an ongoing process that gives "boundary, relevance, and direction"[25] to the work. It was seen as the thinking in problem solving.

Perlman's book reflected a focus on the ego functions of the personality. This is in contrast to the earlier era of the diagnostic approach in which the id, the ego, and the superego were each considered equally important. Adaptation was viewed as one of the important ego functions. In Perlman's work one begins to see the concept of "coping" used relative to adaptation, which would seem to be an aspect of the view of the person in the situation.

Perlman saw casework as a process—a problem-solving process—and she developed the process or movement idea throughout her book. She held that the caseworker-client relationship was essential to the movement or work of problem solving. The professional relationship was perceived as being purposeful, accepting, supportive, and nurturing.

Underlying Perlman's work is the assumption of human competence with a goal of developing this competence. Problems are seen not as pathological but as part of all life. The social-functioning focus of social work began to emerge.

Another trend of this era deserving of mention is the emergence of literature that, rather than addressing cause-function issues or the analysis of a case situation in light of the state of the art, began to identify and specify the theory base underlying practice. This emerging theory base included not only the casework method but also group work and community organization methods.[26] These two methods drew heavily from a sociological theory base. Knowledge of small-group process was a major interest, and the assessment of group interaction was a major concern. The focus of these two methods was in part on growth as a process. Relationship with non-clients began to be considered. The groundwork was being laid to identify the common base of social work practice—those concepts that applied to practice regardless of the system being worked with.

Social work, like the society of which it was a part, was expanded during the 1946–1960 period. This was not a time of great unrest or change but a period of conformity and acceptance of sometimes superficial answers. There was a belief that poverty was being eliminated and thus was not an issue of concern. Much social work energy went into the development of the professional organization and professional education. The majority of clients focused on were not poor but middle-class people who had adjustment problems. This orientation reflected societal demands for conformity and the illusion of an affluent society. It was also a time in social work when the search for a unified profession reflected the spirit of the times. Theory was developed by stating a position (diagnostic or functional) and then defending that position. This expanded the existing theory as well as led to new theory development in the search for a unifying approach. Two legacies of this era are a major concern for the relationship of worker and client and the notion that there is a process aspect of practice.

1961–1975

This era was indeed rich in theory development, just as it was rich in the development of new service possibilities, concern for new problem areas and new client groups, and the use of old methods in new ways. To look at theory development in this era, three focuses will be used: 1) the continuing development of traditional methods; 2) the development of generic or integrated approaches to practice; and 3) the development of new approaches to practice, using new underlying assumptions or for use in service to specific groups of clients.

During the 1960s, both the diagnostic approach (now called the **psychosocial approach**) and the functional approach were further expanded and updated.[27] Both of these formulations were approaching the stage of well-developed theory. These new formulations not only developed the theory and the understanding about the five concepts (assessment, person in the situation, process, relationship, and intervention) but they also incorporated new theory development from the social sciences. Use of social systems theory and communications theory[28] began to appear.

During the early part of this period, important formulations of group work[29] and community organization work became available.[30] These formulations not only continued to develop the practice theory of these methods but made it possible to begin to identify the use of the concepts that were universal to casework, group work, and community organization. It became possible to begin to identify the theoretical commonalities of all types of social work practice.

Of particular interest is the movement from the use of the medical terms *diagnosis* and *treatment* to the more general terms *assessment* and *intervention*. As community organization theory developed, the use of the terms *assessment* and *intervention* was given additional support as commonalities were identified.

Examination of the use of the concept of *process* during the early part of the era indicates that the concept of the problem-solving process was being used in all three traditional methods of social work: casework, group work, and community organization. The casework use of the problem-solving process is reflected in the continued importance of Perlman's approach during this era. Process came to imply movement through time.

The concepts of person in the situation and client-worker relationship were again expanded somewhat later in the era by the application of new social science theory. The 1970s saw a rapid rise in the use of social systems theory as important supportive knowledge for all social work.

The concept of relationship also expanded. Not only was relationship seen as important for work with the client, but the importance of many other relationships was noted in group work and community organization literature. During this era there began to be discussion of **interactional skill,** an idea that was very close to the idea of relationship and that enlarged the scope of the meaning of the concept of relationship.

In 1970, two early attempts to conceptualize social work from an integrative point of view were published. Carol Meyer's *Social Work Practice: A Response to the Urban Crisis* stressed the need for a new conceptual framework because of limitations of current theory in relating to the turmoil on the urban scene of the 1960s.[31] Harriett Bartlett's *The Common Base of Social Work Practice* was written out of the need of the social work profession for specification about the nature of practice.[32] Both books reflected the development of the five concepts being discussed. And although the books focused on the problems of integration rather than on the development of theory, they did introduce several useful concepts. Bartlett identified *social functioning, professional judgment in assessment,* and *interventive action.* Meyer used *process of individualization, interventive points,* and *plan of action.* She saw diagnostic process as a tool of assessment and intervention as having a variety of possibilities known as the *interventive repertoire.* These two books marked a turning point in theory development. No longer was theory to be developed for the traditional methods of casework, group work, and community organization. It was to be developed for the unified social work profession and to respond to particular problems and needs.

During the early 1970s, several textbooks appeared that presented conceptualizations that were integrative in approach.[33] The Pincus and Minahan text received the widest acceptance. In their approach, social work was seen as a planned change with the intervention plan based on a problem assessment. The assessment "identified problems, analyzed dynamics of the social situation, established goals and targets, determined tasks and strategies, and stabilized the change effort."[34] One major aspect of the approach was the use of influence: "effecting the condition of development of a person or system."[35] The use of relationship was seen as part of this process. In the Pincus and Minahan approach the five concepts are used, but they are put together in new ways and new concepts are added. The developing profession was moving toward new ways of thinking about practice, toward new practice conceptualizations.

Given the growing commonality of social work practice, it is not surprising that an important contribution of this era was the effort to develop what came to be known as *integrated methods* or *generalist practice.* This effort was influenced by the fact that during this era, when new services were evolving and new groups of clients were being served, it was discovered that these clients did not fit nicely into traditional casework, group work, or community organization molds. Rather, a combination of methods might be needed to respond to the complex problems and situations these clients were presenting. The efforts of the National Association of Social Workers and others toward the unification of the profession provided a milieu in which these efforts toward commonality of theory could go forward. The federal legislation of the Great Society and the War on Poverty provided training funds that increased the capacity for knowledge building. The rediscovery of rural social work called for a generalist approach. The time was right, both in a societal and a professional sense, for this forward movement in the development of the theory base of social work.

A third trend of this era was the development of many new approaches to practice, most of which focused on specific needs. This trend began in the 1960s as the family became a unit of attention and as approaches for work with the family developed.[36] At about the same time, interest in short-term casework, particularly crisis intervention, also contributed to this trend. As social workers began to work with new problems and new client groups, approaches with a more specific focus were needed for action with and for clients after a generalist approach was used in the early stages of service. Concurrently, examination of current group work and community organization practice yielded the understanding that more than one approach had developed in each of these traditional methods.[37] The 1969 Charlotte Towle Memorial Symposium was a presentation of major theoretical approaches to casework practice.[38]

During this era, other helping professions were also achieving new approaches, and many social workers adopted such approaches as transactional analysis, behavior modification, and reality therapy for use in their practice. The sensitivity-encounter group movement influenced social work with groups. The breaking down of the old alliance with psychoanalysis and the disenchantment with the medical model enabled this trend to develop. Social workers were becoming aware of the other psychological approaches. By using a social systems framework, they were able to incorporate sociological understandings into their framework in a manner heretofore impossible.

In the late 1960s and early 1970s, social workers did not have the degree of agreement about practice approaches they once had. For example, they no longer agreed on the conceptual framework of the person in the situation underlying professional practice. Some of the important new practice approaches that developed were crisis intervention, task-centered casework, and social-behavioral social work. (See Appendix 2–1 for a summary of these and other contemporary approaches of social work practice.) An interventive repertoire was developing that was rich and that gave workers choice. These choices made it possible to respond appropriately to the many new service opportunities and demands. Not only was the intervention repertoire broader, but the intervention strategies were elaborated to a greater degree; they were more specific.

The various approaches, while different, all contained a means of assessment, concern about relationship, a process, and a focus on the client or clients in a situation; and all were a means to influence change (intervention). The degree of emphasis on each concept differed from approach to approach, and the specific interpretation of the concept was different, but the core concepts were present.

A social work practice was emerging in which a general theory base was used for the original response to need and for the assessment of the client in the situation. Then, using a relationship developed in the process, an intervention based on one of the more specific approaches was chosen from the intervention repertoire. This practice reflects the needs and concerns of the times: a broadened client group and new problems to respond to. The essence of generalist practice began to appear. A primary outcome for the understanding of social work practice from this era was that the basis for generalist practice emerged.

1976–1990

This era saw a societal disenchantment with the social welfare system. It was a time of inflation, unemployment, and concern with defense. Within the social work profession, issues that received considerable attention were: the differential roles of the BSW and the MSW worker, development of specialization at the MSW level, and the conceptualization of generalist practice. Considerable attention was paid to identifying the foundation, core, or base that underlies all social work practice. It was a time of concern about the social problems of homelessness, AIDS, substance abuse, and peace and justice.

Assessment was seen as the process that develops the understanding of the person in the situation and as the basis for the action to be taken. Assessment was ongoing and made use of knowledge developed from a number of different sources. Of particular importance was assessment of the effect of cultural and ethnic factors on the behavior of individuals and on the capacity of the individual and family to use help. Also, attention was paid to the effect of gender on individual development and behavior.

The **person in the situation** (or as now referred to, **person in the environment**) construct received considerable attention with the development of the ecological approach to practice.[39] Personal support networks were identified, developed, supported, and used as a part of the helping process. Persons and social systems were both seen as significant in problem solving. The social systems approach was almost universally accepted.

Relationship, both its professional and helping qualities, continued to be seen as the cohesive quality of the action system. Relationships seen as important were not only those with clients but also relationships with significant social systems and with persons influential in those systems.

Process continued to be seen as a recurrent patterning of a sequence of change over time—that is, various stages of the work were specified in the order in which they were the primary focus of practice. Process was conceptualized in different ways by different theorists. **Intervention** was also conceptualized differentially but there was a growing tendency not to accept any one intervention or approach to practice as appropriate for all situations.

1991–1993

While it is too early to discern the future of practice theory as it will develop from contemporary practice, there are some trends that might be considered. In 1986, James K. Whittaker, Steven P. Schinke, and Lewayne D. Gilchrist went so far as to suggest that social workers have moved to a new paradigm, or way of thinking about practice. They further stated that this new way of thinking, the ecological paradigm, is based on two major features; "improving social supports through various forms of environmental helping and on improving personal competencies through the teaching of 'life skills'."[40] This way of thinking is congruent with generalist practice, as discussed in Chapter 1. Generalist practice would, however, also include considering the possibility that the intervention should be focused on environmental change. Subsequent trends seem to confirm this idea. In fact, the growing emphasis on the importance of empowerment as a goal or strategy of practice supports this theory.

Yet the author believes that the emphasis of generalist practice on considering the need for environmental change must not be lost. To empower individuals to change their environment is a noble cause, but the generalist social worker must also be willing to help change the social environment in other ways when this is more appropriate. Thus, it is important for the generalist social worker to continue working with various systems in a variety of ways.

Another paradigm that is being suggested by some social workers is the feminist perspective.[41] This paradigm is based on five principles: eliminating false dichotomies and artificial separations, reconceptualizing power, valuing process equally with product, the validity of renaming, and the personal is political. In other words, it calls for a holistic view, a wide distribution of power, attention to the importance of how goals are implemented, the value of renaming action so as to purge discriminatory language, and the recognition that personal problems are often the result of political injustice and require that the focus of intervention be on change in large systems. It is a paradigm that seems very useful in any situation in which discrimination is of major concern, for example, work with women or minority groups.

Another contemporary trend in social work practice is the continuing development of private practice. In part, this has been in response to possibilities of reimbursement from third-party payors. It is a trend that, to date, has primarily affected the masters-level social worker, and it would seem to be a trend that supports the cause of clinical social work and may detract from the use of a generalist approach to practice. What the long-term effect on social work practice will be remains speculation at this time.

Generalist practice, then, reflects the evolutionary response over the past century to societal concerns and needs and events and thinking. Generalist practice reflects the theoretical heritage of the profession: assessment, person in the situation, relationship, process, and intervention. Social work is an ever-changing and ever-developing professional endeavor. However, its strong emphasis on assessment, a concern for intervention through working *with* rather than doing *to* or *for* a client, its emphasis on the person in the situation, the importance of relationship, and the concern for the process of practice all remain at the heart of social work practice today.

CASE EXAMPLE

In 1912, a social worker was apt to be concerned about a client who was having difficulty adjusting to a new culture and/or was living in poverty. The response was to study the client's situation to determine the cause of the problem and to offer resources that would acculturate the client to middle-class norms.

In 1927, the client might be a person whose adjustment to society was seen as not normal. The response was to study the client from a psychoanalytic point of view, being particularly careful to develop a "good relationship" and to help the client gain insight into her behavior.

In 1933, the client was probably suffering from poverty. The response was to provide economic resources and, if there was time, also to give thought to how the economic insufficiency was affecting the person.

In 1946, the client was apt to be middle class and experiencing psychological discomfort because the "normal happy family life" was illusive. The response was a relationship that would allow for exploration of the functioning person in the situation. Understanding and acceptance of the client led to the client's developing insight.

In 1963, the clients might be a multiproblem family living in poverty; traditional responses did not seem to work. The worker was seeking new responses, such as how to work with seemingly unmotivated clients, how to work with clients who were victims of environmental insufficiency, or how to respond within the culture of a person who was a member of a racial minority group.

In 1990, the client or target for change might be any person, family, group, or community needing help in some aspect of social functioning. Many social workers will use a generalist approach and, thus, assess the person in the situation. A major focus of this assessment will be on the social support in the environment and the client's competencies. The worker will engage the client in the assessment, thereby developing a working relationship with the client. Through this process they will together decide on the intervention and the tasks that need to be accomplished if the client's social functioning is to stabilize.*

SUMMARY

This chapter discusses the nature of a profession and the development of its theory. Social work does meet the criteria of a profession, although it does have

*This description of clients and responses is not meant to indicate that these were the only clients or the only approaches but merely to indicate the predominant focus of practice.

difficulty being recognized as such because of some of its characteristics. The development of a knowledge base is one criterion of a profession. Five concepts (assessment, relationship, person in the situation, process, and intervention) are used to trace the development of social work's knowledge base. This knowledge base developed in response to historical and cultural conditions. An understanding of the historical basis of social work practice provides one way of understanding contemporary practice.

QUESTIONS

1. Who or what gives authority to the social worker to respond to problems of social functioning? Why is social work not given the respect other professions receive?

2. How has the social welfare system been affected by societal trends and events? How has this affected social work practice?

3. How has a changing clientele changed the manner in which social work is practiced?

4. What do you see as problems for the social work profession because of the lack of agreement about practice theory? What are the advantages?

5. How has the development of social work practice enhanced contemporary practice? How has it been an inhibitor to responding to the contemporary situation?

SUGGESTED READINGS

Alexander, Leslie B. "Social Work's Freudian Deluge: Myth or Reality?" *Social Service Review* 46 (December 1972): 517–538.

Balgopal, Pallassana R., and Vassil, Thomas V. *Groups in Social Work: An Ecological Perspective.* New York: Macmillan, 1983 (Chapter 1).

Brieland, Donald. "The Hull House Tradition and the Contemporary Social Worker: Was Jane Addams Really a Social Worker?" *Social Work* 35 (March 1990): 134–138.

Gavin, Charles D., and Cox, Fred M. "A History of Community Organizing Since the Civil War with Special Reference to Oppressed Communities." In Fred M. Cox, John L. Erlich, Jack Rothman, and John E. Tropman, *Strategies of Community Organization*, 3rd ed. Itasca, IL: F. E. Peacock Publishers, 1979 (pp. 45–75).

Germain, Carel B., and Hartman, Ann. "People and Ideas in the History of Social Work Practice." *Social Casework* 61 (June 1980): 323–331.

Gordon, William E. "Social Work Revolution or Evolution?" *Social Work* 28 (May–June 1983): 181–185.

Greenwood, Ernest. "Attributes of a Profession." *Social Work* 2 (July 1957): 45–55.

Hollis, Florence. "On Revisiting Social Work." *Social Casework* 61 (January 1980): 3–10.

Jiménez, Mary Ann. "Historical Evolution and Future Challenges of the Professions" *Families in Society: The Journal of Contemporary Human Services* 71 (January 1990): 3–12.

Johnson, Louise C., and Schwartz, Charles L. *Social Welfare: A Response to Human Need.* Boston: Allyn and Bacon, 1988.

Kendall, Katherine A. A "Sixty-Year Perspective of Social Work." *Social Casework* 63 (September 1982): 424–428.

Kirk, Stuart A., Siporin, Max, and Kutchins, Herb. "The Prognosis for Social Work Diagnosis." *Social Casework* 70 (May 1989): 295–304.

Leiby, James. *A History of Social Welfare and Social Work in the United States.* New York: Columbia University Press, 1978.

Leighninger, Leslie. "The Generalist-Specialist Debate in Social Work." *Social Service Review* (March 1980): 1–12.

Lynn, Kenneth S., and the editors of *Daedalus. The Professions in America.* Boston: Beacon Press, 1965.

Minahan, Anne, Ed. *Encyclopedia of Social Work,* 18th ed., Silver Spring, MD: National Association of Social Workers, 1987 ("History and Evolution of Social Work Practice," "History of Social Work and Social Welfare: Significant Dates," pp. 739–788).

Perlman, Helen Harris. *Looking Back to See Ahead.* Chicago: University of Chicago Press, 1989 (pp. 211–228).

Peterson, K. Jean. "Assessment in the Life Model: A Historical Perspective." *Social Casework* 60 (December 1979): 586–596.

Peti, Christopher. "The Worker-Client Relationship: A General Systems Perspective." *Social Casework* 69 (December 1988): 620–626.

Poteck, Kathleen. "Jane Addams Revisited: Practice Theory and Social Economics." *Social Work with Groups* 11 (No. 4, 1989): 11–26.

Rodwell, Mary K. "Naturalistic Inquiry: An Alternative Model for Social Work Assessments." *Social Service Review* 61 (June 1987): 231–246.

Rozenfeld, Jona M. "The Domain and Expertise of Social Work: A Conceptualization." *Social Work* 28 (May–June 1983): 186–191.

Sands, Roberta G., and Nuccio, Kathleen. "Post-Modern Feminist Theory and Social Work." *Social Work* 37 (November 1992): 489–494.

Specht, Harry. "Social Work and the Popular Psychotherapies." *Social Service Review* 64 (September 1990): 345–357.

Van Den Bergh, Nan, and Cooper, Lynn B. *Feminist Visions for Social Work.* Silver Spring, MD: National Association of Social Workers, 1986.

Vigilante, Florence Wexler, and Maileck, Mildred. "Needs-Resource Evaluation in the Assessment Process." *Social Work* 33 (March–April 1988): 101–104.

Weick, Ann, and Pope, Loren. "Knowing What's Best: A New Look at Self-Determination." *Social Casework* 68 (January 1988): 10–16.

Whittaker, James K., Schinke, Steven P., and Gilchrist, Lewayne D. "The Ecological Paradigm in Child, Youth, and Family Services: Implications for Policy and Practice." *Social Service Review* 60 (December 1986): 483–503.

NOTES

1. For one view of the development of the social welfare system see Louise C. Johnson and Charles L. Schwartz, *Social Welfare: A Response to Human Need,* 3rd ed. (Boston: Allyn and Bacon, 1994).

2. June Gary Hopps and Elaine B. Pinderhughes, "Profession of Social Work: Contemporary Characteristics," in *Encyclopedia of Social Work,* vol. II, 18th ed. Anne Minnahan, Ed. (Silver Spring, MD: National Association of Social Workers, 1987), p. 231.

3. Ernest Greenwood, "Attributes of a Profession," *Social Work* 2 (July 1957): 45–55.

4. Leslie Leighninger, *Social Work Search for Identity* (New York: Greenwood Press, 1987).

5. Gary R. Lowe, Laura Rose Zimmerman, and P. Nelson Reid, "How We See Ourselves: A Critical Review of Text Versions of Social Work's Professional Evolution," unpublished paper.

6. Elizabeth Howe, "Public Professions and the Private Model of Professionalism," *Social Work* 25 (May 1980): 179–191.

7. For an in-depth study of this material see James Leiby, *A History of Social Welfare and Social Work in the United States* (New York: Columbia University Press, 1978). Other useful references include: Clarke A. Chambers, *Seedtime of Reform* (Minneapolis: University of Minnesota Press, 1963); Phillip Klein, *From Philanthropy to Social Welfare* (San Francisco: Jossey-Bass, 1968); Walter Trattner, *From Poor Law to Welfare State,* 2nd ed. (New York: Free Press, 1979); and Nathan Cohen, *Social Work in the American Tradition* (New York: Holt, Rinehart and Winston, 1958).

Useful social history references include: Harvey Wish, *Society and Thought in Modern America* (New York: David McKay, 1962); Morton G. White, *Social Thought in America* (New York: Viking Press, 1962); Eric F. Goldman, *The Crucial Decade—And After, America 1945–1960* (New York: Alfred A. Knopf, 1971); Douglas T. Miller and Marion Nowak, *The Fifties: The Way We Really Were* (Garden City, N.Y.: Doubleday, 1977); and William L. O'Neill, *Coming Apart: An Informal History of America in the 1960s* (Chicago: Quadrangle Books, 1971).

8. Mary E. Richmond, *Social Diagnosis* (New York: Russell Sage Foundation, 1917; reprint, Free Press, 1971).

9. Ibid., p. 357.

10. See Herman Borenzweig, "Social Work and Psychoanalytic Theory: An Historical Analysis," *Social Work* 16 (January 1971): 7–16.

11. Leslie B. Alexander, "Social Work's Freudian Deluge: Myth or Reality?" *Social Service Review* 46 (December 1972): 517–538.

12. *Social Casework: Generic and Specific* (New York: American Association of Social Workers, 1929).

13. Virginia P. Robinson, *A Changing Psychology in Social Case Work* (Chapel Hill: University of North Carolina Press, 1930).

14. Ibid.

15. Gordon Hamilton, *The Theory and Practice of Social Casework* (New York: Columbia University Press, 1940), p. 153.

16. Ibid., p. 35.

17. Ibid., p. 167.

18. Jessie Taft, Ed., *A Functional Approach to Family Casework* (Philadelphia: University of Pennsylvania Press, 1944); and Herbert H. Aptekar, *Basic Concepts in Social Casework* (Chapel Hill: University of North Carolina Press, 1941).

19. Gordon Hamilton, *Theory and Practice of Social Casework,* 2nd ed. rev. (New York: Columbia Press, 1951).

20. Felix P. Biestek, *The Casework Relationship* (Chicago: Loyola University Press, 1957).

21. Ibid., p. 17.

22. Helen Harris Perlman, *Social Casework: A Problem-Solving Process* (Chicago: University of Chicago Press, 1957).

23. Ibid., p. 4.

24. Ibid., p. 171.

25. Ibid.

26. See Grace Longwell Coyle, *Group Work with American Youth* (New York: Harper Brothers, 1948); Gertrude Wilson and Gladys Ryland, *Social Group Work Practice* (Boston: Houghton Mifflin, 1949); Harleigh B. Trecker, *Social Group Work* (New York: Whiteside, 1948); and Murray G. Ross, *Community Organization* (New York: Harper Brothers, 1955).

27. Florence Hollis, *Casework: A Psychosocial Therapy* (New York: Random House, 1964), and Ruth Elizabeth Smalley, *Theory for Social Work Practice* (New York: Columbia University Press, 1967).

28. Florence Hollis, *Casework,* 2nd ed. (1971).

29. Gisela Konopka, *Social Group Work: A Helping Process* (Englewood Cliffs, NJ: Prentice-Hall, 1963), and Helen Northen, *Social Work with Groups* (New York: Columbia University Press, 1969).

30. Murray G. Ross, *Community Organization: Theory, Principles, and Practice,* 2nd ed. (New York: Harper and Row, 1967), and Robert Perlman and Arnold Gurin, *Community Organization and Social Planning* (New York: John Wiley, 1972).

31. Carol H. Meyer, *Social Work Practice: A Response to the Urban Crisis* (New York: Free Press, 1970).

32. Harriett M. Bartlett, *The Common Base of Social Work Practice* (New York: National Association of Social Workers, 1970).

33. Max Siporin, *Introduction to Social Work Practice* (New York: Macmillan, 1975); Beulah Roberts Compton and Burt Galaway, *Social Work Processes* (Homewood, IL: Dorsey Press, 1975); Howard Goldstein, *Social Work Practice: A Unitary Approach* (Columbia: University of South Carolina Press, 1973); and Allen Pincus and Anne Minahan, *Social Work Practice: Model and Method* (Itasca, IL: F. E. Peacock, 1973).

34. Pincus and Minahan, *Social Work Practice,* p. 103.

35. Ibid., p. 247.

36. See Joan Stein, *The Family as a Unit of Study and Treatment* (Seattle: Regional Rehabilitation Research Institute, University of Washington School of Social Work, 1969).

37. See Catherine P. Papell and Beulah Rothman, "Social Group Work Models: Possession and Heritage," *Journal of Education for Social Work* 2 (Fall 1966): 66–77; and Jack Rothman, "Three Models of Community Organization Practice," in *National Conference on Social Welfare Social Work Practice* (New York: Columbia University Press, 1968), pp. 16–47.

38. Robert W. Roberts and Robert H. Nee, Eds., *Theories of Social Casework* (Chicago: University of Chicago Press, 1970).

39. Carel Germain and Alex Gitterman, *The Life Model of Social Work Practice* (New York: Columbia University Press, 1980).

40. James K. Whittaker, Steven P. Schinke, and Lewayne D. Gilchrist, "The Ecological Paradigm in Child, Youth, and Family Services: Implications for Policy and Practice," *Social Service Review* 60 (December 1986): 483–503.

41. Nan Van Den Bergh and Lynn B. Cooper, Eds., *Feminist Visions for Social Work* (Silver Spring, MD: National Association of Social Workers, 1986), Introduction, pp. 1–28.

APPENDIX 2–1 The Development of Social Work in the United States

Societal	Social Welfare	Social Work
1885–1900		
Immigration (new groups); population increase. Industrialization-urbanization puts populations at risk. Closing of the frontier. Big business influence on politics. Agrarian revolt; beginning of trade unions. Beginnings of federal control (commerce and trusts). Social Darwinism vs. Puritan ethic.	Search for cause of poverty and individual breakdown. Emphasis on moral behavior and on affecting individual through personal influence and "neighborliness." Search for improved methods of government responsibility for care of special groups—children, the insane, etc. Emphasis on the "deserving poor." 1873—National Conference of Corrections and Charities.	Concern for urban situations in response to religious motives. Movement from volunteer to paid employment. 1863—First state social welfare board. 1866—First settlement house in the United States. 1887—Charity Organization Society comes to the United States.
1901–1919		
Age of progressives; liberalism; Social Darwinism. Emphasis on the real rather than the ideal. Development of the social sciences as a body of knowledge. Rise of the "Social Gospel." Growth of the Muckrakers. Growth of labor movement—concern for work conditions. Influence of John Dewey and "progressive education." World War I—"Make the world safe for democracy."	Age of philanthropy. Emphasis on environmental improvement and social reform with emphasis on poverty. Concern for labor conditions, safety, hours, wages. Establishment of programs in highly specialized and fragmented form. Concern for the care of dependent children; institutional vs. foster care; establishment of juvenile courts, widows' pensions, child labor laws. Social welfare legislation for special groups. 1909—First White House Conference (Children). 1912—Establishment of the Children's Bureau. Country life movement. Welfare programs for military personnel. Reform legislation: Restriction of immigration. Prohibition (of alcoholic beverages). Women's suffrage.	Beginnings of social work education with emphasis on method. Age of scientific philanthropy. Attempts to establish knowledge base, clarify goals, and establish itself. Social science theory predominant; sociology emphasis. Beginning attempt to establish practice theory with Richmond's *Social Diagnosis*. Development of practice in specialty areas. 1905—Medical social work. 1906—School social work. 1907—Psychiatric social work.

1920—1929

Conservatism returns; disillusionment and dissatisfaction prevalent.
Emphasis on production and distribution; responsiveness to corporations.
"Return to normalcy"; individualism.
Prosperity—national income high, unemployment low.
Reduction in immigration—deportation of alien radicals.
Antisocialism, racial intolerance, upsurge of Ku Klux Klan.
Era of laissez-faire and intolerance.
Urbanism—indifference to social reform, sensationalism, skepticism.
Development of psychology.

Disillusionment with political solutions to social problems.
Marked increase in philanthropic foundations.
Multiplication of service clubs.
Formation of community chests—reorganization of private charities.
Rise of public administration, state agencies, institutions.
Change from "charity and corrections" to "public welfare."
Rise of "child guidance," "mental hygiene," character-building agencies, concern for the prevention of delinquency.
Some state laws on unemployment compensation, mothers' pensions, old age pensions, help for the blind.
County-level organization of rural child welfare services in some states.

Emphasis on function of social work rather than on the social cause. Withdrawal from social responsibility and placing of emphasis on the adjustment of individuals.
Use of casework with middle-class clients.
Milford Conference of 1923–24; search for generic aspects of casework, definition of social casework.
Development of specialized professional organizations; medical, school, and psychiatric social workers as well as the American Association of Social Workers.
Search for a body of knowledge and theoretical framework led to adoption of psychoanalytical theory by an increasing number of workers and educators.
By 1930 twenty-eight schools of social work had been established.

1930—1945

Depression—solutions for economic and social ills in action by the federal government.
Social experimentation—pragmatism.
New Deal; federal regulation of business.
Rise of organized labor.
Mass movement from rural to urban settings.
Collectivist mood for building a new social order.
World War II; revolt against totalitarianism, but an emphasis on unity.
Rise of communism—fear of communism.

Federal government becomes heavily involved in social welfare, relief programs, and public works programs.
Social Security Act of 1935.
Federal funding—state administration of categorical assistance for the unemployable (children, aged, blind).
Federal administration of social insurance against old age.
State-administered unemployment insurance.
1939—social security amendment includes survivor's insurance.

Concern over public-private functions as the major responsibility for relief becomes public.
Redefinition of role of family agency.
In search for casework theory, two approaches develop—diagnostic and functional.
Group work becomes a part of social work; formation of the National Association for the Study of Groups, 1936.
Lane Report on Community Organizations, 1939.
Formation of many national planning organizations; rise of community chests.
Continued growth and development of social work education; minimum curriculum requirements, formal accreditation, need for university affiliation, strong concern that it be graduate education.
Debate over uniqueness of rural social work.

Continued

Societal	Social Welfare	Social Work
1946–1960		
Postwar prosperity; partnership of business and government. Threat of nuclear war—fear of communism. "New conservatism," McCarthyism. Korean War; Cold War. Farm problems; decline of family farm. Gains for labor; higher wages and welfare packages. Population explosion. Growth of metropolitan communities; migration of minorities to cities. Television. "Happy home" illusion; *Growing Up Absurd;* "affluent society."	1946—Hill-Burton Act (hospital survey and construction). 1946—National Mental Health Act. 1950—expansion and strengthening of Social Security; Addition of aid to the disabled. Growth of interest in services and their delivery. Business corporations' and labor unions' support of private philanthropy. Growth of community chests and councils. Growth of national health organizations. 1953—establishment of Department of Health, Education, and Welfare. 1955—Joint Commission on Mental Illness and Health. 1956—amendments to Social Security Act call for services as well as income maintenance. 1956—Federal Housing Act. Growth of national institutes of health. Concern about juvenile correctional institutions and delinquency.	Time for introspection, cooperation, and search for unity. Development of methods of group work, community organization, and research; continued diagnostic-functional dichotomy. Expansion into new settings; new problem areas. 1946—establishment of the National Council on Social Work Education to resolve problems of educational standards. 1952—Hollis-Taylor Report, *Social Work Education in the United States.* 1952—formation of Council on Social Work Education, MSW the professional degree; development of curriculum policy, accreditation standards, 85% of social work students in casework sequence. 1955—NASW formed; adoption of *Code of Ethics;* establishment of ACSW. 1958—eight-volume curriculum study.
1961–1975		
High unemployment; growth slowed. Cold War; Cuban Missile Crisis; Vietnam War. Space program. Desegregation. Growth of government bureaucracy. Kennedy assassination. Concern with consumerism. From civil rights to Black Power; minority rights. Women's Liberation Movement. Counterculture; New Left. Federal support for education. Family farm declines. Concern for law and order.	Discovery of poverty; *The Other America.* War on Poverty; Great Society. Drift toward "universalism." Growing ADC roles; AFDC (1962). 1962—Social Security amendments implement service provision. 1962—Manpower Training Act. 1965—Medicare-Medicaid. 1965—Office of Economic Opportunity. 1965—Older Americans Act. Concern for health care; discussion of income distribution; preoccupation with rehabilitation and accountability.	Growth in number of social workers, in areas of concern, and in knowledge development. Knowledge base expanded; use of social systems theory, lessening of psychoanalytic influence. Return to concern for multiproblem, difficult-to-serve client. Proliferation of new practice modalities. Involvement in social reform, social action, and social policy activity. Emphasis on research and theory development. Concern with manpower and deployment issues. Development of integrated or generalist methods.

1976–1991

Inflation.
Fiscal retrenchment.
Conservatism prevails.
New Realism, New Federalism.
High unemployment.
Changing family structure.
Changing role of women; defeat of ERA.
Aging of the population.
Escalation of health care costs.
New technology, age of computers.
Concern about nuclear energy, defense, and peace issues.
Farm crisis.
	Federal Grants-in-Aid Program; intermingling of public and private sectors; revenue sharing, purchase of service.
	Rent supplement program; food stamps; WIN.
	Separation of income maintenance and services.
	Rebirth of rural concerns.
	1970s—time of doubt about effectiveness; reorganization and accountability themes.
	1972—SSI replaces AA, AB, and AD; federal administration of programs.
	1975—Title XX of Social Security Act; decentralization of services; child support enforcement.
	1975—Original passage of fairly liberal entitlements.
	
	1980s—Saw restrictions which crippled entitlement programs.
	1981—Block grants restrict Title XX.
	Block grants.
	Revenue sharing.
	Civil Service declassification.
	Deinstitutionalization.
	Curtailing of social welfare budget; cost containment.
	Third-party payments.
	Health care planning mechanisms.
	"Workfare" and other "welfare reform."
	Introduction of prospective payment for health care costs for Medicare recipients through Diagnostic Related Groups (DRG's), 1983.
		Reappearance of rural social work.
		Rise of "clinical social work" movement and private practice.
		Tremendous growth in social work education.
		Accreditation of BSW programs; development of doctoral programs; Considerable diversity of educational programs.
		NASW accepts BSW for membership.
		Proliferation of new practice modalities including planned short-term approaches.
		
		Generalist at BSW level; specialization at MSW level.
		Continued tension between BSW and MSW levels.
		Rise of social work in industrial and rural settings.
		Clinical Register; growth of private practice.
		New *Code of Ethics*.
		Emphasis on political involvement.
		Concern with:
		  Child and spouse abuse, displaced homemakers, use of community resources, homelessness, AIDS, substance abuse, and peace and justice.
		Growing support for an ecological paradigm.
		Education:
		  New curriculum policy statement.
		  New accreditation standards.

3

SOCIAL WORK AS A CREATIVE BLENDING OF KNOWLEDGE, VALUES, AND SKILLS

Learning Expectations

1. Understanding of the range of knowledge used by the social worker.
2. Understanding of the nature of values.
3. Knowledge about the value base underlying social work.
4. Understanding of the nature of skills and beginning knowledge of the skills of a generalist social worker.
5. Understanding of the manner in which knowledge, values, and skills are used together in social work.

Social work as a creative blending of knowledge, values, and skills is the third major perspective of social work practice. It relates to the "how" of social work practice. As discussed in Chapter 2, important characteristics of any profession are systematic theory and ethical codes. The development of systematic theory upon which to base practice implies that the practice is grounded in a knowledge base and that practioneers are using that knowledge base in their practice decision making. This practice also is based in an ethical code that in part delineates the value base for practice. The value base also must consider societal, client, and worker values.

Soon after the formation of the National Association of Social Workers (NASW), it became evident that there was a need for definition and clarification of social work practice in order to codify the unifying elements of the profession. The Commission of Social Work Practice of NASW, through the work of a subcommittee chaired by Harriet Bartlett, developed the "Working Definition of Social Work Practice."[1] From this work and the subsequent work of Bartlett and William Gordon,[2] understanding began to evolve about the necessity for further identifying the body of knowledge (ways of knowing) and the set of values (attitudes toward people) that guide practice and are operationalized through a set of skills. This constellation of knowledge, values, and skills is one important means of describing the nature of social work practice. It is used to operationalize the five concepts discussed in Chapter 2: assessment, relationship, person in situation, process, and intervention. It provides an organizing framework for practice regardless of problem, system of focus, worker role, or context of practice. It is the foundation of professional relationships and of the helping process, and gives substance to the concepts of concern and need—the problems of social functioning with which a social worker is confronted.

In some ways knowledge, values, and skills are related to the feeling, thinking, and doing construct introduced in Chapter 1 (see Figure 1–1). Knowledge is a part of the cognitive or thinking component of practice; values are a part of the feeling or emotional component of practice, though in some ways they are also a part of the thinking component. Skills are action, or the doing of social work; they are part of the behavioral component. However, it must be recognized that skills may also be cognitive in nature. That is, development of the capacity to think about a practice situation such as to utilize the broad knowledge base and choose those aspects appropriate to the situation, determine relevant values for consideration, and identify appropriate action is included in the realm of skill as discussed in this book.

It is important to examine the nature of each of these components of social work practice as well as the content of each component. This is not sufficient for understanding this perspective, however. It is also important to consider how these three components are used together in practice, which raises the issue of whether social work is a science or an art. It gives rise to the notion that the connection among the three results from a *creative blending*.[3] Other issues that must be considered are the use of both science and art in considering the relationship of knowledge, values, and skill and the importance of creativity in combining the three into a coherent practice assessment and plan.

KNOWLEDGE

In *The Common Base of Social Work Practice*, Bartlett makes a strong case for the need for social work action to be founded on a strong knowledge base—to be guided by knowledge.[4] **Knowledge** is a term with a broad and varied meaning. Gordon defined knowledge as "the picture man has of the world and his place in it."[5] Max Siporin gives a definition that enhances Gordon's: "Knowledge is cognitive mental content (ideas and beliefs) concerning reality that we take to be true (perceive with certainty, based on adequate evidence), or that we decide is confirmable and has a high probability of truth."[6]

Social work has placed increasing emphasis on knowledge that is scientific as opposed to beliefs in unconfirmed ideas. An attempt has been made to develop a knowledge base that begins to move toward the hardness characteristic of the sciences. Yet the very nature of the social sciences, with their concern for the complex phenomenon of the human being in his social environment, tends to make this difficult and gives a quality of softness to the knowledge base.*

In their struggle to develop the science of sociology, sociologists have experienced problems similar to those of social work. Paul Reynolds identifies a scientific body of knowledge as designed to "describe things and identify why events occur."[7] He perceives this body of knowledge as providing a method for organizing or categorizing things, predicting future events, explaining past events, and giving a sense of understanding about what causes events and the potential for control of events.[8] He goes on to state that knowledge that is accepted as scientific has these attributes:

1. *Abstractness*—independence of time and space.
2. *Intersubjectivity*

    a. *Explicitness*—description in necessary detail and with terms selected to insure that the audience agrees on the meaning of the concepts.
    b. *Rigorousness* (logical rigor)—use of logical systems that are shared and accepted by relevant scientists to insure agreement on the predictions and explanations of theory.

3. *Empirical relevance*—the possibility should always exist that other scientists can evaluate the correspondence between theory and the results of empirical research.[9]

Other sociologists have demonstrated how society determines the presence and content of ideas; how social values define the phenomena to be studied and color interpretations of these phenomena.[10] This leads to the understanding that although knowledge can be tested—can be developed in a scientific manner—the content developed and tested is strongly influenced by the social context in which social work practice takes place. For example, societal values about individuals have influenced the development of knowledge that emphasizes the needs of individuals.

Social work knowledge, particularly the foundation knowledge used for understanding, has been largely borrowed from the social sciences, particularly psychology and sociology, though anthropology, political science, economics, and history as well as the natural sciences of biology and physiology contribute as

---

*It is assumed that students will be exposed to the concept of scientific knowledge in a research course. It is also assumed that they will understand such terms as *concept, theory,* and *hypothesis.* It is not the purpose of this book to consider this material in any depth. This book is concerned with application of knowledge after a judgment is made about its reliability and validity.

well. It is complex, requiring a breadth of knowledge in various disciplines as well as a depth necessary for more than superficial understanding.

Social work knowledge is what is known about people and their social systems. It is relative to the situation in which it was developed. It is descriptive of the phenomena of persons in situations, and it explains the functioning of individuals and their social systems. It is used to gain understanding of persons in situations and of larger social systems and to guide the actions of social workers as they seek to enhance individuals' social functioning. It includes knowledge of human development, human diversity, and social systems theory as discussed in Chapter 1. It is knowledge that directs the response to need and includes knowledge about assessment, relationships, the social work process, and intervention.

The knowledge used to guide the action of the social worker with clients has usually been developed by social workers. Much of this knowledge has not been rigorously tested in a scientific manner. However, a small body of practice knowledge can be identified. Task-centered social work is an example of this type of knowledge.[11] However, the use of only scientifically developed knowledge in social work practice fails to account for much that the practioners know about human beings and how change takes place. Reality is much more than that which has been proven and observed in concrete ways. Ways of knowing other than the narrowly scientific have been referred to as *practice wisdom.* Howard Goldstein has referred to this as "that which we learn from the lives of our clients and from the experiences we share with them."[12] Goldstein also noted that recognition of this knowledge as valid for practice opens up a new range of what are known as generative theories for use in practice.[13]

Thus, the knowledge base developed for social work is eclectic, interdisciplinary, tentative at best, complex, and often subjective. Social work continues to search for the acceptance of common concepts and common frames of reference and to test hypotheses about the nature of practice in the effort to become more scientific. By its very nature, this knowledge base is problematic. Some of these problems include:

1. Problems that come from borrowing knowledge from another discipline. This borrowing often provides yesterday's knowledge rather than the current thinking of the discipline developing the knowledge. Often, such knowledge is given much more certainty by the borrowing discipline than it is given by the developing discipline. Also, borrowing tends to be of a simplified nature.[14] Questionable assumptions may result when borrowed knowledge is improperly used.

2. Problems that arise from separating the knowledge and value elements of practice. Value considerations so influence one's view of reality that observations and facts that conflict with these values are often overlooked. The manner in which knowledge is developed and used contributes to this difficulty.[15]

3. Problems that develop because practice wisdom has often been conceptualized insufficiently to separate fact, perception, ideas, and values. Practice wisdom has often not been tested by applying it to different situations in a controlled manner. Its validity and reliability with respect to different situations has not been examined. Thus, it is difficult to determine if knowledge gained from practice wisdom is appropriate in a given situation.

4. Problems that develop because of the many variables involved in the human situation and in the worker-client interaction. These make it difficult to generalize knowledge for use in determining intervention possibilities. Of particular concern are cultural factors that change perceptions about human behavior and helping situations.

5. Problems that result from a tendency to use terms and concepts without sufficient definition or without agreement as to definition. Without this agreement, the same terms and concepts are sometimes used with different meanings. For example, some social workers define the *service delivery system* as an agency or group of agencies; others may also include in the service delivery system a variety of other resources, like helpers in the community.

6. Problems that result from a tendency to develop insufficient relationships among terms and concepts. Social systems theory has given a framework for doing this, at least in part, with the knowledge used for understanding—the person in the situation. The practice theory knowledge is still very difficult to place in an organized framework except at an abstract level.

Although many problems are inherent in the social work knowledge base, it has a major strength. Because social work takes a broad view of the person in the situation and of social functioning, there is a vast amount of knowledge that can be called on to inform practice. Knowledge that workers have gained from life experiences of their own, observations made about other's life experiences, and understandings developed from a broad liberal arts education are all available for use in practice.

If a worker is to base practice on a knowledge base, he or she must have the ability to evaluate the knowledge available,[16] to use judgment in the choice of knowledge to apply to specific situations, and to keep an open mind as to the tentativeness of the knowledge base and the knowledge about the client in the situation. The worker must be able to think theoretically, systematically, critically, and creatively. Goldstein stated that this is far more an art than an applied science. He further stated: "Reflectively, creatively, and imaginatively, the mind of the practioneer strives to blend and incorporate fragments of theory, information, intuitions, sensations, and other perceptions into something ambiguously called 'understanding.' "[17]

The sources of knowledge used by the social worker are wide and varied, coming from a variety of disciplines. The choice of which understandings to use in which situations is always problematic, and connecting knowledge bits from a variety of sources is difficult. The human condition is a complex phenomenon. It has been explained in a variety of ways. To have a sufficiently broad knowledge base, a social worker needs the following:

1. *A broad liberal arts base*—This includes a knowledge of the social sciences (sociology, psychology, anthropology, history, political science, and economics) to provide explanations about the nature of human society and the human condition. Study of the natural sciences provides tools for scientific thinking and an understanding of the physical aspects of the human condition. Study of the humanities aids in the development of the creative and critical thought processes; it provides an understanding of the nature of the human condition through the examination of creative endeavors and of the cultures of human society. A social worker is a person with a developed and expanded personal capacity gained by exposure to a broad, liberal educational experience.

2. *A sound foundation knowledge about persons, their interactions, and the social situations within which they function*—This includes knowledge about persons from emotional, cognitive, behavioral, and developmental points of view. Such knowledge must consider the diversity of the human condition and the effect of diversity on functioning and development. Understanding of human interaction in depth is also essential. This knowledge includes one-to-one relationships, family relationships, and small group relationships. It also includes understanding of the societal organizations and institutions that are a part of contemporary society and of the social problems that affect human functioning.

3. *Practice theory, with concern for the nature of helping interactions, of the process of helping, and of a variety of intervention strategies appropriate for a variety of situations and systems*—This includes knowledge of professional and societal structures and institutions for delivery of service to individuals in need of help and methods of adapting and developing the service structure for more adequate need fulfillment.[18]

4. *Specialized knowledge needed to work with particular groups of clients and in particular situations*—The choice of knowledge each worker includes in this area is dependent on the practice situations and on career aspirations.

5. The capacity to be reflective, imaginative, and creative in the use of knowledge obtained from a variety of source.

CASE EXAMPLE

When working with an older person, over age 65, there is a great deal of specific knowledge that will help the social worker in understanding the needs of such a client. Biology and physiology will provide knowledge about the physical aging process. In the field of gerontology, a number of theories relative to the aging process have emerged. These include disengagement theory, activity theory, and developmental theory. Developmental theory is particularly congruent with the emphasis of this book and identifies specific tasks that the older person needs to complete if the older adult stage of life is to be a fulfilling one. It is important to have basic knowledge about the many health problems of older persons as well as an understanding about death and dying.

Sociological knowledge provides understanding of the meaning of retirement to individuals as well as the role and function of older persons in our culture. It provides understandings about the social context of both the individual and institutional situations. Cultural and gender differences regarding the view of the aging process are also important. Knowledge about family structure and functioning as they relate to older persons is a needed understanding. Another valuable concept is that of cohort (age group) differences. This is particularly important as societal changes have speeded up to the point that different cohorts have experienced life in very different ways. Knowledge of various social problems that often affect older persons, such as limited financial resources, age discrimination, and isolation and loneliness is also necessary. The social worker should acquaint herself with the various societal and community resources that have been developed to help older persons deal with these problems. An in-depth understanding of social policy as it has developed is another needed knowledge for working with older persons. This knowledge all helps the worker to understand the person in the situation. In order to help that person, knowledge about a wide range of interventive strategies that have proven useful in the past is also needed.

VALUES

Knowledge and values are often confused. It is important to distinguish between these two important components of social work practice. **Knowledge** is at least potentially provable; it is used to explain behavior and to conceptualize practice. **Values** are not provable; they are what is held to be desirable; they are used to identify what is preferred. This includes preferable assumptions about human behavior and preferable ways of helping. Knowledge assumptions and value assumptions are used in different ways in the helping endeavor.[19]

Several definitions of the term *value* are useful for developing an understanding of the term. Muriel Pumphrey has defined values as follows: "Values are formulations of preferred behavior held by individuals or social groups. They imply a usual preference for certain means, ends, and conditions of life, often being accompanied by strong feeling."[20] Herbert Aptekar refines the meaning of value: "A standard or standards held by a significant portion of a society reflected in patterns of institutionalized behavior, and predisposing the participants to act in relation to one another within the framework of commonly understood although not consciously controlled or logically consistent referential system."[21] This definition might be questioned for its requirement that the value be held by a "significant portion of society." It is useful, however, in pointing out the societal aspect of values, or the influence of others in the development of values.

It is also questionable whether in the contemporary diverse society of the United States there are, in fact, any generally agreed upon societal values. What does seem to exist are groups of values that various segments of society *believe* should be the societal values and which they tend to want to impose on everyone.

A source from outside the field of social work is also useful in the search for understanding the term *value*. The literature of value clarification sees values as: 1) guides to behavior, 2) growing out of personal experiences, 3) modified as experiences accumulate, and 4) evolving in nature.[22] This literature provides additional understanding about the nature of values by noting that the conditions in which values operate often have conflicting demands; that is, several values are functioning in the same situation, and each calls for conflicting modes of functioning or end states. One social work example of this is working with a frail older woman. In such a case, the worker is confronted with values of physical safety and self-determination. The older person wants to remain in her own home, but it is not safe as presently set up. Which value should take precedence? A value judgment is called for.

Milton Rokeach defines value as "an enduring belief that a specific mode or end state of existence is personally or socially preferable to an opposite or converse mode or end state of existence."[23] He goes on to state that values, rather than standing alone, exist in systems; that is, individual values are organized in such a manner that they have a relative importance to other values. He construes values as being relatively enduring, as beliefs upon which persons act by preference, and as modes of conduct or end states of existence. Value beliefs are conceptions of what is desirable; there is an emotion or feeling aspect to them; and they lead to action.

There are several types of values. *Ultimate values* are the most abstract and tend to be those most easily agreed upon by large groups of people. They include such values as liberty, worth and dignity of people, progress, and justice. *Proximate values* are more specific as to the desired end. The right to an abortion on demand, freedom to determine how one will do the assignments in a course, and the right to punish one's child in a specific manner are examples of proximate values. There is apt to be disagreement regarding these values. *Instrumental values* are those values that specify the desired means to the end: they are modes of conduct. Self-determination and confidentiality are examples of instrumental values. They are means for maintaining and actualizing the dignity of individuals.

Values originate, in part, from the cultural relationship a person is a part. If individuals are thought of as well-socialized, it can be said that individuals have worth as human beings and as human situation.

Spiritual values are important because, just as religion and spiritual frameworks are important components of human values.

Values are developed as individuals are exposed to the differing value systems of society. The *societal value system* contains values generally held by the dominant segment of society. In American society, some of these values which have been articulated are achievement and success, activity and work, humanitarian responsibility, concern for people who are victims of natural disaster, temporary distress, efficiency and practicality, progress, material comfort, equality, freedom, external conformity, science and secular rationality, nationalism and patriotism, democracy, worth of the individual, and superiority of the dominant group.[24] These values have had their origin in a combination of sources, including: 1) the capitalistic-Puritan ethic; 2) the Judeo-

Christian heritage; and 3) humanistic, positivist, utopian thinking.[25] Conflicts, tensions, and inconsistencies exist among these various sources as well as among societal values, professional values, and personal values of clients and social workers. Tensions and conflicts become more apparent as one moves from ultimate values to the choice of specific goals and means, that is, as one moves from the abstract to the concrete. Some of these tensions arise because of differences between values about needs of individuals and values about needs of groups of which individuals are a part.

Social work practice is based on a set of values that is often expressed in such principles as the worth and dignity of the individual, the right to self-determination, and the right to confidentiality. Gordon expresses these values in the following manner: "It is good and desirable for man to fulfill his potential, to realize himself and to balance this with equal effort to help others fulfill their capacities and realize themselves."[26] Aptekar has expressed these same ultimate values in a slightly different manner: "Worth and dignity of a man as related to the well-being and integrity of the group. . . . Progress and development of individual and society as related to the security of individual and the society."[27] Armando Morales and Bradford Sheafor, using Charles Levy's scheme for organizing values,[28] have identified values held by the social work profession:

Preferred Conceptions of People

1. Social workers believe in inherent worth and dignity.
2. Each person has an inherent capacity and drive toward change which can make life more fulfilling.
3. Each person has responsibility for himself and his fellow human beings—including society.
4. People need to belong.
5. There are human needs common to each person yet each person is unique and different from others.

Preferred Outcomes for People

1. Society must provide opportunities for growth and development that will allow each person to realize his fullest potential.
2. Society must provide resources and services to help people meet their needs and to avoid such problems as hunger, inadequate education, discrimination, illness without care, and inadequate housing.
3. People must have equal opportunity to participate in the molding of society.

Preferred Instrumentalities for Dealing with People

People should be treated with respect and dignity, should have maximum opportunity to determine the direction of their lives, should be urged and helped to interact with other people to build a society responsive to the needs of everyone, and should be recognized as unique individuals rather than put into stereotypes because of some particular characteristic or life experience.[29]

Codes of ethics flow from values; they are values in action, and as such they are preferred instrumentalities for dealing with people. Werner Boehm has stated that values are behavioral expectations and preferences associated with responsibility; they represent consensus regarding the preference in specific situations.[30] Ethical codes specify what ought to be done in professional practice. At the 1979 Delegate Assembly, NASW adopted a new *Code of Ethics,* replacing a code of ethics adopted in 1960 and amended in 1967. Growth and change in the profession of social work as well as shortcomings in the old code made it desirable to develop this new code of ethics (see Table 3–1).[31]

As the social worker attempts to base practice on these values, it is soon apparent that this is not an easy or simple matter. The basing of practice on values leads to several problems:

1. The abstract statements of values are the subject of conflicting interpretations. As the abstract value is operationalized, the guidelines must take into consideration not just one value but several. It is often difficult to decide what action will fulfill the value's imperatives. For example, does a worker enhance a person's worth and dignity by allowing a choice that will clearly lead to the consequence of imprisonment? Can such a client be allowed self-determination?

2. The balance between individual rights and societal responsibility is difficult to maintain. Potential elements of conflict and tension in maintaining this balance are: a) the need to reform the social structure yet help persons cope with the imperfect social structure that exists; b) the responsibility to the consumers of service and at the same time to those who pay for the service; c) the providing for the good of the group and the community; and d) equality for all yet the need to meet individual needs, for in American culture individual self-sufficiency provides a sense of dignity; using help often lowers self-esteem.[32]

3. Henry Miller points out another problem in the application of values to practice: "How is one to minister to man's suffering without robbing him of his dignity?"[33] This is an ongoing question that is always present in social work practice.

4. Alan Keith-Lucas points out yet another problem: How is it possible to use the scientific approach and at the same time use a humanistic approach?[34] Roland Warren looks at this same problem in a somewhat different way. He sees two values that operate in relationship to social change: truth and love. Each seems to lead to different assumptions as to how to bring about change. Truth seems to call for knowing about, reasoning, a task orientation. The relationship with people in this value seems to be that of I-It. It carries the stance of the prophet. Love seems to call for knowledge by acquaintance of intuition and a process orientation. The relationship with people is more in an I-Thou manner. It carries the stance of the reconciler. This is the problem raised by valuing both the use of the scientific method and the worth and dignity of each individual. In his recognition of this

TABLE 3–1   NASW *Code of Ethics*—Summary of Principles

  I. The Social Worker's Conduct and Comportment as a Social Worker
   A. *Propriety*—The social worker should maintain high standards of personal conduct in the capacity or identity of social worker.
   B. *Competence and Professional Development*—The social worker should strive to become and remain proficient in professional practice and the performance of professional functions.
   C. *Service*—The social worker should regard as primary the service obligation of the social work profession.
   D. *Integrity*—The social worker should act in accordance with the highest standards of professional integrity.
   E. *Scholarship and Research*—The social worker engaged in study and research should be guided by the conventions of scholarly inquiry.
 II. The Social Worker's Ethical Responsibility to Clients
   F. *Primacy of Client's Interests*—The social worker's primary responsibility is to clients.
   G. *Rights and Prerogatives of Clients*—The social worker should make every effort to foster maximum self-determination on the part of the clients.
   H. *Confidentiality and Privacy*—The social worker should respect the privacy of clients and hold in confidence all information obtained in the course of professional service.
   I. *Fees*—When setting fees, the social worker should ensure that they are fair, reasonable, considerate, and commensurate with the service performed and with due regard for the client's ability to pay.
III. The Social Worker's Ethical Responsibility to Colleagues
   J. *Respect, Fairness, and Courtesy*—The social worker should treat colleagues with respect, courtesy, fairness, and good faith.
   K. *Dealing with Colleague's Clients*—The social worker has the responsibility to relate to the clients of colleagues with full professional consideration.
 IV. The Social Worker's Ethical Responsibility to Employers and Employing Organizations
   L. *Commitments to Employing Organizations*—The social worker should adhere to commitments made to the employing organizations.
  V. The Social Worker's Ethical Responsibility to the Social Work Profession
   M. *Maintaining the Integrity of the Profession*—The social worker should uphold and advance the values, ethics, knowledge, and mission of the profession.
   N. *Community Service*—The social worker should assist the profession in making social services available to the general public.
   O. *Development of Knowledge*—The social worker should take responsibility for identifying, developing, and fully utilizing knowledge for professional practice.
 VI. The Social Worker's Ethical Responsibility to Society
   P. *Promoting the General Welfare*—The social worker should promote the general welfare of society.

Reprinted with permission from *NASW Code of Ethics*, 1980. Copyright 1979, National Association of Social Workers, Inc.

dilemma, Warren calls for a stance that seeks to persuade but never to coerce the conscience, that does not love but respects, that is concerned with task but not oblivious of process, that seeks to understand but also to experience directly, that has a trace both of the prophet and of the reconciler.[35]

Dealing with values is central to social work practice. The social worker must be concerned with both societal and personal values, with the client's and with her own. The worker also must function within the framework of social work values and ethics. The worker must be comfortable with discomfort as the search continues for congruence between believing and doing and for resolution of conflict among values. This calls for tolerance and humility.

Some of the contemporary issues confronting social work and about which there are conflicting value judgments are: abortion, homosexuality, treatment for AIDS victims, extreme health care measures, and treatment of the chronically mentally ill.

When dealing with ethical issues, there is often not a clear-cut answer to determining the ethical action in a particular situation. For instance, when does a client have a right to privacy in a situation in which a child may be at risk of abuse? If there is a clear indication of abuse, most legal jurisdictions mandate that the abuse be reported. But what about when there is only an *indication* of risk? Or what about the client who makes threats against another person in the course of service? What about the mentally ill person who makes threats on her own life? All of these situations call for a professional judgment as to the seriousness of the situation. Another contemporary dilemma may arise when working with a person who is HIV positive or one who suffers from AIDS. If that person has not informed a sexual partner of the risk, does the social worker have an obligation to do so? The landmark case of Tarasoff v. Regents of the University of California (1976) is often cited regarding the liability of a social worker for failure to warn.[36]

There are no clear-cut answers to any of these situations. The Social Work Code of Ethics states: "the social worker should share with others confidences revealed by clients, without their consent, only for compelling professional reasons." It would then follow that the worker must be sure that a real danger to another person exists before breaching the confidentiality ethic. Yet, when a real danger exists, the worker must intervene on behalf of the at-risk other. A first step would be a careful and fully documented assessment of the situation. Next would be an attempt to persuade the client to self-reveal to the at-risk other. If this fails to occur in a timely manner, the worker, usually after informing the client, should take steps to insure that the other is protected.

Clients should always be aware that there are limits to confidentiality and be informed regarding those limits. The worker should be aware of laws protecting and limiting confidentiality. They also must be aware of liability risks and standard guidelines for informed consent.

Valuing is a common human experience. It allows persons to identify what they hold in high esteem—the objects, instruments, experiences, conditions, qualities, and objectives that are worthy of human effort and interest. It is particularly important for the social worker to engage in the process of valuing. Each worker has developed an individual value system that at least in part is related to the societal and cultural value system of which he is a part. The social work values are also similar to the societal value system in some respects, but there are differences. Social workers must recognize these differences and develop ways of dealing with the tensions and conflicts that result from them. They must be aware of their own values so that unexamined values do not influence their practice.

The social work endeavor is based on the dual values of the worth and dignity of individuals and of social responsibility. These values can be expressed in these principles for action:

1. People should be free to make choices.
2. Individuals are important; individual needs and concerns cannot be totally subjected to community needs.
3. Workers should use a nonjudgmental approach to persons and their concerns, needs, and problems.
4. The social work role is helping or enabling, not controlling.
5. Feelings and personal relationships are important.
6. People have responsibility for others; for their needs and concerns.

CASE EXAMPLE

Understanding one's values is particularly important when working with older persons. In our society, which almost worships youth, health, athletic ability, and beauty in the young body, the negative attitudes toward the aging process and toward aging persons are very prominent. This often affects the older person's feelings of self-worth. A worker may be so influenced by these societal values that she is unaware of how negative feelings toward older people affect her relationships with older clients. Social workers also need to be vigilant that they do not accept the common myths about old age, such as: old people are alike, they are not dependable, they cannot learn. *Agism,* or discriminatory behaviors toward older people, has its roots in values. This discrimination is counter to the Social Work *Code of Ethics.*

The worker must constantly watch that he does not take away the client's rights to self-determination, to confidentiality, that he does not place institutional rules and family desires as more important than the wishes of the client. Quality of life issues are often difficult to sort out, but there must be an assessment as to what the client considers to be quality of life, and whenever possible that must be a guide in service provision.

When working with older persons, values about death and dying often come into play. Many younger workers attempt to avoid this area, but dealing with the process of aging calls for a person to come to grips with their mortality. For a worker to be helpful to older persons around this issue, she needs to have considered it in her own life and have come to some comfort with this topic, which is extremely value laden.

Thus, we see that in working with older people the social worker needs to consider not only social work ethics but societal values, their own values, and the client's values. These values often are not congruent. Strong feelings are often raised because of the discrimination experienced by older people or because of acceptance of societal myths. Often the worker's first task in working with an older client is to identify the value issues that are present in the situation.

SKILLS

Skill is the practice component that brings knowledge and values together and converts them to action as a response to concern and need. A sociological definition of **skill** is also useful in understanding the meaning of the term: a complex organization of behavior (physical or verbal) developed through learning and directed toward a particular goal or centered on a particular activity.[37]

Bartlett uses the term **interventive repertoire** to describe the bringing together of knowledge and values to respond to problems of social functioning. She describes this interventive repertoire as being made up of methods, techniques, and skills. Skill is seen as technical expertise, the ability to use knowledge effectively and readily in performing competently.[38] This formulation seems to encompass two important attributes of this particular component of practice. First, it is necessary to make choices from a variety of possibilities based on knowledge and value considerations. Second, the choices are in regard to action to be taken in relation to a social-functioning problem.

The more recent literature seems to use the term *skill* rather than *interventive repertoire* in discussing the action component of practice. Morales and Sheafor state that "the skill of social work requires both the appropriate selection of techniques for a particular situation and the ability to use techniques effectively." They discuss how this selection is based on a conscious use of knowledge and state that social work values filter this knowledge in determining appropriate skills for use in providing service. They believe that skill is needed both for the selection of appropriate techniques and for the ability to use techniques effectively.[39] They define skill as the social worker's capacity to set in motion—in a relationship with the client (individual, group, community)—guided psychosocial intervention processes of change based on social work values and knowledge in a specific situation relevant to the client. The change that begins to occur as the result of this skilled intervention is effected with the greatest degree of consideration for, and use of, the strengths and capacities of the client.[40] This would seem to point to a consideration of how to enable the client to use these strengths and capacities not only in the helping situation but in other areas of human functioning.

Social work does not have one skill but a wide variety of skills useful for many different situations.[41] It would seem appropriate to use the term *skills* for the action component of practice and to use the term *skillful* in discussing the competent manner in which skills are used.

Several attempts have been made to identify the core, base, or basic skills needed by all social workers. Betty Baer and Ronald Federico have organized the skills component of practice into four areas: 1) information gathering and assessment; 2) the development and use of the professional self; 3) practice activities with individuals, groups, and communities; and 4) evaluations. They listed the needed skill cluster in each of these areas and translated these skills into ten competencies.[42] Based in part on this formulation as well as numerous other statements about the nature of social work practice other formulations have been developed.[43]

The "Curriculum Policy Statement" of the Council on Social Work Education[44] provides the official statement of the skill level expected of baccalaureate and masters-level social work graduates. This is a complex document, but two types of skills are called for (although it is impossible to completely separate them): cognitive skills and interactive or relationship skills. *Cognitive skills* are those used in thinking about persons in situations, in developing understanding about the person and the situation, in identifying the knowledge to be used, in planning for intervention, and in performing evaluation. *Interactive skills* are those used in working jointly with individuals, groups, families, organizations, and communities; in communicating and developing understanding; in joint planning; and in carrying out the plans of action. A social worker must be proficient in both types of skills.

Skillfulness develops over time as a result of practice in the use of the various techniques and methodologies. The development of skillfulness involves not only the application of knowledge and the operationalization of values but also the use of the worker's individual attributes and the development of a personal style of work. A useful analogy in understanding the development of skillfulness (and thus competence and personal style) is the musician. Musicians develop their skills and competence only after long hours of practice, practice that starts with learning such simple basics as fingering, note reading, and time concepts, and then progress to more and more complex techniques and music. The musician's personal style develops in the interpretation of the music. Similarly, it is only as the social worker learns to blend the cognitive and interactive skills that skillfulness develops.

CASE EXAMPLE

The skills a worker might use in working with older persons are many and varied. Certainly all situations will call for assessment skills, problem-solving skills, planning skills, and relationship skills. Different situations may call for skill in working with the individual older person or with a group of older persons, with a family group or with a community group on behalf of older persons, as well as working to develop services for older adults. Some older persons work best through use of activity, such as story telling or painting to express their feelings and thinking; others may be in crisis; some may need support. The worker will choose which skills to apply in each situation depending on the needs, the resources, and the client's desires.

CREATIVE BLENDING OF KNOWLEDGE, VALUES, AND SKILLS

The ability to combine appropriately and creatively the elements of knowledge, values, and skills in the helping situation is indeed an important characteristic of the social worker. This characteristic calls not only for choosing and applying appropriate knowledge, values, and skills but for blending the three elements in such a manner that they fit together and become a helping endeavor that is a consistent whole. This ability involves more than the blending of knowledge, values, and skills; it involves identifying and choosing appropriate, often unrelated bits of knowledge, and using not only social work values but also those of the client and the agency in order to screen the knowledge tentatively chosen for use. It involves skillful application of the knowledge and interactional skill to the situation. Because each person in a situation and each need for help is different, the knowledge, values, and skills to be used are also different. There can be no cookbooks, no standardized procedures that must be adhered to in great detail, though there can be generalized ways of approaching persons in situations. The application of knowledge, values, and skills can be approached only from a creative stance.

The creative stance is often expressed as the *art of social work* as opposed to the *science of social work.* This art is based on hunches and intuition, on previous experience, on very personal attributes of workers that are difficult if not impossible to identify. It is the social worker encountering the knowledge, values, and skills elements; choosing and applying so that the helping endeavor indeed is a unique work of art. Beulah Compton and Burt Galaway have described this art as having an emphasis on feeling, an empathic quality, and a high degree of subjectivity and of self-consciousness. It allows for the creation of new vistas and new perspectives.[45] It should be the essence of each worker's individual style.

Much of Lydia Rapoport's description of creativity is useful for understanding the blending of knowledge, values, and skills. She identifies qualities that creative people possess. These include a kind of nonconformity in opinion and judgment; high motivation and persistence in task performance; openness and receptivity to new information and ideas; a liking for complexity, a high tolerance for ambiguities, a capacity not to seek premature closure; a tolerance for contradiction, obscurity, and conflict; not too deep a commitment to particular theoretical positions; and thorough familiarity with, and knowledge of, all aspects of the problem.[46]

Rollo May has said that creativity is the "encounter of the intensively conscious human being with his world"[47] and adds that it "occurs in an act of encounter and is to be understood with this encounter as its center."[48]

The science and art aspects of social work, rather than being in conflict with one another, are complementary. As science and art are blended creatively in the use of knowledge, values, and skills, the essence of professional social work is expressed.

CASE EXAMPLE

Mrs. Abbott, an eighty-six-year-old woman, has been admitted as a resident to the Sunnyside Nursing Home. She is recovering from a broken hip and displays some confusion.

Her family and doctor have decided that she can no longer live alone and needs nursing care the family cannot provide. The social worker is responsible for helping Mrs. Abbott become comfortable in her new situation and for developing the psychosocial aspect of her care plan. To do this, the social worker will draw on knowledge, values, and skills to develop a relationship with Mrs. Abbott and an understanding of her needs.

First, the social worker will look to knowledge of human behavior with particular concern about knowledge of older individuals. The worker knows that important aspects of the behavior of older individuals includes their ways of coping with change and problems; the ways they relate to other persons, including family members and friends; and how they are functioning in dealing with the psychosocial tasks of aging. The worker will need to determine Mrs. Abbott's coping patterns, values, and skills; the nature of her interpersonal relationships; and her psychosocial development status.

The worker will also look to understandings about crisis and particularly the crisis of needing to leave a home and familiar surroundings. This yields the knowledge that older persons are often confused in new situations. When moving to nursing homes, they need support and help in finding their place in the new situations. In Mrs. Abbott's situation she is also faced with limited mobility because of the broken hip, which adds to the crisis of change. This knowledge not only gives some understanding about Mrs. Abbott's behavior, it also informs the worker about the way to work with her. Knowledge about crisis intervention says that the worker needs to be actively involved with the client as quickly as possible after the onset of the crisis and that the client can use some specific direction and needs to know that someone cares about, and will look after her.

The worker also knows from experience in working with older persons adjusting to the same basic situation that certain tasks need to be accomplished. Mrs. Abbott needs to know what the routine of the home will be and what will be expected of her. She needs to know who will be taking care of her and what resources and activities will be available to her. The worker also knows that Mrs. Abbott needs to maintain her relationships with family and friends and that the family may also need help in this new situation in order to maintain their relationships. The worker knows how Sunnyside Nursing Home functions and what resources it offers its residents. The worker also knows from experience that it is best not to try to gather too much information needed for the social history in one interview. Several short interviews are usually preferable to develop the plan.

The worker applies a social work value base in the work with Mrs. Abbott. It is important that Mrs. Abbott feel that she is still able to make choices about her life; that she maintain as much self-determination as possible. Ways in which this can be done include giving Mrs. Abbott the choice of which of her personal belongings can be brought from her home to have in her room and by allowing her a choice of which activities she will take part in from the total program available to Sunnyside residents.

The worker will recognize Mrs. Abbott's worth and dignity in the way in which past experiences and present feelings are discussed with her. These discussions will take place in a quiet, private area so that confidentiality can be preserved. The worker will strive to understand Mrs. Abbott's feelings and behavior rather than make judgments of "good" and "bad" and rather than plan for Mrs. Abbott before sufficient understanding is gained.

The worker will use skill in relating to Mrs. Abbott so that she will feel comfortable in expressing concerns and feelings. As information is gathered, the worker will skillfully develop a social history that will yield the understanding needed for planning. The worker will use skill in involving Mrs. Abbott and her family in the planning process. The worker will present the psychosocial plan to staff in such a way that they can become a part of the integrated care plan.

The preceding example provides only a portion of the knowledge, values, and skills needed by a social worker in this situation. It does, however, depict the creative blending of knowledge, values, and skills needed in carrying out the task of the social worker in meeting the needs of a client.

SUMMARY

Knowledge, values, and skills are all used in the social work endeavor. Knowledge is that part of reality that is confirmable. The knowledge base of the social worker is complex, partly borrowed from other disciplines. It explains the functioning of persons and social situations. It also directs the response to need. Values are what is preferred or can be considered as a guide for behavior. Values that concern social work are those of the client, the social worker, the profession, as well as the general cultural and societal values of the situation. These values can conflict with one another; in fact, a value system usually has conflicting parts. Social work values contain preferred conceptions of persons, preferred outcomes for persons, and preferred instrumentalities for dealing with persons. The Social Work *Code of Ethics* expresses what ought to be done in professional practice. Skill brings knowledge and values together and converts them into action. Skills must be developed through use over time. Social workers should have a variety of skills for use in practice. Choices are made as to which knowledge, values, and skills are applied in each practice situation. The bringing together of these elements calls for creative blending. The creativity is the art of social work.

QUESTIONS

1. Identify the knowledge you now have that you believe may be helpful to you as a social worker. How did you attain that knowledge? Do you see any incongruities among the various aspects of this knowledge? Identify knowledge you believe you should gain at this time.

2. What values do you hold about people and their relationship to each other? Do these values seem congruent with social work values and with its code of ethics? How will your values affect the manner in which you work with clients and others in social work situations?

3. How are your values congruent or incongruent with societal values as you understand them? How do you deal with situations in which your values and societal values are different?

4. What is the usual manner in which you develop skills in your daily living? How can you use this method in learning social work skills?

5. Discuss the concept of "creativity" as it is used in meeting clients needs.

SUGGESTED READINGS

Abramson, Marcia. "Keeping Secrets: Social Workers and AIDS." *Social Work* 35 (March 1990): 169–173.

Baer, Betty L., and Federico, Ronald C. *Educating the Baccalaureate Social Worker.* Cambridge, MA: Ballinger, 1978 (Chapters 8 and 9, pp. 115–129).

Bartlett, Harriett M. *The Common Base of Social Work Practice.* New York: National Association of Social Workers, 1970 (Chapters 4 and 5).

Canda, E. R. "Conceptualizing Spirituality for Social Work: Insights from Diverse Perspectives." *Social Thought* 14 (1988): 30–46.

DeRoos, Yosikazu S. "Development of Practice Wisdom Through Human Problem Solving Processes." *Social Service Review* 64 (June 1990): 276–287.

Freedberg, Sharon. "Self-Determination: Historical Perspectives and Effects on Current Practice." *Social Work* 34 (January 1989): 33–38.

Gelman, Sheldon. "Risk Management through Client Access to Case Records." *Social Work* 37 (January 1992): 73–99.

Gelfand, Bernard. *The Creative Practitioner: Creative Theory and Method for the Helping Services.* New York: The Haworth Press, 1988 (Chapter 2).

Goldstein, Eda G. "Knowledge Base of Clinical Social Work." *Social Work* 25 (May 1980): 173–178.

Goldstein, Howard. "The Knowledge Base of Social Work Practice: Theory, Wisdom, Analogue, or Art." *Families in Society: The Journal of Contemporary Human Services* 71 (January 1990): 3–12.

———. "The Neglected Moral Link in Social Work Practice." *Social Work* 32 (May–June 1987): 181–186.

Gordon, William E. "Knowledge and Value: Their Distinction and Relationship in Clarifying Social Work Practice." *Social Work* 10 (July 1965): 32–39.

Hartman, Ann. "Many Ways of Knowing." *Social Work* 35 (January 1990): 3–4.

Imre, Roberta Wells. "The Nature of Knowledge in Social Work." *Social Work* 29 (January–February 1984): 41–45.

Kopels, Sandra, and Kagle, Jill D. "Do Social Workers Have a Duty to Warn?" *Social Service Review* 67 (March 1993): 101–126.

Lowenberg, Frank M. *Ethical Decisions for Social Work Practice.* Itasca, IL: F. E. Peacock, 1992.

Morales, Armando, and Sheafor, Bradford W. *Social Work: A Profession of Many Faces,* 4th ed. Boston: Allyn and Bacon, 1987 (Chapters 7, 8, and 9).

Nicholson, Barbara L., and Matross, Gerald N. "Facing Reduced Decision-Making Capacity in Health Care: Methods for Maintaining Client Self Determination." *Social Work* 344 (May 1989): 234–238.

Padilla, Yolanda C. "Social Science Theory on the Mexican American Experience." *Social Service Review* 64 (June 1990): 261–275.

Peile, Colin. "Determinism versus Creativity: Which Way for Social Work?" *Social Work* 38 (March 1993): 127–134.

Reamer, Frederic. "AIDS, Social Work, and the 'Duty to Protect.'" *Social Work* 36 (January 1991): 56–60.

Reamer, Frederic G. "AIDS and Social Work: The Ethics and Civil Liberties Agenda." *Social Work* 38 (July 1993): 412–419.

Reamer, Frederic G. *Ethical Dilemmas in Social Service,* 2nd ed. New York: Columbia University Press, 1990.

Reid, William J. "Mapping the Knowledge Base of Work." *Social Work* 26 (March 1981): 124–132.

Rein, Martin, and White, Sheldon H. "Knowledge for Practice." *Social Service Review* 55 (March 1981): 1–41.

Rhodes, Margaret. "Gilligan's Theory of Moral Development as Applied to Social Work." *Social Work* 30 (March–April 1985): 101–113.

Ross, Judith W. "Are Social Work Ethics Compromised?" *Health and Social Work* 17 (August 1992): 163–165.

Rothman, Jack. "Client Self-Determination: Untangling the Knot." *Social Service Review* 63 (December 1989): 598–612.

Ryan, Caitlin, and Rowe, Mona J. "AIDS: Legal and Ethical Issues." *Social Casework* 69 (June 1988): 324–333.

Schwartz, Gerald. "Confidentiality Revisited." *Social Work* 34 (May 1989): 223–226.

Scott, Dorothy. "Practice Wisdom: The Neglected Source of Practice Research." *Social Work* 35 (November 1990): 364–368.

Sheator, Bradford W., Horejsi, Charles R., and Horejsi, Gloria A. *Techniques and Guidelines for Social Work Practice.* Boston: Allyn and Bacon, 1988 (Part I).

Shulman, Lawrence. "Developing and Testing a Practice Theory: An Interactional Perspective." *Social Work* 38 (January 1993): 91–97.

Siporin, Max. "Clinical Social Work as an Art Form." *Social Casework* 69 (March 1988): 177–183.

————. "Moral Philosophy in Social Work Today." *Social Service Review* (December 1982): 516–539.

Warren, Roland. *Truth, Love, and Social Change.* Chicago: Rand McNally, 1971.

Weick, Ann, and Pope, Loren. "Knowing What's Best: A New Look at Self-Determination." *Social Casework* 69 (January 1988): 10–16.

Wells, Carolyn Cressy. *Social Work Ethics: Day to Day,* 2nd ed. New York: Longman, 1986.

Witkin, Stanley L., and Gottschulk, Shimon. "Alternative Criteria for Theory Evaluation." *Social Service Review* 62 (June 1988): 211–224.

Wetzel, Janice W. "A Feminist World View Conceptual Framework." *Social Casework* 67 (March 1986): 166–173.

Yu, Muriel M., and O'Neal, Brenda. "Issues of Confidentiality When Working with Persons With Aids." *Clinical Social Work Journal* 20 (Winter 1992): 421–443.

Ziefert, Marjorie, and Brown, Kaaren. "Skill Building for Effective Intervention with Homeless Families." *Families in Society* 72 (April 1991): 213–219.

NOTES

1. Harriett M. Bartlett, "Toward Clarification and Improvement of Social Work Practice," *Social Work* 3 (April 1958): 3–9.

2. Harriett M. Bartlett, *The Common Base of Social Work Practice* (New York: National Association of Social Workers, 1970); William E. Gordon, "A Critique of the Working Definition," *Social Work* 7 (October 1962): 12; and *idem,* "Knowledge and Value: Their Distinction and Relationship in Clarifying Social Work Practice," *Social Work* 10 (July 1965): 32–35.

3. For another early formulation of this perspective, see Werner W. Boehm, "The Nature of Social Work," *Social Work* 3 (April 1958): 10–18.

4. Bartlett, *The Common Base,* chap. 5.

5. William E. Gordon, "Notes on the Nature of Knowledge," *Building Social Work Knowledge* (New York: National Association of Social Workers, 1964), p. 70.

6. Max Siporin, *Introduction to Social Work Practice* (New York: Macmillan, 1975), p. 363.

7. Paul Davidson Reynolds, *A Primer in Theory Construction* (Indianapolis, IN: Bobbs Merrill, 1975), p. 4.

8. Ibid.

9. Ibid., p. 18.

10. Peter Berger and Thomas Luckmann, *The Social Construction of Reality* (New York: Doubleday, 1967).

11. For examples of this see: William J. Reed, "Task-Centered Approach." in *Encyclopedia of Social Work,* 18th ed., Anne Minahan, Ed. (Silver Spring, MD: National Association of Social Workers, 1987, pp. 757–765; Scott Briar, "Incorporating Research into Education for Clinical Practice in Social Work: Toward a Clinical Science in Social Work," in *Sourcebook on Research Utilization,* Allen Rubin and Aaron Rosenblatt, Eds. (New York: Council on Social Work Education, 1979); and Martin Bloom, *The Paradox of Helping: An Introduction to the Philosophy of Scientific Practice* (New York: John Wiley, 1975).

12. Howard Goldstein, "The Knowledge Base of Social Work Practice: Theory, Wisdom, Analogue, or Art?" *Families in Society* 71 (January 1990): 41.

13. Ibid., pp. 38–41. Included as humanistic alternatives are Narrative Theory, Social Con-

structionism, Cognitive Theory, Moral Theory, Faith and Spirituality, and Feminist Theory.

14. Based on material in Alfred Kadushin, "The Knowledge Base of Social Work," in *Issues in American Social Work*, Alfred J. Kahn, Ed. (New York: Columbia University Press, 1959), pp. 67 ff.

15. Note Berger and Luckmann, *Social Construction of Reality,* and Gordon, "Knowledge and Value."

16. For a helpful discussion of evaluating knowledge for use in social work, see Florence Hollis, "And What Shall We Teach? The Social Work Educator and Knowledge," *Social Service Review* 42 (June 1968): 184–196.

17. Goldstein, op. cit., p. 41.

18. For another formulation of the knowledge base see Betty L. Baer and Ronald Federico, *Education of the Baccalaureate Social Worker: Report of the Undergraduate Curriculum Project* (Cambridge, MA: Ballinger, 1978), pp. 75–78.

19. For a discussion of these differences see Gordon, "Knowledge and Value."

20. Muriel W. Pumphrey, *The Teaching of Values and Ethics in Social Work Education,* vol. 13 of the Curriculum Study Council on Social Work Education (New York, 1959), p. 23.

21. Herbert Aptekar, "The Values, Functions and Methods of Social Work in an Integrated Report of the Honolulu Seminar," in *An Intercultural Exploration: Universals and Differences in Social Work Values, Functions, and Practice* (New York: Council on Social Work Education, 1967), pp. 3–59.

22. Lewis Raths, Merrill Harmin, and Sidney B. Simon, *Values and Teaching* (Columbus, OH: Charles E. Merrill, 1966).

23. Milton Rokeach, *The Nature of Human Values* (New York: Free Press, 1973), p. 5.

24. From Robin Williams, *American Society: A Sociological Interpretation,* 2nd ed. (New York: Alfred A. Knopf, 1967), as discussed in Charles S. Prigmore and Charles R. Atherton, *Social Welfare Policy: Analysis and Formulation* (Lexington, MA: D.C. Heath, 1979), chap. 2.

25. Alan Keith-Lucas, *Giving and Taking Help* (Chapel Hill: University of North Carolina Press, 1972), chap. 8.

26. Gordon, "A Critique of the Working Definition," p. 7.

27. Aptekar, "Values, Functions, and Methods of Social Work," p. 17.

28. Charles S. Levy, "The Value Base of Social Work," *Journal for Education for Social Work* 9 (Winter 1973): 34–42.

29. Armando Morales and Bradford W. Sheafor, *Social Work, A Profession of Many Faces,* 4th ed. (Boston: Allyn and Bacon, 1987), pp. 205–207.

30. Werner Boehm, "The Nature of Social Work," *Social Work* 3 (April 1958): 10–18.

31. For a discussion of this new code of ethics see *NASW News* (April, May, and June 1980), Washington, D.C.: National Association of Social Workers.

32. For a discussion of balance, see Mary McCormick, "The Role of Values in Social Functioning," *Social Casework* 42 (February 1961): 70–78.

33. Henry Miller, "Value Dilemmas in Social Casework," *Social Work* 13 (January 1968): 27–33.

34. Keith-Lucas, *Giving and Taking Help.*

35. Roland Warren, *Truth, Love and Social Change* (Chicago: Rand McNally, 1971), pp. 273–299.

36. For further discussion, see Frederick G. Reamer, "AIDS, Social Work, and the 'Duty to Protect,' " *Social Work* 36 (January 1991): 56–60; Marcia Abramson, "Keeping Secrets: Social Workers and AIDS." *Social Work* 35 (March 1990): 169–173; and Sandra Kopels and Jill Doner Kagle, "Do Social Workers Have a Duty to Warn?" *Social Service Review* 67 (March 1993): 101–126.

37. George Theodorson and Achilles Theodorson, *A Modern Dictionary of Sociology* (New York: Crowell, 1969), p. 382.

38. Bartlett, *The Common Base,* pp. 80–83.

39. Morales and Sheafor, *Social Work,* chap. 9.

40. Ibid., p. 140.

41. See Naomi I. Brill, *Working with People: The Helping Process,* 2nd ed. (Philadelphia: J. B. Lippincott, 1978), chap. 9; Lawrence Shulman, *The Skills of Helping: Individuals and Groups* (Itasca, IL: F. E. Peacock, 1979); and F. M. Loewenberg, *Fundamentals of Social Intervention* (New York: Columbia University Press, 1977).

42. Baer and Federico, *Education of the Baccalaureate Social Worker,* Chap. 9.

43. One of the more important statements of social work functions and tasks is found in Allen Pincus and Anne Minahan, *Social Work Practice: Model and Method* (Itasca, IL: F. E. Peacock, 1973), chap. 1.

44. Found in *Handbook of Accreditation Standards and Procedures.* (Washington, DC: Council on Social Work Education, 1988 rev.), pp. 119–130.

45. Beulah Roberts Compton and Burt Galaway, *Social Work Process* (Homewood, IL: Dorsey Press, 1979), p. 28.

46. Lydia Rapoport, "Creativity in Social Work," in *Creativity in Social Work: Selected Writing of Lydia Rapoport,* Sanford N. Katz, Ed. (Philadelphia: Temple University Press, 1975), pp. 3–25. *Creativity* is defined as thought and action that leads to the forging of something new. *Artistic* is the ingenious, imaginative, and proficient application of what is already known. It is my position that these two terms can be placed on a continuum and that the blending of knowledge, values, and skills creates a newness because of the unique person in the situation.

47. Rollo May, *The Courage to Create* (New York: W. W. Norton, 1975), p. 51.

48. Ibid., p. 77.

4

SOCIAL WORK AS A
PROBLEM-SOLVING PROCESS

Learning Expectations

1. Knowledge of the nature of the problem-solving process.
2. Understanding of how the problem-solving process is used in social work.

The fourth approach to describing generalist social work practice is as a **problem-solving process,** one of the "hows" of social work practice. It is one of the ways of approaching concern and need, and it is one of the ways of organizing and applying knowledge, values, and skills. A problem-solving approach gives direction to doing something about concerns, or responding to identified need. It is an organized way of thinking about assessment, the person in the situation, relationship, process, and intervention. Assessment and intervention are also a part of the problem-solving process.

In many ways this chapter is an introduction to Part Three of this book. There the process is considered in much more depth. This chapter is placed in Part One to give the reader a sense of the overall process in relationship to the other perspectives considered in this part. It prepares the reader to consider Part Two, The Interactional Process, as embedded in a problem-solving process.

As social work searched for its commonalities in the 1960s, problem solving was one of the concepts found in casework, group work, and community organization. Helen Harris Perlman, in *Social Casework: A Problem-Solving Process,* states: "The casework process is a problem-solving process in that it employs the orderly, systematic methods which are basic to any effective thinking and feeling toward action."[1]

Murray Ross, in *Community Organization: Theory, Principles, and Practice,* discusses the planning process as a key concept in his formulation of community organization.[2] As one examines Ross's formulation, it is evident that the planning process is indeed an adaptation of the classic problem-solving process. Helen Northen, in *Social Work with Groups,* discusses the problem-solving theme in group work.[3] Wide applicability and its use by the diverse parts of the profession seeking unification caused problem solving to become one of the earliest identified commonalities of social work practice. It also became an important concept in developing integrative or generalist practice theory.[4]

Problem solving, of course, is not unique to social work; it is an important approach to human need in many helping endeavors. The problem-solving process is indeed the scientific process. It is one means of addressing the science component of social work practice as contrasted with the creative process, or art, of social work as was discussed in Chapter 3. The scientific process in one of its many formulations is used almost universally by scholars from all disciplines as they seek to develop new understandings of the material they study, and as they conduct formal research studies, indeed as they think about how to set up a study or how to answer questions addressed by their discipline.

Problem solving is the process by which the social worker examines the concern and need and identifies blocks to need fulfillment. This leads to problem identification and formulation and to seeking solutions for problems. There is no assumption that the client or an individual is the source of the block. Rather, all systems involved, including those systems in the environment, are considered as potentials for the source of the blockage. Furthermore, the blockage may come from the interactions of several individuals or systems. The knowledge, values, and skills of social work are used in understanding the nature of the problem and in identifying possible solutions. Creativity is also an important ingredient of the problem-solving endeavor.[5] The problem-solving work is carried out with, not for, the client. While feeling and action are very much a part of problem solving, the emphasis in this perspective is on the thinking or cognitive part of practice. In order to grasp the nature of the problem-solving process in social work, it is important to approach understanding from several perspectives:

1. Definition
2. Understanding of the stages of the problem-solving process as used in the thinking aspects of practice
3. Discussion of the process as used in worker-client endeavor.

PROBLEM

In order to develop a definition of the term *problem-solving process,* it is helpful to look first at the concepts of problem and process. *Problem,* according to *The American Heritage Dictionary,* is "a question or situation that presents uncertainty, perplexity, or difficulty."[6] This definition is rather inadequate without elaboration for defining its use in this chapter. 1) When does a situation become problematic? 2) When does a problematic situation become one appropriate for social work concern? If one looks at a problem in terms of both need and social functioning, clarification of the term becomes somewhat easier. Concern for and need of human systems is the basis of the social work response. When the need is seen as mitigating a block to social functioning, a problem of concern to social work is said to exist. This concern should be understood also to include potential blocks to human functioning so as to include preventive as well as ameliorative con-

cerns. The perplexing situation is the need to the removal of the obstacle
th   olution, goals are related to need
fu

human situation, and solutions are
us   concern of social work is narrowed
to   lily unblock the fulfillment of need
wi   the term *problem* within the larger
co   implies a somewhat more limited
an   on. **Problem** in social work usage,
the   which need fulfillment of any of
the   or has a significant potential for
blo   cannot by themselves remove the
blo

co   protection agency because she is
cry   leaves her four-month-old baby
the   y or more minutes). On talking to
wo   is indeed left to "cry it out." The
a y   understanding of how to care for
the   the child's needs then seems to be
onl   e. It is still uncertain if this is the
of   ersonal needs of the mother, lack
blo   ons and attitudes that might be

PROCESS

The   ocial work definition is used. Sal
Hof   nt patterning of a sequence of
chai   "[7] It is important to note three
qua   r stages, 2) takes place over time,
and   versible). However, this description   rocess, for there is also a cyclical
asp   g process, over time there is a
forw   a tendency to return to earlier

stages and a mixing of certain aspects of various stages. The irreversibility is not that one never returns to an earlier stage but rather that one can never return to an earlier state of sameness, since the input of the process prevents this.

The problem-solving process as used in social work has its source in the classic work of John Dewey[8] and in his description of the thought process used by human beings when confronted with difficult situations. This process has been referred to as "logical thinking" and the "stages of reflective thinking" and is the base for the "scientific process." Problem solving has been defined as finding—by stages over time and in a cyclical and irreversible manner—a way of feeling, thinking, and acting that will satisfy some need or remove some obstacle to achieving some goal.[9]

In the example of the young mother who allows her small baby to "cry it out," the worker would use a problem-solving process to decide what should be done in the situation. First, information must be gathered. The worker would talk with the mother, examine the child, and perhaps talk to the neighbor or other concerned persons. He would determine which needs of the child were not being met and also determine whether the mother, with help, could meet those needs. Plans would be made with the mother about how to best meet the most immediate needs. As this plan is implemented, the worker would continue to gather information such as: What kind of help can this mother use? Can she carry out her part of the plan? And what other needs exist in this situation? This will result in further explanation of the situation and more planning. The process of problem solving would be carried out in an orderly yet cyclical manner, moving toward a goal of meeting the needs of the young child.

Social work problem solving is specifically concerned with social-functioning concerns and needs, especially with those that are blocked and that cannot be met with resources readily available to the concerned persons. Social work problem solving, then, is finding a way through feeling, thinking, and acting. It progresses over time in a cyclical, irreversible manner that is focused on removing blocks to need fulfillment in social functioning that individuals cannot remove with their own resources.

THE STAGES OF THE PROBLEM-SOLVING PROCESS

It should now be apparent that the problem-solving process (as considered in this perspective) limits the concept not only to particular types of problems under particular circumstances but also to a particular process. It should certainly be recognized that all persons face perplexing situations and reach solutions in a variety of ways. However, the social work process is related to a highly organized and reliable manner of reaching solutions.

People in different disciplines for various usages have discussed the problem-solving process and have specified the steps in a variety of ways. The basic process remains the same. One way to specify the steps is as follows:

1. Preliminary statement of the problem
2. Statement of preliminary assumptions about the nature of the problem
3. Selection and collection of information
4. Analysis of information available
5. Development of a plan
6. Implementation of the plan
7. Evaluation of the plan.

In social work, the problem-solving process is somewhat different from the social work process. Problem solving is a part of the social work process, but the social work process is broader than just problem solving. It contains work that is focused on developing and maintaining a relationship and on beginnings and endings. It should also be noted that at each step of the process creativity is an important ingredient. Bernard Gelfand has recently pointed out the necessity of finding novel solutions in social work practice. He further suggests that the creative capacity of the social worker enhances the work to be done. Looking at situations in new ways and not defining plans for action until many ideas and possible plans have been examined are two ways creativity is used in problem solving.[10] Before discussing the social work process, each of these steps in the problem-solving process of the social worker is examined more closely below.

1. *Preliminary statement of the problem*—A clear statement of the problem is necessary before proceeding to subsequent steps. Often problem statements tend to be vague, global, and lacking in precision. This happens when the social worker fails to sufficiently examine a concern and to identify the nature of need or needs involved. For example, school dropouts or unwed mothers are often referred to as problems, but in this vague formulation nothing is said about the needs of individuals or other human systems, and nothing is indicated about how need fulfillment is being blocked. A more adequate formulation in the area of unwed mothers might be: lack of educational resources for teenage pregnant girls. In this statement, the need that is individual and societal is for education. The population having the need is clearly defined, not by a vague term *unwed mother* but by an age group in a particular situation, teenage pregnant girls. The block to meeting the need is identified as a lack of resources, or at least usable resources. The manner in which the problem is stated gives direction to all the stages that follow. Often the key to successful problem solving lies in what is known as **reframing,** stating the concern or problem in a new way, from a different point of view. The more precise the statement and the more individualized the situation, the more relevant and salient can be the goals and desired solutions. Usually, as one proceeds to further steps, the need and opportunity for greater precision of the problem statement arises, and this step is returned to for restatement of the problem.[11]

2. *Statement of preliminary assumptions about the nature of the problem*—This step is necessary to help make explicit the type of information needed for understanding and planning. As the problem is stated, implicit assumptions are made about its nature and cause, which provide indications as to the need in the situation and as to the block to need fulfillment. The social worker's knowledge base is another source for ideas about the cause of a problem. Since the overall goal is the removal of a block to fulfillment of need, it is necessary to examine the assumed block to determine if it is in fact the block. If the assumptions prove untrue, the very determination of this usually leads to new assumptions about the block. A return to an early step is called for, and new assumptions are made explicit so that direction can be established for the information to be sought.

3. *Selection and collection of information*—Determination of what is important to know about any specific situation is a skill. The identification of significant systems in a situation and of the need of each in relation to the problem gives some indication of the information needed. Sources for information should include a variety of perspectives that may be chosen from historical, social-psychological, biological, economic, political, religious, and ethical understandings.

Both the facts of the problem itself and the meaning of the problem to those concerned are important. Information should test the validity of the preliminary assumptions regarding causality, and the information collected should be based on a breadth of knowledge and related to theory appropriate to the situation. The worker's general knowledge base and value systems are influential in determining information to be sought. Hence, capacity for perception of situations as they really are and awareness of one's own prejudices and values are most important. Skill in the collection of information also calls for skill in communication and social interaction with persons who are sources of the information. The validity of such information is determined in part by the nature of both the communication and the social interaction. Creativity should be used in determining information sources. The values of social work call for the client to be a primary source. There is a need to determine and accumulate relevant evidence about the situation, and this evidence needs to be related to the salient features of the situation and to the presented concern of need.

4. *Analysis of information available*—Analysis of information is influenced and directed by the purpose for which the analysis is to be used. Some of these purposes are identification and assessment of the various systems involved in the situation, further definition and explanation of the nature of the problem, identification of additional information needed, and identification and formulation of relevant policy. Other purposes include determination of feasible goals and possible outcomes and of possible plans of action, interpretation of the meaning of the information gathered, and evaluation. The cyclical nature of the process becomes very apparent, for one returns to analysis as an ingredient of each step of the process. The carrying out of the process generates new information. Additional information is often called for at each step.

There are general considerations in analysis regardless of outcome desired. First, it is important to determine the nature of the information. Is it fact or opinion? How reliable is the source of the information? Does it agree or disagree with other information that has been gathered? Conclusions are only as reliable as the information on which they are based. Because reliability of the information available to social workers is often tenuous, it is important that conclusions remain tentative and that additional information be analyzed as the process proceeds.

The determination of salient parts and of the relationship of the various parts to each other and to the whole constitute another important aspect of analysis. The human situation is complex in even a seemingly simple problem. Considerable skill is involved in determining what is important in any particular situation. As the human situation is seldom of a cause-effect or linear nature, a systematic approach to analysis is desirable. This is assessment in social work practice.

5. *Development of a plan*—Information and its analysis lead to understanding of what can be done to remove obstacles blocking need fulfillment. A social worker uses assessment in developing a plan of action. Crucial to any plan is the goal or desired outcome of the problem-solving process. Goals develop out of analysis of the nature of the block to need fulfillment and how this block might be overcome or circumvented. Goals take into consideration how the situation might be coped with in a manner that will minimize the negative aspects of the situation. Goals are best stated in behavioral terms that describe a desired outcome in as specific a manner as possible. For example, a goal might be stated as "The family can discuss conflict and resolve it in a manner agreeable to all members" rather than "The family can get along better." Since the goal should be achievable, analysis of constraints and feasibility is called for.

When considering the matter of feasibility, it becomes apparent that there are constraints on any plan. These constraints arise in the various systems involved and in their environment. The agency and its policy place constraints on the service to be delivered. Availability of time, money, and other needed resources can be very limiting on the nature of the plan. Communities have expectations of the organizations, the individual workers, and the clients. The workers' skill and interests are important constraints. Even more important are the client's expectations, energy available, motivation, and capacity for change. This is not an exhaustive listing of constraints, since each situation is unique. What is important is that relevant constraints of each situation be identified and taken into account as the plan is developed.

Plans develop from a consideration of a variety of possible strategies and techniques. As a plan becomes more specific, the social worker will return to early steps in the process to gather and analyze new information needed for the specifics of planning. Consideration of a variety of plans is important in creative planning. Each plan should be evaluated for possible outcomes, not only in terms of goal fulfillment but in terms of other possible implications for the functioning of the systems involved. The final plan is typically a synthesis of several of the possibilities. The worker uses creativity in developing the synthesis and evaluative strategy.

6. *Implementation of the plan*—In social work, implementation involves interaction between people and is interventive in nature. It is action based on thinking that has its source in feelings about concern or need. In addition, it is action based on substantial knowledge from many sources that explain and predict behavior of persons in the situation.

7. *Evaluation of the plan*—This step may result in redefinition of the problem, expanded information gathering and analysis, or reformulation of the plan. If the goal has been reached, evaluation is an appropriate and necessary climax to the process. Regardless of the outcome of the plan, evaluation of what happened can lead to an understanding that can be transferred to other situations and to more effective problem solving in those situations.

As the social worker develops skill in the problem-solving process, thinking about the phenomena being confronted will begin to take place in orderly steps. These steps appear to be simple but are quite complex in application.

CASE EXAMPLE

1. *Preliminary statement of the problem is:* The child is not receiving adequate care to meet her needs.

2. *Preliminary assumptions about the lack of care include:* a) The mother does not know how to care for the child. b) The mother has needs of her own that are not being met. c) The mother does not have sufficient income to meet the child's needs. d) The community rather than being supportive is hypercritical.

3. The social worker now proceeds to check out the validity of each of these assumptions. He finds that not only does the mother not know how to care for the child but also that she is frustrated by "being cooped up" all the time with no social outlets. She does love the baby and wants to care for it. Her own mother died when she was very young and her grandmother, now dead, raised her. The worker finds that the mother is on Aid to Families with Dependent Children (AFDC). The neighbor reporting the situation is truly concerned for both the child and the mother but does not know how to help them. She is afraid of interfering.

4. In thinking about the information that has been gathered, the worker decides that this mother is motivated to give proper care to the baby but does not know how. She needs instruction in childcare. Some provision is needed for time away from the baby so the mother can socialize with friends. Budgeting help is needed. The mother's relationship with the neighbor needs to be explored (and more information gathered about that). It may prove to be an important resource in this situation. The major problem does seem to be the mother's lack of knowledge about childcare. A secondary problem is the mother's need for meaningful relationships with others.

5. The worker then begins to develop a plan. First he considers a homemaker or public health nurse to provide childcare instruction. He also investigates the young mother's club at a nearby community center (gathering and analyzing information) and discovers that this group would be appropriate in this situation. The group provides an opportunity for young single mothers to receive instruction in childcare, discuss the issues involved for them, and provides childcare during the meetings. This group is chosen because it not only meets the instructional need but to some extent the socialization need. The worker has also discovered that the mother and neighbor can be of help to each other. The neighbor is older and can't do some heavy chores. The mother is willing to do these in return for babysitting one night a week. As the neighbor has come to understand the situation, she has been able to give the mother suggestions and to provide support and companionship.

The mother says the neighbor is good to her like her grandmother was. The plan also includes the worker continuing to see the mother once a week for a three-month period to coordinate services, help with budgeting, and provide support. The neighbor will be involved in these meetings once a month to clarify any concerns. At the end of three months, the situation will be evaluated to see if further help is needed.

SOCIAL WORK PRACTICE AND THE PROBLEM-SOLVING PROCESS

The social work process is carried out in interaction with individuals—worker, client, and significant others. The interaction may be person to person or may involve systems of people. Thus, it is important for the worker not only to have skill in the use of the process in her own thinking but also to be able to carry the process out in interaction with others. Indeed, her role is often to enable or teach others to participate in interactive problem solving. The outstanding characteristic of the problem-solving process in social work practice is the inclusion of the client as much as possible in the work at each step of the process. The client expresses the need or concern that is the source of the problem. The client also furnishes much of the information needed in the process, validates information sought from other sources, participates in developing the plan of action and in implementing and evaluating it, and develops problem-solving skills to use in coping with other life situations.

Problem solving, a creative cognitive process, is used by the worker to think about a social work situation in order to develop understanding of the client in the situation, identify the problem to be worked on, and formulate possible plans and ways of intervening. The social work process, also a problem-solving process, is used with clients and **significant others** (persons with the capacity to affect a client's situation in an important way) to move through study, assessment, planning, action, and termination. Interactional in nature, it complements the cognitive problem-solving process.

One of the important considerations of the social worker when using the problem-solving process is how and when to teach the client how to use the process. When clients begin to use the process for themselves, they are enabled to have greater capacity to resolve other problems they may face in the course of daily living. Thus, we see development of problem-solving skills by clients as one means of enabling the client. Further understanding of this process is gained by considering each step.

1. *Problem or concern brought to worker or agency*—Usually the problem is not well specified when someone comes to an agency with a difficulty of their own or one about which they are concerned for someone else. Usually they are assigned to a worker to explore that concern, to identify the need(s) involved, to identify the blocks to need fulfillment, to formulate the problem to be worked on. Sometimes the concern is such that the worker goes out to a prospective client to determine if there is a need and a willingness to explore it with the worker. Occasionally, the worker and client have a mandate from a legal body to work on a need or problem.

2. *Initial statement of problem and its possible causes by worker and client*—At this point the worker begins to determine with the client if the client sees the need and problem in the same way that the worker does. The worker asks who has the problem. Why does the problem exist? The situation in which the problem takes place and its seriousness are discussed. Necessary clarification and modification occur to see if agreement can be reached. With at least some beginning agreement about the nature of the need and problem to be worked on, worker and client begin to explore together what might be causing the problem. The worker's preliminary assumptions are considered together with the client's thinking about the situation. The client is asked to give feedback on whether these assumptions might be valid. The worker shares with the client what might be happening in the situation. The worker uses his knowledge base to explain the situation and to identify the underlying factors related to the problem. The worker is also making decisions as to how competent the client is; how realistic is his expectation, and whether there is any imminent danger in the situation. The worker explores cultural diversity factors that may be a part of the problem or situation. When exploring causality, social workers look to the client's own behaviors, the situation in which the client is functioning relative to the problems, and environmental factors that may be contributing to the problem.

3. *Determination of desirability of continuation by worker and client*—Worker and client discuss the kind of help the client believes is needed. The worker also discusses with the client the kind of help available and the worker's recommendations. They discuss whether the agency and the worker are the appropriate source for help. Sometimes all a person needs is someone to help formulate their problem or to design the steps to be taken to unblock need fulfillment. In such a situation the client may decide not to continue. In other situations the client does not want to use the help offered, which the client can choose to refuse unless she is mandated to receive service. Sometimes the worker or the agency may not be able to provide the service that is indicated, in which case the worker would refer the client to an appropriate source of help. If no appropriate help is available, the worker may consider some means of resource development for the client or for future clients.

4. *Selection of information to be sought*—If the worker and client decide to continue to work together, the worker discusses with the client the information he needs in order to understand the problem and the situation more fully. If other agencies or professionals may possess needed information, a decision is made about obtaining that information and releases of information are secured. The client is asked to suggest people who may be of help. Family and friends are involved if this is appropriate. The worker may also begin to obtain information about resources that may be useful in this situation. The context of the problem is given particular attention. Problems arise in a particular context and must be solved in that context. Without a thorough understanding of the relationship of the context to the problem and how the context would affect any plan and its implementation, information of vital importance may be missed.

5. *Collection of information*—Once the necessary information is identified, worker and client carry out the tasks needed to collect that information. Wherever possible, the client is used as the primary source for the information. Sometimes clients do not realize the importance of a piece of information so the worker must take responsibility to explore the situation with the client. It is often advisable to solicit similar information from several sources so that validity can be checked.

6. *Assessment of person in situation by worker and client*—After gathering necessary information, the worker uses her knowledge base to consider the meaning of the information. She compares information from various sources, considers the influence of values and biases that may be at work, and develops an explanation of what seems to be happening in the situation. Yosikazu S. DeRoos has pointed out that in problem solving the worker has less than complete information. The worker also has limits on time for collecting and processing information. Thus, any conclusions reached must always be considered as tentative.[12] This is shared with the client and together they explore the client's view of the situation given this assimilated information. Adjustments are made based on any new information the client may provide. The worker and client again determine the desirability of working together.

7. *Determination of goals, outcomes, and constraints of any plan by worker and client*—If the decision is to continue to work together, the worker and client discuss what the outcome of their work together should be. The worker shares his thinking about what might be accomplished together, based upon the worker's cognitive problem solving. They discuss what should be accomplished and how much time and energy both the worker and the client can give to working together on the problem. Any other constraints that may be at work are identified and discussed. Preliminary goals for the work together are developed. A preliminary contract is developed.

8. *Determination of possible plans of action by worker and client*—The worker and client now begin to discuss ways in which they may go about reaching the goals discussed. The worker again shares possibilities based on her use of the cognitive problem-solving process. The worker's knowledge of possible strategies and of resources that might be available is most important at this stage. The worker discusses implications of the use of the various suggested plans. It is also important to be sure the means of the plans relate to the goals; to consider ends before means. Worker and client consider together what they know of the context of the problem and how each of the plans might work in that context. The client expresses reactions to and preferences for the various suggested plans.

9. *Synthesis and choice of plan, including development of detail (tasks, techniques, etc.)*—Together the worker and client now decide on how they are going to proceed in working on the problem at hand. They specify what is to be done, with whom, and by when. Goals are modified if necessary. Usually the final plan is a synthesis of the suggested plans of both the worker and the client.

10. *Agreement between worker and client*—When agreement is reached between the worker and client, a contract may be written or a verbal agreement made. The worker should be sure that the client understands the various parts of the agreement, what the client can expect of the worker, and the client's own responsibilities in the situation. The worker should also explore any negative feelings that the client may have about the contract before it is finalized.

11. *Implementation of the plan*—The worker and the client now can proceed to do what it is they have contracted to do together. The worker only does for the client what the client cannot do for himself. The worker gives the client help, support, and direction in carrying out his tasks.

12. *Evaluation by worker and client*—Whenever it seems appropriate the worker and client stop to assess how their plan is working out. Are expected changes happening? If not, why not? Is there a need to change the plan or the contract? Are the goals feasible or appropriate? This evaluation is particularly important when the tasks laid out in the contract have been accomplished. In that case, the focus is on whether the goals have been reached.

13. *Return to appropriate step or termination*—If the goals have been reached, it is time to move to the termination phase, unless there is some agreement that there are other problems to be worked on. If other problems remain, the process begins anew. If the goals have not been reached, consideration needs to be given as to why they have not been reached. The worker and the client determine together whether to return to some earlier step or to terminate at this point.

Although the social work process is an orderly one with specified steps, it does not proceed in a clear-cut manner. Worker and client are often working simultaneously on two or more steps (and in the process building a cooperative relationship). The social work process is a problem-solving one that combines the rational, cognitive, problem-solving process of the worker with the problem-solving work carried out by the worker and client together. The social work process is also a means to teach clients problem-solving skills so that when they meet other problems in social functioning they will be better able to deal with them.

CASE EXAMPLE

1. *Problem or concern is brought to worker or agency*—Mrs. G, an adult foster home provider for the public social service agency in a small midwestern county seat, informs the worker that she is no longer able to provide care for Mrs. B, who is an agency client placed in Mrs. G's home for supervised living care.

2. *Initial statement of problem and possible cause by worker and client*—Mrs. G states that Mrs. B is lazy and will do nothing for herself. She steals things, including pills from the medicine cabinet. The worker has an uneasy feeling about Mrs. G. She feels that Mrs. G may not be caring for Mrs. B as the agency expected. Her monthly visits have left her unsure about what was going on.

3. *Determination of desirability of continuation by worker and client*—The worker talks to Mrs. B, who says she wants to move. She says Mrs. G is no longer her friend. Mrs. B says she wants the worker to help her find a place where she can live alone in another town.

4. *Selection of information to be sought*—The worker decides she needs a better understanding of Mrs. B and her needs. She wants information about her life history. This would help her understand Mrs. B's strengths and limitations, particularly as they relate to her living alone. She also wants to review why the decision was made for Mrs. B to live with Mrs. G and what has happened since she has been living with Mrs. G.

5. *Collection of information*—The worker reviews the record and finds that Mrs. B has been known to the agency for many years. She was abandoned by her parents before she was five years old. She grew up in ten different foster homes. When she was fifteen, she was sent to the state hospital because of her "peculiar" behavior. She remained in the hospital until she was twenty-one. From that time until two years ago, when she was forty-eight years old and placed with Mrs. G, she has had five more admissions to the state hospital. These were all for excessive use of alcohol. She has been married three times, but none of her marriages lasted more than three years. Her two children by the first marriage were placed in foster care during one of her hospitalizations. They were never returned to her care and have always considered their foster parents as adoptive parents. They live in a distant city and have little contact with their mother. Mrs. B talks about the children but does not seem to want to change the relationship with them. She has been diagnosed as a schizoid personality with moderate retardation.

About two and a half years ago, when she was living in a nursing home, Mrs. B became friends with Mrs. G. Mrs. B was very unhappy in the home. Mrs. G offered to let her live in her basement apartment. The agency agreed to this on the condition that Mrs. G would furnish meals and supervise medication. The agency provided a protective payee for her SSI (Supplemental Security Income) disability payment. In the beginning all seemed to go quite well. Mrs. G is a dominating person and seemed to enjoy giving Mrs. B the supervision she needed. But recently Mrs. G seems to have developed a drinking problem. She also spends considerable time away from home with a man. She says she wants to rent the apartment. There is a housing shortage, and she can get good rent for it.

The worker then talks with Mrs. B to find out how she sees the situation. Mrs. B first talks about how Mrs. G has been treating her and how she wants a new place to live by herself. She talks about Mrs. G's drinking and her awful boyfriend. After Mrs. B has spent some time on this topic, she begins to talk about how good it was when she first came to live with Mrs. G. They had meals together and talked. Sometimes Mrs. G took her shopping. Mrs. B also talked a lot about her many hospitalizations. She showed great fear that Mrs. G would send her back to the hospital. The worker assured Mrs. B that Mrs. G has no power to send her back to the hospital. She asks Mrs. B what it is she would like to happen. Mrs. B says she would like to live alone in an apartment.

6. *Assessment of person in situation*—Mrs. G's needs are no longer being met by caring for Mrs. B. Mrs. B is in a situation where she is not wanted. This is just another rejection in a long series of them. When she had been rejected in the past, she often began to drink. There is the potential for this to happen again. Mrs. B must be moved to a new setting. This must be done in a manner that minimizes feelings of rejection by Mrs. G.

7. *Determination of goals, outcomes, and constraints of the plan*—One of the client's goals seems to be that of living independently. The worker first sees this as unrealistic. Mrs. B has never been able to live independently. However, as the worker talks to Mrs. B (she returns to earlier steps in the process), she discovers that Mrs. B has been preparing her own meals much of the time during the last three months. She has been left alone in the basement apartment for several days at a time. She seems to want to care for herself (Step 5). The worker decides that Mrs. B may be able to live independently if she has a support system to help her ease into this kind of living. The worker believes that to accept Mrs. B's plan would minimize the rejection by Mrs. G (Step 6). The worker also knows that Newtown, about thirty-five miles away, has the potential for such a support system. It is decided to work toward the goal of independent living for Mrs. B in Newtown. The worker discusses the plan with her supervisor, and after some discussion the supervisor agrees to it.

8. *Determination of possible plans of action*—The worker now considers how to set up the support system. Using the problem-solving process, she determines several possible plans. The homemaker service in Newtown could provide a homemaker for part of each day, who would both supervise and teach Mrs. B in her activities of daily living. The public health nurse could also be of help in supervising Mrs. B's activities. As Mrs. B must take medication, a nurse would be a good choice. The worker could plan for daily visits to Mrs. B for the first week, and then several times a week for a period of time.

Mrs. B is going to need to learn to shop for groceries, and she will need help in planning how to use them. The worker knows of a vacant apartment overlooking the town square in Newtown. It will need to be cleaned.

9. *Choice of a plan*—a) To move Mrs. B to an independent living situation in Newtown, and b) to set up a support system for Mrs. B that will gradually allow her to become as independent as possible.

10. *Agreement*—The worker and Mrs. B agree on the plan for independent living. They discuss and agree on specifics. Worker discusses with Mrs. B the kind of help she believes she will need in beginning to live independently. (This has already been discussed. Now the worker and Mrs. B discuss it again to determine the specific supports.) The worker specifies what is to be done to set up these supports.

In this case we see the worker using the problem-solving process to assess a person in a situation and in planning for and with the client. The worker moves from step to step, returning to earlier steps, as new information is needed, becomes known, and as new plans must be made. The client is involved in the entire process. We also see the client enabled to move to a higher level of social functioning and to begin to take control of her life in positive ways.

SUMMARY

The problem-solving process is a means of responding to concern and need and of applying knowledge, values, and skills to work with clients using the concepts of assessment, person in the situation, relationship, process, and intervention. Problems that concern the social worker are those in which needs related to social functioning are blocked and cannot be readily unblocked by the person or persons affected. The problem-solving process is a means of proceeding over time, through stages in a cyclical manner, to unblock the need fulfillment. In social work practice the client is involved in the process to the maximum extent possible. Worker and client together proceed from an initial statement of the problem through information collection to assessment, planning, implementation of the plan, and evaluation of what happened in the work together.

QUESTIONS

1. What is the usual manner you use to solve problems? How is it similar or different from the process described in this chapter?

2. Think of a need of which you are aware. Use the social work problem-solving process to develop a plan for meeting that need.

3. Contrast the problem-solving process presented in this chapter with another formulation you have been presented with in another course.

4. What are the advantages of using a problem-solving approach with a client? What are the disadvantages?

5. Can the social worker always share all of her own cognitive problem solving with the client? If not, why not? How should such a situation be handled?

SUGGESTED READINGS

Brown, Lester B., and Levitt, John L. "A Methodology for Problem-Solving Identification." *Social Casework* 60 (July 1979): 408–415.

Compton, Beulah Roberts, and Galaway, Burt. *Social Work Processes*, 3rd ed. Homewood IL: Dorsey Press, 1984 (Chapter 8).

DeRoos, Yosikazu. "The Development of Practice Wisdom through Human Problem-solving Processes." *Social Services Review* 64 (June 1990): 278–287.

Gelfand, Bernard. *The Creative Practitioner: Creative Theory and Method for the Helping Services.* New York: The Halworth Press, 1988.

Murdach, Allison D. "A Political Perspective in Problem Solving." *Social Work* 27 (September 1982): 417–421.

Perlman, Helen Harris. *Social Casework: A Problem-Solving Process.* Chicago: University of Chicago Press, 1959.

Spitzer, Kurt, and Welsh, Betty. "A Problem Focused Model of Practice." *Social Casework* 50 (July 1969): 323–329.

Sucato, Vincent. "The Problem-Solving Process in Short-Term and Long-Term Service." *Social Service Review* 52 (June 1978): 244–264.

Witkin, Stanley L. "Cognitive Processes in Clinical Practice." *Social Work* 27 (September 1982): 389–395.

NOTES

1. Helen Harris Perlman, *Social Casework: A Problem-Solving Process* (Chicago: University of Chicago Press, 1957), p. 3.

2. Murray Ross, *Community Organization: Theory, Principles, and Practice* (New York: Harper & Row, 1955).

3. Helen Northen, *Social Work with Groups* (New York: Columbia University Press, 1969).

4. See Kurt Spitzer and Betty Welsh, "A Problem Focused Model of Practice," *Social Casework* 50 (June 1969): 323–329. See also Beulah Roberts and Burt Galaway, *Social Work Processes*, 3rd ed. (Homewood, IL: Dorsey Press, 1984), chap. 8.

5. Bernard Gelfand, *The Creative Practitioner: Creative Theory and Method for the Helping Services* (New York: The Halworth Press, 1988), pp. 1–18.

6. *The American Heritage Dictionary of the English Language,* s. v. "problem."

7. Sal Hofstein, "The Nature of Process: Its Implications for Social Work," *Journal of Social Work Process* 14 (1964): 13–53.

8. John Dewey, *How We Think,* rev. ed. (New York: D. C. Heath, 1933).

9. Adapted with additions from John Keltner, *Group Discussion Process* (New York: Longman, Green and Co., 1975), p. 32.

10. Gelfand, *The Creative Practitioner.* The entire book is an excellent resource on the relationship between creativity and problem solving.

11. For further discussion of problem statements, see Lester Brown and John L. Levitt, "A Methodology for Problem-System Identification," *Social Casework* 60 (July 1979): 408–415, and Allen Pincus and Anne Minahan, *Social Work Practice: Model and Method* (Itasca, IL: F. E. Peacock, 1973), chap. 6.

12. Yosikazu S. DeRoos, "The Development of Practice Wisdom through Human Problem-Solving Processes," *Social Service Review* 62 (June 1990): 276–287.

5

SOCIAL WORK AS INTERVENTION INTO HUMAN TRANSACTIONS

Learning Expectations

1. Understanding of the concept of intervention.
2. Understanding of the nature of human transactions.
3. Understanding of the concept of influence.
4. Understanding of the nature of the change sought by the social worker.

Intervention into human transactions is the fifth and last of the perspectives on generalist social work practice to be considered. It is another way of discussing the "what" of social work practice. Discussion of this perspective calls for: 1) consideration of the meaning of intervention, 2) discussion of transactions as the focus of change, 3) influence as a means of intervention, and 4) consideration of the change sought in social work practice. Problem solving is used to determine the nature of the problems of human functioning and the goals of the practice activity. Intervention into transactions is the practice activity related to the process of influencing for change. The two complement each other: both are responses to need and call for the creative blending of knowledge, values, and skills.

This perspective describes a contemporary perspective on the nature of practice based on understandings developed from use of a social systems perspective and from practice wisdom developed by the author. Other contemporary writers seem to be using a similar approach,[1] one that seems particularly useful when practicing in a generalist framework with the multisystem focus.

INTERVENTION

The term *intervention* began to appear in the social work literature in the late 1950s and early 1960s. At first there seemed to be little explanation of the meaning of the term. It was being used in place of the term *treatment* as used in the "study, diagnosis, and treatment" description of the social work process. Usually the use of *intervention* was accompanied by the term *assessment* in place of the more traditional word, *diagnosis*.[2]

This change came about because of a variety of influences and marked the beginning of the contemporary conceptualization of social work practice. Some of the more important influences for this change include:

1. The use of newer conceptualizations of ego psychology, emphasizing coping and social functioning, raised questions regarding continued employment of the medical model. *Diagnosis* and *treatment* are terms that have strong connotations of medicine and illness.

2. Attempts to find the commonality in the practice theory of casework, group work, and community organization increased. Community organization practice and some types of group work practice did not fit into the concept of treatment, so that different terminology became necessary to capture the commonality of practice.

3. The growing diversity of practice modalities, many of which rejected the medical model, entailed new ways of approaching practice situations and new terminology. *Intervention* was a term used in some of the other helping professions, and like many other borrowed terms, social work adopted it for its own use.

4. The use of social systems theory grew. When considering a person or persons in a situation from a social systems point of view, the notion of change coming about from "intervention into social systems" seemed a logical progression.[3] Intervention is congruent with systemic thinking. The social systems framework highlights the importance of relationships among systems and the influence of change in one subsystem on the need for change in other subsystems. Thus, the notion that change in relationships between systems (or subsystems of the larger system) is a valid target for change.

5. A more aggressive practice stance developed. During the 1960s, social work became involved with new problems, new groups of clients, and new situations. Many of these called for aggressive strategies and techniques rather than older strategies and techniques that encouraged clients to develop insight or to think logically and then make their own changes based on their new insights and thinking.

This change represented not just a change of terminology but a change in the way of looking at the person in the situation. It was an indication of the new paradigm discussed in Chapter 2. Assessment began to focus on roles, relationships, and interactions rather than on intrapersonal aspects of the client's life.

It dealt with the environmental factors to a much greater extent than had previously been the case. A great deal of new knowledge was available for use by social workers and this knowledge was ordered in new ways. The focus came to be on relationships of systems rather than on systems as separate entities. This shift in focus called for a new kind of analysis, one that was multidimensional in nature.[4]

Intervention is the activity of the worker in bringing about change in a systemic sense. It represents a leap in social work thinking from understanding a person in a situation to purposefully bringing about change in the person-situation phenomenon. *Intervention*, as conceived of in this work is: specific action by a worker in relation to human systems or processes in order to induce change. The action is guided by knowledge and professional values as well as by the skillfulness (competence level) of the worker. Intervention is purposeful, goal directed, and makes use of the worker's helping repertoire (including his creativity, knowledge, values, and skills).

As used in social work, intervention does not assume control of either the client or the situation. Not only is absolute control impossible in most human situations but it is also contrary to social work values. What is expected is that the worker will move with the "stream of life," the developmental process of the systems in the relationship, and that in so doing the worker, by means of actions and other types of input into the situation, will influence that stream of life. This influence will change the course of events that could be expected if there were no intervention. The course of events is also changed by the reactions and interactions of the client and others in the situation. The change in the course of events can be of a preventive as well as ameliorative nature. The social work input consists of perceptions and understanding about what is happening, identification of needs in a situation, enhancement of problem solving, and knowledge of and help in getting specific resources the worker can bring to bear in the situation to meet needs and solve problems. This approach to intervention places considerable stress on enabling clients not only to engage in the helping endeavor but also on enabling them to become heavily involved in change-producing behaviors of their own.

Intervention, then, is action guided by the worker's knowledge, values, and skill directed toward the achievement of specific ends. Intervention encompasses the concepts of treatment, planned change, and social intervention as they have been used in the social work literature.

CASE EXAMPLE

A social worker in a small rural hospital, on finding that a patient who has AIDS is not receiving needed routine care, decides that intervention is called for. First the social worker, John, asks the patient, Bob, for detailed information about the care he has received in the last twenty-four hours. John also asks who on the staff has come into his room. He finds that Bob has not been given a bath and his room has not been cleaned. Bob is on complete bed rest and yet has been given a urinal to keep by his bed, which has only been emptied twice in the last twenty-four hours. Bob has been given no meal choice, though this would be indicated according to orders on his chart. Based on his knowledge of the usual care given to patients, John believes he now has sufficient information on which to determine that Bob is being discriminated against regarding the provision of care.

John decides that his social work value system indicates that he has a responsibility to intervene so that Bob receives the care that he deserves. John knows that the hospital personnel have not received sufficient education about the nature of AIDS, and that Bob is the first AIDS patient that has been admitted to this hospital. John decides that his next step is to question discreetly the head nurse about the situation. The nurse states that they are very busy on the floor right now with many critically ill patients. Because of this they are having to cut corners, some routine care is just not getting done, at least the patient has a urinal to use without calling a nurse. John senses that Head Nurse is resentful of his questions and not comfortable in caring for Bob. He decides that to probe further might cause more difficulty for Bob.

He next seeks out Bob's doctor and shares his findings. Dr. Blue says he is aware that the staff are afraid of Bob; they resisted his admission but had to allow it when Dr. Blue insisted. He says he has no patience with these people who believe all the scare stories about the dangers of treating an AIDS patient. They just have to take care of him. John asks if the staff has had any training for caring for an AIDS patient; Dr. Blue replies that he assumes they have.

John next seeks out the administrator of the hospital and shares his knowledge about Bob's care with him. Mr. Administrator states that this all happened so fast that the staff has had no preparation for this patient, let alone any special training. He says that it is evident that the staff are scared of this patient, and that there needs to be in-service training that will not only provide them with knowledge of safe treatment techniques but will also deal with their fears. He asks John to help him plan for this. John suggests they call the Head Nurse and ask her help with planning the needed in-service. John believes that this is one way to involve her in the problem and minimize her resistance.

In deciding how to intervene in this situation, John used knowledge he had about the hospital system and the interactions of the various subsystems. He saw his goal as obtaining better care for Bob as well as developing attitudes in the staff that would enable them to care not only for Bob but future AIDS patients without fear of contagion. To do this he knew that he had to work with the dual authority system of doctor and administrator. (He later found out that Dr. Blue had talked to the administrator before John came to him.) John also skillfully gave the message that he was not blaming anyone for the situation but was trying to find out why the problem existed and how he could help in solving it. His intervention was focused on changing relationships among subsystems in the hospital system. He also knew that this approach would enable the staff to look at their own caregiving and make changes they determined helpful.

TRANSACTIONS AS THE FOCUS FOR CHANGE

A major consideration of the interventive approach is determining what change is to be sought. More specifically, what change is possible in any given system? Careful consideration of this question in light of knowledge from social systems theory and from practice wisdom led the author to the conclusion that change of systems is not the target for change; rather, the target is change in the relationships among systems. The relationships among the parts of the systems affect the whole. The person in the situation is a system, a part, and a whole. Parts are systems in their own right. This target of relationships of systems (persons and groups of persons) is also valid when the focus of social work is on social functioning and enabling. Social functioning implies relationships, interactions, and ways of functioning with other persons and with social groups and institutions. If social functioning is the focus of social work, the target of social work intervention should then be the relationship among systems.

Gordon expressed this central focus of social work as "the interface between the meeting place of person and environment. . . . The phenomenon of concern is the interface in the transaction between persons and environment."[5]

Transaction denotes the nature of relationships in the person-situation phenomenon—not just a simple interaction but an interaction influenced by other interactions in the situation. Interactions, then, are affected by other interactions. For example, a mother-child relationship is influenced by a number of factors: the mother's relationship with the father and with other children in the family; by other relationships she may have had in the past, particularly with her mother; by the relationship of the father with the child and with other children in the family; and by a variety of relationships outside the family (see Figure 5–1).

In considering the nature of the family, John Spiegel has described transactions as the interplay among individual, family, and society. His thesis—that everything is connected to everything else—implies that there is a mutual interrelatedness affecting action between any two members of a family. This interrelatedness is also affected by environmental factors and by the mutual interrelatedness as it has extended over time. The individual is seen as filling social roles, having impact on the system, and having impact on other individuals.[6] Spiegel says that "any act of a person in a role must fit into the reciprocal and complementary actions of his role partner."[7] Problems in social functioning develop when these role patterns do not fit.

These understandings about the nature of transactions within the family system are applicable to transactions within any system and between any systems. By focusing on the transactions (the relationships) among systems, the social worker finds a realistic means to influence for change. Social functioning is problematic when the needs of one or more systems in the transaction are not being met. Thus, a transactional focus cannot be on any one system in the transaction but must be on the interplay among the systems in relation to needs. The desired change is one that brings the systems into harmony as they function together. It usually brings about change in the relationships among the systems. These relationships may be affected by issues of power, energy, communication, or motivation, as well as by external impingements on one or more of the systems in the relationship. Obviously, then, the intervention needs to take the transactional nature of relationships into consideration.

The transactional nature of relationships becomes especially important when the practice is with a person from a racial minority group. Often people from minority groups make decisions based on that culture's way of functioning. They may not understand the messages coming from a worker of a different culture or see the importance of any expectations from institutions that reflect the majority

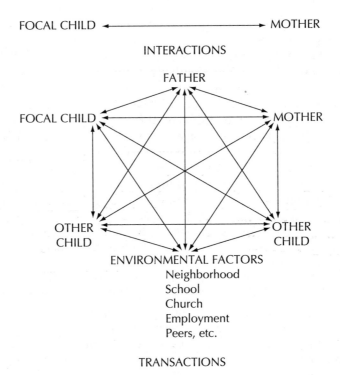

FIGURE 5–1   Interactions and Transactions

culture. In these situations, interactions may yield contradictory messages that add complexity to the transactions. In such situations there is a strong chance that interventions may have a negative effect by raising resistances to change imposed from the outside.

CASE EXAMPLE

The Chicano mother of an eight-year-old girl has been urged by the school nurse to seek medical help for her daughter's skin rash. The mother has not followed up on this recommendation and the school social worker has been asked to see what can be done. The social worker should consider cultural attitudes toward health care; this family's experiences with the school, school nurse, and local health care system; the family's relationships; and the family's decision-making process when assessing this situation. The difficulty or inability to follow through on the recommendation may be influenced by factors arising from any of the areas mentioned above. Difficulties can also arise from a language barrier, a lack of knowledge of health care and financial resources, or other family problems. The relationship of the mother and the school nurse or school social worker should be seen as transactional in nature.

INFLUENCE

Reality demonstrates influence, not control, best describes the worker's impact on a situation. As has been stated, the social worker does not have complete control and cannot guarantee a specific outcome when working from an interventive-transactional stance. Clients and others involved in the situation maintain the ability to decide what their behavior will be in the situation. This ability makes control by the social worker impossible except in those areas where he has been given the authority to control certain aspects of the client's behavior such as in some institutional situations, some work with children, protective service work, and probation and parole work.

Influence has been defined as "the general acts of producing an effect on another person, group, or organization through exercise of a personal or organizational capacity."[8] Influence is powerful. It can produce change, persuade or convince, overcome obstacles, motivate, and bring about attitudinal changes. Use of influence also recognizes resistance as serving a purpose when persons are exposed to new situations and ways of thinking. The social worker's input is to create a climate favorable for the needed work, heighten the motivation of those needing to do the work, "provide a vision"[9] for the work to be done together, and deal with the resistance involved.

An important base for influence is the skill and knowledge of the social worker in developing and using relationships with a variety of persons in a variety of situations. Influence can be exerted by those who know about and can use a planned change process. And influence derives from understandings about human development, human diversity, the variety of social problems, and the availability of services and resources.

Social workers use not only their own base of influence but that of other people with whom they are working. When working for change in situations, in organizations, and in communities, people with influence are very useful. Influential people may be elected or appointed to positions of authority, are respected and looked up to, have control over resources and information, or are involved in the decision making of any situation. They often are people who control from behind the scenes. Values are another important factor to consider in relationship to influence. People are more apt to be influenced for change when the change is within their value system, and provides something which is important for them personally.

Clients do have some choice of whether they will be influenced or not. To be influenced, clients must have at least some motivation for change. Some factors that affect their willingness to be influenced include: discomfort with the situation and a belief that it can be changed, a desire to gain position or resources, a desire to change the situation for someone else.

Nora Gold has stated, "Social workers can be very useful as motivators to their clients by increasing their sense of competence and control and helping them to recognize the power in 'seeing oneself as a potential force in shaping one's ends; and changing oneself with making whatever changes must come about.'"[10] Gold's quote is from none other than Helen Harris Perlman. This statement is very close to describing a process of enabling.[11]

Resistance is the opposite of motivation and is sometimes a sign that other influences on a person are stronger than the need for change. The Chicano mother, for example, may be influenced by the culture and family to such an extent that the influence of the school has little effect. There may be practical barriers of family responsibilities or lack of money influencing the situation. Using knowledge and skill, the social worker may be able to discover what is preventing the mother from seeking the needed medical care for her daughter and, using a problem-solving process, find a way of removing that block.

Barriers to change—to accepting influence—can be cultural in nature. Ideologies, traditions, and values are all a part of cultural influences on situations. Barriers also may be social in nature. The influence of a person's family or peer group, the norms of the situation, or the reputation of the change agent could be social barriers to change. Or the barriers may be organizational in nature: a competitive climate or an organizational climate that considers procedure rather than individuals. Family communication patterns are another important barrier to change. Personal barriers such as fear, selective perception, or lack of energy and skill also affect an individual's capacity to accept influence and to change. All these barriers are part of the transactive nature of relationships in a helping situation.

The influence process is carried out in a relationship with one or more of the systems involved in the transaction. This relationship is transactional in nature, so that it is affected by other relationships. The relationship between the social worker and the system being influenced is a major source of a social worker's influence. A major task in the social work endeavor is to foster the kind of relationships that allow the worker to bring other sources of influence to bear on the situation being dealt with. As the worker applies these various sources of influence to the situation, change takes place in the relationships among the subsystems involved in that situation. The worker's knowledge and skillfulness as well as social work values guide the decisions about what sources of influence to use and how to use them.

There are value considerations regarding the use of influence. Of particular importance are concern about the difference between influence and either manipulation or control. Clients and others typically do not understand the limits of the social worker's span of control and ascribe more authority to the worker than is legally allowed. Clients may think that the worker can withhold an income maintenance check if they do not do what they think the worker wants them to do. Situations of this kind can become quite complex when the client is acting according to what she believes the worker wants rather than because of anything the worker has said. Workers can use their ascribed authority to control clients. However, this negates the value of self-determination, and it also raises concerns about who has the right to do what and on what grounds.[12] Three questions can be used to determine if the use of influence is being used within social work values (all three must be considered).

1. Whose needs are being met by the use of the influence? If it is the client's needs, it is within the social work value system. If it is the worker's needs, it is not.
2. Whose goals are being used to determine the desired outcome for the use of the influence? If the goals have been established by worker and client together, it is within the social work value system.
3. Has freedom of choice for all concerned been maintained? If so, it is within the social work value system.

Influence is the major base for the social worker to use in intervening in the transactions among people and their systems. It is not used to guarantee a specific change but to allow the persons and systems involved to make choices as to how to change the relationships between and among themselves so that all can function in such a manner that the needs of all are met. Influence thus serves an enabling function.

CASE EXAMPLE

Using the example in which the social worker is working on behalf of the eight-year-old Chicano girl, the worker can influence the situation in several ways. She can discuss the cultural implications with the school nurse to see if the nurse's recommendations can be given in a manner that is more congruent with the Chicano culture. In doing this she is changing the situation by working for a change in the relationship between the nurse and the mother, thus changing the transactional nature of the situation. The social worker could influence the mother to follow the nurse's recommendations by either explaining their importance or by enabling the mother in seeking the health care needed, perhaps making a referral to an affordable health clinic or even taking the mother and daughter to the first appointment. If a Chicano aide is available, the worker could explain to this aide why the care is needed and ask her to work with the mother in obtaining the care, thus influencing a third party, who in turn will influence the mother. If the worker has seen several similar situations, she might work for change in the school system by such means as staff education about the Chicano culture or by influencing the health care system as to ways to make that system more useable by these clients. The social worker can also influence the educational system to be more responsive to the needs of all Chicano children and their parents.

CHANGES SOUGHT BY THE SOCIAL WORKER

Over the course of its history, the focus of social work in its role of enabling social functioning has been the subject of much discussion and debate. One of the earliest of these debates was referred to as cause-function.[13] This can be translated into: Is the change to be sought that of the larger social system, or is it the change of individuals from within? In discussing the change sought and social functioning, Harriett Bartlett has used the terminology "people coping" and "environmental demands." She states that "these ideas must be brought together within the same dimension and it is the idea of 'social interaction' that the writer thinks accomplishes this."[14]

People must cope within an environmental context. In coping they engage in relationships with the environment or, more specifically, with people in their environment. Thus, by changing relationships or enabling the development of new relationships, the desired change takes place. In the earlier example of the Chicano mother, the social worker may find that the mother does not understand the seriousness of her daughter's skin rash. The mother may not be able to explain the situation to other family members, especially her husband, who must be involved in the decision to seek help. She also may not be aware of resources available to provide the medical treatment indicated. Here the social worker might use a teaching/learning strategy to influence the situation. She could do this by telling the mother about two or three specific resources and explaining to her procedures for obtaining service from each resource or helping her to relate appropriately to the environment.

After the family has an opportunity to consider what it is they want to do, the worker might use an action strategy of going with the mother and child to the medical facility to obtain the needed treatment if she decides that the mother's discomfort in new situations might also be a block. In all that is done, the worker will be particularly sensitive to cultural diversity as it affects the situation.

In this example, the social worker could bring about change in the larger system of the school by providing information about the blocks to change. This might take the form of talking to the school nurse and discussing the need for the mother to have a better understanding of the seriousness of the situation and how a language barrier needs to be overcome. This would hopefully lead to the nurse being more sensitive in the future with other Chicano mothers. The social worker might sense a lack of understanding of Chicano culture by the school staff and discuss with the principal the need for in-service training for the staff.

Whereas change in relationships is the major focus of intervention, change in individuals and systems involved in the relationship must also be considered, for the means of change in relationships—the desired end state—is often change in individuals and in systems. Oxley has identified five ways in which positive individual growth takes place: 1) maturation, 2) interaction, 3) action, 4) learning, and 5) crisis.[15] This formulation is helpful for the purposes of this discussion because it looks to the **life processes** of individuals and the change that takes place over time as an individual lives out life (participates in relationships). The interventive-transactive approach looks to the life process, or relationships, and seeks to influence that life process for change. Enabling or enhancing maturation, interaction, action, learning, and crisis management are means of influencing the relationships (the life processes).

Change in larger systems takes place with change in the roles of people and the structure of their relationships in the system. This would include change both in the communication patterns and in the decision-making process. Change also takes place as subsystems are added or taken away from the larger system. Change takes place as new ways of functioning or carrying out tasks develop. All these changes call for individuals to change, and all involve the life process of the larger system. The social worker can be involved by enabling, enhancing, and managing change in relationships. The decision to choose a specific intervention is made by determining which changes within both the individuals and the larger systems involved can enable the needed relationship change.

Schwartz has described the role of the social worker as that of mediator. In his view, the worker's function is "to mediate the process through which the individual and his society reach out for each other through a mutual need for fulfillment."[16] It is through relationships that people grow, learn, and resolve problems and crises and that larger systems carry out their functions in society. The relationships between people and systems are important aspects of the helping process in mediating or enabling the resolution of problems of social functioning. Also important are the relationships between the social worker and the people and systems involved. As the social worker fills the mediation role, there is a strengthening and supporting of the efforts of individuals and systems to function in a mutually fulfilling manner. This enables not only more effective social functioning but growth of individuals as well. In intervening in the transactions among persons and situations, the social worker must be concerned with change in the nature of relationships. This calls for concern with individual change and larger system change.

The National Association of Social Workers Publication Committee and the Editorial Board of *Social Work* sponsored a project for study and debate about the purpose and objects of social work. One product of this debate was a "Working Statement on the Purpose of Social Work" (see Figure 5–2). The transactional nature of social work practice is supported by this statement, which also specifies the kinds of change the social worker seeks when working with clients and significant others.

CASE EXAMPLE

The treatment team in an adolescent psychiatric institution became concerned about the unrest that existed in the living facility. This state facility had twenty girls in residence ranging from thirteen to sixteen years of age. The girls had mixed psychiatric diagnoses. Some had been placed because there was no other available placement for them, some for diagnostic purposes, and others for treatment. One of the causes of the unrest was the placement of girls with this variety of needs in the same setting. Efforts were being made to transfer to another facility those girls who did not need a psychiatric setting, but in the meantime something had to be done to deal with the unrest. Part of the difficulty seemed to stem from a few girls who were constantly complaining about the way staff were treating them. They were aggressive and generally uncooperative. There was some indication that a few girls were involved together in an "extortion ring." They were apparently demanding money, cigarettes, and clothing from other girls on the unit in return for not physically abusing them. The staff seemed unable to control this situation.

After considerable discussion the treatment team agreed to allow the social worker to develop a discussion group with six girls on the unit. The focus of this group was to discuss the situation as it existed and seek the group members' ideas as to how the

Working Statement on the

Purpose of Social Work

(Developed by participants at the second meeting on conceptual frameworks)

The purpose of social work is to promote or restore a mutually beneficial interaction between individuals and society in order to improve the quality of life for everyone. Social workers hold the following beliefs:

— The environment (social, physical, organizational) should provide the opportunity and resources for the maximum realization of the potential and aspirations of all individuals, and should provide for their common human needs and for the alleviation of distress and suffering.
— Individuals should contribute as effectively as they can to their own well-being and to the social welfare of others in their immediate environment as well as to the collective society.
— Transactions between individuals and others in their environment should enhance dignity, individuality, and self-determination of everyone. People should be treated humanely and with justice.

Clients of social workers may be an individual, a family, a group, a community, or an organization.

Objectives

Social workers focus on person-and-environment *in interaction*. To carry out their purpose, they work with people to achieve the following objectives.

— Help people enlarge their competence and increase their problem-solving and coping abilities.
— Help people obtain resources.
— Make organizations responsive to people.
— Facilitate interaction between individuals and others in their environment.
— Influence interactions between organizations and institutions.
— Influence social and environmental policy.

To achieve these objectives, social workers work with other people. At different times, the target of change varies—it may be the client, others in the environment, or both.

FIGURE 5–2

Reprinted with permission from *Social Work*, Volume 26, Number 1, p. 6, January 1981. Copyright 1981, National Association of Social Workers, Inc.

problem might be resolved. All six girls chosen to participate were either leaders or had the potential for being leaders on the unit and were among the highest functioning girls on the unit. They included:

1. Mary, a fifteen-year-old black girl. She was considered the leader. She had been placed on the unit because no other placement had been found for her. She had been in several foster homes previous to coming to the unit. She was not mentally ill.
2. Alice, a fifteen-year-old white girl. Her mother had recently remarried and could no longer tolerate her in the home because of acting-out behavior. Alice exhibited much anger about this. She had been placed for diagnostic purposes.

3. Betty, a fourteen-year-old white girl. She had spent three years in a private psychiatric setting and had been placed in the state setting because she was considered untreatable. She was bright, manipulative, and constantly complaining about the staff and the other girls on the unit. She had an intact adoptive family who was very concerned about and involved with her.

4. Jo, a fourteen-year-old black girl. She was awaiting a more suitable placement. She had little contact with her family and had previously been placed in two different institutions. She had been removed when these institutions believed that they could not meet her needs.

5. Jane, a sixteen-year-old black girl. She had been removed from an unsuitable home at age thirteen, and had been unable to adjust to any subsequent setting. Her family had left the state after placement, and their residence was unknown to Jane or the institution. She was extremely angry and had no relationships with any adult. Staff were unable to determine her needs because of her resistance to communicating with any adult. She got along well with the other girls on the unit.

6. Terry, a fourteen-year-old white girl. She came from a middle-class home. Her behavior had become very unstable after her father died suddenly two years before placement. The family physician had recommended institutionalization. She functioned quite well at times, at other times her judgment was poor and she seemed confused.

The transactions in this relationship situation were complex, for there was not only the relationship system among the six girls but also the relationships with other girls and staff on the unit. In addition, each girl brought influences and ways of relating from very troubled life situations. Some of the girls came from a culture that was dominated by "street society" in which might ruled and weak persons were exploited.

The worker identified the desired intervention as one in which the six girls would discuss what the situation was that existed on the unit. In addition, they would be helped to consider what they might do to improve it. They would be asked to take responsibility for improving the situation rather than continuing to blame each other, the other girls on the unit, and the staff of the unit. The worker had to work with other staff to see that they understood the goal and to inform the staff that the focus was on the girls' behavior, not the staff's. The goal was a new relationship structure on the unit.

The group met weekly for two months. Though the discussion in the group remained superficial, the unit became quieter. The worker felt that a good deal of discussion about the situation by the girls in the group was going on outside the group meetings. The girls suggested several unit activities that they would like, and some of them were implemented. One that was particularly important was a role-playing activity. Staff played the role of girls, and the girls played the role of staff. Both the staff and the girls felt that they saw each other's behavior in a different light after this.

The group was terminated at the end of two months. Two members had been discharged. The unit was not as disturbed, and the extortion seemed to have stopped. The remaining girls were involved in other aspects of their treatment. Two, Jane and Betty, developed treatment relationships; previously, they had not been able to do so.

The intervention was into the transactions of a group of six girls. These transactions were affected by their former experiences and by the situation (system of the unit) in which they were living. The change in the transactions of the six girls also brought about a change in the system of which they were a part and in their other relationships. The worker's intervention was to facilitate discussion of a dysfunctional situation among persons who could take some responsibility for improving the situation. It involved a demand for social responsibility. The worker mediated between the girls and the unit on which they lived. The worker helped the group carry out some of their own plans for improving the situation. It enabled a change in relationships.

SUMMARY

Intervention is specific action by a social worker in relation to human systems or processes in order to induce change. It is purposeful and goal directed. It does not assume worker control of any situation but rather implies moving with and influencing the stream of life. Human interaction is transactional in nature; that is, all interactions are affected by other interactions. Social work intervention focuses on these transactions in order to influence for change when social functioning is problematic in meeting needs of one or more elements in the transactions. Influence brings about change by the exercise of the social worker's capacity. This capacity has a base in the worker's knowledge, skill, and reputation, among other factors.

The interventive-transactive approach calls for the social worker to identify needs and problems in social functioning; to apply knowledge, professional values, and skills, including the problem-solving process and creativity; and to influence the ongoing transactions relative to the needs and problems so as to bring about a change in the transactions. The change sought is the development of relationships that are need-fulfilling for all parties of the relationship. This development may result in new relationships or in a change in existing ones. In order to participate in the change process, the worker engages in two types of activity: 1) the development of helping relationships with the transactional system that is the focus of change (Part II) and 2) the carrying out of the helping process with the transactional system that is the focus of change (Part III).

QUESTIONS

1. What do you see as advantages and disadvantages of using the term *diagnosis* in the medical model in social work practice? Why do you think some social workers believe *intervention* is a more appropriate term?

2. Think about a situation in which you interacted with someone else. Identify all the influences that affected that interaction.

3. List value considerations that the term *influence* brings to your mind.

4. What do you think are ways you influence situations in your own life?

5. How is the view of social work presented in this chapter similar to your present understanding of social work practice? How is it different?

SUGGESTED READINGS

Anderson, Joseph D. "Toward Generic Practice: The Interactional Approach." *Social Casework* 65 (June 1984): 323–329.

Cimmarusti, Rocco A. "Family Preservation Practice Based on a Multisystems Approach."

Child Welfare LXXXI (May–June 1992): 241–256.

Germain, Carel B., and Gitterman Alex. "Ecological Perspective." in *Encyclopedia of Social Work,* 18th ed., Ann Minahan, Ed. (Silver

Spring, MD: National Association of Social Workers, 1987).

Gold, Nora. "Motivation: The Crucial but Unexplored Component of Social Work Practice." *Social Work* 35 (January 1990): 49–56.

Monkman, Marjorie McQueen. "Outcome Objectives in Social Work Practice: Person and Environment." *Social Work* 36 (May 1991): 253–257.

Monkman, Marjorie McQueen, and Kagle, Jill Doner. "The Transactions Between People and Environment Framework: Focusing Social Work Intervention in Health Care." *Social Work in Health Care* 8 (Winter 1982): 105–116.

Reamer, Frederic G. "Ethical Dilemmas in Social Work Practice." *Social Work* 28 (January 1983): 31–35.

Shulman, Lawrence. *Interactional Social Work Practice: Toward an Empirical Theory* (Itasca, IL: F. E. Peacock, 1991.

Simons, Ronald L. "Strategies for Exercising Influence." *Social Work* 27 (May 1982): 268–274.

Social Work 26 (January 1981). Second Special Issue on Conceptual Frameworks.

NOTES

1. See readings for examples of this.

2. See Carol H. Meyer, *Social Work Practice: The Changing Landscape,* 2nd ed. (New York: Free Press, 1976), chap. 5, for a discussion of the change in the use of terms.

3. For early formulations using this notion, see Gordon Hearn (Ed.), *The General Systems Approach: Contributions Toward an Holistic Conception of Social Work* (New York: Council on Social Work Education, 1969), and Charles R. Atherton, Sancha T. Mitchell, and Edna Biehl Schein, "Locating Points of Intervention" and "Using Points of Intervention," *Social Casework* 52 (March and April 1971): 131–141 and 223–228.

4. For a practice model that has this multidimensional focus, see Carel B. Germain and Alex Gitterman, *The Life Model of Social Work Practice* (New York: Columbia University Press, 1980).

5. William E. Gordon, "Basic Constructs for an Integrated and Generative Conception of Social Work," in Hearn, *The General Systems Approach,* p. 7.

6. John Spiegel, *Transactions: The Interplay Between Individual, Family, and Society* (New York: Science House, 1971). For another view of these ideas, see also Roy H. Rogers, *Family Interaction and Transaction* (Englewood Cliffs, NJ: Prentice-Hall, 1973).

7. Ibid., p. 96.

8. Irving Spergel, *Community Problem Solving* (Chicago: University of Chicago Press, 1969), p. 106.

9. William Schwartz, "The Social Worker in the Group," in *The Social Welfare Forum Proceedings* (New York: Columbia University Press, 1961), p. 157.

10. Nora Gold, "Motivation: The Crucial but Unexplored Component of Social Work Practice." *Social Work* 35 (January 1990): 49–56.

11. Helen Harris Perlman, *Social Casework* (Chicago: University of Chicago Press, 1957).

12. See Charles S. Levy, "Values and Planned Change," *Social Casework* 53 (October 1972): 488–493, for another discussion of these factors.

13. Porter R. Lee, "Social Work: Cause and Function," *Proceedings of the National Conference on Social Welfare, 1929.* See also the section entitled "Cause-Function Debate" in Chapter 1 of this text for a previous discussion of this idea.

14. Harriett M. Bartlett, *The Common Base of Social Work Practice* (New York: National Association of Social Workers, 1970), p. 100.

15. Genevieve B. Oxley, "A Life Model Approach to Change," *Social Casework* 52 (December 1971): 627–633.

16. Schwartz, "The Social Worker in the Group," pp. 154–155.

TWO

THE INTERACTIONAL PROCESS

Based on the overview of generalist practice presented in Part One, specific processes integral to the social work endeavor will be considered. In Part Two, the interactional process is explored.

In the simplest sense, the generalist social worker is a provider of services which vary in nature. They include provision of concrete services (such as income maintenance), assistance in problem solving, developmental services (such as group work in a settlement house), intervention into crisis situations (such as illness or loss of loved ones), and certain therapeutic services. It is not the service but the focus of the service and how that service is given that defines generalist social work. The service focuses on social functioning—the interaction of persons and social systems in meeting human needs.

In order to provide services that focus on social functioning, the worker must interact with individuals and social systems. How the service is provided has two dimensions: 1) the interactions of the worker and other people and social systems as service is provided and 2) the process of service provision. The interactions and service provision are simultaneous, intertwined processes. In this text they are artificially separated to enable students to develop in-depth understanding of each process. Part Two focuses on interactions. It also considers development of understanding of individual, group, agency, and community functioning as each affects the interactional process. In-depth understanding of these systems and their functioning usually has been obtained from courses in sociology, psychology, anthropology, and human biology, as well as from courses titled Human Behavior in the Social Environment, or something similar. Discussion in Part Two focuses on the use of this knowledge, including means of organizing it in service of the interactional process. In other words, understanding of the system both from a global and particular frame of reference is deemed essential for professional relationships. Part Three will treat the process of service provision.

A basic interactional approach is used regardless of the service being offered, although there are modifications and adaptations of that interactional approach depending on the service.

In its simplest form, the components of the interactional process are the worker and client interacting in an environment. However, the generalist social worker often is part of a multiperson worker system (e.g., a team) and often works with a multiperson client system (e.g., a small group or family). Thus, Part Two will also explore these kinds of interactions.

Chapter 6 discusses the worker component and considers five concepts: knowledge of self, the helping person, responsibility and authority, helping skills of the worker, and the multiperson worker. This chapter further develops the concept of common human needs.

Chapter 7 discusses the client component and considers three concepts: becoming a client, understanding the individual client, and understanding the family as a multiperson client. The concept of human diversity is expanded.

Chapter 8 discusses the interaction between one worker and one client by considering formation of a one-to-one action system, relationship, communication, and the interview as interactional tools.

Chapter 9 discusses the interaction when a multiperson worker or client is involved. The focus of this chapter is on the small group as a social system. The chapter also discusses the social worker as a member of a group, with a multiperson client, and with a family group.

Chapter 10 discusses the environment in which the interaction takes place. This environment includes the community from which the client comes and the community where the service takes place. It also includes the agency offering the service. Also discussed is the worker as an agency employee. This material is also relevant to working with organizational and community systems as the focus for change.

6

THE WORKER

Learning Expectations

1. Development of a framework for a continuous process of developing knowledge of self.
2. A beginning of the process of self-knowledge needed in the practice of social work.
3. Understanding of human need at various stages of the human development process.
4. Identification of the student's personal needs that arise from human development, human diversity, and membership in social systems.
5. Knowledge about the characteristics of a helping person.
6. Identification of the student's own motivation for being a helping person and of the attitudes and knowledge needed for the student to become a helping person. Identification of some of the helping skills the student needs to develop.
7. Understanding of the student's concepts of authority and responsibility and their relationship to the values of self-determination and social responsibility.
8. Understanding of the term *multiperson worker* and of its various manifestations.
9. Identification of the knowledge and skills that need to be developed in order for the social worker to function in the multiperson worker situation.

In the interaction of generalist social worker and client, the social worker is first a person with life experiences, human needs, and a personal lifestyle and value system. The worker is also a helping person with skills for interacting with individuals and groups and for developing relationships.

The worker brings to the helping situation a knowledge base that provides understandings about persons in situations, knowledge of helping methods and of means for implementing those methods, and knowledge gained from other helping situations. The worker also brings a value system based on professional values, agency and community values, and his own personal values.

In a complex society with complex social problems and multiple human needs, it is sometimes advantageous for the worker to become part of a **multiperson helping system.** A multiperson helping system consists of several workers who are involved in providing the needed service in a collaborative manner. Each worker has special knowledge or skill that is necessary for goal attainment. To explore the meaning of the concept of worker, three topics will be considered: 1) the worker as a person, or knowledge of self; 2) the helping person; and 3) the multiperson helping system.

KNOWLEDGE OF SELF

It has been said that the most important tool a social worker possesses is herself. To use that tool skillfully and knowledgeably, a worker must have considerable self-knowledge. This calls for a kind of introspective stance that seeks to bring personal concerns, attitudes, and values into the area of conscious thought. It calls for a continuous search for self-understanding and for a reasonable degree of comfort with the discovered self.

Social workers develop this self-knowledge in a variety of ways. The process of supervision or discussion of practice situations and problems with peers has always been an important means of developing self-knowledge. Others can often see how our unrecognized concerns, attitudes, and values affect our interaction with others and our helping capacity. Social workers need to be open to help from others as a means of developing self-understanding.

Another way social workers develop self-understanding is through the study of human behavior. Psychological, sociological, anthropological, and biological knowledge that explains human functioning can be the source of considerable self-understanding. It is important to recognize one's self as having imperfections, but it is equally important to keep such awareness within the limits of reality. Medical students tend to believe that they have a disease they are studying. Social work students sometimes believe that the dysfunctional situations they are studying are operational in their own functioning and see symptoms, pathology, or a deviance in themselves. If this is realistic, it can be very helpful to self-understanding. Care needs to be taken, however, not to become overly introspective and to assume dysfunctioning that is not really there. A balance needs to be reached so that introspection is sufficient to gain the needed self-knowledge, but not so much as to become overwhelming. Self-knowledge cannot be developed all at once; it needs to grow over a period of time. It is also important to learn to deal with the recognition of one's imperfection in a manner that supports self-worth and dignity.

Another useful way for a beginning social worker to develop self-knowledge is to conduct an organized self-study. This would entail thinking about one's lifestyle and philosophy of life, moral code and value system, roots, life experiences, personal needs, and personal functioning.

Lifestyle and Philosophy of Life

People are different because of both heredity and environment. Such differences affect the manner in which life is lived and how life's problems are dealt with. Some people are practical and matter of fact; others are sympathetic and friendly; others are enthusiastic and insightful; still others are logical and well organized. Some people prefer to deal with technical facts and objects; others prefer to give practical help and services to people; some like to understand and communicate with people; others like to deal with technical and theoretical developments.[1] Some people are physically strong with no disabling handicaps; others may have limited sight or physical stamina or other handicaps. People differ according to gender, socioeconomic class, cultural group, and religious beliefs. People differ in the ways they learn and in their capacity for learning. They have different energy levels. All these factors affect lifestyle. **Lifestyle** is the manner in which we function in meeting our human needs; in interaction with others; and in our patterns of work, play, and rest. It is important not only to describe lifestyle but to be aware of why a particular lifestyle is preferred.

A philosophy of life—although related to lifestyle in that one's lifestyle is in part affected by one's philosophy of life—is even more basic to self-understanding. One's **philosophy of life** includes beliefs about people and society and about human life, its purpose, and how it should be lived. In identifying one's philosophy of life, some questions to be asked are: What are my beliefs about the nature of humanity? Is humanity innately good or evil? What should be the relationship between men and women? What is the place of work, family, and recreation in a person's life? When is dependence on another person acceptable? What responsibility does each person have for the well-being of his or her fellow human beings? What is the relationship of persons to a higher being, to God? What is the relationship of persons to the natural world? One's philosophy of life affects all we are, feel, think, and do. A philosophy of life is often strongly dependent on religious teachings or beliefs to which a person has been exposed. This influence can result in rejection, adherence, or commitments. It is important that a philosophy of life be well thought out and a reflection of the person each of us is. One's philosophy of life changes with growth and with new experiences.

Moral Code and Value System

A moral code and value system are closely related to one's philosophy of life. A **moral code** is a specification of that which is considered to be right and that which is considered to be wrong in terms of behavior. One's *value system* includes what is considered desirable or preferred. The actions and things we consider valuable are also placed in priority positions so that a system of values exists. A person's moral code and value system are affected by cultural heritage, family influences, group affiliations including religious affiliation, and personal and educational experiences. For some people, the moral code is prescribed and fixed regardless of the situation. For others, the moral code is determined by a set of principles that guides moral and value decisions but that allows for some degree of flexibility; for still others, these decisions are made depending upon the situation in which they find themselves.[2]

Florence Kluckholm and Fred Strodtbeck have discussed value orientations and identified several dimensions along which people develop a value system.

1. *Human nature:* Is it evil, neutral, mixture of good and evil, or Good?
2. *Relationship of individual to nature:* Should it be subjugation to nature, harmony with nature, or mastery over nature?
3. *Time orientation:* Is the emphasis placed on past, present, or future?
4. *Activity:* Should activity focus on being, being in becoming, or doing?
5. *Relationality:* Should its nature be one of lineality, collaborability, or individuality?[3]

Identification of one's position on each of these five dimensions can give some indication of one's basic values—of one's way of responding to needs, problems, and situations in which one finds oneself. For example, if a person sees people as basically evil, his or her response to problems may be to punish in order to exact good behavior. Such a presupposition carries a belief that a person's inclination is to be bad and punishment is needed to curb undesirable behavior. On the other hand, seeing people as good carries a belief that people will try to do what is right, will consider others and their needs, and will work for what is right. The stance that human nature is good seems more in keeping with social work values than the one that human nature is bad.

Value conflicts that exist between the dominant society and an ethnic group can often be identified through examination of the value orientation of the ethnic group. Hispanic people often carry a belief that a person's relationship to nature is one of subjugation to nature. For some Hispanics, then, natural disasters such as floods or hurricanes are seen as indications that the forces of nature (or the gods) are punishing them for some misdoing. Native Americans have a value system based on harmony with nature. For them, natural disasters may be an indication that in some way they are out of harmony with the forces of nature. For example, floods may be the result of misuse of the land. The response of the dominant American culture tends to reflect a belief in mastery over nature. The response to a flood is to attempt to control future floods with dams and other flood-control mechanisms. These differences often explain why individuals view the same situation differently.

Time orientations also are responsible for value conflicts. Some people are heavily influenced by how things have been done in the past. They tend to make decisions based on "how it has always been done." Others are focused on the future. These people place considerable emphasis on planning ahead, "saving for a rainy day," on the needs of their children and grandchildren. Still others focus on the here and now. They tend to live a day at a time, to not save money, to expect children to make their own way. Often persons who must use all their energy just providing for their basic needs—the poverty-stricken—will have this kind of orientation. Again, differences in decisions made about similar situations can often be explained by the value difference of time orientation.

Many Americans emphasize activity that results in observable accomplishment. However, there are always people who see value in *being,* that is, in activity that is not outcome oriented. This stance places more emphasis on the person than on the outcome or the production. *Being in becoming* also places emphasis on the person, but it stresses activity as a vehicle for the growth of individuals. A social worker's belief about the purpose and value of activity will have an important influence on how she practices social work and on her goals with clients. As it is important to work within methods that are congruent with one's value system, it is also important to identify beliefs affecting that value system so that methods can be chosen that are congruent with the worker's value system.

Another way in which people view the world is in the way they see the relationships among various events or parts of the situation. This relates to the Kluckholm and Strodtbeck dimension of rationality. Relationships are sometimes explained in a cause-effect, or linearity, manner. This explanation is not congruent with contemporary generalist social work thinking, which calls for a transactional approach (see Chapter 5). The transactional approach seems more in the manner of collaborality, that is, seeing the interaction of a number of factors as influencing behavior in a situation. Others see each situation as unique and do not see a relationship with other situations, past or present. This would be considered the individuality manner of reaching conclusions about the nature of situations. These varying views of relationships among events are often due to different value orientations.

Often people operate from moral codes and value systems of which they are only partly aware. They may have accepted these without fully exploring the meaning of or implications of adhering to a particular code or system. Sometimes one's various beliefs are in contradiction with one another, and sometimes one is not aware of the priorities of his value system. The self-knowledge needed by the social worker calls for specification and understanding of one's moral code and value system. The needed understanding includes identification of the source of one's moral code and values as well as recognition of priorities and the degree of flexibility possible regarding priorities.

Roots

As a person thinks about lifestyle, philosophy of life, moral code, and value system, the importance of her roots—cultural and family background—should become clear. Individuals have different reactions to their roots. Some feel very comfortable continuing the traditions and lifestyle of past generations; others reject all or a part of that way of life. Many become confused and are uncertain about what should be continued and what should be rejected; others find a balance between using that part of their roots they find useful and making adaptations and changes needed to be functional in their present life situation.

One method of gaining understanding about one's cultural heritage is to spend time studying that heritage. This can be done through formal courses; reading novels about people and their life who belong to that culture; reading books about a cultural heritage; and talking with family members about family customs and about their lives and beliefs. An attempt should also be made to understand a cultural heritage as a response to historical events and situations. Many people are finding a journey into their cultural heritage rewarding and yielding considerable self-understanding.

The **genogram,** a family tree that specifies significant information about each individual for at least three generations, is a useful tool for gaining understanding of one's family.* From studying a genogram one can identify the effect of such things as death, size of family, birth position in family, naming patterns, and major family behavior patterns, to name a few of the issues. This method of studying the family as a system can yield much previously unrecognized information and help a person see not only the place one has filled in a family but also how one has been influenced by the family.[4]

There are other ways of considering family influence that also aid in the quest for self-knowledge. The study of one's family from a sociological and psychological point of view gives a person insight into his family. Discussions with family members about important events in the life of the family are another useful method for gaining deeper understanding about the family and its ways of functioning.

The search for one's roots can be a lifelong journey, yielding many fascinating facts. It can also open old wounds and thus be painful. Yet, recognizing and dealing with the pain can often result in a person being more sensitive to others' pain and a more effective helping person. Most of all, it can lead to greater understanding of self, to knowledge of who one is and why one is the unique person one is.

Life Experiences

The study of one's roots yields some understanding of important experiences in shaping the person. In addition to experiences within the family, other experiences are important to each person. These include educational experience—the experience of learning, the knowledge that has been learned in one's educational experience, and attitudes toward learning. Other meaningful experiences include those with one's peers and those in one's community and neighborhood with all kinds of people—with those who are different because of age, race, ethnic background, and mental or physical handicaps. Experiences in organized group situ-

---

*See page 111 for an example.

ations, in religious activities, and experiences related to illness, disability, poverty, or abundance of economic resources are also important.

Identification of those life experiences that have significant impact upon one as a person is yet another way of developing self-knowledge. It is also helpful to evaluate how each of these significant life experiences relates to other life experiences and how they affect ways of thinking, feeling, and acting. Also to be considered is how an experience is the result of a particular set of previous life experiences.

Personal Needs

Another area of self-knowledge is understanding one's needs and how they are dealt with. This includes personal needs related to common human needs, needs that arise because of human diversity, and needs that arise from relationships with social systems. (See Chapter 1.)

In thinking about common human needs, consideration of our need for food, clothing, shelter, care, safety, belongingness, and opportunity for growth and learning are the focus. An understanding of personal need includes giving thought to how needs are met and the adequacy of the need provision. In thinking about human need it is useful to consider personal developmental patterns in the area of physical development. An understanding of human development provides information about the development expected at a specific age, and it is important to reflect on the development expected in relation to that which has taken place at each specific age. Also involved is the concept of biological needs. This includes such issues as health and wellness, disease and disability, physical strengths and limitations, and changes in the body and its functioning due to aging, and the need for physical closeness.[5]

Identification of the present developmental stage is necessary before consideration can be given to the needs of individuals. For example, during the period of rapid physical growth and development in early adolescence, a person has a need for additional food to support the growing body.

Erik Erikson and others have identified psychosocial need at various stages of human development. Identification of these needs gives rise to developmental tasks that must be accomplished if psychosocial need during each stage is to be fulfilled. See Table 6–1 for a summary of these tasks. For example, as the young child develops cognitively, there is a need for toys and activities that allow for the exploration necessary for learning.

Recently, several persons have questioned the validity for women of Erikson's formulation of human development.[6] While new formulations about differences in male and female development are only now emerging, these new theoretical developments should be noted and given consideration. In considering psychosocial need, it is useful not only to determine need because of present stage of development but also to take into account unmet need in earlier stages. Present functioning is in part affected by the way need has been met in the past. Thus, identification of unmet need is one means of gaining self-understanding.

TABLE 6–1 Psychosocial Tasks to be Accomplished in the Stages of Human Development

Stage I Trust vs. Mistrust (Infancy)

Development of a sense of being cared for through the provision of food, comfortable surroundings, and adult care.

Development of feelings that basic needs will be met and that the adult caretaker can be trusted.

Stage II Autonomy vs. Shame and Doubt (Early Preschool Child)

Development of a sense of self as a separate individual.

Development of the realization that self can assert itself and control parts of personal functioning yet still need adult control because of limited ability to care for self.

Stage III Initiative vs. Guilt (Late Preschool Child)

Development of the ability to plan and carry out activities. To do this there must be opportunities to try new things and to test new powers.

Development of the capacity to maintain a balance between joy in doing and responsibility for what is done.

Stage IV Industry vs. Inferiority (Grade-school Child)

Development of skills necessary to function in a particular culture and society. To do this there needs to be opportunities to produce and to feel good about the production.

Development of a positive self-image and friendships with other persons.

Stage V Identity vs. Role Confusion (Adolescence)

Opportunity to integrate and consolidate psychosocial growth from earlier stages.

Development of a sense of personal identity.

Acceptance of sexuality and of self as an independent person with personalized needs and desires.

Development of a sense of self in relationship with other persons.

Time and opportunity to examine how the person (or self) fits into the world and opportunity to develop a personal value system.

Stage VI Intimacy vs. Isolation (Young Adulthood)

Opportunity to make decisions about lifestyle and career.

Opportunity to make commitments and to develop relationships of an intimate nature with other persons.

Development of adult relationships with family of orientation.

Stage VII Generativity vs. Stagnation (Middle Adulthood)

Involvement in establishing and guiding the next generation and in concern for others.

Development of an outlook on life that values wisdom rather than physical power.

Development of relationships that are socializing rather than sexualizing.

Development of flexibility and openness in thinking about life.

Stage VIII Ego Integrity vs. Despair (Older Adulthood)

Development of some order in own life in a spiritual sense.

Acceptance of life as lived without regret for what might have been.

Differentiation of self from work role.

Acceptance of physical decline.

Separation of self-worth from body preoccupation.

Opportunity to deal with the reality of own death.

Sources: Based largely on work of Erik Erikson, *Childhood and Society,* (New York: W. W. Norton, 1950). Stages VII and VIII are also based on the work of Robert C. Peck, "Psychological Developments in the Second Half of Life," in Bernice L. Neugarten, Ed., *Middle Age and Aging* (Chicago: University of Chicago Press, 1968).

Another dimension of human functioning from which needs arise is the spiritual. This is often ignored by social workers because there is little agreement about its nature and content. There has been little research in this area. Spiritual development has often been considered to be a part of religious development, which it is for many people, but it has broader implications. Carlton Cornett defined spirituality as "The individual's understanding of and response to meaning in life; time and morality; expectations regarding what, if anything, follows death; and belief or non-belief in a 'higher power.'"[7] It follows, then, that spiritual development is the process a person goes through in developing as a spiritual being. This is an area to which social work has paid little attention, but is one that is extremely important in understanding the formation of a value system and philosophy of life. It is of particular importance to the self-knowledge of a social worker in the development of a professional value base. To date, some of the most helpful materials are those developed concerning moral development by Lawrence Kohlberg and Carol Gilligan[8] and faith development by James W. Fowler and Sharon Parks.[9]

It is also useful to reflect on how one's cultural group usually meets the psychosocial needs of its members. Doing this yields some understanding as to whether personal experience has been typical or atypical for one's cultural group.

The second area of personal need arises because of human diversity. Examination of need because of diversity looks at how identification or affiliation with a particular group has affected the person. Institutional racism, prejudice, and discrimination all have serious impact on human functioning. Because of this impact, individuals who are a part of certain groups (racial minorities, handicapped persons, etc.) have distinctive needs. Differences in language, physical appearance, and mental ability tend to separate people from some resources and opportunities for meeting need. Responses to societal expectations and responsibilities are different as are coping mechanisms. Any understanding of personal need should take into account needs that arise because of different lifestyles and the stresses that arise from such differences.

A third area of personal need arises because of each person's interrelatedness with other persons—his or her membership in social systems. Systems such as the family, peer groups, institutions of work and education, organizations persons belong to, the neighborhood and community, and cultural groups all place expectations and responsibilities on their members. People have a need to respond to these expectations and responsibilities. Their response can be acceptance of the expectations and responsibilities; the response can also be one of negotiating with the system for modification of expectations and responsibilities.

Making an inventory of personal needs is another useful way of developing self-knowledge (see Table 6–2). As one comes to understand one's personal needs, an understanding of one's behavior, feelings, and responses to a variety of life experiences also develops. This is a necessary aspect of true self-knowledge. It not only has psychosocial dimensions but biological and spiritual dimensions as well.

TABLE 6–2   A Guide for Thinking about Personal Need

My Common Human Needs

1. What are my needs for food, shelter, and clothing? How do I meet these needs?
2. What are my needs for safety so as to avoid pain and physical damage to self? How do I meet these needs?
3. What are my health care needs? How do I meet these needs?
4. What are my needs for love and belongingness? How do I meet these needs?
5. What are my needs for acceptance and status? How do I meet these needs?
6. What are my needs for developing my capacity and potentiality? How do I meet these needs?
7. What are my needs for understanding myself and the world in which I live? How do I meet these needs?
8. What other biological needs do I have?
9. How do I describe my spiritual development? What are major sources for this development? What are my present needs in this area?

My Developmental Needs

1. What are my needs because of my experience in developing physically? How do I meet these needs?
2. What are my needs in relation to my cognitive development? How do I meet these needs?
3. What is my present stage of psychosocial development?
4. What are my needs because of the development tasks of my current stage of development?
5. How well have I accomplished the tasks of earlier developmental stages?
6. What present needs do I have because of problems related to not accomplishing these tasks?

My Needs Arising from Human Diversity

1. What in my lifestyle is "diverse" from the dominant lifestyle of my community?
2. What is the basis of the diversity—race, cultural group, gender, religion, handicapping conditions, other?
3. What is the meaning of this diversity to me? How do I feel about myself in relation to this diversity?
4. What is the meaning of this diversity to my immediate environment? How does the environment deal with me as a diverse person?
5. How do I deal with the stresses and strains that exist because of diversity?
6. What special needs do I have because of my diversity?

My Needs Arising from Social Systems of Which I Am a Part

1. What expectations do the various social systems of which I am a part have of me? (These include family, peer group, school or work, organizations of which I am a member, neighborhood or cultural group, etc.)
2. What do I see as my responsibility toward the social systems of which I am a part?
3. What needs do I have in relation to these social systems, including the expectations and responsibilities related to them?

Personal Functioning

Self-knowledge includes not only identification and understanding of one's life-style, philosophy of life, moral code, value system, roots, and personal needs, it also includes an understanding of how these affect day-to-day functioning. This involves identification of how one learns, how one shares self with others, how one responds to a variety of situations, and of one's biases and prejudices. Also important is how one feels about self and how this affects day-to-day functioning. Self-knowledge also includes understanding of how one meets personal needs; how one deals with freedom and restrictions; how one accepts change both in one's self and in one's environment; how one views one's responsibility toward the social system of which one is a part; and what one's role is in those systems.

The kind of self-knowledge that has been discussed is not easy to develop. It takes time for introspection, for observation of self in a variety of circumstances, for seeking out other's observations about self. It also requires risk taking, since there may be a cost for self-knowledge: dissatisfaction with the self that is found, pain about past experiences, or anger about one's place and role in society. It is a lifelong journey toward self-knowledge and self-acceptance. It is also a journey that is necessary if the helping person is to be able to use a major tool—the self—skillfully, fully, and with maximal results.

CASE EXAMPLE

I am Janie Bryan, a twenty-year-old junior social work student. I grew up in Cornerville, a small town of 10,000 in the upper midwestern state, Iotota. I am the middle of five children in a family that has lived in the same community all of my life. My oldest brother is five years older than I am, married, and a news announcer in Nearby City. My twenty-two-year-old sister married her high-school boyfriend, lives in our hometown, and has a three-year-old daughter and a one-year-old son. My sister Mary, who is four years younger than I am, is moderately mentally retarded and is still at home, as is our baby brother, who is now eleven years old.

I see myself as enthusiastic and insightful. I really get excited about a lot of things and seem to have the ability to sense what is happening in many situations. I seem to understand my friends and their needs and problems. I think I am also logical and ingenious. I like to have time to think about things and to decide what is the logical way to do something, step by step. I guess I like to see where I am going when I start something, but I also like to brainstorm about what can be done and come up with new ideas about how to reach my goals.

It's very easy for me to talk to people. People seem to like me. I have to be careful, however, that I don't try to second-guess where others are coming from based on my experiences. I'm learning to find out from them why they think and feel as they do. In fact, right now I'm trying to learn as much as I can about a lot of different kinds of people. They have really interesting stories and seem to enjoy telling them to me. Also, I'm fascinated with the different kinds of experiences some of my fellow students have had. I am finding I really need to know something about other people to understand why they think the way they do.

I don't consider myself to have any handicaps, though some of my friends think being a woman is a handicap. I am very optimistic that my generation will not have to put up with all the old hangups, so I just plan that I can do anything I want to do. My family has always been middle class, never a lot of money but always comfortable. We have had what we needed. Dad has owned a small business for as long as I can remember. He is respected by everyone, and I have always been respected as his daughter. We are Methodists, and the church and its activities are important to our family, though now that I'm away from home I don't go to church very often. I'm not sure why; guess I should think about that.

I have always done well in school. I was usually on the honor roll in high school as well as being active in cheerleaders, drama, and music. When I got to college, my first semester was not too good. I was too busy talking to people and partying. Also, I was not used to the kinds of assignments and tests given here at college. But then I seemed to kind of get the hang of it. I did some structuring of my time and organizing myself, and now I'm getting A's and B's with a C once in awhile when I don't like the subject or the instructor. I learn best when I am exploring new ideas and when I'm challenged to think and express my own thinking. I'm enjoying not being in structured extracurricular activities and just spending my play time with friends. We enjoy just sitting around and talking. This year I'm living in an apartment with three other girls. This is great after living in the dorm, but we did have some trouble at first keeping the place livable and getting the cooking done.

I am a positive thinker, optimistic. People are good. I think if you really work at it you can get along with almost anyone. I do like some people better than others, though. I hate to spend too much time discussing all the bad things that are happening and hearing about people's worries over things like tests next week, etcetera. I want to be independent, and it bothers me that I'm still financially dependent on my family. Yet I wonder if I'm not also dependent on my friends, too. I do hope it's in a way that they can count on me when they need it. I really care about other people and want to help them feel good about themselves. So many students seem to not have a lot of self-confidence or feel good about what's happening to them. I wish I could help them.

I guess I see the relationship of man and nature as one of harmony. I am a doer and seem to focus on the present rather than the past or future, though I am concerned about what I will do when I get out of school. I want to see some of the world, maybe work in a big city, though that is scary too. I would rather work alone but know some things must be done with others. Guess I should develop more skills for working with others.

I've never thought much about my family. Dad's side came from Germany about four generations ago, and Mother's people just moved out from the East about the same time. We seem to have sort of taken each other for granted. My mother's brother is really angry at my mother for letting my grandmother live in a nursing home, but Mom just can't handle her and my sister Mary. Dad is so busy at the store that he can't be much help. He really was the one to insist that Mom can't care for Grandma now. The folks really worry about what is going to happen to Mary. I've learned some things in my social work classes that might help. Last time I was home we talked about this, and I felt real good that the folks said it sure helped. I don't know much about Dad's family. That's something I want to find out more about.

The genogram (see Figure 6–1) helps me see that as a middle child I seem to have been more of a helper than the other children. I think this may be because Mary does need special attention and my little brother is so much younger. Mom has had her hands full with them. My older brother and sister sort of left home and got out of the helping. I think maybe I'm more mature because of this experience in my family. These family experiences and the real good experience I had in high school seem to have really prepared me for dealing with college life. I had to learn to use time well if I wanted to do all I did in high school.

As I look at my "common human needs," they all seem to have been met by my family. Mom and Dad still provide part of the money I need to go to school, and I've gotten loans and worked in the summer. Now I have to plan for myself how to deal with the day-to-day needs like eating right; sometimes I don't do so well here. Also, I never thought about health care. Mom has always sent me to the dentist and doctor. I think it's time I took some responsibility for this. I'm going to school to develop my ability to earn money and take care of myself but also to help others. I'm meeting that need by using the opportunities here at school.

I think I've developed normally, but with my sister's problems I understand that this can be a problem for her. I've just never thought about having needs in this area. I'm

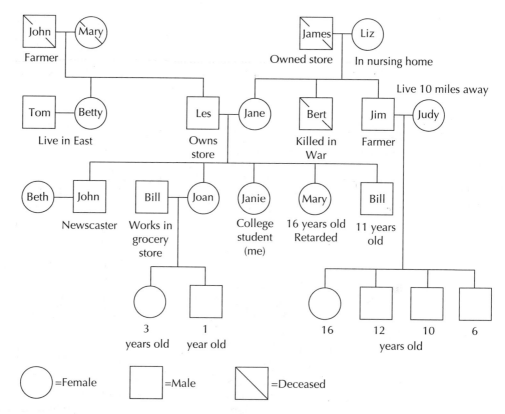

FIGURE 6–1   Janie's Genogram

moving into Stage VI. I'm not yet ready to make any long-term commitments with a man. I want to live a bit and see some of the world first. But I do feel real close to my roommates and sometimes have wondered if they were taking the place of my family. I'm not sure where I am in this area. Maybe this is a sign I am struggling with a developmental task. I guess I need to test myself out as an independent adult person. I'm not sure I really have completed all the tasks of Stage V. I never thought of it, but I've known some role confusion. At home I play mother to my little brother, and I'm not sure what my relationship with Mary should be. I need to think about this and perhaps talk with Mom about it. Otherwise I seem to have gone through the other psychological stages pretty well. I trust people (usually); I feel good about myself; I like to do things and am fairly responsible; I have lots of friends.

I've never thought about diversity. I seem so average. Yet maybe that is my "diversity." Almost everyone I know is different in some way. They have had bad growing-up experiences and now have problems. I've really been lucky. Also, I don't know many people of different races. I need to think about what it means to be different in this way.

Because I'm so fortunate I have a lot of responsibility. Maybe that's part of my reason for wanting to be a social worker. Social systems do expect things of me. My parents want me to come home oftener than I really want to. I need to talk with them about this rather than just let the problem go on. My instructors place lots of expectations for reading and papers on me. My friends want me to spend time with them. Sometimes it's hard to handle all this and still have the time I need to be alone. I need to work for a good balance. Maybe I need to set up some kind of a schedule for myself.

Overall I see myself as doing pretty well, but there are some things I need to do:

1. I need to continue to find out where others are coming from and to realize everyone has not had the opportunities and experiences I have had. I need to listen.
2. I need to plan for some alone time so I can get to know myself better. This means I need to structure my time better so I can meet all my obligations.
3. I need to get to know more about my extended family. I don't seem to know them very well.
4. I need to talk to my parents about my feelings of growing up and being independent. I'm not at all sure of my role in the family. We need to discuss this.
5. I need to increase my capacity for working cooperatively with others.

THE HELPING PERSON

The generalist social worker is a helper who can effectively use self with other persons to enable those persons to meet needs or solve problems more adequately. The helping focuses on needs and social-functioning problems. Thus, the generalist social worker must develop the interactional skills necessary for productive interaction with individuals and groups of individuals.

As the social worker approaches the helping situation, he brings first and foremost self. This self brings concern for others; a knowledge base, both substantive and experiential; values, those of the profession and those of self; a view of the nature of change; and skills, both cognitive and interactive. The self is the major tool for working with others.

Many of these skills are characteristic of the helping person. A distinction between a helping person and a helping professional needs to be made for purposes of this discussion. The social work professional is a helping person and the helping is done in the context of using the knowledge, values, and skills of the social work profession. One major difference between helping and professional helping is that the help given is based firmly in and with conscious use of an identifiable knowledge and value base. Another characteristic of professional helping is that the help is nonreciprocal. That is, help is given with no expectation that the helped will in turn provide help for the helper.

Characteristics of a Helping Person

There have been many descriptions of the helping person. Arthur Combs, Donald Avila, and William Purkey, in a research study, found that the belief system of the worker was an important characteristic of helping. The effective helper believes that people are:

1. More able than unable,
2. Friendly rather than unfriendly,
3. Worthy rather than unworthy,

4. Internally motivated rather than externally motivated,
5. Dependable rather than undependable, and
6. Helpful rather than hindering.

They found that the worker's beliefs about self were also important. The effective worker sees self as 1) identified with people, 2) adequate, 3) trustworthy, 4) wanted, and 5) worthy. Some additional traits of the helping person, according to these researchers, are 1) freeing rather than controlling, 2) being concerned about larger issues rather than smaller ones, 3) self-revealing rather than self-concealing, 4) being involved rather than alienated, 5) being process oriented rather than goal oriented, and 6) being altruistic rather than narcissistic. Effective workers approach a task in terms of people rather than things and from a perceptual rather than an objective viewpoint.[10]

Beulah Compton and Burt Galaway see maturity as another characteristic of helping persons. In their view, maturity consists of the capacities to be creative and to observe self in interaction with others, of a desire to help, and of having the qualities of courage and sensibility.[11] This mature person would seem to be one who is free enough of his or her own life problems to experiment, to risk, and to give of self in service of another. The quality of sensibility can be expressed as good judgment. Used in this sense, good judgment means the ability to make good decisions that serve the client and her needs rather than the worker's.

David Johnson sees the helping person as having another set of attributes.[12] First is the ability to self-disclose while being self-aware and showing concern for what the other person feels about what the worker says or does. This attribute has a quality of honesty, genuineness, and authenticity. Second is the capacity to trust, which entails warmth, acceptance, support, and the capacity to check for meaning. Third is skill in communication. This includes the ability to send messages so that the other can understand, to listen, to respond appropriately, and to clarify what is misunderstood. Fourth is the ability to express feeling; fifth is the ability to accept self and others; sixth is the ability to confront others constructively; and seventh is the capacity to reinforce and model appropriate behavior.

The helping person can be described as one who

1. Has a generally positive view of individuals and their behavior;
2. Is concerned about others and their well-being for the sake of the other, not for self-centered purposes;
3. Is open, trusting, warm, friendly, and honest;
4. Works with persons being helped, not for them;
5. Responds to people rather than supports the use of a particular technique;
6. Is mature, has good judgment, and is willing to risk in the service of others; and
7. Is realistic about human situations, the amount of change possible, and the time it takes to change.

Anthony Maluccio has reported research that examined the factors influencing outcomes of treatment from both the client's and the worker's perspectives.[13]

He found agreement between the workers' and clients' perspective in respect to the following as desirable worker characteristics: acceptance, interest, warmth, and supportiveness. In addition, the clients saw these characteristics as helpful: being human and understanding; caring, trusting, and friendly; encouraging work together; looking for solutions; giving advice and suggestions; and releasing anxiety.

In discussing worker styles, Edward Mullen describes the helping person as one who exerts personal influence rather than as one who applies techniques.[14] This indicates that it is the worker, as he uses self, that is the major factor in helping. Thus, a primary task in becoming a helping person is a fine tuning of characteristics that are a part of everyday human interaction. Techniques can be useful tools, but only when used by a person who knows how to use personal influence (self).

The worker is not a cold, objective student of humanity who knows about rather than feels with; or one who has a strong personal need to control, to satisfy his own conscience, to feel superior to other persons, or to be liked. The worker is not an overly confirmed optimist or a person who has solved his own problems but forgotten the personal cost, nor a person whose own solutions to life problems are so precarious that the solutions take on a moralistic character. The worker is not afraid of feelings, his own or others. The worker uses knowledge and experience for understanding. This understanding is more than intellectual; it has emotional, or feeling, aspects as well. It is an understanding that leads to sensitive and realistic response to human need.

The helping worker is one who can defer his own needs and both recognizes and is not afraid of those needs; is not impulsive and is aware of his own feelings so they do not cause impulsiveness; is responsible for self and his own tasks in the helping endeavor; is growth facilitating and empathic; and is able to communicate clearly and effectively—concretely and specifically. This worker can clarify roles, status, values, and intentions with the client.

Responsibility and Authority

Two characteristics of a helping person—responsibility and authority—are particularly troublesome to the social worker. These two characteristics are related because each is a part of the personal influence aspect of the helping situation. They are also related in that they often become confused with value judgments related to the right of self-determination. Each worker must learn to manage these two characteristics in relationships with clients.

It is very easy for the social worker to take on responsibilities that do not belong to her. Often the worker perceives that self-destructive behavior is a client's way out, and the client is unwilling or unable to change the behavior or to take another way out. The worker begins to feel inadequate because she cannot "get the client to see what is best for him." Societal pressures also place a worker in a position of feeling responsible for the client's behaviors. Friends, public officials, and the person on the street ask why the social worker does not "make clients" do something or the other. The worker again begins to accept inappropriate responsibility. Often the worker can see the consequences of a client's behavior and has a great desire to "save the client from self." The right of self-determination includes not only the right to make one's own choices; it also includes the right to suffer the consequences of those choices.

If the worker is not responsible for the client's choices in the helping situation, what, then, is the nature of the worker's responsibility? The worker is responsible for self in the helping situation, which includes

1. Understanding the person in the situation as far as possible, given the circumstances of the helping situation;
2. Use of self in the way that will be most helpful to this client in this situation;
3. Creating a climate that makes it possible for the client to use the help;
4. Providing a perspective to the client's need or problems, based on the worker's knowledge and experience;
5. Providing structure for thinking about the need or problem, including focusing on, and skillful use of, the problem-solving process; and
6. Providing information about needed resources and assistance in obtaining those resources.

The worker and client share responsibility for the outcome of the work together. The worker provides resources and opportunities for work on the problem of meeting need. The client must make use of the opportunities and resources. If the worker carries out the responsibility for providing the opportunity and resources and the client chooses not to use those opportunities and resources, that is not the worker's responsibility.

Regardless of the nature of the worker's responsibility, the client views the worker as a person with authority. Robert Foren and Royston Bailey, in discussing the authority clients ascribe to workers, identify the following as aspects of that authority:

1. Power to enforce standards of child care,
2. Personal attributes, social class, education,
3. Association with parental figures,
4. Knowledge and skill, and
5. Fantasy-magical power.[15]

It is important for social workers to recognize that such authority has been ascribed to them. In accepting the value of the right of self-determination, many workers will deny this authority or be very uncomfortable with it. They see the right to self-determination and the exercise of authority as contradictory, but an in-depth examination of the nature of social work authority reveals that this is not necessarily true. Denial of authority is not useful; the helping person must recognize and become comfortable with the ascribed authority. For example, a worker can examine with a client the exact nature of the worker's authority so that a client knows that the worker will not impose inappropriate standards.

It is also important to help the client become aware of unrealistic authority expectations and free him to be self-determining. Some functions performed by social workers indeed carry a kind of legal authority, which are the means by which certain of society's social control functions are carried out. These include the areas of protective service for children, the mentally impaired, the aged, and probation and parole work. The needs of the social systems must be recognized; and persons cannot be allowed to act destructively to others, particularly when others cannot protect themselves. The worker needs to learn to be comfortable with the ascribed authority. There are limits to self-determination.

It is important to help clients understand not only their right of self-determination but also their social responsibility (another social work value). Self-determination, or choice, is limited by social responsibility. If people decide not to be socially responsible, then they choose to take the consequences of their behavior. Social workers must use their authority in helping clients understand the consequences of behavior so that their choices regarding social responsibility are truly self-determining. Workers also must accept responsibility for those who cannot protect themselves, children, the frail aged, the abused and the victims of crime.

To be helping persons, social workers must accept responsibility for those areas of the situation for which they are in fact responsible, but not for responsibilities that belong to the client. Social workers also must accept the realistic authority that goes with their role. In exercising this ascribed authority, they must constantly be guided by the values of both self-determination and social responsibility.

Helping Skills

The effective social worker develops helping skills. These skills are not mystical or esoteric; they are the skills of well-functioning human beings. However, they are used with people who are having difficulties in social functioning and cannot fulfill the usual responsibilities in human interaction. They are used with people whose sociocultural context for interaction may be different from that of the worker. These factors place greater responsibility for the interaction on the worker than is true in day-to-day interaction with people of similar backgrounds. Thus, the skills for human interaction must be finely tuned, be brought into the conscious awareness of the worker. The skills that need to be developed include the following:

1. *Skills needed for understanding, including understanding of the person in the situation and helping other people understand themselves in the situation*—Skills needed in this area are listening, leading the person to express self, reflecting on what has been said, summarizing what has been said, confronting the person with the realities of situations, interpreting the facts as presented, and informing the person of facts.

2. *Skills needed for developing a climate that encourages helpful interaction*—Skills that are used in making people comfortable in strange or new situations include skill in supporting persons, in crisis intervention, in focusing so as to ease a sense of being overwhelmed, and in constructing a comfortable physical and emotional climate.

3. *Skills needed in acting on the problems of the client*—These include skills in problem solving, decision making, planning, referring, modeling, teaching, and using activity. They also include the skills necessary to any practice strategy the worker may be using.

4. *Skills used in communicating and relating to others*—These include skills in listening and attending to the communication of others, in paraphrasing, clarifying, and checking perceptions; skills in getting started, encouraging, elaborating, focusing, and questioning; and skills in responding to feelings and to others' experiences, in summarizing and pulling thoughts together, and in interpreting and informing.[16]

This summary of skills is not meant to be all-inclusive but it is meant to give some idea of the breadth of skills the social worker needs to have. Skill development is a continuous task for all social workers if they are to grow as helping persons.

CASE EXAMPLE

As Janie Bryan thinks of herself as a helping person, she is aware that there is a part of her that always seemed to be concerned about other people. She also knows that many people have come to her when they were perplexed or having problems and that she seemed to be able to help them find a means to deal with these situations. After her experience in a social work program in college, she knows that sometimes the help she gave contained too much advice and that she often jumped in to do for others before she adequately understood the situation. Sometimes she had difficulty understanding why a person might not take her advice and yet seemed to solve the problem in another way. Now she understands that help is not telling someone what she would do in that situation.

Janie now has a firm knowledge base on which to base her helping. She has become aware of her value system and of many different lifestyles and the value bases they reflect. A part of her value base now is the ethical code of the social work profession. She has developed skills for developing understanding of people and their situations, for relating to a wide variety of people, and for influencing for change. She has a sense that she has developed into a helping professional person, though she knows this development will be a lifelong experience.

Now that she has her social work degree she is concerned about what kind of authority she will have with her clients. This idea troubles her for she has never wanted to be an authority figure; she just wants to help people. What kind of authority can she exercise with a parent who is having difficulty with a child when she has never had a child, when she is so much younger than the mother? She knows that though she does not have the authority of experience, she does have the authority of knowledge. She is concerned that her clients know that they can make choices even if she does carry some legal authority in some cases. For example, she knows her caseload will contain some situations where the parent has abused a child. She sees her function as providing the parent with different ways to deal with difficult situations so as not to be abusive to the child. She does know that at times this will not happen, and then she will have to exercise her responsibility toward the child and society in general and recommend removing the child from his or her home. She hopes this will not happen too often. Janie knows she has been a helping person for a long time, and now she is excited at the prospect of being a helping professional person.

THE MULTIPERSON HELPING SYSTEM

The social work endeavor is usually discussed from the perspective of one worker helping a human system that can consist of an individual, a family, a small group, an organization, or a community. In a complex society, which among other things is characterized by the knowledge explosion of the last thirty years and with a great deal of specialization, providing such help is not always possible. The worker is often part of a multiperson system. Susan Lonsdale, Adrian Webb, and Thomas Briggs have stated: "Individual problems [are] interconnected, do not always neatly divide along discipline lines and ... the expertise required for effective interaction may elude the solo practitioner, or a single profession for that matter."[17] Contemporary social work often requires the coordinated work of several persons—several social workers, a social worker and paraprofessionals or volunteers, or social workers and persons from other professions.

Allan Pincus and Anne Minahan define several systems involved in the social work endeavor: the client system, the change agent system, the target system, and the action system. The action system is made up of those involved in the change process. The target system is the system toward which the change activity is aimed. The conceptualization of change agent system does carry the implication that the change agent, or worker, can be a multiperson system.[18]

The *multiperson helping system* manifests itself in a number of ways. In a sense, the worker-supervisor activity is a multiworker system. The supervisor is generally an experienced person who can provide the worker with technical assistance, a perspective for considering the worker-client interaction, and help that the worker may need in order to deliver the service. Other manifestations of the multiworker system are the use of consultation, collaboration, or referral. In each of these situations one worker is using the expertise of another worker to meet client needs. In **consultation,** the worker uses the help of another social worker or a person of another professional background to better understand the client and the client's needs to consider possible interventive strategies, or to enable the worker to carry out the interventive strategy more adequately. Although the worker is free to accept the help given or to reject or adapt it, the consultant is nevertheless a part of the action system. **Collaboration** is a situation in which two or more helping persons are each responsible for certain aspects of service to a client. They may represent a single agency or several agencies; they may all be social workers, or they may represent several professional disciplines. The collaboration is a means of integrating the various services being delivered, of defining roles and services to be offered by each participant, and of insuring that conflicting messages are not given to clients.

Referral is the process by which a client is enabled to use additional services, either in conjunction with, or instead of, services presently being provided. It calls for the sharing of information about the client and the client's needs, interpretation of the nature of the new service to the client, and enabling the client to use resources. Ideally, the initial worker should also follow through to insure that the new service is meeting the client's needs. Referral when the worker will continue to provide some service to the client might be thought of as a special case of collaboration.

Often the multiworker system is formalized so that it serves more than one client. It then becomes an ongoing system and is often called a **team.** Lonsdale, Webb, and Briggs have identified four kinds of teams with which social workers are involved: 1) a team in which the workers represent different organizations and agencies, 2) a team composed of persons from different professions, 3) a team of social workers employed in the same agency, and 4) a team that includes not only professional workers but also clients and community members.[19]

The team that represents different organizations and agencies is used when these institutions tend to serve many of the same individuals. Such would be the case when health or mental health agencies and the public social service agency are serving clients from a particular area. Agencies that are often concerned with services for children may include not only public social services, health, and mental health agencies but the school, the juvenile justice agency, and a community recreation center. Cooperative planning and collaborating for specific clients are goals of this kind of team. Sometimes such a team also considers preventive and program-planning issues. They often function through what is known as a **case conference,** in which members of the team share knowledge about clients or the nature of the service to a particular client the agencies are providing. In addition, a case conference can result in joint planning for service to the client.

The team of members from different professional disciplines was first manifested in mental health settings where psychiatry, psychology, and social work collaborated in provision of service to clients. Medical settings also make use of the interdisciplinary team approach in providing for both the psychosocial and the physical needs of the patients; diagnostic centers also make considerable use of this type of team. The range of professions that may be represented on the team is very broad and depends on both the setting and the client's needs.

Interdisciplinary practice calls for the social worker to gain knowledge about, and to develop understanding of, the disciplines being worked with. This knowledge and understanding should include

1. The role and function of that profession from its point of view, including the normal way of carrying out the tasks of the profession;
2. The profession's value system or code of ethics;
3. Something of that profession's knowledge base;
4. How the profession is sanctioned—its educational levels and specialties;
5. Current issues that face that profession; and
6. Areas of overlap and tension with social work.

This knowledge and understanding can be gained in several ways: by talking with representatives of the profession, by working together on teams, and by reading the literature of the professions. Rosalie Kane has identified two types of interdisciplinary teams: the coordinative and the integrative. On the *coordinative team* the professions maintain distinct professional roles; there is designated leadership, nonconsensual decision making, little concern for the process of the team, formal communication, and an emphasis on the assessment phase of service. On the *integrative team* there is deliberate role blurring, consensual decision making, high interdependence among the team members, and much attention to process.[20] Most interdisciplinary teams probably combine elements of the coordinative and integrative teams along a continuum, being nearer one type or the other.

The team made up of employees of a social service agency is known as a *social work team*. The team can include paraprofessional and nonprofessional persons who are carrying out parts of the social work task. It may be led by a worker with a master's degree or by an experienced worker with a bachelor's degree. It may be a group of social service workers who divide the tasks of providing service to clients. For example, in a mental hospital one worker may be responsible for geriatric patients and nursing home placements, another for a specific ward or group of patients from a particular geographic area, another for group services, and so on. Briggs says of this type of team: "Every agency has varying types-levels of personnel and must deploy a rational scheme for division of labor that delivers service consistent with goals and priorities while maintaining adequate standards and levels of accountability."[21]

The team made up of professionals and community persons resembles the change agent system described by Pincus and Minahan. It is used when these persons work together to change something within a community or institution, to develop a new resource or programs, or to influence policy or legislation. The child protection team found in some communities is an example of this type of team.

There has been considerable discussion about the use of the team. Gene Hooyman, in discussing the reasons for using teams and the problems in using teams, says that most of the problems seem to come about because of poorly functioning teams.[22] Teamwork can be time consuming. Teams differ from each other just as persons do. Because of the complex needs and problems of clients and the complex social systems that impact on them, participation on teams must often be a part of the service delivery of social workers. The worker must develop skill in functioning on a team.

Another type of multiperson worker that is only beginning to be recognized by social workers is one in which the social worker, as a representative of the formal helping system, works with the natural helping system. The natural helping system is those supportive persons used in the process of living. This system includes family, friends, coworkers, and certain persons to whom people turn for help who do not have professional training or an assigned helping role. This type of multiperson worker represents a formal, often bureaucratic system interacting with an informal, often primary-group system. Because these two systems function in very different ways, it is problematic for them to work together. Jonathan Baker has stated "unless the professional or 'outsider' sees his role as supporting the efforts of the indigenous (or accepted) informal network . . . he will end up trying to substitute for it."[23] The social worker must carry out tasks and functions so as not to undermine the informal helping network. Also, conflicting value systems and norms must be clarified.

Another problem that can develop when using a multiperson worker is the exclusion of the client in the helping endeavor. The workers must spend time developing their relationship, and this can easily lead to the development of a system that excludes client input or participation. The planning can develop as planning for, rather than planning with, the client. This is a particularly difficult issue when working with other professionals who do not value working with the client but prefer doing to or for the client. One solution has been to include the client on the team, but this is not always possible or desirable. Clients who are overwhelmed with needs or problems and who have low self-esteem do not feel comfortable in a group of professionals.

Another problem in using a multiperson worker is the amount of time involved in developing the worker system. Some teams lose sight of their primary purpose—service to the client—and focus on the team functioning as the goal rather than as a means to an end. Time does need to be used in developing the team and monitoring its function; but the time spent on team-functioning activity should be kept to a minimum and, when possible, carried out as a part of the task focus of the team. Despite the fact that working as a team is often difficult and time consuming, in some situations a team can provide service to a client that is not possible for one worker to give.

In any multiworker situation the individual social worker is in an interdependent situation. In order to function in service of the client in multiworker situations, the individual must have developed a set of knowledge, values, and skills specific to such situations. Knowledge needed includes considerable understanding of small-group process and of group problem solving. (See Chapter 9.) It includes knowledge of methods of working with others in a cooperative and collaborative manner and an understanding of other disciplines and of the natural helping system. The worker must incorporate into his value system a positive attitude toward cooperative and collaborative efforts and be comfortable in interdependent situations. Willingness to share and trust other workers is important, as are flexibility and tolerance for disagreement. Skills that are important include the ability to facilitate team process and to develop and maintain cooperative and collaborative relationships.

CASE EXAMPLE

As Janie Bryan became familiar with her caseload in her first job as a social worker she had particular difficulty working with one client. She found that she needed much help from her supervisor in deciding how to approach this mother who was not properly caring for her one-year-old son. Ms. M, a single parent, did not seem to understand how to care for the child. She expected Joe to feed himself, use the potty, and obey her commands. She also seemed to be having a great deal of difficulty with his attempts to be self-assertive. As Janie and her supervisor discussed this situation, it became clear that Ms. M had little understanding of the needs of small children. She had no family and no contact with Joe's father. In fact, she was isolated and beginning to feel angry about being tied down to caring for this small child. There was danger of serious child abuse in this situation.

Janie decided to refer Ms. M to a community center that had a program for single parents. This program provided instruction in childcare and socialization experiences with other single-parent mothers. Janie continued to work with Ms. M because of the potential for child abuse (her agency was responsible for working with abusing parents). Later, the director of the single-parent program suggested that Ms. M seemed to have some personal problems that needed attention from a mental health worker. In planning for this service, Janie collaborated with the single-parent program director and a social worker from the local mental health center to plan ongoing services for Ms. M. They were particularly careful to note who would work with Ms. M around which problems. They planned ongoing contact to share what each was doing, to share any pertinent information they had obtained, and to set ongoing goals for this situation. The three workers became a team as they helped Ms. M with her concerns, needs, and problems.

SUMMARY

The interactions of worker and client are at the center of the social work endeavor. The worker must develop a high level of self-understanding if he or she is to maximize the helping interactions. The development of self-understanding, which is never complete, is an ongoing endeavor that involves assessing one's values, lifestyle, roots, personal needs, and culture.

The worker's use of self is a major tool in the helping endeavor. Some of the characteristics of the helping person are concern for others, acceptance of others, warmth, supportiveness, and maturity. The helping professional person is one who is grounded in a knowledge base and who uses a professional code of ethics as a guide to the helping endeavor. Good judgment also is a very important factor. The helping person needs to develop skills for understanding clients and their situations, for creating a climate that encourages interaction, for acting on the client's problems, and for communicating with and relating to others. The social worker also needs to develop a degree of comfort with the authority and responsibility that are inherent in the professional helping role.

Sometimes more than one person or worker needs to be involved in the helping situation. This may take the form of consultation, referral, or collaboration. Functioning in a team situation is an important skill for social workers. Teams take many forms: sometimes they are made up of persons from different professions, sometimes of social workers from a variety of agencies or with a variety of skills. Regardless of the type of team, functioning with others in a cooperative, collaborative manner is imperative.

QUESTIONS

1. What areas of self-knowledge should you examine in order to develop greater helping capacity?

2. What is the difference between a philosophy of life and a value system?

3. What do you see as your strengths as a helping person? Your limitations? What can you do to mitigate your limitations?

4. How well do you believe you have dealt with issues of authority in your life experience? With issues of responsibility?

5. Discuss the conflict between responsibility and self-determination. How do you think this conflict can best be resolved?

6. What do you see as problems you may have in working in a multiworker situation?

SUGGESTED READINGS

Abraham, Julie S. "Making Teams Work." *Social Work with Groups* 12 (no. 4, 1989): 45–63.

Cohler, Bertram. "The Human Studies and Life History: The Social Service Review Lecture." *Social Service Review* 62 (December 1986): 552–575.

Cornett, Carlton. "Toward a More Comprehensive Personology: Integrating a Spiritual Perspective into Social Work Practice." *Social Work* (March 1992): 101–102.

Erikson, V. Lois, and Martin, Joshua. "The Changing Adult: An Integrated Approach." *Social Casework* 65 (March 1984): 162–171.

Floren, Robert, and Barley, Royston. *Authority in Social Casework.* Oxford, England: Pergamon Press, 1968.

Garvin, Charles D., and Reed, Beth Glover, "Gender Issues in Social Group Work: An Overview." *Social Work with Groups* 6 (Fall/Winter 1983): 5–18.

Hartman, Ann, and Laird, Joan. *Family-Centered Social Work Practice.* New York: Free Press, 1983 (Chapter 10).

Joseph, M. Vincentia. "Religion and Social Work Practice." *Social Casework* 69 (September 1988): 443–452.

Lonsdale, Susan, Webb, Adrian, and Briggs, Thomas L. *Teamwork in the Personal Social Services: British and American Perspectives.* Syracuse, NY: Syracuse University School of Social Work, 1980.

Paradis, Bruce A. "An Intergrated Team Approach to Community Mental Health." *Social Work* 32 (March–April 1987): 101–104.

Scott, Dorothy. "Meaning Construction and Social Work Practice." *Social Service Review* 63 (March 1989): 39–51.

Sotomayer, Marta. "Language, Culture and Ethnicity in Developing Self-Concept." *Social Casework* 58 (April 1977): 195–203.

Toseland, Roland W., and Rivas, Robert F. *An Introduction to Group Work Practice.* New York: MacMillan, 1984 (Chapter 1).

Tropp, Emanual. "Three Problematic Concepts: 'Client,' 'Help,' 'Worker.'" *Social Casework* 55 (January 1974): 19–29.

NOTES

1. Adapted from the work of Isabel Briggs Myers, *Introduction to Type* (Gainsville, FL: Center for Application of Psychological Type, 1976).

2. For development of this idea from a Christian viewpoint, see Joseph F. Fletcher, *Situational Ethics: A New Morality* (Philadelphia: Westminster Press, 1966).

3. Florence Rockwood Kluckholm and Fred L. Strodtbeck, *Variations in Value Orientations* (Evanston, IL: Row Peterson, 1961), pp. 10–20.

4. Ann Hartman and Joan Laird, *Family-Centered Social Work Practice* (New York: Free Press, 1983), chap. 10.

5. See Dennis Saleeby, "Biology's Challenge to Social Work: Embodying the Person-in-Environment Perspective." *Social Work* 37 (March 1992): 112–117.

6. See Carol Gilligan, *In a Different Voice* (Cambridge, MA: Harvard University Press, 1982); Jean Baker Miller, *Toward a New Psychology of Women* (Boston: Beacon Press, 1976); and Alice S. Rossi, "Life-Span Theories and Women's Lives," *Signs* 6 (Autumn 1980): 4–32.

7. Carlton Cornett, "Toward a More Comprehensive Personology: Integrating a Spiritual Perspective into Social Work Practice." *Social Work* 37 (March 1992): 101–102.

8. For a discussion of moral development in a social work frame of reference see Wayne A. Chess and Julia M. Norlin, *Human Development and the Social Environment,* 2nd ed. (Boston: Allyn and Bacon, 1991), pp. 231–237; Charles Zastrow and Karen Kirst-Ashman, *Understanding Human Behavior and the Social Environment* (Chicago: Nelson-Hall, 1988), pp. 205–212; and John F. Longres, *Human Behavior in the Social Environment* (Itasca, IL: F. E. Peacock, 1990), pp. 474–481.

9. James W. Fowler, *Stages of Faith* (San Francisco: Harper, 1981); and Sharon Parks, *The Critical Years: The Young Adult Search for a Faith to Live By* (San Francisco: Harper and Row, 1986).

10. Arthur W. Combs, Donald Avila, and William W. Purkey, *Helping Relationships: Basic Concepts for the Helping Professions* (Boston: Allyn and Bacon, 1971).

11. Beulah Roberts Compton and Burt Galaway, *Social Work Processes,* 3rd ed. (Homewood, IL: Dorsey Press, 1984), pp. 245–248.

12. David W. Johnson, *Reaching Out: Interpersonal Effectiveness and Self-Actualization* (Englewood Cliffs, NJ: Prentice-Hall, 1972).

13. Anthony N. Maluccio, *Learning from Clients: Interpersonal Helping as Viewed by Clients and Social Workers* (New York: Free Press, 1979).

14. Edward Mullen, "Differences in Worker Style in Casework." *Social Casework* 50 (June 1969): 347–353.

15. Robert Foren and Royston Bailey, *Authority in Social Casework* (Oxford, England: Pergamon Press, 1968), p. 19.

16. Based in part on Lawrence M. Brammer, *The Helping Relationship: Process and Skills,* 2nd ed. (Englewood Cliffs, NJ: Prentice-Hall, 1979).

17. Susan Lonsdale, Adrian Webb, and Thomas L. Briggs, *Teamwork in the Personal Social Services and Health Services: British and American Perspectives* (Syracuse, NY: Syracuse University School of Social Work, 1980), p. 1.

18. Allen Pincus and Anne Minahan, *Social Work Practice: Model and Method* (Itasca, IL: F. E. Peacock, 1973), chap. 3.

19. Lonsdale, Webb, and Briggs, *Teamwork in the Social Services.*

20. Rosalie A. Kane, "Multi-Disciplinary Teamwork in the United States: Trends, Issues and Implications for Social Workers," in Lonsdale, Webb, and Briggs, op. cit., pp. 138–150.

21. Thomas L. Briggs, "Social Work Teams in the United States of America," in Lonsdale, Webb, and Briggs, *Teamwork in the Social Services*, pp. 75–93.

22. Gene Hooyman, "Team Building in the Human Services," in Compton and Galaway, op. cit., pp. 465–478.

23. Jonathan Baker, "The Relationship of 'Informal' Care to 'Formal' Social Services: Who Helps People Deal with Social and Health Problems If They Arise in Old Age," in Lonsdale, Webb, and Briggs, *Teamwork in the Social Services*, pp. 159–176.

7

THE CLIENT

Learning Expectations

1. Understanding of the term *client* and familiarity with other terms used that convey a similar meaning.
2. Understanding of the meaning of seeking help from a social agency in U.S. society.
3. Understanding of the process a person must go through in becoming a client.
4. Understanding of and the beginning ability to develop a social history of an individual.
5. Understanding of the influence of diversity upon the needs of individuals.
6. Development of knowledge of what factors about any culture a social worker must understand in providing service to a client of that culture.
7. Knowledge about the family as a social system.
8. Appreciation of the need to focus sometimes on the multiperson system as client.

The term **client** in social work usually refers to a person, family, or group that is the focus of the social worker's helping activity. In the generalist approach, this term may be somewhat inaccurate because as the social worker assesses the situation and develops plans, the focus may not be on an individual or on a system that has requested help. The focus for change may be on a system that is blocking the need fulfillment of an individual(s) or a family(s); the focus for change may be on groups, communities, or institutions/agencies. Nevertheless, the generalist social worker's knowledge base contains understandings about all of the systems upon which change might be focused. This chapter focuses on the individual and family as client, on people seeking help. Later in the book, material on engaging larger systems in the helping process and on assessing those systems is developed.

The person seeking help brings to the helping situation concerns, needs, and problems. The person comes to the helping situation sometimes seeking help, sometimes being required to use help, and sometimes not realizing the nature of the help offered or the reason it is being offered. The person comes with concerns, unmet needs, and problems of social functioning. She comes from a societal and cultural milieu, a set of life experiences, and a set of transactions with other persons that make the person unique yet sharing the commonalities of human-kind.

Regardless of the client's reason for coming for help, the client brings much more than concern, need, or problems to the helping situation. The client brings the total self as a biological, psychosocial, cultural, and spiritual being. This includes the resources of self and the personal environment and also environmental constraints. What the client brings includes perceptions of self and the situation and patterns of coping with stress and patterns of interpersonal relationships. The client's present need and/or problem is affected in part by the way developmental needs have been met and by needs arising from the diverse aspects of the client's lifestyle and from the expectations of the client's environment.

One of the major tasks of the worker-client interaction is the understanding of the client as a unique person in a unique situation. There can never be total knowledge about a client; that is impossible. The worker seeks knowledge about the client that is needed for giving the service to be delivered. The client is the major source of the facts used to develop the understanding of the person in the situation.

The social worker must also understand the meaning of seeking and using help, which is a first step to understanding the person seeking help. Understanding of the client also must include consideration of the multiperson client system. In this chapter, the family as a client is discussed as an example of a multiperson client system. Other multiperson systems will be considered in later chapters.

BECOMING A CLIENT

Emanual Tropp sees the client as one who seeks professional help, one who employs the help of another, or one who is served by a social agency or institution. In discussing each of these definitions, Tropp points out that there are inconsistencies. These inconsistencies also permeate the way workers, agencies, and community persons view clients. Several questions arise from these definitions: Is the client a customer or a dependent person? Is the client seen as a charge or ward, a person not worthy of respect? Is the client seen as a generally self-reliant person, able to make decisions? Must a client seek help, or may the person who is involuntarily referred be considered a client until she voluntarily seeks the help provided?[1]

Scott Briar and Henry Miller discuss the client in terms of his social role. A social role has normative expectations for the behavior of the person filling the role. These expectations are held by social agencies, reference groups, and the general public.[2]

Allen Pincus and Anne Minahan use the term *client* in a somewhat limited sense. The client system is that system which asks for help; the system that needs to change is known as the target system. The system asking for help may not be the system needing to change. A target system may become a client system by realizing a need for change and asking for help.[3]

In the context of this book, the client is one who has either sought the help of a social worker or is served by an agency employing a social worker. When the client has not sought the help, it is assumed that one of the tasks of the worker is to engage the client in a helping relationship that enables the client to understand the reason the help is offered and the implications for using the help or rejecting it. It is further assumed that the client's role calls for active participation in the helping endeavor, which includes furnishing appropriate information to inform the decision-making process, participation in the decision-making process to the limits of the client's ability and capacity, and the carrying out of mutually agreed upon tasks.

The client is either a person or a social system. Clients are of several types:

1. Those who ask for appropriate help for themselves;
2. Those who ask for help for another person or system;
3. Those who do not seek help but are in some way blocking or threatening the social functioning of another person (e.g., the neglectful parent in a child protection case);
4. Those who seek or use help as a means to reach their own goals or ends (e.g., a client the court has ordered to receive service in order to avoid more severe sanctions); and
5. Those who seek help, but for inappropriate goals.

Identification of client type is a first step in the delivery of service, for the worker-client relationship and interaction will vary depending on the type of client and the nature of the help sought.

The client is a person with both needs and a problem or problems. The problem may be related to a person the client has a responsibility for; for example, a parent becomes a client when seeking help for problems a child may have. The client may be the victim of the problem; the problem may be aggravated by other conditions; or the client may be the cause of the problem.[4] The social-functioning problem may rest in interpersonal relationships, in negotiating with systems in the environment, or in role performance. The problem may be one of deficiency or the lack of material means or personal capacity (temporary or permanent) or of the knowledge or preparation needed to carry out social roles. It may be due to disturbance or disorder resulting in intrapsychic turmoil, constriction, or distortion; it may be a result of discrepancies between expectations of a person and the demands of various segments of that person's environment or between environmental expectations and demands and personal needs.[5]

For example, a client may be having difficulty because of inadequate income due to a layoff at her place of employment; she is a victim of the problem of the workplace. Or she may be a single parent who is having some difficulty with parenting a young child yet still managing to cope with the help of a good childcare provider. When that provider suddenly becomes seriously ill and is no longer able to help, the parent's difficulty is aggravated by outside conditions over which she has no control. Or the client may not be able to hold a steady job due to excessive use of alcohol and thus be the cause of the problem.

The social-functioning problem may rest in interpersonal relationships; for example, the inability of a parent to understand an adolescent child's needs and, thus, is so strict that the relationship between parent and child is at the point where there is open rebellion and an inability to discuss the situation. The problem may rest in an inability to negotiate with systems in the environment; for example, a patient in a hospital is unable to ask the doctor the questions that are bothering that patient or to make his concerns known to the doctor. Or the problem may rest in inadequate or inappropriate role performance; for example, the parent does not meet the nutritional needs of the child or maintain a suitable home for that child.

The problem may be one of deficiency; that is, an individual does not have either the material means or the personal capacity (temporary or permanent) to carry out the tasks needed for coping with a situation. An older person with a limited income and limited physical capacity may not be able to maintain a home or fix nutritious meals. The problem may also be one of not having the preparation needed to carry out a social role. The mother who did not have adequate mothering as a child and has received no instruction in childcare may not be able to properly care for her child because she just does not know how to care for small children.

Some problems are due to disturbance or disorder resulting in intrapsychic turmoil, constriction, or distortion. In these situations, the person may be mentally ill or have some perceptual difficulty, which results in using inappropriate or ineffective means for coping with life situations. There may be problems as a result of discrepancies between expectations of a person and the demands of various segments of that person's environment. For example, an individual expects that food, clothing, and shelter will be provided by a community social agency without work on his part, but the agency can only provide partially for those needs and then only if work is performed for the community. Other problems may be due to discrepancies between environmental demands and personal needs. For example, a teenage girl whose mother is ill is expected to care for younger siblings, but she needs time for completing her education and for socialization with her peers.

In practice, a number of terms are used for the client role. The term used depends in part on the setting for practice and carries with it additional meanings. Social agencies generally use the term *client,* but in medical and mental health settings the term **patient** is often used. When using the term *patient,* a social worker might see the client in a more traditional patient role, as sick and dependent rather than as an interdependent client. In a school setting and certain institutions for youth, the client is called a *student.* This can lead to an instructor-learner relationship and to a superordinate-subordinate relationship. Social workers in advocate roles sometimes see the client as victims. The relationship may then be based on compensating for the wrongs of others and on doing for. Whatever name is used for the client, the person occupying the client role should be seen not in a superordinate-subordinate relationship but in a collaborating role and as having specific tasks and responsibilities that result in more effective social functioning for the client when carried out in cooperation with a person filling the worker role.

The worker, the client, and the environment all have expectations about how the client will fill the client role. The worker and the agency supplying the service have expectations about appointments, use of the time during helping sessions, time and place of these sessions, and the client's sharing of information and involvement in the helping process. The community's expectations of clients often center around being grateful for the help provided. The community also has expectations concerning drinking, sexual behavior, childcare practices, and money management concerns. Clients often do not understand what is expected of them in the helping situation. They may expect to be told what to do or to receive certain kinds of advice and help; they may expect to be treated as second-rate persons because they need help. Clients usually come for help at times of powerlessness and a lowered sense of self-worth, and with anxiety about the unknown helper and the helping situation. Seeking help and taking on the client role can add to the stress of an already stressful situation.

Before a person seeks help from a social agency, he or she has usually attempted to deal with the problem in a way that has worked with previous problems (commonly known as **coping**). "Coping is a person's effort to deal with some new, and often problematic, situation or encounter or to deal in some new way with an old problem."[6] Coping results not only in solving problems but in the reduction of tension and anxiety. But if the coping is not successful, a person may then turn to his or her natural helping network. Going to a social agency may be a last resort. Thus, individuals often come to the agency after a period of unsuccessful attempts to deal with their problem. Going to an agency or being unable to cope can result in anxiety and in feelings of low self-worth or of anger.

When persons from a culture different from those providing service come for help, another stress is added. For example, when a black person must seek help from an agency staffed by white people, the black person may bring feelings of resentment and anger toward whites because of discriminatory practices she has experienced in other situations. She may be unsure that a white social worker can understand her or her situation because the white worker does not have sufficient knowledge about black culture.

Before coming to a social agency, most people will have attempted to meet the need or solve the problem first with their own resources and then with the resources of their natural support system (e.g., friends, relatives, associates). If this has not been successful, they may have sought advice or help from a helping person they are familiar with, a pastor, a teacher, a doctor.[7]

People come to agencies in varying ways. F. M. Lowenberg has identified the pathways to help as 1) an informal referral by a neighbor or acquaintance, 2) knowledge of the work of the agency in one's social circle, 3) self-referral, 4) a formal request or referral from another professional or agency, 5) outreach the agency has done to identify persons with needs and encourage these persons to accept service, and 6) mandated participation by a court or some other authority.[8] Lowenberg goes on to note that becoming a client requires a person to admit that he has a problem and to express willingness to give up a behavior if necessary and to cooperate with a relatively unknown person in an often misunderstood process in an unknown place.

People may resist the acceptance of help from a social agency because of discomfort with strange people and strange or new situations. They may resist because of cultural norms regarding the use of help. Cultural groups prescribe helping mechanisms, attitudes toward the use of help, and the kinds of situations for which one may receive help. People also may resist asking for help because they feel that no help is possible.

David Landy has identified the process a person goes through in seeking help, or in becoming a client:

1. The help seeker must decide something is wrong.
2. The help seeker must face the probability that family, friends, and neighbors will know of his disability.
3. The help seeker must decide to admit to a helper he is in distress, failed or is not capable of handling his own problem.
4. The help seeker must decide to surrender enough sovereignty and autonomy to place himself in a dependent role.
5. The help seeker must decide to direct his search for help among persons and resources known to him.
6. The help seeker must decide whether to take time off a job or from other responsibilities to receive help.
7. The help seeker may realize that in receiving help other of his relationships may be threatened.[9]

In a recent study of farm families and the use of social services, Emilia Martinez-Brawley and Joan Blundall explored attitudes and preferences in help seeking. They note that help seeking and help acceptance are very complex processes. The study found that some of the major barriers to seeking or receiving help are concern about community reputation, lack of knowledge about services, feelings about the use of help that originate in the community culture, distrust of workers, and pride.[10] Although the study is limited in size of the population studied, it does provide information about the importance of culture and context in understanding help-seeking feelings and behaviors. It also leads to a conclusion that it is important for workers to consider not only the present context or situation of a client but also the client's historical context. For example, many farm families have had to migrate to metropolitan areas because of recent problems in agricultural communities. In the new setting, stresses and strains have often affected the social functioning of individuals and families. Although there may be a need for social services, attitudes and ways of functioning brought from the rural setting are apt to be present, which affect the capacity to seek help.

The role of client is not an easy one to take on. Social and cultural groups have norms that mitigate against easy assumption of the role. Personal feelings of adequacy and self-worth are often threatened in assuming the role. There usually exists considerable discomfort, anxiety, and stress; there may even be a state of crisis when a person enters a social agency. The acceptance of this role also calls for energy when the personal system may have already depleted its energy supply in attempting to cope with the problem or meet the need. The worker must understand the phenomena of asking for help and be ready to support the person through the process of becoming a client.

CASE EXAMPLE

Mrs. P has been caring for her husband, who is suffering residuals from a stroke two years ago. Mr. P is confined to a wheelchair and has only minimal speech. He is very demanding of Mrs. P and does not want her to leave his side. A home health nurse helped with his care for a while, but when the Medicare benefits were used up, Mrs. P decided they could no longer afford this service. Mr. and Mrs. P have two children who live at considerable distance from the parents and have growing families. They visit occasionally and this has given Mrs. P some help. The family doctor has suggested placing Mr. P in a nursing home, but Mrs. P cannot bring herself to do this. Besides, she has no idea where the money would come from for this expensive care. Mrs. P is able to get an old family friend to come in for two hours a week so she can do grocery shopping and other errands, but she feels that she should not depend on friends to give any but the most necessary help.

Last month their daughter came for a visit and was struck by how tired her mother appeared. She discussed this with her mother, who admitted that it was becoming increasingly difficult for her to care for Mr. P. The daughter discussed the situation with the family pastor, but he didn't have any suggestions, saying they had rejected any help the church had offered them.

The daughter then visited a nearby senior center and asked if they knew of any help that might be available. She found that the center had just developed an Adult Senior Day Care center, which might give some respite to Mrs. P and might be able to encourage some new activity and perhaps provide some therapy for Mr. P. The social worker at the center encouraged the daughter to discuss the possibility with her parents and to stress the fact that the program could improve the quality of Mr. P's life. They would work with him to help him develop as much capacity to take care of himself as possible.

At first Mrs. P completely rejected the notion of senior day care. She, again, was concerned about the cost. The daughter suggested that the Day Care social worker be allowed to visit them and discuss this as well as talk to them about the program that could be offered. Reluctantly her parents agreed, saying that they really did need some kind of help if Mrs. P was to continue to care for Mr. P in the home.

The social worker visited the family and engaged Mr. P in the discussion. She seemed to know just how to communicate with someone who had his disabilities. The social worker also discussed how the cost of day care might be met. She noted that, given their limited income, they would be eligible for help with the funding from the state. Mr. and Mrs. P were somewhat hesitant, but said they were at a point where they could no longer be proud and would have to take the help. The worker suggested that they visit the center before making a final decision; she would arrange for an agency van, which had a wheelchair ramp, to pick them up in a couple of days. After this visit, both Mr. and Mrs. P and their daughter were quite enthusiastic about Mr. P spending three half-days at the center with the possibility of expanding this later if he could benefit from more time. Mrs. P found that with these three mornings a week and the suggestions the day care center made about his care, her care-giving tasks were now within her capacity to cope. Mr. and Mrs. P both became clients of the Adult Day Care Center.

UNDERSTANDING THE INDIVIDUAL CLIENT

Before a worker can adequately respond to an individual's need, develop a working relationship, or engage in problem solving with a client, it is necessary to understand that client and her situation. Although there are commonalities among people, there are also differences. These differences include ones that are related to the developmental stage and to present and past adequacy in meeting the individual's common human needs and developmental needs. Differences are the result of hereditary and environmental factors.

The human condition is very complex. It must be remembered that each person is a unique bio-psycho-social-spiritual being. When the person in the situation is examined from a systemic point of view, the various aspects—of both the person and the person's situation—are seen to interact with each other. The outcome of these transactions is a unique person who perceives the world in a unique manner, who reacts to common human needs and developmental needs in an individualized way. The understanding of the person in the situation is crucial to all of social work practice.

Just as the worker must develop knowledge of self, the worker must also develop knowledge of the client. Some of the same tools used for self-knowledge are useful in gaining understanding of the client. The identification of a client's lifestyle, philosophy of life, moral code, and value system is possible only insofar as the client is willing to share of self with the worker and as the worker is able to make assumptions based on the worker's knowledge of the client's background, cultural identification, and life experiences and share these assumptions with the client for confirmation. The extent to which the worker needs to understand these factors about a client depends to a degree on the client's needs and the service to be offered.

Understanding the client's roots, that is, his cultural background, is often crucial in providing service. The worker can use some of the same tools available for understanding her own culture to understand the client. It is most important that the client not be stereotyped because of membership in a particular racial or ethnic group; there are many variations within each of these groups. To gain the needed understanding of any member of a racial or ethnic group, it is necessary to individualize that person.

An understanding of the client's family structure and functioning and of the client's place in the family is very important. Family influences are some of the strongest in any person's life. Sometimes reactions to these influences are to accept and conform to the family's lifestyle; other times the person rejects what the family expects. In both situations, understanding of a client's family is needed to understand the client's needs, desires, and problems. The genogram is a useful tool to use with clients when developing the needed understanding of family influences for both worker and client.

An understanding of client needs and ways of functioning is very important in providing services. Such understandings need to be developed to the extent necessary for providing the needed service. Thus, the worker will be selective about the information to be sought and will individualize the nature and depth of the understanding, depending on the client need and the service being provided.

The method used for attaining this needed understanding is often referred to as a **social history.** Table 7–1 is a schema for the development of a social history of an individual. Not all of the material called for will be important or available for all clients. In some agencies, for some situations and some clients, other information will be important for either all clients or for some clients. For example, in a nursing home it is important for the social worker to have information about the resident's avocational interests and friendship ties to enable the resident to remain active and involved with other people. Often religious ties and experiences will be important. In working with an adolescent who was adopted at age seven, it is helpful to know something about the adoption and the client's attitude and feeling about the adoption. The schema in Table 7–1 is not meant to be a fixed outline of what must be included in all social histories but is meant as a guide to be modified and adapted, depending on agency practice, client need, and the service being sought. The schema has three major parts: 1) a description of the person in the situation; 2) an identification of concern, needs, and problems related to the concern and needs; and 3) a description of the strengths and limitations of the client in the situation. The social history should be descriptive rather than evaluative. For example, family relationship should be described in terms of who relates to whom and in what manner rather than stating that the family relationships are "good." Strengths and limitations should be stated as facts rather than as value judgments.

Vital Roles

Any social history should pay particular attention to vital roles—the roles of work, marriage, and parenting.[11] With children and youth, attention is paid to

TABLE 7–1   Schema for Development of a Social History: Individual

I. The Person
  A. Identifying information (as needed by agency): name, address, date and place of birth, marital status, religion, race, referred by whom and why.
  B. Family
    1. Parents: names, dates of birth, dates of death, place or places of residence.
    2. Siblings: names, dates of birth, places of residence.
    3. Children; names, ages, dates of birth, places of residence.
    4. Resources in the family for client—expectations for client.
  C. Education and work experience
    1. Last grade of school completed, degrees if any, special knowledge or training. Attitudes toward educational experiences. Resources and expectations of educational system for client.
    2. Work history—jobs held, dates, reasons for leaving. Attitudes toward work experiences. Resources and expectations of work system for client.
  D. Diversity
    1. Handicapping factors—physical, mental health history, current functioning.
    2. Cultural and ethnic identification, importance to client.
    3. Other diversity factors (include religious affiliation or spiritual factors, if any).
    4. Resources and expectations related to diversity characteristics of client.
  E. Environmental factors
    1. Significant relationships outside family, resources and expectations for client.
    2. Significant neighborhood and community factors, resources and expectations for client.
II. The Concern, Need, Problem
  A. Reason for request for service
  B. History of concern, need, or problem; onset of concern, need, or problem; nature and results of coping attempts; factors that seem to be contributing to concern, need, or problem.
  C. Capacity to carry "vital roles"
  D. Needs of client (general)
    1. Needs based on common human need/development.
      a. Stage of physical, cognitive, and psychosocial development.
      b. Adequacy of need fulfillment in previous stages.
      c. Present needs (needs for developmental stage and compensation for previous stage deficiency).
    2. Needs based on diversity factors
      a. What dominant societal factors and attitudes affect the way people of this diversity meet common human/developmental needs?
      b. What cultural group factors affect the way people of this diversity meet common human/developmental needs?
      c. Individualize client within the diverse group. What are this client's attitudes toward diversity, means of coping with diversity, adaptation or lifestyle within diverse group, coping or adaptation relative to dominant societal expectations?
      d. What incongruities exist between this client's way of functioning and the societal expectations due to diversity?
      e. What needs does this person have because of dominant societal attitudes and expectations, because of cultural factors related to common human need/human development, because of individual factors of attitudes toward the diversity and dominant societal expectations and impingements, or because of incongruities between the client's way of functioning and societal expectations due to diversity?
    3. Needs based on environmental expectations.
      a. Client's responsibilities toward family, peer group, work, organizations, community.
      b. Other environmental expectations of client. Client's attitudes toward these expectations.

TABLE 7–1   *Continued*

  c.   Are responsibilities and expectations of the client realistic?
  d.   Client needs because of the responsibilities and expectations.
  4.   Need of client in relation to the request for service.
    a.   What general needs of the client have bearing on the request for service?
    b.   What is the specific need of the client in relation to the request?
    c.   What factors seem to be blocking the fulfillment of that need?
III. Strengths and Limitations for Helping
  A.   What does the client expect to happen during and as a result of the service to be provided?
  B.   What are the client's ideas, interests, and plans that are relevant to the service?
  C.   What is the client's motivation for using the service and for change?
  D.   What is the client's capacity for coping and for change? What might impinge? What are the individual's internal resources for change?
  E.   What are the client's strengths?
  F.   What are the environmental resources and the environmental responsibilities and impingements that could support or mitigate against coping or change?
  G.   Are there any other factors that affect the client's motivation, capacity, or opportunity for change?
  H.   What is the nature of the stress factor?
  I.   Are the client's expectations realistic?
  J.   Summarize the strengths and the limitations of the client in the situation as they relate to meeting need and/or problem solving.

how they are being parented and how they are preparing for the work role (education). With older persons past retirement age, or after the loss of the mate, attention is given to how past functioning affects present functioning. It is because of difficulty in one or more of these vital roles that most individuals' social-functioning problems come to the attention of social agencies and social workers.

Human Diversity

The area of human diversity is another factor that merits special concern in developing the understanding of individuals. Before a worker can understand the influence of culture on any specific client, he or she must understand that person's cultural group generally. It takes special effort to gain such understanding, but it is the obligation of all social workers to have a knowledge of the general characteristics of any diverse group with which they are working. It is also important to evaluate the individuality of each person in the context of his or her diversity. Table 7–2 outlines the factors about any culture that a social worker should understand in order to understand a client from that particular cultural group.[12] As important as this understanding is, it is not sufficient; the worker must also understand how the dominant society has impacted on individuals of a particular group with diverse characteristics. A person's diverse needs arise from the expectations of the cultural group and from the attitudes of, and relationships with, the dominant society. In addition, restrictions on the diverse group that arise from the dominant society must be understood. A third

TABLE 7–2   Human Diversity: Factors That Should Be Considered in Identifying Needs Because of Diversity

A. Cultural factors
   1. Values
      Attitudes about: things, time use, dominant culture, authority, work, display of feeling or emotion, etc.
      Past, present, future orientation
      Taboos
   2. Relationships—ways of relating
      With other persons
      To the physical world
      To the spiritual world
   3. Family structure
      Nature of family relationships
      Content of family life
      Variety and change possible
      Decision making
      Generational factors—age, sex considerations
      Child-rearing and housekeeping practices
   4. History—migrations
      Of relationship to dominant culture
      Of change-development-meaning to the group
   5. Communication patterns—language
      Usage, idioms, colloquialisms, labels, dialects, symbols, grammar, breadth of expression
      Nonverbal aspects
      Patterns—use of small talk, time, etc.
   6. Community structure
      Political, economic, educational, religious
      Means of mutual assistance, socialization, social control
      Social, cultural, and religious activities
      Health care
      Resources for individuals and families
   7. Coping mechanisms
      Adaptation, compensation, reaction to stress, adjustment to new situations and environments
B. Factors related to dominant societal attitudes and behaviors
   1. Issues of prejudice, discrimination, stigmatization, stratification, and stereotyping
   2. Ethnic consciousness
   3. Relationship to majority culture
      Amount of distance, majority expectations, exploitation, minority hyper-sensitivity, pain and suspicion, power relationships
   4. Quality-of-life issues
   5. Group identity and expectation of group relative to majority group
   6. How difference is valued
   7. Opportunity provision or restriction
C. Individual differences
   1. Orientation—traditional, assimilated, adapting, confused relative to culture
   2. Attitude toward self, others of same minority, difference minorities, and dominant groups
   3. Self-concept, coping and adaptation mechanisms, use of language and other communication mechanisms
   4. Relationships with family and/or cultural groups, responsibility or resources in the relationships
   5. Significant life experiences as a member of the cultural group
   6. Dynamics of self affected by diverse status, impact of diversity on self

group of understandings about any diverse group includes the range of differences that exist in any cultural group. Cultural understanding recognizes the uniqueness of persons in situations that operates within any diverse group just as it operates in all of human experience.

The influence of social class is one factor that must be taken into account in individualizing within a culture. In developing an understanding of an ethnic culture, it is important to separate culture from social class. In other words: How much of the diversity is due to membership in a cultural group, and how much is due to the fact that the person lives in poverty? John Longres states that minority status is not just a matter of cultural difference but also is related to relative power, privilege, advantage and prestige of a group within society (social class is an important consideration here). He also points out that these factors lead to the individual's perception of her place in society and her identity. This leads to help seeking and using behaviors, and influences the ways persons of minority status perceive problems.[13] Kenneth L. Chau notes that, unless "impediments to individual progress are taken into consideration in needs assessment, the meaning and significance of the client's attempt to solve problems may not be properly understood."[14]

Human diversity is not only ethnic or racial; we are diverse because of age, gender, physical or mental ability, physical appearance, religious affiliation, sexual preference, and socioeconomic standing. When persons with a diversity form an identifiable group with a common culture, then factors of cultural diversity exist, and worker understanding of that culture is important.

Some types of diversity do not exist as a cultural group. For example, a physically handicapped person may not identify with other physically handicapped persons; nevertheless, that person may be subject to discrimination, stereotyping, expectations, exploitation, opportunity restriction, and the like. The societal attitudes and behaviors toward the diverse person are important in identifying need because of diversity; also important is the diverse person's attitude toward self as a diverse person.

One group that has received considerable attention in terms of diversity is women. Women are not a cultural group, though there is a sense of culture in subgroups of women such as the women's liberation groups and right-to-life groups. It is important to see women as having a particular kind of diversity and as having been impacted by social factors that often lead to undermining their capabilities, opportunities, and self-perceptions.[15] During times of social change it is particularly important to determine an individual's orientation toward that change. This includes identification of attitudes and self-image in relation to change issues. Currently, major social change is taking place with respect to the role and function of women. Thus, social workers should be aware of a particular woman client's orientation toward this change, of how she perceives society impacting on her as an individual, and of her personal desires about her role and function as a woman. It is especially important that women social workers not assume that all women have or should have the same attitudes toward the women's movement that they may hold.

Motivation, Capacity, and Opportunity

In determining a client's strengths and limitations, a useful framework is one that assesses a client's motivation, capacity, and opportunity.[16] Motivation is influenced by what a person wants and how much that person wants it. It is assumed that for a person to work on the problem or use an offered service that person must want to work on the problem or use the service. Factors that seem to be important for motivation include the push of discomfort, the pull of hope that something can be done to relieve the problem or accomplish a task, and internal pressures and drives toward reaching a goal.

Capacity can be broken down into three categories: relationship, problem solving, and physical capacity. In considering relationship capacity, the factor to be determined is the ability of the client to form relationships with a worker or other persons who might be used as resources for helping. Problem-solving capacity is related in part to the cognitive development of the client. The ability of the client to engage in a problem-solving process either independently or with the assistance of a worker is the factor to be determined. A person's physical capacity is affected by certain handicapping conditions and age.

Opportunity refers to two factors. First is whether the client's environment will allow the client to use the service or to change. A part of this opportunity would be whether the client has sufficient energy for the problem-solving or change activity after the energy expenditure required to satisfy environmental and personal responsibilities. For example, a woman who is a single parent and the breadwinner in a family may not have sufficient energy to engage in an after-work educational activity that would prepare her for work that would yield a higher income. Opportunity also refers to the availability of resources and services needed to support problem solving or the needed change. Attention needs to be paid to whether the particular client can use available resources and services. Cultural or other factors may preclude the usability of resources and services by clients. This results in a lack of opportunity even though the resources or services exist. This conceptualization can also relate to workers' motivation (to work with this client), capacity (in terms of knowledge, skill, and energy), and opportunity (size of caseload, agency sanction, etc.).

Recently Nora Gold has pointed out the importance of considering motivation when developing an understanding of clients. She has pointed out that two factors seem to be of prime importance. One is **locus of control.** This concern is whether motivation comes from within, an internal process, or from influences in a person's environment, an external process. Also of importance and related to locus of control is the capacity of the individual for self-determination. Here the concern is whether the individual desires or is given the opportunity to make decisions based on internal factors (personal preferences) or external factors (situational imperatives and controls). According to Gold, motivational considerations affect the manner in which people select and define goals, which in turn are influenced by value issues.[17] An emerging goal for change is empowerment (see the section entitled "Empowerment" in Chapter 13). If the worker is concerned with empowering the individual, then it would seem that understanding that individual's motivations would be very important.

Stress and Crisis Determination

In considering a client's strengths and limitations, another factor to take into account is the degree and nature of the stress the client is experiencing. Stress exists when any internal or external event or condition impacts on a person or social system so as to upset its usual steady state or way of functioning. Usually, coping and problem-solving mechanisms are used, and the steady state is reestablished. If these mechanisms do not result in some modifications that enable reestablishment of the steady state, or if the severity of the problem or the number of events to be coped with becomes too great, a state of crisis may result.

The crisis state is marked by disequilibrium and disorganization.[18] A true crisis exists when a person who has usually functioned and coped relatively well is rather suddenly in a state of disequilibrium and disorganization. It is important to differentiate between a state of crisis and chronic disorganization. Another factor to examine is how previous crises have been resolved. Sometimes a crisis is resolved in a manner that is dysfunctional for later social functioning. Dysfunctional resolution of a crisis may stifle growth or cause negative relationships or feelings to develop.

Strengths and Uniqueness of Clients

Before leaving the discussion of the person as a client, there are two more considerations. All people have strengths that must be identified and called into play in the helping endeavor, some of which have already been discussed with regard to motivation, capacity, and opportunity. Other strengths become apparent when past problem-solving or coping mechanisms are examined. Strengths also exist in the individual's surrounding network. Elizabeth M. Tracy and James Whittaker developed an assessment instrument relative to the social supports of individuals and families.[19] With this instrument, they determine the components of a network, its capabilities, and its nonsupportive aspects, among other factors.

When using a schema such as the one presented in this chapter (Table 7–1), it is easy to miss the unique qualities of a particular individual or family. Jackie E. Pray declared that, it is important to assume, "at the outset that the client will differ from all others." She also calls for the use of the practitioner's practice wisdom and tacit knowledge in considering client uniqueness.[20] Also of importance is the development of mutual understanding between worker and client about the situation and the client, particularly the meaning of the experience to the client based on the client's personal beliefs and life experiences. Thus, the worker must be sensitive to information and understandings not called for in the schema and allow for the inclusion of this material when developing understanding about clients.

Social workers often become involved with clients after considerable effort has been made to cope with a situation, solve a problem, or meet a need. The client may be experiencing a high level of stress, be in danger of a crisis, or even be in crisis. Social workers should determine the stress level so that appropriate responses to need can be made.

CASE EXAMPLE

Social Study: Individual

Though the following case example is dated because of the enactment of the Indian Child Welfare Act of 1978, it has been retained because it so clearly portrays the necessity for providing service within the framework of the client's culture and experience.

A. Identifying information:
    Name: Lucinda Deer Kill   *Address:* 204 Main, Any Town
    Sex: Female   *Date of birth:* May 8, 1955, Rosebud, South Dakota
    Ethnic identification: Sioux Indian, Rosebud Tribe
    Marital status: Divorced 1977   *Date of marriage:* April 1973
    Husband's name: Tony Deer Kill
    Date of first service—nature of service: June 9, 1978—Removal of children to foster care. Children found alone at 1:00 A.M. Attempts to find Lucinda unsuccessful for one week. Children placed under emergency custody with Department of Social Services on June 11. Custody given to the department on August 3 after attempts to work with Lucinda unsuccessful. Father of children deceased April 1978 in auto accident.

B. Family:
    1. Children: Joe, born December 9, 1973.
        Linda, born January 16, 1975.
    2. Parents: Bill and Mary Buffalo, deceased since childhood. Lucinda was raised by maternal grandmother, Mary Many Moons; deceased February 1974.
    3. Brothers and sisters: three brothers and two sisters. Two brothers dead; one in auto accident ten years ago, one of unknown causes in childhood. Brother George resides on reservation, five years older than client. Sister Mary resides in Any Town, one year younger than client, married, has two preschool children. Sister Paula, two years older than client, divorced, has three children ages three, four, and five, now in foster care.
    4. Resources and expectations: Brother and sisters willing to help as in Indian tradition (sharing with family and friends what a person has even if it means giving up something that is needed). However, all three families already seem overburdened. George has been unemployed six months, has a drinking problem, and has four children of his own to support. Client lived for six months, two years ago, with Mary, who provides considerable emotional support for client. Mary has had several separations from her husband. The problems seem resolved at this time. One of these problems was Lucinda's living in Mary's home.
        Client now lives with Paula, who also is seeking to regain custody of her children. At this point the two sisters are close and seem to get great strength from each other. They are taking responsibility for each other.

C. Education: Completed eighth grade at Benton Country School. Basic skills in reading seem limited.

D. Work experience: Is now working as a maid at ABC Motel. Has held job for past six months. Sister works at same motel. Source of support ADC (Aid to Dependent Children) prior to removal of children. Source of support from time of removal of children to six months ago, sporadic jobs as maid in motels and dependence on Indian community.

E. Diversity factors: Community and self-identification, Indian. Seems to fall into category of confused regarding culture. Reference point for childcare: Indian culture and family. Children are given freedom at an early age. Older children care for younger ones at an early age. Indian community helps in care of children. Children may be left alone with expectation that community will care for them if needed. Does not want to return to the reservation at this time, as there is no work there. Has great difficulty negotiating in the majority society.

F. Environmental factors: Has used the local Indian Service Center in obtaining present employment and as an advocate for return of children. Occasionally misses work when she becomes involved with Indian friends.

G. History of need or problem: Children were found unattended by police on night of June 9, 1978. Her children and her sister Paula's children had been left in the care of Paula's boyfriend. He was called away and asked a neighbor to watch the children. The neighbor called the police. Police notified the Protective Services worker on call who placed all five children in temporary foster care.

　　Lucinda made no attempt to contact agency and was not found for one week. At that point she was intoxicated. Indian Service Center advocate states that Lucinda was afraid to contact agency; a friend had told her she would be put in jail. She did not understand her rights in the situation. Record states she was uncooperative with agency. This is not described.

　　Eight months ago, due to the new requirements of the Indian Child Welfare Act and a need for permanency planning for children, the agency reached out to Lucinda to determine her interest in the children and her ability to care for them. The local Indian Service Center was contacted. This center has been working with Lucinda and Paula to help them establish a home for the children. They report that Lucinda cares a great deal about the children and that the removal took place because of a lack of agency understanding of Indian culture and because Lucinda did not know how to negotiate with the agency system about the return of the children. The center worker feels both Lucinda and Paula have worked very hard to try to establish a home for the children. They have held jobs for the past six months and now have the privilege of having the children on days off. Visits have gone well. They recommend return of the children to Lucinda.

　　A major problem in this situation seems to be incongruities between societal expectations for childcare and the traditional Indian childcare customs. Another problem seems to have been Lucinda's inability to relate to the formal societal institutions of the community. With help, she seems able to do this to some degree.

H. Needs of client: Lucinda seems to have not successfully negotiated the Identity Stage of psychosocial development. She needs to develop a sense of who she is as an Indian person. She has also been unsuccessful in negotiating the Intimacy Stage, though there is growth in her family relationships at this time. She does have a steady boyfriend who seems supportive of her plans for the children. She is being asked to parent children as a single parent and has not been successful at this, though there is growth in this area at this time. She needs support in her growth efforts, a sense of success, and opportunities to help her develop a positive self-image. She also needs stability in the provision of basic food and shelter needs. Her problem-solving skills are poor, and she needs help appropriate to her culture in this area. Her childcare practices are somewhat incongruent with those of the dominant culture. She needs help in understanding the consequences of leaving the children alone and in finding ways to provide for the children's care while also providing for her own social needs.

This seems to be a situation in which lack of cultural understanding has prevented appropriate service being given to Lucinda. Her lack of understanding of the dominant culture and her lack of ability to negotiate with the social agency further added to the problem of providing appropriate service.

I.   Strengths and limitations for helping:
1.   Strengths
    a.   The client loves and cares for her children. She has a desire to provide for them. She wants them returned to her care.
    b.   The client has been able to use the services of the Indian Services Center. They are willing to continue to work with her on the parenting and work roles.
    c.   The client has a concerned extended family. Relationships with sisters and boyfriend are positive.
    d.   The client has been able to hold a job for six months and has established a home for her children.
2.   Limitations
    a.   The client has a very limited education and poor problem-solving skills.
    b.   The client is a single parent with unmet personal needs that may get in the way of meeting the needs of her children.
    c.   The client has limited financial capacity to support the children.
    d.   The client has limited capacity to negotiate with the dominant society, yet chooses to live in Any Town where this capacity is important.
    e.   The client has received inappropriate services that have led to an extended separation of mother and children and to angry feelings toward the agency and the dominant society. It is hard for her to use the services of the agency.
    f.   The client has not worked out adequate childcare plans for the children when she is working or socializing with friends.

UNDERSTANDING THE MULTICLIENT SYSTEM: THE FAMILY

When the client is a multiperson system, the worker must understand not only the persons who are members of the system but the subsystems that exist within the system and the system itself. This includes understanding the relationships among the individuals and subsystems. Social systems theory provides one means for describing multiperson systems. All social systems have structural, functional, and developmental aspects. An analogy from photography helps to differentiate these three aspects. Structure may be seen as a snap-shot; it describes the parts and their relationship to one another at a given point in time. Functioning may be seen as the movie; functioning describes the nature of the process of the system. Development may be seen as time-lapse photography; development describes stages of family functioning and is also concerned with roots and history and with significant past events in the life of the system.

Systems that may be multiperson clients are the family, the small group, organizations, institutions, agencies, neighborhoods, and communities. Each of these kinds of systems has unique characteristics that must be considered in understanding the worker-client relationship with a specific system of that kind. In this chapter, the understanding of the family system is developed. (Chapter 9 will discuss the small group; Chapter 10 will discuss the agency and community.)

The family is the system that is most apt to influence the functioning of the individual; it is the primary system responsible for providing for needs of individuals. Problems in individual functioning often arise from family functioning, past or present. Often, without change in the family system, the needs of individuals cannot be provided for and the problems of individual functioning cannot be solved. To bring about this change in the family system, it is necessary to understand the family as a social system. Knowing about an individual's place in his family system is also often necessary for understanding that individual. When the change needed is in transactions among members of the family system, the family becomes the unit of attention, or the client. The social worker determines the family system's motivation, capacity, and opportunity for change and engages the family system in the helping process. The family goes through the process of becoming a client.

Just as the use of a social history is useful in gaining an understanding of individuals, so a family social history is also useful in achieving an understanding of the family system. (See Table 7–3 for a family schema.) The family schema contains four parts: necessary identifying information; a description of the family as a system; the identification of concerns, needs, and problems of the family system; and identification of the strengths and limitations of the family system for meeting needs and solving problems.

In studying the structure of the family, it is useful to understand each family member in considerable depth. Use of appropriate parts of Table 7–1 would be a helpful tool for development of such understanding. The family should be considered as a system. System members are those persons who have stronger relationships among themselves than with other persons. The boundary of the family—the separation of the family from the environment—should be drawn so as to include other significant persons.

Thus, the family system may include some members of the extended family who may or may not be living in the home, such as a grandparent or an aunt. It may include an unrelated person living in the home or a neighbor. The children who have left the home for whatever reason need to be considered, depending on the nature of their functioning with the family system. Attention should be paid to absent family members—those who have died or left the family through divorce. Their influence on the family system and its functioning should be ascertained. The determination of who is in a family system is particularly difficult in the case of a blended family. The *blended family* is one in which the parents have had previous marriages and have children from these marriages.

Another part of the structure of the family is its subsystems—the martial, the parental, the sibling, and the parent-child subsystems. The marital subsystem includes the husband and wife as marriage partners. Their relationship should be described in terms of separation from each partner's family of origin and the ability of each partner to support and validate the other partner. The parental subsystem includes the mother and father and their interactions as parents of a child or children. The understanding of the sibling subsystem is concerned with how the children relate to one another. The parent-child subsystem is intergen-

TABLE 7–3   Schema for Development of a Social History: Family

I. Identifying Information (as needed by agency)
   A. Names and birthdates of family members, dates of death
   B. Dates of marriage, dates of previous marriages
   C. Religion, race, cultural background
   D. Language spoken in the home
   E. Date of first contact, referred by whom
II. The Family as a System
   A. Family structure
      1. Identify all persons within the functioning family system. Include members of extended family and nonrelated persons if they function as part of the system. Describe each person using appropriate parts of "Schema for Development of a Social History: Individual" (Table 7–1).
      2. Subsystems—Describe the relationships and functioning of the marital, parental, sibling, and parent-child subsystems or other subsystems.
      3. Family cohesiveness—Describe the manner in which the family maintains its system, boundary, and relatedness. This should include the issue of connectedness and separateness among family members, specification of family rules and norms, and emotional climate.
      4. The family's environment. Describe the family's:
         a. Living situation
         b. Socioeconomic status
         c. Nature of community or neighborhood and the family's relationship with the community or neighborhood. Include community organizations and institutions important for the family and the nature of the relationship with these. Describe community and neighborhood resources, and responsibilities and impingements for this family in this community.
         d. Extended family: involvement with; significant persons in the extended family; strength of the influence of this family system; and resources, responsibility, and impingements from it.
   B. Family Functioning
      1. Communication patterns
      2. Decision-making patterns
      3. Role performance
         a. Work and housekeeping standards and practices
         b. Parenting and child care standards and practices
         c. System member support; growth encouragement, care, and concern
      4. Family's customary adaptive and coping mechanisms
      5. Construct an eco-map for the family. (See example in Figure 7–1.)
   C. Family development—history
      1. Roots, influence of cultural group and previous generations on the family system
      2. Significant event in the life of the family
      3. Developmental stage of family life
      4. Construct a genogram
III. The Concern, Need, Problem
   A. Why did this family come to the agency? What service is requested?
   B. Needs of individual family members. (See Table 7–1.)
   C. Needs of subsystems within the family. (Particular attention should be paid to the marital system and the parental system.) Identification of resources and other assistance or change needed for appropriate functioning.
   D. Needs and problems of the family system. Consider how the needs of individuals and subsystems impact on the family system. Also consider environmental responsibilities, expectations, and any diversity factors that impact on the family as a system. Identify problems and blocks to the family system's meeting these needs.

TABLE 7-3   *Continued*

IV. Strengths and Limitations for Meeting Needs
    A. What does this family want to happen as a result of the service provided?
    B. What are the family's ideas, interests, and plans that are relevant to the service?
    C. What is the family's motivation for using the service or for change?
    D. What is the family's capacity for coping and change? What might impinge?
    E. What are the family's resources for change (internal to the system)?
    F. What are the environmental resources, responsibilities, and impingements on this family that could support or mitigate against change?
    G. Are there any other factors that affect the family system's motivation, capacity, or opportunity for change?
    H. Are the system's and the environment's expectations realistic for this family?
    I. What are the strengths and limitations for the family in the situation as they relate to meeting need and to problem solving?

erational in nature; of particular concern is how limits of authority and responsibility are drawn between the generations.[21] Other subsystems may exist in a family, and these should be identified and the nature of relationships in these subsystems described. Ann Hartman and Joan Laird have pointed out that an intergenerational perspective is very helpful in developing understanding of the family system. To do this, they suggest the use of a genogram.[22] (This technique was introduced in Chapter 6.)

A third consideration in describing family structure is cohesiveness. This is the stuff that binds the family together. It involves the emotional or feeling tone of the family, the we-ness of the family; it is the connectedness of family members with one another. Healthy family relationships allow for both connectedness and separateness.[23] The mechanisms for both connectedness and separateness should be described. Family rules and norms (the way this family does things or behaves) are means of expressing cohesiveness. Description of what is allowed and under what circumstances is another means of discovering the interrelatedness of family members.

The family system is part of a larger environment. That environment has expectations for the family, which involve both those for the functioning of the family as a system internally and for responsibility toward other systems in the environment. In a society of cultural diversity, there are often conflicting expectations, and these conflicting expectations should be identified. Also, impacts such as prejudice and discrimination because of family diversity should be identified. It is important to determine the nature and extent of the influence of systems such as church, school, cultural group, extended family, and the like that impinge upon the family or have expectations of responsibility for the family. It is also useful to identify environmental systems that may be a resource to the family. As one way of gathering this information, Hartman and Laird have developed the technique of developing an eco-map. (An illustration of this technique is found in the case example that follows.)[24]

Important features to consider with regard to the ways a family functions are the communication patterns, the manner in which decisions are made, and the way in which roles delegated to family members are carried out. Families having functional difficulty often have dysfunctional communication patterns. Some of these patterns may involve parents communicating through children, lack of freedom to communicate, and conflicting messages.[25] Identification of these communication patterns is important in understanding the functioning of the system.

In understanding the functioning of any social system it is important to know how decisions are made in that system. This includes identifying which decisions are individual ones, which are made in the subsystem, and which belong to the total system. It also includes influences on the decisions and how those decisions are communicated, performed, and enforced.

The family is one of the major institutions of society. For any society to be functional, families must carry out the roles delegated to them by society. These functions include the primary provision of common human needs for individuals, the care and nurturing of children, and the continuance of the culture. In order to perform these functions, the adult members of the family carry work roles including the homemaking role, the income-providing role, the parenting role, and the childcare role. These are vital roles in meeting the common human needs and the developmental needs of all family members. Through the carrying out of work, parenting, and marriage roles, the family provides the support, encouragement of growth, and the care of and concern for all family members. Knowing how these roles are filled provides an understanding of family functioning.

Change is a part of all human functioning. The family is subject to change because of growth of family members; because of birth, children leaving the family home, death, and divorce; because of changed functioning of family members due to illness or disability; or because of changed environmental resources, impacts, or responsibilities. All systems develop mechanisms for coping with changes or for adapting to changing conditions. These adaptive and coping mechanisms should be identified and examined for their contribution to appropriate flexibility of the family system in meeting changes both within the social system and in the environment.

A final area for understanding the family as a social system is the development of the family, which begins in a family's roots. Current structure and functioning are in part a product of its roots. Again, the genogram is a useful tool to use with a family in considering these roots. Also important is an understanding of the family's cultural background (see Table 7–2). Events that have called for significant change, adaptation, and coping within the family system are also important in understanding a family's development.

All families go through stages as the composition and needs of family members change. Sonya Rhodes has identified seven stages of family life:

1. *Intimacy vs. idealization or disillusionment*—The dyadic relationship of husband and wife is formed. Developmental task involves developing a realistic appreciation of one's partner.

2. *Replenishment vs. turning inward*—The stage between the birth of the first child until the last child enters school. Developmental task involves developing nurturing patterns for family members.

3. *Individualization of family members vs. pseudomutual organization*—The stage where the family has school-age children. Tasks include parents separating their own identity from that of the child and the enabling of the development of support and opportunities for individual family members outside the family system. Another task is the individualization of each family member.

4. *Companionship vs. isolation*—The stage of teenage children in the family. Important themes are separation and sexuality. The tasks are development of parent-child relationships based on the knowledge of the child's growing independence and a marital relationship based on companionship.

5. *Regrouping vs. binding or expulsion*—This is the stage of the children leaving home. The task is a regrouping on generational lines and development of an adult-to-adult relationship between parents and children.

6. *Recovery vs. despair*—The couple renegotiates a relationship that does not involve parenting children in the home. Parent-child relationships are also changed. The task then is renegotiation of relationships.

7. *Mutual aid vs. uselessness*—Parents are now retired. Couple often are grandparents. The task is to develop a mutual-aid system among the generations.[26]

A study of the family as a social system also includes the identification of that system's concerns, needs, and problems. Though the needs of individual members and subsystems contribute to the family system needs and problems, the needs and problems of the family system are different from those of the parts. The needs and problems of the family system relate to what will enable the family to maintain itself as a system and still fulfill its responsibility to its members and to its environment.

Of particular importance when working with families in which ethnicity and social class must be considered is use of a multisystem model. Here the focus is on the interacting level of family functioning (within the family, within the extended family, and with the various formal helping agencies involved). This type of approach will lead the worker toward more appropriate interventive strategies, whether it be strategies better suited to a particular ethnic situation or toward a choice that will bring about change in the larger system within which the family is finding negative impacts for healthy functioning.[27]

It is also important to identify the strengths and limitations of the family in the situation as a base for developing a professional relationship and for considering intervention into the transactions among family members and of the family and its environment. It is through intervention into these transactions that the social worker can enable families to meet the needs of the family as a system, as well as those of the individual members, and to help families solve social-functioning problems. The understanding of the family as a social system is a means of identifying its strengths and limitations and of planning for intervention.

CASE EXAMPLE

Social Study: Family

In the situation of the A family discussed in Chapter 1, if the family is considered the client, an assessment of that family might look as follows:

I. Identifying Information
    A. Names and birthdates of family members:
        Father: Henry A   Born: June 12, 1956
        Mother: Sally A   Born: April 21, 1957
        Children: Henry Jr.   Born: November 3, 1976
                    John   Born: September 10, 1979
                    Mary   Born: February 16, 1982
    B. Marriage: June 24, 1975. First marriage for both parents. Parents had dated steadily in high school.
    C. Religion: Methodist; do not attend regularly.
    D. Cultural/racial background: Caucasian, mixed German and Scandinavian.
    E. Language spoken at home: English
    F. Date of first contact with agency: March 1991, referred by school because of John's adjustment problem.
II. The Family as a System
    A. Family structure
        Henry finished high school and went to work full time in the hardware store that his father owned, and which he now manages. Due to economic problems in the community, this store is not doing as well as it once did, though, through hard work and long hours, Henry has managed to provide for his family and provide his widowed mother with an income. He says he has little time for his family but is looking forward to one of the boys coming into the business and lightening the load. Henry does belong to a local service club and is active in the businessmen's association. He says this is necessary if he is to stay in business. He says there was never any question but that he would work in the store. He just wants John to behave himself and stop upsetting his mother.
        Sally is also a high school graduate. She and Henry were married soon after she graduated, and she has always stayed at home and cared for the children. Occasionally she helps in the store and enjoys getting out of the house to do this but believes her husband does not want her to become too involved in the business. It is her job to see that the children behave themselves. She has no trouble with Henry Jr. or Mary but has always found John a difficult child.
        Henry Jr. is a freshman in high school. He has always been a good student. He has been active in Boy Scouts and is looking forward to getting into athletics in high school.
        John is in seventh grade and has always found school difficult. He thinks everyone wants him to be exactly like his big brother. He says he tries but he just can't do it and is giving up. He does not like Scouts and prefers to hang around with a group of friends. All these boys are entering adolescence and seem to be rebelling against school and parental control.
        Mary is in fifth grade and is a good student. She enjoys helping her mother around the house and has one very close girlfriend. She wishes she could take dancing lessons but has not been able to because of the cost.
        There seems to be little communication between the marital pair. Each has a well-specified area of responsibility in the family. Mr. A does not believe the family needs to be concerned with his business. He wants to find a clean house,

well-cooked meals, and well-behaved children when he comes home. The couple have been hesitant to discuss their sexual life, though the worker suspects that this reticence could be overcome. Mrs. A would like some help with the children, especially John, but says, "He (Mr. A) is the way he is and won't change. I just have to find a way to get John to behave." There seem to be an increasing number of fights between the couple, which seem to be related to John's behavior and to Mrs. A's desire to engage in some activity outside of the home.

The children seem to go their own ways. When the boys were younger, John tried to become involved with Henry Jr.'s activities, but Henry Jr. refused to have this. John seemed to give up and find his own friends. Now Henry Jr. is very critical of John's friends. Neither boy has much to do with Mary. When she was born, John had a very hard time for a while and seemed to feel he was being replaced. As the family seldom does anything together, the children have had little opportunity to form a close system.

The parent-child system is primarily focused on mother-children relationships. She seems to be having increasing difficulty understanding the needs of her growing sons. There is little father-son relationship. Henry Jr. seems to find role models in the men he knows through scouting. John seems to be seeking male attention but has not been successful in getting it; occasionally, if his behavior is particularly bad his father gives him a yelling. Mary and her mother seem to have a very close relationship.

In this family there seems to be an expectation of traditional family roles and ways of functioning. No one seems free to discuss what any one member of the family wants. The cohesiveness that exists is related to this traditionalism which seems to be questioned by at least John and to some degree his mother. There does seem to be considerable concern about what outsiders are thinking when one member of the family fails to function in expected ways. The economic difficulties in the business and John's recent problems have seemed to engender a tenseness in the climate of the family. Mr. A and Henry Jr. seem to deal with this by absenting themselves from family life. Mrs. A and Mary seem to find a great deal of satisfaction in their relationship and do not seem particularly distressed by the absences. John seems to be reacting to the tenseness in ways that are not acceptable to the family.

The family lives in a comfortable older house in a well-kept part of town. Each of the children has his or her own bedroom. The home looks lived in but is clean. The family is of lower middle-class economic status.

The neighborhood is changing. In the past there were many older couples. Mrs. A used to spend time with these older women and enjoyed that very much. Now, she says, younger families are moving in, and the women work and have no time for neighborhood get togethers. Also, some of these young couples are having loud parties and don't take pride in their home or neighborhood.

Mrs. A's parents died within four months of each other about two years ago. She states she was very close to her mother and misses her very much. She has one brother and one sister; they live at a distance and she is not close to either of them. Mr. A's father died four years ago after a long bout with cancer. He remained close to the business until his last days. Mr. A feels strongly that his father had a great influence on him and expected him to keep the business going so that it will provide an income for his mother, who lives in the community. She has recently moved into an elderly housing complex and is having difficulty adjusting. She often calls Mr. A at work about her needs. Mrs. A states that she tries to help her mother-in-law but finds that her help is not appreciated. Mr. A has one sister; he has never gotten along with her. She lives in town and is always telling him what he ought to be doing for their mother. She also has been very critical of John's recent behavior.

B. Family functioning (see Figure 7–1)

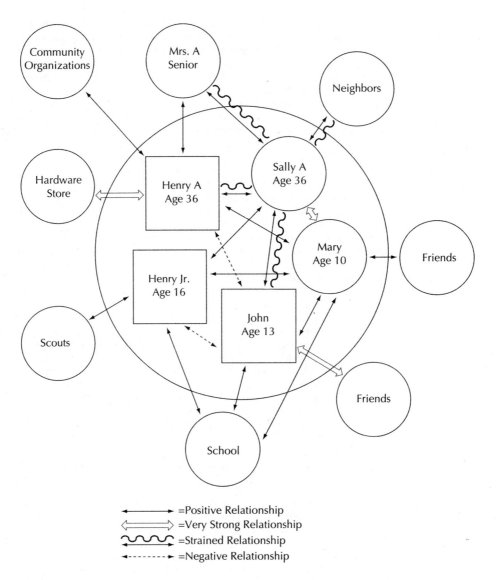

Community Organizations

Mrs. A Senior

Neighbors

Hardware Store

Sally A Age 36

Henry A Age 36

Mary Age 10

Friends

Henry Jr. Age 16

John Age 13

Scouts

Friends

School

⟵——————▶ =Positive Relationship
⟸==========⟹ =Very Strong Relationship
∿∿∿∿∿ =Strained Relationship
◀- - - - - -▶ =Negative Relationship

FIGURE 7–1   Eco-Map

There seems to be minimal communication in this family around needs and desires of individuals. Mr. A communicates his desires to Mrs. A. He does not communicate his concerns about the business. He is annoyed that Mrs. A does not understand his mother and relate to her needs. There is good communication between Mrs. A and Mary. Communication among children seems primarily of a negative nature. Mr. A is distant from the children.

Mr. A makes all financial decisions. He also decides on the roles of each family member. Mrs. A is expected to make all decisions about the children and running of the household. There seems to be an expectation that each person will know what the other wants. Children are excluded from family decision making.

Housekeeping standards are high and carried out. Mr. A works hard and provides an adequate financial support for the family. Parenting is left to Mrs. A. She has high expectations for herself. The emotional aspect is missing except between Mrs. A and Mary. Mr. A shows approval for Henry Jr. and disapproval for John.

When adapting or coping with change, this family seems to revert to a set of guidelines that relate to traditional roles, hard work, and doing what is right. They seem to have little skill in adapting to change or individual needs.

C. Family development history (see Figure 7–2)

This couple seems tightly tied to their parents. They adhere to the lifestyle with which they grew up. There appears to be little conflict between the lifestyle of the two families of orientation. Neither partner seems to have a sense of their grandparents, as all died when they were very young; they had little contact with aunts and uncles. They cannot identify any specific cultural influences, saying they are just plain people who have always worked hard and kept to themselves. The death of parents seems to be a critical point of change for this couple.

They seem to be in the individualization of family members vs. pseudomutual organization stage. It appears that the balance is more toward pseudomutual organization. In earlier stages, it can be suspected that there was more turning inward than replenishment, and that intimacy was not well established, but rather they may have used idealization.

III. Concern, Need, Problem

Family was referred to agency for help because John had been involved in a minor stealing episode (candy bar at a local store) and because of increasing school difficulty. School suspects family difficulties. Mrs. A says she wants help in dealing with

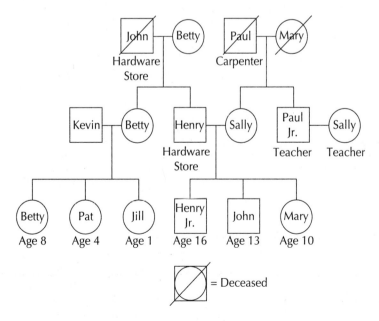

FIGURE 7–2   Genogram

John. Mr. A says he wants John to be straightened out. John says he wants to be allowed to be himself and not always be yelled at.

Mr. A seems to need help in understanding the needs of other family members. He also may need someone to talk to about concerns around the business and his relationship with his mother.

Mrs. A needs help in communicating her needs to her husband. She is very unsure of her parenting ability with her sons. She may need help in coming to grips with the death of her parents and of the changing nature of her community. She seems to need some interest or activity outside the home.

Henry Jr. appears to be the best adjusted member of the family. He might benefit from greater interaction with his father. John needs a relationship with his father that focuses on his positive attributes. His behavior seems to be a call for help for this family, thus, he needs to be relieved of the role of trouble maker by having a better functioning family. His school difficulty also may be an area to explore. Why has he always had difficulty in school? Does he have a minimal learning difficulty that could be corrected? He needs positive relationships with boys his own age and with other men. He also could use some help in understanding the adolescent process and how it is affecting him. Mary probably needs help in beginning to break away from the family and not being overly dependent on her mother.

This couple seems to need help with both the marital and parental relationship. There is a question as to how much intimacy exists in this relationship. They need help in learning to express needs to each other and in how to respond to these needs in a manner that brings satisfaction to the individual. They seem to have limited understanding of the needs of adolescent children. The children could use help in discovering their commonality and developing meaningful relationships with each other.

This family needs to explore their self-defined lifestyle to determine if it is meeting the needs of the family and its individual members. To do this it will be necessary to help them develop greater communication, particularly around feelings. Also, there should probably be emphasis placed on hearing about the needs of others. The family is very isolated from its environment, and greater participation, individually and perhaps as a family, seems indicated.

IV. Strengths and Limitations in Meeting Needs

The family seems to be asking that John's problems be solved. They do not seem to realize that the problem rests in family functioning. Mrs. A seems ready to participate in a treatment experience. Mr. A may be resistant. The children will take their cues from the parents. The family's capacity to participate remains to be seen as does their capacity for change. It would seem that pressure from the school to relate to John's needs might be something the parents could respond to. If they can begin to openly express feelings and needs, this experience could well motivate them to work on their problems. They seem very concerned about the children, and Mrs. A, at least, realizes she needs help in parenting. This may mean they would do well in a parenting group situation. This would also provide exposure to people outside the family.

SUMMARY

The client is an individual or social system requesting help or receiving service from a social worker. The client's capacity to request or use help is affected by his culture's attitudes toward receiving help, the client's past experiences in using help, and pressures and constraints of the context in which the help is given. It is important for a social worker to understand how attitudes about seeking and receiving help affect a client's capacity to function in the helping situation.

Understanding a client's past and present functioning and the various factors that affect the functioning is a key skill of a social worker. This understanding is often expressed through the development of a social history. Factors that are particularly important to consider are how the client fills the vital roles of work, marriage, and parenting; how human diversity affects the social functioning of the individual; the motivation that the client brings to the helping endeavor; and the extent of the crisis and stress the client is experiencing.

Understanding a client also extends to understanding multiclient systems. Of prime importance is understanding the family as a client from a structural, functional, and developmental point of view. Understanding the client system is of vital importance when developing a professional relationship with that client.

QUESTIONS

1. What image do the terms *patient, client,* and *consumer* bring to mind? How do you think terminology may affect the way help is given?

2. What experiences do you believe help people seek assistance from social workers? What experiences make it difficult to seek help?

3. In what ways are people socialized to use or avoid using help by their culture?

4. Develop a social study for someone you have recently helped in some way.

5. Using a cultural group different from your own and with which you have had considerable contact, identify factors that you need to find out about to have sufficient knowledge to work as a social worker with people from that culture group.

6. Discuss the differences in the family structure and functioning in two families other than your own. Use families with whom you have had considerable contact.

SUGGESTED READINGS

Alcabes, Abraham, and Jones, James A. "Structural Determinants of Clienthood." *Social Work* 30 (January–February 1985): 49–53.

Anderson, Joseph D. "Family-Centered Practice in the 1990's: A Multicultural Perspective." *Journal of Multicultural Social Work,* 1 (No. 4, 1992): 17–29.

Canda, Edward R. "Spirituality, Religious Diversity, and Social Work Practice." *Social Casework* 69 (April 1988): 238–247.

Chau, Kenneth L. "Social Work with Ethnic Minorities: Practice Issues and Potentials." *Journal of Multicultural Social Work* 1 (No. 1, 1991): 23–39.

Cimmarusti, Rocco A. "Family Preservation Practices Based upon a Multisystems Approach." *Child Welfare* 71 (May–June 1992): 241–256.

Conway, Pat. "Losses and Grief in Old Age." *Social Casework* 69 (November 1988); 341–349.

Coulton, Claudia J. "Person-Environment Fit as the Focus in Health Care." *Social Work* 26 (January 1981): 26–34.

De Anda, Diane. "Bicultural Socialization: Factors Affecting the Minority Experience." *Social Work* 29 (March–April 1984): 101–107.

DeHoyos, Genevieve, DeHoyos, Arturo, and Anderson, Christian B. "Sociocultural Dislocation: Beyond the Dual Perspective." *Social Work* 31 (January–February 1986): 61–67.

Dubray, Wynne Hanson. "American Indian Values: Critical Factors in Casework." *Social Casework* 66 (January 1985): 30–37.

Gelfand, Donald E., and Fandetti, Donald V. "The Emergent Nature of Ethnicity: Dilemmas in Assessment." *Social Casework* 67 (November 1986): 542–550.

Gold, Nora. "Motivation: The Crucial But Unexplored Component of Social Work Practice." *Social Work* 35 (January 1990): 49–56.

Goldstein, Howard. "Starting Where the Client Is." *Social Casework* 64 (May 1983): 267–275.

Green, James W. *Cultural Awareness in the Human Services.* Englewood Cliffs, NJ: Prentice-Hall, 1982.

Hardy-Fanta, Carol, and MacMahon-Heuera, Elizabeth. "Adapting Family Therapy to the Hispanic Family." *Social Casework* 62 (March 1981): 138–148.

Harrison, Dianne F., Wodarski, John S., and Thyer, Bruce A. Eds. *Cultural Diversity and Social Work Practice.* (Springfield, IL: C. C. Thomas, 1992).

Hartman, Ann, and Laird, Joan. *Family-Centered Social Work Practice.* New York: Free Press, 1983.

Jayaratne, Srinika, and Irey, Karen V. "Gender Differences in the Perceptions of Social Workers." *Social Casework* 62 (September 1981): 405–412.

Katlin, Fay. "The Impact of Ethnicity." *Social Casework* 63 (March 1982): 168–171.

Keith-Lucus, Alan. *Giving and Taking Help.* Chapel Hill: University of North Carolina Press, 1972.

Kuhn, Daniel. "The Normative Crises of Families Confronting Dementia." *Families in Society* 71 (October 1990): 451–459.

Landy, David. "Problems of the Person Seeking Help in Our Culture." In Mayer N. Zald, Ed., *Social Welfare Institutions: A Sociological Reader.* New York: John Wiley, 1965 (pp. 559–574).

Loewenstein, Sophie Freud. "Understanding Lesbian Women." *Social Casework* 61 (January 1980): 29–38.

Logan, Sadye L. "Race, Identity, and Black Children: A Developmental Perspective." *Social Casework* 62 (January 1981): 47–56.

Longres, John F. "Toward a Status Model of Ethnic Sensitive Practice." *Journal of Multicultural Social Work* 1 (No. 1, 1991): 41–56.

Martinez-Brawley, Emilia E., and Blundall, Joan. "Farm Families' Preferences Toward Personal Social Services." *Social Work* 34 (November 1989): 513–522.

McGoldrick, Monica, Pearce, John, and Giordano, Joseph. *Ethnicity and Family Therapy.* New York: Gilford Press, 1982.

McMahon, Anthony, and Allen-Meares, Paula. "Is Social Work Racist? A Content Analysis of Recent Literature." *Social Work* 37 (November 1992): 533–539.

Pray, Jackie E. "Respecting the Uniqueness of the Individual: Social Work Practice within a Reflective Model." *Social Work* 36 (January 1991): 81–85.

Rhodes, Sonya L. "A Developmental Approach to the Life Cycle of the Family." *Social Casework* 58 (May 1977): 301–311.

Robinson, Jeanne B. "Clinical Treatment of Black Families: Issues and Strategies." *Social Work* 34 (July 1989): 323–329.

Rothman, Jack, Gant, Larry M., and Hnat, Stephen A. "Mexican-American Family Culture." *Social Service Review* 59 (June 1985): 197–215.

Ryan, Angela. "Cultural Factors in Casework with Chinese-Americans." *Social Casework* 66 (June 1985): 333–340.

Saleeby, Dennis. *The Strengths Perspective in Social Work Practice.* New York: Longman, 1992.

Sheafor, Bradford W., Horejsi, Charles R., and Horejsi, Gloria A. *Techniques and Guidelines for Social Work Practice.* Boston: Allyn and Bacon, 1988 (Chapter 9).

Sotomayor, Marta. "Language, Culture and Ethnicity in Developing Self-Concept." *Social Casework* 58 (April 1977): 195–203.

Timberlake, Elizabeth, and Cook, Kim Dank. "Social Work and the Vietnamese Refugee." *Social Work* 29 (March–April 1984): 108–113.

Tracy, Elizabeth M., and Whittaker, James K. "The Social Network Map: Assessing Social Support in Clinical Practice." *Families in Society* 71 (October 1990): 461–470.

Weick, Ann. "A Growth-Task Model of Human Development." *Social Casework* 64 (March 1983): 131–137.

Whittaker, James K., and Tracy, Elizabeth. *Social Treatment*, 2nd ed. New York: Aldine DeGruyer, 1989, (Chapter 14).

Williams, Sharon E., and Wright, Dolores Finger. "Empowerment: The Strengths of Black Families Revisited." *Journal of Multicultural Social Work* 2 (No. 4, 1992): 23–37.

Young-Eisendrath, Pauline. "Ego Development: Inferring the Client's Frame of Reference." *Social Casework* 63 (June 1982): 323–332.

Zimmerman, Shirley L. "The Family: Building Block or Anachronism?" *Social Casework* 61 (April 1980): 195–204.

NOTES

1. Emanual Tropp, "Three Problematic Concepts: 'Clients,' 'Help,' 'Worker,'" *Social Casework* 55 (January 1974): 19–29.

2. Scott Briar and Henry Miller, *Problems and Issues in Social Casework* (New York: Columbia University Press, 1971), chap. 6.

3. Allen Pincus and Anne Minahan, *Social Work Practice: Model and Method* (Itasca, IL: F. E. Peacock, 1973), chap. 3.

4. F. M. Lowenberg, *Fundamentals of Social Intervention: Core Concepts and Skills for Social Work Practice* (New York: Columbia University Press, 1977), chap. 5.

5. Helen Harris Perlman, *Persona* (Chicago: University of Chicago Press, 1968), p. 207.

6. Helen Harris Perlman, "In Quest of Coping," *Social Casework* 56 (April 1975): 213–225.

7. For a report of research regarding help-seeking behavior see John B. McKinlay, "Social Networks, Lay Consultation and Help-Seeking Behavior," *Social Forces* 51 (March 1973): 275–292.

8. Lowenberg, *Fundamentals of Social Intervention.*

9. David Landy, "Problems of the Person Seeking Help in Our Culture," in *Social Welfare Institutions: A Sociological Reader,* Mayer N. Zald, Ed. (New York: John Wiley, 1965), pp. 559–574.

10. Emilia E. Martinez-Brawley and Joan Blundall, "Farm Families' Preferences Toward Personal Social Services," *Social Work* 34 (November 1989): 513–522.

11. Perlman, *Persona,* pp. 207–211.

12. An excellent resource for the study of a diverse culture is Ann Templeman Brownlee, *Community, Culture, and Care* (St. Louis: C. V. Mosby, 1978). This book specifies questions to ask, resources to use, and reasons for gaining the various kinds of information. Also, Emelicia Mizio and Anita L. Delaney, Eds., *Training for Service Delivery to Minority Clients* (New York: Family Service Association of America, 1981), discusses the impact of the majority society on Blacks and Puerto Ricans.

13. John F. Longres, "Toward a Status Model of Ethnic Sensitive Practice," *Journal of Multicultural Social Work* 1 (No. 1 1991): 41–56.

14. Kenneth L. Chau, "Social Work with Ethnic Minorities: Practice Issues and Potentials," *Journal of Multicultural Social Work* 1 (No. 1 1991): 23–39.

15. Sharon Berlin, "Better Work with Women Clients," *Social Work* 21 (November 1976): 492–497.

16. Lillian Ripple, Ernestina Alexander, and Bernice P. Polemis, *Motivation, Capacity, and Opportunity: Studies in Casework Theory and Practice,* Social Service Monographs, Second Series (Chicago: School of Social Service Administration, University of Chicago, 1964).

17. Nora Gold, "Motivation: The Crucial But Unexplored Component of Social Work Practice," *Social Work* 35 (January 1990): 49–56.

18. Howard J. Parad, "Crisis Intervention," in *Encyclopedia of Social Work*, 17th issue, John B. Turner, Ed. (Washington, D.C.: National Association of Social Workers, 1977), pp. 228–237.

19. Elizabeth M. Tracy and James K. Whittaker, "The Social Network Map: Assessing Social Support in Clinical Practice," *Families in Society* (October 1990): 461–470.

20. Jackie E. Pray, "Respecting the Uniqueness of the Individual: Social Work Practice within a Reflective Model," *Social Work* 36 (January 1991): 80–85.

21. For further discussion, see Curtis Janzen and Oliver Harris, *Family Treatment in Social Work Practice* (Itasca, IL: F. E. Peacock, 1980), pp. 6–12.

22. Ann Hartman and Joan Laird, *Family Centered Social Work Practice* (New York: The Free Press, 1983), chap. 10.

23. Janzen and Harris, pp. 12–16.

24. Hartman and Laird, chap. 8.

25. Janzen and Harris, pp. 15–20.

26. Based on Sonya L. Rhodes, "A Developmental Approach to the Life Cycle of the Family," *Social Casework* 58 (May 1977): 301–311.

27. See Joseph D. Anderson, "Family-Centered Practice in the 1990's: A Multicultural Perspective," *Journal of Multicultural Social Work* 1 (No. 4, 1992): 17–29; and Rocco A. Cimmarusti, "Family Preservation Practice Based upon a Multisystems Approach," *Child Welfare* 71 (May–June 1992): 241–256.

8

INTERACTION
WITH INDIVIDUALS

Learning Expectations

1. An understanding of the one-to-one action system as one context for delivering social work services.
2. An understanding of what goes into the formation of such a system.
3. An understanding of the concept of relationship and of its importance in the one-to-one action system.
4. An understanding of the specific characteristics of a professional relationship.
5. An understanding of the characteristics of a helping relationship.
6. An appreciation of the complexity of cross-cultural relationships.
7. An understanding of the communication process and of some common blocks to that process in the professional helping relationship.
8. Knowledge about the use of the interview as a tool in social work practice.
9. Knowledge about the ways to prepare for an interview and of the stages in an interview.
10. Knowledge about the skills needed when working in a one-to-one action system and the beginning ability to use some of these skills in everyday communication.

The social work endeavor takes place in an interpersonal interactional process. This interaction is more than an exchange between a worker and a client; the worker also interacts with colleagues, community persons, and any other professionals and people who are significant to the helping situation (significant others). The interaction can be one-to-one, between the worker and another person, or it can take place in multiperson situations such as a family, a team, or a small group. Although there are similarities between the process of interaction of one individual to another and the interaction with multiperson systems, there are also

159

differences. This chapter considers the interaction of the social worker with one other person. Chapter 9 will consider the interaction in multiperson situations.

Because the worker-client interaction is the core of the social work endeavor, it will receive primary focus. Much of the knowledge base relative to the worker-client interaction also applies to the interactions a worker has with other persons. Issues that are important in understanding the one-to-one interaction are 1) formation of a one-to-one system, 2) the nature of relationship, and 3) communication. Techniques to enhance relationship and communications are also important, as they can improve the quality of interactions.

FORMATION OF A ONE-TO-ONE ACTION SYSTEM

An action system is formed because of the work to be done and because the tasks to be carried out require more than one person. The worker collaborates with a colleague because each may have special areas of expertise relative to the work at hand or because the worker may profit from another view of the situation. The worker interacts with a significant other when that other person has some information needed for helping a client or can serve as a support or resource for the client's efforts in meeting needs or solving problems. In the worker-client interaction, the efforts of both are also necessary in the helping endeavor. The worker brings to the interaction a professional knowledge base and a professional set of values and skills for helping. The worker also brings the total self, finely tuned, to be used by the client as is appropriate to the needs of the helping situation and worker's capacity. The worker brings in skill in understanding situations, identifying needs, focusing problems, and developing interventions. The client brings needs or problems, a perception of the situation, life experiences that influence this perception, and capacity for dealing with the situation. The client also brings motivational forces for work on the problem or for change of self or the situation. In the work to be done, the roles of the worker and of the client emerge from what each brings to the interaction.

Felix Biestek has identified seven needs of clients as they come to the helping situation:

1. To be dealt with as an individual rather than a type or category.
2. To express feelings both positive and negative.
3. To be accepted as a person of worth, a person with innate dignity.
4. Sympathetic understanding of and response to feelings expressed.
5. To be neither judged nor condemned for the difficulty in which the client finds himself.
6. To make own choices and decisions concerning one's own life.
7. To help keep confidential information about self as secret as possible.[1]

The first encounter is crucial in forming the action system, determining as it does much that will happen in subsequent sessions. The nature of the interaction, its kind and quality, begins to form at this point. The client will be making decisions as to whether the worker can provide the needed help, whether the worker can be trusted, and whether the worker has the capacity to understand the client in the situation.

The initial contact takes place at the point that someone comes to the agency for help, either with regard to a need or problem of her own or with a concern about someone else; or it occurs at the point when the worker reaches out to someone to help with a need or a problem. In preparation for the first contact, when possible, it is helpful for the worker to collect and review any available information to determine what is known about the prospective client. Consideration of possible needs this client might bring is another useful preparation. The worker can also get in touch with feelings he might have about the particular client in her particular situation and about possible feelings of the client. Social workers disagree about whether new workers should read records of a previous worker before meeting the client. Records may present stereotypes or invalid assumptions that can color the thinking of the new worker. But if records can be read with an open mind and an eye for facts, they can be good preparation for meeting with a client for the first time. The worker needs to be careful not to develop unsupported preconceptions about the client and the situation. Unsupported preconceptions can endanger the formation of the action system.

Based on the preliminary understanding of the client in the situation, the worker can plan to structure the first encounter to make the client feel comfortable. This structuring will also involve environmental factors related to the time and place of the encounter—for example, the nature of the worker's greeting as the client enters the agency and meets the worker, the placement of desks so as not to be barriers between worker and client, and comfort in terms of temperature and privacy for the encounter. Choice of a time for the client is also important.

At the point of contact the worker will attempt to make the client as comfortable as possible. Cultural factors need to be taken into consideration. If the client comes from a culture where small talk is used before getting on with the task at hand, the worker should engage in a bit of small talk. If, on the other hand, the client is anxious about the purpose of the interaction and comes from a culture that wastes few words, the worker will quickly explain what is to be done together. In other words, it is important to structure the initial contact from the interactional framework of the client, not from the worker's framework. The worker should demonstrate to the client what will happen in the work together as soon as possible and to the extent possible. The worker does this by

1. Being attentive to what the client is saying and being receptive to the client's feelings;

2. Demonstrating a real desire to help the client and giving the client some indication that the worker knows how to help;

3. Actively asking the client to share his perceptions of the situation and the problem (asking the client about the significance of the problem, about the onset and attempts at coping, and about the solutions desired are other ways to involve the client and demonstrate the way of working together);

4. Attempting to answer any unspoken questions the client may have (e.g., the client may not be sure of whether the information being shared will be available to anyone else);

5. Explaining something about the way the agency delivers service, the kind of help it gives, and the procedures for using that help; and

6. Trying to reach for the feelings the client is having about what is happening.

In other words, the worker does as much as possible to enable the client to become engaged in helping herself in the need-meeting, problem-solving activity. In addition, attention should be given to supporting and developing self-esteem in the client. Part of this is the realization by the client that she is capable of participating in the search for solutions. Under no circumstances should the worker give unrealistic assurances about the outcome of the service.

As the worker is demonstrating to the client the way in which both can work together, he is also gathering information, understanding client functioning and the need as seen by the client, and enabling the client to think about the situation and perhaps see it in a new perspective. The social history is begun. The worker also encourages a climate of trust to develop. Until the client can trust the worker, the relationship is tenuous and the interaction is influenced by the client's concerns about the trustworthiness of the worker. As the client experiences the concern, understanding, and expertise of the worker, there is usually a reduction of these concerns and a strengthening of the relationship. A sense of trust develops.

During this exploratory phase of the initial contact, the worker's task is to test out ideas about the nature of the problem; to gather information about the client in the situation; and to define expectations for the client about the nature of service, relationships, and behaviors. The worker is nonauthoritarian, genuine, accepting, and empathic. The client is gathering information about the agency, its services, and the helping process and is also providing information needed to give the worker understanding. The goal is to develop what Nick F. Coady identifies as a "therapeutic alliance." He defines therapeutic alliance as, "an observable ability of the worker and client to work together in a realistic collaborative relationship based on mutual liking, trust, respect, and commitment to the work of counseling."[2]

Sometimes the client presents an angry, hostile, and resistive front. Carl Hartman and Diane Reynolds believe this front is used when the client is frightened and hurting, and lacks trust in the worker and in the process of help. They suggest using an approach that they identify as confrontation, interpretation, and alliance. After searching for the source of the feelings and associated behaviors, the worker first confronts the client about the behavior with questions or other means that communicate that the worker recognizes the feelings and the resistance to help. Immediately thereafter the worker provides the client with an interpretation of the meaning or source of the feelings and associated behaviors.

Then the worker provides the client with support and encouragement.[3] This approach often allows the client to feel accepted, which leads to a trusting and working relationship.

When the worker decides that sufficient understanding has been developed, he refocuses the discussion to negotiation concerning service delivery. During this next stage, the worker and the client discuss whether the problem as the client sees it is one that this worker in this agency can work on with this client. They also discuss whether the client is willing to work on the problem in the way expected by the agency if this seems appropriate. The worker and client will discuss other possibilities for need fulfillment and problem solution. The worker attempts to partialize the problem for the client so that it does not seem overwhelming. The worker also presents the realities of what the client can expect from the service.

During this phase the worker and client decide whether 1) they can work together on the concern, need, or problem brought by the client; 2) some other need or problem should be worked on; 3) the service needed by the client is better delivered by another resource; and 4) the client does not desire to use further service. There are times when all a client needs is to discuss a problem and gain a new perspective or knowledge of unthought-of resources. The client can then cope without further service.

In deciding whether to continue to work together (to form an action system), the worker and client need to make explicit the expectations of each person, the possible goals and expected outcomes of the service, the role of each person, and the ways of working together. The worker reaches for feelings the client may have and brings negative feelings and disagreements out into the open so they can be examined and discussed. It is very important to discuss the limits of confidentiality connected with the service. The worker should be sure that all terms being used are understood by the client.

If the decision is made to work together, a preliminary contract may be developed that states the next steps of the work together as well as the responsibility of both worker and client and time frames for accomplishing the needed task. The contract should also indicate hoped-for outcomes of the service. (The concept of contract will be developed in Chapter 11.)

During the negotiation and contract stage, the worker openly faces and deals with resistance. Edith Ankersmit, in discussing contracting in probation settings, has suggested that in dealing with resistance it is useful to help the client discuss two questions: Why am I here? How do I feel about being here? This discussion will allow the client to ventilate hostile feelings. The worker must not deny the existence of such feelings; rather, the worker should actively listen and point out the reality of such feelings. Ankersmit also says it is important to point out the power the worker has in the situation and particularly note its limits and the power the client maintains. This discussion can communicate to clients that they do have responsibility for their own behavior.[4]

Charles Horejsi calls for a motivation, capacity, and opportunity approach in probation. He points out that it is particularly important to try to identify the problem from the client's point of view and then decide with the client if the problem as seen in this way is something that can be worked on together. He also points out that the client must believe that there is hope for a solution of the problem and recognize a feeling of discomfort about the problem. The balance between hope for relief and recognition of discomfort is very important; both must be present, yet neither should overwhelm the other. He points out that there is discomfort in change. This must be considered when determining the client's capacity for change. Workers should attempt to lessen the discomfort concerning change as one means of lowering resistance. One source of resistance may be environmental factors at work in the situation. For example, if a person's peers are supporting delinquent behavior, it can be difficult for her to give it up. The discomfort of losing the companionship of one's peers may be so great that the change carries too great a price for the client.[5]

During this stage, the worker attempts to provide a climate that allows for productive discussion and a focus for the work together and to identify behavioral, cognitive, and emotional responses of the client to the work at hand and possible future work together. The worker also needs to keep in touch with her own feelings and to share these, as appropriate, with the client.

When agreement about the work together is reached, the worker should summarize what has happened in the previous stages of exploration and negotiation. It is also important to be sure that the next steps, the next session together, and any tasks to be accomplished before the next session are clearly understood.

The formation of the action system may be accomplished in one session, or it may take several sessions. During this formation the worker is attempting to bridge gaps in understanding; set the tone for the work; develop client involvement in the work to be done; maintain a focus on the work; and tune in to the client's feelings, way of functioning, and concerns. In carrying out the worker role, the worker is sensitive to the readiness of the client to move from one stage of work to another.

Several blocks can prevent the formation of a functional worker-client system. The worker should be aware of these and attempt to prevent them from interfering with the system's functioning. First, there is the complexity of human functioning. Relationships between persons with different life experiences and cultural backgrounds are particularly difficult. Misunderstandings happen easily. Bias and prejudice are often present. These lead to differences in perception of what is happening in the work together.

A second block arises from the client's fears. He or she may fear depersonalization, powerlessness, being judged, or having irrelevant goals placed upon him. These fears can lead to feelings of anger. They may also cause the client to keep a distance between himself and the worker or to avoid appropriate involvement in the work together. The fears may result from prejudices and unrealistic expectations on the part of the client.

A third block arises because the worker is often an employee of a bureaucratic organization. The complexity of rules and regulations and the inability of an organization to individualize for clients often gets in the way of the worker providing the service needed by the client. The worker may have feelings of powerlessness and may not feel appreciated by the agency. This can lead to frustrations that get in the way of responding to the client appropriately.

A fourth block relates to inadequate communication, which is also related to the differing cultures of worker and client. Because of poor communication, the client may not understand what is expected in the work together. The client also may not be able to sense the worker's interest and readiness to help. And the client may not see the worker as competent.

A fifth block relates to the worker's sense of purpose. If the worker has unrealistic expectations for self and clients, the client may sense this and avoid engagement in the tasks at hand. Workers sometimes aspire to heal all, know all, and love all; this leads to unrealistic expectations. Other workers have strong nurturing drives and tend to place clients in overly dependent relationships. Still other workers tend to avoid conflict, anger, and aggressive behavior. This may stifle the expression of feelings that need to be expressed in the development of the action system.

A final block is the underlying assumptions or theory base chosen by the worker for explaining the situation. For example, if the assumptions label the client as sick, the worker may be hesitant to demand work from the client and this may lead to more dependency in the relationship than is merited. If the assumptions assume blame as in the situation of a family of a mentally ill young adult, this will impact the worker's relationship with that family.

When working with the nonvoluntary client, it is particularly important to pay attention to these blocks. Unwilling clients often do not see the need for service, do not believe help is possible, or have difficulty in developing a relationship with the worker. In this situation, workers can sometimes overcome resistance by pointing out the reason for the concern or the consequences of a lack of change. A caring, nonjudgmental approach that focuses on the client's concerns and desires can often provide the nonvoluntary client with a unique helping experience and reduce resistance to help.

The worker has a responsibility to attempt to engage a resistant client when services have been mandated by a societal institution or when the client or a person for whom the client is responsible is in danger of significant harm. In doing this, the worker should try to relate as much as possible to the client's frame of reference. The worker should attempt to use the client's communication patterns and should not catch the client unaware. The worker should say why there is a problem and what the consequences of not resolving the problem might be. The worker should openly deal with either hostility or quiet inertia and should support the client's strengths. In working with a resistive client, the worker must be reasonably comfortable with the authority carried and be reasonable and supportive in its use. Often the resistant client misunderstands the nature of the service, has unmet needs that mitigate against dealing with the problem, has inadequate cognitive capacity to deal with the problem, or is influenced by the environment in a way that prevents need fulfillment or problem solution. In working with a resistant client, the worker should determine the source of the resistance and attempt to overcome it if possible; otherwise, a functioning action system may not form.

Often a bargaining strategy can be used; that is, the worker can make individuals who are resisting services aware of benefits they can receive from working with the social worker. For example, a neglecting mother can come to understand that cooperation with the worker may prevent removal of her children from her care. A juvenile delinquent can come to see that cooperation with the worker can prevent placement in an institution. An institutionalized youth can see that by adhering to certain rules and carrying out prescribed tasks she can gain desired privileges.

The development of the action system may be limited by the time available to the worker and client, by the skill of the worker, by ethical considerations, by the agency function, and by the client's desires. The worker and client must decide together on the desirability and the ways of working together.

Another type of two-person action system that social workers are often involved in is one made up of a social worker and a non-client person. The non-client can be a significant other in a client's life, a resource provider, or an individual who is or could be involved in a helping endeavor. The individual might be a community influential, a person who is or could be involved in action plans focused on community or organizational change or a person whom the worker is seeking to educate about some aspect of service delivery or the social welfare system.

While worker-nonclient relationships are somewhat different, the worker also needs to pay attention to the formation of the action system. The same principles apply to these systems as apply to the worker-client systems. If a worker uses the process of precontact, exploration, negotiation, and agreement, both parties are more aware of the reason for the work together and of the responsibility of each party for that work. These non-client individuals may also display resistance. Exploration of the reasons for the resistance is a first step in overcoming it and in deciding if it is possible to form a functional action system.

CASE EXAMPLE

Tim Brown is a BSW social worker in a community hospital. He has received a referral for Mrs. Hughes. Protocol calls for a worker in this hospital to see the patient within twenty-four hours after the referral. Tim begins service to this client by reviewing the referral. It is from Dr. White, a family practice physician. Tim has not worked with him before so he does not know what his approach to this situation might be. He notes that Mrs. Hughes is seventy-five years old and has been living alone. She is hospitalized because of pneumonia. Dr. White has requested that nursing home placement be made within three days. No other information is given. Tim knows the DRG days for pneumonia are limited but wonders about the three-day limit. He also flags the request for nursing home placement, which seems extreme unless there are factors other than the illness to be considered.

Next, Tim goes to the chart to review Mrs. Hughes' medical history. She has been in the hospital two days. She was admitted after going to the doctor's office for what she felt was a bad cold. She is progressing nicely and there seem to be no complications. Tim decides to consult with the head nurse on the floor. He knows this nurse can be very brusk and short with social workers and decides to anticipate resistance and try to overcome it by careful preparation for this interaction. He knows the head nurse is overworked and so chooses a time when she will be less busy. He formulates a few questions that, if answered, should give him the information he needs. First, he wants to know what the nurses have found out about Mrs. Hughes and her living situation. Second, he wants to know who has been visiting Mrs. Hughes; he is particularly interested in whether there have been any family members. Tim finds that Mrs. Hughes has been a very compliant patient who has shared little with the nurses; they do know that she lives alone. Her pastor has been in to see her, but the only other visitor has been a neighbor who brought her a few personal things she needed. There have been phone calls every day from a daughter who lives at some distance. The daughter is expected to arrive sometime tomorrow. The nurse refuses to discuss whether she believes nursing home placement is appropriate for Mrs. Hughes, saying the doctor's orders are to be followed. Tim decides not to push for more information as he needs to maintain a working relationship with the head nurse and he senses that he has obtained all the information that she is willing to give at this time.

Tim then begins to plan his first visit with Mrs. Hughes. He considers the hospital schedule and chooses a time when patient care will not interrupt the interview. He knows he will have to conduct the interview in Mrs. Hughes' room and that she has a roommate, so he plans to sit by her bed in a manner that will make the conversation as private as possible. He decides that he needs to explore several areas with Mrs. Hughes. She is probably very fearful of going to a nursing home. He needs to get these fears out in the open and communicate to her that he is there to find out what she wants to happen and what resources she needs when she leaves the hospital. He needs to show her that she indeed has some input into the decision-making process. He also needs to find out when the daughter is coming and get Mrs. Hughes' permission to talk to her daughter. He needs to get a better feel for her present living situation and for her support network. With this preparation he is ready to meet with Mrs. Hughes.

RELATIONSHIP

Relationship is the cohesive quality of the action system. It is the product of interaction between two persons. *Relationship* is a term of considerable historical significance in social work practice (see Chapter 2). It has often been expressed as "good rapport" with the client. The development of a good relationship has been seen as a necessary ingredient of the helping endeavor. Helen Harris Perlman has provided a description of relationship and its importance: "Relationship is a catalyst, an enabling dynamism in the support, nurture and freeing of people's energies and motivation toward problem solving and the use of help."[6] She saw relationship as an emotional bond and as the means for humanizing help. She further stated: "'Good' relationship is held to be so in that it provides stimulus and nurture. . . . [It] respects and nourishes the self-hood of the other. . . . [It] provides a sense of security and at-oneness."[7]

The social work relationship is both a professional and a helping relationship. A **professional relationship** is one in which there is an agreed-upon purpose; one that has a specific time frame; one in which the worker devotes self to the interests of the client; and one that carries the authority of specialized knowledge, a professional code of ethics, and specialized skill. In addition, a professional relationship is controlled in that the worker attempts to maintain objectivity toward the work at hand and to be aware and in charge of her own feelings, reactions, and impulses.[8]

The Helping Relationship

A great deal has been written about the nature of helping relationships.[9] The characteristics that appear most often in these discussions include the following:

1. *Concern for others*—An attitude that reflects warmth, sincere liking, friendliness, support, and an interest in the client. It communicates a real desire to understand the client in the situation.

2. *Commitment and obligation*—A sense of responsibility for the helping situation. Dependability and consistency are also involved. The worker must have a willingness to enter into the world of others, with its hurts and joys, its frustrations and commitments.

3. *Acceptance*—A nonjudgmental, noncritical attitude on the part of the worker, as well as a realistic trust of the client and respect for the client's feelings. Belief that the client can handle his own problems and can take charge of his own life.

4. *Empathy*—An ability to communicate to the client that the worker cares, has concern for the client, is hearing what the client is perceiving, wants to understand, and is hearing and understanding.

5. *Clear communication*—The capacity to communicate to the client in ways that enable the client to fully understand the message being sent.

6. *Genuineness*—The worker's honesty about self and his own feelings. An ability to separate the experiences and the feelings of the worker from those of the client. Genuineness on the part of the worker allows the client to become what the client wants to be. It is present when the worker's communication is understood and comfortable for the client. The worker's personal style of helping should not be an inflexible use of technique.

7. *Authority and power*—The expectation that the client will work to fulfill needs and responsibilities and will want to solve problems. This expectation involves encouraging the client to go beyond the present level of functioning as well as providing guidance and resources so that goals can be reached. It involves insistence that the client do what she can for herself. The worker's knowledge and skills are a base for authority and power.

8. *Purpose*—The helping relationship has a purpose known to, and accepted by, both worker and client. According to Beulah Compton and Burt Galaway, this is the most important characteristic of all.[10]

There is some disagreement about the place of advice giving in helping. Traditionally, social workers have thought it unhelpful to give advice; advice was seen as the worker's solution for the client and not the product of mutual problem solving and thus was not useful for the client. Clients, however, indicate that they expect and are looking for advice.[11] Advice is tangible evidence of help. If advice is given selectively and as a result of mutual problem solving by worker and client and in a nondemanding manner as something that might be tried, leaving the final decision for its use to the client, advice may well be a useful tool for helping.

Another characteristic of the helping situation is that help can be given by the client to the worker. When the client helps the worker understand his situation or culture, this is help and should be recognized as such. When the client evaluates the usefulness of various means of help and the appropriateness of various goals, this is help. Such a view of help enables the client to see the roles as interdependent rather than as superordinal to subordinal. An interdependent relationship encourages growth rather than dependency and is more helpful to the client.

Biestek's classic seven principles of a casework relationship and the worker's role in using each principle are one way of defining the responsibility of the social worker in a worker-client interaction or action system.

- *Principle I: Individualization*—This principle is "the recognition and understanding of each client's unique qualities and the differential use of principles and methods." The worker uses this principle when functioning from a nonbiased nonprejudicial stance; when applying knowledge of human diversity; when listening and observing to better understand the client; when moving at the client's pace; and when empathizing with the client.
- *Principle II: Purposeful expression of feelings*—This principle is concerned with "the client's need to express his or her feelings freely, especially negative feelings." The worker uses this principle when creating an environment in which the client is comfortable, when expressing the desire to be of help, when encouraging the client to express feeling and then listening to the expression of the feeling, and when avoiding providing advice and solutions before the client's situation is understood.
- *Principle III: Controlled emotional response*—This principle calls for "sensitivity to the client's feelings; an understanding of their meaning; and a purposeful, appropriate response to the client's feelings." The worker uses this principle when responding to the client on a feeling level in a purposefully selective manner, using her self-knowledge to direct her response to the needs of the client.
- *Principle IV: Acceptance*—This principle calls for perceiving and dealing with the client as he really is. It entails recognizing and using the client's strengths and limitations, congenial and uncongenial qualities, positive and negative feelings, and constructive and destructive attitudes and behaviors.
- *Principle V: Nonjudgmental attitude*—This principle "is based on a conviction that the [social work] function excludes assigning guilt, innocence, or degree of client responsibility for causation of the problems or needs" of the situation.
- *Principle VI: Client self-determination*—This principle recognizes the "right and need of clients to freedom in making their own choices and decisions in the [social work] process." The worker carries out this principle by helping the

client see problems and needs clearly and with perspective, by acquainting the client with appropriate community resources, and by creating an environment in which worker and client can work together.

- *Principle VII: Confidentiality*—This principle asserts the right of the client to preservation of secret information concerning self that is disclosed in the professional relationship. It is the worker's role to explain the limits of confidentiality and rights of the worker and client within the framework of professional and legal obligations.[12]

These principles are used to guide the professional helping relationship. They help promote a climate in which the client-worker action system can have an opportunity for fulfilling client needs and/or solving problems. The principles can also be applied selectively to other two-person action systems.

Special Influences on the Helping Relationship

There are a few situations in which a client's or worker's personal characteristics have a special influence on the action system's functioning. These include situations in which the worker and the client come from different ethnic or racial backgrounds and those in which the gender of the worker affects the interaction with the client and the environment in which the action takes place.

Several obstacles seem to be prevalent in cross-cultural helping relationships:

1. *Mutual unknowingness*—Because of a lack of knowledge about the other's culture on the part of both the worker and the client, there is a tendency toward stereotyping. Fear of the other is also a result of lack of knowledge and understanding. Inappropriate "good" or "bad" judgments may be made. Social distance that does not allow for the sharing and the trust necessary in the helping endeavor is often present. Of particular importance is lack of knowledge about a client's traditional communication patterns.

2. *Attitudes toward the other culture*—Negative attitudes may have developed from limited knowledge about a different culture. These attitudes may also have developed from negative experiences with persons who belong to the same cultural or ethnic group as the person being interacted with.

3. *Availability of different opportunities*—Members of different cultural groups have different opportunities. When the social worker does not understand this difference of opportunity he can have unrealistic expectations about how clients should use the help offered. This fact can also relate to the use of appropriate resources. Some resources are just not usable for a particular cultural group. For example, a culture that does not allow expression of feeling or that uses limited verbal expression and is action oriented will have considerable difficulty in using a traditional talk therapy. Some resources are available to, and traditionally useful for, particular ethnic groups. For example, American Indians traditionally use the tribe's medicine man or elders as a resource. Indians also have the support and financial aid resources of the Bureau of Indian Affairs at their disposal.

4. *Conflicts between societal and cultural expectations*—These often are difficult to resolve around the helping situation. Clients may have difficulty in identifying these conflicts, and the worker may not be aware of them.

In addition, minority clients often have a low sense of self-worth that results in low expectations for resolution of problems, in special relationship needs, and in lack of appreciation of their own culture. There may be a different world view, different expectations for the use of time, and different expectations of male and female behavior. These can get in the way of developing working relationships. The minority client may have a low trust level toward persons of other cultures; this may be the result of past relationships that produced pain and anger. A client with a low level of trust may use concealment mechanisms that hinder the helping endeavor. Different mechanisms for showing respect can result in misunderstandings. Different mechanisms for expressing ideas and feelings and different communication patterns can be particularly troublesome. Ann Brownlee has identified some of the communication differences that may exist, which include the appropriate situations for the communication of specific information, the tempo of communication, taboos, norms for confidentiality, the ways of expressing emotions and feelings, the ways to express appreciation, the meaning of silence, the form and content of nonverbal communication, and the style of persuasion or explanation.[13]

In order to work effectively in cross-cultural situations, the worker should develop both an understanding of diverse needs and a tolerance for difference, understand the complexities of cross-cultural communication, understand her own biases and prejudices, and develop considerable skill in accurate perception.

Gender is another factor that affects relationships. Social work literature contains little discussion of the influence of the worker's gender on the helping endeavor. There seems to be an assumption that a skilled worker should be able to work with both male and female clients. While this is probably true, social workers should become more aware of gender factors in professional relationships. One study has found that when male and female workers make assessments about women clients, male workers see these clients as less mature and less intelligent than do female workers. Female workers see women as having greater need for emotional expression and less need of home and family involvement than do male workers.[14] Differences in perceptions between men and women social workers, then, seem to exist. The different perceptions are probably a result of sex-role socialization, and these perceptions can affect professional relationships.

Joanne Mermelstein and Paul Sundet have found differences in client expectations in rural areas due to gender factors. In the female worker–female client situation, the client expects nurturing, mothering, and friendship. In the female worker–male client situation, the client sees taking help from a woman as counter to his definition of manhood. The interaction is also affected by taboos about what is to be discussed with women. In the situation of male worker and female client, the male worker is seen as performing a traditional female nurturing role.

The female client expects the male worker to support her, to give her moral guidance and clear direction. In the male client–male worker situation, the male client expects the male worker to prove his masculinity.[15]

Louise Johnson, Dale Crawford, and Lorraine Rousseau found that in traditional Sioux Indian culture it is a mistake for a male worker to go alone to a female client's home. The male worker should go through a male relative, for in traditional culture a female speaks through a male relative.[16]

Social workers should examine the expectations for male and female behaviors from the client's perspective and take these into consideration in developing action systems and in understanding and using relationships within these systems. Attention also must be given to the influence of gender of both worker and client on practice, on the functioning of the action systems. Workers also need to develop an understanding of how their own gender expectations influence their professional relationships.

Other differences that may exist between worker and client are young workers with old clients; unmarried workers with experienced parents; well-educated, middle-class workers with illiterate, poor clients; and upright, well-behaved workers with norm violators. These and other differences all influence the functioning of the action system, the helping relationship.

Little attention has been given to how the context of the social work endeavor affects practice, particularly the relationship factors of practice. A growing body of literature relative to the practice of social work in rural areas has pointed out the need to pay attention to the context of practice. Again, the work of Sundet and Mermelstein provides an indication of the influence of context on practice. They have found that social work roles that call for little risk on the part of the client are most effective when an outside worker is entering a new rural community.[17] It may be that this experience provides a useful principle for situations where cultural distance exists between the worker and the client. Confidentiality is an aspect of relationship that takes on new features when examined in a rural setting. People are more visible in rural settings. In some situations, it is in the client's best interest that certain aspects of the service be known so that misinterpretations about the service do not develop.[18] The effect of the context of practice on the social work interaction will be explored in Chapter 10.

Social workers have given little attention to the understanding of the two-person relationship in an action system that does not involve a client, for example, relationships with other professionals, such as a teacher or a pastor, or relationships with community leaders. Yet workers often use this type of action system in serving clients. In discussing this type of system from an interactional viewpoint, Yvonne Fraley has suggested that mutual problem solving is more effective if this type of relationship is assessed using these six variables: 1) the position of the worker ("actor one"); that is, the location of actor one in an agency or community system; 2) the goal of actor one in the relationship; 3) the position of the other ("actor two"); 4) the goal of the other; 5) the form of communication being used (verbal, written, nonverbal media, etc.); and 6) the method of influence being used by each actor (problem solving, teacher-learner, helper-helpee, etc.).[19] This kind of analysis points out that in the non-client action system there needs to be some reason for the two actors to work together. If the goals of each are compatible, if one actor does not feel threatened by the position of the other, and if the form of communication and the method of influence are carefully chosen, there is a better chance for gaining the desired outcome.

Regardless of the nature of the action system, the characteristics of the actors (worker-client or other), and the situation in which the interaction is taking place, the relationship of the two persons is a crucial factor in whether the work together produces the desired outcomes. Each person brings much to the system that can aid in, or detract from, the relationship and the work to be done. The social worker must be aware of these factors and use them to further the work by developing functional working relationships with other people. (See Figure 8–1.)

Relationship is not the end-state goal of the helping endeavor or the action system; it is the glue that holds the action system together and as such is a necessary ingredient of a well-functioning action system. It is not a relationship in which there is no conflict and all is happiness and goodwill, nor is it an overly dependent relationship. It is a relationship in which conflict is open and examined and in which there is respect for the position of the other. It is a working relationship, and the purpose of the relationship is the accomplishment of tasks needed to fulfill client need or solve client problems.

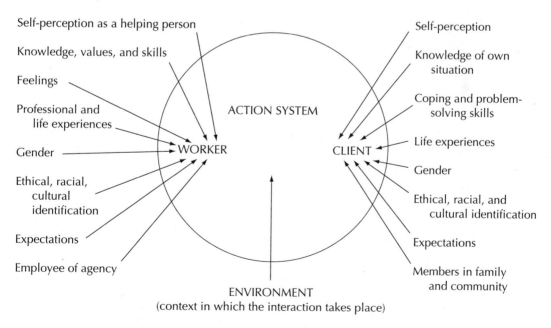

FIGURE 8–1   Relationship

CASE EXAMPLE

When Tim went to Mrs. Hughes' room he found that she had company. He introduced himself and said he would come back and asked when it would be convenient (recognizing the need for confidentiality). He found the visitor was a neighbor who was just leaving. He left the room briefly so that they could say good-bye. In about five minutes he saw the neighbor leave and returned to Mrs. Hughes' room. He placed a chair near to the bed so that Mrs. Hughes could see his face and so neither of their voices would project to the neighboring bed. He tested out Mrs. Hughes' hearing ability by asking if she had had a good visit with the neighbor. (Here he individualized by finding out if Mrs. Hughes had a hearing problem rather than assuming as much because of her age.) He found that she seemed very able to understand him if he spoke clearly. He then told her who he was and that her doctor had asked him to see her and discuss plans for when she was able to leave the hospital. (He did not want to bring up the nursing home or mention any specific date until the relationship was better formed.) Mrs. Hughes then said her doctor had told her someone would be in to see her about going to a nursing home. Tim noted that her affect was somewhat sad and almost like she was giving up. He then said that a nursing home was certainly one possibility, but he needed to know more about what she wanted before he could say that a nursing home was the most desirable plan for her care after leaving the hospital. He told Mrs. Hughes that he had not talked to the doctor and thus did not know why the doctor had decided she needed a nursing home. He wanted to talk to her first and find out a little about her and her desires. Then, if there were a better plan he would suggest this to the doctor. He also told Mrs. Hughes that she would have to make the decision about whether she went to a nursing home (client self-determination). Mrs. Hughes said that she didn't think there was any choice. Tim responded by saying that maybe the nursing home would be recommended to her, but they needed to see if there were other possibilities. (During this conversation Tim was attempting to communicate to Mrs. Hughes that she did have some choice in the matter, and that he wanted to know how she felt about the situation. He was using this discussion to demonstrate the way the work together could proceed.)

After this, Mrs. Hughes began to be less sad and in fact became somewhat agitated as she talked about her fear of going into a nursing home. She said that she was able to take care of herself and wanted to get back to her apartment. After expressing these negative feelings for awhile, she became quiet. (During this time Tim had tried to maintain a stance of accepting her negative feelings and listening to her concerns. He controlled his emotional response by not responding to her in a way that showed any displeasure with her agitation because he knew that at this point these feelings needed to be expressed before the work could proceed.)

Tim then said that before he could make any suggestions he needed to know more about her and her situation. He told her that there was also some information that he needed to get for the hospital records. At this point Tim asked for some factual information, but as Mrs. Hughes gave this he explored to obtain more detail where it was needed and to get a sense of Mrs. Hughes' feelings about her situation. For instance, when he asked about the details of her living situation he found she was living in the same apartment she had lived in for twenty years. It was on the second floor and the steps were becoming difficult for her. She had been thinking about making a move but just did not know how to go about finding a more suitable place to live. Many of her friends had died or gone into nursing homes in the last few years, so she did not have friends around her as she once had. The neighbor who visited was much younger, had just retired, and traveled a lot. She was willing to help in an emergency, but Mrs. Hughes did not feel she should depend on her for any other help. (During this discussion Mrs. Hughes seemed much more involved in the work together. Tim sensed that the relationship had started to form.)

He then began questioning her about her family. She was a little more reluctant to discuss this area, saying her children all had their own lives to live and she did not want to burden them. Tim asked about the daughter who was coming to visit. Mrs. Hughes said that she was closest to her. The daughter had arranged things so she could spend about ten days and would help care for her when she was discharged from the hospital. Tim asked if she wanted some help in explaining to the doctor that this could be a short-term plan until Mrs. Hughes and her daughter could discuss alternative future plans. Mrs. Hughes brightened up and said, "Oh yes, I don't seem to be able to get him to listen to me." Then Tim asked her if he could talk to her daughter when she came. He told Mrs. Hughes that perhaps the daughter also might need someone to talk to about her feelings regarding what was happening with her mother. Mrs. Hughes said, " Yes, it was hard for her to talk about this, and I do want my daughter to help me think about what I should do." (At this point Tim felt that he had developed a relationship sufficient for the work at hand. He had made a tentative assessment that Mrs. Hughes did not need a nursing home placement, especially if her daughter was to stay with her for a time. He also suspected that the mother and daughter needed some help in discussing long-term plans for Mrs. Hughes. He felt Mrs. Hughes was almost ready to change her living situation but did not know what resources were available to help her maintain her independence in the community. His next step would be to discuss the situation with the doctor and to make contact with the daughter to get her view of the situation.)

COMMUNICATION

Because effective communication is such an important ingredient of the functioning action system, it is important for all social workers to develop good communication skills. Communication is the sending and receiving of messages between two or more persons. Effective communication occurs when the persons involved in a situation accurately perceive the messages of the other person and in which the messages are sent in a way that allows the receiver to take action or respond to the sender in ways that facilitate the purposes of the communication. The purposes of communication in the social work interaction include

1. Gathering information needed for the helping endeavor;
2. Exploring ideas, feelings, and possible ways to meet need and solve problems;
3. Expressing feelings or thoughts;
4. Structuring the work of the action system; and
5. Informing, advising, encouraging, and giving necessary directions.

Communication is a process. The *sender* conceptualizes the message and through a *transmitter* (the voice or visual production) sends the message through a *channel* (sensory and modern technological means) to a *receiver* that interprets the message cognitively and affectively. This results in a *response*, another message and/or an action. The response may result in *feedback*, a means for the sender to evaluate the effectiveness of the message. One other factor of the process is *interference* or noise. Interference consists of those influences from outside the process that affect the message while it is in the channel and cause *distortion* of the message as it reaches the receiver. (See Figure 8–2.)

Each part of the process has a particular function and special problems that can interfere with the effectiveness of the communication. The sender must conceptualize the message in a way that is understandable to the receiver. This requires understanding how the receiver deals with and interprets ideas and information. The transmission of the message takes place not only through verbalization but also through nonverbal means. Nonverbal communication takes place through vocal tone and behaviors, such as gestures and body position. The motivation, needs, feelings, and attitudes of the sender influence the manner in which the message is transmitted. The message has content—the specific words used—and it has meaning—how that content is treated. The choice of words, the order of ideas and words, the use of humor and silence all contribute to the quality of the message.

As the message travels through the channel, the possibility of distortion is great. Previous experiences, cultural and societal demands, and attitudes and feelings of the receiver can distort the message. Distractions such as additional stimuli, concerns, and responsibilities can distort the message. The recognition of distortion and noise is a recognition of the transactional nature of communication.

The manner in which the message is received also influences the effectiveness of the message. The receiver may perceive or interpret the message in a manner different from the intention of the sender. The receiver may not comprehend the meaning of the message as intended or may receive only a part of the message. Feedback is the means of ascertaining if the message received and the message intended by the sender are sufficiently similar to make the communication effective. Feedback is sending a message about a received message to the sender of that message. The feedback is also subject to the problems of the original message.

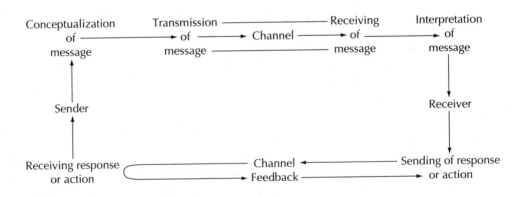

FIGURE 8–2   Communication

Effective communication is communication in which the outcome is the accomplishment of the purpose intended by the sender. Messages that have the best chance of being effective are those in which

1. The verbal and nonverbal messages are congruent;
2. The message is simple, specific, and intelligible to the receiver;
3. The receiver can understand what is meant by the sender;
4. There is sufficient repetition for the receiver to sense the importance of this message from among other messages being received simultaneously; and
5. There has been sufficient reduction of both psychological and actual noise.

Effectiveness in communication is affected by the credibility and honesty of the sender of the message. The receiver who has reason to trust the competence and reliability of the sender will tend to be receptive to the message and its expectations. Effective communicators tune into and are sensitive to the feelings and situations of those they are communicating with. They are assertive without being overly aggressive or confrontational.

Often the one-to-one communication is not with the client but with other professionals, with significant others in the client's environment, or with people who may in some way be involved in situations that are blocking client need fulfillment. These relationships are particularly important when the focus is on organizational or community change. The principles of communication discussed in this section (regarding clients) apply to interactions with non-clients even though they may be of a bargaining or adversarial nature (discussed in Chapter 15). When social workers find themselves in situations where the viewpoint of the other may be different from their own, clear communication is imperative. Sometimes the differences can be resolved through clarification of messages. Other times a clear understanding of the differences allows the work to progress despite the differences.

Brett Seabury has identified several problems that confront social workers in their communications with clients and significant others.

1. *Double messages*—Two contradictory messages are received simultaneously or in close succession.
2. *Ambiguous messages*—These messages have little meaning or several possible messages for the receiver.
3. *Referent confusion*—The words have different meanings to each person or they may be professional jargon not understood by the other person involved in the communication.
4. *Selective attention and interpretation*—This causes distortion of the message or confusion as to meaning.
5. *Overload*—This is the receiving of more messages than a receiver can interpret and respond to at any one time.
6. *Ritual or order incongruence*—This is the failure of the message sequence to follow expected or habitual behavioral patterns.

tor incompatibility—The use of eye contact and patterns of speaking and _ning which regulate the communication of one party in the interchange are not known to, used by, or are unacceptable to another party in the interchange.[20]

Other barriers to effective communication are inattentiveness, assuming the understanding of meanings, and using the communication for purposes different from those of others in the interchange (having hidden agendas). Cross-cultural communication is particularly problematic because the structure of messages differs from culture to culture. Even if the same language is used, words are used differently or have different meanings. Each culture has its own idioms and expressions, and the syntax (form) of the language may be different. The differences make it difficult to listen to the messages and make the likelihood of misunderstanding great. It is a responsibility of the social worker to overcome the barriers to effective communication as one way of enabling the action system to develop relationships that permit it to carry out its task and reach its goals. In social work, communication is dialogue. The worker and client openly talk together and seek mutual understanding. Floyd Matson and Ashley Montagu, in the introduction to *The Human Dialogue,* describe communication as:

> Not to "command" but to "commune" and that knowledge of the highest order (whether of the world, of oneself, or of other) is to be sought and found not through detachment but through connection, not by objectivity but by intersubjectivity, not in a state of estranged aloofness but in something resembling the act of love.[21]

This is the essence of communication in its most effective form. It is the kind of communication that adds vitality to and nourishes and sustains the process of working together, the interaction.

CASE EXAMPLE

Tim next seeks out Mrs. Hughes' doctor. He introduces himself as the social worker assigned to Mrs. Hughes. The doctor immediately asks in a brusk, hurried manner, "When can she go to the nursing home?" (This manner of communication could have easily turned Tim off. He could have developed a block to listening. On the other hand, the doctor may be assuming that what Tim had to say to him related to sending Mrs. Hughes to the nursing home. Thus, he was not ready to hear the message to be given.) Tim said that Mrs. Hughes' daughter would arrive tomorrow and that it seemed as if she was prepared to care for her mother for a time. He wondered if Mrs. Hughes' condition was such that this would be a workable plan for now. (Tim could have told the doctor outright that he did not think a nursing home was the desirable plan. This could have set up further communication blocks as the doctor might see his authority as being challenged. Instead, Tim chooses to give the doctor new information and involve him in deciding if a different plan might be better in light of that new information.)

The doctor said yes, if someone stayed with her she could go home, but he did ı.
want her to live alone, as it is just too risky for seventy-five-year-old women to live alon␖
(This statement led Tim to suspect that the doctor's plan was not related to Mrs. Hughes'
specific medical condition but to his preconceived ideas about seventy-five-year-old
women. This was interfering with the discussion about Mrs. Hughes and her specific
needs.) Tim then told the doctor that he was going to find out how the daughter was
prepared to help her mother. He said he thought Mrs. Hughes was ready to make a change
in living situation and that he could refer the mother and daughter to someone who could
help them make long-range plans. (Tim wanted to communicate to the doctor that there
were resources other than nursing homes for seventy-five-year-old women living alone.
He knew he would have to go slow in challenging the preconceived ideas, so he decided
to just try and get Mrs. Hughes home and help the mother and daughter find the help they
needed.)

Tim then asked the doctor when he thought Mrs. Hughes would be ready for discharge and what specific care she would need for the first few days after discharge. The
doctor indicated she could go tomorrow and that she would need to continue some
medication and have plenty of rest and a nutritious diet. Tim wondered if the day after
tomorrow might not be better so the daughter would have a day to settle in and prepare
for her mother's homecoming. The doctor reluctantly agreed. Tim said he would let the
doctor know how his interview with the daughter went and if the plan was satisfactory
with her. (Tim wanted to communicate to the doctor that he needed time to work with this
patient and that he would keep the doctor informed. He felt that he had at least made a
start in this direction. He hoped the daughter would indeed care for her mother for a time,
but if that did not work, he had several alternatives that would avoid permanent nursing
home placement. Tim also was aware that he needed to find a way to discuss with the
doctor his concerns about inappropriate referrals for nursing home placement. He
planned to discuss the issue with the other social workers in the hospital and urge that
together they develop plans to address the problem.)

THE INTERVIEW: AN INTERACTIONAL TOOL

The interview is a primary tool of the social worker. It is the structure for operationalizing the interaction between a worker and a client. Each social worker
develops her own interviewing style. Interviewing is an art and skill, and learning how to interview is learned by doing it. Some guides to interviewing can be
helpful to the person learning to interview. These guides include preparing for an
interview, the stages of an interview, and skills used by the worker during the
interview.

Each interview should have a specific purpose or goal. Generally, this purpose may be to obtain the information needed for carrying out some task or
function, or to work together to meet a client's need or solve a client's problem.
The purpose of a specific interview will depend upon the stage of work together,
the agency function and the method of service, and the client's needs and/or the
nature of the problem or problems to be solved. In addition to purpose, several
types of variables, listed below, affect the nature of the interview.

  1. *How the interview is initiated.* Is it a voluntary activity on the part of the client?
     Is it a formal, planned, regular interview or a walk-in request of the client?

it a life-space contact (one that takes place in the process of the client's ..y activities)?

2. *Where the interview takes place.* Does the interview take place in an office, a home, a hospital room, or some other setting?

3. *The experience of the worker and client with each other.* Have this worker and this client had previous contact with each other? Is this encounter a part of a time-limited or long-term plan?

Each interview will be different. The worker needs to be flexible in structuring and guiding the interview, depending on the interview's purpose and the needs of the client. It should be carried out in a manner that encourages interaction and relationship.

Preparing for an Interview

In preparing for any interview the worker has three tasks: 1) planning the environment for the interview, 2) planning the content of the interview, and 3) tuning in. Each of these tasks is carried out before the contact with the client.

The worker thinks about the physical conditions of the interview. If the interview takes place in an office, the worker arranges the office so as to encourage the work together. This can be done by giving some thought to the placement of desk and chairs (sitting behind a desk may place a barrier between worker and client). An office that is comfortable and does not have too many distracting features is ideal. The worker tries to prevent interruptions such as phone calls and knocks on the door. If the worker plans to take notes or use a tape recorder, arrangements are made so this can be done with full knowledge of the client but in a manner that does not distract from the work at hand. The worker also tries to provide a place for the interview where the conversation will not be overheard by others. Attention is given to the time of the interview so that neither worker nor client will be hurried, but the interview will also not be overly long. The worker will think about the impact of his dress on the client. If the interview is held outside the office, the worker will choose a time that is convenient for the client and when the fewest interruptions are likely to take place. For instance, an interview with a mother in the home might best take place when the children are in school.

In planning for the content of the interview, the worker will recall the goal and the purpose of the service and will identify the goal for this particular interview. The tasks to be accomplished will be considered. Any additional knowledge or information needed will be obtained. The worker might review notes about the previous interview if there has been one. The structure of the interview and questions to be asked will be considered. This planning is done to give form and focus to the interview, but the worker is prepared to be flexible and make changes if the client has unanticipated needs.

In tuning in, the worker first tries to anticipate the client's needs and feelings in the interview and to think about his own response to those feelings and needs.[22] The worker tries to become aware of his own feelings and attitudes that might interfere with effective communication. Such awareness should minimize the impact of these feelings and attitudes on the interview. The worker also needs to prepare to help by dealing with personal needs and any work-related attitudes that might interfere with the work of the interview.

Preparation for the interview is one way to promote worker readiness, which communicates to the client that she is important and that the work to be done together is important. Worker readiness prepares the way for effective interviewing.

The Stages of an Interview

All interviews have three stages: 1) the opening or beginning stage, 2) the middle or working-together stage, and 3) the ending stage. Each stage has a different focus and different tasks. Some time is spent during each interview in each stage, but the amount of time spent in each stage may differ depending on the work at hand and the relationship of the worker and client.

The beginning stage starts when the worker greets the client by name and does whatever seems in order to make the client comfortable. The worker tries to reduce any tensions and discuss any hostilities that may exist and reaches out to the client to help him or her become an active participant in the interview. This can be done by asking the client to share any significant events since the last session.

During the beginning stage, the worker will define the purpose of the interview or recall plans made in a previous session. The client is given an opportunity to discuss this purpose and any special needs he might have at this time. The worker reaches for the client's feelings about the work to be done and accepts the client's sense of purpose and need by modifying the purpose and plan of the interview if necessary.

When the worker senses that the client is ready to proceed to the work to be done, the worker changes the focus of the interview. The worker may have to "demand this work."[23] The middle phase has then begun. The content of this phase depends on the task at hand. The worker needs to maintain a sense of timing attuned to the client's pace of work, to refocus if the content strays from the task, or to renegotiate the purpose if that is indicated. The worker also should monitor the communication for its effectiveness.

Before the agreed upon time for ending an interview is reached or when the purpose of the interview has been fulfilled, the worker again shifts the focus. In bringing the interview to an end, the worker summarizes what has happened during the interview and how it fits into the service being offered. The worker and the client together plan the next steps, which will include work to be done by each before the next interview and the purpose, goal, time, and place of the next interview. If this is a single interview or a final interview, the client is helped to say good-bye and given permission to come again if other needs arise or problems develop.

Skills Used by the Worker During the Interview

As a means of guiding and supporting the work together and of promoting relationship and effective communication, the worker uses five groups of skills during an interview: observation skills; listening skills; questioning skills; focusing, guiding, and interpreting skills; and climate-setting skills. The skill of interviewing is in part skill in selecting and using the appropriate response at the appropriate time. Like all skills, these must be developed through use over a period of time. Many exercises have been developed that are useful in beginning to acquire these skills, but it is only as they are used in actual client situations that skill development reaches the professional level.

Observation Skills

Clients give information and express feeling in nonverbal, behavioral ways. They also provide information and express feeling in the way in which other information is given and discussed. Sensitivity to this nonverbal material is useful for tuning in to where the client really is in relation to the material being discussed, for checking the validity of the client's verbal expression, and for feedback purposes. Workers should observe the following:

   1. *Body language*—What is the client communicating by the way he or she sits, by behaviors such as thumping on the desk with the fingers, by facial expression?
   2. *The content of opening and closing sentences*—These sentences tend to contain particularly significant material. They also may give cues about the client's attitudes toward self and the environment.
   3. *Shifts in conversation*—These shifts, particularly when always related to similar topics, can indicate that a particular topic is painful, taboo, or something the client does not want to discuss.
   4. *Association of ideas*—Observing which ideas the client seems to associate with which other ideas can often give the worker an indication of unspoken feelings.
   5. *Recurrent references*—When the client continues to bring up a subject, it indicates that it is a subject of importance to the client or one with which the client would like help.
   6. *Inconsistencies or gaps*—When these are present, it is an indication either that the material being discussed is threatening to the client or that the client is unwilling to openly share in this area.
   7. *Points of stress or conflict*—In cross-cultural action systems, stress and conflict may indicate areas of inadequate knowledge about cultural aspects of the client's functioning. This may also indicate misunderstanding on the part of the client or areas of client bias or prejudice.

Listening Skills

Of vital importance in any interview situation is listening—listening to what the client has to say and how the client responds to questions and responses. Beginning workers often place primary emphasis on the questions to be asked and on what they say. Good questioning does enable clients to provide necessary information, to consider alternatives, to work on the problem at hand. However, if the worker's listening skills are deficient, the full value of the interview will not be realized. Active listening—being with the client in her struggle to deal with difficulties and problems—is the appropriate response at many points in the interview.

Another reason to develop listening skills is because social workers are often in communication with persons whose language expression is somewhat different from their own. In listening, it is important to try to understand what the client is attempting to communicate. To do this the worker seeks to understand what the words mean to the client. The worker maintains focus on what the client is saying even though there is a tendency to shut out the communication because it is strange and difficult to listen to. It is important to note feeling words and how they are expressed. Listening reflects an attitude of openness and acceptance, and it involves a sense of timing that allows the worker to focus on the client and what is being said and does not shut off the communication by premature evaluation or advice.

Questioning Skills

The essence of this group of skills is knowing the various types of questions to ask and the usefulness of each type of question. A first category of questions includes open- and closed-ended questions. A closed-ended question calls for a specific answer. An example would be: "What is your age?" These are used to gain factual information. An open-ended question is one that enables the client to define, discuss, or answer the question in any way they choose. An example would be: "What do you think is the reason why your child is doing poorly in school?" The open-ended question allows expression of feeling and gives the worker the client's perception of the subject at hand. In developing a social history, it is usually advisable to mix open- and closed-ended questions, which allows for discussion between the worker and the client about the facts as well as about the client's life experiences.

There are leading and responding questions. A leading question is used when it is desirable for a client to continue to explore the subject at hand. An example would be: "You have tried to cope with this problem, haven't you?" A responding question follows the lead of the client's response. An example would be when a client has been discussing how he has tried to cope with a problem and the worker responds: "Tell me more about how you went about helping your child."

In an answer-and-agree question, the client is expected to answer in such a way as to agree with the worker. An example would be: "You are feeling much better today, aren't you?" This usually is not a good form of questioning to use because it blocks discussion and imposes the worker's ideas on the client.

With most clients, it is better to ask questions so that they contain single, rather than several, ideas. A question with a number of ideas might be used when the worker is attempting to help the client recognize connections between the ideas. Whether to ask very broad questions or a very specific one depends on the work at hand and on the worker's style. Some workers like to gain a broad picture first and then explore details. Other workers believe it is more helpful for clients to consider small parts of the situation and then look at the broader picture later. Questioning is one of the means used by a social worker to enhance relationships and communication.

Focusing, Guiding, and Interpreting Skills

This group of skills comprises those used by the worker to enable the action system to accomplish the tasks necessary to reach the agreed upon objectives. It includes the capacity to paraphrase and summarize what has been said, to reflect feelings and ideas, to confront, and to elaborate. The effective use of these skills includes a sense of timing as to when to focus, when to interpret, and when to direct.

Paraphrasing and summarizing often clarify what has been said. Clarification and elaboration enhance understanding. With understanding of issues and facts, the work can progress as a truly joint effort.

Confrontation and silence are often difficult for the worker. Confrontation is the bringing out into the open feelings, issues, and disagreements. It involves looking at these elements and attempting to find ways to deal with them. If feelings, issues, and disagreements remain hidden, they may interfere with the work at hand. Silence may indicate resistance, frustration, or anger, but it also can provide a time for worker and client to be reflective. Rather than just being uncomfortable with silence, a worker can attempt to understand the nature of the silence and use it appropriately. Times of reflection are useful in the work together. Silence related to resistance can be used to develop sufficient discomfort on the part of the client so that she will have to do something. It can be used as a means to focus on the work together. The worker who senses frustration and anger can bring it out into the open, confront the client, and thus deal with it so that the work can proceed.

It is the worker's responsibility to direct the interview but not to control it. The worker takes whatever material and expression of feeling is given by the client and, by focusing, guiding, and directing, enables the process of the work together to proceed toward the desired outcome.

Climate-Setting Skills

Three attributes have been identified as characteristics of interpersonal situations that seem to produce understanding, openness, and honesty, which are enabling factors in the work of the action system. These three characteristics are empathy, genuineness, and nonpossessive warmth.[24]

Empathy is the capacity to communicate to the client that the worker accepts and cares for the client. Empathy communicates that at this point in time the client's welfare is to be considered before the worker's. Empathy is expressed by openly receiving and recognizing the feelings of the client, by accurately perceiving the client's messages, and by providing the client with concrete feedback about messages.

Genuineness is the capacity of the worker to communicate to the client that the worker is trustworthy. It is expressed by being willing to let the client know the worker as a person in ways that meet the client's need for such information. It also expresses congruence between the worker's verbal and nonverbal messages. In addition, genuineness involves informing the client when the worker disagrees with the client and when the client's behavior and communication are inconsistent. This skill calls for honesty, but honesty communicated in a manner that is sensitive to the client's feelings and concerns.

Nonpossessive warmth is the capacity to communicate to the client both a concern and a desire for an intimacy that allows the client to make decisions, to have feelings negative and positive, and to feel worthwhile. It has qualities of nonblame, closeness, and nondefensiveness. A warmth that is nonpossessive is displayed through positive regard and respect for the client and through thoughtfulness and kindness as well as appreciation for, and pleasure at, the client's growth and well-being.

The climate of all interpersonal endeavors greatly affects the nature of the relationship and the quality of the communication. Skills in developing and maintaining an accepting, growth-producing climate are an important part of the worker's repertoire.

Interviewing is just one form of communication. The skills used in the interview can also be used in the less formal social work interactions. They are the same skills that encourage relationships to form and to be used and maintained. In the social work endeavor, in the one-to-one action system, it is the responsibility of the social worker to move toward the client so that relationships may form and a common ground for communication may be established. To do this the social worker must understand the client and be willing to work with the client in meeting the client's needs and in solving the client's social-functioning problems.

CASE EXAMPLE

An Interview

This is a report of an interview with a fifteen-year-old girl who has been in foster care for the last year. The worker and Mary, the client, have been working on plans for Mary to return home. Mary's mother is a single parent who has five other children ranging in age from six to eighteen. Mary is the third from the oldest and the oldest girl. At thirteen, Mary became uncontrollable; she was skipping school and remaining away from home for several days at a time. Mary began to skip school when she had not completed homework assignments; when this behavior became chronic, she was placed in a juvenile shelter at her mother's request for a short time. Placement in a foster home was made when it was determined that Mary's mother was making excessive demands on her to help with the care of the younger children. The goal of foster care was to give Mary a period of time in which to grow without these excessive demands and to provide a relationship with an adult who could help her sort out what she wanted to happen to her. Mary has now decided she wants to return home. She feels she understands why her mother expects so much from her. The worker and Mary are now discussing how Mary can respond if her mother's demands become overwhelming to her again.

Preparation

Mary and the worker have a 2:30 appointment. They have been meeting in an office provided in the school for such meetings. They chose 2:30 because this is Mary's study hall time. The worker called the school in the morning to be sure the schedule for the use of the room was clear. The worker had agreed to get Mary some information on part-time jobs and has this information in hand. The worker also reviewed her notes on the last session. The worker arrived at school at 2:15, went to the meeting place, and did some minor rearranging of the chairs by bringing the worker's chair out from behind the desk. The worker then spent the time remaining until Mary came thinking about Mary and her situation.

Beginning Stage

As Mary entered the room the worker said, "Hi, Mary, how goes it today?" Mary replied, "Okay." However, the tone of her voice indicated that Mary was a little down. The worker replied, "You seem a little down. Anything the matter?" Mary said, "Well, I just had a history test; I'm not sure I did too well." The worker asked Mary why she did not feel she did well and discussed the test with Mary, her preparation for the test, and her concern about whether studying history would be of any use in her getting a job.

When Mary seemed to have released her feelings concerning the test, the worker changed the subject to the plans for today. The worker reminded Mary that they were going to discuss two things. First, was the possibility of Mary getting a part-time job. Mary thought that if she was working, her mother would not be so apt to depend on her to take care of the younger children when she went home. Second, was how Mary could deal with situations in which her mother puts what Mary considers too heavy a responsibility on her. The worker said she also would like to know about her weekend at home with her mother and brothers and sister. The worker had intended to use this as a means for beginning the session today but changed her plans when it became apparent that Mary was concerned about the history test.

Middle Stage

Mary's whole manner changed, and she became bright and lively while telling the worker about how good the weekend had been. Things had gone well, but what was really great was that her mother had asked her if she minded watching her youngest brother while she went out. Mary had told her mother she really wanted to spend time with her; her mother seemed astonished but said she just needed to get out of the house—the kids got her down. The worker asked her what had happened then. Mary said that she and her mother had really talked about how Mary felt about taking care of the kids and that her mother shared with her some of her frustrations about raising six children alone. Then they decided that the whole family would go to the park together.

The worker asked Mary how she felt when she told her mother she did not want to take care of her younger brother. Mary said, "Scared." Then she said, "I just had to do it. If I hadn't, things would have just gotten started all over again. I am learning that if I don't tell people how I feel, they will never know." The worker said, "Yes, I think you have learned a lot, Mary." Then they talked about how Mary had changed and grown in the last year. The worker asked Mary if she had thought about other ways she could handle frustrations when she went home. This was also discussed. Mary then said, "I don't think I want a job just now. I only wanted one to get out of the house and avoid certain things. I think I can deal with these things by talking about what I don't like. It's not going to be easy, because Mom doesn't talk much, but maybe we can keep up what we started to work on last weekend. She told me you had suggested that the three of us might like to talk together before I go home." Mary continued to talk about these ideas. She said she thought it might be good for her and Mom and the worker to get together and talk.

Ending Stage

As the time of the interview was almost over, the worker said they certainly had talked about some important ideas today, but she thought it was most important that they begin to plan for a time for Mary to go home for good. She also wondered what more Mary wanted to happen before she went home. Mary said she really wanted to get started on the idea of her and Mom meeting with the worker. The worker suggested that before the next session with Mary, she would talk with her mother to see if this could be arranged. The worker said, "Next week let's plan on deciding on a date for you to go home for good." Mary almost floated out of the room.

SUMMARY

The emphasis in this chapter is on one-to-one (worker-client) interaction that takes place in an action system. The formation of the action system requires understanding of the client and skill on the part of the worker. Special consideration must be given in developing action systems with resistant clients.

Relationship is the cohesive quality of the action system and is for the purpose of helping clients. It is influenced by the life experiences of both the client and the worker. Cross-cultural relationships have special characteristics that the worker must understand.

Communication is an important ingredient of the action system. The process of communication can become blocked in a variety of ways. Social workers need to be aware of these blocks and of the means for dealing with them.

The interview is an important interactional tool for use in the one-to-one action system. It is important to prepare for interviews. They should be goal directed. Each interview has three stages: a beginning, a middle, and an ending. Workers use a variety of skills in the interview. These include observation; listening; questioning; focusing, guiding, and interpreting; and climate setting.

The same principles and skills used in one-to-one interaction with clients are also used when working with significant persons in the situation, with those who may be able to provide resources for the client, or with a variety of community persons. The capacity for forming and using one-to-one relationships is a core social work skill.

QUESTIONS

1. How can the client's needs best be met in the interview situation?

2. What are some of the ways to facilitate the development of a professional relationship?

3. Why is the development of a relationship so essential to the helping situation?

4. How do the three phases of interviewing differ? How are they similar?

5. What are some ways to encourage nonvoluntary clients to engage in the helping process?

6. How should resistance be viewed in any helping situation?

7. Discuss each of Biestek's principles of relationship relative to operationalizing them in the interview situation.

8. Why is it difficult to communicate across cultural boundaries? How can social workers facilitate such communication?

9. Discuss the needed balance between questioning and listening in a social work interview.

SUGGESTED READINGS

Anderson, Gary B. "Enhancing Listening Skills for Work with Abusing Parents." *Social Casework* 60 (December 1979): 602–608.

Bloom, Allan A. "Social Work and the English Language." *Social Casework* 61 (June 1980): 332–338.

Brammer, Lawrence M. *The Helping Relationship: Process and Skills,* 2nd ed. Englewood Cliffs, NJ: Prentice-Hall, 1979.

Coady, Nick G. "The Worker-Client Relationship Revisited." *Families in Society* 74 (May 1993): 291–298.

Compton, Beulah Roberts, and Galaway, Burt. *Social Work Processes,* 3rd ed. Homewood, IL: Dorsey Press, 1984. Chapters 6 and 7.

Fortune, Anne E. "Communication Processes in Social Work Practice," *Social Service Review* 55 (March 1981): 93–128.

Gitterman, Alex. "Uses of Resistance: A Transactional View," *Social Work* 28 (March–April 1983): 127–131.

Hartman, Carl, and Reynolds, Diane. "Resistant Clients: Confrontation, Interpretation, and Alliance." *Social Casework* 68 (April 1987): 205–213.

Hasenfeld, Yeheskel. "Power in Social Work Practice." *Social Service Review* 61 (September 1987): 469–483.

Hepworth, Dean H., and Larsen, Jo Ann. *Direct Social Work Practice: Theory and Skills,* 2nd ed.

Homewood, IL: The Dorsey Press, 1986. Chapters 5, 6, 7, 18, 19 and 20.

Hutchinson, Elizabeth D. "Use of Authority in Direct Social Work Practice." *Social Service Review* 61 (December 1987): 581–598.

Kadushin, Alfred. *The Social Work Interview,* 3rd ed. New York: Columbia University Press, 1990.

Keefe, Thomas. "Empathy, Skill and Critical Consciousness." *Social Casework* 61 (September 1980): 387–393.

———, and Maypole, Donald E. *Relationships in Social Service Practice.* Monterey, CA: Brooks/Cole Publishing, 1983.

Lowenberg, F. M. *Fundamentals of Social Intervention: Core Concepts and Skills in Social Work Practice.* New York: Columbia University Press, 1977. Chapter 8, "Interviewing, Observing, and Writing"; Chapter 10, "Engagement Skills"; and Chapter 12, "Communication Skills."

Macarov, David. "Empathy: The Charismatic Chimera." *Journal of Education for Social Work* 14 (Fall 1978): 86–92.

Marziali, Elsa. "The First Session: An Interpersonal Encounter." *Social Casework* 69 (January 1988): 23–27.

Nelson, Judith. "Dealing with Resistance in Social Work Practice." *Social Casework* 56 (December 1975): 587–592.

Perlman, Helen Harris. *Relationship: The Heart of Helping People.* Chicago: University of Chicago Press, 1979.

Pinderhughes, Elaine B. "Teaching Empathy in Cross-Cultural Social Work." *Social Work* 24 (July 1979): 312–316.

Proctor, Enola K. "Defining the Worker-Client Relationship." *Social Work* 27 (September 1982): 430–435.

Raines, James C. "Empathy in Clinical Social Work." *Clinical Social Work Journal* 18 (Spring 1990): 57–72.

Rooney, Ronald H. "Socialization Strategies for Involuntary Clients." *Social Casework* 69 (March 1988): 131–140.

Rumelhart, Marilyn Austin. "When Understanding the Situation is the Real Problem." *Social Casework* 65 (January 1984): 27–33.

Sands, Roberta G. "Sociolinguistic Analysis of a Mental Health Interview." *Social Work* 33 (March–April 1988): 149–154.

Schubert, Margaret. *Interviewing in Social Work Practice.* New York: Council on Social Work Education, 1982.

Shulman, Lawrence. *The Skills of Helping: Individuals and Groups,* 2nd ed. Itasca, IL: F. E. Peacock, 1984. (Part I, "A Model of the Helping Process".)

Seabury, Brett A. "Communication Problems in Social Work Practice." *Social Work* 25 (January 1980): 40–44.

Velasquez, Joan, McClure, Marilyn E. Vigil, and Beavides, Eustolio. "A Framework for Establishing Social Work Relationships Across Racial and Ethnic Lines." In Beulah Roberts Compton and Burt Galaway, Eds., *Social Work Processes,* 3rd ed. Homewood, IL: Dorsey Press, 1984.

Wilson, Suanne J. *Confidentiality in Social Work: Issues and Principles.* New York: Free Press, 1978.

NOTES

1. Felix P. Biestek, *The Casework Relationship* (Chicago: Loyola University Press, 1957).

2. Nick F. Coady, "The Worker-Client Relationship Revisited," *Families in Society* 74 (May 1993): 293.

3. Carl Hartman and Diane Reynolds, "Resistant Clients: Confrontation, Interpretation, and Alliance," *Social Casework* 68 (April 1987): 205–213.

4. Edith Ankersmit, "Setting the Contract in Probation," *Federal Probation* 40 (June 1976): 28–33.

5. Charles R. Horejsi, "Training for the Direct-Service Volunteer in Probation," *Federal Probation* 37 (September 1973): 38–41.

6. Helen Harris Perlman, *Relationship: The Heart of Helping People* (Chicago: University of Chicago Press, 1978), p. 2.

7. Ibid., p. 24.

8. Ibid., p. 62.

9. See Lawrence M. Brammer, *The Helping Relationship: Process and Skills,* 3rd ed. (Englewood Cliffs, NJ: Prentice-Hall, 1984), and Beulah Roberts Compton and Burt Galaway, *Social Work Processes,* rev. ed. (Homewood, IL: Dorsey Press, 1979), chap. 6.

10. Compton and Galaway, *Social Work Processes,* p. 224.

11. See Anthony N. Maluccio, *Learning from Clients: Interpersonal Helping as Viewed by Clients and Social Workers* (New York: Free Press, 1979).

12. Quoted material in this list from Biestek, *The Casework Relationship,* pp. 25, 35, 50, 72, 90, and 103, respectively.

13. Ann Templeton Brownlee, *Community, Culture and Care* (St. Louis, MO: C. V. Mosby, 1978), chap. 3.

14. Joel Fischer, Diane D. Dulaney, Rosemary T. Frazio, Mary T. Hadakand, and Ethyl Zivotosky, "Are Social Workers Sexists?" *Social Work* 21 (November 1976): 428–433.

15. Joanne Mermelstein and Paul Sundet, "Education for Social Work in the Rural Context," in *Educating for Social Work in Rural Areas,* A Report on Rural Child Welfare and Family Service Project of the School of Social Work, Lynn R.

Hulen, project coordinator (Fresno: California State University, June 1978).

16. Louise C. Johnson, Dale Crawford, and Lorraine Rousseau, "Understandings Needed to Work with Sioux Indian Clients" (unpublished paper).

17. Joanne Mermelstein and Paul Sundet, "Worker Acceptance and Credibility in the Rural Environment," in *Rural Human Services: A Book of Readings*, H. Wayne Johnson, Ed. (Itasca, IL: F. E. Peacock, 1980), pp. 174–178.

18. Janet Kirkland and Karen Irey, "Confidentiality: Issues and Dilemmas in Rural Practice," in *2nd National Institute on Social Work in Rural Areas Reader*, Edward B. Buxton, Ed. (Madison, WI: University of Wisconsin—Extension Center for Social Studies, 1978), pp. 142–149.

19. Yvonne L. Fraley, "A Role Model for Practice," *Social Service Review* 43 (June 1969): 145–154.

20. Adapted from Brett A. Seabury, "Communication Problems in Social Work Practice," *Social Work* 25, No. 1 (January 1980): 40–44.

21. Floyd W. Matson and Ashley Montagu, *The Human Dialogue: Perspectives on Communication* (New York: Free Press, 1967), p. 6.

22. See Lawrence Shulman, *The Skills of Helping: Individuals and Groups*, 2nd ed. (Itasca, IL: F. E. Peacock, 1984), chaps. 2 and 4.

23. See Ibid., pp. 65–72, for discussion of this task.

24. This triad is based on the work of C. B. Truax and R. R. Carkhuff, *Toward Effective Counseling and Psychotherapy* (Chicago: Aldine, 1967). For an excellent discussion of this material, see Eveline D. Schulman, *Intervention in the Human Services*, 2nd ed. (St. Louis, MO: C. V. Mosby, 1978), chap. 8, "Traux Triad."

9

MULTIPERSON INTERACTION

Learning Expectations

1. An understanding of group process so as to be able to recognize its various aspects in the functioning of a small group.
2. An understanding of the importance of the small group in generalist social work practice.
3. An understanding of how the social worker can influence the work and process of any small group of which he is a member.
4. A beginning skill in small-group interaction as a member of a group.
5. A knowledge of the role and function of the generalist social worker with a multiperson client.
6. An understanding of the nature of the generalist social worker's interaction with the family system in the various forms that the family takes in U.S. society.

The social worker is often called on to interact with more than one person at the same time, particularly when working from a generalist approach. This happens when the client is a family, a small group, an institution, an agency, or a community. When the agency, institution, or community system is the client, the interaction is usually with groups of people within the system.[1] When the focus is on the development of new resources, task groups are usually involved. The social worker works with more than one person at the same time when she is functioning on a team or a case conference or as a member of a committee or a planning group. These groups can have a fact-finding, evaluation, policy-making, planning, education, problem-solving, or therapeutic purpose; they can be casual, appointed, ongoing, or self-formed. Multiperson interaction is used when people share a common task or purpose and when the situation does not lend itself to one-to-one interaction. Situations that often call for the use of the group include the following:

1. Those in which individuals cannot reach their goal except in working with others (e.g., when a group of persons works for some environmental change);
2. Those in which individuals cannot function on a one-to-one basis with a professional person but can function with peers (e.g., a group of delinquent adolescents);
3. Those in which the group has considerable influence over the individual (e.g., the family influence on individual functioning);
4. Those in which the task or purpose needs the contribution of several persons (e.g., the interdisciplinary team); and
5. Those in which persons are faced with similar needs or problems (e.g., parents of retarded children).

Much of what was discussed in Chapter 8 about the one-to-one interaction also applies to group interaction. Relationships between persons are important for the facilitation of the tasks to be accomplished. Group process and task accomplishment are also facilitated by effective communication. The relationships and the communications become more complex because of the additional people involved, so that the transactional nature of the interaction must receive greater attention. In effect, the interview becomes group discussion. Thus, many of the techniques useful in facilitating the interview are also useful in facilitating group discussion.

In order for the social worker to be effective in multiclient and multiworker interactions, three kinds of understandings are important:

1. *The small group as a social system*—This chapter considers client groups (unrelated persons), community and professional groups, and family groups. The family is a special case of the small group. Because of the intensity and the long-term nature of the relationships, the family has qualities not found in other small groups.

2. *The social worker as a member of a small group*—When the social worker is a member of a team or participates in a community committee or an agency task force, the worker is a member of a small group. Although the social worker is not always the designated leader of these groups, he can use knowledge about small-group interaction and skill in interaction to influence group process so that the group can effectively carry out its function and tasks.

3. *The social worker and the multiclient system*—Often the social worker does not become a member of the group when working with the multiclient system. Rather, the social worker influences the group process from a point outside the group. Doing this entails a differential use of interactional skills.

THE SMALL GROUP AS A SOCIAL SYSTEM

The term **group** is often used in an imprecise, broad sense. The definition of the small group as a social system places some limitation on the term. As a social system, a small group is composed of three or more persons who have something in common and who use face-to-face interaction to share that commonality and work to fulfill needs and solve common problems, their own or others. An effective small group allows each person in the group to have an impact on every other person in the group. The group is an entity or system that is identifiable, and it is more than the sum of its parts. For best results, the group should not exceed twelve to fifteen members. Groups, like all social systems, have structure, the form of a system at any point in time; a way of functioning or behaving in order to accomplish tasks; and development that takes place in stages over time.[2] (See Table 9–1.) To develop sufficient understanding for effective interaction in and with a small group, a social worker needs to assess all three of these dimensions.

Structure

Three major dimensions of structure are boundary, relationship framework, and bond. **Boundary,** in a social system, is the point at which the system of interaction around a function no longer has the intensity that the interaction among the members has. Sometimes membership in a group is clearly defined; at other times, the determination of boundary may be difficult to establish. For example, a community group may have sporadic attendance. There may seem to be a real involvement in the task at hand by only a few persons. Some of the persons who only occasionally attend meetings probably are not members of the group, but others may be quietly influencing the group's action in ways other than attending meetings. These people may be group members. When considering boundary, it is important to take into account who the group members are. All members have a personal history, current needs, and responsibilities toward other systems of which they are a part. These affect each person's functioning in the group. Each group member receives certain rewards for participating in the group; these need to be identified. The history of the group, how and why it was formed, and any change in focus, membership, or way of functioning as it influences current structure is important for a group assessment.

The worker's role in the group is another component of relationship. Henry Maier has identified three orientations to member-worker interactions. Type A relationship has a strict boundary between the work of the group and the larger life situations. The worker is considered an expert and as such functions from a position of separation from the rest of the group yet exercises considerable control over the functioning of the group. Type B relationship finds the worker more a part of the group yet with a distinctive role of facilitator of group functioning. Type C relationship finds the worker as one member of the group with no

TABLE 9–1   A Schema for the Study of the Small Group as a Social System

---

I. Structure
  A. Boundary
  1. What is the purpose, mission, or task of this group?
  2. Identify members of the group. Describe them as persons. (Use appropriate parts of Table 7–1.)
  3. What are the factors that separate these persons from other persons? How were the members chosen? Under what circumstances would a person no longer be a member of this group?
  4. What is the history of this group? How and why was it formed? How long has it been meeting?
  5. What is the position of the worker with this group?
  6. What is the influence of the environment on this group and its functioning? Include environmental expectations, impingements, and resources.
  7. Describe the open/closed character of the boundary. Include communication and energy exchange and openness to new ideas and ways of functioning.
  B. Relationship framework
  1. Describe any rating/ranking of group members.
  2. Draw a sociogram.
  3. Describe the manner in which members fill roles. Are all needed roles filled? Are any roles overfilled? Which members fill several roles?
  C. Bond
  1. What is it that holds members of the group together? Note common interests and friendships.
  2. Describe the climate of the group.
  3. What are the goals of the group? Are they explicit and known to, and accepted by, all group members?
  4. What are the norms or rules for functioning in this group? How did they develop? Are they known to, and accepted by, all group members?
  5. What are the rewards of membership in this group?
  6. What priority do members give to the group?
II. Functioning
  A. Balance/stability
  1. How does this group adapt to changing conditions? Consider change both in the environment and within the group.
  2. How much time is spent on group maintenance and how much on group task? Is this balance appropriate?
  B. Decision making
  1. How does this group make decisions about norms, goals, and plans for work?
  2. Describe group problem-solving mechanisms. Do any members engage in diversionary or blocking tactics that inhibit problem solving?
  3. Describe leadership as it facilitates or inhibits the group's decision making.
  4. How do group members influence group decisions?
  5. How is conflict resolved? Is it recognized and kept in the open?
  C. Communication
  1. Describe communication patterns of the group.
  2. Does the group have adequate feedback mechanisms? Is attention paid to nonverbal communication?
  3. Do all group members have adequate opportunity to communicate? Do any members tend to overcommunicate?
  4. Are there any content areas that seem to be troublesome when communicating?
  5. Is attention paid to communication difficulties that arise from cross-cultural or cross-professional interaction?

TABLE 9–1   *Continued*

    D. Task implementation
        1. Describe the manner in which the group carries out its tasks. Describe the quality of interaction in carrying out tasks.
        2. Do any members engage in diversionary or blocking tactics that inhibit the carrying out of plans?
III. Development
    A. Identify the stage of development in which the group is operating.
    B. Describe any factors that may be inhibiting continued group development.
IV. Strengths and Limitations
    A. What are the strengths of the group?
    B. What are the limitations of the group?

---

differentiation between roles. Type C would seem to be the relationship found in work with groups such as community groups or interdisciplinary teams.[3]

The environment of the group also affects the group's functioning. The environment places expectations on, and furnishes resources for, the group. The boundary may be relatively open or closed. When a group has an open boundary, it is fairly easy for persons to join the group, and the group is open to new ideas and other communication from the environment.

The *relationships* among the members can be examined in several ways, three of which include:

1. *The rating-ranking pattern*—In some groups one (or more) member clearly has higher status than others. When examining relationships from this perspective, it is important to look not only at the status hierarchy but at the reason for members' status as well.

2. *The sociogram*—This **sociogram** shows patterns of liking and nonliking.[4] It can also show subgrouping and strength of relationships in a group. Figure 9–1 describes a friendship group in a settlement house. A, B, and C form a strong subgroup. E and I are isolates. G seems to be a central figure and may be a leader.

3. *The role structure*—Kenneth Benne and Paul Sheats have identified three categories of roles that may develop in groups: group task roles, group-building or maintenance roles, and individual roles.[5] **Group task roles** are related to the accomplishment of the function or task of the group. In discussion groups, roles include the initiator or contributor of ideas, the information seeker, the clarifier of ideas, the information giver, the opinion giver, the opinion seeker, and the orienter. **Group-building or maintenance roles** are those that focus on the maintenance of the group as a system. Roles that fall into this category include the encourager, the harmonizer, the compromiser, and the gatekeeper. The gatekeeper is the one who controls the flow of communication by allowing, encouraging, and blocking messages from the various group members. The third category comprises the **individual roles** that satisfy individual need but detract from the work of the group. These roles include the dominator, the special-interest pleader, and the blocker.

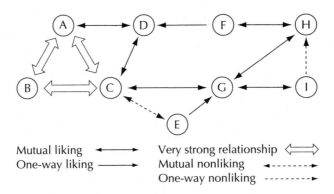

FIGURE 9–1   **Sociogram of a Friendship Group in a Settlement House**

Many times, leadership is considered to be a role. **Leadership** can be thought of as the attribute of filling a number of roles, particularly of those needed for effective group functioning. The identification of who fills which roles, which roles are not being filled, and which members tend to carry many or crucial roles explains an important aspect of group structure.

Bond is the cohesive quality of the group; it is a quality that is expressed in a "we feeling" as opposed to an "I-he-she feeling." It is expressed in common group goals, in norms for group behavior, and in common values held by group members. In systems terms, steady state is a related concept. *Steady state* is a particular configuration of parts that is self-maintaining and self-repairing. In other words, it is a state of systems that leads to both stability and adaptability. The functional group needs to maintain stability while still being adaptable to changing conditions and situations.

Description of the bond existing in a group identifies what holds the group together: common interests or tasks, friendships, desire for relationships, and the like. Also important is the identification of group goals, norms, and values, as well as the ability of the group to adapt to changing conditions and situations.

The structure of the group is described by identifying the aspects of boundary, relationship structure, and bond. The structure changes as the group interacts and carries out its function over time. The social worker strives to enable the group to develop a structure that enhances the quality of the interaction of its members.

Functioning

Group interaction is a complex process influenced by the actions of group members and by the interactions among the various members. These actions and interactions in turn are influenced by the group members' needs and responsibilities. The process is also influenced by the needs of the group as an entity accomplishing tasks and maintaining itself. The situation or environment in which the group functions also influences the functioning. This functioning, which is quite complex, is transactional in nature.

One way of describing group functioning is in terms of *the use of energy*. Every system has a limited amount of energy and there is always a state of tension as to the way the energy will be used. Tensions may be expressed in terms of energy allotted to group tasks or to group building. They may be expressed in terms of stability versus change or adaptability issues. Each group develops ways of dealing with these energy issues.

Another aspect of the group's functioning is its *decision-making and communication processes*. Groups make decisions about which roles and tasks belong to which team members, about how to communicate and implement group decisions, and about the use of energy. Decisions are made in different ways in different groups. Sometimes a rational or problem-solving process is used; sometimes compromise is a method; sometimes one or more group members impose their will on the rest of the group. Often groups merely function on the basis of past experience.

Closely related to decision making are issues of leadership, power control, and conflict. Conflict is often viewed as a negative ingredient of group interaction. Properly managed, however, it can be a force that enhances group creativity and problem solving. Conflict is expected in a situation when people of varying backgrounds seek to work together. **Conflict** is the struggle for something that is scarce or thought to be scarce. In a group, this may be attention, power, status, influence, the right to fill a role, and so on. Groups make decisions about how conflicts will be resolved. One of the tasks of a social worker in fostering group interaction is to identify conflict areas and help the group work toward healthy resolution of the conflict.

Communication is the heart of the process of group interaction and thus a most important aspect of its functioning. Through communication, information, decisions, and directives are transferred among group members. Communication is the means of forming and modifying opinions and attitudes. The communication process is described by focusing on who communicates to whom and about what.

Another way of describing the group's functioning is to note the task implementation process, that is, how the group accomplishes its task. The task implementation process is concerned with who does what and whether or not individuals carry out delegated tasks.

The functioning of the group is simply movement in carrying out the group's function. The structure changes as the movement takes place. This change is related to the development of greater organization, which results in specialization and stabilization. As the worker in and with the group strives to influence the group's interaction he enables the group to carry out its function and tasks.

Development

As the group functions and the structure changes it passes through a series of expected identifiable stages. At each stage, the group has differing group maintenance needs. The capacity for the group to fulfill its function grows as it progresses through the stages of development. Groups develop at different rates. Factors that encourage group development include:

1. The strength of the members' commitment to the group's function, tasks, and goals;
2. The satisfaction of the mutual needs of the members;
3. The liking or caring that the members feel for one another;
4. Reciprocation rather than competition for roles;
5. Respect for diversity among group members;
6. The amount of time the group spends together;
7. Interaction that encourages individual growth;
8. A degree of homogeneity that allows group norms and goals to form; and
9. A degree of heterogeneity that provides different ideas and points of view among the members.

The stages of group development may be conceptualized as follows:

1. *The orientation stage*—Members come together for the first time, seek similarities in interest, and make an initial commitment to the group. There is also an approach-avoidance mechanism at work. Patterns of functioning around tasks begin to develop. Task roles begin to emerge. Emphasis is on activity and orientation to the situation. Individuals make decisions about the desirability of belonging to the group and whether to become dependent on other group members.

2. *The authority stage*—There is challenge to the influence and control of the group by individual members. Conflict develops; members rebel and search for individual autonomy; power control is an issue; there may be dropouts. Structure and patterns of functioning are revised. Members share ideas and feelings about what the group should do and how the group should function. Norms and values develop through this sharing.

3. *The negotiation stage*—The group confronts, differs, and engages in conflict resolution. Goals, roles, and tasks are designated and accepted. Group traditions are stronger; norms develop; personal involvement intensifies. Group cohesion is stronger, and members are freer in sharing information and opinions.

4. *The functional stage*—A high level of group integration is reached. There is little conflict about structure, and ways of functioning have been established. Roles are differentially assigned to members and accepted by all. Communication channels are open and functional; goals and norms are known and accepted. The group has the capacity to change and adapt. Conflict and tension are managed with minimal energy use; a problem-solving capacity develops. Members are interdependent. Plans are implemented, tasks are completed, and goals are reached. The group can evaluate itself and its work. Few groups reach this stage in its ultimate form.

5. *The disintegration stage*—At any of the first four stages, a group may begin to disintegrate. Signs of disintegration include the lessening of the bond and a reduction in the frequency and strength of group interaction, in common norms or values for group members, and in the group's strength of influence on members.

Identifying a group's stage of development allows a worker to respond to that group with greater understanding about the structure and functioning of the group. It also provides an informed response to that group's functioning, which is a means for enhancing the interactional processes of the group.

Understanding the small group as a social system is a prerequisite to effective work as a group member or to working with the multiclient system. This understanding is a guide for the worker's interaction and interventions when working in and with groups.

CASE EXAMPLE

Women's Career Exploration Group

  I. Structure
    A. Boundary
      1. Purpose: The WCEG is sponsored by the Women's Center of State College. It was formed at the request of a group of nontraditional women students who felt a need for help in exploring career possibilities when they finished their undergraduate degrees.
      2. Group members: There are five members in the group.

        Carol is a diploma nurse. Her goal is to complete her general education requirements at the college and transfer to an institution that has a baccalaureate program in nursing. She is questioning this decision but does not know what other possibilities there are for her. She is recently divorced after a very stormy marriage. She has custody of two children, a boy and a girl.

        Joan is an English major who is a freshman. She has been divorced six years. During this time she has worked as a receptionist in a doctor's office. She has three adolescent sons who live with her. She is exploring job possibilities after graduation. Joan and Carol have been friends for years.

        Patty is a psychology major and a junior. She is a commuting student. She remains in her marriage, though she has some doubts as to how long she will want to do this. She has three children, two in college and one in high school.

        Bev is a history major and a senior. She is divorced and has no children. She works part time in the library and is exploring whether she wants to take a full-time job there or seek other employment. She is concerned about the job market for history majors who do not have qualifications to teach.

        Mary, in her mid-thirties, is divorced with one early-teenage daughter. She has a degree in English and works in the college library but is seeking a position in which she can use her potential to a greater degree. She is the only member of the group who is not a full-time student. Bev and Mary are close friends.

3. Why these women constitute a group: This is a self-chosen group. All but Mary are nontraditional students. All are concerned about career issues. All usually eat lunch together. They are a part of a group of nontraditional students who study together and offer each other support in their academic endeavors. This group, by agreement, is to last six sessions. All have agreed to attend all the sessions, so one would lose membership in the group if she failed to attend a session without a good reason. Also, to be a member of this group an individual needs to be a female nontraditional student or else very close to the academic scene. Another requirement is that the group member be seriously considering career options.

4. History of the group: The group has met for four sessions. Because it is nearing the end of the semester, it plans two more sessions. All members have attended all sessions.

5. Worker and the group: The worker, a social work faculty member, was asked to facilitate the group by the prospective members. The worker in this group has a combination of B and C characteristics (see Maier's Types). She has had some of the experiences that group members are having—she is divorced and had returned to school as a nontraditional student. She shares her experience with the group when it is useful to the group members. This would place her in a C stance. However, because these experiences are some years past—she is now established in a career and is clearly identified as a helping professional—she is separated from the group members. This places her in a B stance. Her role in the group is to provide group members with help in exploring possibilities and to enable the group members to help each other in this exploration through encouragement of group process.

6. Environmental influences: The major influence is the academic setting. Scheduling of meetings must consider class and work schedules of each group member. Each member's choice of major also influences the content of the sessions as the group explores possibilities for careers for each member. Also influencing the group is the marital status of the group members. All but one are divorced and trying to establish themselves as single women. All but one have children. Four of the members have long-standing friendships with another group member.

7. Meeting arrangements: The group meets in a small conference room on the campus at 2:00 on Tuesdays. This was the most convenient place and time and was chosen by the group at its first session. Six sessions are planned; this choice was made by the group due to timing of the first session in the spring semester.

8. Open/closedness: After the group formation, no new members will be added. Each member of the group and the worker bring ideas from their experience to the group. The group, however, is characterized as having a fairly closed boundary.

B. Relationship framework

1. Ranking: There is no rating and ranking in this group. All are seen as equal and ideas from all are accepted.

2. Sociogram (see Figure 9–2): It should be noted that there is a positive relationship among all group members but that there are two dyads and one relative outsider.

3. Roles: Joan is the organizer who seems to remind everyone of the meetings. She seems to have the least input in the career discussion except when her own situation is being discussed.

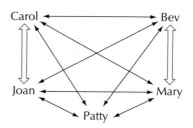

FIGURE 9–2   Sociogram of Women's Career Exploration Group

Mary tends to keep the group on task. She is very good about questioning others about what they are thinking and offering suggestions for them to think about.

Carol notices when a member of the group is troubled by the discussion. She then attempts to help them communicate their feelings to the group. She also helps the group listen to each member of the group.

Patty is a questioner. She often seems to be stalling group discussion, but what she is really doing is asking the group to look more deeply at whatever is being discussed.

Bev is a listener. She makes her contribution by working on her own agenda but sharing her work with the group for their comments. In this way she really models for the rest of the group the work to be done.

C. Bond
   1. What it is: The commonality of their situation of being nontraditional students is a major component of the bond. The fact that they are friends and self-selected themselves into the group is also important. The task of the group is of major importance.
   2. Climate: The climate is comfortable with everyone wanting to work on the identified task of the group.
   3. Goals of the group: The group goal is for each member to receive help in moving toward a career choice. This goal was made explicit in the group formation process.
   4. Norms of the group: In the first meeting the group made its norms explicit. These norms include attendance at all meetings, which last an hour and a half; members will be on time; the material discussed is confidential and will not be discussed elsewhere; the group will not spend time discussing family or marital problems other than as they affect career choices. The worker tried to impose a norm of outside homework. Though the group verbally agreed, this norm was not adhered to by members of the group.
   5. Priority of group: Group members give priority to the group for the time of the group session. This is demonstrated by perfect attendance at the sessions. They do not give high priority to preparation time outside the group as demonstrated by their failure to do any requested preparation.

II. Functioning
  A. Balance/stability
   1. Adaptation: The group has had a stable environment and stable membership so has not had an opportunity to demonstrate this quality. It should be noted

that each member of the group has been making changes in her thinking about career possibilities and has been able to adjust to those changes easily.

2. Maintenance vs. task: During the first meeting the group spent considerable time on maintenance. There was much discussion as to how the group would proceed in its work together. There was also a contract developed detailing this work and the number of sessions that would be held. Since that meeting, minimal time is spent on group maintenance. Usually either at the beginning or end of each meeting there is some discussion about number of sessions left and how well the group is fulfilling its contract with each other. As the group is working well together and all members are making progress on their individual goals, the balance can be deemed appropriate.

B. Decision making

1. Method: Decisions are made by consensus. For example, when discussing the meeting time or a technique to use in carrying out the group task, all members discussed several possibilities and as a group decided on the specific time for the meeting and the technique to be used.

2. Problem solving: Problems considered other than group procedures tend to relate to a particular group member's struggle to make career decisions. The pattern of problem solving is for members to throw out ideas as to possible solutions and then together consider each solution. Group solutions are then implemented after consensual decision making. There have been no diversionary tactics. Decision making and implementation regarding a member's career decisions are left to that member to make as she sees fit.

3. Leadership: Joan and Mary tend to share the leadership role. Both tend to be facilitative leaders. At times Carol calls for the worker to take this role by asking the worker to be more directive and tell them what to do. Joan and Carol are usually able to take the worker's cues and call for the group to work on the task together using input from the worker as part of the material to work on.

4. Influence on decision making: Group members all have influence on the decisions through their contributions to discussion. Joan and Mary seem to have the most influence because of the quality of their contributions.

5. Conflict: Conflict is denied by group members. The worker notes that when the group recognizes a conflict, they tend to ask for input from her as to a decision or task. They refuse to recognize this as a mechanism of avoiding conflict, even when it is pointed out to them by the worker. However, after this denial, they work as a group in a problem-solving mode to resolve the differences.

C. Communication

1. Patterns: The group gives each person an opportunity to discuss each issue. There are no blocks, as group members are aware of the communication process and of the need for listening as well as talking. Occasionally, Carol and Joan or Bev and Mary will get into a side conversation. Other members of the group will call attention to this and that ends the intrusion into the work of the group.

2. Feedback: The group members often ask each other for feedback about topics being discussed. Carol is particularly active in noting nonverbal communication and pointing it out to other members of the group.

3. Opportunity: All group members are encouraged to add their thinking to the group discussion. If one member gets off on a tangent and holds the floor too long, someone will step in and bring the discussion back to the subject at hand.

    4. Troublesome content areas: Within the focus of the group there seems to be no troublesome areas except for conflict. This is dealt with in only a nondirect manner.

    5. Cross-cultural factors: There are none; group is homogeneous culturally.

  D. Task implementation

    1. How tasks are carried out: The only concrete tasks carried out by the group are exercises provided by the worker to trigger thinking and discussion. These are engaged in willingly, with much discussion as they are carried out. Members are expected to carry out their own tasks relative to career exploration, which are being postponed, seemingly, until the dissolution of the group.

    2. Blocking tactics: None other than failure to do homework.

III. Development

  A. Stage: The group is in the negotiation stage, though in some ways they appear to be in the functional stage. The reason they are in the negotiation stage is that they still have not dealt with hidden conflicts about leadership and power in the group in an open manner.

  B. Inhibiting factors: The denial of conflict is the major block. Group members have a deep-seated cultural norm against conflict. They are afraid of open expression of conflict and have not learned to deal with conflict in an open manner.

IV. Strengths and Limitations

  A. Strengths: The group is self-organized with a well-focused task. The relationship framework, bond, decision-making process, and use of the problem-solving process are all very functional for the task at hand. Communication is good.

  B. Limitations: The group's inability to deal with conflict situations in an open manner is the major limitation. Another limitation that places constraints on how much work can be done is the time factor (six sessions) and the lack of motivation (or energy) to work on the task outside of the meetings.

THE SOCIAL WORKER AS A GROUP MEMBER

The responsibility for the interactions of a small group rests with the members of that group. This is particularly true when members are professional and the focus is on the concerns and needs of clients. This responsibility for the interaction cannot be carried by any one member; it is a responsibility shared by all. Persons who understand small-group process and the factors that contribute to effective group functioning, however, can be quite helpful to groups of which they are members. Social workers can use their knowledge of human interaction in both one-to-one and small-group situations in fulfilling this responsibility of group membership. When enabling teams and other agency and community groups to reach their goals and accomplish tasks that relate to client service, the social worker is also serving the client.

Group Enabling

Four factors are particularly helpful in enhancing interaction so as to enable the group to reach its goals and to carry out its tasks or functions: 1) member involvement; 2) decision making about norms, goals, and roles; 3) group discussion skills; and 4) structuring of meetings.

Member involvement is a prerequisite to effective decision making and problem solving. The climate of the group is a major contributor to member involvement. The ideal group climate encourages participation; is friendly and accepting; and is supportive of, and sensitive to, the needs of individual members. The group climate is one where effectiveness is expected and self-actualization and innovation are encouraged. There is a stress on inclusion and trust. Members seek to collaborate with each other. The ideal group distributes the influence and power among the members rather than relying on an authoritarian power figure. Influence and power rest in the knowledge and skills of the members. Conflict is not suppressed but is dealt with in the discussion process. Members engage in periodic evaluation of the work of the group.

A troublesome area in relation to involvement is bringing a new group member on board. An effective group does this in an organized manner so that the new member understands how the group functions, what its goals are, and what is expected of the new member. The new member needs time to get to know the group and its members, and the group needs time to get to know the new member.

A second contributor to effective functioning is *the manner in which decisions are made.* In making decisions about norms, goals, and roles, it is important that all members be involved in the decision-making process and that consensus be reached whenever possible. Not all group decisions must be made in this way. After norms and goals are set, some decisions can be made by individual members with permission from the group.

The process of developing norms is known as **norming**—the process by which implicit norms or expected ways of behaving are made explicit. The norms are examined to discover if they are appropriate to the task. Periodically, the norms should be evaluated to determine their usefulness. Changes are made in the norms as necessary. Norms that are most useful to group functioning are those that allow recognition in decision making, and that support individuals and the cohesiveness of the group. Another important norm is that feelings are valid information.

The *development of goals* is another shared responsibility. Goals should be clear to, and accepted by, all group members. Whenever possible, a match should be sought between individual and group goals. Goals should not be imposed on the group. It is helpful if the goals are prioritized.

Role definition also belongs to the total group. No member should automatically take on a specific role without permission from the group. Messages should be clear to all members about the acceptability of members filling roles. A conflict over roles—the desire of two or more persons to fill the same role—should be openly negotiated and alternatives sought. Compromise is an appropriate mechanism in resolving role conflict. No one person should have a role overload, that is, be filling too many of the needed roles. One means of encouraging participation is to spread the roles among the members. Periodic evaluation to determine how roles are filled is helpful.

A third characteristic of good group functioning is *skill in group discussion.* Group discussion is to the small group what interviewing is to the one-on-one action system: it is a means for structuring communication. One definition of group discussion is: "Two or more people talking with one another in order to achieve mutually satisfactory understanding of each other's images or beliefs or a solution to a problem."[6] Cooperative interaction is influenced by each individual's perception of the topic under discussion and the group process. Two factors are particularly important for good group discussion: good communication and the use of the problem-solving process as a guide to group thinking.

Good communication calls for skill in sending messages and receiving messages so that all can know what is happening. No one person monopolizes the conversation. The feedback is

1. Descriptive rather than evaluative,
2. Specific rather than general,
3. Such that it considers the needs of all persons involved,
4. Directed toward that which the receiver has control over, and
5. Well timed.

Group thinking involves several different persons, each of whom may be at different stages in his or her consideration of the problem. Use of the problem-solving process in group discussion is a means of structuring the group thinking so that each member is aware of the stage of the discussion. In order to use this means, all members of the group should understand the problem-solving process and be aware of which step in the process the group is using. In this way, group thinking can progress from problem identification and formulation to analysis of the problem, to identification of possible solutions, to analysis of the possibilities, and to choice of solution. Thus, the solution becomes the property of the group rather than the contribution of an individual member.

Several areas that often give groups difficulty as they attempt to solve problems are

1. Lack of clarity in stating the problem;
2. Lack of necessary information;
3. A critical, evaluative climate;
4. Pressure for conformity; and
5. Premature choice of a solution.

If a plan for implementation is a result of group thinking, there is a better chance that the plan will be carried out than if the plan is imposed by a group member.

Some attention should be paid to the structure of group meetings to further enhance the group's capacity. There needs to be preparation for group meetings, just as there needs to be preparation for an interview. Various members should be responsible for bringing needed information to the meeting. Someone should take the responsibility for insuring that the meeting room is comfortable and arranged so that each member can have eye contact with each other member. Someone should also be responsible for seeing that agendas and other needed printed materials are available and for keeping minutes or recording decisions in some way.

The planned agenda should be reviewed and revisions made if necessary at the beginning of each meeting. Everyone should know what the meeting is intended to accomplish and what the time limitations are.

The middle part of the meeting is spent on the task of the day. When necessary, the group should deal with any group maintenance issues that seem to be impeding the work at hand. An indication that group maintenance should be attended to is when it does not feel good to the members. Discussion should focus on tasks or goals or on the process of carrying out these tasks or goals. All members should be urged to participate. One member of the group should be responsible for keeping the group on task and helping it move through the problem-solving process in an orderly manner. Before the allotted time is over, the group should review what has been accomplished at the meeting, and plans should be made for the next meeting.

In helping the group involve members, make decisions, have productive discussions, and structure the discussion, social workers can be a valuable resource for the group. Knowledge of group process and of the problem-solving process and skill in group discussion form the base of effective membership as a group member.

Issues in Group Participation

Several issues of group participation are of particular concern to social workers when they participate as members of small groups, including 1) the use of the team, particularly the interdisciplinary team, as a means of service; 2) leadership in its delegated form; and 3) conflict management. Each of these issues confronts the social worker and, if not understood, can block effective group functioning.

Use of the Team

Although the well-functioning team can be very effective in providing service to clients, there are often problems that cause some social workers and agency administrators to question the team approach. These problems need to be understood and some ways for overcoming them considered.

The team has been defined as "joining the essentially dissimilar skills which colleagues in diverse occupations bring to bear upon different aspects of a common problem."[7] The definition is most applicable to the interdisciplinary team, and it is the interdisciplinary team that presents the greatest hazards for working together. The dissimilarity of backgrounds and work expectations is a major cause of these hazards. Another important cause of the difficulty is overlap of the expertise of the various helping professions. This can lead to conflict over turf.

Some of the most frequent problems encountered by teams are:

1. *The time and energy needed for team building*—The task of the team is to provide service to clients. Often the immediacy of the need for service and number of clients needing service place expectations on the team that mitigate against the use of team time and energy for team building. These expectations may come from within the team or from the agency within which the team or any of its members operate. Yet effective team functioning does require time and energy from the team members. The allocation of time and energy for team building can be problematic.

2. *Communication*—The use of technical language by any member of the team that is not understood by all other members of the team blocks communication. Persons from different disciplines often use the same terms but with somewhat different meanings. When this happens, there are problems in communication.

3. *Decision-making traditions*—Professions and agencies develop traditions as to how decisions are made. In bureaucratic organizations decisions are often made from above, and lower-status persons are expected to implement the decisions. A team in such an organization may have a leader appointed by administration; the appointed leader may assume an authoritative stance. In health care, the high-status professional, the doctor, has traditionally used this authoritative stance. This stance is needed in an operating room, but it is not helpful in a protective service situation. Other decision-making models may call for everyone to have equal decision-making power about all aspects of service. All team members may not have equal knowledge or understanding of certain aspects of the team's service. One of the purposes of a team is to allow differing types of expertise to be used in service of the client. The decision-making process needs to allow for this diversity of understanding yet facilitate the process so that it is reasonably expedient.

4. *Use of the problem-solving process*—As with all small groups, goals need to be accepted by all. Differences in goals among team members can arise from inadequate problem identification. If different team members see the problem differently and do not understand or accept the team goals, hidden agendas can develop. Also, if different team members are functioning at different stages of the problem-solving process, confusion in planning results.

5. *Implementation of plans and carrying out tasks*—Team members usually have other tasks and other influences on how they prioritize their work. Often this results in assigned tasks not being carried out, particularly when those tasks are imposed on team members.

6. *Functioning within a complex organization*—Sometimes organizations institute or sanction the use of the team approach without full understanding of the implications of teamwork. The organization may not allow sufficient time for team functioning, may impose leadership that does not enable team functioning to develop, or may interfere with the team's ability to function in other ways.

Each team is unique and must discover its own best way of functioning. For some teams this will be in a cooperative manner where an integrated approach to client service is the mode. Other teams will use a collaborative approach in which the team decides on the services needed; appropriate team members then provide those services in an autonomous manner. Other teams will use various combinations of the two approaches.

Regardless of approach, teams that function best have members who are dedicated and share a common ideal and have confidence in one another. Members also have a willingness to work together, to learn from one another, and to share clients. They have a cooperative rather than a competitive climate, flexibility, and good communication and problem-solving processes. They also have the support of the agency of which they are a part.

Social workers who are members of teams can help to resolve problems in functioning by helping the team to identify the issues confronting the team so that it can work for resolution.

Leadership

Because leadership has differing meanings for different persons, it is often the source of problems in group functioning. Some people perceive a leader as being one who tells everyone else what to do. Other people see the leader as one who consults with the other group members but in the end makes the decisions. Still others see the leader as the one who enables the group to function. Some people who carry the title "leader" are appointed, some elected; others emerge from the group. Some people resent leadership or leadership by certain people or professions; others expect the leader to take full responsibility for the group or expect a member of a particular profession to automatically be the leader.

More and more leadership is being understood as "interpersonal influence," and it is in this sense that the meaning of leadership as used here is captured. Such influence can be exerted in a variety of ways, some of which are more helpful in furthering the functioning of the group than others. The idea that only one person, elected or emergent, carries the entire leadership responsibility is fallacious.

If the group members understand leadership as a shared responsibility, much interpersonal conflict can be avoided. The group can then use the knowledge and skills of all group members, for the leadership can change from person to person, depending on the task at hand.

As a group member, the social worker can influence, or enable, the group to carry out its task and function. Some of the tasks involved in this enabling include:

1. See that decisions are made (but not making them for the group);
2. Be sure the group knows what it is doing: Are there goals? Are they known to all the members? Does the group know its reason for being? Are group norms explicit?

3. Make certain the group knows how it is doing: What stage of problem solving is the group functioning in? Are the essential roles in the group being filled? Are all group members' contributions accepted? Is communication open and understood by all?
4. Be sure when things are not going well or feeling good, the group stops to evaluate what is wrong.

Social workers with a knowledge of group process can carry out these tasks for any group of which they are members regardless of their position in the group. To do this they must use good judgment about how and when to exercise this kind of influence. In doing so they exercise leadership and influence the outcome of the group's functioning.

Conflict

For many persons conflict is frightening. There is a feeling that disagreements can lead to fighting, and it is the fear of uncontrolled fighting that explains, in part, the fear of conflict. Other persons believe that conflict can result in nothing positive and thus attempt to avoid it. Conflict does not need to result in uncontrolled fighting, and it can result in the development of new ways of functioning that give rise to new ideas.

Conflict is to be expected when people of different backgrounds and differing experiences interact with one another. Conflict in small groups is not to be avoided; it is to be managed. Differences about what the task and function of the group is, who would fill roles, and what the norms of the group should be are to be discussed and negotiated. Negotiation is a process in which each party to a conflict states his or her point of view and the reasons for that point of view. These points of view are then examined to discover if there is any faulty thinking and if there are any aspects of the points of view the parties are willing to give on; attempts are then made to reconcile the disagreement. Often faulty communication is a part of the disagreement. Usually each point of view has something that can contribute to the work of the group. Conflict is not to be avoided but brought into the open and dealt with by the total group.

Following are some aids to the resolution of conflict:

1. Define the conflict, not as one person's problem, but as belonging to the group.
2. Listen to each person's point of view and seek to identify similarities as well as differences among them.
3. Seek clarification so that each point of view is fully understood.
4. Try to avoid win-or-lose solutions.
5. Do not ignore cues that conflict exists; check them out.
6. Work for a cooperative rather than a competitive climate.

Because social workers have skills in understanding persons and their behavior, the worker who is a group member can often help the group recognize conflict. The recognition of conflict is the first step toward its management and resolution. When conflict is *not* recognized, it can be most destructive to the group's interaction.

Social Work Tasks

Social workers who are group members are qualified to carry out three tasks that can be very useful for the group in its functioning: consultation, facilitation, and coordination. The *consultation task* calls for the worker to ask for and offer information and suggestions. Consultation does not place any demands that the suggestion be accepted. The consultation provides an expectation that all group members will examine the information and suggestions in light of their particular perspective, and provide feedback on the usefulness and validity of the social worker's contributions. This type of consultation is a means of enabling the group to engage in a joint assessment of clients in situations and for considering alternatives for developing the solutions to problems and developing plans for action. It is through consultation that the social worker contributes the expertise she brings to the group. This expertise can be in the area of group functioning, or it can be in the form of contributions to the task of the group.

The *facilitation task* is one that enables others to function. Facilitation of the group process is one form of this task. Social workers can carry out this task in a number of ways. They can support helpful behaviors of other group members, model useful behaviors, ask appropriate questions, or provide appropriate observations and feelings about the group. They can teach other group members information about group process and functioning. Other means of facilitating are helping members stay on the topic, summarizing what has been said or decided, and letting other members know their feelings are O.K. Because of their problem-solving skills, social workers can help the group state problems so that they can be worked on. They can partialize problems, which is done by breaking a problem into parts and prioritizing as to which part should be worked on and/or deciding the order for working on the various parts of the problem.

Some behaviors to avoid are criticizing others or their values, forcing ideas on the group, making decisions that belong to the group, and talking too much. The social worker studies the group and its functioning and decides what will most help the group at any point in time.

A third task, the *coordination task,* calls for monitoring to learn if all members are carrying out their assigned tasks and that, in the carrying out of the tasks, the work of each group member is done in a way that complements those of other members. Coordinating insures that the work of various members does not conflict but complements the work of other group members. Social workers are especially able to perform this role because of their broad view of personal and social functioning. They are able to view the various parts of a plan and ascertain how the parts fit together and, where misfit exists, to identify means of modifying misfitting plans.

Much of this coordination is done by building relationships. The social worker attempts to understand the position of every other group member and to gain an appreciation of the needs of each member in relation to the group's task. Through relationships with group members, the social worker can attempt to mediate differences and to provide observations about the group functioning. In this way, the social worker assists the group in its work together and helps the group coordinate its work.

Social workers can contribute a great deal to groups of which they are members. Knowledge of group process; understanding of issues that can inhibit group functioning; and skill in carrying out the tasks of consultation, facilitation, and coordination provide the social worker with a firm base for making this contribution.

CASE EXAMPLE

A Team Meeting

Setting

An interdisciplinary diagnostic center for the developmentally disabled. The practice of this team is for each professional discipline to see the client and the family or person responsible for the client individually. Then the team meeting is held to present and discuss findings of each discipline, to develop a group assessment, and to make recommendations to the family and/or the referring agency. One team member serves as coordinator for the client.

Client

Name: John Jones   *Age:* 4 years, 6 months
Client's living situation: lives with mother; parents divorced; father in jail
School: Head Start program, Anytown
Presenting problem: Down's syndrome; behavior problem; mother requesting placement

Information Available

(Information known to each team member before individual interview.)

1. Report from the Department of Social Services (state agency),
2. Report from local physician,
3. Report of Head Start teacher, and
4. Report of psychologist.

Referral made by Department of Social Service (DSS) for help in planning for John. The mother is overwhelmed by child and is asking for placement outside the home. DSS would like information about

1. Current functioning and potential of John,
2. Placement recommendations, and
3. Recommendations for long-term planning for John.

John is a Down's syndrome child who has been exhibiting increasingly destructive behavior. He has little speech. He is a behavior management problem at home. He wanders at night, gets into the refrigerator, and throws food at and hits his siblings.

Records indicate a normal full-term pregnancy and delivery. The Down's syndrome was diagnosed immediately. Child had difficulty thriving in the first year for no apparent reason. Eating was a problem. Development lagged. Sat alone at eighteen months, crawled at twenty-four months, walked alone at thirty-six months, fed self (spoon) at thirty months, cut first tooth at twenty-four months.

School

Child is enrolled in local Head Start program. Must be watched in group situation because of disruptive behaviors. Responds to one-to-one involvement well. Mother has difficulty getting child to school because of distance and transportation. Averages one day a week attendance. Child works with form board, pegboard, and stacking cubes. Responds to language development by making sounds. Has some success at this. School is working on motor development, throwing ball, and standing on one foot.

Family

Parents divorced three years ago. Father has been in and out of jail. Three other children— a son, seven years old, and two daughters, six and two. Mother reports no problems with other children.

Other agency involvement: Mother has received ADC since separating from husband soon after John's birth. Youngest child, while conceived after divorce, is seemingly of same father as other children. Mother is afraid of father. Recently she requested placement for John. She seems unable to provide for him any longer.

Psychologist's report centers around service mother requested last year for help with older brother, who was refusing to attend school. Mother and son came for one session; did not continue service. Psychologist's impression is that mother and son are overly involved with one another.

Team Meeting

Attending: Educational psychologist (team leader), social worker, pediatrician, speech therapist, clinical psychology student, nursing student (observing students).

The educational psychologist opened the meeting by introducing each staff member and his or her role. He also explained how the team functioned. This was primarily for the observing students. He then began to call on each team member for a report of his or her findings.

The social worker reviewed the material known before the evaluation began and discussed his interview with the mother. The mother cares about the child but has become overwhelmed by his behavior. She feels the other children are suffering. She has started to work part time and is enjoying this but says that childcare help is almost impossible to find. Relatives are helping, but this is only temporary. In observing mother and child together, the mother seems unable to discipline him and is somewhat cold and removed. The mother seems to have little understanding of the special needs of the child and resists attempts by the social worker to give such understanding. She states that the father blames her for child's condition. He is in jail for assault and battery. He is violent and she is afraid of him. He is due to be released in two months. She wants to move so he can't find her. Social worker stated that the mother is overwhelmed by all the demands placed on her by the family. At this time she is probably unable to meet child's needs without help. The other children may be at risk. The older brother's school problems are an indication of this. If she gets help with the family problems and develops greater understanding of the child's needs, she may be able to care for him in the future. She seems ready to cooperate with placement plans. (Consultation.)

The pediatrician stated that this is a typical Down's syndrome child. She can find no physical reasons for behavior problems. After giving her report, she left the meeting for a time.

The DSS worker entered the room at this time and was introduced.

The speech therapist reported that it was impossible to test the child in any but the most general way because of hyperactivity. The child has a vocabulary of about twelve words and uses them in ways that indicate understanding of meaning. The child did attempt to imitate sounds and was successful with quite a few. It appears that John is not receiving sufficient stimulation for developing his speech potential.

The clinical psychology student saw both the mother and the child. He feels the family needs some kind of therapy, as their relationship seems disturbed.

The nursing student was asked for her observations. She said the mother tried to discipline John but became very anxious when he did not respond. John responded to her attention when she worked with him apart from the mother, but when the mother entered the room it was impossible to hold his attention.

The educational psychologist said that he concurred in much that had been said. The child seemed very tired and was impossible to test. However, he did perform some tests when the mother was not in the room. It is estimated he is performing on a one-year, four-month level but has a somewhat greater potential. The problem does seem to rest in the behavior and the mother-child relationship, not in the retardation.

The educational psychologist then asked the DSS worker if she would like to add anything or had any questions about anything that had been said. She said she had nothing more to add and needed a definite recommendation if she was to place this child.

The team then began to discuss the findings. The educational psychologist structured this discussion by asking each team member for recommendations and listing them on the blackboard. First he asked the pediatrician, who had returned, what her recommendations would be. She said she had none except routine care. The social worker asked if genetic counseling would be advisable. (Facilitation.) The pediatrician said, "The parents are divorced, I don't see any necessity." The educational psychologist pointed out that there had been a child born since the divorce. The pediatrician replied, "Well, if you want to, all right," in a sort of detached manner and left the room.

The speech therapist suggested that John receive speech therapy and that the mother be helped to reinforce this at home. A long discussion ensued about resources for this therapy. The social worker said that he wondered if the specifics should not be postponed until it was decided what was to be done about the mother's request for placement. If the child is to be placed, the availability of speech therapy should be considered when choosing the specific placement. (Facilitation and Consultation.)

The team discussed the clinical psychology plan for therapy and decided that the family would not be able to use formal therapy at this time.

The educational psychologist recommended that placement be considered, as the mother seemed unable to meet the child's needs at this time. The placement should be one that would have a quality special preschool education program available and that could carry out a behavior management program.

The social worker was then asked what programs might be available. The social worker stated that first the team needed to consider if there was any chance this child could remain in his own home. (Facilitation.) After much discussion, mostly about the limitations of the home, it was decided that a period of respite for both John and his mother was in order. During this discussion, the social worker pointed out the importance of a family to a child and discussed how this mother seemed not to have received very much help in understanding the special needs of John. The social worker also discussed the dynamics of this family and the needs of the mother as a single parent. (Consultation.) The staff discussion slowly began to change. They began to talk about trying once more to maintain John in his own home. The social worker was asked what kind of services might be available for this family. He asked the DSS worker what might be available. The DSS worker said she had heard of a new concept called in-home treatment and wished this were available for this family. The other team members asked the DSS worker to tell them about this idea. The DSS worker described the concept of providing an intensive therapeutic experience in the home for a fairly short period of time. In this situation the mother would be shown how to manage John and provide him with some of the experiences he needed in order to grow. This service would be provided at times during the day when it is most needed, such as early in the morning or at dinnertime.

The team social worker asked if there was any way for the family to receive this kind of service. The DSS worker said she was not sure but would be willing to work on it if the team could identify some possible ways of managing John so he would not be so disruptive.

It was suggested that if his attendance at the Head Start program were more regular, more could be done in that program. There followed a discussion of why John might not be getting to Head Start.

As the time allotted for the team meeting was about over, the team leader asked the two social workers if they would try to develop a plan for in-home treatment. He would help with management techniques. The plan should be reported back to the team in a week.

THE WORKER AND THE MULTIPERSON CLIENT

In many multiperson situations the social worker interacts as a worker with the system rather than as a member of the system (see page 193). When working in and with a group the worker's interaction with the group depends on the situation. Where the situation is clearly a multiclient one, the worker is usually not seen as a part of the group but rather as a professional helper. In other situations, such as when serving as a staff assistant to a board or a committee, the worker is seen more as a resource person who helps the group members carry out the work of the group.

In order to function as a worker with a group, the social worker must understand group process and must develop interactional skills for working with groups. The worker uses many of the enabling skills used when a member of a group.

The Worker and Group Interaction

When a social worker works with a group of unrelated persons, the focus is on the group interaction. Because the system may not have formed, in the early stages the worker may be involved in interaction that enables the group system to form. Again the interactions are to enable individuals to become part of the group and to function in the group. The major focus is on the group interaction, not on the worker-individual member interaction; otherwise, the worker is not working with the group system but with individuals in the presence of other individuals.

The worker influences the process of the system in a number of ways, including:

1. *Acceptance*—The worker accepts individual members with their feelings, attitudes, ideas, and behaviors. Through such acceptance, other members come to see the member's contribution, to realize that feelings are O.K., and to appreciate difference. In being accepted by the worker, group members gain strength to carry out their roles in the group.

2. *Relationships*—The worker helps each group member to relate to other members and to gain interactional skill. The worker also uses relationship to help the members find their commonalities.

3. *Enabling and supporting*—The worker helps members to accept themselves and others, to express themselves, to have a feeling of accomplishment, and to involve themselves in the activity and the decision making of the group. In addition, the worker helps the group and its members gain understanding of their group process and how it may be modified. The worker contributes facts and understanding that enable the group to function.

4. *Limiting behavior*—When behavior of individual members is harmful to themselves and particularly to others or is destructive of property or relationships, then the worker helps the group or the individual members to limit such behavior.

5. *Guiding*—The worker helps the group by providing guidance for the discussion process, such as helping the group keep on focus or task, teaching effective problem solving, and so on. The worker also guides the activity and the movement of the group in its process.

6. *Alleviation*—The worker relieves tensions, conflicts, fears, anxiety, or guilt that may be interfering with group functioning.

7. *Interpreting*—The worker helps the group to understand the function of the agency and of the worker in relation to the group's task. The worker may also interpret the meaning of the feelings or actions of the group or its members.

8. *Observation and evaluation*—The worker is constantly trying to understand what is happening in the group and why it is happening.

9. *Planning and preparation*—The worker plans for the group as needed to enable the group to function and carry out its purposes.[8]

The role of the social worker with the group is to help the members reach out to one another in such a way that they can help one another in meeting the needs of individual group members of that group or can in some way influence the environment so that group and individual needs are better met. Helping the group as a system to carry out its task is the focus of the social worker when working with a multiclient system.

The social worker's role is influenced both by the stage of group development and by the stage of individual development of the group members. During the orientation stage the worker is very active with the group. The worker helps the group members to share their needs and concerns relative to that function; structures group meetings so the members can get a vision of how the group can function; enables group members to maintain a distance while making decisions about the group and their role in the group; and attempts to maintain a comfortable, accepting climate.

As the group moves to the authority stage, the worker allows members to challenge ideas and ways of functioning. The worker helps the members recognize and deal with conflict. The worker supports the group and its members as they struggle to find ways to work together.

As the group begins to negotiate differences, the worker supports this negotiation and continues to help the group deal with conflict. The group is helped to identify norms and values, to establish goals, and to negotiate roles. The worker clarifies feelings and ideas.

In the functional stage, the worker allows the group to function as independently as possible. The worker serves as a resource person and as an observer and helps the group evaluate its process. During this stage the worker's contribution to the group's process and work depends on what will be useful as the group engages in its work together.

When a worker senses the onset of disintegration, a decision should be made with the group as to whether the group has served its purpose and the disintegration should be allowed to progress or an attempt should be made to help the group reverse the disintegration. If the decision is to reverse, the worker's role is to help the group determine the reasons for the disintegration and to take those steps needed to solve the problem. A problem-solving process is used with the group. If the group has served its purpose, then the worker helps the group to understand what is happening and to feel good about the group's accomplishments.

Three areas of understanding are needed by the social worker in working with groups. These are the process of group formation, group discussion leadership, and the use of structure and activity to facilitate group functioning.

Group Formation

While social workers sometimes work with already formed systems or groups, at times it is necessary to form a group. Persons who are considered for group membership may not be acquainted with one another. The way in which the formation process is done is an important factor in whether or not the group will be able to function to meet its goals. There are four stages to the formation of a group: 1) establishing the group's purpose, 2) selecting members, 3) making the first contacts with prospective members, and 4) holding the first meeting of the group.

The group's purpose may develop from client request or from an agency staff decision that there is a need that can be met through developing a group. Some of the reasons for forming a group are 1) identification of several persons facing similar situations who can benefit from a sharing of experiences; 2) when group influence on individuals is great, such as during the teen years when individuals need to develop social skills; 3) when the target for change is in the environment, such as development of a new community service; 4) when a natural group exists; and 5) when individuals are having difficulty in relating to others or with authority figures, or are having problems of social isolation. The group is an excellent vehicle to use for reality testing for it is a social microcosm of the larger society. Groups should not be used as timesavers, when a common goal or purpose does not exist, when an individual is in danger of being overwhelmed by the group, when there is insufficient commonality for a cohesive climate to develop, or when the environment will impinge on the group's functioning or not allow it to reach its goals. Groups can work together on individual needs, on relationships within or outside of the group, on problem solving or task achievement, or on targeting for change in the larger community.

For a group to be functional, the group members must have some commonality (in part, the purpose and function provide the commonality). At this stage of the formation process, the worker and agency identify a common need and translate the need to the purpose for the prospective group. The worker formulates tentative group goals. Based on the purpose and the tentative goals, the worker begins the selection of members. Consideration is given to how many persons should be in the group. For persons who have good interactional skills, the number can go as high as fifteen and still allow for interaction among all the members. For clients with little interactional capacity, the size of the group should be limited to perhaps four or five persons.

The commonality is in part based on the attractiveness the prospective members have for one another. People are attracted to other people because they admire them, because they hold common values, because they respect them, or because they support their functioning in some way. People feel most comfortable with those who are similar to themselves. For a group to be productive, however, it is necessary for the members to have sufficient difference so that different contributions are made by the group members. The worker must determine how much commonality is necessary for the group to be attractive to prospective members and how much difference is necessary to carry out the function of the group.

In choosing prospective members the worker also evaluates how well a person can be expected to function in the group and what his or her contribution to the group might be. The choice of persons as prospective members is based on multiple factors that relate to the need for balance and the individual qualities of prospective members.

Other factors in forming a group are the resources and expectations that arise from the prospective group's environment. These factors affect the prospective member's ability to function in the group, and they also affect the manner in which the group can function.

When the worker has completed the process of choosing prospective members, the next step is an initial contact with each person. During the initial contact, the worker explains the purpose of the group and the reason for considering the person for group membership. Together they explore how the group may function and come to a decision about the prospective member joining the group. In many ways, this session is similar to the worker's initial interview with an individual client. The major purpose of the session is to begin to engage the member in the group and to orient the member to the group.

The first meeting of the group is crucial for group formation. The group function and the way of operating are discussed again. The worker enables each member to share with other members his or her reason for joining the group and his or her individual goals with respect to the group. The worker facilitates communication among the members and helps them to begin formulating group norms and goals. The group begins to work on the tasks of carrying out the function of the group. Every attempt is made for this first session to be a positive experience for all members.

Adequate group formation is time consuming, but if properly done it saves time later. It reduces the chances of having a mismatch of group members, and it prepares the members for functioning in the group. In this way, the time in the group can be spent on its function and tasks, not on unrelated individual needs.

Discussion Leadership

Discussion is the means of communicating within the group. The worker carries the task of enabling the discussion to develop until such time as leadership emerges in the group. This enabling takes place through:

1. *Climate setting*—The worker pays attention to the physical atmosphere. Placement of chairs so that all members can have eye contact and are neither too close nor too far apart is important. The atmosphere should be warm, friendly, and relaxed.

2. *Stimulating*—The worker knows that encouragement of the sharing of ideas is important. The worker also helps group members to disagree without developing hostility.

3. *Encouraging mutual respect and understanding*—The worker helps the members understand their commonalities and differences. The right of persons to be different is considered. The worker demonstrates respect for all members and their ideas. This modeling often helps members respect one another.

4. *Reducing overdependence*—The worker encourages the group to develop its way of functioning. The worker seeks ideas and facts from the members and helps group members to fill the essential roles.

5. *Drawing in nonparticipants*—The worker helps a member who is not active in the discussion to contribute by asking questions or suggesting information she may have.

6. *Checking overaggressive participants*—The worker points out to the group the need for each member to have an opportunity to participate.

7. *Helping the group define and verbalize goals and problems*—The worker stimulates group thinking and helps the group in problem solving.

8. *Helping the group in other ways*—The worker clarifies issues, analyzes problems, discovers and describes possible solutions, evaluates solutions, and carries out decisions. Also, the worker helps the group focus when it gets off course and summarizes as appropriate.

9. *Helping the group deal with conflict*—The worker points out symptoms of conflict, helps individuals clarify viewpoints and state positions and seeks commonalities.

In providing discussion leadership to a group, the worker is also teaching members of the group how to take over the responsibility for their own leadership. The worker needs to help the group avoid placing undue pressure for conformity or dependency on its members, harmful and unsupportive responses to vulnerable members, and allowing assertive and talkative members to receive all the attention. As soon as group members are able to carry any part of that responsibility, the worker encourages the discussion leadership to begin to rest in the group members and fills the enabler role.

Structuring Group Activity

The group can be enabled to function through the use of activity. Activity can be tasks the group does together, such as games, crafts, or other program materials, or structured exercises. The way in which a worker structures these activities can enable the group to develop. Activity can also give the group data on which to make decisions about its functioning. Another part of structuring is the use of the physical facility and the time and place of the meeting. (See the section entitled "Use of Activity as an Interventive Strategy" in Chapter 13 for further discussion of this kind of action.)

When working with the multiperson client, the worker has four primary tools: 1) the worker and the way he uses self, 2) the use of group process, 3) discussion as a means of communication, and 4) structures and activity. Through the use of these tools the worker enables the group to function and carry out the tasks that lead to goal fulfillment.

The generalist social worker's interactive repertoire includes skill in working in and with small groups as well as in one-to-one interaction. To develop this skill the worker needs knowledge of group process, means for influencing groups of which she is a member, and means for enabling the functioning of the multiperson client group.

CASE EXAMPLE

Session Summaries of Women's Career Exploration Group

Session 1: Carol and Joan immediately took over leadership of a discussion about meeting times and place. Members immediately began to point out all the obligations each has: classes, home responsibilities, etc. Worker moved into a clarifying role, asking questions about the meaning of the points being discussed. She pointed out the availability of the room at the time the group wanted to meet. Worker then moved to clarify the purpose of the group by stating the goal as she understood it: for the group to gain greater understanding of possible jobs and of the educational qualification for those jobs. Carol stated that she was a nurse and didn't see that as the goal, she just wanted to know how to get a degree in nursing when the school didn't offer a BS in Nursing. Bev said she was finishing her history degree and wanted to know what she could do with it. Joan wanted to know what she could do with an English degree. The worker stated that she was not sure the group could answer these specific questions but felt that she could help the individuals come to understand themselves so they would be in a better position to answer the questions for themselves. She then shared with the group a little of her own experience in going back to school and how her career goals evolved. There was then some discussion about how they had been treated as nontraditional students. The worker acknowledged this discussion and suggested that right now the goal of the group seemed to be for each individual to gain help in identifying her personal goals rather than on changing the situation in which they found themselves. The worker told the group that if they wanted to work on changing the system she would be glad to help them in another situation. The worker and the group then discussed the subject of confidentiality. As it was almost time for the session to end, the worker handed out an individual assessment instrument and asked members to fill this in before next week, when it would be discussed. The group then did their own summary of what had happened regarding plans for the group and confidentiality. The worker felt they understood the goal and were accepting of it.

Session 2: After the group had gathered and there had been some sharing of what was going on with each member, the worker asked if the plans for the group they had made last week still seemed to be workable for each of them. Everyone agreed that they were. The worker then asked what their reaction was to the work on the instrument she had given them last week. She found that no one had filled it out, but all had it with them. There followed another time of sharing how busy they were and that they really didn't know what the worker wanted. The worker explained that she thought this would be a good way for them to identify their interests, strengths, and limitations, which in turn would give them information on which to base career decisions. The group seemed to have a better understanding of the purpose of the activity. The worker suggested that they take some time and fill out the instrument now. Questions were asked about the meaning of material from time to time. Each member was asked to share what she had learned about herself and the others from working on the instrument. Everyone came up with something they had learned. This began an interchange among group members about how they saw each other. Worker suggested that next time they could look at the needed characteristics for various careers and see how chosen careers fit with the information they had gained about themselves today.

Session 3: As the group gathered, they were very anxious to share with the worker some thinking they now had about what they had learned from the inventories last week. It was obvious they had been discussing this with each other outside of the group sessions. The difference in the discussion this week from last week was that rather than talking about how they saw each other, individuals were talking about self. Carol said she was not sure that she wanted to be a bed-side nurse. Mary said the inventory had helped her see why she was so unhappy in her present job. Patty seemed to be questioning whether her psychology major was the right choice. Joan said maybe she didn't even belong in school and would do better in managing a small business, but then where would she get the money to buy a business. After allowing free discussion for about half the session, the worker suggested that the group now fill out another inventory that looked at interests and skills related to various career opportunities. She did this to get the group thinking along these lines for next session. The group freely commented on what they were finding out as they worked on the inventory. As it took most of the rest of session to finish it, the worker suggested taking it home and studying it and bringing it back next week for discussion. The worker also pointed out that half of the planned sessions were now completed.

Session 4: The group engaged in its usual bringing each other up to date about the latest in their lives. The worker then asked the group about their reactions to the job inventory that was done last week. There seemed to be some hesitancy to discuss this material. Finally, Patty began to talk about the reaction of faculty members to the nontraditional students. The worker reminded the group that this was an area they as a group might want to work on at another time. Carol then said that if faculty were not receptive to students there was no use working on that major, as they would not be able to get a job in that area. There also was discussion about how it's nice to know what career areas seem to be most congruent with one's personality, but if there were no jobs in that area, what good would it do anyway to choose that major. The worker said it sounded like the group was changing the focus of the group to job finding. There were activities they could engage in that would prepare them for a job search, but the group would need to meet more sessions. The group agreed that they could not add any sessions as the school year was coming to an end. Perhaps they should look at what kind of jobs would best meet their needs now. Carol then said that maybe she did have some options other than nursing and she wanted to look at that. Mary seemed very serious in looking at career options she might have, and said she liked the idea of getting work with a women's center. The group looked at how this might be done locally. Patty said she would like to explore with the worker the idea of a double major in social work. The worker suggested that before next week the group interview a faculty member of a department they might consider as a major about job possibilities. As time for the meeting was up, the group noted there were only two more meetings. The worker wondered if they would reach the goal of the group in that time. The group was not ready to discuss this.

Session 5: The worker opened the group by stating that in thinking about last week's session, she sensed some dissatisfaction with what the group was doing. She thought members had hoped to have answers to their questions about a career route. The group hesitantly acknowledged this. Then Joan spoke up and said that may have been what they wanted, but she now saw it was a much more complicated process than she realized. It's too bad the school year was coming to an end so they couldn't continue as a group but she did think she'd made a lot of progress. She said, "I have a lot to think about and I need time. Right now, with the school year ending and all the tests and papers, I just don't have that time." Others seemed relieved at this expression of feeling and began to talk about all they had to do. Carol then said she had not gone to check out a major as had been requested last week because she just didn't have time. Patty said that would have to come later. The worker asked about the desire for job-finding skills—would they want a group on this next year? The group was not ready to commit themselves on this, so the worker dropped the subject. She then asked them how they wanted to use their last session next week. They said they felt there needed to be more discussion about personality characteristics and job match. The worker said she would also like them to evaluate the usefulness of the group and what they would have liked to have been different.

Session 6: The group began with everyone acknowledging that this was the last meeting. There seemed to be some relief about this from group members, as they all seemed very busy with the end of the school year. The worker pointed out that last week they decided to use this session to discuss a bit more how career choices are tied to personality characteristics and then to evaluate the group experience together. The group members immediately pointed out how the group had helped them individually. They said that they wished there had been more time, but thought that they now had some direction in their career search. They really did not want to discuss anything of substance and seemed in a hurry to get the session over with so they could get back to writing papers and studying. The worker acknowledged this and told the group that this was O.K. She told the group that if they as a group or individually wanted her to help them in the future, to get in touch with her and she would see what could be done. The group left early, but with a sense of closure.

Followup: Discussion with each group member at later times indicated that each was indeed able to use the content of the group and continue on her individual search for her life work.

THE WORKER AND THE FAMILY GROUP

Many approaches to working with the family as a system have been developed, several of which are summarized in the Appendix. It is beyond the scope of this book to consider any one of these in depth; rather, what will be presented about working with the family as a group will be understandings and principles of action that enable the worker-family interactional process to develop. A first principle of working with families is that the social history of the family unit be developed (see Table 7–3) so that the worker develops the necessary understandings of the family.

The family group is seen as a system using knowledge of social systems, small-group processes, and family structure and functioning. The family group has many of the same characteristics as the small group. The family, however, is a special small group—one that is usually intergenerational, exists over an extended period of time, and has very strong bonds because of both the amount of time spent together and the strength of the influence a family has upon its members. The family has its own developmental process that is related to the developmental stages of the family members.

A second principle is that a caring, understanding relationship be developed with the total family unit, not just with certain individuals within that unit. The social worker must recognize that the family is a well-established system. The social worker should not become entangled with that system nor should the worker take sides with individual family members. The contribution of all family members is sought and valued. Each family member is respected as an individual.

A third principle is that problems are to be owned by the family—not blamed on individual family members. When confronting families with the realities of the situation—the responsibility of the total family for family related problems—it is important to do so gradually. This can be done by conveying an explorative approach toward the presented problem. It can also help if the worker can convey to the family that problems are often an indication of a blockage in the growth of the family. Anxiety can often be relieved by explaining and clarifying the situation. Most important, the family needs to understand that the helping situation is a safe place in which to work on its problems. By demonstrating a nonblaming attitude that respects the rights of each family member, the worker is providing them with a model of how they might begin to work together on the family's problems.

Next, he helps the family take responsibility for the problem as a total system rather than blame the problem on one family member. The family is then expected to develop and carry out plans for meeting unmet needs and alleviating problems. The worker's role is an enabling one.

A fourth related principle is that blame and guilt are to be avoided because they place responsibility on specific family members. When working with the family as the client, the focus is on how the family structure and functioning contribute to the problem. The influence of environmental factors and lack of skill in meeting family needs are also stressed when appropriate.

When working with the family group, the worker demands that each person be allowed to speak for himself or herself. The worker demonstrates to the family how the work will be done and how communication is to take place. Each family member is given the feeling that this is a safe place to work on their problems. Attention is paid to the physical setting in which the work takes place. If young children are involved, provision is made for them to move around and play quietly. The expectations and problem definitions of each family member are clarified so that each family member understands those of every other family member. The worker seeks to help the family develop consensus about the nature of the difficulty. Negotiation among the family members about not only the nature of the difficulty but about the purpose, goal, and strategy of the work together is very important. The worker helps the family develop a contract among the members as well as a family contract with the worker about what needs to be done and who should do it. The worker uses an educational approach when members of the family lack understanding and skill necessary for effective family functioning. Skill in dealing with resistance to change is most important because families often have entrenched ways of functioning that are the source of problems of social functioning but that also are very hard for individual members to give up.

When working with the family as the unit of attention, social workers often encounter difficulty because they either are not aware of or have not resolved some of their concerns and feelings about their own families of orientation (the family they grew up in). Workers may also make unfounded assumptions about the functioning of families based on their personal experience. Thus, an important prerequisite to working with family groups is recognition and resolution of how the worker has been affected by her own family.[9]

Often the assumption is made that a family consists of two parents and two or more children. In contemporary American society this is often not the case. Many couples choose to remain childless, more couples are living longer after their children have left home, and the number of single-parent families is growing. Social workers need to adapt the models for work with family groups to these situations. Couple or marital therapy may provide understandings when working with a family made up of only husband and wife. When working with older persons, either as couples or with adult children and their families, consideration must be given to the developmental tasks of the later years. Role reversal of parents and adult children is to be avoided. Unresolved or poorly resolved issues from the past may need to be dealt with. Two tasks that often are important for families with older persons are 1) to help the family find and use community resources that will allow older persons to live in the least restrictive environment possible and 2) to help families maintain supportive, helpful relationships that do not overburden any family member.

When working with the single-parent family, it is important to consider the influence of the absent parent. Different concerns may be present if the absent parent is dead, a divorce has taken place, or there has never been a marriage. The father or mother may be the custodial parent, or there may be a joint-custody agreement. When working with the single-parent family, it is particularly important to consider role overload and the needs of the single parent. There may be unresolved feelings or problems resulting from death or divorce. Inappropriate expectations of family members may be present. Children may be filling the role of the absent parent in a way that places too much stress or responsibility on the child. Often this type of family has a need for supportive community resources.

Many of the families that social workers work with are known as multiproblem or chaotic families. Both child abuse and spouse abuse are often the problems that bring multiproblem families to the social agency. These families usually do not come to social workers voluntarily but are ordered by the court or some other authority to seek service. When working in these very difficult situations, a first step must be the development of a relationship based on trust of the worker. To do this, the worker must be consistent and flexible and avoid any type of retaliation. The worker must be honest with the family about why they are there and what the consequences of lack of cooperation may be. Concern and empathy expressed in a nonjudgmental manner are very important. These families often need help in setting priorities and in developing skills of social functioning. Their communication skills may be limited. It is most important that these families develop a sense of competency.

The worker must understand the differences in family functioning and structure within different cultural groups. When working with families from a minority cultural group, workers should presume ignorance until they have checked out with a family how it functions within its cultural group. Usually meeting with families in their home, using short-term, action-oriented modes, is most successful. The worker helps the family work out its own solution in a manner that is supportive of the extended family and immediate ethnic community system. Often work with minority-group families involves helping them deal with the external dominate society system and its institutions. Advocacy with individuals, groups, and institutions within the majority culture may be needed. An important goal when working with all families, but particularly with families who have experienced discrimination in its various forms, is enabling the family and its members to take control of their own lives and work toward changing the situation in which they find themselves. (Enabling as a practice strategy will be discussed in Chapter 13.)

The social worker needs to develop understanding of the various forms that families take in our society. Workers need to develop skill in assessing a family and its situation and then creatively developing means for working with the family—skill in interacting with the family so as to provide the needed information and to enable participation in the planning and work necessary for need fulfillment and enhanced social functioning.

CASE EXAMPLE

Summary of the First Session with the A Family
(see Chapter 7, pages 150–154)

The worker had arranged the chairs in a circle. He had deliberately provided one more chair than there would be people involved to give some indication of separations in this family as they seated themselves. Mrs. A and Mary sat next to each other, Mr. A left one chair between himself and Mrs. A, and Henry Jr. sat on the other side of him. John hesitated for some time as to where to sit and he sat next to Henry Jr. but moved his chair somewhat away from his brother. The worker chose to sit next to John with Mary on the other side. Mr. A immediately seemed to try and take over the situation by announcing that he had to get back to work at 3:00 and he didn't see why all of them had to be involved because John couldn't behave himself. The worker replied that in order to understand the family situation, he preferred to talk to the entire family together. He also stated that when one member of a family is having difficulty there is a family difficulty. Mr. A responded, "That is true, each of us is being affected by John's behavior." (The worker chose to ignore this as he did not think Mr. A was ready for further confrontation at this time.)

The worker then said that he would like to know what each family member saw as the way in which the family solved problems. He would like to start with John. In going around the circle, the worker noted that the children commented that Mr. A decided how things should be and expected Mrs. A to see that things went that way. Mrs. A stated that she tried to handle as many of the problems as possible, but that the boys (particularly John) were just beyond her capacity, so she asked her husband for help. Mr. A stated that he had to make decisions in his business, and that he felt comfortable that he knew what was best for the family, but he did not want to have to make all the day-to-day decisions. He thought his wife knew what he wanted and should be able to see to it that things were done that way. The worker noted that the children were uneasy but he needed to probe further in order to understand how the family functioned.

Next he asked each family member what they would like to see happen in the family. Henry Jr. was first to answer and he began to blame John for all the trouble. The worker interrupted and said he did not ask what was wrong and he did not think it would help to blame anyone; rather, it would be more useful to talk about what the family wanted for itself. Henry said, "Well, I just wish the fighting would stop." The worker asked for clarification about fighting. This led to a discussion of parents fighting and the fact it wasn't always over John. The worker then returned to family members telling what they wanted for the family. Some of the areas brought up were: Mary wished Henry Jr. would stop teasing her. John wished they could do some things together. Mrs. A said she wished they could discuss things calmly and that people would listen to each other. Mr. A then launched into a monologue about how hard he worked for his family and that no one seemed to appreciate how hard he worked. The worker let this go on because he felt those feelings had not been expressed before and needed to be heard by other family members. Henry then said, "But Dad you never give us a chance to help and you never listen to us, you just talk."

At this point the worker noted that time was almost up. He thought sufficient issues had been raised for discussion in another session, and that it was time to plan ahead. He told the family that they seemed to have some issues that needed discussion and wondered if they would be willing to come back for three more sessions after which the family would decide if they wanted further help with their problems. Mr. A said he guessed they had better come back, he hadn't realized how unhappy the family members were and would like to talk more about that. The rest of the family agreed with him.

SUMMARY

Multiperson interaction is an important part of generalist social work activity. In order to be effective in multiperson interaction, a social worker should understand the small group as a social system. Understanding the structure, functioning, and development of any small group gives the social worker direction for effective interaction.

Social workers participate as members of small groups as they carry out tasks and serve clients. They can enable these groups to function by 1) helping all group members to participate in the group, 2) clarifying the decision-making process, 3) stimulating the discussion process, and 4) structuring group meetings. One type of group in which social workers often participate is the team. Teams have special characteristics and problems in functioning. Social workers with knowledge of small-group functioning can help to resolve team problems.

Leadership and conflict are also important aspects of small-group functioning for the social worker to understand. The social worker can carry out three tasks as they enable small-group functioning: consultation, facilitation, and coordination.

Generalist social workers also work with multiperson clients (groups and families). The social worker is not a member of the system but rather enables the system to function. In doing this, the social worker helps groups to form and uses group discussion techniques and activity to facilitate group functioning.

The tools a social worker uses to work in and with small groups are self, group process, discussion, and activity. It is important for social workers to have skill in using these tools.

A family group is a system that already exists. Thus, when a social worker works with a family group, he or she does not become a part of the system but remains outside the boundary. Interactions with an individual family member are for the purpose of enabling that person to interact with other family members more adequately. The focus is on the family interaction.

QUESTIONS

1. Using the schema for study of a small group, describe a group of which you have been a part. How does this kind of analysis help you understand what was happening in that group?

2. Think about groups of which you are now a part. How do you think you might enable that group to function more effectively?

3. Identify a conflict situation in a group with which you are familiar. What was the cause of the conflict? How did the group handle the conflict? Was there a better way to handle the conflict?

4. How would you justify to an agency administrator the amount of time needed for good group formation?

5. Identify ways that you can use to develop your skill in group participation and in group leadership. What do you see as the difference between group participation and group leadership?

6. What issues do you think you should consider when working with a family group? Identify those issues that may be unresolved or important to you personally in your own family situation, which may get in the way as you work with a family.

7. Discuss the differences when working with the family as a system as contrasted with working with individuals who may be family members. Why is it important to work with the family as a system rather than work with individuals in a family?

SUGGESTED READINGS

Bakalensky, Rosalie. "The Small Group in Community Organization Practice." *Social Work with Groups* 7 (Summer 1984): 87–96.

Bercher, Harvey. "Effective Group Membership." *Social Work with Groups* 10 (Summer 1987): 57–67.

Berman-Rossi, Toby. "The Tasks and Skills of the Social Worker Across Stages of Group Development." *Social Work with Groups* 16 (No. 1, 1993): 69–71.

Brown, Leonard. "Group Work and the Environmental Systems Approach." *Social Work with Groups* 16 (No. 1/2, 1993): 83–95.

Edwards, E. Daniel, and Edwards, Margie E. "American Indians: Working with Individuals and Groups." *Social Casework* 61 (October 1980): 498–506.

Farley, Joan E. "Family Developmental Task Assessment: A Prerequisite to Family Treatment." *Clinical Social Work Journal* 18 (Spring 1990): 85–98.

Friedman, Robert. "Techniques for Rapid Engagement in Family Therapy." *Child Welfare* 56 (July 1977): 509–517.

Gitterman, Alex, and Shulman, Lawrence. *Mutual Aid Groups and the Life Cycle,* 2nd ed. New York: Columbia University Press, 1994.

Glassman, Urania. "The Social Work Group and Its Distinct Healing Qualities in the Health Care Setting." *Health and Social Work* 16 (August 1991): 203–212.

Gourse, Judith E., and Chescheir, Martha W. "Authority Issues in Treating Resistant Families." *Social Casework* 62 (February 1981): 67–73.

Hardy-Fanta, Carol, and MacMahon-Herrera, Elizabeth, "Adapting Family Therapy to the Hispanic Family." *Social Casework* 62 (March 1981): 138–148.

Hepworth, Dean H., and Larsen, Jo Ann. *Direct Social Work Practice: Theory and Skills,* 2nd ed. Chicago: Dorsey Press, 1986 (Chapter 11).

Janzen, Curtis, and Harris, Oliver. *Family Treatment in Social Work Practice.* Itasca, IL: F. E. Peacock, 1980.

Kane, Rosalie. *Training for Teamwork.* Manpower Monograph No. 9. Syracuse, NY: Syracuse University School of Social Work, Division of Continuing Education and Manpower Development, 1975.

Lowy, Louis. *Social Work with the Aging,* 2nd ed. New York: Longman, 1985 (Chapter 12).

Minahan, Anne, Ed. *Encyclopedia of Social Work,* 18th ed. Silver Spring, MD: National Association of Social Workers, 1987 ("Family Practice," "Group Theory and Research," and "Social Work Practice with Groups").

Pinderhughes, Elaine B. "Family Functioning of Afro-Americans." *Social Work* 27 (January 1982): 91–96.

Rubin, Irwin, Fry, Ronald, and Plovick, Mark. *Making Health Teams Work.* Cambridge, MA: Ballinger, 1975.

Shulman, Lawrence. *The Skills of Helping: Individuals and Groups,* 3rd ed. Itasca, IL: F. E. Peacock, 1992 (Part II and Chapter 6).

Simons, Ronald L., and Aigner, Stephen M. *Practice Principles: A Problem-Solving Approach to Social Work.* New York: MacMillan, 1985 (Chapter 5).

Thorman, George. *Helping Troubled Families.* New York: Aldine Publishing, 1982.

Toseland, Ronald W., and Rivas, Robert F. *An Introduction to Group Work Practice.* New York: MacMillan, 1984.

Toseland, Ronald W, and Rivas, Robert F. "Structured Methods for Working with Task Groups." *Administration in Social Work* 8 (Summer 1984): 49–58.

Toseland, Ronald W., Palmer-Ganes, Joan, and Chapman, Dennis. "Teamwork in Psychiatric Settings." *Social Work* 31 (January–February 1986): 46–52.

Tropman, John E. *Effective Meetings.* Beverly Hills, CA: Sage Publications, 1980.

Tropman, John E. Effective Meetings: Some Provisional Rules and Needed Research." *Social Work with Groups* 10 (Summer 1987): 41–55.

Wells, Susan J. "A Model of Therapy with Abusive and Neglectful Families." *Social Work* 26 (March 1981): 113.

NOTES

1. See Steve Burghaidt, "The Tactical Use of Group Structure and Process in Community Organization," in *Strategies of Community Organization: A Book of Readings,* 3rd ed., Fred M. Cox, John L. Erlich, Jack Rothman, and John E. Tropman, Eds. (Itasca, IL: F. E. Peacock, 1979).

2. This discussion of the small group as a social system is a synthesis of knowledge about small groups primarily based on three schools of thought: 1) *Field theory or group dynamics.* The work of Kurt Lewin is the original source. Darwin Cartwright and Alvin Zander, *Group Dynamics: Research and Theory* (Evanston, IL: Row Peterson and Co., 1960), is another source. 2) *Interactional process analysis.* Paul A. Hare, Edgar F. Borgotta, and Robert E. Bales, *Small Groups: Studies in Social Interaction* (New York: Alfred A. Knopf, 1965), is a source for this school of thought. 3) *Homans's systems theory.* George Homans, *The Human Group* (New York: Harcourt, Brace and World, 1960) is the third primary source. Another excellent source on group process is Margaret E. Hartford, *Groups in Social Work* (New York: Columbia University Press, 1972).

3. Henry W. Maier, "Models of Intervention in Work with Groups: Which One Is Yours," *Social Work with Groups,* 4 (Fall/Winter 1981): 21–34.

4. For a full description of this technique, see Mary L. Northway, *A Primer of Sociometry,* 2nd ed. (Toronto: University of Toronto Press, 1967).

5. Kenneth D. Benne and Paul Sheats, "Functional Roles of Group Members," *Journal of Social Issues* 4 (1948): 41–49.

6. John K. Brilhart, *Effective Group Discussion* (Dubuque, IA: Wm. C. Brown, 1974), p. 5.

7. John J. Horwitz, *Team Practice and the Specialist* (Springfield, IL: Charles C. Thomas, 1970), p. 10.

8. Based on a formulation developed by Henriette Etta Soloshin, "Development of an Instrument for the Analysis of Social Group Work Method in Therapeutic Settings," Ph.D. diss. March 1954, University of Minnesota, Minneapolis. Also see William Schwartz, "The Social Worker in the Group," in *Social Welfare Forum 1961* (New York: Columbia University Press, 1961), pp. 146–171.

9. Two excellent references for work with families are Curtis Janzen and Oliver Harris, *Family Treatment in Social Work Practice* (Itasca, IL: F. E. Peacock, 1980), and George Thorman, *Helping Troubled Families* (New York: Aldine Publishing, 1982).

10

ENVIRONMENT

Learning Expectations

1. An understanding of the importance of the influence of the environment on the worker-client interaction.
2. An understanding of the community as a social system.
3. A beginning skill in studying a community.
4. An understanding of the social service agency as a social system.
5. A beginning skill in studying a social agency.
6. An understanding of the skill needed for working in a bureaucracy.

The environment of the helping interaction, that is, of the social work endeavor, is the community and the social agency. The client comes from a community or neighborhood, which has both expectations and resources that must be considered in the helping. The worker is usually an agency employee and thus has expectations and resources from that agency. The agency is also a part of a community. The community has expectations about the services being delivered by the agency. It also provides resources. The community of the client and agency may or may not be the same. In order to understand the influence of both the community and the agency upon the helping endeavor, the worker can use a social systems approach as an organizing framework. The helping endeavor takes place not in a vacuum but in an environment. Because of the transactional nature of human interaction, understanding of that environment and its impact is essential for effective service. Sometimes the community or the agency impacts on individuals and clients in such a negative manner that either might be considered as targets for change. As generalist social workers develop understandings and assess agencies and communities, they must be alert to identify situations in which the agency or the community is the appropriate unit of attention. Strategies for working toward change in these systems are discussed in Chapter 14.

THE COMMUNITY AS A SOCIAL SYSTEM

The **community** is the environment of the worker, the client, and the agency. Different units of that community will have different impacts and influences on each. The interaction of worker and client is influenced by the transactions of the community. The service delivery is a part of the community system. Understanding these impacts and these influences is an important aspect of generalist social work knowledge. To gain this kind of understanding, it is first necessary for the worker to acquire an understanding of the community as a social system.[1] This understanding is important not only for understanding the environment that influences the worker-client interaction but, in generalist social work, the community may also be the target for intervention. In the latter case, the worker usually works with individuals and small groups to bring about change in the community structure and functioning. For the generalist social worker, this is usually focused on changing or developing a community resource that will in turn enhance the functioning of individuals and families.

At a minimum, such knowledge calls for awareness of the boundaries of the community, its component parts (individuals, families, associations, neighborhoods, organizations, institutions, etc.), and its environment. The worker also needs to be aware of the way the community functions and of its historical development.

The identification of a community's boundaries poses a substantial problem in a society of large cities and multiple institutional catchment areas. Is an agency's community a geographical place, the catchment area from which the clients come? Is a group of persons who support and sanction the agency its community? Is it the immediate geographic neighborhood in which it is located? Should the entire metropolitan area be considered a community? Or are community and neighborhood the same? Each of these questions may be answered affirmatively under certain circumstances.

There is also a time element in the concept of community. The *community system* functions in relation to issues and to provide services (e.g., education). The *community units* may interact only when dealing with those issues and in providing services. Community units are groups, both formal and informal, organizations, institutions, and other social systems that function within the boundaries of the community. Thus, the community system also has a time element; it exists only under certain circumstances.

The community may be seen as a geographical place. In addition, *community* is a term also used to describe "nonplace" associations such as the professional community or the religious community. When considering the kinship group, the extended family, or certain cultural groups, community is a related concept. It would seem that the community system can have a wide variety of forms, all of which are relevant for social work. All impact on the transactions among individuals, families, and small groups.

Sociology furnishes us with several ways of considering a community. Ferdinand Tönnies saw a change in the relationships among people with the industrialization of society. He described this change as one from *Gemeinschaft* (rural "we-ness") to *Gesellschaft* (individuals related through structures in the community).[2] These differences among communities still exist. Rural or small communities function rather informally; urban or large communities tend to function more through formal structures. In searching for understanding of a community, a worker will find it useful to determine the kind of relationships that exist in the community. Usually there are different kinds of relationships, depending on the community functions involved.

Understanding the use of land adds another dimension to the study of a community. One method of using this concept is to draw maps of a community showing retail stores, wholesale businesses; industry (light and heavy); schools, churches, and other institutions; various types of residential dwellings; and where various ethnic and social economic groups live.

Floyd Hunter's studies of community power are also useful.[3] The location of the community power structure is particularly important when trying to develop new services or to change existing services. This power structure may be formal or informal; elected or assigned control. The impact of the power is varied depending on how the power holder and others perceive the power. It is exercised through initiating activity, legitimizing activity, giving approval to ideas and plans, implementing decisions, or blocking discussion of issues and of decisions. Usually the impact of a particular power holder depends on the issue at hand. There are some power persons who tend to have greater influence over economic issues than over social welfare issues. In larger communities, where power is more dispersed, there is a greater chance that the power is related to specific segments of community life than in smaller communities where power tends to be held in one small group of people. Identification of not only the individuals in the power structure but how they exercise that power and over what issues they have significant influence is another important ingredient of any community assessment.

Eugene Litwak's work on the significance of the neighborhood points out its importance for the individual in meeting need. He has identified several types of neighborhoods and their effectiveness in meeting need. The *mobile neighborhood* is one in which there is rapid turnover of residents but manages to retain its cohesion. The *traditional neighborhood* is one that has residents who are long term and that maintains stability. The *mass neighborhood* is one in which there is no mechanism of integration.[4] Understanding the kind of neighborhood a client lives in helps a worker understand a client and the resources that may be available for that client.

Roland Warren's work, which considers the community as a social system, is especially useful. He identifies the locally relevant functions of a community as: 1) production-distribution-consumption, 2) socialization, 3) social control, 4) social participation, and 5) mutual support. Each community has community units that carry out these functions. The business community has a major responsibility for production, distribution, and consumption. The schools are involved in socialization. Government is concerned with social control. Various clubs and organizations fulfill social participation needs. The social welfare organizations are involved in mutual support. Warren also notes that many community units have ties with structures and systems outside the community. These links are known as *vertical patterns;* relationships within the community are known as *horizontal patterns.* An example of this conceptualization as it relates to a church (a community unit) would be that the horizontal link would be a local council of churches or ministerial group; the vertical link would be to a denominational body. Warren sees the exploration of these patterns as a primary means for studying a community.[5]

There are differences among communities, just as there are among types of any category of social system. It is almost impossible to develop a scheme for classifying communities because of the many variables involved. Dennis Poplin has identified three areas that seem important when considering differences among communities: size, the nature of a community's hinterland, and social-cultural features.[6]

Differences in size usually have been discussed on a rural-urban continuum. The U.S. Census Bureau uses a population of 2,500 as the division point between rural and urban. This leaves many different types of communities in the urban category. Another division point frequently used is 50,000, or the population necessary for a Standard Metropolitan Statistical Area. In looking at nonmetropolitan community service delivery systems, Louise Johnson has identified four types of communities: the small city (15,000 to 20,000), the small town (between 8,000 and 20,000), the rural community (under 10,000), and the reservation community.[7]

In subsequent work, Johnson identified two additional types of small communities: the bedroom community and the institutional community. The bedroom community is found near a larger community that furnishes jobs and often a variety of services for residents of the bedroom community. The institutional community contains a large institution, such as a state mental hospital, an educational institution, or a government site (state capital), which is the major employer in that community. She also found that community characteristics are heavily influenced by the distance between communities that contain services (e.g., medical, social, and retail). In other words, small communities that are at considerable distance from services in another community have a richer service system than do communities of the same size that are near communities from which they can obtain services.[8]

Metropolitan areas contain communities that differ: there are the central city, the suburban community, and the satellite city. In addition, some communities are inhabited by the upper class (Grosse Point, Michigan, for example). Some may have a reputation for being inhabited by bohemian, intellectual, or artistic persons, such as Greenwich Village; others are middle-class communities. There also are the ghettos and the barrio communities that have always been a particular concern of social workers.[9] Ethnic communities have particular characteristics that come in part from the culture of the groups occupying them (Chinatown or Little Italy).[10] A social worker should possess an understanding of the characteristics of the particular kind of community with which she is working.

A community, then, can be considered as a social system that has a population, shared institutions and values, and significant social interactions between the individuals and the institutions. The institutions perform major social functions. It usually but not always occupies space or a geographic area. It has many forms. In modern society several communities may overlap. Communities differ in the amount of autonomy they have and the extent to which persons living in the community identify with their community.[11] When considering the community as a social system, understanding from many sources can be used to provide a theoretical base or point to characteristics that should be considered in specific communities. In other words, different communities, because of differing characteristics, often call for different choices as to what is important to include in a community study.

In trying to attain understanding about a community and its impact on people, agencies, and institutions, a social worker faces two major problems. First is the identification of the system itself, which varies, depending on the situation. Often a political unit is the defined system; this is a fairly easy way to define boundaries, but it is artificial and does not really consider parts of the community system that may lie outside the political boundaries. When looking at the neighborhood system, it is difficult to define boundaries.

Understanding a community calls for identifying the boundaries of the unit to be considered. Too large an area makes the study unwieldy; too small an area makes it too limited. In nonmetropolitan areas the choice may be a small city or town. In metropolitan areas the choice may better be a neighborhood or some other manageable unit. Creativity is necessary in deciding how to define the community.

Social workers function in many different kinds of communities: large metropolitan areas, neighborhood settings, small cities, rural communities, large institutions, Indian reservations, and so on. Each kind of community has different characteristics. The study of any community as a social system provides understandings which can lead to greater degrees of client congruent culture, to better use of available resources, to identification of when the community should be the focus of change, and to better identification of which work strategy is best suited to a particular situation.

Second, the information that can be collected about any community is vast. It is never possible to obtain complete information. Some decisions must be made as to when there is sufficient information for understanding. Care needs to be taken to insure that the information is representative of all units in a community. Some information can be found in a library, including local history books, census reports, directories, and the like. Other helpful written material can be obtained from chambers of commerce, local government units, and volunteer organizations. Other information is not so easy to obtain; it may be known within the community but not shared with outsiders. This includes information about relationships among people and institutions and the community's decision-making and power structure. Information about norms and values may be obtainable only after observing and being a part of the community for some period of time.

In order to understand community interaction, gathering information from many individuals and small groups is essential. The generalist social worker uses both formal and informal interviews and observes and participates in small groups. The worker carefully observes a wide range of community interactions in order to develop understanding about the community and its impact on the functioning of individuals, groups, and families.

Because of the amount of material in terms of both volume and variety, it is helpful if an organized plan is developed for gathering such material. Social workers can begin to gather some material before entering a new community. They also need to add to this material as long as they work in the community. As with all social systems, the community system continues to change. Table 10–1 presents one means of organizing a community study. It considers major subsystems that are related to Warren's locally relevant functions. It seeks to identify possible impacts, influences, and resources in the community system and looks for both horizontal and vertical relationships. Table 10–1 provides a social worker with a guide for developing a working understanding of a community.

Once a social worker has the necessary information, it becomes possible to identify and understand current concerns in the community, the community decision-making process, and the manner in which that community usually solves its problems. Issues relative to community autonomy become clearer, as do differing service areas for different community agencies and institutions; for instance, the school district, the political boundaries, and the shopping service area are often different. Also, at this point it is possible to identify strengths and limitations of the community system. Because of the size and diversity of the units (subsystems) within the community system, different parts of the system will show different strengths and different limitations. One way of focusing the consideration of strengths and limitations is to consider the overall quality of life as perceived by community residents.

A community study should include at least some consideration of the strengths and limitations of the community system, the manner in which that community solves its problems, and the capacity and motivation for change. Communities that seem most able to fulfill their functions and meet people's needs have the following characteristics:

1. At least some primary relationships exist,
2. They are comparatively autonomous (not overly impacted by outside influences),
3. They have the capacity to face problems and engage in efforts to solve those problems,

TABLE 10–1 Schema for the Study of a Geographic Community

I. Setting, History, Demography
    A. Physical setting
        1. Location, ecology, size
        2. Relationship to other geographic entities
            a. ecological, political, economic, social
            b. transportation, mass media from outside the community
    B. Historical development
        1. Settlement, significant events, change over time, cultural factors
    C. Demography
        1. Population
            a. age and sex distribution
            b. cultural, ethnic, racial groups
            c. socioeconomic distribution
        2. Physical structure
            a. who lives where?
            b. location of businesses, industry, institutions
        3. Other
            a. mobility
            b. housing conditions
    D. Cultural setting
        1. Community norms, values, and expectations
        2. Community traditions and events
II. Economic System
    A. Employment
        1. Industry: nature, who employed, number of employees, influence from outside community, relationship to community and employees
        2. Distribution-consumption: retail and wholesale business, kind, location, ownership, employees, trade territory
        3. Institutions that employ large numbers of persons: nature, number of employees, types of employees, relationship to community, influence from outside community
    B. Other economic factors
        1. Stability of economy
        2. Leading business persons
        3. Organizations of business or organizations that influence the economic system
III. Political System
    A. Government units (structure and functioning)
        1. Span of control
        2. Personnel, elected and appointed
        3. Financial information
        4. Way of functioning—meetings, etc.
    B. Law enforcement, including court system
    C. Party politics: dominant party and history of recent elections
    D. Influence on social service system
    E. Services provided
IV. Educational System
    A. Structure and administration (all levels)
    B. Financing, buildings
    C. Students
        1. Numbers at each level or other divisions
        2. Attendance and dropout rates

Continued

TABLE 10–1   *Continued*

    D. Instructional factors
       1. Teacher-student ratio
       2. Subjects available, curriculum philosophy
       3. Provisions for special-needs students
    E. Extracurricular activity
    F. Community relations
  V. Social-Cultural System
    A. Recreational-cultural activities, events
       1. Parks, public recreation programs
       2. Cultural resources: libraries, museums, theaters, concerts
       3. Commercial recreation
    B. Religious institutions and activities
       1. Churches: kind, location, membership, activities, leadership
       2. Attitudes: values, concern for social welfare issues, concern for own members
       3. Influence on community
    C. Associations and organizations
       1. Kind, membership, purpose, and goals
       2. Activities, ways of functioning, leadership
       3. Intergroup organizations and linkage within and without the community
       4. Resources available
    D. Mass media in community
       1. Radio, TV, newspapers
    E. Ethnic, racial, and other diverse groups
       1. Way of life, customs, child-rearing patterns, etc.
       2. Relationship to larger community
       3. Structure and functioning of group
    F. Community persons
       1. Power persons; how power is manifest
       2. Leadership and respected persons
 VI. Human Service System
    A. Health care services and institutions
       1. Doctors, dentists, and other professionals
       2. Hospitals, clinics, nursing homes
       3. Public health services
       4. Responsiveness of health care system to needs of people
    B. Formal social welfare system
       1. Agencies in community: function, persons eligible for service, how supported and how
          sanctioned, staff, location
       2. Agencies from outside that serve community, location: services available, conditions of
          service, control of agency
       3. Conflicts among, overlaps, complementary factors of social welfare agencies
    C. Informal helping system
       1. Individuals and organizations
       2. How help is given, to whom
       3. Relationship to formal system
    D. Planning bodies
       1. Fundraising, regulatory, consultative
VII. General Considerations
    A. Current concerns of community. Who is concerned? Why? What has been done about the
       concern.
    B. Customary ways of solving community problems. Who needs to be involved?

TABLE 10–1   *Continued*

C. Community decision-making process
D. How autonomous is the community? Do various service areas coincide or are they different? How strong is the psychological identification with the community?
E. Strengths of community in terms of "quality of life"
F. Limitations of community in terms of "quality of life"

4. There is a broad distribution of power,
5. Citizens have a commitment to the community,
6. Citizen participation is possible and encouraged,
7. There are more homogeneous than heterogeneous relationships, and
8. They have developed ways of dealing with conflict.

It is difficult for a community to meet citizen need when: 1) the problems lie beyond the capacity of the community to solve, 2) the organizations and institutions of the community lack sufficient autonomy, and 3) the citizens lack identification with the community. These community characteristics should be considered when identifying strengths and limitations of any community system.

The community can be a nebulous entity that is often understood only intuitively. It can also be a defined system understood through an organized study. In fact, through organized study a social worker is most apt to grasp the impacts and influences the community has on the social work endeavor.

Skill in understanding a community includes:

1. A framework to organize information,
2. The ability to locate information and resources,
3. The ability to identify the information needed in specific situations,
4. The ability to analyze the information obtained and to identify linkages and relationships among information and among subsystems in the community system,
5. The ability to interact with individuals and small groups for purposes of developing relationships and gathering information about a community, and
6. The ability for careful observation of community functioning.

It is also through organized study that the social worker gains knowledge about the resources that a community provides for all members of that community. Knowledge of impacts, influences, and resources leads to effective practice with individuals, families, and small groups. It also leads to a practice that considers interventions into the system of the community and/or its subsystems when these larger systems impact on individuals, families, and small groups. Negative impacts, then, may become legitimate targets for change.

One community-centered model model of practice, described by Padi Gulati and Geoffrey Guest, is based on experience in Quebec, Canada. It grew out of a conviction that poverty could not be addressed apart from social justice and social rights and that alternatives to exiting service delivery structures should be explored. It contains a strong preventative element and addresses the delivery of both community health and social services. Major features in the model include: use of multidisciplinary teams, universality of service provision, use of community networks, user participation in policy and service delivery, and egalitarianism in the work place. While this model developed using a community organization approach to improve services to individuals in a particular political and social environment, it shows that such approaches hold considerable potential in other settings. Generalist social workers with an understanding of community functioning cannot fail to develop the view that the community delivery system might be an appropriate focus for change.[12] (Chapter 14 discusses specific strategies that might be used in such practice.)

The community is a social system. Like any social system, it has a structure, a way of functioning, and a history. It has energy and organization. The functioning of the helping system cannot be fully understood apart from the environment in which it functions, the community.

CASE EXAMPLE

Helen, a new BSW graduate, faced her first job with both anticipation and anxiety. She had been hired by the Family and Children's Division of a Department of Social Services in a state adjacent to the one where she had lived all her life and gone to school. Having done her field experience in a similar setting in her home state, she had some idea about how such an agency functioned. However, she was also aware of differences. In her home state the Department of Human Services was organized on a district basis. Her new job was in a state that had county administration.

She had spent about a week in Pringvale, the community where she would be working, getting settled in her new apartment. She was glad she could have this time to get settled and to begin to learn something about the community. It would be the community in which she would be living as well as working. She had discovered where the grocery stores were and how to get her utilities turned on. A neighbor who was also an employee of the department had told her about some groups she might want to join.

She had taken time to stop by the library. The librarian had been very helpful in providing her with the resources from which she could begin to develop her understanding of the community. She was really glad that her social work class had done a community study and that she knew what to look for and what to ask about. Census directories, community reports, and books about the community were all available. The librarian had recommended one good history, which she had brought home.

She had stopped by the chamber of commerce office and had gotten a lot of information, and the local tourist office also gave her some material. She had started to get the local paper. Now that she was settled in, she wanted to get going on her new job.

Helen knew she had made a good start in developing her understanding of the community. She also knew there was a great deal more she would have to learn about it. She knew it would take time, but she already had an outline of the information she needed, and by seeking out that information and asking questions of those she worked with or met at community activities, she would enhance her now sketchy understanding.

UNDERSTANDING THE AGENCY

Social work is an agency-based profession. The **agency** is the immediate environment of the worker-client interaction. This interaction often takes place in an office or building identified as "the agency." The influence of the agency is strong even when the interaction takes place elsewhere in the community. As an employee, the worker is a part of the agency system, and because of this the worker is accountable to the agency. The form and content of the service offered must be within the agency's purview and guidelines. The manner in which the agency is structured and functions greatly influences the nature of the worker-client interaction. The agency also provides resources for both the worker and the client. To work in and use the agency in service of the client, the social worker must first understand the agency and its way of functioning.

Social workers not only need to understand the agency in which they are employed but they also need to be able to understand other social agencies. This is important if the worker is to help the clients use the resources and services of other agencies. In addition, where needed resources are not available or usable, an understanding of the agency is a prerequisite to bringing about needed change. (See Chapter 14.)

Agencies in which social workers are employed vary as to type and organization. Some are exclusively social work agencies. They provide social services delivered by professional social workers (MSW or BSW). A family service agency might be an example of this. The family service agency may, however, have a homemaker service or use other than professional workers in other ways. A family service agency is a voluntary agency; that is, it has a governing board of citizens and raises money for its support in the community (either separately or with other agencies). Once voluntary agencies did not use governmental funds, but since public funds have been used to purchase service from private agencies, this is no longer true.

Other social workers are employed by a variety of governmental agencies. They are in what is known as the *public sector*. These agencies are often state and/or federally funded. The worker is regulated by law and by governmental policies and regulations. Other social workers are employed in what is known as *host* or *secondary* settings. In this kind of setting, the primary function of the setting is not social service; social services are used to enhance the primary service. The social worker in a hospital is an example of this kind of setting. In other settings the social worker is part of an interdisciplinary team. The prime focus may be social service, or it may be some other service. Work in a community mental health center is an example of this kind of setting.

It has been pointed out by Barbara Oberhofer Dane and Barbara L. Simon that social workers in host settings have predictable issues which they must address. These include: value discrepancies between social workers and those who are the primary discipline in an agency, an often marginal status assigned to social work in such settings; devaluing social work as woman's work; and role ambiguity and role strain.[13] Thus, agencies vary with respect to several dimensions: size, means of support and governance, nature of the primary service offered, and range of people who are employed.

Another differential aspect of social service agencies is the **field of practice,** or the problem area on which the service focuses. Some fields are clearly identified, such as medical social work, school social work, and social work in corrections. Others are more difficult to differentiate. For example, where does child welfare end and children's and family services begin? The important differentiation in terms of understanding the agency is what field of practice the agency sees itself within. Related to that is how the community sees the problems with which the field of practice is concerned. Does it perceive people who have these problems as sick, deviant, or inadequate, or as persons who deserve some help over a rough spot? Community attitudes impact the agency and its capacity to deliver service.

These attitudes lead to another differential that can be described as people-processing, people-sustaining, or people-changing agencies.[14] At the people-processing end of the continuum would be the provision of an information-and-referral service with little followup. The goal is to give information. At the people-changing end of the continuum is the highly skilled social work clinician in a mental health agency. Many social services have varying amounts of both people processing and people changing involved. The people-changing focus of an agency may be seen as socialization or growth oriented, or it may be seen as rehabilitation or treatment oriented. One common problem of service delivery is when worker, agency, and community have different views of the mix of people processing and people serving. This leads to incongruent expectations for the outcome of the service.

The community provides financial and other support and sanction for the agency. It also has expectations for the nature and outcome of services. These resources and expectations vary, depending on the nature of the agency structure and on the service the agency offers. These impacts also vary from community to community because the agency is one unit in the community system. As changes take place in the larger system, change will be inevitable in the agency system. Social workers who understand this relationship of agency and community are better able to understand and use the agency system in service of the client.

The social service agency is an organization. In its larger forms it is a complex organization or a bureaucracy. This complex organization is made up of subunits, small groups, and individuals. The agency is a social system with distinctive qualities that affect the way it functions:

1. The goals are external to the system. They are not primarily self-satisfying for those who are employed by the agency.

2. They are people serving, not product producing. This service function differentiates social agencies from organizations, the goal of which is the production and marketing of a product.

3. The goals are change in knowledge, beliefs, attitudes, and skills. The means to achieve these goals are complex, and the measurement of the outcome is also complex.

4. A major component of the agency is professional people. The professional functions with a degree of autonomy and a commitment to the client that often conflicts with the classic and efficient functioning of organizations.

Because of these distinctive characteristics of social service organizations, social workers find themselves functioning with two different kinds of expectations: the professional and the bureaucratic. The larger the organization, the greater the differences. Bureaucratic expectations call for loyalty to the organization; acceptance of authority from above; working within rules and regulations; formal relationships; and an emphasis on achievement of goals, on specialization, and on efficiency. Professional expectations call for commitment to professional values and to the service of clients; ability to have a broad span of decision-making power; collegial relationships; and an emphasis on meeting client need and allowing for client self-determination and individualization. These two kinds of expectations lead to tensions in service delivery and are manifest in such issues as: 1) How is the competence of the worker to be determined? From a bureaucratic perspective or from a professional perspective? 2) Should workers specialize or be generalists? 3) Should the focus be client need or societal need? 4) What range of professional judgment is to be allowed workers? 5) Are certain services and tasks performed best by professional workers or by technicians? 6) Should service be a clearly identifiable activity, or is there a "mystical something that happens"?

Before a worker can effectively deliver service as a professional in a bureaucratic organization, the worker must first understand the organization. A social systems approach, again, is a means for developing that understanding.

The first task in understanding an agency is to define its boundaries. The entity that operates with a great enough degree of autonomy so that a unique structure and ways of functioning have developed—in which the influences within the structure are stronger than those without—might be identified as the agency. In a Veterans Administration hospital the social services department might be the choice as the primary system for focus if interaction among departments is limited largely to department heads. If the interaction is greater within a team of doctor, nurse, and social worker, then the unit team might be considered the agency. Because both kinds of interaction are important, however, the total institution might be the better choice. None of these answers is completely adequate. Whatever set of boundaries is used, it should be one that defines the entity with the greatest influence on the worker-client interaction.

The second task is to determine environmental factors that influence the structure and functioning of the agency. These influences involve other social systems and broad socioeconomic factors, including those that impact the agency either by providing resources or by placing expectations.

Some of the social systems that may need to be considered include:

1. Any organization or system of which the agency is part (e.g., a national membership organization, a statewide organization, or an institution of which the social services department is a part);

2. The community (or communities) from which clients come or that provides support for the agency;

3. Professional organizations to which the workers belong;

4. Foundations or other sources of support;

5. Community planning and funding bodies;

6. Governmental bodies that regulate or supply support for the services;

7. Colleges and universities that educate for the professions employed;

8. Other social agencies;

9. Individuals and families who are clients or potential clients; and

10. Organizations such as churches and service clubs that may be resources to the agency or its clients.

Socioeconomic forces that should be considered include:

1. Economic trends,
2. Societal trends,
3. Community expectations,
4. Community need,
5. Political forces,
6. Governmental policies or regulations, and
7. Cultural diversity needs within the community.

The third task is to understand the structure and functioning of the agency system. The factors involved include:

1. *The purposes, objectives, and values of the system*—These are spelled out in articles of incorporation, enabling legislation, agency handbooks, and other official documents. Also important is how these formal expressions are interpreted and implemented in actual service delivery. The agency's value priorities influence this interpretation and implementation. The history of the agency is important in determining how the purposes, objectives, and values developed.

2. *Agency resources, including financial resources*—Resources include the funds provided by the community, through either gifts or tax money; the building or other physical structures the agency leases or owns; and the people resources, both paid and volunteer, including professional and supportive staff.

3. *The traditional ways of working*—Each agency tends to use particular approaches in its service (such as long-term counseling, crisis intervention, provision of specific resources, group-work activity). This can also include specific theoretical approaches, such as task centered, psychoanalytic, and so on. Agencies tend to work with particular systems, individuals, families, groups, or communities. They tend to hire workers with particular educational backgrounds for specific tasks (e.g., MSW, BSW, college graduates, persons indigenous to the community). They have particular patterns of work (e.g., teams, cotherapy).

4. *Boards or other governing bodies*—An important consideration is the method of sanctioning the agency (public or private). If public, identify the laws, policies,

and other regulations that govern the agency and the organizational structure of the larger organization of which the agency is a part. If private, the structure and functioning of the board of directors is the focus. Members of the board and their motivations and needs are also important, as is the relationship of the governing body to the agency and its staff. Another element is the committee structure and functioning. This structure can be one of the board, the staff, or a combination of the two. It is often in committees that new ideas are formulated, that the work of the organization is carried out.

5. *The organizational structure*—This includes both the formal and informal structure, the administrative style, the accepted norms and values, the decision-making and communication processes, and the power and control patterns.

6. *The staff*—Important considerations are: who they are as both persons and professionals; the relationships among staff (formal and informal); and the relationship of staff, clients, administration, and governing body. The professional identification and qualifications of staff should also be considered.

7. *The clients*—Often the clients are overlooked as a part of the agency system. Without them the agency would have no reason for existence. In an age of consumer advocacy, this aspect of agency functioning takes on new importance. Consideration should be given to client needs, expectations, and ways of relating to the agency. The status, designation (patient or student, etc.), and values relating to clients should also be considered.

Each of these aspects of the structure and functioning of the agency system may overlap with other aspects. In developing understanding of an agency, workers should be aware of these overlaps and of the relationships and linkages between the various aspects. Workers also need to be aware of any special aspects of their agency that affect its structure and functioning. In order to gather the information needed for understanding an agency, an organized framework is often useful, such as Table 10–2.

It should now be apparent that there are several subsystems that function within the agency. First there are *persons*. Each person in the system brings personal and sometimes professional attributes. As these persons interact in carrying on the work of the agency, their attributes influence interactions. Second, those persons fill *roles*. Some of the roles are defined in job descriptions. Roles imply relationships to other roles. This relationship structure also influences other interactions. Third, there are *small groups*. These small groups may be formal work groups or informal social groups. The functioning of these small groups is another influence on interactions within the agency. Fourth, there is the *formal structure*, which includes the formal lines of authority outlined by the organizational chart. The chart defines the hierarchical relationships: who is responsible to whom and/or how the various parts of the organization are related. Fifth, there is the *power system*—the system of decision making.[15] It is important to know who makes decisions and how those decisions are influenced in understanding an agency. Each of these systems is important in the functioning of the agency. An understanding of all is necessary for understanding the agency

TABLE 10–2   A Schema for the Study of a Social Agency

A. Identify the boundaries of the agency.
B. Discuss the history of the agency.
C. Discuss the structure and function of the agency.
   1. The purposes, objectives, and value priorities of the agency
   2. The agency resources: financial—sources and amount; physical property, staff—paid and volunteer.
   3. The traditional way of working with clients
   4. The sanctioning of the agency (public or private). If public, identify the laws, policy, and regulations that impact on the agency functioning. Identify the organizational structure of any larger organization of which the agency is a part. Note means of citizen involvement and input. If private, describe the structure and functioning of the board of directors. Who serves on the board? (Describe them as persons.) What are the roles and responsibilities of the board (both internal to the board and with the rest of the agency)? Describe committee structure and functioning.
   5. The organizational structure of the agency. Describe formal and informal functioning of the agency. What are the accepted norms and values? How are decisions made? What is the communication process? Describe power and control aspects.
   6. The staff, as persons and as professionals, their relationships, roles, and ways of working with each other, clients, administration, and governing boards. Identify formal and informal staff groups and describe their functioning.
   7. The clients, their needs, characteristics, expectations, role, and status
D. Identify the strengths and limitations of the agency.
   1. What are the strengths of the agency in terms of serving clients?
   2. What are the limitations of the agency in terms of serving clients?

as a social system. It is also necessary if the worker is to work effectively for needed changes in the agency's structure or way of working. (Specific strategies for working with agencies in an effort to change the agency will be discussed in Chapter 14.)

CASE EXAMPLE

The first morning on the job Helen dressed very carefully, for she knew that first impressions are very important. She decided that she would wear a good wool skirt with a blouse and sweater and shoes with just a small heel. She thought this outfit would look neat and businesslike but wouldn't be too dressy. She didn't know whether or not she would see a client that first day, but she wanted to be prepared and felt that too dressy an appearance might make a client feel uncomfortable.

When she got to the office one of the secretaries showed her her desk and got her some office supplies—pencils, pens, paper, and so on. She found out there were three other workers in the unit besides herself and her supervisor. One of the workers stopped by her desk and introduced himself. About that time her supervisor, whom she had already met, came in and said she had an emergency and wouldn't be able to see her until about ten-thirty; she gave Helen the manual and five case folders for her to read and dashed off.

Helen looked at the manual first. It was somewhat different from the one she had known as a student. She looked at the table of organization and began to find out how the department was organized. While she was reading, she also observed what was going on in the office and tried to identify who the various people were. Two of the secretaries came over, and she introduced herself. As she read the manual she jotted down questions that she had. She was certainly glad for her social welfare policy course, for she at least knew what the programs were and the federal laws that related to them.

About ten o'clock another of the workers came in and introduced herself. She said it was coffee time and invited Helen to join the staff. There were about ten people in the coffee room. Helen was introduced and asked each person what he or she did. She found that some worked in other units, such as income maintenance. She made a mental note to ask her supervisor to brief her on all the people who worked in the office and on what they did. After an hour and a half with the manual, it was good to talk with someone.

At 10:30 A.M. her supervisor came in and said, "Let me grab a cup of coffee and then we can talk." Helen got her pad with her list of questions and the case records, which she had only looked at long enough to find out who they were about. The supervisor told her she was sorry to leave her as she had this morning but that a client needed her. The supervisor told her something about the situation and why she felt it so important to go to the client immediately. Then the supervisor asked her if she had read any of the cases yet. Helen told her she had just looked at them but had been reading the manual. The supervisor told her that she could begin to work with these five cases immediately. One was a ten-year-old child in a foster home. Helen was to make an appointment to see both the child and the foster parent as soon as possible, as no one had been able to see them for some time. She was to find out if the mother had visited and how things were going, and then they would decide what needed to be done.

The second case was a single-parent mother who had been seen on a regular basis by a former worker for about a year because she was having trouble with her twelve-year-old son. They were doing better, but the mother still needed someone to talk to; Helen was to see her and be ready to talk about what goals should be set in this case.

The other three cases were similarly discussed. Then Helen asked her questions about the manual and the material she had read. She asked about supervision, what was expected of her, and how often she would see her supervisor. The supervisor said that for the first month or so she would try to see her twice a week but that sometimes it might not be at a set time. Then they would decide what to do about supervision. The supervisor told her that there would be more case assignments later that week. She said she wanted Helen to go with other workers two or three times on child abuse investigations before she went on one of her own. She should be prepared to do these as they came up. The supervisor also told Helen she had an appointment with the county director right after lunch. Then Helen was given a lot of employment forms that she was to fill out and give to the supervisor tomorrow.

Helen asked the supervisor if she had any suggestions for getting to know the community and the agency. The supervisor said, "Oh, that just happens, but maybe you would like to go to the interagency luncheon meeting with me on Wednesday." Helen asked if there were some kind of directory of the other agencies in the community. The supervisor told her that the one they had was really out of date, but that one of the secretaries had a good list of the agencies and it might be a good idea to look at it. The supervisor told her she'd need a map too. Helen told the supervisor she had already gotten one.

It was lunchtime, and another worker she had met at coffee asked her to join her for lunch. Helen noticed that people in each unit seemed to sort of hang together and that the secretaries had their own group.

After lunch, Helen and her supervisor went to meet with the county director. Helen had met her when she interviewed for the job. The county director greeted her and asked if she was getting settled in. Helen said yes. They then talked a little about the community and some of its problems. A new dam was being built nearby, and there were lots of construction workers in the community. Most of them were living in mobile home courts on the west side of town. There was some tension among the town residents and the construction workers. The county director was involved in a project to try to ease some of this tension. One way the presence of these new people was impacting on the agency was in a rise in child abuse reports. Many were coming from schoolteachers. They were having difficulty fitting these new children into their classes. The county director said the community expected the agency to work with these families, yet didn't seem to want to provide any resources. Many of the informal resources used by the agency's clients didn't seem to be available to these new clients. The county director also talked about how important it was to keep the community happy.

Just as Helen was returning to her office, Bob, another one of the unit workers, told her he had to investigate a child abuse report and asked if she would like to come along. As they drove out to the M home, Bob told her that this was a family the agency had worked with in the past. The community was quick to report the mother, who was somewhat mentally retarded but tried to take care of her children. A neighbor called to say that the six-year-old was home from school taking care of a four-year-old. The mother went off with the baby at about ten o'clock.

While they were driving to see this family, Bob pointed out a number of things to Helen and talked about the west side of town where many of the agency's clients lived. Helen asked questions about the kinds of problems these clients had and noted that many of them stemmed from lack of resources.

When they got to the M home, Mrs. M had returned. She had taken the baby to the doctor and thought she would be back by eleven-thirty, but the doctor was late getting in and they made her wait because the baby had a very bad cold. She said she just didn't know what to do. It was so hard to take the four-year-old along, and she had no one to leave him with. Bob suggested that maybe some other mothers had that same problem. He would be willing to get together a group he knew of who had this problem and help them try to set something up so they could exchange child care. Mrs. M said that sure would help.

By the time they got back to the office it was almost four o'clock. Helen spent the rest of the day reading records and thinking about how to approach each client.

When she got home, she took stock of what had happened that first day and what she needed to do.

1. She was beginning to get a feel of the community. No one seemed to have all the information she wanted. She would just keep her eyes and ears open and jot down what she had learned each night. After a couple of weeks she would check to see what information she needed to seek out in other ways.
2. The information about the agency was a little easier to get. She would continue to ask questions and sit back and watch until she got the hang of things.
3. She liked the way her supervisor was letting her get started. She intended to try to see all five of her cases this week. Then she would make plans about what to do with each one. She thought that this way she could preserve her power of discretion. She was glad she had some clients to work with right away and could go ahead on her own.
4. It seemed that resources were a real problem. She had some ideas from her classes at school she wanted to explore in this area. She thought that by doing this she not only might be of help to the clients but also demonstrate that she wanted to make a contribution to the agency.

WORKING IN A BUREAUCRACY

With the growth of a service society, many social workers find employment in bureaucratic settings. They are confronted with the conflict between professional and bureaucratic expectations—with human need, human pain, and societal injustices and with agency policy, rules, and regulations. They are confronted with the slowness of change, the seeming unresponsiveness of the system, and demands for accountability by the bureaucratic agency. They are also confronted with the need to find ways to use the agency and its resources to meet the needs of clients. This calls for a set of skills for functioning in a bureaucracy.

Ralph Morgan has identified five role conceptions that social workers have adopted in bureaucratic organizations:

1. *Functional bureaucrats*—These workers just happen to be working in a bureaucratic organization. Their major orientation and loyalty is toward the profession and its values. They look for interaction with, and recognition from, professional peers. There is resistance to interaction in and with the bureaucracy. These workers are usually very competent practitioners whose services are valued by the agency, so that the agency overlooks their lack of bureaucratic loyalty.

2. *Service bureaucrats*—These workers are oriented toward the client but also see themselves as part of the bureaucratic structure. They maintain relationships with both professional peers and agency staff. They are ambivalent about their identification with the agency but believe the agency is the means to help clients reach their goals and to obtain needed resources.

3. *Specialist bureaucrats*—These workers attempt to reconcile "bureaucracy to humans and humans to the bureaucracy." They use the rules and regulations but are also guided by professional judgment. They understand that the human condition is so complex that it can never be encompassed by rules and regulations. They seek means of using professional discretion so as to make the system work in service of the client. They realize that, like all human endeavors, the agency is imperfect. They have a strong professional identification.

4. *Executive bureaucrats*—These workers' major orientation is toward the exercise of power. They are innovators, infighters, and risk takers who tend to enforce bureaucratic norms. They like to manage people, money, and materials.

5. *Job bureaucrats*—These workers have a considerable investment in a bureaucratic career. They seek job security. Their primary orientation is to the agency. They adhere to rules and regulations. They also live by the agency norms.[16]

When working in a bureaucratic setting, a combination of characteristics of the functional bureaucrat, the service bureaucrat, the specialist bureaucrat, and the executive bureaucrat seems most effective. This combination of characteristics would include a professional loyalty, a client orientation, a mediation stance, a sense of realism, a search for areas of discretionary freedom, a respect for rules and regulations, and an innovative approach to services. This is a tall order for a young, inexperienced worker but one that can be sought after. It would seem, then, that the issue is not professional versus bureaucratic but rather a search for means to combine the best of the professional with the best of the bureaucratic.

Robert Pruger has pointed out the necessity for learning bureaucratic skills at a time when it is increasingly impossible to deliver professional service without being a bureaucrat. He points out that one can be a "good bureaucrat." A first step to developing these skills is the realization and acceptance of the reality that a career in social work will involve work in and with bureaucracies. He sees the key to being effective in a bureaucracy as maintaining the greatest amount of discretion possible. To maintain this discretionary power a worker must be self-directive. The worker who expects to be told every move to make soon loses this power. The good bureaucrat also knows how to negotiate stresses, opportunities, and constraints. According to Pruger, the worker does this by

1. Staying with it, not giving up on the first try;
2. Maintaining vitality and independence of thought;
3. Being responsible by understanding legitimate authority; and
4. Conserving energy, working only on some issues and choosing issues that are worth the effort.[17]

The bureaucracy, like all human institutions, is meant to serve society's needs. The social worker who can help the social service bureaucracy meet the needs of people can become a valuable employee. This can give the worker leverage to obtain the needed discretion. Another means of gaining this leverage is to gain the competence the agency sees as important. For example, if the agency is developing the case management approach to working with some clients, then seek information, go to workshops, and collect material about this way of working with clients. In order to maintain discretionary power it is important for a social worker to demonstrate good judgment. Part of this good judgment is the ability to make decisions that are in compliance with agency rules and regulations, that do not cause negative community reactions, and that lead to effective service to clients. Another part of good judgment is doing the right thing at the right time. The attributes of self-directedness and good judgment are possible when social workers have a realistic sense of their professional self, when they use a knowledge base in making decisions, and when they develop a repertoire of skills.

There are a number of ways in which workers can enhance their effectiveness.

1. Don't seek blame; rather, spend the energy available on seeking solutions.
2. Learn to do a lot with a little. Be realistic about the resources available and make them stretch as far as possible.
3. Be comfortable with uncertainty, ambiguity, and inconsistency. When these are present discretion is necessary.
4. Be self-confident, creative, and responsible.

The use of supervision can be an effective means of becoming a good bureaucrat. The supervisor can provide a great deal of information about the agency, about what is happening, and about what is allowable. The worker can negotiate with the supervisor for a degree of discretion. The supervisor can be a sounding board for new ideas. To use the supervisory process effectively, the worker must take responsibility for bringing questions and problems to the supervisor. The supervisor needs to have some knowledge of the problems that exist for the worker and the ideas of the worker in order to defend him when questions arise from other parts of the system.

Social workers get into difficulty in a bureaucracy when they make unfounded decisions or do not determine the feasibility of plans they make. Problems also develop if their concerns are not focused but take the form of vague complaints. The expectation that change will take place overnight also can cause difficulty. An understanding of what the agency is trying to do and what is expected of the worker are a base upon which to develop effective service. A thorough understanding of the agency as a social system is a prerequisite for being a good bureaucrat.

One phenomenon that has recently received considerable attention is *worker burnout.* Christina Maslach has described it as "helping professionals losing positive feelings, sympathy, and respect for their clients or patients."[18] Burnout may be a symptom of stress in the agency system. It interferes with a worker's capacity to interact with clients and others in a professional capacity. Martha Bramhall and Susan Ezell have described some of the symptoms of burnout as feeling unappreciated, loss of the ability to laugh, being literally sick and tired (suffering from headaches, backaches, stomachaches), feeling exhausted, dreading going to work, or having trouble sleeping.[19] Some people seem particularly susceptible to burnout. They tend to be people who take on too much for long periods of time, in a very intense manner. They are often young and enthusiastic about their work. Another group susceptible to burnout are those who use relationships in the work situation to compensate for a lack of meaningful relationships in their private lives. Workers who feel they cannot achieve their objectives or believe they lack control over their activities also seem particularly vulnerable to burnout.

Social workers need to be sensitive to their functioning and to symptoms of burnout. If they are developing, they should engage in a plan to overcome the burnout. Although stress within the agency system can be a source of burnout, the worker can develop lifestyle changes that allow the worker to function within the system. Identification of the condition is the first step. Once burnout is identified as the source of the difficulty, the worker needs to pay attention to personal needs that have been slighted. A regimen that includes sufficient rest, exercise, good diet, and other self-care tasks needs to be undertaken. The worker should develop a network of personal resources that can help in meeting personal need. Having a person who can serve as a sounding board and help in analyzing the situation is particularly useful.[20]

Prevention of burnout should be a goal for all social workers. Preventive measures include providing time and energy for personal needs—the pacing of one's self with a time to work and a time for self is important. Developing the skills of a good bureaucrat is also important. This includes taking responsibility for maintaining and enhancing one's sphere of discretion.

CASE EXAMPLE

During her second month of working, Helen found she had a client who no longer was eligible for service by the agency. This client still had many personal problems that she needed help with. Helen thought about continuing to give the needed service and just ignoring the ineligibility. She also considered telling the client that since she was no longer eligible for service she would have to stop seeing her. Neither solution seemed right to Helen. Helen reviewed the material she had collected about other agencies in the community; she also reviewed the relevant agency policy to see if there was any way to get around the ineligibility. She found one resource that might provide the service needed, but knew it would take a little time to facilitate a referral to that agency. She also noted in the regulations that service eligibility did not terminate until the end of the month in which the client became ineligible. As it now was the fifteenth of the month, she knew she had at least two weeks to work with this client.

Helen's next step was to discuss the situation with her supervisor. The supervisor told her that with the kind of plan she was developing she could see the client for a few widely spaced sessions over the next month or two. Helen and her supervisor discussed how these sessions might be used for the benefit of the client. This would give her time to make the referral and arrange an orderly transfer of service.

Helen wished she did not have to terminate with the client because she really liked working with her and felt they were making progress. She also knew she did not want to jeopardize the client's growth by having to terminate suddenly. She was glad that a way had been found to use the agency and community systems in service of the client. As she thought about the situation she knew she was learning to work in a bureaucracy.

SUMMARY

This chapter considers the environment of the helping endeavor, the community and the agency. Both can be understood from a social systems perspective. The transactional nature of human functioning makes it essential that social workers understand the influence of these two systems on the functioning of both worker and client.

If the worker is to be a generalist, this understanding is essential in making decisions as to the target for change and the mode of intervention. If the target is to be the community or agency system, the worker needs in-depth understanding of that target. Communities and agencies are complex systems that must be understood in considerable depth before they become a target for change.

Most social workers are employed in bureaucratic settings. Conflicts between professional and bureaucratic demands are often confronted by the social worker in these settings. It is important that social workers develop skills for dealing with these conflicts and become "good bureaucrats." Social workers are also prone to burnout and need to develop means of protecting themselves against this occupational hazard.

QUESTIONS

1. Identify explanations of community functioning that you have been exposed to in sociology courses.

2. How does conceptualizing the community as a social system enhance a social worker's understanding of any community?

3. Using a community with which you are familiar and the material presented in this chapter, identify information you should obtain if you are to develop greater understanding of the community. Where would you go to obtain that information?

4. What factors do you consider the most important influences on the manner in which an agency functions?

5. What are the differences in agencies where social work is the primary profession and those in which some other profession is primary?

6. How would you go about gathering the information needed to understand any agency in which you might be employed?

7. Using the Morgan classification (page 247), identify the preferred way for a social worker to function in a bureaucracy. Why did you make the choice?

8. What do you think are some of the ways a social worker can avoid burnout?

SUGGESTED READINGS

Abramson, Julie S. "Orienting Social Work Employees in Interdisciplinary Settings: Shaping Professional and Organizational Perspectives." *Social Work* 38 (March 1993): 152–157.

Arches, Joan. "Social Structure, Burnout, and Job Satisfaction." *Social Work* 36 (May 1991): 208–206.

Berg, William E. "Evolution of Leadership Style in Social Agencies: A Theoretical Analysis." *Social Casework* 62 (January 1980): 22–28.

Borland, James J. "Burnout Among Workers and Administrators." *Health and Social Work* 6 (February 1981): 73–78.

Cherniss, Cary. *Staff Burnout: Job Stress in the Human Services.* Beverly Hills, CA: Sage Publications, 1980.

Cox, Fred M. "Communities: Alternative Conceptions of Community: Implications for Community Organization Practice." In Fred M. Cox, John L. Erlich, Jack Rothman, and John E. Tropman, Eds., *Strategies of Community Organization: A Book of Readings,* 4th ed. Itasca, IL: F. E. Peacock, 1987 (pp. 213–231).

———. "Community Problem Solving: A Guide to Practice with Comments." In Fred M. Cox, John L. Erlich, Jack Rothman, and John E. Tropman, Eds., *Strategies of Community Organization: A Book of Readings,* 4th ed. Itasca, IL: F. E. Peacock, 1987 (pp. 150–167).

Cox, Fred M., Erlich, John L., Rothman, Jack, and Tropman, John E. *Tactics and Techniques of Community Practice.* Itasca, IL: F. E. Peacock, 1977 (Chapter 1, "What's Going On: Assessing the Situation").

Dane, Barbara Oberhofer and Simon, Barbara L. "Resident Guests: Social Workers in Host Settings." *Social Work* 36 (May 1991): 208–213.

Davidson, Jeffrey L. "Balancing Required Resources and Neighborhood Opposition in Community-Based Treatment Center Neighborhoods." *Social Service Review* 56 (March 1982): 55–71.

Fellin, Phillip. *The Community and the Social Worker.* Itasca, IL: F. E. Peacock, 1987.

Fellin, Phillip, and Litwak, Eugene. "The Neighborhood in Urban American Society." *Social Work* 13 (July 1968): 72–80.

Finn, Janet L. "Burnout in the Human Services: A Feminist Perspective." *Affilia* 5 (Winter 1990): 55–71.

Gilbert, Neil, Miller, Henry, and Specht, Harry. *An Introduction to Social Work Practice.* Englewood Cliffs, NJ: Prentice-Hall, 1980 (Chapter 8, "Organizational Setting: Theoretical Perspectives," and Chapter 9, "Bureaucratic Competence; Roles and Guidelines").

Gitterman, Alex, and Miller, Irving. "The Influence of the Organization on Clinical Practice." *Clinical Social Work Journal* 17 (Summer 1989): 151–164.

Gulati, Padi, and Guest, Geoffrey. "The Community-Centered Model: A Garden Variety Approach or a Radical Transformation of Community Practice?" *Social Work* 35 (January 1990): 63–68.

Holland, Thomas P., and Cook, Martha A. "Organizations and Values in Human Services." *Social Service Review* 57 (March 1983): 59–77.

Indyk, Debbie, Belville, Renate, Lackapelle, Sister Susanne, Gordon, Gaul, and Deward, Tracy. "A Community-Based Approach to HIV: Case Management: Systematizing the Unmanageable." *Social Work* 38 (July 1993): 380–387.

Katan, Joseph. "Role Formation and Division of Work in Multi-Professional Human Service Organizations." *Administration in Social Work* 8 (Spring 1984): 73–87.

Lauffer, Armand, Nybell, Lynn, Overberger, Carla, Reed, Beth, and Zeff, Lawrence. *Understanding Your Social Agency.* Beverly Hills, CA: Sage Publications, 1977.

Lightman, Ernie S. "Professionalization, Bureaucratization, and Unionization in Social Work." *Social Service Review* 56 (March 1982): 131–143.

Minahan, Anne, Ed. *Encyclopedia of Social Work,* 18th ed. Silver Spring, MD: National Association of Social Workers, 1987 ("Administration," "Environmental Aspects," and "Community Theory and Research").

———. "Burnout and Organizational Change." [editorial]. *Social Work* 25 (March 1980): 87.

Pruger, Robert. "The Good Bureaucrat." *Social Work* 18 (July 1973): 26–32.

Ratliff, Nancy. "Stress and Burnout in the Helping Professions." *Social Casework* 69 (March 1988): 147–154.

Reed, Henry. "Burnout and Self-Reliance." *Public Welfare* 40 (Summer 1982): 29–35.

Rivera, Felix G. and Erlich, John L. *Community Organizing in a Diverse Society.* (Boston: Allyn and Bacon, 1992).

Ruff, Elizabeth. "The Community as Client in Rural Social Work." *Human Services in the Rural Environment* 14 (Spring 1991): 21–25.

Sheaford, Bradford W., Horejsi, Charles R., and Horejsi, Gloria A. *Techniques and Guidelines for Social Work Practice.* Boston: Allyn and Bacon, 1988 (Chapters 7, 8, 14, and 15).

Stein, Herman D. "The Concept of Human Service Organizations: A Critique." *Administration in Social Work* 4 (Summer 1980): 1–11.

Walsh, Joseph A. "Burnout and Values in the Social Service Profession." *Social Casework* 68 (May 1987): 279–283.

NOTES

1. For two other views of the importance of environment, see Carel B. Germain and Alex Gitterman, *The Life Model of Social Work Practice* (New York: Columbia University Press, 1980), particu-

larly chap. 1, and Max Siporin, *Introduction to Social Work Practice* (New York: Macmillan, 1975), pp. 176–178.

2. Ferdinand Tönnies, *Fundamental Concepts of Sociology* (Gemeinschaft und Gesellschaft), trans. Charles P. Loomis (New York: American Books, 1940).

3. Floyd Hunter, *Community Power Structure* (Chapel Hill: University of North Carolina Press, 1953).

4. Eugene Litwak and Ivan Szelenyi, "Primary Group Structures and their Function: Kin, Neighbors, and Friends," *American Sociological Review* 34 (August 1969): 465–481; Phillip Fellin and Eugene Litwak, "The Neighborhood in Urban American Society," *Social Work* 13 (July 1968): 72–80; and Eugene Litwak, *Helping the Elderly* (New York: Guilford Press, 1985), chap. 8.

5. Roland L. Warren, *The Community in America* (Chicago: Rand-McNally, 1963).

6. Dennis E. Poplin, *Communities,* 2nd ed. (New York: Macmillan, 1979), chap. 2, "Community Types."

7. Louise C. Johnson, "Human Service Delivery Patterns in Non-Metropolitan Communities," in H. Wayne Johnson (Ed.), *Rural Human Services: A Book of Readings* (Itasca, IL: F. E. Peacock, 1980), pp. 55–64.

8. Louise C. Johnson, "Services to the Aged: Non-Metropolitan Service Delivery" (Unpublished paper delivered at NASW Symposium, Chicago, IL, November 1985).

9. For a good discussion of this type of community, see Gerald D. Suttles, *The Social Order of the Slum* (Chicago: University of Chicago Press, 1968).

10. Joseph Bensman and Arthur J. Vidick, *Metropolitan Communities* (New York: New Viewpoints, 1975), is a collection of articles discussing characteristics of different kinds of metropolitan communities. Roland L. Warren (Ed.), *Perspectives on the American Community: A Book of Readings,* 2nd ed. (Chicago: Rand-McNally, 1973), is another useful source for material about different kinds of communities.

11. A useful resource when developing a community study is Roland L. Warren, *Studying Your Community* (New York: Free Press, 1955). For other conceptualizations of community see: Fred M. Cox, "Communities: Alternative Conceptions of Community: Implications for Community Organization Practice" in *Strategies of Community Organization,* 4th ed, Fred M. Cox, John L. Erlich, Jack Rothman, and John E. Tropman, Eds. (Itasca, IL: F. E. Peacock, 1987), pp. 213–231.

12. Padi Gulati and Geoffrey Guest, "The Community-Centered Model: A Garden Variety Approach or a Radical Transformation of Community Practice?" *Social Work* 35 (January 1990): 63–68.

13. Barbara Oberhofer Dane and Barbara L. Simon, "Resident Guests: Social Workers in Host Settings," *Social Work* 35 (January 1990: 63–68.

14. See Phillip Fellin, *The Community and the Social Worker* (Itasca, IL: F. E. Peacock, 1987), chap. 9.

15. This identification of systems is based on Armand Lauffer, Lynn Nybell, Carla Overbeiger, Beth Reed, and Lawrence Zeff, *Understanding Your Social Agency* (Beverly Hills, CA: Sage Publications, 1977).

16. Ralph Morgan, "Role Performance in a Bureaucracy," in *Social Work Practice* 1962 (New York: Columbia University Press, 1962), pp. 115–125.

17. See Robert Pruger, "The Good Bureaucrat," *Social Work* 18 (July 1973): 26–32, and "Bureaucratic Functioning as a Social Work Skill," in *Educating for Baccalaureat Social Work: Report of the Undergraduate Social Work Curriculum Development Project,* Betty L. Baer and Ronald Federico, Eds. (Cambridge, MA: Ballinger, 1978), pp. 149–168.

18. Christina Maslach, "Job Burnout: How People Cope," *Public Welfare* 36 (Spring 1978): 56–58.

19. Martha Bramhall and Susan Ezell, "How Burned Out Are You?" *Public Welfare* 39 (Winter 1981): 23–27.

20. These ideas are further developed in Martha Bramhall and Susan Ezell, "Working Your Way Out of Burnout," *Public Welfare* 39 (Spring 1981): 32–39.

PART THREE

THE SOCIAL WORK PROCESS

The content of the service process—the process of the work of the client and worker in meeting need and solving problems—is the focus of Part Three. This process of the work can be separated from the interactional process only for purposes of study. Interaction and service are two ways of looking at the professional response to need. The generalist social work process, as developed in this book, is a problem-solving one based on knowledge, values, and skill. It is intervention into the transactions of human systems. Part Three will build on material presented in Parts One and Two, offering more depth regarding already-introduced concepts. It will present another facet of the social work endeavor.

The process can be conceptualized as having four major components: assessment, planning, action, and termination. Although assessment precedes planning, planning precedes action, and action precedes termination, the process is cyclical in nature. Planning often leads to the need for new or different understanding of the person in the situation (assessment). Action often produces new information for use in understanding or demonstrates the need for additional planning. Evaluation, the assessment of what has happened as a result of action, is ongoing in the process and leads to new understanding and sometimes to new plans and action. Thus, all four stages are always present, but at various points in the work one or more may be the focus and receive the most attention.

All four stages as well as the interactional process constitute intervention. All can influence change in the transactions between clients and the systems in their environment. All can influence the social functioning of individuals and social systems. Figure 1 depicts the social work process.

Chapter 11 considers the content of the assessment phase. In addition, attention is given to the place of the problem-solving process in assessment, to the nature of transactional assessment, and to the strategy of needs assessment.

Chapter 12 discusses planning. It presents a means for developing a plan of action that includes goals and objectives, units of attention, strategy, roles, tasks,

FIGURE 1   The Social Work Process

and techniques. It looks at factors that affect the plan of action. In addition, there is a discussion of the agreement between worker and client about the plan, including consideration of the use of a contract.

Chapter 13 identifies and discusses important actions used in direct practice with clients by the generalist social worker. The specific actions identified and discussed are 1) use of resources, including a discussion of the nature of the service delivery system, referral, broker and advocate roles, and empowerment of clients; 2) crisis intervention; 3) supportive social work; 4) use of activity; and 5) mediation.

Chapter 14 discusses indirect practice, that is, actions taken by social workers on behalf of clients. Actions discussed include 1) work with influentials; 2) coordination of services, including the strategy of case management; 3) program planning and resource development, including development of a volunteer program and work with self-help groups; 4) environmental manipulation; 5) work toward changing organizations from within; and 6) cause advocacy.

In Chapters 13 and 14 the focus is on presenting a variety of strategies so that the reader gains a sense of the variety of actions available for use by social workers. The strategies presented are developed so that the reader can gain an understanding of the more important aspects of the strategy and of situations in which these strategies might be useful. No attempt has been made to present a comprehensive discussion of the strategies. That is best done by study of the primary sources for each strategy.

Chapter 15 discusses evaluation and its importance in contemporary American social work practice, which places considerable emphasis on accountability. This chapter presents issues related to evaluation as well as tools used by social workers for evaluation.

Chapter 16 considers termination and discusses various situations in which termination takes place. It discusses the process of termination and its relationship to evaluation.

11

ASSESSMENT

Learning Expectations

1. An in-depth understanding of assessment as a complex process.
2. Skill in assessing individuals, families, small groups, organizations, and communities.
3. An appreciation for the need to involve the client in the assessment process.
4. The ability to choose and apply appropriate knowledge to the assessment process.
5. The ability to tolerate the uncertainty of incomplete assessment.
6. Skill in judgment or decision making.
7. Skill in identifying needs and blocks to their fulfillment.
8. Skill in choosing assessment tools most useful in a given situation.
9. Skill in problem formulation.
10. Skill in transactional assessment.
11. Understanding of the needs assessment process.

The first step in the generalist social work process is **assessment,** sometimes referred to as *diagnosis.* Interviews (discussed in Chapter 8) are a very important source of information in assessing the problem. The assessment phase of the social work process also includes the study aspect of "study, diagnosis, and treatment," the classic description of the social work process. Assessment is the phase being discussed when the term *analysis* is used. The development of understanding about individuals, families, small groups, agencies, and communities is an important aspect of assessment. The same understanding about any system that is requisite for professional interaction with that system is the core of the assessment stage of the interventive or service process. A social study is an assessment. The content of group meetings (discussed in Chapter 9) is another important source of information. Observations of individual and group behavior in the community are also important sources. Questionnaires and other research tools are sometimes used to gather needed information as are various psychological tests. Assessment is an essential ingredient for the individualization of people and social systems.

Max Siporin defines *assessment* as "a process and a product of understanding on which action is based."[1] It is the collection and analysis of information, the fitting together of available facts so they yield meaning. Within the perspective of this book, it does not include planning, which is seen as a separate step.

In a recent article Mark A. Mattaini and Stuart A. Kirk reviewed various assessment approaches used by social workers. These include the psychosocial, classification systems, and behavioral approaches often used in clinical social work; computerized assessment instruments; ecosystems perspective, and expert systems. The approach which most nearly approximates that presented for use in generalist social work in this book is the ecosystems approach. Mattaini and Kirk characterize it as a way of organizing complex assessment data and suggest that it does significantly expand the breadth of assessment without a loss of depth.[2]

Four ideas will be discussed in the further development of the concept of assessment: 1) the content of the assessment phase, 2) the use of the problem-solving process in assessment, 3) transactional assessment, and 4) needs assessment.

THE CONTENT OF THE ASSESSMENT PHASE

Assessment is a complex process at the core of the service process. The need for development of an understanding of clients, whether they are individuals, families, or small groups, and of the systems in the client's environment was discussed in Part Two of this book in relation to the interactional process. These schemas are tools for gathering information. They provide a structure for information gathering, but care must be taken that relevant information that falls outside the schema is not overlooked. Assessment, although a creative process, is also scientific in that it is a manifestation of the problem-solving (scientific) process. Some of its most important characteristics are:

1. *It is ongoing.* Assessment takes place throughout the life of the helping endeavor. During the early stages it is a primary focus. However, during later stages when the work of doing something about need, of solving the problem, of intervening into transactions among systems takes place, assessment is also a concern. As the client and worker engage in their work together, new information becomes available and new understandings emerge. These then become a part of the ongoing assessment. The ongoing assessment process leads to greater understanding about persons and situations as the social work process—the working together of worker and client—progresses.

2. *Assessment is twofold, focusing both on understanding the client in the situation and on providing a base for planning and action.* Information must be gathered about the people and systems involved, about their interrelationship and their environment. Information should be collected about the need, block to need fulfillment, the problem, and the people and systems significant to the need and problem. It is also important to determine strengths, limitations, motivation for change, and resistance to change that are applicable to the persons and systems involved. When dealing with large systems, it is important to gather information about the demography of the situation and the problem being considered. Also it may be important to gather information about interagency relationships, coordination, and cooperation; funding and other resources available or potentially available; attitudes, values, and cultural factors that may affect the problem-solving work.

This information is gathered in many different ways. Of prime importance is the client's perceptions and feelings about the problem and the situation. The manner in which the client tells the story, including observation of nonverbal communication, provides important information. Judgments about the consistency of the story, patterns of interaction and behavior and the client's cognitive capacity, judgment, and coping mechanisms can develop from listening to the story. Other sources of information may be previous case records and reports from other interested persons. If a worker uses information sources other than the client, the client should be aware of the use of the resources and give suggestions about sources for such information and permission for the worker to obtain the information from other people. When gathering information about large systems, such as a community, both key persons in the community and those involved with the problem should be used as informants. The information being collected should always be information clearly connected to the problem being worked on.

In addition, understanding the actual and potential resources, expectations of the various concerned systems for the outcome of service, and limitations or impingements that arise from the client's environment are also important. They are an important part of the information base used in planning for intervention.

3. *Assessment is a mutual process involving both client and worker.* The client is involved in all aspects of assessment to the maximum of her capacity. The primary content to be assessed arises from the worker-client interaction in the interview or in group discussions. Content also arises from the information provided as the worker observes the client in the interview or in group discussion. It arises from observations of the client in life situations. (*Life situations* are those opportunities a worker has to observe clients in interaction with other persons in either a natural environment, such as the home or the hospital ward, or in constructed situations such as an activity group.) The worker discusses observations and other information and knowledge with the client in establishing the meaning of the facts or the understanding of *client in situation.* The client's response is an important and valid part of the information to be obtained. The client is also made aware of the relationship of the understanding and the interventive planning possibilities and limitations. The use of a mutual process in assessment is one means of empowering clients for it provides them with a sense of self-worth and demonstrates that what they think and believe is important and that they are now passive recipients of help but important partners in the work to be done.

4. *There is movement within the assessment process.* This movement usually is from observation of parts of the service situation, to identification of information needed for understanding, to collection of facts about parts of the service situation, to explanation of the meaning of the facts collected, to putting together facts and their meanings about various parts in order to understand the total situation. The initial observation is usually through the eyes of the client. As the client describes these observations to the worker, the worker adds additional observations. Together, the worker and client identify the parts of the situation. The parts identified include those that are impacting on the situation in any significant way. The worker and client then identify the information they need to understand the situation. Understanding of parts can never result in complete understanding of wholes. To understand the situation it is necessary to look at interactions and relationships among the parts.

5. *Both horizontal and vertical exploration are important.* In early stages of assessment it is usually helpful to look at the situation horizontally: the situation is examined in breadth to identify all possible parts, interactions, and relationships. The purpose of this horizontal exploration is to determine the block to need fulfillment (the nature of the problem). Later, those parts identified as most important to the situation or to the solution of the problem are examined vertically or in depth. The information-gathering process can move from horizontal to vertical and back to horizontal several times as the worker and client explore the need, problem, and the situation. Social workers should develop skill in determining when a horizontal approach is most appropriate and when a vertical approach is the one to use.

6. *The knowledge base is used in developing understanding.* The worker uses his knowledge base as one means for developing understanding of the client in the situation. The understanding of an individual takes into consideration factors of human development and human diversity. The understanding of a family is related to what is known about family structure and family process. The understanding of an agency considers knowledge of bureaucratic structures. The understanding of community functioning calls for knowledge of economics and political science. The understanding of a family with a retarded child calls for knowledge about mental retardation and family reactions to having a developmentally disabled family member. The worker also makes use of knowledge developed from relevant research projects. When appropriate, the social worker uses research techniques to gather needed information.

7. *Assessment identifies needs in life situations, defines problems, and explains their meaning and patterns.* Assessment makes use of the problem-solving process in specifying the need and what is blocking need fulfillment. (This idea is discussed more fully later in this chapter.)

8. *Assessment is individualized.* Human situations are complex; no two are exactly the same. Each assessment is different and is related to the differential situation of the client. It takes into consideration the different parts of the situation and relates these to the unique whole that emerges.

9. *Judgment is important.* Many decisions must be made regarding each assessment. Decisions include what parts to consider, which parts of the knowledge base to apply, how to involve the client, and how to define the problem. The kinds of decisions that are made greatly affect the content and the interpretation of that content.

10. *There are limits to the understanding that can be developed.* No assessment is ever complete. Not only is it impossible to gain complete understanding of any situation but it is also undesirable. Understanding takes time. Clients in need are seeking help, and this help often must be given quickly. The worker must decide what understanding is necessary to give that help and then be aware of new understandings that develop in giving the help. The worker also must be comfortable with the uncertainty of limited understanding.

Recently social work literature is also drawing attention to the fact that strengths need to be identified in assessments.[3] This calls for identifying client aspirations and capabilities in the broad range of that client's social-functioning arenas. It also calls for identification of resources that may be present in both the immediate client system and in the immediate environment or situation.

The tasks of assessment, then, are: 1) identification of the need or problem, 2) identification of the information needed to further understand the need or problem and to determine appropriate means for dealing with the need or problem, and 3) collection and analysis of information.

Decision making includes interpreting meanings and ordering information as well as discovering relationships among parts of the situation. Decision making considers persons, problems, situations, and relationships.

Judgment

Because judgment is such an important component of assessment, there needs to be additional discussion of its meaning. Judgment is decision making. Harriett Bartlett has said, "Professional judgment provides the bridge between knowledge and value, on one hand, and interventive action on the other. Assessment is its first application in practice."[4]

Although the discussion of characteristics of assessment may seem to focus on small systems (individuals, families, and small groups), the same characteristics apply to larger system (organizational and community) assessment. As individuals, families and small groups are subsystems of the large systems; any assessment of a large system involves assessing the subsystems. The schemas provided in Chapter 9 provide frameworks for large system assessments. The schemas should, of course, be adapted and individualized depending on the particular system and the understanding needed for the specific service at hand. An important characteristic of the generalist social worker is knowledge and skill in assessing both large and small systems.

Values are very influential in the decision-making process. Our perceptions and thinking are affected by our values. Values affect how much of a situation and what parts of a situation are perceived. We tend to screen out that which is not congruent with our values or our thinking. Our biases about how things should be affect how we perceive situations. Because it is easiest for us to perceive that with which we are familiar, we may miss the unfamiliar or the different. When working with people from different backgrounds, it is particularly important for the worker to be aware of how values influence his or her decisions. Decisions about the meaning of information made from a worker's value perspective are often invalid when seen in the client's perspective.

For example, a worker using a personality theory that places a major emphasis on the individual when working with a client such as an American Indian (whose major orientation is to the extended family and to the tribe) would probably lead to the worker and client viewing the situation differently. The worker might determine that the client was not being given appropriate opportunities for self-determination, whereas the client might view the situation as one in which the worker did not care about the client's responsibilities to family and tribe. The worker would be viewing the situation through her value perspective that considers individual rights of prime importance. The client would be viewing self-determination as irrelevant and be more concerned with how he could better the lot of the collective group. Different value systems can lead to viewing the same situation in very different ways. Some resolution of this difference must take place before a worker and client can productively work together.

Harriet A. Feiner and Harriet Katz have pointed out how deeply held beliefs relating to women and family structure influence the judgments that are made in practice situations.[5] They note that commonly held myths, such as women should not compete with men and women carry the nurturing role, can be very detrimental when working with women clients who are struggling to become competent individuals.

Decision making is an important ingredient in professional judgment. These judgments are decisions based on reason and evidence. They identify what is fact, what is an assumption, and what is an inference. The influence that values may have on assumptions and inferences is then considered. Perceptions are tested.

In applying a knowledge base to the explanation of a phenomenon it is important to check to see if the appropriate knowledge has been chosen. Florence Hollis has given three criteria to use for choosing knowledge for social work education.[6] These criteria can also be used in considering knowledge for application to specific practice situations.

1. The choice should be related to phenomena being assessed and the situation being considered. In working with a small task group it would be inappropriate to use knowledge about groups that has been developed in working with a therapeutic group in a mental health situation unless that knowledge has been tested to learn if it is valid with a task group. (A task group is formed to accomplish a specific task, as contrasted with a group where treatment issues are of prime importance; for example, a community group that forms around an interest in developing a community service.) In looking at the small-group literature, the worker should be aware that much of that literature has been developed from observations of groups of students. Again, the worker would want to know if that knowledge has been tested with other kinds of task groups.

2. The choice should be related to whether or not the knowledge is useful in a social work context. Social work has a particular view of the human situation that perceives persons as self-determining. Thus, some knowledge that is very deterministic in nature is not appropriate for social work because it gives little hope for change. Determinism negates the idea that people have choices and that by making different choices they can more adequately deal with situations and problems. Without hope for change or the possibility of choice, the social work process is unworkable.

3. Consideration should be given to the nature of the power the knowledge possesses. Knowledge developed from working with a small sample of people in one kind of situation does not have the power that knowledge developed by testing a hypothesis under different sets of circumstances with a large sample does. In other words, what has worked with one client may not work with another client because the worker may fail to take into consideration the power of the knowledge being used.

Choices need to be made with the client's needs and preferences as a primary consideration. The identification of these needs and preferences is an important aspect of all assessment. Principles that can be used when making judgments in assessments include:

1. *Individualization*—Each person and system in a situation is different. In order to assess effectively, the unique aspects of the system need to be identified and understood.
2. *Participation*—Client participation in the assessment process is an important means of developing an assessment that recognizes the client's needs and preferences.
3. *Human development*—The assessment recognizes the developmental process of an individual and a social system as a means to further the understanding of that person or system.
4. *Human diversity*—Recognition of the diverse aspects of individuals, systems, and cultural groups is another important component of assessment.
5. *Purposeful behavior*—Recognition that all behavior is purposeful leads to a search for understanding of the purposes of behavior in the assessment process.

6. *Systemic transactions*—The assessment process identifies stressful life transactions, maladapative interpersonal processes, and environmental unresponsiveness in seeking understanding of persons in situations.

7. *Strengths and resources*—Identification of client capabilities and resources in the environment is important.

Through using the principles of individualization, participation, human development, human diversity, purposeful behavior, systemic transactions, and strengths and resources, the worker identifies with the client, the client's needs, and the client's preferences about what needs to be done. This, combined with an awareness of value influences and an appropriate choice of the knowledge to apply, leads to an assessment that yields a valid understanding of the client in the situation that is useful for planning intervention. Mary K. Rodwell, in presenting a model for assessment based on the naturalistic paradigm of research, seems to be describing a model very similar to the one discussed in this chapter. She states, "The naturalistic framework frees social work to reach a deeper understanding of person-situation through a holistic assessment style and promotes a sophisticated inquiry into human relationships with social and physical environments."[7]

CASE EXAMPLE

A school social worker requests that Mrs. P come to see her. Of her three school-age children, two are having school-related problems. Jimmy, age ten, is not performing up to his capacity and is becoming a management problem in the classroom. Ann, age six, has excessive absences and gives the excuse that she is staying with her aunt. John, age eight, seems to have no problems. He is seen as a bright, well-adjusted child. The worker knows that the children's father died very suddenly about six months ago. In using the principles of assessment the worker:

1. *Individualizes*—Although she knows the children's problems may relate to stress from the father's death and the need for reorganization in the family, she also knows that the impact on this family is felt uniquely. She already is aware that the three children seem to be reacting in quite different ways. She wants to explore to find out if there are other stresses that may be contributing to the problems.

2. *Allows for client participation*—The worker asks Mrs. P to discuss the situation as she sees it. She also questions Mrs. P about the areas that are not clear to her. She is careful to find out from Mrs. P what kind of help she would like. She discovers that Mrs. P is very overwhelmed by her responsibility for the family. She is working for the first time, feels very guilty about neglecting her children, and does not understand her own continuing grief reaction.

The worker also interviews each of the children, after receiving the mother's permission, in order to discover each child's perception of the situation. Ann has a great deal of difficulty talking about her absences from school. She becomes teary when the worker tries to draw out her feelings about her father's death and says she does not want to talk about it. When the worker suggests she must like her aunt a great deal, Ann smiles. The worker probes a bit to find out why. Ann finally quietly says that her aunt plays with her and takes care of her. The worker then says she wonders if Ann misses someone to play with her at home. Ann again withdraws and becomes restless. The worker decides not to probe further at this time.

In the interview with John, the worker asks how he sees things at home since his father's death. John says that his mother always seems either very busy or very sad, and that she has so much to do now. He believes his mother misses his father a great deal, as he does. He tries to help his mother by "being good." He also says he wishes his brother would stop causing her so much trouble. When the worker asks what he means by this, he talks about how Jimmy just seems to pick fights with everyone. He says he tries to stay out of Jimmy's way.

Jimmy proved to be very difficult to interview. He just sat and ignored the worker's questions. Finally he told her that it was none of her business. She assured him that she was interested in helping his mother and just wants to know how he feels. As he still refuses to talk, she decides to terminate the interview.

3. *Considers human development*—Each member of the family is considered in relation to his or her developmental stage. Mrs. P (Mary), age thirty, seems to still be in the Intimacy vs. Isolation stage of development. (See Table 6–1 in Chapter 6.) During her marriage she seemed to have almost completed this stage, but the death of her husband has upset this resolution and thrown her into a state of isolation. She has also lost her identity as a wife and is having to return to the Identity vs. Role Confusion stage and consider who she is as a person in her new state of widowhood.

The three children are all in the Industry vs. Inferiority stage, but each is having different experiences in this stage. Six-year-old Ann is just moving into the stage, and her reaction to the death of her father was to cling more closely to her mother. The worker knows that her situation needs careful consideration so that she does not regress and develop feelings of inferiority, thus endangering her ability to develop the skills she needs to function independently. John, eight, seems to be progressing through this stage in good fashion. He feels good about himself and is developing the needed skills, but he, too, may need help with the loss of his father.

Jimmy, ten, is not doing so well, certainly a reaction, at least in part, to the death of his father, with whom he spent a great deal of time. But as the worker talks with Mrs. P she discovers that Jimmy has never liked school. He had a great deal of difficulty learning to read in first grade and still does not read very well. The worker notes that perhaps there needs to be some testing to find out the nature of the difficulty. Jimmy seems to have developed his self-image as a wise guy. His father thought this was funny and encouraged it.

The family development was in the stage of individualization of family members vs. pseudomutual organization at the time the father died (see Chapter 7, page188). His death not only upset the steady state of the family system, it removed an important source of support for both mother and Jimmy. This family is in danger of moving to a pseudomutual organization.

4. *Considers human diversity*—This is a white, lower middle-class family who seems to have no ethnic ties. They also have no religious ties. The thing that is most important to remember in terms of diversity is that they are a single-parent family.

5. *Considers purposeful behavior*—The worker knows that both Ann's and Jimmy's behavior is purposeful and at least in part related to their reactions to the death of their father. Ann is probably clinging to her mother and her aunt because she is afraid she might also lose them. At this stage of her development this takes the form of wanting them not out of her sight. Thus, she needs help with understanding that they will not intentionally leave her and that she will be cared for. Jimmy, on the other hand, is reacting to broken relationships and problematic behaviors (mother overwhelmed and asking him to become the man of the house to meet her needs and a frustrated teacher who is also female) by seeking the companionship of a group of boys he considers "free and male." To be accepted by this group he must participate in their sometimes antisocial behavior. He needs some way to develop his maleness through positive relationships with male figures. While John is not displaying any negative behaviors, he, too, may be reacting to his father's death by being "too good." His need for help in dealing with his loss should also be explored.

6. *Considers systemic transactions*—At least a part of the difficulty in this family is due to the death of the father. This stress has impacted the mother and thus lessened her parenting capacity. Stress that was already present in the school situation for Jimmy has been exacerbated by the new stress.

7. *Identifies strengths and resources*—Mrs. P is very concerned about her children and wants to meet their needs. She is aware each is responding in a different manner to the loss of their father. She seems to be accepting of help. The aunt can also be considered another concerned adult and thus a resource to both the mother and the children. The family relationships seem to have been positive for the most part, and the memories of the father are good ones.

THE USE OF THE PROBLEM-SOLVING PROCESS IN ASSESSMENT

There are two ways the worker uses the problem-solving process in the assessment activities of the helping process. First, the worker uses the early steps of the problem-solving process with the client as they work together at the task of assessing the client's situation. The steps of the process (see Chapter 4) used in the assessment phase are

1. Preliminary statement of the problem,
2. Statement of preliminary assumptions about the nature of the problem,
3. Selection and collection of information, and
4. Analysis of information available.

The worker must decide how the client is to be involved in the problem solving. This decision depends in part on how much energy and desire the client has at any point in time for working on the problem. It hinges on the client's capacity, both cognitive and emotional, to problem solve. For example, in a crisis situation when the need for action is great, and when the client is already overwhelmed, the worker will be more active in the work than in a situation where there is less pressure for an early solution. It is not that the client in crisis is not involved in resolving the crisis; rather, it is how the worker involves the client and to what extent the process is made explicit to the client. Teaching the problem-solving process is often a strategy.

A second use of the problem-solving process by the worker is as a means of developing an assessment that is then checked out with the client. This latter use will be discussed in the remainder of this chapter. The worker must develop skill in problem solving before using the process with clients or before attempting to teach the process to clients.

One of the more difficult tasks in problem solving is the specification of the problem; that is, what the first four steps of the problem-solving process are all about. The preliminary statement is often the problem that the client brings to the helping situation. Based on material discussed in the first few contacts with the client, the worker may realize that the presenting problem is not the actual problem. As the worker makes explicit the reasons for formulating the preliminary problem, the underlying assumptions about the problem become more explicit. Identification of theoretical knowledge to use in thinking about the client in the situation is another way in which assumptions become explicit. As the assumptions are made explicit, it is possible to identify information that will be needed in order to verify the preliminary problem formulation and to restate it if necessary. The problem to be worked on is formulated after understanding of the client in the situation is developed and after the available information has been analyzed.

Problem formulation is the base for planning and assessment. Planning and action can be enhanced by thorough and appropriate problem formulation. Three steps to problem formulation are 1) identification of need, 2) identification of blocks to need fulfillment, and 3) formulation of the problem in terms of removing the blocks to need fulfillment. It should also be remembered that the needs and problems that concern the social worker are those that relate to social functioning.

Identification of Need

The first source of material for the identification of need is how the client tells his story. The worker not only listens to the verbal content but also looks for nonverbal communication. The pronouns that are used, the tense of verbs, the words used, and the way they are used all give clues as to the meaning of the need to the client. The worker also can note what is not said, what is omitted.

The skillful worker often begins to have hunches about what is wrong. These hunches are in the artistic realm of social work; they are a part of the worker's creativity. Hunches are very useful, but they should be checked out before they are given the power of facts. Usually they are checked out with the client or the system concerned.

As the worker begins to identify the client's need by using the material provided by the client, hunches or ideas that derive from the knowledge base being used, and information that may be available to the worker from other sources, other systems that are significant to this situation are identified. The needs of these systems in relation to the situation being considered should also be identified. Systems that are significant to a situation are those that are affected by the lack of need fulfillment, those that impact on the situation, and those that may have resources for meeting the need.

One of the areas that bears attention at this point is the agency and the service delivery system. If the function of the agency does not include services that can enable the client to fulfill the identified need or needs, the client should be made aware of this. The nature of the service delivery system is sometimes an important factor in the lack of need fulfillment.

Identification of Blocks to Need Fulfillment

Once the need is identified, it is then possible to consider why that need is not being fulfilled. Past experience, values, and particular theoretical frameworks provide assumptions about the reasons for the blockage. These preliminary assumptions must be checked out.

Additional information about the client and the situation may be needed. The client and the significant systems should be given an opportunity to provide their points of view. Written materials such as case records or descriptions of social systems involved may be useful.

From a social-functioning point of view, the location of the blockage is sought in the relationships among the significant systems. In this way, the needs of all systems are recognized, and the problem is not placed as the responsibility of just one system but is seen as interactive in nature.

Carel Germain has identified three situations that seem most likely to lead to problems in social functioning: 1) stressful life transitions, 2) communication and relationship difficulties, and 3) environmental unresponsiveness.[8] Assessment of the client in the situation to see if one of these situations exists is one means of determining the nature of the blockage of need fulfillment.

Stressful life transitions can be the result of problems in carrying out the tasks of the developmental stages of individuals and other social systems. Thus, the assessment must be concerned with identifying the developmental stage and identifying the tasks that have not been carried out or in which there is difficulty in carrying them out. These difficulties may be the result of lack of opportunity, including opportunities to fulfill tasks in ways that are congruent with one's cultural group (recognition of human diversity).

Another potentially stressful life transition is a status change. This includes such events as the death of a spouse and becoming a widow or widower, loss of a job and becoming unemployed, graduation or dropping out of school, and becoming part of the work force. New statuses make new role demands on people. Often there has been no preparation for these new demands; or the new demands may place additional expectations on people. The widow with young children who returns to the work force confronts not only the demands of being a single parent and helping the family adapt to the loss of a father but also the demands of a job. Demands of the single-parent role and the work role may conflict or be overwhelming and thus cause stress.

Closely related to stressful situations are crisis situations. When change is so great that persons and systems cannot cope and maintain their steady state, a crisis can result. The need in such a situation is not only for the resolution of the problem but also for the system to regain its steady state in such a manner that it can meet the expectations of its environment.

Other social-functioning problems develop because a person or social system is not effectively communicating with, and relating to, other persons and social systems. Some persons from diverse cultures have considerable difficulty in relating to the institutions of society. For example, the school may be unaware of the needs of children from diverse cultures. This lack of understanding and the inability of parents to relate to the school can result in a situation where children's developmental needs are not being fulfilled. Another way of stating this is that the individual or family may not be able to use existing resources or they may not even know about them. Also the institutions may not be able to identify the strengths of the individual or family because of lack of understanding about cultural factors. The core of the matter then lies in lack of accurate communication, which results in relationship problems.

The problems of children from diverse cultures may also be the result of the school's unresponsiveness to their needs. This environmental unresponsiveness is a third cause of stress and coping failure. Environmental unresponsiveness can take two forms: lack of provision of a needed service or failure to provide the needed service in a manner in which it can be used by certain clients. Examples of this latter failure include unrealistic expectations for the client on the part of the social worker, such as obtaining transportation to an office under certain circumstances; providing the service in a way that asks persons to violate cultural values and norms; and expecting clients to function with ease in a culturally foreign milieu.

Formulation of the Problem

Once the blockage to the need is identified, it is possible to formulate the problem. The problem formulation considers the need that is not being fulfilled, the block or blocks to the fulfillment of that need, and factors contributing to the block. It is important to be as specific as possible yet to recognize the transactional nature of social functioning.

The specification of need may be made in several ways. It may be a demonstration that a concrete resource or service is lacking, such as sufficient income to meet needs (e.g., a nutritious diet or health care). Need can also be specified in terms of psychosocial development needs. An example of this would be that of a physically challenged ten-year-old child not having the opportunity to develop skills of daily living. This might take place when there is lack of understanding of the child's need to feel competent or because the mother is compensating for her own guilt over the child's condition by "overcaring." Need can also be specified in terms of inadequate role fulfillment in the roles of parenting, marriage, or work. It can also be specified in terms of difficulty in life transitions. Another way of specifying need is in terms of relationships among people and social systems, which is often used when working with organizations and communities.

Next in the formulation of the problem is a statement about what seems to be blocking the need fulfillment. This includes a recognition of relationships with potential resources. This needs to be clearly stated and must recognize the transactional aspects of the blockage.

To illustrate the formulation of the problem, the example of a young widow with three school-age children can be used. The need arises from a lack of ability to cope with the demands of work and parenting as a single parent. It is a life-transition need. The block is conflicting demands in carrying out the two roles. One of the children is in trouble in school; another does not want to go to school. The school is demanding that the client take time off the job for conferences. She is employed in a low-paying secretarial job, and her employer is threatening to fire her for taking too much time off the job. When the cause of the blockage is examined, several factors seem to be contributing to her inability to cope:

1. In the six months since her husband's death, she has not completed the grief work.
2. She does not know how to manage the family finances, which is causing her to be tense and cranky with the children.
3. She does not know how to fill the role of the single parent. She is overly demanding of herself and feels sorry for her children.
4. Because of financial deficiencies, she does not have adequate childcare.
5. She does not know about resources available to her.
6. She does not have skills that would lead to a higher-paying job.
7. One son, the oldest child, misses his father and is very difficult to manage.
8. The youngest child, a daughter, is not happy with the after-school babysitter who lives in the neighborhood. When she stays home from school, she is taken to her aunt's home across town where she is happy.
9. The school is overcrowded and does not have the resources to deal with children who are having problems.

The source of a blockage may be in attitudes and values, in knowledge and understanding, in behavior, in coping skills, in role overload, in environmental expectations, in not recognizing available resources, or in lack of usable resources. Usually the source is not just one but a combination of circumstances, and it is the combination that causes the stress and blocks need fulfillment. The problem formulation should recognize this complexity as it states need and specifies blockage to need fulfillment. The problem-solving process is particularly useful in formulating the problem.

When working in a psychiatric setting, the classification of *DSM-III-R (Diagnostic and Statistical Manual of Mental Disorders* of the American Psychiatric Association, 1987) may be used. Social workers have also developed a variety of classifications of problems and needs. Some social workers believe that the use of classifications leads to stereotyping and labeling and interferes with individualized assessments.[9]

Some believe that the use of a problem focus in assessment leads to individualistic assessment rather than social-environmental explanations, which can lead to a "blaming of the victim." They see a problem focus as giving an illusion of a solution or remedy when none is possible.[10]

Including identification of resources and strengths in the collection and analysis of data is an important ingredient of the assessment process. This part of the assessment allows the problem-solving activity to consider the situational factors involved in the problem. It leads to the identification of environmental factors that are a part of the problematic situation. These factors may either be a source of the problem or may support the continuance of the problematic situation. It is a mark of the generalist social work approach to problem solving.

CASE EXAMPLE

The problem in the example of the P family can be formulated in different ways for the various members of this family. It can be seen as a widow not having had an opportunity to complete grief work because of demands from family and job. It can be seen as a widow who lacks knowledge needed to manage the family finances. The problem can be seen as a lack of skills needed for obtaining employment that will adequately support the family. The problem can be related to the oldest son and formulated as: the son is misbehaving owing to anger over his father's death. The problem can also be related to the daughter and stated as: the daughter is not receiving the needed care from her mother and babysitter. The problem can be formulated relative to the total family. In this case it can be stated as: the family organization and functioning has been upset by the death of the father. The problem can also be formulated as: this family lacks the resources it needs to function. The way the problem is ultimately formulated will depend on which system is seen as the client and what is seen as that system's most pressing problem.

TRANSACTIONAL ASSESSMENT

The transactional nature of human interaction is very complex, and this causes difficulty in assessment. Given the present state of social work knowledge about transactional assessment, there are only tools or guidelines for doing such an assessment. Transactional assessment depends to a great extent on the worker's creativity and ability to look at a complex situation and bring order and meaning to that complexity. Transactional assessment is particularly useful when considering possible plans of action and the effect those plans might have on the various systems involved in the situation of concern. Recently some frameworks for transactional assessment have appeared. An example is the eco-systems framework developed by Paula Allen-Meares and Bruce A. Lane. They identify variables to be considered and place them in a three-dimensional framework. The three dimensions are kinds of data, data source, and the system to which the data are related. Examination of the framework leads to the conclusion that, in order to obtain the breadth of understanding needed for assessment, it is important to collect and place a wide variety of data in some kind of framework that shows at least some relationships among the data.[11]

When considering the nature of transactional assessment it also becomes apparent that the generalist social worker needs tools for use in assessing the functioning, needs, and problems of individuals, families, small groups, organizations, and communities. Four tools that can be useful in transactional assessment include 1) using a dual perspective, 2) mapping, 3) social support network analysis, and 4) social impact assessment. The use of genograms, as discussed in Chapter 6, is another transactional assessment technique.

The Dual Perspective

Dolores Norton has developed the concept of *dual perspective* to depict the plight of many minority persons. It is "a conscious and systematic process of perceiving, understanding, and comparing simultaneously the values, attitudes, and behavior of the larger social system with those of the client's immediate family and community system."[12] This conceptualization holds that every individual is a part of two systems: 1) the societal system that functions within the norms and values of the dominant groups within society and 2) the smaller system that functions in a person's immediate environment. This latter system can be the cultural system. When the two systems are not congruent in terms of norms, values, expectations, and ways of functioning, problems develop for individuals, families, and cultural groups.

In making an assessment using the dual perspective, the worker looks for points of difference, especially for conflicting expectations between the two systems. The degree of difference and the number of characteristics that are different are important in judging the incongruity between the systems. Also important is how the systems perceive the difference and how the difference affects their functioning. This kind of an assessment calls not just for a general intellectual understanding of a specific cultural group but for an understanding of a specific, immediate environmental system of any person or group of persons. The dual perspective is a particularly useful tool in assessing the transactions of any specific cultural group or of persons from a minority culture with the larger, dominant society.

Whenever a worker deals with clients and situations with values, culture, and ways of functioning that are different from the generally dominant culture, it would seem wise to use a dual perspective approach as a part of the assessment process. Some determination of the extent of the difference and the impact of the difference on individuals and systems should be made. Where the difference is great or the impact significant, it is important to determine motivations, resistances, and appropriate interventive points to bring about adjustments in dominant society systems that impact on the situation or affect need fulfillment. It is also important to determine, with clients affected by incongruencies between the two systems, if there are coping mechanisms that would be helpful in the situation.

Use of the dual perspective can be illustrated by looking at some of the characteristics of Puerto Rican culture. Sonia Ghali has identified these as an extended family structure with kinship through godparents; the importance of virginity for an unmarried woman; an emphasis on individualism and inner integrity; a fatalistic, submissive-passive approach to life situations; use of family, friends, and neighbors as the first sources of help; high respect for the advice of pastors and teachers of their own group; use of spiritualism; expectation that helping persons will use authority; belief in mysticism; use of the Spanish language; and an expectation that the wealthy will be paternalistic and benevolent toward the poor.[13] It is, of course, important to determine if these characteristics hold true for a particular Puerto Rican client. When these characteristics are compared with the characteristics of the majority society, a number of incongruities become apparent. These include a different language, different expectations about the source of respect, different usage of egression, and so on. An assessment of the incongruities gives an understanding of the transactional influences on a Puerto Rican person.

Mapping

Mapping is a tool for pictorially representing the relationships of the significant parts of any situation. (See Figure 11–1 in the following case example.) It is a variation of the sociogram discussed in Chapter 9. First, the client or focal point of a situation is depicted with a circle. If this focal point is a multiperson system, the relationships of the person in that system are shown in the circle just as they are in the sociogram.

The other significant systems in the situation are placed around the circle representing the focal system. Various kinds of relationships are drawn, noting which individual in the focal system carries the relationship to these systems.[14]

Mapping can also be useful in assessing the role structure of a situation. The map can be examined for incongruities in role expectations, either within the focal system, or with systems in the environment of that focal system. The map can be examined for role overloads and for missing roles.

Use of mapping makes apparent the transactional nature of the problematic situation. It can also be useful in identifying strengths and resources available to the helping situation. It can be useful when working with an organizational system or a community system in developing understanding about the relationships among the parts of those systems. It also can be used to depict the relationships among key persons in these larger systems.

CASE EXAMPLE

Mapping yields several understandings about the P family and its transactions. (See Figure 11–1).

1. The mother seems to have only one supportive relationship, her sister. (Relationships with children and work are asking more of her than they give.) She seems to be surrounded by negative, problematic, and broken relationships.
2. The oldest son, who was very close to his father, is also surrounded by problematic, negative, and broken relationships.
3. The daughter has a strong relationship with the mother and a good relationship with her aunt. Her relationships to the school and to the babysitter are negative. This

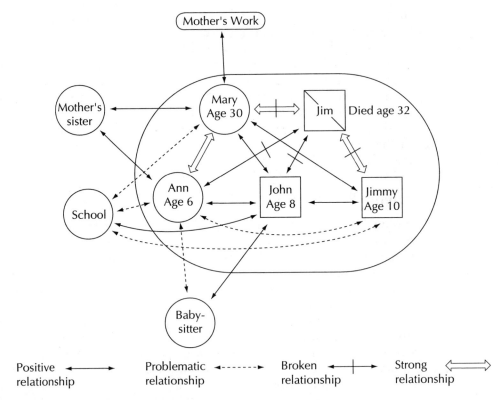

FIGURE 11–1   **Map of a Family and Their Situation**

relationship pattern may hold an answer to the school problem. It may be that the strong relationship to the mother and the dislike of the babysitter cause her to want to go to her aunt's rather than to school.

4. The middle son seems to have more positive relationships, and he is the child not exhibiting problematic behavior.

From this analysis it would seem that one way of fulfilling need in this family would be to find a means to develop a positive relationship network with resources outside the family system. Before proceeding, however, more information needs to be obtained about other relationships the family may have or about the relationships that may have been broken by the father's death. Another possible intervention might be with the school and the babysitter relationships. These two relationships are affecting more than one member of the family; thus, they are quite significant.

Social Support Network Analysis

Closely related to the technique of mapping is the analysis of the social support network of an individual or family. Mapping allows for the identification of significant social support resources. A **social support network analysis** allows for specification about the nature of the supports. It complements the map in the assessment process.

James K. Whittaker and Elizabeth M. Tracy recently developed a Social Network Grid for use in a research project. This grid can also be useful in assessing the social support network of an individual or family. Areas to be considered in such an assessment include the area of life in which the support is given (e.g., work, school, etc.); the kind of support (e.g., concrete, emotional, informational, etc.); how often the support is given; whether the support is critical of or problematic to the support receiver; whether the support is in a reciprocal relationship with the support receiver; the closeness of the support to the support receiver; how often there is contact between the provider and receiver; and how long the receiver has known the support provider.[15]

With a concern for identifying and using resources or social supports that are either available or potentially available to individuals and families, generalist social workers must develop assessment tools for analysis of social support networks. This is a developing area for practice knowledge development.[16]

Social Impact Assessment

Social impact assessment is an interdisciplinary movement that is developed as a response to the need for social as well as environmental assessment of possible impacts of proposed new dams, highways, power plants, and other changes in land usage. It is the application of research techniques to the problems of predicting what the impact of a proposed change will be on the social interactions or social functioning of people. It can be a helpful technique for social workers in predicting services that may be needed when a change in a larger system is proposed. One aspect of assessment is evaluating the possible impact of any proposed change on systems and their parts.[17]

A social impact assessment is a situational assessment. Data are collected using several research techniques, depending on the data to be gathered. The activity depends on the worker's knowledge, skill, and creativity. The data collected describe the situation as it exists and as it is projected to exist with the change.

Some social impact assessments use a process of profiling, projecting, displaying, and mitigating. *Profiling* is the identification of individuals and systems that will be impacted by the change; in this stage, it is important to identify as many systems as possible. Later, this group of systems can be limited. The second step is *projecting,* which is a process of describing the implications of the change on the identified systems. *Displaying* is an analysis of the options available to avoid the negative impacts that have been identified. *Mitigation* is choosing the option or options that will be used to prevent or lessen the negative impacts of proposed change.

When doing a social impact assessment, the practitioner goes through the steps several times. During the first go-throughs many systems are considered, and the work is largely cognitive. As the work progresses, the number of systems considered decreases and the work moves to the use of research technology to collect data.

CASE EXAMPLE

A Social Impact Assessment

For some time rumors were heard in the local community that the local office of the Department of Human Services would be closed. The department was organized on a district basis in the state. Service to the local community would come from a district office in a neighboring county. A local social worker decided to use social impact assessment techniques to determine the impact of such a change.

In the profiling step, three systems were identified as those most apt to be impacted by the change: 1) the clients, 2) the workers, and 3) the community, particularly those segments of the community that might refer clients or provide services to persons who were clients of the agency; others considered were those persons who might be resources for clients and persons who supported the agency in a variety of ways.

In projecting the possible impacts, initial thinking brought the following assumptions:

1. *The clients*—The social service office would be less accessible. More time would be needed to reach the office, so that transportation could prove to be a problem. Additional cost for or lack of availability of transportation would lead to difficulty in coming to the office.

2. *The workers*—More time would be spent traveling to visit clients and to confer with significant individuals and community members. Workers would be less available to clients.

3. *The community*—The community might have less concern for the agency. Community members might feel that the agency no longer belonged to the community and be less inclined to refer persons to the agency or to contact the agency about working cooperatively in service of clients. Community resources might be less known to workers.

Before accepting these preliminary assumptions as fact, some data needed to be collected. Three kinds of data were collected:

1. A record was kept for one week of all phone calls that came into the agency. They were classified by which of the agency's services they related to and by who was calling: client, significant other, other persons. It was found that very few clients called the agency. Most of the phone calls came from significant others and concerned community members. At the same time, a record was kept of the persons who came to the agency. Again it was found that very few of the clients came in except for initial applications for food stamps or income maintenance. There also were few community members coming into the agency.

2. The county was matched with a neighboring county of similar size. Census and statistical records of the department relative to the number of persons receiving services were examined to determine if the two counties were similar; they were found to be similar. The matched county did not have an office of the agency in the county. Income maintenance and food stamp workers held office hours at the county seat one day a week. Service workers serving the two counties were asked to keep time studies for one month; the time studies included time on the road, time in the office, the nature of the tasks performed in the office, time spent in clients' homes, and time spent in the community with community members. There was virtually no difference in the time studies of workers in the two counties. From this information it became apparent that the method of service delivery was such that neither the worker nor the clients would be significantly impacted by the closing of the office if the present pattern of service delivery were maintained.

3. An information-gathering interview using a schedule was held with fifteen community members, chosen as those who occupied positions in the community that would make them apt to have contact with the agency, either as referral persons, cooperating or coordinating persons, or as resources for the agency to use. They included the police chief, the probation officer, the county sheriff, the school coordinator of special services, the mayor, a Community Action Program worker, the director of the Senior Citizens Center, a member of the county board of supervisors, the Rec Center Director, two women who were leaders in an organization sponsoring a used-clothing store and numerous local helping endeavors, and three ministers of local churches. These persons were asked what their contact with the local office of the agency had been, what knowledge they had of the services provided by the agency, and what kind of contact they would have with the agency if it were not located in the community. It was found that most of these significant persons had limited knowledge about the services of the agency; only about a third of them worked with the agency; most of those who worked with the agency spontaneously discussed negative feelings they had about the agency; and almost all said that they would have little or no contact with the agency if it were not in the community.

Assessment of this information indicates that the agency has serious relationship problems with its community. Community support is necessary for any agency not only because community resources are needed for clients but because without community understanding of the programs and services offered by the agency, optimal community-agency relationships do not exist. Removing the agency from the community would make it very difficult to establish the needed relationships.

In carrying out the displaying step, three options seemed possible:

1. Do nothing but continue service as now being delivered;
2. Close the office because it's not going to affect the clients or workers anyway; or
3. Leave the office open for a time and attempt to develop the potential community linkages and support.

An unexpected understanding was developed from the assessment. This understanding indicated a quite different problem relative to delivery of services needed by the clients. Development of community relationships and the associated resources and support could be an important input from the agency's environment that could enhance the service capacity of the agency.

If the choice was to close the office in the mitigation stage, then two steps should be taken to mitigate some impacts. First, a nontoll phone system to the office serving the community should be developed. Second, additional efforts should be made with the community to help it understand the agency's services and to develop linkages. If the choice was to develop the community linkages while remaining in the community, then additional assessment should be made to determine the source of the difficulty and possible means to alleviate it.

Note: The worker was very knowledgeable about the agency and the community and based assessment decisions on that knowledge.

NEEDS ASSESSMENT

Assessment of a community and its resources or assessment of a client in a situation may result in the realization that resources that are needed are not available. Social workers have a responsibility for working toward the development of needed resources. One of the first steps in doing this is carrying out a needs assessment. Funding sources usually require that some data relative to the nature and extent of need are available before they are willing to support new projects or programs. Some governmental funding agencies and some accreditation bodies also require a needs assessment as part of their on going review of programs. In addition, well-designed needs assessments are an excellent means for involving community members, users, and potential users of services in developing awareness of needs in a community.

The assessment can be carried out in several ways. First, general opinions about the service or the need for service can be obtained from various segments of the community, such as service providers, consumers, and community influentials. A major problem with this type of information gathering is that it represents opinions, not hard facts. However, this mechanism can provide information that may not be obtainable through other mechanisms; it can be used as a preliminary step to designing an assessment instrument that captures a complete picture of the problem; and it can be used as a means for involving the community in the assessment. When obtaining information from service providers, it is important to recognize that sometimes they do not allow for the fact that there are some people who do not want the services provided by the formal system and who are able to meet their needs in other ways.

A second mechanism for needs assessment is to survey current users of service. Often professionals forget that the *I need* perspective is just as important as the *they need* perspective. Individuals and families are more apt to use services that they believe are needed. Involving users in needs assessments may provide important information about the design of services. However, it is not always possible for users to articulate their needs, so the mechanism may not provide a complete picture of the need. For example, it has been found by the author that older people have a good deal of difficulty admitting to need. They feel that the admission of limitations may force them into a nursing home or force them to come to grips with the aging process in ways they prefer to avoid.

Another mechanism of determining need is through the use of statistical data. For example, if community population figures for the number of handicapped persons are high compared to similar size communities, this would probably indicate a high level of need. If a community has a high percentage (compared to similar communities) of older people or people below the poverty level, then it can be assumed that there are needs not being met. The worker must be careful in using these data, as the use of this mechanism may lead to assumptions which later prove unfounded.

Usually in designing a needs assessment it is desirable to use several means for collecting data. Need can be identified in several different ways: gaps in services, redundancy of services, availability of services to various groups of people, accessibility of services to those who are in need, and usability of service (e.g., is it provided within a framework that can be used by various cultural groups?).

Before designing a needs assessment instrument, it is important to be thoroughly familiar with the community, the need area, and the population to be targeted. Involving community influentials or community organizations can also be very helpful in the planning of the assessment. These people can help interpret the need for the assessment, give it community sanction, and give input to its construction, which will make the assessment acceptable to the community and thus result in a greater chance of accurate response. Other social systems significant to the study also need to be identified, as well as all possible data sources. In the latter category, one should search out demographic statistical profiles, key informants (those in direct contact with persons experiencing problems), consumers of service, and individuals with problems or having potential for problems; the general public is also a source. A preliminary statement of the problem should be developed at this stage and assumptions about the nature of the problem stated.

When the needed background information has been gathered, the worker is ready to begin the design of the needs assessment. Decisions must be made about the type of data needed, the individuals who can best provide the information, and the most appropriate means for gathering that information. Information can be gathered in person or by phone interviews, mailed questionnaire, or by using already gathered data such as agency records or census data. Generally, it is wise to develop an instrument that will allow the collection of the same information from each respondent. Information sought may include: demographic data, such as race, gender, age, marital status, educational level, and length of residence in the community; perceived problems; where information about services is obtained; factors that hinder the seeking of help; and services needed. The development of the needs assessment design calls for creativity on the part of the designer so that it individualizes the situation for which it is designed.

As the needs assessment design is being developed, two other areas need attention. First is the development of a publicity campaign. Public knowledge of the assessment and its purpose is necessary if people are to respond in the manner necessary for the obtaining of accurate information. This campaign can include news releases, television and radio spots, posters, and announcements at meetings and community activities. It can also make use of the community people who have been involved in the development of the needs assessment; they can give sanction and lend credibility to the effort. When considering a needs assessment that will involve community people, it is important to consider timing of the survey. The worker must be aware of other activities going on in the community and plan the assessment for a time when the community has the energy and time to be involved.

Another necessary consideration relates to the confidentiality of information obtained, or the human rights concern. All publicity should indicate how the information obtained will be used, and assurances of confidentiality must be provided. Interviewers must be trained not only in confidentiality but in how to conduct the interview. Often, it is helpful to first test an instrument with a small sample of people that are representative of those who will be contacted during the assessment. This can alert the designer to questions that are problematic and apt to be misinterpreted or not answered. In short, it allows for greater certainty that the outcome of the assessment will be accurate. The evaluation and interpretation of information gathered depends on the particular information, and these functions are part of the assessment design. Once this has taken place, it is important to share the findings with those who have participated in the assessment. Needs assessment, when properly carried out, is an involved process, but one that can lead to greater possibility for meeting the needs of individuals and families.

CASE EXAMPLE

Sally Jones is an adult services worker in a public social services agency in an area where about 18 percent of the population are over sixty-five years of age. The agency is concerned about the unmet needs of these older people. It has developed a program that involves workers and communities working together to discover unmet needs and develop resources to meet those needs. The program provides guidelines but allows workers and communities to make adaptations as determined by the community.

Sally has been working for about a year with this community, which has a population of about 5,000. She has already carried out a very thorough community study (see pages 235–237) and knows that it is important to involve the community in the needs assessment as soon as possible. She knows that it is important to find out if this community recognizes the needs and accepts responsibility for the senior citizens who live here. She has found that there is an active senior citizens center and several very active women's church groups that are interested in community projects. Because Sally does not live in this community, she needs sanction for the project from the community.

As a first step, Sally makes appointments with the president of the senior citizens center and the presidents of three church women's groups. She learns these presidents are concerned and they acknowledge that they have never thought of a formal or systematic means of trying to identify needs. Sally then introduces the idea of a formal needs assessment. She has some guidelines from the state office on carrying out an assessment. She also has some information on what some other similar communities have done as a result of their needs assessment, and she shares these in each of the interviews. She states her belief that the community could benefit from such a process and asks if the organization each individual represents would be willing to help. Sally could have worked with just one organization, but she knows it will be important to have a broadly based community organization to work with later on if plans for community projects are developed based on the needs assessment. She believes that by beginning to develop this broad base early in the process, through using several groups to do the needs assessment, there will be a better chance of services being developed.

Each of the group leaders expresses interest for their group as long as there is not too much time demanded. Sally explains that if several groups work on the project it should not call for a great deal of time. The guidelines from the state office indicate that 100 calls to senior citizens and 100 to the general public will give the information needed. She hopes for a total of twenty volunteers, five from each organization, so that each would only have to make ten phone calls in a two-week period. She also told the president of the senior citizens center that she would need some help in identifying those over age sixty in the phone book for the random sampling of that group. The president says they have a meeting in two weeks and asks Sally to come and talk to them about the project. She also says that the center has been concerned about several people in the community but did not know how to go about meeting their needs. Sally replies that she can also discuss the resources that are already available from her agency.

The first church group president wants to discuss the project with the members and get back to Sally. She does this in a month's time and says they are ready to help. The second church group president says she will have to talk to the pastor and see if he approves of the project, and she will then get back to Sally. She never does and is very evasive when Sally calls her back. Sally does not pursue this group as she has found another group of women in the community who are anxious to be included in the project; they have ten members who want to be involved. The third church group president says that her group is just too busy on their own projects to help right now, but she does want to be informed about the results.

The design for this assessment has been developed in the state office. Phone calls are made to a random sample of the general community and those over age sixty in the community; an instrument has been developed for use with each group. The community sample is asked opinions about need in the community around five areas; loneliness and isolation, ability to care for a home, nutrition, transportation, and activities of daily living. Those over age sixty are asked about their needs in these areas. Respondents are also asked their age, whether they have family living within a thirty-mile radius, and how they would rate their health. Once the surveys are completed they are sent to the state office for computer tabulation.

Sally goes over this with the group of volunteers and asks if they would add any other questions that are unique to people living in this community. She explains that this assessment is their attempt to understand their own town and it needs to reflect what they want to know. She says that any data they collect that are not appropriate for state office analysis will be gone over by her and any of the volunteers that want to help.

When it becomes apparent that community groups will be able to obtain the needed volunteers, and when a date for the survey has been set, Sally begins a public relations campaign. This campaign is designed to inform the community of the upcoming survey and its purpose. The use of the information is carefully discussed, noting the confidentiality of individual answers and how the findings will be shared with the community through news releases to the local weekly newspaper and public meetings. The campaign also uses announcements at meetings of various organizations.

When all the community respondents have been identified and the senior citizens have completed their identification of those over age sixty in the community, and when Sally has chosen the random sample to be called, a meeting is held with the volunteers. At this meeting Sally passes out the instrument to be used in collecting data during the phone call. She suggests that the telephone volunteers jot down any remarks or questions that respondents make about needs or present services. She tells the group that after the forms have been sent to the state office for tabulation they will get together to discuss the experience and the remarks and questions of the respondents. She notes that this information may reveal additional needs in the community and of older persons, as well as providing responses to the survey questions. She carefully goes over all details and stresses confidentiality of the information obtained. She discusses how to handle various situations that may be encountered and has the group engage in role-play of the phone call.

Each volunteer is then given ten names to call with three alternates if they cannot complete the first ten calls. Sally stresses the need for trying to get all the calls completed in a two-week period. She tells them to be sure and get in touch with her if they have any problems, and that she will check with them at the end of a week and collect their forms at the end of two weeks. As a result of Sally's thorough knowledge of the community and her careful planning with community leaders and volunteers, all but five of the calls are completed in the two-week period. Two volunteers agree to complete the remaining calls, which one volunteer with unexpected family stress could not finish. A month after sending the data to the state office for analysis, Sally received the results. Sally is aware that the true meaning of the data will only be determined within the context of this specific community. She knows that the volunteers and club officers are the real experts on this community. Thus, she calls a meeting of the involved individuals that they may begin the work of data analysis, trying to determine what are the unmet needs of the elderly and move toward deciding what to do about those needs.

SUMMARY

A social work assessment is a picture (however incomplete) made up of all available facts, fit together within a particular frame of reference for a particular purpose. It contains the following elements:

1. Identification of all the entities involved in the situation;
2. Development of the needed understanding about each of these entities;
3. Ordering or arranging these entities in such a manner that the role and relationship structure becomes apparent, that the transactional nature in the situation is seen;
4. Identification of the need in the situation and of the blockage to need fulfillment;
5. Identification of strengths and resources of individuals and systems present in situations;
6. Formulation of the problem from a transactional point of view;
7. Identification of additional information needed, of the knowledge base to be used to enhance understanding, and of the values that are operating in the situation;
8. Evaluation of the information available;
9. Identification of relevant social policy, of constraints in the situation, of expectations of all involved, and of actual and potential resources in the situation; and
10. Identification of possible impacts of potential change in the situation on all systems involved.

Assessment is a core skill for any social worker. Like any other skill, it must be practiced if it is to be developed. Professional interaction and professional helping both are heavily dependent on skill in assessment.

QUESTIONS

1. Review the Case Example in Chapter 9, pages 211–214. Identify all of the information you would seek if you were asked to make an assessment of this situation. What would you use as sources for each piece of information you have identified?

2. Review the material on interviewing in Chapter 8. How do you see the interviewing process used to assess the need, problem, and situation with the client?

3. Consider the concept of *professional judgment.* What are the strengths you now have for operationalizing this concept? What are your current concerns about operationalizing this concept?

4. What is the place of "hunches" or "gut feelings" in the problem-solving process?

5. Think of someone you know who comes from a cultural background somewhat diverse from the commonly accepted majority group. Use the dual perspective to assess congruencies and incongruencies between that person's cultural or sustaining system and the societal system. Do you have any suggestions for dealing with incongruencies?

6. Use the mapping technique to develop a picture of some problematic situation of which you are aware. What did you learn from the map that might be of use in solving the problem?

7. Discuss the advantages of using a strengths perspective rather than only identifying needs and problems in the assessment process.

SUGGESTED READINGS

Allen-Meares, Paula, and Lane, Bruce A. "Grounding Social Work Practice in Theory: Ecosystems. " *Social Casework* 68 (November 1987): 315–321.

Cheung, Kam-fong Monit. "Needs Assessment Experience Among Area Agencies on Aging." *Journal of Gerontological Social Work* 19 (No. 3/4, 1993): 77–93.

Cox, Fred M., Erlich, John L., Rothman, Jack, and Tropman, John E., Eds. *Strategies of Community Organization,* 4th ed. Itasca, IL: F. E. Peacock, 1987.

Feiner, Harriet A., and Katz, Harriet. "Stronger Women—Stronger Families." *Affilia* 1 (Winter 1986): 49–58.

Germain, Carel B., and Gitterman, Alex. *The Life Model of Social Work Practice.* New York: Columbia University Press, 1980 (Chapter 1, "Introduction to the Life Model").

Hartman, Ann, and Laird, Joan. *Family-Centered Social Work Practice.* New York: Free Press, 1983 (Chapters 8–14).

Lauffer, Armand. *Assessment Tools for Practitioners, Managers, and Trainers.* Beverly Hills, CA: Sage Publications, 1982.

Marrow-Howell, Nancy. "Multidimensional Assessment of the Elderly Client." *Families in Society* 73 (September 1992): 395–406.

Mattaini, Mark A. "Contextual Behavior Analysis in the Assessment Process." *Families in Society* 71 (April 1990): 236–245.

Mattaini, Mark A., and Kirk, Stuart A. "Assessing Assessment in Social Work." *Social Work* 36 (May 1991): 260–266.

McPhatter, Anna R. "Assessment Revisited: A Comprehensive Approach to Understanding Family Dynamics." *Families in Society* 72 (January 1991): 11–21.

Meyer, Carol H. *Assessment in Social Work Practice.* New York: Columbia University Press, 1993.

Minahan, Anne, Ed. *Encyclopedia of Social Work,* 18th ed. Silver Spring, MD: National Association of Social Workers, 1987 ("Assessment in Direct Practice" and "Diagnostic and Statistical Manual [DSM]").

Monkman, Marjorie, and Allen-Meares, Paula. "The TIE Framework: A Conceptual Map for Social Work Assessment." *Arete* 10 (Spring 1985): 41–49.

Neuber, Keith A. *Needs Assessment: A Model for Community Planning.* Beverly Hills, CA: Sage Publications, 1980.

Paquin, Gary W., and Bushoni, Robert J. "Family Treatment Assessment for Novices." *Families in Society* 72 (June 1991): 353–359.

Peterson, K. Jean. "Assessment in the Life Model: A Historical Perspective." *Social Casework* 60 (December 1979): 586–596.

Rodwell, Mary K. "Naturalistic Inquiry: An Alternative Model for Social Work Assessments." *Social Service Review* 61 (June 1987): 231–246.

Sheafor, Bradford W., Horejsi, Charles R., and Horejsi, Gloria A. *Techniques and Guidelines for Social Work Practice.* Boston: Allyn and Bacon, 1988 (Chapter 10 and pp. 422–426).

Siegel, Larry M., Attkisson, Clifford, and Carson, Linda G. "Need Identification and Program Planning in the Community." In Fred M. Cox, John L. Erlich, Jack Rothman, and John E. Tropman, Eds., *Strategies of Community Organization,* 4th ed. Itasca, IL: F. E. Peacock, 1987 (pp. 71–97).

Simons, Ronald, and Aigner, Stephen M. *Practice Principles: A Problem-Solving Approach to Social Work.* New York: Macmillan, 1985 (Chapters 2 and 3).

Siporin, Max. *Introduction to Social Work Practice.* New York: Macmillan, 1975 (Chapter 9, "Assessment").

Stiles, Evelyn, Donner, Susan, Giovannie, Jean, Lochte, Elizabeth, and Reetz, Rebecca. "Hear It Like It Is." *Social Casework* 53 (May 1972): 292–299.

Sundel, Martin, Raden, Norma, and Churchill, Sallie R. "Diagnosis in Group Work." In Paul Glasser, Rosemary Sarri, and Robert Vinter, Eds. *Individual Change Through Small Groups.* New York: Free Press, 1974 (pp. 105–125).

Tracy, Elizabeth M. "Identifying Social Support Resources of At-Risk Families." *Social Work* 35 (May 1990): 252–258.

Tracy, Elizabeth M., and Whittaker, James K. "The Social Network Map: Assessing Social Support in Clinical Practice." *Families in Society* 71 (October 1971): 461–470.

Vigilante, Florence Wexler, and Marlick, Mildred D. "Needs-Resource Evaluation in the Assessment Process." *Social Work* 33 (March–April 1988): 101–104.

Weick, Ann, Rapp, Charles, Sullivan, W. Patrick, and Kisthardt, Walter. "A Strengths Perspective for Social Work Practice." *Social Work* 34 (July 1989): 350–354.

Ziter, Mary Lou. "Culturally Sensitive Treatment of Black Alcoholic Families." *Social Work* 32 (March–April 1987): 130–135.

NOTES

1. Max Siporin, *Introduction to Social Work Practice* (New York: Macmillan, 1975), p. 219.

2. Mark A. Mattaini and Stuart A. Kirk, "Assessing Assessment in Social Work," *Social Work* 36 (May 1991): 260–266.

3. Ann Weick, Charles Rapp, W. Patrick Sullivan, and Walter Kisthardt, "A Strengths Perspective for Social Work Practice," *Social Work* 34 (July 1989): 350–354; and Florence Wexler Vigilante and Mildred Maileck, "Needs-Resource Evaluation in the Assessment Process," *Social Work* 33 (March–April 1988): 101–104.

4. Harriet Bartlett, *The Common Base of Social Work Practice* (New York: National Association of Social Workers, 1970), p. 159.

5. Harriet A. Feiner and Harriet Katz, "Stronger Women—Stronger Families," *Affilia* 1 (Winter 1986): 49–57.

6. Adapted from Florence Hollis, "And What Shall We Teach? Social Work Education and Knowledge," *Social Service Review* 42 (June 1968): 184–196.

7. Mary K. Rodwell. "Naturalistic Inquiry: An Alternative Model for Social Work Assessment." *Social Service Review* 61 (June 1987): 231–246.

8. Carel B. Germain and Alex Gitterman, *The Life Model of Social Work Practice* (New York: Columbia University Press, 1980), chap. 1.

9. Helen Northen, "Assessment in Direct Practice," in Anne Minahan, Ed. *Encyclopedia of Social Work,* 18th ed. (Silver Spring, MD: National Association of Social Workers, 1987), pp. 171–183.

10. Weick, Rapp, Sullivan, and Kisthardt, "A Strengths Perspective. "

11. Paula Allen-Meares and Bruce A. Lane, "Grounding Social Work Practice in Theory: Ecosystems," *Social Casework* 68 (November 1987): 315–321.

12. Dolores Norton, *The Dual Perspective* (New York: Council on Social Work Education, 1978), p. 3. Also see Dolores G. Norton, "Diversity, Early Socialization, and Temporal Development: The Dual Perspective Revisited," *Social Work* 38 (January 1993): 82–90.

13. Sonia Badillo Ghali, "Culture Sensitivity and the Puerto Rican Client," *Social Casework* 58 (October 1977): 459–468.

14. Ann Hartman and Joan Laird, *Family-Centered Social Work Practice* (New York: Free Press, 1983), chap. 11.

15. Elizabeth M. Tracy, "Identifying Social Support Resources of At-Risk Families," *Social Work* 35 (May 1990): 252–258; and Elizabeth M. Tracy and James K. Whittaker, "The Social Network Map: Assessing Social Support in Clinical Practice," *Families in Society* 71 (October 1990): 461–470.

16. Also see Charles Froland, Diane L. Pancoast, Nancy J. Chapmen, and Priscilla J. Kimboko, *Helping Networks and Human Services* (Beverly Hills, CA: Sage Publications, 1981); and James K. Whittaker and James Garbarino, *Social Support Networks: Informal Helping in the Human Services* (New York: Aldine Publishing Co., 1983).

17. Kurt Finsterbusch and C. P. Wolf, *Methodology of Social Impact Assessment* (Stroudberry, PA: Dowden, Hutchinson and Ross, 1977).

12

PLANNING

Learning Expectations

1. An understanding of the nature of strategic thinking in the planning process.
2. Skill in planning.
3. An understanding of the nature of goals in social work and skill in developing goals and objectives.
4. Skill in choosing units of attention.
5. Skill in identifying strategies to use in specific practice situations. This includes choice of roles and tasks.
6. An understanding of the factors that affect a plan of action and skill in identification of the impact of these factors on the specific practice situations.
7. An understanding of the nature of the contract in social work practice and of the skill needed to negotiate a contract.
8. Skill in identifying resources for use in planning.

Planning is the bridge between assessment and activity focused on change. Often it is seen as a part of the assessment process. Although planning considerations are important in assessment, the emphasis at that stage is on assessing possible planning resources. Planning and assessment are both such important aspects of the total process that each deserves separate consideration. Planning is based on assessment and is the outcome of assessment. It is part of the problem-solving process, and as such it cannot be separated from other aspects of the generalist social work process except for study purposes. Planning is based on deliberate rational choices and thus involves judgments about a range of possibilities.

The assessment process develops understanding of the person in the situation and identifies potential resources. The planning process translates the assessment content into a goal statement that describes the desired results. It also is concerned with identifying the means to reaching goals, which includes identifying the focal system or unit of attention and the strategies, roles, and tasks to be used. It sequences tasks, specifies a time frame, and considers the costs involved.

Planning, when related to social functioning, involves activity designed to enhance people's growth potential and adaptive capacity. It also is designed to increase the capacity of environments to respond to people's needs and problems in social functioning.

Strategic thinking is the cognitive source of the plan. This implies a complicated process of developing a plan with parts that fit together, not by chance, but by choice. It considers alternatives, evaluates their usefulness, and predicts outcomes of each. Through the problem-solving process a plan is developed that is a synthesis of several plans. The plan considers both process and outcomes by specifying intermediate objectives as well as end goals.

Planning is a skill. The specification of this phase of the generalist social work process at first view seems straightforward and simple, but this is not the case. The work of the process calls for a complex set of decisions. These decisions are informed by a broad body of knowledge about the nature of human systems and their functioning and of possible interventive strategies. In addition, social work, client, and community values must be considered. The worker's experiences in similar situations also inform the decisions. Planning moves from problem definition to seeking problem solution; it links purpose to action. Intervention into the transactions between people and social systems is the context of planning. The end goal is planned change. The plan is composed of specified, interrelated parts that have a logical relationship. The reason for each action is specified. An often used way of involving the client or clients in the planning process is through use of a contract. The contract specifies agreed upon goals and the responsibilities of both worker and client in work aimed toward goal attainment.

Because of the nature of the human condition and the complexity of the social situation, it is virtually impossible to predict with certainty the outcome of a plan. However, a well-developed plan—one developed with flexibility for change as the process develops—has a better chance of the desired outcome than action not based on such a process. Planning does make it possible to predict probable outcomes and consequences.

A plan specifies the reason for each component and action in the plan. Accountability has become very important in social work practice. A well-developed plan that specifies what is to be done and why it is to be done is a means of fulfilling the responsibility for accountability to clients, agencies, and the supporting public.

COMPONENTS OF A PLAN

Because a **plan of action** relates to a complex human situation dealt with over time, identification of the components of a plan helps to manage the complexity of the plan. One formulation of a plan specifies three components: goals and objectives, units of attention, and strategies that include the roles of worker and client and the tasks to be performed.

Goals and Objectives

The **goal** is the overall, long-range expected outcome of the endeavor. Because of the complexity of the overall plan, this goal is usually reached only after intermediate goals or **objectives** have been attained. These objectives may relate to several different persons or social systems involved in the situation. Goals and objectives develop out of assessment related to the need or needs of the various systems involved and the identifications of the blockage or blockages to need fulfillment. They are generally related to the removal of a blockage or to developing new means of need fulfillment, or to developing means for coping to fulfill needs with situations so as to enhance social functioning.

When developing goals, one danger rests in setting goals that are too broad and general. Broad goals do not lead to the precision that is possible when the objectives are more specific. It is helpful to specify a rather general goal that is a statement of the desired end state; then develop specific short-term objectives. These short-term objectives can be placed in a time order to facilitate a plan; that is, the first objective must be reached before working on the second and third objectives. Objectives can relate to a specific desired change of individuals or social systems involved in the total situation. In effect, a mini-plan, or a plan within a plan, is developed. This approach allows for evaluation of the progress toward the general goal and for adjusting the plan in progress because of change in the situation or previously unrecognized influences and consequences.

Care must be taken to express the objectives in terms of the behavioral outcome desired rather than of how the goal will be reached. Also, each goal and objective should have a specified date for its accomplishment. For example, in setting a goal for Mrs. C, a chronically mentally ill woman, the goal could be stated: Mrs. C will live in her own apartment by December 1. Objectives for reaching this goal could include 1) Mrs. C will be able to manage her own personal hygiene by August 1, 2) Mrs. C will be responsible for taking her medication by September 1, 3) Mrs. C will attend classes in home management September 1 to November 15, and 4) Staff and Mrs. C will find a suitable apartment by December 1. Other objectives would also be identified in this situation. Goals and objectives established in this way give direction to the work to be done by both the worker and the client. Goals and objectives should be specific, concrete, and measurable, if possible.

Goals should be reasonably feasible; that is, there should be a good chance of reaching them. In thinking about feasibility, consideration needs to be given to time and energy factors. Some of the questions that should be asked are: Do the worker and the client have the time available to work toward the specified goals? Is sufficient energy available to work toward the goals? Are the needed resources available? Wherever possible it is wise to state goals in positive rather than negative terms. That is, goals should be stated as "John will" rather than "John will not."

Clients can often be most helpful in evaluating the feasibility of a goal, thus they should be involved in setting goals. The setting of the goals can often motivate a client for the work needed to reach that goal. As clients see small goals reached, they can gain hope for reaching the overall goals. This, of course, enables clients by giving hope and teaching means for dealing with other problems.

As with all decisions in the social work process, decisions regarding goals are influenced by value judgments. The choice of goals or end states is based on what is desirable. What is desirable is a value judgment. Social work values also influence the means to the end, or the process and the objectives involved in the process. Because persons are seen as having the right to make decisions about themselves, workers will not use means in reaching goals that go against the client's desires and values. Workers should respect lifestyle and cultural factors in the development of goals and objectives. The worker should constantly evaluate whether or not the chosen goals are appropriate. There also must be flexibility to adjust the goals to changing situations as the plan is implemented.

Different situations call for different kinds of change and different kinds of goals. Kinds of change that should be considered are:

1. *A sustaining relationship*—used when it appears that there is no chance to change the person in the situation and when the person lacks a significant other who can give needed support;

2. *Specific behavioral change*—used when a client is troubled by a specific symptom or behavior pattern and is generally otherwise satisfied with his or her situation;

3. *Relationship change*—used when the problem is a troublesome relationship or there is recognition that another person is a part of the problem;

4. *Environmental change*—used when it is recognized that a part of the problem is the lack of responsiveness of some segment of the environment and there is a possibility of bringing about such a change; and

5. *Directional change*—used when values are conflicting or unclear, when a client system is unclear about goals or direction of effort, or when aspirations are blocked in a manner that makes unblocking very difficult or impossible.

When setting goals, it is important to consider expectations of the client, significant others in the client's environment, and of the worker. These three sets of goals may be different because each party may see the situation differently or may have identified the need differently. The consistency and inconsistency among these goals must be identified and some reconciliation obtained. The client's goals are to be considered of prime importance, with the worker pointing out to the client the environmental expectations and the consequences of not meeting these expectations. The worker's goals can be discussed and incorporated or discarded as jointly determined by the worker and the client.

In summary, goals and objectives should relate to meeting a need or solving a problem. They should be stated in terms of an outcome, be specific, and be measurable. They should be feasible and positive in direction and developed with the client to reflect the client's desires.

Units of Attention

The unit of attention, or focal system, is the system being focused upon. This is generally in relation to the overall goals, but there may be different units of attention in relation to specific objectives. A unit of attention is either a person or a social system. It may be the client or a significant influence on the situation. In other words, units of attention are systems that are the focus of the change activity.

The unit of attention can be an individual client; it can be several clients (a small group) working on a common problem or on similar individual problems; it can be an individual who in some way is impacting on the client and her problem; or it can be a group of persons in a community concerned about services to meet the needs of a category of clients.[1]

As the change process is divided into activity related to more specific objectives, several objectives and mini-plans are often worked on at the same time. It is important to specify the specific unit of attention related to each mini-plan. For example, the overall goal may be one of a particular kind of desirable living situation for a client. It may be necessary to have an objective that relates to understanding the client's situation. To develop this understanding, the focal system may be the client or the present landlord as a source of needed information. Another objective may be that a potential landlord be prepared to meet the special needs of the client. The potential landlord then becomes a focal system. Other objectives may relate to the provision of service by certain community service agencies. These agencies also become units of attention.

Units of attention may be individuals, family groups, small groups of unrelated persons, organizations, or communities. Table 12–1 gives some indications and counter-indications for the choice of each kind of system. It is important to specify appropriate units of attention for every goal and objective. Units of attention may be clients or other persons and social systems involved in the situation.

Strategy

Strategy is an overall approach to change in the situation. It contains roles for worker and client, tasks to be done by each, and methods and techniques to use. It has been defined as "an orchestrated attempt to influence persons or systems in relation to some goals."[2] The term originated in a military context and relates to a battle plan. It also is used in a game context. Action in the game depends on the action of others, as contrasted with "games of chance." There is an implication

TABLE 12–1   Indications and Counterindications with Units of Attention

	Indications	Counterindications
Individuals	Information giving. Information gathering. Concrete service. Referral service. Need relates primarily to an individual without significant family. No other involvement feasible. Intrapsychic problems. Individual who with help can involve significant systems in problem solving and the change process Individual choice.	Cannot function in a one-to-one helping relationship. Action-oriented service needed. Focus on interactional aspects of family or peer group needed. Need fulfillment best reached by change in larger system.
Family	Major problem seems to exist in family interaction. One family member undercuts change efforts of other members. Individual dysfunction is symptom of family problem. Need for understanding family interaction to understand individual functioning. Family needs to examine role functioning or communication. Chaotic families where there is a need to restore order. Family choice.	Irreversible trend toward family breakup. Where significant impairment of individual family member prevents participation. Where the need for individual help precludes work with family. Where there is no common concern or goal. Where the worker cannot deal with destructive interactions.
Small group	Individuals face similar situations and can benefit from interchange. Group influence on the individual is great. Development of socialization skills is indicated. Use of activity is desirable. Focus on environmental change. Usable natural groups.	Individual overwhelmed by the group. Individual destructive to group. A common purpose or goal does not exist. Sufficient cohesive factors do not exist. The environment will not allow the group to function. The environment will not allow the group to reach its goal to at least some extent.
Organization	Problem related to organizational functioning. Number of individuals are affected, and needs are not being met because of organizational factors. Workers are overconstrained from providing service to clients.	The dangers of further negative results to clients are great. Client service will be neglected or negated.
Community	Lack of needed resources and services. Lack of coordination of services. Community influence on organization or family prevents meeting of need. Community functioning is affecting a large number of individuals and families negatively.	Same as organization.

of multiple cause. Action is dependent on the action of others; that is, there is anticipation and assessment of the actions and reactions of others rather than reliance on independent action. There is a recognition of the transactional nature of human social functioning.

When a general strategy is used in many situations it gains a name. Some that have been identified are *consensus strategy, conflict strategy, demonstration strategy,* and *bargaining strategy.* Social work has developed a variety of approaches to practice. These may be called theories of practice or models of practice. These conceptualizations of practice (e.g., crisis intervention, conjoint family therapy, locality development) provide an overall approach to practice and thus may be considered as strategies.

Some strategies provide a philosophic approach to the situation. For example, a social action approach assumes a lack of balance in the power structure and assumes that a conflict strategy must be used to redistribute the power. Value judgments as to the desirability of power redistribution in part guide the choice of this strategy. Other strategies have a theoretical base. The socialization model based in socialization theory is an example of this. Most strategies have both value assumptions and knowledge assumptions. They also have identifiable practice theory. Strategies are one means of tying the knowledge and value aspects of practice to the action. (See the Appendix for summaries of often-used strategies or models of practice.)

In choosing strategies it is important for the worker to decide if the value and knowledge base of a particular strategy are congruent to his own values and view of people. It is also important for the worker to determine if he possesses the knowledge called for in using the strategy. Another decision is to determine if the values, explicit and implicit, in the strategy are congruent with those of the client and her situation.

Strategies should have the capacity not only of meeting the client's need but also be in keeping with the client's lifestyle. Much has been written about the understanding of minority clients and their culture and of the necessity of this understanding for service to the minority client. This literature supports decisions that match the helping to the lifestyle of the client.

For example, in discussing services for blacks and Puerto Ricans, Mizio and Delaney indicate that it is important to use strategies that recognize the impact of racism and discrimination as they impact the lives of minority people. They believe this calls for the use of advocacy as a core strategy and the use of counseling strategies based on ecological and systems knowledge.[3] The author's Native American students indicate that Siporin's situational approach and the functional approach are appropriate for their culture. (See the Appendix for summary of these two approaches.)

Different strategies and different kinds of service call for the social worker to fill different roles. The term *role* is being used here in a somewhat different manner from the strict pattern-of-behaviors sense. Rather, the definition used is that of Robert Teare and Harold McPheeters: "A cluster of altruistic activities that are performed toward a common objective [goal]."[4] The role is the way the worker uses self in the specific helping situation. Role is further dependent on the function of the worker and the particular agency offering the service and its function. For example, in a short-term, crisis-focused service the caregiver role will be minimally used, whereas in a nursing home this may be an often-used role.

Teare and McPheeters have identified twelve roles that may be part of the generalist repertoire that social workers fill:

1. *Outreach worker*—Identifying need by reaching out to clients in the community. Usually involves referral to services.
2. *Broker*—Enabling persons to reach appropriate services by providing information, after assessing need of individual and nature of resources. Also includes contact and follow-up.
3. *Advocate*—Helping clients obtain services in situations in which they may be rejected. Helping expand services to persons having a particular need.
4. *Evaluation*—Gathering information and assessing client and/or community problems. Considering alternatives and planning for action.
5. *Teacher*—Teaching facts and skills.
6. *Behavior changer*—Activities aimed at specific behavior change.
7. *Mobilizer*—Helping to mobilize resources to develop new services or programs.
8. *Consultant*—Working with other professionals to increase their skill and understanding.
9. *Community planner*—Helping communities to plan for ways to meet human need.
10. *Caregiver*—Providing support and/or care to persons when problems cannot be resolved.
11. *Data manager*—Collecting and analyzing data used in decision making.
12. *Administrator*—Planning and implementing services and programs.[5]

There seems to be one additional role, that of coordination. The coordinator enables several social workers, other professionals, or other service providers to function so that services are provided in a synchronized manner. The coordinator sees that all involved are aware of and take into consideration the work of all others as they provide service. This role may also be identified as the *case manager role*. (This will be discussed in Chapter 13.) Another role which has emerged recently is the enabler role. (See Chapter 13 for a full discussion of enabling as a strategy.)

Ronald Simons and Stephen Aiger have discussed role choice in terms of client characteristics and needs.[6] The four client characteristics they see as important to consider when choosing the worker role are: 1) the needs and desires of the client, 2) the resources of the client, 3) the expectations of the client and of the worker regarding the client, and 4) the client's perceived expectations of the worker. While they define roles somewhat differently than do Teare and McPheeters, they identify particular situations and clients' problems in which particular roles are important. A lack of resources calls for the broker role; a lack of opportunity, the advocate role; role inadequacy, the teacher role; unrealistic role expectations or behavior, the confronter role; conflicting role expectations, the mediator role; role transition stress, an empathic listener; role indecision, the clarifier role.

Usually, role and task are discussed in relation to the worker and the worker's functioning. However, role implies action and interaction by and with the client—a reciprocal relationship. Thus, attention needs to be paid to the client's functioning and tasks in carrying out the plan. The plan should specify the role or roles of the worker and consider the reciprocal role of the client. The tasks to be completed by the client and the worker should be specified. **Task** is a specific action or activity; it is the specification of what needs to be done.

The strategy, including the role and task specification, is developed after tentative goals and units of attention relative to the goals have been identified. After the strategy has been identified, it is possible to develop the operational goal or goals and objectives and to become more specific about tasks. Tasks and objectives are often related.

The tasks that have been identified should be sequenced and a time for the completion of each established. This results in an overall time frame or *time line* for the service. It is also important to specify the resources needed to carry out the plan and to indicate how those resources are to be obtained. This would include the time investment of the worker and client. Any fiscal investment, such as client fees or agency funds, should be specified. Other needed resources could be the use of an agency or community facility or service or the inclusion of other persons in the action system.

The plan is always based on the information collected and the assessment of that information. It is always developed with the fullest possible participation of the client. The plan often results in a contract with the client outlining what the worker will do and what the client's responsibility in the endeavor is.

All plans of action should contain some mechanism for evaluating how well the goals of the plan were met. Evaluation, which is ongoing in the entire interventive process, is the focus of Chapter 15.

Plans should also contain some mechanism for specifying when various objectives are to be met or when specific tasks are to be completed. This can be as simple as specifying a date for the completion of each objective. When working on complex goals it is often useful to use a task-flow mechanism. Figure 12–1 shows an example of this type of time line.

The plan must be flexible. As the implementation of the plan progresses, new information or assessments may be added, which may result in a change of plan. The development of the plan may seem to call for a great deal of specifity. However, it is the belief of the author that such plans lead to service that is directed toward client needs and desires and that enhance accountability. They allow for a breadth of possible decisions about the components of the plan, a mark of generalist social work as developed in this text.

When developing plans of action, it is usually advisable to consider several different plans and make choices based on an analysis of each plan and its suitability for the specific situation. This involves considering strengths and limi-

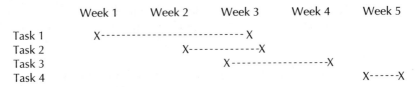

FIGURE 12–1   Time Line

tations of each plan. The chosen plan may be a synthesis of parts of several of the considered plans.

CASE EXAMPLE

Plan of Action

The school contacted the Community Services office because of problems they were having with Bob and John Smith, Jane Jones's children. They were also concerned because the children's clothing and cleanliness were deplorable and other children at school were picking on them for this.

Bob and John are Jane's children by a former marriage. She married Jerry Jones six years ago and they have had four more children, ages six months to five years. Jerry is reluctant to take an active role in parenting any of the children, but particularly Bob and John.

Because of the immediate need to sustain Bob and John in school, that problem was the immediate focus of the plan. After determining that no dangerous child abuse is present, other plans could focus on the family situation, especially the care of the children. Also considered was whether other children were having difficulty in school and the community because of attitudes toward children from families that deviate from accepted norms.

The Plan of Action:

Goal: Bob and John will not disrupt the classroom by misbehavior by April 15.

   Objective 1: The boys will come to school clean and dressed appropriately by March 30.

   Objective 2: The boys will not fight with classmates by April 15.

Unit of Attention: The school is the client in many ways, as it requested help with the children and for the family. The school has high expectations for the children, as the teachers do not understand the differences in family backgrounds. The school, as it is in many small communities, is one of the systems the town functions around and so follows the expectations and norms of the community. The school does have a good staff that can be used as a resource.

Bob and John are also the clients, or units of attention, as they are the ones causing the conflict. In many ways, the boys are bringing to school behavior that they use at home to get attention. They are also expected by their classmates to be the rowdy ones, and they have lived up to this expectation. The boys are average students and have responded to adults working with them before. They are fortunate in that their mother does care for her children very much and is willing to help with the boys.

Strategy: As for strategies, the social services worker, Maria, is an advocate for John, Bob, and their family at the school, as everyone seems to have given up hope that the situation can improve. Maria is using knowledge of child rearing to get Jane to try some new things with her children in regard to discipline and encouragement. Maria is using a teaching strategy and is also a mediator between Jane and the school. She is enabling Jane to parent the boys better.

Maria's tasks are to contact school personnel and talk with them about the problems at school, encouraging them and giving them suggestions about how they might work with the boys. Maria also can explain a little of the boys' background without violating the Joneses' right to privacy to help the teachers understand the problem a little better. Another task is to inform Jane of the problem and ask her to help with the cleanliness problem. It is Maria's task to encourage Jane and one of the teachers to get together and talk about the misbehavior at school. It is also her job to keep in touch with the school and Jane each week in case anything comes up that they can work on together. Maria feels she can influence the guidance counselor and teachers to have a more realistic understanding of the family's strengths and limitations and that this will affect how they treat the boys.

Jane's tasks are to check the boys each morning before school to make sure that they are leaving home clean. She has also agreed to keep their clothes a little cleaner and to meet with the guidance counselor. It is also her task to find out from the children what is happening at school and to encourage them to behave.

The teacher's tasks are to keep trying to motivate the boys and to support any improvement they make in behavior or cleanliness.

The guidance counselor's tasks are to work with the boys at school when they misbehave and to support them when they are doing well. It is also his task to help the boys trust him as an adult and a friend, to meet with Jane and talk with her about the boys, and to initiate some activities for Bob and John.

Bob's and John's tasks are to stay clean after they have washed in the morning until they get to school, to behave for their teacher, and to go to the guidance counselor or teacher when they need to talk.

The principal's tasks are to let Maria and/or Jane know if anything important happens in regard to the classroom and schoolyard behavior and to support the teacher's efforts with the boys.

The plan will be evaluated by observing whether the two objectives are met within the time framework noted in the objectives.

FACTORS AFFECTING A PLAN OF ACTION

Plans of action reflect the differential nature of social work. Each plan is specific to a situation and to the persons involved. Each plan of action, with its component parts, should be different from every other plan of action. It is important to specify not only the components of a plan but also the various factors that have affected the development of that plan. Five factors that have considerable influence on the plan are: 1) the community in which it is being carried out, 2) the agency sanctioning the plan, 3) the social problem that the plan is a response to, 4) the worker involved in the plan, and 5) the client involved in the plan.

The Community

The community as a system is an important influence on the differential plan of action. The client is a part of a community; as such, the client reflects its characteristics. The community has expectations for the client. Any plan of action needs to consider the environment in which the plan takes place. What is feasible in one community may not be feasible in another.

The culture of a community is important to consider in planning. Attitudes about receiving help are particularly important, as are accepted coping mechanisms. In communities where self-help and neighborliness are highly valued, the chosen plan of action may be one that strengthens and enables the natural helping system to function well rather than an extended casework service.

The community's service delivery system is another factor to be considered. An assumption is often made that the ideal service delivery system is that of a large urban community with many specialized services. This has led to the development of strategies for use in such situations. But these strategies are sometimes inappropriate for small nonmetropolitan settings where the service delivery system is different.[7]

The Agency

In considering the influence of the agency upon the plan of action, the worker is influenced by constraints and resources within the agency. Constraints may take the form of the kinds of service that can be offered, fiscal considerations, time priority factors, and the manner in which the agency is organized. Resources to be considered include people (staff expertise), structures, money, and expendable supplies that can be used by the worker and client to enhance the social work process or make goal realization possible. Skillful use of the agency system in service of the client is an important attribute of planning.

The agency is a component part of the community and as such it is an integral subunit of the community system. It is sanctioned by the community and thus must, at least in part, express its will. The agency is dependent upon the community for resources. Social agencies seldom function without financial support from the community, which may be in the form of contributions or taxation. Other kinds of resources and support are also vital to giving services to clients. Planning must take into consideration the influence of community needs, values, and intentions for the service being delivered by the agency. It is important for the planning process to recognize the influence of agency structure and functioning on service to clients. This recognition gives both the worker and the client a sense of realities involved in the provision of service.

The Social Problem

Societal attitudes and expectations about social problems vary. In sanctioning or developing means for problem control, amelioration, or prevention, these attitudes and expectations influence the task assigned to the agency structure. Some problems are seen as illness, some as deviance, and some as the result of environmental influences.

Elliot Studt has expressed this idea in her conceptualization of the *field of practice*. She sees "three organizing dimensions for describing a field of practice: social problem, social task, and social service system."[8] In thinking about the social problem it is helpful to consider why the problem concerns the community and other social systems. Important are such questions as: How does the problem affect the general welfare of the community? Why does a community see a need for action? What is the condition of central concern? Also important is how the problem affects the social functioning of individuals and families. As these questions are answered and as social policy and programs are developed, the social tasks related to the specific social problems develop. The social task is what the community sees as needing to be done in order to control the social problem. Social tasks also include work needed to be done in order to help the individual affected by the social problem. These tasks develop in part from the expectations of the various segments of the community: taxpayers, professionals, legislators, agents of social control, commercial interests, and so on. Thus, the social task is often unclear and made up of conflicting expectations. This is one of the reasons that accountability is difficult and that goal expectations are unclear.

For example, quite different attitudes are held about someone with a problem in social functioning that leads to breaking the law and someone whose problem in social functioning is the result of sudden illness. One enters the corrections field of practice; the other the health field of practice. Social control concerns are greater in the corrections field; thus, punishment is often the expected strategy. The strategy used must protect the community from further threat of danger from lawbreaking. Treatment of illness is the prime concern in the medical setting, and concern with social functioning is always in relationship to the illness. Society has considerable compassion for the person whose social-functioning problems arise from sudden illness. The strategy chosen must allow for the treatment of the illness and provide means for coping with the resulting problems in social functioning. Social policy is often a reflection of societal concerns and attitudes about social problems. Relevant social policy must always be considered in developing plans of action. Societal and individual attitudes toward the social problem related to the problems being worked on by the worker and client are important influences on the planning process.

The Worker

Each worker is first a unique person. The worker's primary tool is the self. The worker brings herself as a person, as a professional, as an agency employee, and as a member of the community to the social work endeavor. The self is another factor influencing the plan of action.

Because of workers' individuality, because there is no one theory about the human situation, and because there is no one way to achieve social work goals, workers have preferences as to how they explain the human situation and how they prefer to practice social work. One worker may find ego psychology a helpful theory and use psychosocial casework extensively. Another worker may use a more eclectic theory base and find problem-solving social work and reme-dial group work useful. Plans of action, though developed by worker and client together, reflect the worker's preferences, priorities, and skills.

As an agency employee, the worker is both constrained and supported. The worker is responsible and accountable to the agency for her work. The worker must function within the agency structure and is interdependent with others employed by the agency. As a member of the community, the worker is subject to pressures from that community. The worker's preferences and influences on the worker from both the agency and the community also affect the planning process.

The Client

The client in his uniqueness brings much to the worker-client interaction. The client comes from a community, a neighborhood, a particular diverse group, and a particular family. The client brings the biological, psychosocial, spiritual being. The client has a self-image, roles in family and community, values, hopes, and expectations. The client has rights—the right to service, the right to participate, the right to fail. The client carries a reference group's expectations as well as the results of interactions with meaningful persons in meaningful situations. The client has strengths, modes of adaptation, and ways of coping. The client brings a particular set of motivations, capacities, and opportunities. The uniqueness will support some interventive strategies and mitigate against others. Even more important, the client will have unique expectations and goals for the service. The client may have preferences about the way of working on the problem with the worker. The client's need is unique, and the plan must be unique in its response to that need.

The client's role in the plan depends on several factors. Among these factors are the client's roles in his life situation (parent, child, employee, etc.), the client's role in the agency or organization (patient, inmate, student, etc.), and the role the worker has chosen (the client's must be reciprocal to it). The client is a vital part of the factors influencing the plan of action.

CASE EXAMPLE

Before working on a plan for the Joneses, Maria had to take into consideration the ABS School System and the community. The town of Abbott is very small and quite conserva-tive, and everyone knows everyone else's business. There is only one other family in town of the same economic and social status as the Joneses; the family sticks out like a sore thumb. Most Abbott citizens are working-class, middle-income people who do not under-stand problems arising from a small income supporting a large family. The community frowns on the type of entertainment the Joneses seek and expects the children to dress the same as other children and to act in an accepted manner. Community persons have bad feelings toward the family. They do not really expect the children to achieve. They disap-prove of the Joneses' house and yard, the way the children are disciplined, and the general methods of child rearing. The problem of the boys' behavior at school affects the classroom because it disrupts the class. The other children probably also go home and talk about the children's antics at school, thereby causing the town to have worse feelings toward the Smith children. If they are dirty and smell badly, the other children do not want to play with them or associate with them when they are mischievous. This adds to the problem, as the children need peer interaction and acceptance. Although there seem to be some good-hearted people in the community who would like to help this family, they want to help the Joneses to be like the rest of the Abbott people.

The Community Services office has had contact with this family before. It is their responsibility to intervene when a child is being neglected physically or emotionally. Because it is a state agency and supported by taxpayers' money, many people in the community feel that there are no limits as to what a social services agency can do to or with a client. They seem to feel that it would take only a snap of the fingers to take the children out of the family and place them with foster parents. It is the agency's desire to support this family and keep them united. As a worker in this agency, Maria felt that she could draw on others' experiences with this family and the Abbott community to know how to go about helping the school and the family. Because they are under state and federal regulations, workers need to comply with the laws that are written to protect the family's and the school's interests.

The worker's contribution to this situation is her knowledge base and her ability to interact with various persons in the community.

AGREEMENT BETWEEN WORKER AND CLIENT

When the worker and client have worked together in assessment and in developing the plan of action, an *agreement* develops between them as to what needs to be done and who should do it. This agreement may take the form of a contract. This **contract** may merely be an understanding between worker and client; or it may be a formal, written, signed agreement. The form the agreement takes will be dependent in part on what is best for a particular client and in part on agency practice and policy.

Contracting is an accepted part of the worker-client interaction in many agencies. Recently, however, the use of contracts has been challenged in two ways. Pamela Miller believes the use of contracts fails to recognize that the service provider is a professional using empathy as an important ingredient of the service. She calls for a covenant approach, which implies that the worker has a gift of service for the client.[9]

Tom Croxton has pointed out that the use of *contract* is inaccurate as it is used in social work because its use lacks an important ingredient—the legal implications. He believes this inaccurate use can lead to misunderstandings, vagueness, and even conflict.[10]

Given these points of view, rather than using *contract* as the term for the final expression for the plan for use as agreed upon by the worker and client, an overarching term, *agreement,* may best describe the worker-client decision. However, *contract,* as used in social work, has never been defined as a legal contract. The concept as developed in social work literature seems best to describe the agreement about the plan in the generalist social work approach presented in this book. It can be thought of as an understanding between the worker and the client as to the work to be done. It is not necessarily a written document, though in some situations this is the case.

A contract, as used in social work, is a promissory agreement between people. It implies agreement and mutuality about what is to be done, influences the nature of the interaction between those persons, and considers the transactional nature of the interaction. It should be as specific and clear as possible.

The use of contracts became a part of social work practice during the 1970s, brought about by a growing acceptance of the necessity for agreement between the worker and the client about the work together. As the practice of involving the client in the assessment phase of the process developed, the necessity of involving the client in planning also developed. The use of contracts is an outgrowth of these trends.

The client's role was changing from passive (one in which something was done to or for a client) to active (one in which the worker and client participate together). As worker and client worked together on a more mutual basis, some agreement about what was to take place naturally became necessary. The use of contracts was supported by the tendency toward short-term and goal-oriented practice. Task-centered and behaviorally oriented models of practice also provided techniques for the development of contracts.

The push for accountability has also encouraged the use of contracts. Substantiating that contracts have been fulfilled has become one method for demonstrating what can happen in the social work endeavor. Contracts add specificity about what takes place in situations in which considerable ambiguity once existed.

Contracts are essentially plans of action. They arise from a mutual determination of needs, blocks to need fulfillment, and problems. The mutual work includes prioritization of needs or problems to be worked on, a specification of the change needed, and an outlining of the methods to be used in working toward that change. The contract includes a problem statement, goals and objectives (the desired change and steps in reaching that change), and a specification of tasks to be carried out by worker and client. It also contains a time frame for carrying out tasks and meeting goals and objectives.

The contract has a slightly different form from a plan of action as presented earlier in this chapter. The plan of action represents the worker's thinking and is more complex than the contract developed with the client. The two, however, must be congruent. The contract is a simplification of the plan of action.

The contract is not a legal document. It is binding only within the worker-client relationship and thus is only valid to that relationship. Also, it contains more flexibility than a legal document for it can be changed by agreement between the worker and the client. This flexibility is essential if indicated changes in plans of action are to take place when new information is identified that points to a need for a change in the plan of action and the contract.

Theodore Stein has suggested that there are two parts to every contract. The first part specifies the client's objectives, the goals for the service, a statement of agreement by the worker with the client's objectives, a statement of potential consequences of the service, and a time limit. The second part is a specification of treatment methods. It includes steps to be taken, tasks of the client and others who may be involved, environmental resources, and the role of the worker.[11] This represents another way of writing a contract.

The use of contracts in social work enhances the motivation of many clients for work on problems and tasks because it gives structure, specificity, and a sense of participation to the client. The reaching of agreed upon goals and objectives through the client's own actions (at least in part) enhances self-esteem and the sense of being able to affect a situation. The choices involved in developing a plan give clients a sense of some control over their problem and situation.

Clients should understand all parts of the plan or contract. They need to know explicitly what their responsibility is in carrying out the plan. It is particularly important to help clients understand the transactional nature of situations. They need to understand how the unanticipated outcomes and implications for outcomes can affect and be affected by community, agency, and other persons and systems related to the situation at hand. Attitudes, values, policies, and ways of functioning are all important when considering spinoffs and implications of change efforts. It is also important that the client understand the implications of completion or noncompletion of the contract.

The worker should identify disagreements between self and the client. These disagreements should include those that are actual, potential, and latent. The worker must develop skill in negotiating to resolve disagreement as a part of the planning or contracting process. The worker should remember that the client's wishes have precedence whenever possible. It is the worker's responsibility to help the client do what she wants to do and what she cannot do without help. When workers have hidden agendas the client can become confused about responses received from workers and their work together can be jeopardized.

So far our discussion has been about contracts with individual clients. When working with multiperson situations, such as a small group, family, or community group, the same principles are used. The major difference is that agreement about goals and what is to be done must take place between all the persons involved. For example, when working with a husband and wife, the worker would ask each to identify what he or she sees as the problem and then the worker would help both of them negotiate an agreement as to what the problem is, giving input as appropriate. All would then move to identification of goals and methods. When working with a therapy group, the worker first identifies needs, problems, and goals with each member individually. At the group's first meeting these are shared and commonality is identified. From this commonality a contract between members of the group and between the group and the worker can be developed through group discussion.

Contracts are easiest to develop with motivated, trusting clients. They are very useful with disorganized or forgetful clients who need reminding about the work to be done or their responsibility for carrying out tasks. Sometimes contracts are more effective if written, but sometimes this is not necessary or even desirable. For the resistant or distrustful client the signed paper may be a barrier, while a verbal commitment would be a help. For clients in crisis it may be best to quickly get to the work of helping and delay or eliminate the development of a formal contract. A quick verbal agreement may be all that is necessary. The contract should be flexible and appropriate to the specific client and situation. It should be a tool to enhance the work together, not a mechanistic procedure to fulfill some outside, imposed requirement.

Planning and contracting are means for making clear the who, what, why, and how of the social work endeavor. They are means for individualizing the social work process to the person in the situation. They provide tools for accountability and evaluation. Planning and contracting tie knowledge about the person in the situation to the work of doing something to change the situation for the client. Planning expands opportunity for accomplishing the desired change.

CASE EXAMPLE

Name: Jane Jones
Problem to be worked on: Appearance of sons, Bob and John.
Goal: John and Bob will arrive at school in clothes that are clean and mended by April 15. These clothes will be appropriate for school.
Objectives: 1. Jane will wash school clothes twice a week by March 15.
2. Jane will have obtained four appropriate sets of school clothes for Bob and John by April 1.
3. Jane will mend usable school clothes so there are no tears or missing buttons by April 15.
Worker's tasks: 1. Discuss with Jane ways to take care of Bob's and John's school clothes by March 15.
2. Work with Jane to make a list of clothes the boys need for school by March 20.
3. Accompany Jane to used clothing store on March 30.
4. Evaluate with Jane progress made in reaching the goal on April 15.
Jane's tasks: 1. Gather together and inspect Bob's and John's school clothes. Sort into three piles: those that are not able to be repaired, those that can be mended, those that need no repairs and are usable by March 15.
2. With worker make a list of the clothes that the boys need in order to have four changes for school by March 20.
3. Wash all clothes that are usable by March 20.
4. Set up a weekly routine for caring for Bob's and John's clothes so they always have a clean set by March 20.
5. Establish a separate place for storing clean and dirty school clothes by March 20.
6. Go to used clothing store and obtain needed clothing using developed list. Worker will accompany on March 30.
7. Mend clothes that need it by April 15.
8. Evaluate the progress made with the worker on April 15.
SIGNED: Worker: Maria Smith   Client: Jane Jones
Date: March 1

SUMMARY

The following principles for developing a plan of action can give guidance to the planning process:

1. Each plan of action is a part of an overall social work process. This implies:
   - It is based on personal-social need.
   - It is developed through a problem-solving process.
   - It is dynamic, changing as new knowledge leads to reassessment of situations; reformulation of need and problem; and new goals strategies and tasks.
2. Each plan of action should clearly indicate:
   - The goal toward which it is aimed. This goal should be directly related to personal-social need. Objectives should be clearly stated.
   - The unit(s) of attention that are included in the plan.
   - The strategy to be used and the role of worker, client, and others and the tasks to be performed by all concerned.
3. The plan of action takes into consideration the community in which the action system functions. This would involve the awareness of community expectations, norms, values, service delivery system, and resources.
4. The plan of action reflects the agency or organization "way of doing business." Community influences and agency organization structure, functioning, and development all contribute to this "way of doing business."
5. The nature of the social problem is recognized as an important variable in the development of the plan of action.
6. The worker's contribution to the plan of action is based on professional knowledge, values, and skill. It involves ability to assess and determine the usefulness of various resources, as well as the capacity for professional judgment, and to make appropriate choices from among various possibilities.
7. The client brings uniqueness to the situation. This includes a perception of the need and the problem, a set of values, unique motivation, capacity, opportunity, and goals.
8. The plan of action is the outgrowth of the worker-client interaction. Each contributes from his or her perspective regarding the client in the situation. Planning sometimes results in a contract between worker and client.
9. The plan of action considers the availability of the resources needed to carry out the plan and the feasibility of reaching the goals.
10. The plan of action contains a time line.
11. The plan contains a means for evaluation.

The plan of action is a dynamic concept. No plan is developed as *the plan;* rather, there is an overall plan that changes as the work progresses. This plan develops as worker and client interact in a joint endeavor. There are many plans within plans.

QUESTIONS

1. Set a goal for yourself that you can reach in a week. Write it in outcome terms and identify three objectives that relate to the goal.

2. Discuss the difference between process, method, and goals.

3. What do you see as the advantages of being very clear about the identification of the unit of attention?

4. With three of the roles identified by Teare and McPheeters, discuss the complementary client role and possible tasks for client and worker.

5. In developing a plan of action for a client, discuss some considerations that exist in a community with which you are familiar.

6. What are the implications for planning for a young person who has engaged in destructive behavior if he or she has been labeled as delinquent? As mentally ill? Discuss differences in planning under the two circumstances.

7. What are some ways for developing a contract with a resistant client?

SUGGESTED READINGS

Chau, Kenneth L. "Social Cultural Dissonance Among Ethnic Minority Populations." *Social Casework* 7 (April 1989): 224–230.

Cox, Fred M. "Community Problem Solving: A Guide to Practice with Comments." In Fred M. Cox, John L. Erlich, Jack Rothman, and John E. Tropman, Eds. *Strategies of Community Organization,* 4th ed. Itasca, IL: F. E. Peacock, 1987 (pp. 150–167).

Cox, Fred M., Erlich, John L., Rothman, Jack, and Tropman, John E. *Strategies of Community Organization,* 4th ed. Itasca, IL: F. E. Peacock, 1987 (Part III, "Strategies").

Croxton, Tom A. "Caveats on Contract." *Social Work* 34 (March–April 1988): 169–171.

Miller, Pamela. "Covenant Model for Professional Relationships: An Alternative to the Contract Model." *Social Work* 35 (March 1990): 121–125.

Mizio, Emelicia, and Delaney, Anita J., Eds. *Training for Service Delivery to Minority Clients.* New York: Family Service Association of America, 1981.

Parsons, Ruth J., Hernadex, Santos H., and Jorgensen, James D. "Integrated Practice: A Framework for Problem Solving." *Social Work* 33 (September–October 1988): 417–421.

Rosen, Aaron, Proctor, Enola K., and Livne, Shula. "Planning and Direct Practice." *Social Service Review* 59 (June 1985): 161–177.

Seabury, Brett A. "Contracting and Engagement in Direct Practice." In Anne Minahan, Ed., *Encyclopedia of Social Work,* 18th ed. Silver Springs, MD: National Association of Social Workers, 1987 (Vol. I, pp. 339–344).

Sheafor, Bradford W., Horejsi, Charles R., and Horejsi, Gloria A. *Techniques and Guidelines for Social Work Practice.* Boston: Allyn and Bacon, 1988 (Chapter 11 and pp. 426–430).

Simons, Ronald L., and Aigner, Stephen M. *Practice Principles: A Problem-Solving Approach to Social Work.* New York: Macmillan, 1985 (Chapter 4).

Zayas, Luis H., and Katch, Michael. "Contracting with Adolescents: An Ego-Psychological Approach." *Social Casework* 70 (January 1989): 3–9.

NOTES

1. This formulation is similar but not identical to a format developed by Ruth R. Middleman and Gale Goldberg, *Social Service Delivery: A Structural Approach to Social Work Practice* (New York: Columbia University Press, 1974), chap. 1, "A Frame of Reference."

2. Fred M. Cox, John L. Erlich, Jack Rothman, and John E. Tropman, Eds., *Strategies of Community Organization,* 4th ed. (Itasca, IL: F. E. Peacock, 1987), p. 258.

3. Emelicia Mizio and Anita J. Delaney, Eds., *Training for Service Delivery to Minority Clients* (New York: Family Service Association of America, 1981).

4. Robert J. Teare and Harold L. McPheeters, *Manpower Utilization in Social Welfare* (Atlanta, GA: Southern Regional Education Board, 1970), p. 34.

5. Ibid.

6. Ronald L. Simons and Stephen M. Aiger, "Facilitating an Eclectic Use of Practice Theory," *Social Casework* 60 (April 1979): 201–208.

7. For a discussion of nonmetropolitan service delivery, see Louise C. Johnson, "Human Service Delivery Patterns in Non-Metropolitan Communities." in H. Wayne Johnson, Ed., *Rural Human Services: A Book of Readings* (Itasca, IL: F. E. Peacock, 1980), pp. 55–64.

8. Elliot Studt, *A Conceptual Approach to Teaching Materials* (New York: Council on Social Work Education, 1965), pp. 4–18.

9. Pamela Miller, "Covenant Model for Professional Relationships: An Alternative to the Contract Model," *Social Work* 35 (March 1990): 121–125.

10. Tom A. Croxton, "Caveats on Contract," *Social Work* 34 (March–April 1988): 169–171.

11. Theodore J. Stein, Eileen D. Gambrill, and Kermit T. Wiltse, "Foster Care: The Use of Contracts," *Public Welfare* 32 (Fall 1974): 20–25.

13

DIRECT PRACTICE ACTIONS

Learning Expectations

1. An understanding of the need to match the action taken to the needs of the client.
2. A knowledge of the various kinds of action that may be used to help clients.
3. An understanding of principles that should be used in making choices about the action to be taken.
4. An understanding of how to enable clients to use available resources.
5. An understanding of strategies for empowering clients.
6. A knowledge of the range of resources that can be used to help clients.
7. A knowledge of the referral process.
8. An understanding of the nature of crisis.
9. A knowledge of the crisis intervention process.
10. An understanding of the nature of support.
11. An understanding of the place and use of activity in helping clients.
12. An understanding of the use of mediation in helping clients.

Following planning, the next step in the generalist social work service process is action. Different clients with different needs in different situations require different kinds of action on the part of the worker. For some situations the actions of the assessment and planning phase provide the help that is needed so that the client can then take the action that is needed for change. Sometimes help comes through the development of the worker-client relationship. This relationship then frees the client to engage in problem-solving activity with the worker. In other situations, other action on the part of the worker is required. This action can be very helpful in the development of relationship and in assessment. The social worker may also use various kinds of activity with people and with systems other than client systems as a part of the helping process.

The actions of social workers in helping clients have been classified by the theory, approach to practice, or method used in the helping.[1] This means of classification does not describe all the kinds of help used in meeting client need. It is more a means of considering the theory base underlying the helping of clients and of relating the helping response of that theory. Social workers do need to be aware of the variety of theories available to guide their helping efforts. An in-depth study of these theories is best done by study of the original source of that theory, which is beyond the scope of this book. The Appendix, however, gives a short summary of the better known theories, approaches, and models used by social workers. Various other attempts have been made to classify the actions of social workers,[2] but none is completely satisfactory nor developed in any depth.

One of the marks of a generalist practitioner is the capacity to choose from a wide variety of possibilities the action that is most appropriate for the specific situation. Social work action falls into two primary classifications: **direct practice** (action with clients) and **indirect practice** (action with systems other than clients). Direct practice involves primarily action with individuals, families, and small groups focused on change in either the transactions within the family or small-group system or in the manner in which individuals, families, and small groups function in relation to persons and societal institutions in their environment.

Indirect practice involves those actions taken with persons other than clients in order to help clients. These actions may be taken with individuals, small groups, organizations, or communities as the unit of attention. This type of help will be discussed in Chapter 14.

Direct practice seems to fall within the following categories:

1. Action taken to enable development of relationships,
2. Action taken to enable development of understanding of persons in situations,
3. Action taken in the planning process,
4. Action taken to enable the client to know and use resources available,
5. Action that empowers clients,
6. Action taken in crisis situations,
7. Action taken to support the social functioning of clients,
8. Action taken that uses activity with clients as the base of help,
9. Action taken to mediate between clients and a system in their environment, and
10. Action taken in using a clinical model of social work.

In this chapter, action related to the use of resources, to empowerment of people, to crisis intervention, to support, to the use of activity, and to mediating is discussed. Action taken to enable the development of relationships, action taken to enable the development of understanding of the person in the situation, and action taken in the planning process have already been discussed. Action taken in using clinical models of social work is beyond the scope of this book.

Action also depends on the skills of the worker. Depending on the service goals and the usual ways the agency uses to deliver service, workers tend to use one or more kinds of action more often than other kinds of action. Skill in using the various types of action develops through use over time. In order to help clients with a variety of needs from a variety of situations, social workers can be most effective when they possess skill in using a variety of actions and choose the action best suited to the particular client and situation. The generalist practitioner has within her repertoire actions for use in working with individuals, groups, families, organizations, and communities. Often several types of action are needed to reach identified goals. There is overlap among possible actions or strategies and often the worker creatively combines strategies or makes alterations in them so as to better respond to specific situations. The art of social work is important when action becomes the focus of service.

When a social worker is deciding about which kinds of action to take in a particular situation, there are principles that can be used, which include:

1. *Economy*—The action chosen should be that which requires the least expenditure of time and energy by both client and worker. Generally, a worker helps the client do for himself whatever is possible to do with help, and does for a client only what the client cannot do for himself.

2. *Self-determination of clients*—The action that is most desirable to the client should be used whenever possible. The action of the worker is planned with the client during the planning phase of the helping process.

3. *Individualization*—Any action taken should be differentially adapted to the needs and characteristics of the particular client system with which it is to be used. This calls for the worker to adapt the action, depending on the client's characteristics and situation, and to be creative in the use of any action.

4. *Development*—The action of the worker depends in part on the developmental stage of the client system. At different stages of development the individual, family, and small group each requires different kinds of help.

5. *Interdependence*—The action of the worker depends in part on the action of the client. There is always consideration of the activity of the client and of the client's capacity to change. The actions of the worker and client should be complementary.

6. *Focus on service goals*—All action should be related to the goals for the service as developed by the worker and client together during the planning stage.

ACTION TO ENABLE CLIENTS TO USE AVAILABLE RESOURCES

For some clients the major block to meeting need is a lack of resources. Sometimes these resources are available but the client is not aware of them or does not know how to use them. Sometimes the resource is not responsive to some clients. In a complex and diverse society all resources are not responsible to all clients. One part of the generalist social worker's understanding of a community is knowing which resource can meet the needs of which clients. An important part of the social worker's interventive repertoire, then, is the ability to match client and resource and to enable the client to use the resources available to her.

In order to help clients use the resources that may be available to them, workers should have knowledge and skill in four areas: 1) they should have a thorough knowledge of the service delivery systems of the community in which they practice and the community in which the client lives and functions; 2) they should have knowledge of, and skill in, the use of the referral process; 3) they should understand the appropriate use of the broker and advocate roles and have skills in filling these roles; and 4) they should know how to empower clients to take charge of their life situation. When the social worker is taking action to enable clients to use the resources available, the function of the social worker is to link people to the resources they can use in meeting their needs and thus enhance their social functioning and coping capacity.

The Service Delivery System

When identifying components of the service delivery system, workers usually begin by identifying social service agencies and services provided by other professionals. A far broader view needs to be considered. Within many neighborhoods, communities, and ethnic groups, a helping network outside the formal system exists. This "natural helping system" is becoming known to social workers as they attempt to stretch the scarce resources of the formal systems in a time of economic stress. There is, however, much that needs to be learned about how to work cooperatively with this system.

The **natural helping system** is made up of a client's family, friends, and coworkers. These are the people to whom a person in need goes for help first. When clients come to a social worker, they have probably tried to get help from these persons first. Social workers can sometimes strengthen or support the natural helping attempts rather than take over the helping completely. The extended family has always been an important part of the helping system for many ethnic groups and in small towns and rural areas. For example, among the American Indians the extended family is so important that if a social worker fails to involve this system in the planning process the client may not be able to use any help offered. Ross Speck and Carolyn Attneave have developed a method of working with extended families, called Network Therapy, which involves and supports the extended family in helping a family member in need.[3]

The work of Eugene Litwak and Ivan Szelenyi supports the use of family, neighbors, and kin as a helping resource.[4] They describe neighborhood ties as useful because of the speed of response to need. The person seeking help has face-to-face contact that is immediately available. The person in need is continually observed, and help is provided quickly when situations change. Family or kin are particularly helpful bec~~ ~~ ~~ ~~g-term relationship that exists. For example, they are a r~~ ~~ldren when a parent dies or when persons f~~ ~~nalization. Friendship groups are ~~ ~~ship among friends has strong ~~ ~~e provision of support.

~~ ~~natural helpers in the commu-
~~ ~~**tural helpers** are those persons ~~ ~~he context of mutual relation-
s~~ ~~; a part of their everyday life.
T~~ ~~being able to change; mature,
fri~~ ~~m as those they are helping;
tru~~ ~~re a sense of mutuality with
oth~~ ~~and have similar values as
the ~~ ~~t of neighborhoods, small
com~~ ~~e persons are. However, it
is ofte~~ ~~without help from those
who a~~ ~~

Al~~ ~~ctive methods for working wit~~ ~~s should not try to train
natural~~ ~~social workers should
recogniz~~ ~~t them in their unique
ways of ~~ ~~helpers' capacity and
competen~~ ~~

Comm~~ ~~or someone who has had a
catastrophe~~ ~~ of a family member and is another
example of~~ ~~g system at work.

Self-hel~~ ~~ups may also be considered a part of the natural helping system. Mutual aid is related to the responsibility people feel for each other. One means of carrying out this responsibility is the voluntary small group, often of sponta- neous origin, that develops for people who have similar problems. Groups are useful in developing connectedness to others at a time when isolation may be a felt problem. They are useful in encouraging growth and redefinition of self. Some also work for social change regarding social impacts that affect the resolu- tion of the common problem of the group members. These groups involve per- sons who have lived through problems helping those who currently have the problem to find their own solutions. Help is given by modeling, positive rein- forcement, and emphasis on the here and now. Examples of these groups are the anonymous groups like Alcoholics Anonymous; cancer-support groups; and life- transition groups, like widow-to-widow groups.[6]

The relationship between self-help groups and the formal human service organizations is often problematic because of different ways of functioning. Such variables as the client group on which service is focused, the need for resources from outside the system, and the relationships of helper and those receiving help are usually quite different. Also, relationships between self-help groups and human service organizations vary. Yeheskel Hasenfeld and Benjamin Gidron identified five relational patterns: competition, referral, coordination, coalition, and cooptation. The ideal relationship would be one of coordination and/or coalition.[7] Regardless of relational patterns, in order to maximize the use of self-help groups, social workers must be aware of the relational pattern that exists and, when appropriate, work to facilitate a different pattern.

In working with all natural helping systems, social workers must be aware that these systems are primary groups that use an informal, personal means of interaction. To attempt to work with natural helping systems using the strategies and techniques of formal bureaucratic systems often blocks any meaningful interaction or coordination. Two results that take place are: 1) the natural helping system may give up its help and allow the formal system to do the helping—in this situation the natural helping system is destroyed; 2) the natural helping system may withdraw from the formal system and go underground—in this situation the social worker is unable to coordinate and cooperate, and the two systems may offer help that does not allow clients to use both systems effectively. The consultative, enabling stance seems to be the most appropriate way of functioning with natural helping systems. Social workers must be creative and seek means of linking formal and informal networks if the use of the resources of the natural helping system is to be maximized. The most important consideration in this linkage is maintenance of communication without undue interference with the functioning of either the formal or informal systems.

The formal service delivery system includes not only the social service agencies but organizations that either have an interest in specific projects or have resources for their members. The American Legion may be able to provide certain resources for a veteran or his family, particularly if that veteran is a member of the organization. The Lions Club has always concerned itself with visual problems; this organization might be a resource for obtaining glasses for a client. Other organizations may have projects, such as used clothing stores, that can provide a resource for clients. The knowledge a social worker needs of any community in which she works includes knowledge of these organization resources.

In order to help clients use the resources of the various community institutions and professionals, the social worker needs a good understanding of the institutions, the services, and the resources they have available and how clients can best avail themselves of those resources. Acquaintance with other professionals—such as teachers, ministers, and doctors—also helps the worker know of resources available. Skill in coordination, consultation, and team functioning, as discussed in Chapter 11, is often important in helping clients to use resources.

Service delivery by social service agencies takes many different forms. Agencies use many kinds of workers to deliver different kinds of services. MSWs deliver clinical services; BSWs are used in many ways to support clients, to help with problem solving, and to provide concrete services; paraprofessionals may also be used to provide some services. Indigenous workers who have special skills for working with cultural groups of which they are a part may be another resource. Indigenous workers come from the sociocultural group being helped.

They often have no formal education relative to the job. Homemaker or chore service may be provided by paraprofessionals or indigenous workers. Volunteers may also provide some services.

Service may be provided in an agency office only, or workers may reach out to people in need. Agencies may provide only counseling or clinical social work, or they may provide concrete services or resources like food or money. Some agencies have workers stationed in small communities or in neighborhoods not easily accessible to the main office. Other agencies use a "circuit-riding" approach to servicing clients in remote areas. In this approach, the worker goes into an area one day a week or biweekly or monthly to meet with clients. In some small population areas or for some kinds of highly specialized services, the client must leave the community to obtain service. The social worker must have knowledge of how agencies deliver services and what resources they have if they are to enable clients to find the resources they need. Some agencies may not deliver services in a manner that is usable by some clients. Workers need to be aware of these agency limitations so that they do not further add to clients' frustration by referring them to services they cannot use or that will not be responsive to their needs.

The first step in enabling clients to use resources is a thorough knowledge of the resources available. The second step is choosing the appropriate resource for the client. This choice is based on matching client need and client lifestyle with a resource that can meet the need and provide help in a manner congruent with the client's lifestyle. Client involvement in the choice is important for obtaining the desired match—for linking the client to the resource. In addition, workers may use indirect practice strategies to work for change in the relational patterns between various segments of the service delivery system so that client need can be better met. (See Chapter 14.)

Referral

Referral is the process by which a social worker enables a client to become aware of another service resource and to make contact with that resource. In addition, the referral process involves providing the referral agency with information that may be helpful in providing service to the client (with the client's permission) and followup as to the usefulness of the service to the client. The referral service may be used in conjunction with the service a worker is providing or as the primary service. Referral is used when the client's needs cannot be met with services provided by the agency that employs the worker or when a more appropriate service is provided by another agency.

The worker uses knowledge of the potential resources and knowledge of the way service is delivered to match potential clients and potential services so that the service is acceptable to, and usable by, clients.

Referrals are made only with permission of clients. The worker and client together discuss the potential service, and the worker helps the client make the initial contact with the new agency if this is necessary. This can be done by giving a phone number or directions for reaching the new agency; it can also be done by making suggestions about how to approach the new agency. Sometimes it is helpful for a worker to call the new agency for the client or go to the agency with the client for the first contact.

The worker and client also discuss the kind of information that would be helpful to the new agency. After receiving the client's permission, usually in writing, a worker provides that information to the agency. It is often helpful if the two workers know each other and can discuss the client's needs.

A last and often overlooked step in referral is followup. In determining whether the client is receiving the services sought, the worker gains information about the appropriateness of the service for the client and other persons who may be in need of similar services (which enables the worker to make appropriate referrals in the future). If the client has not been able to use the service, then the worker may want to follow up with that client in helping the client to receive the needed service elsewhere or to determine why the client was unable to use the service. Skill in referral is a necessary tool for all social workers.[8]

Broker and Advocate Roles

In enabling clients to use available resources, primarily two roles are used: the **broker role** and the **advocate role.** It is important for the social worker to understand the difference between these two roles and to choose the one most appropriate to the situation. The broker helps a person or family get needed services. This includes assessing the situation, knowing the alternative resources, preparing and counseling the person, contacting the appropriate service, and assuring that the client gets to the help and uses it.[9] The major thrust is to expedite the client linkage to the needed resource. It involves giving information and support and teaching clients how to use resources. There is also some negotiation with the agency to which the client is referred.

The role of the advocate is "pleading and fighting for services for clients who the service system would otherwise reject."[10] It involves seeking different interpretations or exceptions to rules and regulations, pointing out clients' rights to services, and pointing out blockages to clients receiving or using an agency's services. In carrying out this role the worker is speaking on behalf of a client. Before engaging in advocacy a worker must first be sure that the client desires the worker to intervene in this manner. The client should clearly understand the risks involved and be motivated to use the service if it is obtained. Second, the worker must carefully assess the risks involved for the client if advocacy is used. This would include the consideration of any action that might be taken that could cause further problems for the client and the probability of a usable resource being obtained. **Case advocacy,** advocacy for a single client, is most effective when used to obtain concrete resources for which the client is eligible. It is also useful when persons and systems are impinging on a client's functioning in ways they are not aware of. To fill an advocate role, social workers must be comfortable with conflict situations and knowledgeable about the means for conflict management. They must be willing to negotiate and be sensitive to the need for withdrawal if the best interests of the client are not being served. Clients usually must have considerable trust in the worker before they will be willing for the worker to use advocacy on their behalf.

The worker uses the advocate role only when the broker role is not effective. There are times, however, when an advocate stance must be taken in order to enable clients to obtain needed services.

CASE EXAMPLE

The social worker in a pediatric intensive care unit has been working with the Norton family since their prematurely born son, Bobby, was a few hours old and placed on the unit. Bobby is now three months old and is ready to be discharged to his home in a community 100 miles away. The family is still having some emotional reaction to having a premature baby. The parents have been able to visit only once a week because of the distance and the fact that they have three other children, aged two to six. Bonding is still somewhat of a problem and Mrs. Norton seems very frightened of what she sees as a very fragile baby. Bobby is showing more than the usual developmental delays of a premature baby and needs an infant stimulation program as well as continued monitoring of his physical condition.

The social worker knows that if this child is to continue to progress when he is discharged from the hospital, it is important that the Nortons use a variety of resources. Because they live in a small city, the social worker knows that she will have to be creative in finding what is needed. She calls the social worker in the small hospital that sent Bobby to the intensive care unit (after receiving permission from the Nortons) and finds that there is a local child welfare agency that can serve as a resource to help the Nortons with their feelings about Bobby, his prematurity, and his delayed development. The worker on the intensive care unit then discusses with the Nortons a referral to the agency. She shares her concern that they have the support they need in the next few months so that Bobby is able to continue his development. She informs them that the child welfare agency can also help the Nortons work with the school district to set up an infant stimulation program. The Nortons agree that they would like to have someone to talk to about their concerns regarding Bobby and agree that the social worker can call the agency and discuss the needs of the family and of Bobby.

When the social worker calls the agency she finds that they are indeed willing to work with the Nortons. The agency worker says that she will get in touch with the Nortons before Bobby is discharged to help them in the transition period. (She feels it important to reach out now, so the relationship can develop before the Nortons become overwhelmed with their feelings about Bobby's care.) The worker also says that she is aware of several mothers of premature children who she thinks can use a group. She is willing to get them together to see if they want to develop a group. This group could also use resource persons to help them understand the needs of their children. The agency worker asks about the extended family and finds that this family has no relatives in the state. She says she may suggest that the family use the services of an older woman in the community who is very good in helping families who need a grandmotherly type of relationship.

The intensive care worker now feels she can work with the Nortons around the details of Bobby's discharge. She feels comfortable that the child welfare agency can meet the needs of this family, both through their own services and through referral to other community resources.

Empowerment

Some clients need more than referral, brokering, or advocacy if they are to make use of available resources. Other clients can benefit from being able to take an active role in changing the situations impinging on their functioning.

Empowerment is "a process of increasing personal, interpersonal, or political power so that individuals can take action to improve their life situation."[11] Empowerment has been suggested as a strategy of choice when working with members of minority groups and with women.[12] In the contemporary world where power is an all-pervasive issue, where the gap between haves and have-nots is growing dramatically, it is a strategy to be considered when working with any client caught in the throes of powerlessness.

Enabling or helping clients and others do what they want to do may seem to be a similar strategy. Although it may seem that enabling and empowering are synonymous, there are subtle differences. **Enabling,** the broader term, refers to making it possible for an individual or system to be able to carry out some activity they might not be able to engage in without support or help. This term recently has taken on negative connotations when used with regard to alcohol and other addictions. (E.g, spouse whose actions support the addictive behaviors is called an enabler.) As used in this book, enabling has a positive connotation. (That is, the action being supported is a desirable one.) **Empowering,** while a kind of enabling, means providing clients with the supports, skills, and understanding needed to allow them to take charge, to become powerful in situations in which they have been powerless.

However, those caught in powerlessness not only lack knowledge of how to negotiate the system, but they are hopeless that any change is possible and lack the self-esteem necessary for engaging in change activity. Empowerment involves not only enabling clients but also motivating, teaching, and raising self-esteem so that clients can believe they are competent individuals, that they have the skills needed for negotiating community systems, and that they deserve the resources necessary for healthy social functioning. It makes it more possible for clients to receive the benefits of society, and gives people the capacity to work toward the resolution of conditions that are preventing them from providing for their needs.

According to Ruth J. Parsons, a search of the literature confirms that the important ingredients of an empowerment strategy are: support, mutual aid, and validation of the client's perceptions and experiences. When these ingredients are present there is a heightened degree of client self-esteem, more self-confidence, and a experience of a greater capacity to make changes or to do for self. She sees the use of an empowerment strategy as calling for building collectives; working with others in similar situations; educating for critical thinking through support, mutual aid, and collective action; and competency assessment or identification of strengths and coping skills.[13]

Thus, it appears that the use of groups is necessary for this action strategy. Silvia Staub-Bernasconi pointed this out and called for a focus on consciousness development, social and coping skills training, and networking and mediation. Also, she noted that empowerment calls for work with power sources and power structures.[14] This strategy is congruent with the generalist social work model presented in this text. The strong emphasis on maximal client involvement in assessment, planning, and action to meet goals is an important ingredient of empowerment. Teaching clients how to problem solve and about the nature of various systems in their environment is a part of empowerment.

The nature of the relationship between the worker and the client is an important consideration when using this strategy. There must be mutual respect and trust. As the worker demonstrates belief in the client and points out existing competencies, the client gains a sense of self-worth and a belief that he has the ability to bring about the change that he defines as needed.

Another valuable technique that has been suggested for use when using an empowerment strategy is work focused on reduction of self-blame. The client needs to be helped to see that the problems he is facing often have their source in the functioning of systems in his environment. Tied to the reduction of self-blame is the assistance needed to help clients take responsibility for changing the impacting environment. Here, the worker teaches the client specific skills for environmental change. Although the worker may also work for environmental change through advocacy and mobilization of resources, it is important that the client accept major responsibility; otherwise, a feeling of personal incapacity may be further reinforced.[15]

Consciousness raising has been suggested as a technique for use with the empowerment strategy. This involves giving the client information about the nature of the situation, particularly the functioning of various environmental forces, as they impact the client's functioning. It heightens the client's understanding of self in relationship to others. Workers must feel comfortable with the anger that can evolve as a result of this technique and be able to help clients use the energy of that anger in ways that further the work at hand. When the time is appropriate, it is also important for the worker to help clients move beyond anger into other responses to injustices. What is hoped is that the client can gain a more realistic view of the situation and then can take advantage of change possibilities as they develop.

Groups have been found to be a powerful adjunct to consciousness raising. It is helpful to the client to see others struggle with the new understandings. Indeed, the work of a group can result in the development of those understandings. The group can become involved in collective action and thus enhance the sense of power within the individual. The group also becomes a support system for mutual aid. Participation in the group can lead to enhanced self-esteem. It can be a place where clients learn new skills.

Empowerment is not a strategy that is used in isolation from other strategies. Rather, it is a strategy that points to a goal of reduced helplessness—a goal of clients taking charge of their own lives in less than ideal situations. It encompasses ingredients from many other strategies, using them in ways that allow clients to sense the full force of their own competence.

Generalist workers with a thorough knowledge of available resources, and with skill in making referrals, in filling the broker and advocate roles, and in empowering clients, are prepared to take action that enables clients to use needed resources. This is sometimes the strategy of choice.

CASE EXAMPLE

Mary Jones moved to Anytown from the projects in Large City to avoid having her children grow up in a crime-ridden, drug-saturated area with poor educational opportunities. After a period of homelessness, she found herself living in an area of subsidized housing with many other single parents. The area was becoming a high-crime area, with drug dealers from Large City frequent visitors. In addition, Mary and many other African Americans found that their children, who were considered to be doing well in Large City schools, were having difficulty adjusting to the new schools. They had trouble keeping up with the standards set in this system, and also were apparently not expected to do well. In addition, the racially integrated schools presented many challenges associated with dealing with the discriminatory behaviors of other students. Mary was becoming discouraged and worried that the move was not resulting in the better life she dreamed of for her children.

The school social work staff noted that many of the African American parents did not respond to requests from the school to become involved when their children were not doing well, were not attending school regularly, or were involved in interpersonal difficulties. At a meeting to discuss the situation, they identified a number of reasons why these children were having difficulty and the parents were not involved with the school in the problems' resolution. Some of the important reasons were: the school was seen "as a white people institution" where the students and the parents feel threatened, believe unrealistic expectations are placed upon them, and do not understand what is happening or know how to respond. Another problem was lack of transportation. The children are bused a considerable distance to school, and the parents have neither an easy means of transportation nor, at times, money to pay for it. Also, the social work staff noted that many of the teachers had no understanding of either the culture or the educational background of the students. They also were frightened of them and had little understanding of the students' everyday struggles just to get along both in the new and strange school environment and in the neighborhood.

It was decided that this situation required a many focused approach. Some of the strategies called for were a staff development thrust by the teachers, advocating for greater police protection for the area, and development of a range of services for the families and children in the neighborhood. The social work staff also saw that the involvement of parents in the schools was very important. It was determined that the parents needed to be empowered to work with the schools in finding ways to increase the children's chances for success.

Because Mary had called the school recently to inquire about her son Bob's low grades, the staff decided she might be an ideal person to help with the plan. The social worker, using Mary's request for information as an entree, made an appointment to see her in her home. During this contact she found that Mary was very concerned, not only about Bob's grades but about the danger he encountered from the drugs and crime to which he was being exposed. Mary and the social worker identified several areas that seemed to make school very difficult for him and discussed Mary's fear of coming to school and the fact that she had no way to get there. The social worker also asked if Mary thought other mothers would like a discussion group in their neighborhood in which together they could discover means of interacting with the schools.

The group of mothers began to meet with the social worker. After some time, a teacher visited the group and talked about the problems from her point of view. The group sought help in going to the school as a group to talk to the principal and, eventually, to individual teachers. The social worker helped the teachers to provide the parents with activities they could carry out with the children that would enhance the school situation and communicate to the children the importance of getting an education. Eventually, the group was formalized into an advisory board for the school on the education of children from their neighborhood, and individual parents became active in helping teachers in the classrooms. In addition, this group became active in working with city authorities and the police in developing a neighborhood crime-stopping program. The results were that the children seemed more comfortable in school and, on average, performed at a higher level; the school had much more understanding of these at-risk children and felt more comfortable working with them; other children in the school became more tolerant of diversity; the parents were very involved and proud of their accomplishments; and the neighborhood began slowly to take responsibility for maintaining itself as a good place to raise children.

ACTION IN RESPONSE TO CRISIS

Clients tend to use many coping mechanisms as well as the resources of the natural helping systems and community institutions before coming to a social worker. They often are under considerable stress and may be in a state of crisis. If the client is in a state of crisis, it is important that the social worker be able to recognize this situation and respond appropriately. Crisis intervention is a model of social work practice that provides a knowledge base and guidelines for such a response. All generalist social workers should develop some knowledge and skill for working with people in crisis.

The major goal of action in response to crisis (crisis intervention) is resolution of the crisis and restored social functioning. If after this goal is reached the worker and the client then decide there is some other goal they want to work on together, some other kind of action is taken.

Recognizing Crisis

A **crisis** exists when, because of a stressful situation and/or a precipitating event, a system, such as an individual or family, that has had a satisfactory level of social functioning develops a state of disequilibrium, or loses its steady state. Coping mechanisms that have worked in past situations no longer are working, although there is usually some considerable struggle to cope. It is not a crisis situation when a person or family is continually in a state of disorganization; work with such problems requires a different kind of action.

Crisis can be and usually is a part of the life experience of all persons. The crisis situation can develop because of situational and developmental factors. Situational factors include illness (self or close family members), death of a close family member, separation or divorce, change of living situation or lifestyle, and loss of a job. These situational factors call either for assuming new roles or additional responsibilities or for changing the established way of functioning with other persons. Sometimes these factors only cause considerable stress that, after a period of instability and trying new methods of coping, results in a new and comfortable way of functioning. At other times, an additional stressful situation precipitates the crisis situation.

Developmental stress arises from the unsettled or stressful feelings that may occur as persons move from one developmental stage into another. This movement calls for new ways of functioning. Adolescence is a time of stress when new concerns and needs may not be fulfilled. As young persons must deal with their sexual drives, make career decisions, and develop new relationships with parents, they may become overwhelmed, and crisis can develop. Families also experience a crisis as they move from one stage to another. The birth of the first child calls for new patterns of social functioning, thus creating additional stress and sometimes crisis.

Figure 13–1 provides an overall view of the crisis process. The hazardous state, the vulnerable state, and the increased upset are precrisis states that are often resolved by persons using usual means of coping and with help from their personal support system. When these means do not bring about resolution, persons move into a crisis state and crisis intervention becomes an appropriate strategy for action.

Responding to Crisis

When working with individuals in crisis, the worker needs to be aware of the time element of crisis. The true crisis situation lasts from four to eight weeks. After that time individuals do find new ways of coping. Without appropriate help during the crisis stage, the result may be a reduced capacity for effective social functioning. Thus, help for individuals in crisis must be immediate and sometimes fairly intensive.

The worker has two immediate tasks: 1) development of understanding about the person in crisis and what precipitated the crisis and 2) development of the helping relationship. In developing the understanding, the worker searches for the precipitating event—the event that pushed the person into crisis as well as the nature of the underlying stressful situation. The worker also determines what the client has tried to do to resolve the stress (the coping mechanisms used) and enables the client to share how she feels about the situation.

The worker enables the formation of a helping relationship by actively responding to the client's concern and need. Together they explore the reality of the situation and determine the reality of the client's perceptions. The worker supports the client in giving credit for the coping attempts and makes specific suggestions for other means of coping that can be tried. The worker shares with the client the understanding of the situation as he sees it. The worker communicates a sense of realistic hope that the crisis can be resolved and that the worker will help the client through this difficult time. The client is encouraged to express feelings about the situation. The worker is sensitive to the client's anxiety and to the possibility of depression. If excessive anxiety or depression develops, the

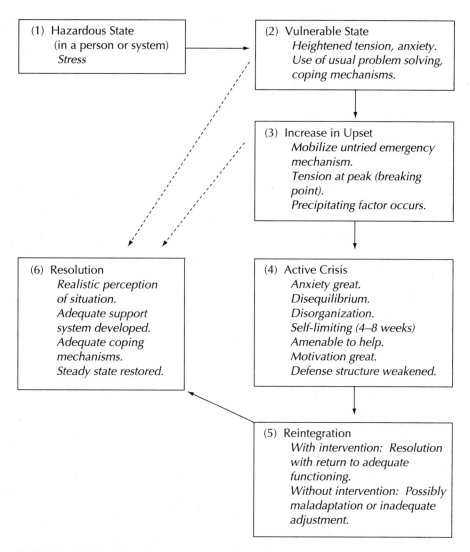

FIGURE 13–1   The Process of Crisis

Note: Dotted lines indicate that Resolution can occur after states 2, 3, or 5.

worker helps the client seek the services of a competent mental health professional who is skilled in dealing with these disorders. The worker also links the client to other needed resources.

Through the work together in the four- to eight-week period of crisis, the client usually discovers new coping mechanisms, and the crisis is resolved. In the later part of this period, the worker can often enhance the client's problem solving and thus prevent future crisis. Working with clients in an intensive, fairly directive manner during the crisis prevents future social-functioning problems and restores the client to a state in which she can manage life in an effective and satisfying manner.

When family systems experience crisis, the use of crisis intervention is also appropriate. Sometimes it is possible to work with persons in crisis in small groups. When the worker has several clients in crisis situations, it can be helpful for these persons to share perceptions and experiences as a part of the response to crisis. Some crisis groups are open ended, with people in the later stages of crisis receiving help by helping those in the early stages of crisis.[16]

CASE EXAMPLE

When Mrs. Norton (in previous case example) came to see her newborn premature son for the first time, the social worker immediately noted that she was exhibiting considerable stress. She seemed unusually anxious, was very hesitant to go into the nursery, and had to be encouraged to touch the baby. The social worker spent some time with the Nortons before they went in to see the baby. She tried to prepare them for the sight of the newborn, with many tubes inserted into various spots of his body. The social worker knew that the birth of a premature baby can be a cause of stress, which can push a family or parent into crisis.

After the Nortons had seen their son, the social worker invited them into her office. She first allowed them to talk about their reactions to seeing the baby. Mrs. Norton remarked that she felt like she was falling apart. She exhibited a great deal of guilt about not being able to carry the baby to term. Then she said, "This is really another piece of bad luck." The social worker asked her what she meant by that. Mrs. Norton then burst into tears and said that this year everything seemed to be going wrong. The worker asked what beside the premature birth had gone wrong. Mrs. Norton said it all started with the serious illness of her four-year-old child when she was three months pregnant. She had done a lot of lifting during that period and wondered if that could have led to the new baby being born prematurely. The social worker said she didn't know but wondered if Mrs. Norton should feel guilty about caring for her sick child. She then asked if there was anything else that had gone wrong. Mrs. Norton started to cry again and said that two months ago her mother had died very suddenly. She had planned to visit when the new baby was born and help with the other children. After the social worker inquired as to the functioning of this family prior to the stressful events and found that they had indeed functioned adequately, she knew that Mrs. Norton, at least, and perhaps the family were in a state of crisis. She sensed that Mrs. Norton was in a hazardous state when her mother died due to the illness of her child and her own pregnancy. She also believed that the death of Mrs. Norton's mother added to this stress and that she was very vulnerable to crisis. She doubted that Mrs. Norton had yet recovered from the death of her mother, when a new stress appeared with the birth of the fourth child prematurely.

In planning the work with the Nortons, the worker saw several tasks that needed immediate attention. Mrs. Norton needed an opportunity to talk about her feelings around both the death of her mother and the birth of the child. She needed relief from the guilt she was feeling about her responsibility for the premature birth. She needed help in placing all of these stressful events in some perspective. She got the Nortons' permission to talk to the doctor who delivered the baby to see if he could discuss the reasons for the premature birth with the Nortons. She knew she needed to help Mr. Norton be aware of the reasons for his wife's distress and her need for support at this time. She asked if the family had a pastor they could talk to. They stated they did, and he had been very helpful when Mrs. Norton's mother died. The worker suggested they get in touch with him, as she felt Mrs. Norton could still use some help around that event. She told them that it often takes time to deal with such a sudden death. She told them this was something they could work on while their son was in the hospital. She also discussed the need for frequent visits to the baby, and she set up an appointment for them to see the attending physician later that day to discuss the baby's progress. The Nortons stated they could only visit once a week as they lived at such a distance. The worker made arrangements for them to see her again on their next visit.

ACTION THAT IS SUPPORTIVE

Support has been a universal part of helping. As Lois Selby so accurately has said, "It is as old as man's humanity to man."[17] Supportive means are a part of every generalist social worker's repertoire, yet support is a concept that has received little attention in social work literature. Selby and Beulah Roberts Compton point out that social work attitudes toward support historically have limited its use to chronic clients or to those for whom no other treatment is possible.[18] There is a prevailing notion that support is hardly worth the social worker's time. This seems to have developed as social workers emulated psychiatry and its attitudes.

Florence Hollis identifies sustainment as one of the procedures of social work practice.[19] Her usage of the term *sustainment* seems very close to the notion of support. She sees sustainment as heavily expressed by nonverbal means. Hollis identifies some of the components or techniques of sustainment as expression of the client's abilities and competencies as they exist, expression of interest, a desire to help, understanding of a client's situation and feelings about that situation, and use of encouragement and reassurance. There is a need for reassurance to be realistic. Emphasis is on the feeling component and support for the acceptability of having feelings about the situation the client finds himself in.

Contemporary social work, then, seems to see support as a more acceptable function. Social work literature recognizes the use of support as a means of helping persons cope with difficult situations and, through successful coping, helping clients grow. Yet little has been written that identifies the nature of that support; there seems to be an assumption that social workers know what support is. The use of support seems to be an idea that is in the domain of practice wisdom of social work knowledge.

Judith Nelson has defined supportive procedures as "those intended to help clients feel better, stronger, or more comfortable in some immediate way."[20] She has also identified four kinds of support: 1) *protection,* which includes giving directions and advice, setting limits, and giving structure to complex or overwhelming situations; 2) *acceptance,* which includes making the clients aware that the worker is with them in their struggles, confirming the worthwhileness of the person, and communicating understanding of their feelings and situation; 3) *validation,* which includes showing clients ways they are effective and competent persons, giving feedback to clients, giving hope, praise, and approval, and encouraging clients in their coping efforts and role performance; and 4) *education,* which includes teaching clients how to cope and how to function effectively, providing the client with needed information, socializing clients to new roles, and helping clients develop self-knowledge. One of the ways of teaching is modeling effective methods of coping.

Not only is it useful to use Nelson's classification to identify which kind of support will best meet a client's needs at any particular point in time, it also is important to identify which aspects of a client's functioning the worker desires to support. Selby and Compton discuss support as relating to a client's ego functioning. Two other useful ways to identify the specific area of social functioning that needs support might be in terms of coping tasks or life roles. Using the coping-task approach, the worker would identify the task or tasks a client is confronted with when coping with a life situation (e.g., acceptance of the limitations of chronic illness). Using the life-role approach, the worker would identify limitations, problems, and strengths a client has in carrying out a life role. For example, if the parenting role is troublesome and the worker identifies that discipline is an area in which the client seems to have limited skill, the worker would teach discipline techniques and give praise when the client uses these techniques instead of the previously used ineffective behaviors.

When using support as an interventive strategy, the worker identifies the client's need (as in all social work practice). This assessment emphasizes the client's perception of the situation and the client's realistic experiences in attempting to fulfill the need. Feelings of threat or deprivation are particularly important to note. The assessment should also consider the client's capacity to hope, the client's strengths, and the support the environment is capable of providing to the client.

The worker then decides what behaviors and attitudes can be supported to enable the client to have the unmet needs met. A decision is made about the specific kind of support to provide. Sometimes it is useful to provide the client with concrete resources or tangible services as a means of demonstrating the worker's care and concern. The worker using a supportive approach tries to develop a climate for helping that is accepting, understanding, comfortable, and validating. It is a climate in which the client feels free to discuss concerns and feelings openly. The worker expresses interest and concern, encourages and praises the client for appropriate efforts, expresses realistic confidence in the client's ability to cope and to carry out life tasks, guides the client, and provides needed structure for the client's work.

There can be problems in the inappropriate use of support. There is always a danger that the client will become overly dependent on the worker. Thus, the worker must guard against unrealistic expectations on the part of the client and avoid helping when the client can help himself or when the environment can provide the support. Workers need to be aware of tendencies to be overly protective of clients or to make up for all the wrongs they have suffered. The worker also needs to be aware that evaluative feelings can lead to a lack of acceptance and thus be counter to a supportive stance.

Small groups (support groups) have been found to be effective for providing support. This form of support is of particular value for use with caregivers,[21] those who have family members suffering from chronic or life-threatening conditions,[22] and those who have had a common debilitating experience.[23]

Properly used, support can be growth producing, not just maintaining the status quo, as has often been thought. It is positive reinforcement. It gives clients strength to live and to grow in difficult situations. It should be a part of the generalist social worker's interventive repertoire.

CASE EXAMPLE

Mrs. Jones is a sixty-year-old widow who has no children. She recently found out that the cancer she suffers from is terminal and she probably has about eight months left to live; she has been referred to a hospice team. The social worker on the team has determined three foci for work with Mrs. Jones: 1) to see that the resources she needs are provided in such a way that the highest quality of life can be maintained, 2) to help Mrs. Jones problem solve and decide how she wants to live the life left to her and what she wants to happen after she dies (funeral arrangements and disposal of her material possessions), and 3) to provide the support that she so badly needs. In fact, supportive action is the primary focus of the work to be done.

The worker develops a relationship with Mrs. Jones and is careful to let her know what they can do together to make her life more comfortable. She explains the purpose of hospice and how volunteers will be assigned to visit with her and help her with both the activities of daily living and her task of bringing her life to a satisfying close. The worker will also be available to the volunteers to give them support as they provide service to Mrs. Jones.

USE OF ACTIVITY AS AN INTERVENTIVE STRATEGY

Activity is doing something or performing tasks as opposed to talking about what to do or about feelings and ideas. Activity can be in the form of helping clients to carry out normal life tasks. It can also take the form of activity constructed by the worker in order to enhance the helping process, such as role-playing a difficult situation or, in a small group, using an activity that demands cooperation.

Activity can be a powerful means for influencing change in the ways systems or individuals function. It is through action that individuals learn many of the skills needed for adequate social functioning. Socialization of persons to the ways of their society and culture, that is, life experience, relies heavily on the use of action. Activity is a means for developing social-functioning skills. It is also a means for enhancing self-awareness. Activity leads to accomplishment, which in turn enhances self-esteem, including a positive sense of self and a sense of competence. Activity also has usefulness in developing an assessment. As a worker observes the client in action, the client's interactional and communication patterns become evident. The worker can also assess the client's competence in functioning and the quality of the functioning by observing the person in action.

Activity has traditionally been used in certain segments of social work. Notable has been the use of games and crafts in social group work. The use of play therapy with children has been another use of activity. Milieu therapy (use of the setting) used in institutions makes use of activity. Some family therapists make use of opportunity for families to plan family activity. Workers dealing with chaotic families have found activity to be very useful.[24] Recent literature on the ways people learn places emphasis on experiential learning that uses activity. Use of activity has been a major means of working with children. More recently, it has been seen as valuable for working with "action-oriented" persons. It can also be useful in a variety of other helping situations.

Activity can be used as a technique for meeting many needs of clients. It enhances physical development and neuromuscular control and stimulates intellectual growth. Activity can be an acceptable release for feelings and emotions, teach patterns of behaviors and provide discipline for behavior, enable acceptance by peers, and increase status. It can provide opportunity for making and carrying out decisions, for forming relationships, and for resolving conflict. It can also provide for the development of new interests, skills, and competencies.

Activity can enhance the social functioning by enabling movement along the normal growth processes. It can be useful with persons who may be at risk of not developing in some manner. This risk is often related to lack of opportunity, and activity can provide the needed opportunities. In this sense, it can be a preventive approach.

Activity is a tool social workers need to plan for carefully. This calls for an expanded knowledge of the nature of action and skill in its use. Robert Vinter has identified three aspects of activity: 1) the physical space and social objects involved in the activity, 2) the behaviors essential to carry out the activity, and 3) the expected respondent behavior because of the activity.[25] Before deciding to use any activity, a worker should determine these three aspects as they relate to the specific activity. Some dimensions discussed by Vinter that influence the action include: 1) its prescriptiveness as to what the actors are expected to do, 2) the kinds of rules and other controls that govern the activity, 3) the provision the activity makes for physical activity, 4) the competence required for persons to engage in the activity, 5) the nature of participation and interaction required, and 6) the nature of rewards that are inherent in the activity.

It is also important to consider the clients and their use of the activity. Areas that are particularly important to consider include:

1. *The client's particular need and interests*—Need should be identified before the decision to use activity is considered. Interest can be identified by considering the client's stated desires, skills, and interests.

2. *The capacity of the particular client to perform the tasks required in the activity*—An understanding of age-group characteristics is important, as is understanding of the usual activities of a client's cultural or other diversity subgroup.

3. *The client's motivation and readiness to use the particular activity*—Some clients cannot use certain activities because of cultural taboos. Others, who are work oriented, may not be able to use activity that appears to be play. Clients need to have an opportunity to make choices among possible alternatives. Activity that is relevant to the client's lifestyle is usually the activity most useful to the client.

4. *The ability of the client's support system and community to accept and support the activity being used*—Consideration should also be given to these factors.

A third kind of analysis that workers using activity should carry out is related to its use in a specific situation. This analysis includes:

1. The materials, equipment, and resources needed to carry out the activity;
2. The time and the capacity required of the worker to work with the client in carrying out the activity;
3. The climate and environment in which the activity will be carried out (the environment's ability to allow the activity and its supports for carrying out the activity can enable or prevent such activity);
4. Directions for carrying out the activity;
5. Precautions and safety measures that need to be taken in carrying out the activity; and
6. Adaptations of the activity that may be needed.

Based on the three kinds of assessments discussed above, a decision is made to use a particular activity. In preparing to implement the activity, the following tasks may need to be carried out:

1. An activity may need to be tested or carried out to determine if all aspects are understood. It is usually best not to use an activity with clients that the worker has not pretested. Adaptations should be made as necessary.
2. All supplies and equipment must be obtained. Rooms or other areas must be obtained. Responsibility is allocated for specific tasks to either the worker, other staff, or clients.

As the activity is taking place, the worker should be supportive and positive, show rather than tell, and set appropriate limits. It is also important to discuss the process and outcome of the activity with the client after its conclusion.

In using activity as an interventive strategy, the criteria for "good activity" should be kept in mind.

1. Good activity grows out of the needs and interests of the client(s).
2. Good activity takes into consideration age, cultural background, and other diversity factors of the clients.
3. Good activity provides experiences that enable or enhance the physical and psychosocial development of clients.

4. Good activity is flexible and offers a maximum opportunity for client participation.

Because the possibilities for the use of activity are vast and varied, it is
beyond the scope of this book to provide information about the use of specific
activity. Social workers can make use of literature from the field of recreation,
structured group experiences, and social group work to gain knowledge about
the use of specific activity.[26]

In using activity the worker employs a creative approach and adapts the
activity to the particular client's need. The creative use of activity can be a
powerful influence for helping clients. Its use calls for skill and understanding on
the part of social workers.

CASE EXAMPLES

A ten-year-old girl is having difficulty expressing feelings. The worker gives her paper and
crayons to draw a picture about her feelings. The picture is of a boat that she then destroys
with black crayon marks. The worker is then able to help the girl verbalize some of her
feelings of fear and insecurity, which the picture represents.

A group of mothers of young children is meeting in a settlement house. The goal is for the
mothers to interact with their children in teaching preschool skills. These mothers have
little money for books. The worker chooses the making of picture books for the mothers
to use with their children as the activity. As the books are worked on, the conversation
revolves around appropriateness of pictures and how the books will be used.

A family is having difficulty understanding how family members see themselves in the
family group. The social worker uses "family sculpturing" to draw out the needed information. Each family member places the other family members in the physical pattern that
most nearly depicts the sense of the family as she sees it. This active method gives new
understanding and enables the family to discuss changes they want to bring about.

ACTION AS MEDIATION

Sometimes as the worker and client explore the client's needs, problems, and
situation, it becomes apparent that the way in which a client and a system in the
client's environment are interacting is not functional. Often the situation is of a
conflictual nature. For example, a mother seems unable to communicate with a
probation officer so that they can work together in setting limits for her son. The
mother is frightened of the authority of the probation officer and does not seem
to respond to his suggestions. The probation officer is frustrated and believes the
mother is indifferent to her son's need for limits. The worker knows this is not the
case. In such a situation a mediation strategy can be useful.

William Schwartz describes this strategy as "to mediate the process through which the individual and his society reach out for each other through a mutual need for self-fulfillment.[27] Later he describes it as "helping people negotiate difficult environments."[28] The worker's concern—and the focus of the mediation action—is the social functioning of both the client and the system. The transaction between the two is the concern, the target for change.

Schwartz and Zalba and Lawrence Shulman have written extensively about this type of action and strategy.[29] Shulman has identified three blocks in the interactions of individuals with environmental systems:

1. *The complexity of systems*—The development of institutions and the bureaucratizing of their functioning has made it less possible for individuals to understand how to approach these systems or to use the resources they provide. These complex systems seem strange, impersonal, and often overwhelming to many clients.

2. *Self-interest*—The self-interest of systems often is in conflict with the interests of others or of the larger system of which they are a part. When such self-interest is predominant, it is necessary to make that system aware of the interdependence, and thus of the mutual interest, that is necessary for the functioning of the larger system.

3. *Communication problems*—Often, the inability of systems to work together is a result of a lack of communication or of inaccurate communication, and thus of misconceptions about the other.[30]

In overcoming these blocks or problems the worker and client each have tasks. The purpose of mediation is not for the worker to be an advocate and challenge one or the other system but to help the two systems reach out to each other so that together they can reach a common goal. The worker helps or enables each of the two systems to accomplish the tasks necessary but does not do the work necessary to reach the goal. That belongs to the client and the environmental system.

The worker has three major tasks to accomplish: 1) to help the client reach out to the environmental system, 2) to help the environmental system respond to the client, and 3) to demand that both the client and the environmental system do the work needed to reach the common goal.

In helping the client to reach out to the environmental system, the worker first points out to the client the common interests and goals of the client and the environmental system. The worker also identifies the blocks that seem to be preventing the client from reaching these goals. The worker challenges these blocks by pointing out ways they can be overcome and the advantages to the client of overcoming them. The worker tries to give the client a vision of what can happen if the client and the environmental system find a means for working together. In doing this, the worker reveals her own commitment and hopes for a society in which people and institutions work together for the common good.

Through this the worker gives hope to the client. The worker also helps the client define what needs to be done in the reaching out, and together they decide how the client is to do it. The worker is also careful to define the limits of what may be expected so that the client does not develop unrealistic expectations.

When helping the environmental system to respond to the client's reaching out, the worker points out their common interest and concerns and the obstacles that seem to be preventing cooperative functioning. The worker tries to help the environmental system mobilize its concern for the situation and its resources for helping. Where appropriate, the worker can provide the environmental system with information that will enhance its understanding of the situation. In a sense, both the original client and the environmental system are clients. In some situations (e.g., divorce) a social worker may be engaged as a mediator on initial contact. Both parties immediately are seen as clients under these circumstances.

In using this strategy, the worker negotiates a contract with the client and, where possible, with the environmental system as to the work (tasks) each will do in attempting to overcome the blocks and problems. The worker helps both to carry out their tasks by helping them adhere to the contract, by clarifying what is expected in the situation, and, in a sense, by demanding that they do their tasks.

Schwartz and Zalba have identified a four-step process for working with a client when using a mediative strategy:

1. *"Tuning in"*—The worker gets ready to enter the process of transactions in the situation.
2. *Beginning together*—The worker helps the various individuals involved to reach out to one another and identify what needs to be done. Contracts are negotiated.
3. *Work*—This is doing what needs to be done.
4. *Transitions and endings*—This is leaving the situation, ending the work together, the worker separating from the situation.[31]

Ernesto Gomez has adapted the four steps or phases of work for use with Chicano clients. He places particular emphasis on the tuning in phase. He notes that in this phase it is very important to "tune in" to the culture by focusing on how culture may be affecting the client in the situation. This includes concern for linguistic and other cultural practices as they relate to the specific client's needs in the situation for which help is sought. As worker and client begin together, a cultural assessment helps to focus on how cultural factors are contributing to the problem and how the culture can provide resources for dealing with the problem.[32] This approach would be useful when working with any minority group.

When working in a mediation mode, the units of attention are both the original client and the environmental systems involved. Each are helped to accept their common interests and to become aware of the feelings, needs, and demands of all persons involved. This requires that the worker be aware of the rules and roles within the situation. The worker provides focus and structure for the work to be done. Based on his knowledge and understanding, the worker also provides ideas and suggestions to the systems as to how they might better work together. Clarification and problem solving are important tools of the endeavor.

While the mediation strategy was developed to use with small groups, it has proven equally effective in working with individuals and is particularly useful with institutionalized individuals.[33] It can also be used with family groups. It is often a useful strategy in situations where empowerment is a goal.

CASE EXAMPLE

On Monday morning Bob Green, a social worker in the family and children's division of the Ford County Department of Social Service, received a report on an incident that had happened over the weekend in the Brown family. The report stated that the oldest child in the family, twenty-one-year-old Karen, who is not living at home, had called to file a child abuse complaint on behalf of her fifteen-year-old brother, Joe. She reported that her mother had scratched and bitten Joe in trying to restrain him from leaving home after she had forbidden him from going roller-skating.

The Brown family has been a part of Bob Green's caseload for the last two months. They became a client of the agency when Karen made a child abuse complaint on behalf of her thirteen-year-old sister, Gerry, after Gerry had been bruised under the eyes in a fight with her mother. This fight developed because the mother felt that Gerry was doing too much babysitting. Another issue between Gerry and Mrs. Brown seemed to be the fact that Mrs. Brown was opposed to Gerry using tampons. Karen demanded that Gerry be removed from the home. Gerry does not want this. Karen has retained a lawyer. Despite a recommendation from both the Department of Social Services (DSS) and from the assistant county attorney that no court order was warranted, the judge declared Gerry a child in need of assistance and ordered DSS to work with the family.

The family has a history of moving continuously from county to county. They moved to Ford County eight months ago and live in a mobile home about three miles from town. Bob has gained the following information about this family in his previous contacts with them:

Family Composition

Father, John, forty-five years old, is a truck driver. Has been labeled an alcoholic and convicted for driving under the influence. The worker believes he has a drinking problem but is not an alcoholic because he can control his drinking, which takes place when he is home and over weekends. He is out of home all week. He has a history of ulcers; two thirds of his stomach has been removed.

Mother, Sharon, forty-two years old, works from 11 P.M. to 7 A.M. at an assembly-line job in light industry. She has been hospitalized two times in the last year in the mental health unit of a general hospital. She describes herself as very emotional and nervous and is taking tranquilizers.

Karen, twenty-one, has not lived at home since she was sixteen. She is working as a cocktail waitress, and it is suspected she may also be a prostitute. She was removed from the home after being hit and bruised by her father. She lived in a series of foster homes for the next two years. Family therapy was ordered, but the family failed to follow through on this. Karen always moves to the new community when the family moves.

Henry, nineteen, is a school dropout, having left school after eleventh grade. He did not return to school after the family's last move. He manages a chain food store on the

10:30 P.M. to 6:30 A.M. shift. He says he plans to obtain a general education degree (GED) and go to vocational-technical school.

Joe, fifteen, has been labeled as mentally disabled. He is in an educable mentally retarded class at school. He has received outpatient mental health services that have been discontinued because the family failed to pay the minimal fee requested. The worker has been working with the family and the agency (mediating) to have this problem resolved. The family has made a partial payment on the outstanding bill, and treatment is scheduled to resume this week.

Gerry, thirteen, is either learning-disabled or emotionally disabled; the school has not been able to determine which. She has problems in processing information, and this seems the basis of her learning problems.

Family Functioning

Hitting seems to be an established reaction to stress; Mr. and Mrs. Brown both use this method. Tensions seem to build when Mr. Brown is on the road. The end of the week just before he returns home seems to be the time the mother is most apt to lose control. The father seems to avoid dealing with the problems. He did not return home for the court hearings regarding Gerry. He also seems to sabotage any attempt to work with the family as a unit in a therapy situation. Karen seems to get into every difficult situation that develops between Mrs. Brown and one of the younger children. She seems to see herself as a "rescuer." Henry seems to attempt to help Mrs. Brown in controlling the younger children, but his help is at times inappropriate.

As Bob Green thought about this family and what action he might take to ease this situation, he had the following ideas:

1. This was not a crisis situation. This family has a long history of poor social functioning in the area of parenting and also a history of running from problems. They might be characterized as a chaotic family.

2. Henry seems to be functioning best of all the children. He seems to be truly concerned about his mother and younger brother and sister but his response to that concern is inappropriate. Bob has mixed feelings about working with and through Henry. Henry might, with help, be able to become more constructive in helping his mother. However, Bob does not think it wise to expect him to accept responsibility for the family. For the time being, he decides not to work through or with Henry.

3. Both Mr. and Mrs. Brown are concerned about the family but also seem unable to parent the children appropriately. Bob wonders if they know how. One means of helping the family might be teaching them skills in parenting Joe and Gerry, both of whom seem to have some degree of mental disability.

4. Mrs. Brown may be overwhelmed by working full time while also dealing alone with her two adolescent children most of the time. Her own problems may also add to this overload. Perhaps some kind of support would be useful. Bob wonders if a suitable volunteer might be found to provide this support.

5. Karen seems to exacerbate the family problems. She seems to resent the parenting the younger children are getting and wants them removed from the home as she was. Bob is not sure just what can be done about this. He plans to discuss this with his supervisor.

In helping this family, Bob considered the following actions:

1. *Use of resources*—If there were younger children involved, providing homemaker service toward the end of the week might be desirable. Because of the children's ages and the fact that the homemakers available have little skill in teaching parenting of the adolescent, this is not an action to be considered. Also, the housekeeping standards, while not the best, are within acceptable levels. Family therapy at the mental health center has been tried and, because of Mr. Brown's resistance, has not been successful. Mrs. Brown and Joe have each been involved in individual mental health treatment. Bob decides that for now he needs to continue to encourage them to participate. Joe and Gerry also might benefit from participating in the activities of the local youth center where there is a director who is sensitive to the growing-up problems of adolescents and to parent-child relationships. Joint planning with the special education programs Joe and Gerry are involved in should be considered.

2. *Support*—This should be an important ingredient of any plan that is developed. Both parents, but particularly Mrs. Brown, care and are attempting to parent the children. They seem to have considerable difficulty when the children reach adolescence. Perhaps they have little understanding of the needs of the adolescent person. They have also had a bad experience with their oldest daughter, Karen, who continues to cause problems for the family. Bob thinks that if he arranges visits to the family toward the end of the week, when things seem most tense, he could help the family to think about new solutions for the difficulties that arise. He also should visit over the weekend to attempt to involve Mr. Brown in planning and in an attempt to break down his resistance to receiving help. He plans to use educative support as he focuses on adolescent parent-child relationships. Bob is very uncertain at this point whether to include Karen or to work with the family to minimize her influence.

3. *Activity*—Bob plans to suggest that the family sessions include some role-playing of different ways to solve family problems. He believes this is an action-oriented family and that doing will be very useful for them.

4. *Mediation*—This type of action will also be important. There are many disagreements in the family, especially between Mrs. Brown and the children. Mediation has been useful in the past in Bob's work with the Browns. Bob also believes he may need to make use of mediation between the family and the school, as there seems to be little interaction at best, and what interaction there is between Mr. and Mrs. Brown and the school is negative.

As Bob left the office to go see Mrs. Brown and discuss the problems, he felt he had at least some ideas about what might be tried in helping this family. He planned to confront Mrs. Brown with the implications of the continued family problems (further court intervention). He planned to discuss the options he had to suggest. He then would set up two further sessions in the next week. One would be with Mrs. Brown and the children at the end of the week to discuss how it was going; the second would be over the weekend when Mr. Brown was home, for the family to discuss the kind of help they thought would be most useful to them. Bob hoped to demonstrate that he could be helpful by offering concrete suggestions and helping the family decide what would be most helpful for them.

Because the human services system has had many negative experiences with this family, it will be important to help both the family and agencies serving the family to communicate with each other and develop new understanding about how to work together on the problems impacting the Browns. It would seem that mediation will be the primary strategy, with use of resources, support, and activity strategies to support the mediation process.

SUMMARY

The choice of which kind of action generalist social workers take with a client should be based in part on the principles of economy, self-determination, individualization, development, interdependence, and focus on service goals. The choice also depends on the skill of the worker and the worker's interventive repertoire.

Action to enable clients to use resources available requires a thorough knowledge of the service delivery system, skill in use of the referral process, and skill in the use of the broker and advocate roles. The service delivery system contains the informal helping network as well as the formal system.

Action in response to crisis calls for skill in recognizing a crisis situation. Response to a crisis should be immediate and active.

Action which enables the client(s) to find means for bringing about change in their environment and its institutions allows for empowerment of powerless people.

Action that is primarily supportive is focused on particular positive behaviors and attitudes. It guards against overdependence. It can promote growth.

Activity is especially useful when working with action-oriented persons. It is a tool. When using activity, the worker considers the client's lifestyle and characteristics. Also to be considered are the inherent characteristics of the activity and the process for carrying it out.

Action can have a mediation purpose, a good approach when the client and environment are not interacting in a functional manner. The worker helps client and environment reach out to each other so they can fulfill common needs.

QUESTIONS

1. What are some factors you would consider when making a choice about the kind of action to take with a client?

2. As a representative of a formal system (an agency), how would you go about helping a client use an informal system to obtain a resource she needs?

3. Empowerment has been considered of particular importance when working with women and people of color. Why do you think empowerment is important in such situations?

4. Describe the crisis process in a situation in which you have been involved. What was most helpful in the resolution of the crisis?

5. Name some situations in which you believe support is an appropriate action for a social worker to take.

6. Choose an activity that you think will be helpful in a specific situation. How did you go about choosing this activity? How should it be structured and presented?

7. In what kinds of situations would the mediating model be appropriate? When would it not be appropriate?

SUGGESTED READINGS

Auslander, Brian A., and Auslander, Gail K. "Self-help Groups and the Family Service Agency." *Social Casework* 69 (February 1988): 74–80.

Brown, James S. Toby, and Furstenberg, Anne-Linda. "Restoring Control: Empowering Older Patients and Their Families During Health Crisis." *Social Work in Health Care* 17 (4, 1992): 81–101.

Brown, Karen Strauch, and Ziefert, Marjorie. "A Feminist Approach to Working With Homeless Women." *Affilia* 5 (Spring 1990): 6–20.

Brown, Sam. "Self-Help: An Old Idea Whose Time Has Come." *Public Welfare* 39 (Winter 1981): 13–17.

Compton, Beulah Roberts. "An Attempt to Examine the Use of Support in Social Work Practice." In Beulah Roberts Compton and Burt Galaway, Eds., *Social Work Processes,* 3rd ed. Homewood, IL: Dorsey Press, 1984 (pp. 477–485).

Connaway, Ronda S., and Gentry, Martha E. *Social Work Practice.* Englewood Cliffs, NJ: Prentice Hall, 1988 (Chapter 10).

Coplan, Jennifer, and Strull, Judith. "Roles of the Professional in Mutual Aid Groups. " *Social Casework* 64 (May 1983): 259–275.

Cox, Enid Opal. "The Critical Role of Social Action in Empowerment Oriented Groups. *Social Work with Groups* 14 (2, 1991): 77–90.

Dixon, Samuel L., and Sands, Roberta G. "Identity and the Experience of Crisis." *Social Casework* 64 (April 1983): 223–230.

Ferris, Patricia, and Marshall, Catherine, A. "A Model Project for Families of the Chronically Mentally Ill." *Social Work* 32 (March–April 1987): 110–114.

Gibelman, Margaret, and Demone, Harold W. "The Social Worker as Mediator in the Legal System." *Social Casework* 70 (January 1989): 28–36.

Gibson, Guadalupe, Ed. *Our Kingdom Stands on Brittle Glass.* Silver Spring, MD: National Association of Social Workers, 1983.

Gitterman, Alex, and Shulman, Lawrence. *Mutual Aid Groups and the Life Cycle.* Itasca, IL: F. E. Peacock, 1986.

Golan, Naomi. "Crisis Theory." In Frances J. Turner, Ed., *Social Work Treatment: Interlocking Theoretical Approaches,* 4th ed. New York: Free Press, 1986 (pp. 296–340).

———. "Intervention at Times of Transition: Services and Forms of Help." *Social Casework* 61 (May 1980): 259–266.

Greenberg, Shirley. "The Supportive Approach to Therapy." *Clinical Social Work Journal* 14 (Spring 1986): 6–13.

Gutierrez, Lorraine M. "Working with Women of Color: An Empowerment Perspective." *Social Work* 35 (March 1990): 149–153.

Hasenfeld, Yeheskel, and Gidron, Benjamin. "Self-Help Groups and Human Service Organizations: An Interorganizational Perspective." *Social Service Review* 67 (June 1993): 217–236.

Hirayama, Hisashi, and Cetingok, Muammer. "Enpowerment: A Social Work Approach for Asian Immigrants." *Social Casework* 69 (January 1988): 41–47.

Kelley, James, and Sykes, Pamela. "Helping the Helpers: A Support Group for Family Members of Persons with AIDS." *Social Work* 34 (May 1989): 239–242.

Knight, Carolyn. "Use of Support Groups with Adult Female Survivors of Child Sexual Abuse." *Social Work* 35 (May 1990): 202–206.

Krishef, Curtis H., and Yoelin, Michael L. "Differential Use of Informal and Formal Helping Networks Among Rural Elderly Black and White Floridians." *Journal of Gerontological Social Work* 3 (Spring 1981): 45–59.

Land, Helen, and Harangody, George. "A Support Group for Partners of Persons with AIDS." *Families in Society* 71 (October 1990): 471–481.

Lukton, Rosemary Creed. "Myths and Realities of Crisis Intervention." *Social Casework* 63 (May 1982): 276–285.

Maguire, Lambert. *Understanding Social Networks.* Beverly Hills, CA: Sage Publications, 1983.

Maluccio, Anthony N. "Action as a Tool in Casework Practice." *Social Casework* 55 (January 1974): 30–35.

Middleman, Ruth R., Ed. "Activities and Action in Groupwork." Special Issue, *Social Work with Groups* 6 (Spring 1983).

———. "The Use of Program: Review and Update." *Social Work with Groups* 3 (Fall 1980): 5–23.

Minahan, Anne, Ed. *Encyclopedia of Social Work,* 18th ed. Silver Spring, MD: National Association of Social Workers, 1987 ("Crisis Intervention," "Mutual Help Groups," and "Natural Helping Networks").

Nelson, Judith C. "Support: A Necessary Condition for Change." *Social Work* 25 (September 1980): 388–392.

Parsons, Ruth J. "Empowerment: Purpose and Practice Principle in Social Work." *Social Work with Groups* 14 (2, 1991): 7–21.

Parsons, Ruth J. "The Mediator Role in Social Work Practice." *Social Work* 36 (November 1991): 483–487.

Parsons, Ruth J., and Cox, Enid V. "Family Mediation in Elder Caregiving Decisions: An Empowerment Intervention." *Social Work* 34 (March 1989): 122–126.

Rubenstein, Hiasaura, and Lawler, Sharene K. "Toward the Psychosocial Empowerment of Women." *Affilia* 5 (Fall 1990): 27–38.

Rose, Stephen M., ed. *Case Management and Social Work Practice.* New York: Longman, 1992.

Schlosberg, Shirley B., and Kagan, Richard M. "Practice Strategies for Engaging Chronic Multiproblem Families." *Social Casework* 69 (January 1988): 3–9.

Sheafor, Bradford W., Horejsi, Charles R., and Horejsi, Gloria A. *Techniques and Guidelines for Social Work Practice.* Boston: Allyn and Bacon, 1988 (Chapter 12).

Shulman, Lawrence. *Mutual Aid Groups, Vulnerable Populations and the Life Cycle,* 2nd ed. New York: Columbia University Press, 1993.

Shulman, Lawrence. *The Skills of Helping: Individual and Group,* 2nd ed. Itasca, IL: F. E. Peacock, 1984.

Solomon, Barbara Bryant. "How Do We Really Empower Families? New Strategies for Social Work Practioners." In Beulah Roberts Compton and Bert Galaway, Eds., *Social Work Processes,* 4th ed. Belmont, CA: Wadsworth, 1989 (pp. 529–532).

Solomon, Barbara Bryant. "Social Work Values and Skills to Empower Women." In Ann Weick and Susan T. Vandiver, Eds., *Women, Power, and Change.* Washington, DC: National Association of Social Workers, 1980 (pp. 197–205).

Staub-Bernasconi, Silvia. "Social Action, Empowerment and Social Work—An Integrative Theoretical Framework for Social Work and Social Work with Groups." *Social Work with Groups* 14 (2, 1991): 35–51.

Tobias, Mark. "Validator: A Key Role in Empowering the Chronically Mentally Ill." *Social Work* 35 (July 1990): 357–359.

Whittaker, James K., and Garbarino, James. *Social Support Networks: Informal Helping in the Human Services.* New York: Aldine Publishing, 1983.

Wilson, Paul A. "Toward More Effective Intervention in Natural Helping Networks." *Social Work in Health Care* 9 (Winter 1983): 81–88.

Wood, Gale Goldberg, and Middleman, Ruth A. "Groups to Empower Battered Women. *Affilia* 7 (Winter 1992): 82–95.

NOTES

1. For a discussion of the difference between theory, approach to practice, and method, see Louise C. Johnson, "Social Work Practice Models: Teaching and the Differential Aspects of Practice," in *Teaching Competence in the Delivery of Direct Service* (New York: Council on Social Work Education, 1976), p. 41. Sources that have identi-fied theories, models, or approaches include: Robert W. Roberts and Robert Nee, Eds., *Theories of Social Casework* (Chicago: University of Chicago Press, 1970); Robert W. Roberts and Helen Northen, Eds., *Theories of Social Work with Groups* (New York: Columbia University Press, 1976); Joan Stein, *The Family as a Unit of Study and Treat-*

ment (Seattle: University of Washington, School of Social Work, 1969); and Jack Rothman, "Three Models of Community Organization Practice," in *Social Work Practice 1968* (New York: Columbia University Press, 1968), pp. 16–47.

2. See Charles R. Atherton, Sandra T. Michelle, and Edna Biehl Schein, "Locating Points for Intervention," *Social Casework* 52 (March 1971): 131–141, and "Using Points for Intervention," Social Casework 52 (April 1971); Herbert Bisno, "A Theoretical Framework for Teaching Social Work Methods and Skills with Particular Reference to Undergraduate Social Work Education," *Journal of Education for Social Work* 5 (Fall 1969): 5–17; Genevieve B. Oxley, "A Life Model Approach to Change," *Social Casework* 52 (December 1971): 627–633; and Robert J. Teare and Harold L. McPheeters, *Manpower Utilization in Social Welfare* (Atlanta, GA: Southern Regional Education Board, 1970).

3. Ross V. Speck and Carolyn L. Attneave, *Family Networks* (New York: Pantheon, 1973).

4. Eugene Litwak and Ivan Szelenyi, "Primary Group Structures and Their Function: Kin, Neighbors, and Friends," *American Sociological Review* 34 (August 1969): 465–481.

5. Alice H. Collins and Diane L. Pancoast, *Natural Helping Networks: A Strategy for Intervention* (Washington, DC: National Association of Social Workers, 1974).

6. Alan Gartner and Frank Riessman, *Self Help in the Human Services* (San Francisco: Jossey-Bass, 1977).

7. Yeheskel Hasenfeld and Benjamin Gidron, "Self-help Groups and Human Service Organizations: An Interorganizational Perspective," *Social Service Review* 67 (June 1993): 217–236.

8. For a good discussion of effective referral, see Elizabeth Nicholas, *A Primer of Social Casework* (New York: Columbia University Press, 1960), chap. 9, "How to Make an Effective Referral."

9. Teare and McPheeters, *Manpower Utilization*, p. 34.

10. Ibid.

11. Lorraine M. Gutierrez, "Working with Women of Color: An Empowerment Perspective," *Social Work* 35 (March 1990): 149–153.

12. Barbara Bryant Solomon, *Black Empowerment: Social Work in Oppressed Communities* (New York: Columbia University Press, 1976), and "Social Work Values and Skills to Empower Women," in Ann Weick and Susan T. Vandiver, Eds., *Women, Power, and Change* (Washington, DC: National Association of Social Workers, 1980), pp. 206–214.

13. Ruth J. Parsons, "Empowerment: Purpose and Practice Principle in Social Work," *Social Work with Groups* 14 (2, 1991): 7–21. Also, contains an excellent case example.

14. Silvia Staub-Bernasconi, "Social Action, Empowerment and Social Work—An Integrative Theoretical Framework for Social Work and Social Work with Groups," *Social Work with Groups* 14 (2, 1991): 35–51.

15. Good discussions of techniques are found in Gutierrez, "Working with Women" and in Solomon, "Social Work Values," op. cit.

16. See the Appendix for an outline of this model. Other excellent sources include: Lydia Rapoport, "Crisis Intervention as a Mode of Brief Treatment," in Roberts and Nee, *Theories of Social Casework*, pp. 267–311; Naomi Golan, *Treatment in Crisis Situations* (New York: Free Press, 1978); Samuel Dixon, *Working with People in Crisis* (St. Louis: C. V. Mosby, 1978); and Larry L. Smith, "A Review of Crisis Intervention Theory," *Social Casework* 59 (July 1978): 396–401.

17. Lois G. Selby, "Supportive Treatment: The Development of a Concept and a Helping Method," *Social Service Review* 30 (December 1956): 400–414.

18. Lois G. Selby and Beulah Roberts Compton, "An Attempt to Examine the Use of Support in Social Work Practice," in *Social Work Processes*, 2nd ed., Beulah Roberts Compton and Burt Galaway, Eds. (Homewood, IL: Dorsey Press, 1979), pp. 378–386.

19. Florence Hollis, *Casework: A Psychosocial Therapy* (New York: Random House, 1972), pp. 89–95.

20. Judith C. Nelson, "Support: A Necessary Condition for Change," *Social Work* 25 (September 1980): 388–392.

21. Patricia Ferris and Catherine A. Marshall, "A Model Project for Families of the Chroni-

cally Mentally Ill," *Social Work* 32 (March–April 1987): 110–114.

22. James Kelley and Pamelia Sykes, "Helping the Helpers: A Support Group for Family Members of Persons with AIDS," *Social Work* 34 (May 1989): 239–242.

23. Carolyn Knight, "Use of Support Groups with Adult Female Survivors of Child Sexual Abuse," *Social Work* 35 (May 1990): 202–206.

24. See Elizabeth McBroom, "Socialization and Social Casework," in Roberts and Nee, *Theories of Social Casework*, pp. 315–351.

25. Robert Vinter, "Program Activities: An Analysis of Their Effects on Participant Behavior," in Robert Vinter, Ed., *Readings in Group Work Practice* (Ann Arbor, MI.: Campus Publishers, 1967).

26. See Ruth R. Middleman, "The Use of Program: Review and Update," *Social Work with Groups* 3 (Fall 1980): 5–23. The Suggested Readings in this text contain many important sources for this material as well.

27. William Schwartz, "The Worker in the Group," in *Social Welfare Forum* 1961 (New York: Columbia University Press, 1961), p. 154.

28. William Schwartz, "On The Use of Groups in Social Work Practice," in William Schwartz and Serapio R. Zalba, *The Practice of Group Work* (New York: Columbia University Press, 1971), p. 5.

29. See Schwartz and Zalba, *The Practice of Group Work;* and Lawrence Shulman, *A Casebook of Social Work with Groups: The Mediating Model* (New York: Council on Social Work Education, 1968), and *The Skills of Helping Individuals and Groups*, 2nd ed., (Itasca, IL: F. E. Peacock, 1984).

30. See Shulman, *The Skills of Helping Individuals and Groups*, pp. 9–10.

31. Schwartz and Zalba, *The Practice of Group Work.*

32. Ernesto Gomez, "The San Antonio Model: A Culture-Oriented Approach," in *Our Kingdom Stands on Brittle Glass*, Guadalupe Gibson, Ed. (Silver Spring, MD: National Association of Social Workers, 1983), pp. 96–111.

33. See Shulman, *A Casebook of Social Work with Groups.*

14

INDIRECT PRACTICE ACTIONS

Learning Expectations

1. An understanding of the need to engage in action with those other than clients.
2. An understanding of influence and its use.
3. An understanding of action to coordinate services.
4. An appreciation of the usefulness of a program-planning and development strategy.
5. An understanding of environmental manipulation as a strategy.
6. An understanding of the change-from-within strategy (an organization).
7. An appreciation of the need to engage in cause advocacy.

In the generalist approach to social work practice, the worker is not only involved in direct work with clients (as discussed in the last chapter) but is also involved in work with individuals, small groups, agencies, and communities on behalf of individual and family clients. This work has often been characterized as indirect practice. It is very often work with the agency and community systems, sometimes described as *mezzo* or *macro practice*.

In Chapter 1, the discussion of need pointed out the historic cause-function debate in social work. That discussion also noted two kinds of need: private troubles and public issues. Work with individuals and families usually falls in the function and private-trouble domain of response to need, whereas work focused on agencies and communities tends to fall in the cause and public-issue domain.

One of the identifying characteristics of the generalist social worker is the worker's ability to respond to both private troubles and public issues. Furthermore, the generalist social worker identifies both the private troubles and the public issues inherent in any practice situation and then decides the appropriate focus of the action for change. This focus may be on the private-trouble (individuals and families) or on the social-issue (agency and community) concerns. Often the focus may call for work with both the private and the public. Thus, the generalist practitioner must possess knowledge and skills for indirect as well as direct practice and be able to combine the two when appropriate.

When working for large-system change, the generalist social worker may be able to engage in assessment and planning with the system of focus and thus use a collaborative strategy. If this is not possible, then bargaining or even conflict strategies may be needed.

This chapter discusses six approaches that may be used in indirect practice:

1. Action that involves influentials,
2. Action relative to coordination of services,
3. Action for program planning and development,
4. Action designed to change the environment,
5. Action taken to change organizations, and
6. Cause advocacy action.

Before discussing each of these approaches to action, attention will be given to influence as it relates to action on behalf of clients. As the social worker works with clients, the influence for change is heavily based on the worker-client interaction, particularly on the relationship between worker and client. In indirect practice, the worker often works through individuals and small groups in order to meet needs of clients either as small systems (individuals and families) or as collectives (particularly community segments impacted by a dysfunctional delivery system or a social problem). Relationship remains an important aspect of influence, though other factors such as the knowledge and expertise of the worker and the material resources and services the worker might have available are also important. The worker's status and reputation are also important sources of influence. All these influences are used when the work together is collaborative and cooperative in nature. Sometimes persuasive techniques must be used for the other system or systems involved to become convinced that a collaborative or cooperative approach is of value to all concerned. Sometimes cooperation and collaboration are not possible, and confrontation, bargaining, and even coercion are necessary to reach the desired goals.

Sometimes the social worker initiates and participates in the action on behalf of clients. Sometimes mediation between systems is called for. At other times the social worker stimulates others to carry out the action. Regardless of who takes the action, some means of legitimizing any action taken must be sought. The social worker does not act in isolation but as a representative of an agency. Sometimes the social worker can act with or through an organization to which she belongs. Without the support of legitimization, the worker lacks the influence needed to support the change effort. Ethical issues come into play.

INVOLVEMENT OF INFLUENTIALS

One means of gaining support is through the involvement of **influentials**—persons within a community or an organization who have power and/or authority. Persons may have power because they have a reputation that assigns power to them. They may have power because they are in a position to make crucial decisions, such as which projects get funded, who sees the top administrators, or how the regulations will be written. Other persons have power assigned to them because of a specific role or function they fill that involves control over ideas, information, fiscal resources, and so on.

Influentials have the ability to use power to affect the actions of others. They are persons who can persuade others to act in specific ways. They can gain allegiance from others for their point of view or way of functioning. They can effect compliance with desired ways of functioning. They are persons who have control of needed resources (money, manpower, etc.). They can reward or punish other persons. They can effectively block action they do not favor. Persons may be influential in all aspects of an organization or community, or they may be influential in only certain segments of the system's functioning. Influentials relate to one another in patterns that are known as the power structure.

In working for change, social workers work with influentials in several ways:

1. Sometimes approval for projects or programs must be obtained from influentials in order to facilitate development of the projects or programs.
2. Sometimes an attempt is made to have the influential initiate the action in order to gain the support of others.
3. Sometimes the influentials must be given understanding about what is being planned and why to prevent them from blocking a project.

In order to work with influentials, it is first necessary to identify these persons. This can be done by asking persons who know the system well—"system knowledgeables" who have the reputation of being influential or who must be included in any decision making. Influentials are not always the persons who hold the authority positions; often, they are less visible and function behind the scenes in the informal system. An understanding of the community and its power structure is essential when working with influentials.

As social workers work with influentials, they need to be very clear about the desired change and why it is needed. They can then present facts in a convincing, logical manner. It is often useful to show the influential how the desired change is in the influential's self-interest. This is a first step for involving influentials. It allows influentials to sense that the social worker can sometimes be their ally in carrying out community projects in which they are interested. Social workers should remain open and flexible when working with influentials. Of particular importance is the incorporation of appropriate input from the influentials into the plan. Persuasion skills sometimes are important when working with influentials.

The art of **opportunity seizing** is another important skill when working with influentials. This involves a keen sense of timing and a capacity to sense when influentials are ready to become involved in a desired activity and when they are ready to make use of a social worker's help and expertise. Involvement in the activities of the community can provide social workers with opportunities to get to know influentials and for influentials to get to know them.

Persuasion skills are important when working with influentials. They often can be used to help an influential understand the desirability of working for change. Social workers need to learn how to work with and utilize influentials as a means of affecting change in organizations and communities.

CASE EXAMPLE

Joe, a social worker who is employed in a community residential facility for developmentally disabled adults, was asked after church one Sunday morning by a community influential why these clients were seen wandering around the streets on Saturday with no supervision. Joe pointed out that they have Saturday off from their sheltered workshop jobs, just as many other people do. He said the clients were fairly high functioning and able to be on their own, but that they experienced difficulty because they felt they were discriminated against by local merchants. He informed the influential that the agency lacked staff who could plan recreational activity over the weekend.

Several other people became involved in the conversation and asked Joe if there was anything that the church could do about the situation. Joe replied that he felt there were things that could be done and he would be glad to meet with a group to explore the situation. One of the individuals who was involved in the conversation was the local newspaper editor. He asked Joe to stop in to see him sometime during the week; perhaps he could help with a human interest story in his paper.

As a result of this initial contact with these influentials, a program was set up that resulted in activities for the clients on weekends. The newspaper gave extensive coverage to the program as well as running a series of stories on the agency and its clients. All of this activity resulted in changed attitudes toward the developmentally disabled in the community.

COORDINATION OF SERVICES

Coordination is the working together of two or more service providers. Coordination of activity can be focused on a client, such as an individual or family (*micro-level coordination*), or it can be focused on persons in a particular category, such as the aged or the developmentally disabled (*macro-level coordination*).

Collaboration and coordination are often used as if they were synonymous, but as used in this book, there is a difference. *Collaboration* is a working together of two or more helpers using a common plan of action. It implies teamwork. Coordination does not imply a common plan of action; in fact, there may be two or more plans of action. Collaboration and teamwork are two kinds of coordination. Since they have been discussed in Chapter 9, they will not be discussed again. In this section several other methods of coordination will be presented.

For coordination to be effective, there must be a spirit of working together toward a desirable end. This end may be a common goal, such as maintaining a chronically mentally ill person in the community, which requires different services provided by different agencies such as socialization services and vocational rehabilitation services, as well as help in obtaining appropriate housing, medical monitoring services, income maintenance services, and the like. Public social services, a mental health center, vocational rehabilitation, and perhaps other agencies would all need to be involved.

The end may also be a common goal of providing a range of services to a particular community that would make it possible for the needs of aging persons to be met. This might involve coordination of the services of a senior citizens center, a public health nursing agency, public social services, and a wide variety of other services that may be available in a community. The goals of this coordination would include not only those relating to specific older clients but also those relating to helping existing services become appropriately responsive to the needs of all older persons. The common end would be a network of needed services that are usable by a broad range of older persons.

An important aspect of coordination is the mutual satisfaction of all concerned. The persons or agencies involved need to believe that it is advantageous to coordinate their services with others. This leads to open exchange and to feelings of satisfaction so necessary for productive relationships. Coordination can involve a range of resources much broader than those of the formal social service agencies. It can involve professionals from a variety of disciplines—service providers connected to community institutions such as schools and churches, community self-help group leaders, and the informal resources of friends, family, and work colleagues.

One factor that sometimes hinders coordination is related to the differing perspectives on the client and the client's needs and problems by persons of different professional disciplines. A doctor may see an older person's frail health status or danger of broken bones from falling as the primary problem. A social worker might see this same older person's lack of a support system as the major problem. A senior citizens center director might identify the problem as isolation. Each professional would then also advocate for a different solution for the client. The physician might push for a nursing home placement. The senior citizens director might want to involve the client in the activities of the center. The social worker might want to attempt to develop an individualized support system after ascertaining the client's desires.

Each profession has its own societal task to perform; each has its own way of functioning, its own values and knowledge base. When social workers are working with other disciplines, it is important for them to have an understanding of the perspectives of the other professions before attempting to coordinate with them. Issues of concern to other professions and areas of overlapping interest and service should also be identified. The social worker should also be aware of potential tensions among professionals. (Working with other professions has also been discussed in Chapter 6.)

The expectation that every professional thinks or should think in the same ways about a client or a client's needs and problems is a major block to coordination. Understanding differences is a first step to working together in a coordinated manner. This understanding leads to identifying the distinctive capacities each professional may have that can be used in developing a coordinative relationship and can lead to respect and acceptance. Respect for, and acceptance of, another profession's contribution are necessary components of coordinative action.

When coordinating resources and activities from the informal arena, it is important to be aware of the differing ways of functioning between formal and informal resources. Eugene Litwak and Henry Meyer have pointed out the differences in functioning of the primary group or natural systems and the bureaucracy or formal system. Primary systems are diffuse, personal, have an affective bond, and call for face-to-face contact. They can best deal with nonuniform, relatively unique events. They are adaptable and flexible and have the capacity to respond quickly. Bureaucratic systems tend to be impersonal, specific as to what they can do, and operate within rules and regulations. They function with professional and technical expertise and deal with large numbers of persons in an impartial manner. Both kinds of service systems are important and should be coordinated.

An important contribution of Litwak and Meyer is what they call the *balance theory of coordination*. They believe that the important aspect of coordination is communication. If the two types of systems (formal and informal) are too far apart, communication does not take place. Because of their different ways of functioning, if they are too close together they hinder each other's functioning. Litwak and Meyer believe that there is a midpoint of social distance between the two systems at which each system can function best.[1] (The midpoint is the point where the two systems can communicate with each other but are not so close that the functioning of either system is impaired.)

Social workers who get to know community influentials and natural helpers in relatively informal community groups can develop relationships that will facilitate coordination with the informal system. If persons who function in the informal system know the social worker, they will be more apt to consult with her or to refer someone to her. Social workers in turn can discuss common concerns with persons in the informal system in the informal settings where these helpers are more comfortable.

Another consideration is the difference between the ways in which men and women communicate. The natural helping system seems to be more often a female system. The formal systems, while staffed with both men and women, seem to function in a formalized manner that is more akin to traditional male communication. Male social workers should be particularly aware of this difference in communication styles when working with the informal helping system.

Coordination has been carried out through several mechanisms. One has been to locate those who serve a similar population in a common setting, often called a multiservice center. This can be done by locating entire agencies in a common setting or by locating individual service deliverers (e.g., family service worker, a community health nurse, an income maintenance worker) representing a variety of agencies in a common setting close to those needing service. It is assumed not only that this will make services more accessible to clients but that close proximity will also encourage sharing among the professionals.

Another means of linking services has been an information-and-referral service, which can serve as a coordinative mechanism, depending on its means of functioning and on the capacity of those who staff it. If the emphasis is on providing information about services, the coordinative function will probably not be carried out. If the emphasis is on referral and enabling persons to reach the needed services, then a coordinative service is enhanced by followup and evaluation of the service delivered. Evaluation can also lead to identification of unmet needs and of needed services that are not available and thus to program development. Two coordination approaches that merit special consideration are case management and networking.

Case Management

Case management has recently received considerable attention as a coordinative approach to service delivery. It has been found to be useful in the fields of child welfare, mental health (particularly with the chronically mentally ill), developmental disabilities, and gerontology. Its use is often indicated where a client needs a range of services from several social service or health providers. It should also be noted that provision for such services is supported by recent federal legislation.[2]

Although the process of case management has been identified in a varying manner from field to field, a common thread seems to be emerging. According to Karen Orloff Kaplan, that process contains five components: 1) case identification; 2) assessment and planning; 3) coordination and referral; 4) implementation of services; and 5) monitoring, evaluation, and reassessment.[3]

Assessment and planning involve consideration not only of client needs but also of the resources available within that client's informal network of relationships and in the immediate community. The assessment is carried out with maximal client input. It also involves identifying the needed resources and weaving the need-fulfilling resources into a plan that is congruent with the client's desires and lifestyle. This weaving together can be described as developing a complementary resource pattern. That is, the case manager provides an integration so that resources are not duplicating each other or working at cross-purposes, so that the client can sense a holistic concern for need fulfillment.

The case manager reaches out to the various resources to obtain their cooperative input and to provide the information they need for the coordinated services. The case manager may need to creatively develop a new resource or help to modify an existing resource. Often the case manager provides a part of the needed service. Regular monitoring is another task of the case manager.

Several case management models have been developed, usually addressing service in a particular field of practice (e.g., child welfare, services to older adults). One developed by Jack Rothman seems to depict the process most thoroughly and clearly. This model begins with access to agency through outreach or referral and proceeds through intake and an assessment, which may have both short- and long-term psychological, social, and medical components to goal setting. From this point a variety of options are possible: intervention planning, resource identification and indexing, and linking clients to formal agencies or informally to families and others. Counseling, therapy, advocacy, and interagency coordination, including policy considerations, may also be used, but are outside the process loop and are used only when needed. Monitoring, reassessment, and outcome evaluation are also within the loop. Rothman also notes that the process is meant to be used flexibly and is cyclical in nature.[4]

Two goals are often discussed in relation to the approach: continuity of care and maximal level of functioning. *Continuity of care* is important because many of the clients who benefit from the use of this approach need services for an extended period of time, if not for the rest of their lives. This care may need to be provided in a range of different community and institutional settings. A holistic plan for services is considered desirable. Case managers can often provide the desired continuity. *Maximal level of functioning* is important because many clients with whom this approach is used function at less than a level of independent functioning. Because of the multiple problems involved, they may not be functioning at the highest level of which they are capable. A case management approach provides the overview that can lead to planning, which encourages a maximal level of functioning.

Stephen P. Moore notes that case management should be an enabling and facilitating activity. A major thrust is to insure that formal service complements family care and other informal helping rather than competing with or substituting for such care. Of course, this can add to the complexity of the service as the case manager may need to consider not only the current and potential strengths, limitations, and ways of functioning of the informal care system, but may need to spend time developing a potential for help within these systems. He may also need to provide support and other services to the informal system to enable it to be the needed resource. It is important to always be aware of the stresses and strains on the informal system as well as the needs of the helping system.[5]

Case management calls for the social worker to use both direct and indirect approaches. It is truly generalist social work practice as it weaves together a variety of strategies so that the range of needs of clients with multiple problems can be met. Coordination is a major concern of the case manager.

CASE EXAMPLE

Larry is a 35-year-old developmentally disabled man who has spent the last 15 years in an institution. He was originally placed because his parents' advancing age made it impossible for them to care for him. He had several trials in group homes, but his anger over being separated from his parents and the demands placed on him in the group living facilities led to combative behavior that could not be controlled. Over the years, this combative behavior has decreased and increasing demands have been placed on him for more independent functioning. It has now been determined that Larry is ready to live in a protected situation in the community.

A case manager for the agency to which Larry has been referred for placement carefully considered the comprehensive assessment of the institution. As he has worked with a number of referrals from this institution and found the assessments accurate, he decides to depend primarily on this assessment for the initial planning. In addition, he talks to Larry about possibilities for community living. The case manager sets as a short-term goal that Larry adjust to community living with involvement in sheltered work and recreational activities. Because Larry's parents have died and there is no other involved family, the worker chooses a group home in a small town with a sheltered workshop. The case manager believes that Larry should not have to adjust to big-city life, which might be confusing at this time. He also knows a couple of the group home's current residents who were also placed from Larry's present institution. The staff of this facility has been very successful in working with long-term institutionalized persons.

The case manager discusses Larry's interests and experiences derived from work assignments in the institution with the sheltered workshop staff, who make suggestions about work assignments and ways of working with Larry. The community into which Larry is to be placed is particularly rich in recreational activities as it is a college town and students are available to work with group home residents. The group home director and the case manager make specific plans for using this resource. The case manager also needs to help Larry apply for SSI. He will need help in learning to manage money when he begins to get his checks.

During the initial placement stage, the case manager plans to monitor the situation carefully with weekly contacts with Larry, the group home, and the sheltered workshop. The group home manager will take responsibility for setting up the recreational program. After a period of adjustment, the case manager hopes that monitoring can be less frequent. At such a time, it will be important to set up long-term goals for Larry.

Networking

Networking also is a form of coordination.[6] It is the development and maintenance of communication and of ways of working together among persons of diverse interests and orientations. It is a technique that can facilitate macro-level coordination. Networking holds promise as a means for persons from formal helping systems and those from informal systems (natural helpers) to work together. The technique of networking calls for developing some means of face-to-face communication among people who have the potential for developing a relationship based on a common interest.

One technique used to develop a network is "a fair." Persons delivering services in a particular area (such as to women) are invited to set up displays and provide an informed person to be present to discuss informally the services provided. The fair is usually seen as an opportunity for community persons to find out about services. In the informal, open discussion at a fair, professional persons and other helpers also discover commonalities of interest and concern. From this discussion decisions begin to be made about working together. A sensitive facilitator then encourages further planning for activity that will strengthen the network.

Another technique is a monthly meeting of community agencies that is expanded to include a wide range of community resources. Agendas for these meetings can consist of various agencies presenting their programs and services to those present. However, time needs to be provided for informal discussion and discussion of current community problems. Over time, the goal is for relationships to develop among the participants and for a network to emerge.

Because of the differing patterns of functioning and communicating, the formal systems must not expect the informal systems to accept their patterns. Networking calls for the establishment of innovative patterns that allow both formal and informal systems to function together. Informality must not be stifled but rather respected and encouraged when using this form of coordination.

When coordinating with natural helpers, it is important not to place professional expectations upon them. Professionals tend to place these persons in a paraprofessional capacity and take a supervisory stance in the relationship. This is not appropriate. First, it may destroy any chance of developing the relationship because of the threat to the natural helper in such a relationship. Second, it may destroy the natural helper's distinctive ways of helping and thus his distinctive contribution to the situation.[7] Professionals who use a consultative stance are most apt to develop coordinative relationships with natural helpers.

Blocks to effective coordination include lack of respect for, or confidence in, the other helpers involved; lack of adequate sharing of information among the helpers; differing perspectives or values about what is to be done regarding clients; lack of capacity to share and work together; lack of time to develop cooperative relationships; and lack of agency sanction and support for coordination. When mutual understanding, shared goals, a feeling that it is advantageous to work cooperatively, a capacity to work together, and the sanction needed to develop cooperative relationships are present, a productive, satisfying coordination is possible.

Three social work skills are useful for social workers to employ in facilitating coordination: 1) skill in sensing commonalities and differences and in communicating them appropriately to those involved in the situation; 2) skill in facilitating communication among the participants; and 3) skill in exciting and motivating helping persons in relation to the advantages of coordination of services for the client. Underlying these skills is the capacity to develop opportunities creatively for open and relaxed communication.

Much has been said about the need for, and the advantages of, coordination in interorganizational and interprofessional relationships. Less has been identified with respect to the means (skills and techniques) of developing and maintaining those relationships. The application of understandings about the nature of other types of relationships and means for encouraging and maintaining them can provide some of the needed knowledge base. Coordination is needed for providing complex services in complex situations. Coordination depends on functional relationships among helping people.

CASE EXAMPLE

Lucille is a social worker who is a member of a board of directors of an information-and-referral service in a medium-sized city. She becomes aware of the fact that there are a number of groups providing services to senior citizens. There are three senior citizens centers, a RSVP program, a day-care center, five nursing homes, and two nutrition sites. In addition, the Department of Social Services provides social services and homemaker services to income-eligible persons, and the public health agency provides in-home nursing care. There are two private agencies and a mental health center that have counseling services available to senior citizens. Many of these agencies have transportation services for use in attending that agency's activities. There is, however, no centralized transportation service that can be used for shopping and keeping medical appointments. There is one small low-income elderly housing project, but there is a demand for additional low-income housing appropriate for the elderly. To date, the realtors have been able to prevent additional housing from being provided. They have done this through their influence on the City Council because they believe these housing units are not in their best interest.

As a social worker, Lucille is concerned that there is no coordination among these services. In fact, they seem to be competing with one another. Transportation seems to be a particularly sensitive issue. Each group refuses to use their vans for any programs but their own, yet the vans are parked a good part of the day. Also, several different vans pick up in the same area at about the same time.

Another thing that concerns Lucille and other service providers is an imminent cutback in funding for several of the programs. There is a feeling that services could be maintained if some means could be found to eliminate duplication of administrative costs. Each agency claims that it is willing to take on new services but cannot allow the services it provides to go to another agency. Competition for resources is becoming a big issue.

Lucille believes something must be done to better coordinate the services for the elderly in the community. She is aware of the key persons in each agency and their stance. She also knows several community persons who are very interested in doing something about the problem, and she discusses the situation with them. Two are former state legislators, older persons who are highly respected in the community. One is a natural helper who also is well known. Another is a member of the City Council. She calls together a small group of service providers, choosing those who are most inclined to try a cooperative venture. In this group she includes several social workers from the Department of Social Services because she is aware that the department (the agency administering Older Americans Act funds) is interested in encouraging cooperative planning.

At the meeting, a small group of service deliverers decides that a larger meeting to discuss coordination should be called. Invitations should go to all those who provide service to senior citizens and other persons who have been identified as having a special interest in senior citizens. A list of about one hundred persons is made. The group thinks that a structured program should be put forth with some persons from outside the community presenting information about coordination of services. The suggestion is made that the state Office on Aging (Department of Social Services) be consulted. They also decide (Lucille influences here) that Mr. Black, one of the former legislators, would be a good person to chair the meeting. He knows how to do this and has not been involved heavily in any one of the programs. He is respected by all. Lucille agrees to see if the Office on Aging has any ideas for speakers.

Lucille contacts the Office on Aging and finds it to be most helpful. The office is interested in this kind of project as a demonstration project. Personnel there are trying to identify means for developing coordination of services for senior citizens. They are willing to fund the bringing of two persons to speak at the meeting. They suggest the director of a Senior Citizens Center in a community that has a successful coordinative program. They also suggest a faculty member from the School of Social Work at the State University who is working in the area of coordination of services and has some good ideas. The state program director for aging would also be willing to come and discuss what the state office is doing in the area of coordination.

Lucille decides that her next move is to support Mr. Black in calling a small group together and to help it develop a mechanism to maintain the networking. She also believes that it is important to keep the city council member involved because the support of senior citizen projects by the council will be needed. Perhaps he can even help to counteract the influence of the realtors regarding low-income housing for the elderly.

PROGRAM PLANNING AND RESOURCE DEVELOPMENT

When individual workers or coordinating groups of workers survey the resources available, they sometimes discover that the needed resources are not available. This may be because the need has never been identified or because financial resources to support the resources are not available. Social workers can sometimes use program planning to mobilize different and creative kinds of resources that are relatively inexpensive (financially). Two resources that fall into this category are volunteers and self-help groups.

Program development uses the planning process developed in Chapter 12. As the plan is developed, special attention must be given to means of generating support for the plan. Support must come not only from the agencies involved (both workers and administration) but from the community. Most programs needing community resources cannot be developed without community support.

Usually in developing a new program it is advisable to begin small or to serve at first only a portion of the population that might benefit from the program. It is also advisable to begin with that portion of the population with which the chances of success are the greatest. If done in this way, it is easier to find and correct the deficiencies in the plan. Another point to remember is that it is easier to obtain support for small programs that relate to popular causes.

Jack Rothman, John Erlich, and Joseph Teresa discuss promoting an innovation in an agency.[8] This same idea can be related to planning new community programs. They point out that the literature on the "diffusion of innovations" supports the advisability of beginning small and of demonstrating the new program before planning for widespread use. They give three guidelines that are helpful when planning programs that develop or mobilize new resources:

1. Develop and rely on good relationships,
2. Clarify goals and plans for developing the program, and
3. Be realistic about the resources that may be available to the program.

Program planning can take place within an existing agency structure or from a community base. If the program is to function within an existing agency structure, the support and involvement of the agency administration and staff are crucial.

If the program is to develop from a community base, community persons will carry primary responsibility for its functioning. These persons need to be involved in the planning as early as possible. Usually it is important to discuss the proposed plan with several community influentials as a first step in planning. This discussion will provide the social worker with information that is needed in developing the plan. It also involves these very important persons in developing the support needed for the project. Often it is advisable for a community person to call and conduct a meeting to discuss the project. The social worker may need to identify and motivate a suitable leader. The worker then facilitates by preparing the person providing leadership for the meeting, by making the arrangements for a place to have the meeting, by attending to the details involved in such a meeting, and by evaluating with the leadership after the meeting.

If the decision is made to develop a program, some kind of structure should be set up to do the work necessary for developing the program. This structure can be a provisional board or a planning committee, and it should allow for appropriate involvement of community persons in the planning process. The designated structure may find it useful to establish the extent of the need that the proposed program will address. A needs assessment is an excellent means for doing this. In addition to individual needs, agency and community factors should be considered. It should also be involved in the development of the structure and policy of the program. Another task of such a group is to obtain the needed support for the proposed program, which may involve grant writing and other fundraising activity. Recruitment and hiring of personnel is another task of this group. Development of volunteer programs and focusing on the functioning of the planning group process are other tasks that often are involved.

Sometimes the program becomes a community effort rather than an agency program. In this situation the social worker can fill the role of an enabler by helping the community group reach the goals it has adopted. Also, the worker can fill the role of technical expert by providing information about how to accomplish certain tasks.[9]

Sometimes an already established community group becomes aware of a need and wishes to do something about it. In this situation a social worker can help the group document the need, obtain support (money, people, etc.), and move to develop a program or resource needed by the community. An example of this is a community group concerned with services for the elderly. A social worker helped the group carry out a needs assessment that indicated that housing for single women was a prime need in this community. The group was able to interest a local realtor in focusing on this need, and the group worked with the realtor to develop understanding of housing needs of older women and plans for making more suitable housing available for them.

At other times, groups of people interested in a particular problem emerge. Social workers can also work with these groups in developing community resources to deal with problems. An example of this would be a group of women concerned about battered women. This group contained some professional women. The social worker's function in the group was to provide understanding about battered women and their needs. This group talked to women who had worked on the problem in other communities. They set up a training program, developed a telephone response service, a safe house, and a self-help group.

As has been shown in these examples, grassroots groups can be a useful resource when developing community resources for clients. When working with such groups, social workers do not take over the planning; they respect the group's way of functioning and facilitate the work of the group. Workers must gain and maintain the trust of the group. They enable individuals to carry out the necessary tasks, they suggest ways of proceeding and resources to be tapped, and they mediate the group's difficulties with professionals and other community groups. This latter task is sometimes necessary because already established services or other professionals may be threatened by grassroots groups or they may be concerned about the ability of a grassroots group to provide quality service. In a time of shrinking federal and state resources, the maximizing of local resources is necessary if human need is to be met. Program planning and resource development with grassroots groups thus becomes an important task for social workers.

CASE EXAMPLE

A group of people began to discuss the need for a hospice program in their community (of 10,000 people) after several cancer deaths where the family could have used supportive help. A social worker became involved with this group as a technical expert in process. The group was able to involve several community influentials in the planning process, including a lawyer, a physician, the superintendent of schools, and two pastors. The group, which also included nurses and a representative of the local cancer society, involved about fifteen people. They developed a legal structure and applied for nonprofit status. They worked with the local hospital and obtained office space in the hospital. The organizing group became the original Board of Directors. During this phase the social worker used her understanding of group process and the technical aspects of forming an organization as a contributing member of the group. She also obtained materials from another forming hospice, which provided some guidance in the group's deliberations. A lawyer took major responsibility for the legal aspects of the group's formation.

The next step was to develop a number of working papers, such as job descriptions and forms covering the various aspects of service (e.g., request for service, nursing and psychosocial assessments, doctors' orders, care plan). A service flow chart was developed. The social worker was very active in this activity helping the group to adapt materials that had been developed by other hospices for the local situation.

Another task was the recruitment and training of volunteers. The social worker, again, was active in planning and coordinating a very successful training program, which resulted in an attendance of over fifty persons at each session and thirty individuals recruited as volunteers for the program. The success of the training program was due in part to an excellent public relations campaign. The social worker did not need to be involved in this, as other members of the board were skilled in this area. Several members of the board were very successful in fundraising. Funds were obtained from several community groups, as memorials, from the county commissioners, and from the local United Way. One task that proved difficult, but with persistence was accomplished, was the obtaining of liability insurance.

After nine months the program was operational, though still needing refinement of its procedures and policies. Patients were being referred and service was being provided to patients and their families through the bereavement stage. The social worker was serving as coordinator of social services and working with others who provided the service to the patients and their families. The board was functional and planning monthly training sessions for the volunteers. An active public relations program continued to be carried out so as to heighten community awareness of the service and to recruit additional volunteers. Plans were underway to develop closer ties with the health care network of the community.

Developing a Volunteer Program

Volunteers are a resource that have historically been very important in the delivery of social services. Before the development of the social work profession, most social services were delivered by volunteers. In fact, the early social workers were volunteers. In recent years less emphasis has been placed on this resource. Professionals have believed they were best suited to deliver services. Issues of competence, confidentiality, and dependability have been raised when considering the volunteer as a resource. Also, volunteers have changed. Many women (traditionally the volunteers in the social work domain) are now in the work force and are not available for volunteer roles or during agency work hours. The increasing numbers of retired persons are now seen as an important source of volunteer effort.

Effective use of the volunteer resource calls for the development of a volunteer program. Someone must be responsible for helping to identify the roles and tasks suitable for volunteers to carry out in an agency or a community. Job descriptions and agency policy must be written. To carry out these tasks a volunteer manager must develop an understanding of clients and the services they require and of the factors that motivate persons to volunteer their time and energy in helping others. The volunteer manager also should be able to work with staff persons in identifying services volunteers can be used to provide. Skill in motivating people is also needed.

A volunteer program should have an identified means for recruiting and screening volunteers, matching volunteer with job, and orienting and training volunteers. Provision must also be made for supervising and recruiting volunteers.

The volunteer coordinator or manager is not the only person involved in planning for the development of a volunteer program. Prior to the identification of such a person, some group must be involved in determining the need and focus of such a program and determining goals and objectives for it. The group should be representative of agency staff, concerned community persons, influentials, possible volunteers, and perhaps clients to be served. This group can then serve as a board of directors or advisory group when the program manager is chosen; the group should have input into, or responsibility for, choosing that manager.

When an understanding is developed of what a functional volunteer program entails and the planning process is used in developing such a program, the resources of volunteers can be added to those already available to clients. Clients thus can be better served.[10]

CASE EXAMPLE

A local state social service agency that has two divisions, child protection and services to older adults, is often called upon to help in the distribution of Thanksgiving baskets and Christmas gifts. The agency is located in a small city which has several churches that want to help but do not know the best way to contact "needy families." The workers in the agency are already overburdened and find this seasonal demand from the community unreasonable. After considerable discussion, a supervisor of the child protection unit wondered if a volunteer could be used to coordinate this project. A job description was written and staff discussed how they could best protect the clients' confidentiality. It was decided that workers would identify those who might like to receive this help, and then determine from the clients if they truly wanted the help and, if so, exactly what food and gifts would be most suitable.

Staff suggested several people in the community who might be interested in this short-term volunteer project. The supervisor decided to contact one she believed particularly qualified. Using the job description, she carefully described what needed to be done to the prospective volunteer. Together, they decided this was indeed a job the individual would like to do. The Volunteer Director of Holiday Projects then suggested several individuals who could be assistants, and the supervisor helped in the development of job descriptions for these assistants. It was decided to limit the number to four. The Director assumed responsibility for recruiting the assistants and for planning the project, which involved communication with churches and other organizations regarding needs and ways to process their donations, as well as work with the agency employees in identifying those who needed help. The agency provided office space and a telephone as well as space for short-term storage and sorting of the donations. Distribution was shared by volunteers and agency workers depending on the situation and need for worker involvement and client confidentiality.

After the holiday time, the workers and Volunteer Director evaluated the project. The workers said that it really was a big help to them, and the Volunteer Director, while having several suggestions for improvement, said she would be glad to serve again the following year. As the staff talked about the success of the project in the following months, they began to suggest other areas in which volunteers could be used. The agency then moved to setting up a more comprehensive volunteer program.

Self-Help Groups

Another resource that social workers can help develop is that of self-help groups. These voluntary small groups, which often spontaneously develop, have been a component of mutual aid that has always been a part of human functioning. In the modern world where people feel alienated and isolated from one another, however, it is not always possible on one's own to find a group that is supportive.

Social workers can help those with similar life situations and problems find each other and provide this mutual aid to one another.

Because people facing a new situation or problem often feel helpless, it is advisable to include individuals who have had some opportunity to work on the problem or adjust to the situation. They often are glad to help others, for doing this further facilitates their return to more stable functioning.

The widow-to-widow program is a good example of a useful self-help group. Newly widowed persons can be visited by persons who have been widowed for a year or more; the visitor can then encourage participation in a group. In the group, the newly widowed person finds others who can give help with the many concerns and decisions they face. Much needed information is also shared.

Brian A. Auslander and Gail K. Auslander have suggested that a consultation model is appropriate when working with self-help groups. They identify three roles for the consultant: 1) discussion of client-related problems and possible interventions, 2) discussion of the self-help group's policies and procedures in the hope of obtaining desired change, and 3) a link between resources that the group or individuals in the group may need.[11] The latter role would include the provision of information about and consultation as to procedures for accessing needed resources. Information as to how similar groups function could also be provided.

Self-help groups are not the answer for all clients. Some self-help groups foster an inappropriate dependence or encourage simplistic solutions to complex situations. Some self-help groups develop a strong antiprofessional bias. Some of these negative characteristics can be avoided if, in the process of development, an ongoing consultative role for the social worker can be planned.[12] Some of the ways social workers can support self-help groups are: helping groups find a meeting place, helping them find needed financial resources, providing them with information and training, referring appropriate persons to them, helping the group develop credibility with the community and with professionals, and providing social and emotional support.

ENVIRONMENTAL CHANGE

Environmental manipulation is the strategy that brings about alteration in the environment of a client as a means of enhancing the client's social functioning. Specifically, three factors in the environment will be considered as appropriate targets for change: space, time, and relationships.

Environmental change has been a strategy of social work since the time of Mary Richmond. The term **environmental treatment** appears in the work of Florence Hollis who discusses treatment of the environment as bringing about change in the situation of the client.[13] Max Siporin discusses situational intervention as "actions that alter structural, cultural and functional patterns."[14] In discussing "change in behavioral setting," Siporin points out that "an environment has profound effects on the behavior, feelings, and self-images of the people who inhabit or use that setting."[15]

Richard Grinnel and Nancy Kyte report a study of the use of environmental modification as a technique used by social workers in a large public agency. They state that it is a much more intricate technique than is widely believed.[16] This may be related in part to the fact that the environment is a complex system that transacts with clients and impinges on their functioning.

Environmental psychology, a fairly new area of study, provides some of the knowledge needed to understand the impact of the environment on individuals.[17] This knowledge relates the effects of crowding on persons, individuals' need for privacy, distance as it relates to different kinds of relationships, territoriality, and other effects of the environment on individual functioning. As more knowledge is developed in this field, it should give social workers more understanding about the use of this strategy.

Carel Germain and Alex Gitterman, in *The Life Model of Social Work Practice*, place considerable emphasis on the ecological aspects of human functioning.[18] They differentiate between the social and physical environments. They point out that people in the environment not only can provide resources for clients but that they also can affect the client's behavior by their responses to that behavior. When considering the physical environment, both the "built world" and the "natural world" are included. Germain and Gitterman have provided social work with a beginning knowledge base to use when manipulating the environment. Although social workers have long used the strategy of environmental manipulation, the knowledge base has remained in the realm of practice wisdom or common sense.

When a social worker working with a group arranges the chairs in order to bring about interpersonal interaction, a manipulation of space has taken place. The way the physical environment of a social agency is arranged can cause clients to feel comfortable or uncomfortable. It can cause undesirable behavior or enable constructive activity to take place. It can sometimes make the difference in whether the client makes use of the services offered or does not have his need met.[19]

Placement of a child in a residential treatment facility is a form of environmental change. That facility uses the milieu (the arrangement of the space, program, and staff relationships) to help that child. Milieu therapy involves attitudes and relationships of the persons who occupy the space as a therapeutic tool. Hospitals, nursing homes, and other institutions can make use of milieu therapy.[20]

Any environmental change should be preceded by a thorough study and assessment of the situation with particular emphasis on relationship, space, and time factors that may be impeding the client's social functioning. Attention should be given to how culture and lifestyle prescribe the use of the physical environment and time so that any plans do not conflict with a client's culture and lifestyle.

When planning for change of the environment, a worker can use the variables of relationship, space, and time as a framework. Relationships should be influenced to enhance the competence of the client. This can be illustrated by considering the situation of a physically handicapped person. If those persons in the handicapped person's environment provide care in such a manner that the client makes few decisions and has little opportunity to use the physical capacity she possesses, there is little opportunity to feel competent. If the caregivers encourage appropriate self-reliance, however, competence is enhanced.[21]

Changes can be made in the spatial aspects of a client's environment. The space needs to be appropriate for the person who occupies it. According to Irene A. Gutheil, some of the factors important when considering physical space are the features of a space, whether they are fixed and cannot be changed or whether the space can be modified with regard to the design of the building and the place-ment of furniture. Also important are issues of territory, personal space, crowd-ing, and privacy.[22] These concerns are particularly important in residential situations, but should also be considered in evaluating offices and other areas where services are provided.

In the case of the handicapped person, it is easy to see how physical barriers can prevent a person from being relatively self-sufficient. The sense of compe-tence is enhanced if the barriers are removed. Physical environmental features should provide for the privacy a person needs. Color and light can influence feelings and behavior.

Not only should the person in the environment be considered, but the activity that is to take place in that space is important as well. This may involve the manner in which people interact during the activity. There must be provision for appropriate closeness of people. It is important to remember that being too close can lead to discomfort that causes persons to withdraw, while being too far apart also allows for withdrawal.

Spatial arrangement that allows for eye contact is important in some situ-ations. A circle encourages persons to talk to each other, as each can see every other person. Room arrangements that have all persons facing a speaker discour-age group interaction and encourage all attention being given to the speaker. Social workers can use their understanding of clients and their need and of spatial arrangements to determine how space can be changed to enable persons to function more adequately.[23]

Time factors can be changed in service of clients by the manner in which social workers schedule activity. There is a time for physical or mental activity and a time for quiet in people's lives. By considering client need at various times, the social worker can use the time allotted in ways that are congruent with the client's need. For example, when children have been in school all day, they are usually ready for physical activity rather than for sitting quietly. When working with a mother, the worker should realize that the times when family demand is high are not times when she can reflect on her own needs. The time for appoint-ments should take into consideration the time rhythms of the client's life. Institu-tions often develop schedules to meet staff desires rather than considering usual life-cycle rhythms of those being served. Social workers can be alert to these time elements and work for changes in schedules so that they can be of service to clients rather than becoming one more block to successful functioning.[24]

When using the strategy of environmental manipulation, the worker assesses the situation and plans to bring about change in relationships, in space, and in the use of time. In planning for change it is essential that the worker use the understandings that have developed about relationships, space, and time. The social worker also should be creative in structuring environments so that they support clients' efforts in social functioning.

CASE EXAMPLE

A social worker in a nursing home notes that some patients who must share rooms with another resident because of funding policies need an opportunity to be alone for parts of the day. These same residents seem to need a private place to visit with those who come to see them. The social worker brings this need to the weekly staff meeting. At first the staff takes the attitude that this is just the way it is and states there is no space for a private space. The social worker makes a tour of the facility in order to identify space that may not be used 100 percent of the daytime and early evening hours. She finds a craft facility that is only used two hours each morning and afternoon. She also finds a couple of alcoves in hallways that could hold a couple of comfortable chairs. In addition, she notes that there is outdoor space that, in nice weather, could be used for visiting if comfortable seating were provided. At the next staff meeting she presents her findings. The administrator then asks who is going to provide the needed furniture. The activities director states that she would welcome a comfortable corner in the craft room. She also says that the auxiliary has been looking for a project and wonders if this would not be a good one for them. Within a couple of months the identified space is converted to comfortable private space and the residents have been involved in developing guidelines for its use.

CHANGING ORGANIZATIONS FROM WITHIN

Until recently, consideration of the organization as a target for change has received little attention in the social work literature. Yet in working with clients, workers (particularly in the public sector) are well aware that the functioning of the agency (policy, procedures, etc.) often is a source of blockage to client need fulfillment. It follows that social workers should develop a means for influencing for agency change. Organizational change as a strategy can be defined as "a means of enhancing the effectiveness of human service organizations in their relations with clients. . . . [It] is a set of interrelated activities . . . for the purpose of modifying the formal policies, programs, procedures, or management practices. . . . The intended outcome . . . [is] to increase the effectiveness of the services provided and/or to remove organizational conditions that are deleterious to the client population served."[25] This strategy focuses on those means of change that arise from within the organization. It is carried out by persons in middle or lower levels of the organizational structure.[26]

As with any strategy, the social worker's use of that strategy begins with assessment. Some of the understandings a worker must develop when using a change-from-within strategy are:

1. The agency as a social system (see Chapter 10 for a discussion of a schema for developing this understanding);
2. The source of the block for need fulfillment (Is it in policy or procedure? Is it because of a lack of agency resources? Is it because of methods used in delivering service?);
3. The forces within the agency and the community that influence the agency functioning in relation to the need;
4. The usual processes used to bring about change in the agency;
5. The source of decision making in the areas needing to be changed;
6. Any influences to which the decision-making source is particularly sensitive; and
7. The decision maker's receptivity and resistance to the change sought.

The assessment process should identify what requires changing if client needs are to be fulfilled. It is not sufficient to say that change must take place. It is important that both the place where the change should take place and the desirable change at that site be specified. The assessment also should specify what change is possible and what is impossible to change. There should be some consideration of timing factors that may need to be taken into account in planning for change.[27] For example, if management is under great stress because of changes being imposed from a central office, the chances that management will be receptive to a discussion of other changes from line staff is doubtful. However, if management has become concerned with a problem of service delivery, they may be very receptive to discussion of a possible change that could not only result in better service to clients but that would also alleviate the identified problem.

Herman Resnick and Rino Patti see the change process as:

1. Practitioner's perception of a problem in agency functioning;
2. Discussion of problem among practitioner and like-minded colleagues, including an assessment of change potential;
3. Commitment to the change effort by persons who have been doing the assessment;
4. Formulation of the goal to be sought;
5. Analysis of resistance to change;
6. Development of an action system; mobilization of resources (needed persons added; group development takes place);
7. Formulation of a plan of action; and
8. Submission of proposal to the decision makers; other action taken as needed.

At this point the change is either accepted, rejected, or modified. At each step goals may change as new information is gained or input from additional persons becomes part of the process.[28]

An important consideration is which persons to include in the change effort. At least some persons should have a good understanding of the agency functioning. Some persons should be respected, valuable members of the agency staff. Some may be persons who have the capacity to influence the decision makers; some should have skills in negotiation and mediation; some should have skills in carrying out the particular change being called for. Agency change can originate from the efforts of one person, but to carry out a change-from-within strategy, other persons possessing the characteristics and skills needed must be involved.

Depending on the change being sought, a number of techniques or methods can be used to bring about change in organizations. Patti and Resnick have identified eight collaborative and nine adversarial activities. Collaborative activities are: 1) provide information, 2) present alternative courses of action, 3) request support for experimentation, 4) establish a study committee, 5) create new opportunities for interaction, 6) make appeals to conscience or professional ethics, 7) use logical argument and data, and 8) point out negative consequences. Adversarial activities are: 1) submit petitions, 2) confront in open meetings, 3) bring sanctions against the agency, 4) engage in public criticism through use of communication media, 5) encourage noncompliance, 6) strike, 7) picket, 8) litigate, and 9) bargain.[29]

Collaborative activities should always be tried first. The use of adversarial activities should be restricted to situations in which collaborative activities have not worked. Before using adversarial activities workers should determine if such strategies will bring harm to clients and if they are willing to take the personal risks involved.

Rothman, Erlich, and Teresa have identified four means of bringing about change in organizations:

1. *Promoting an innovation*—This is carried out by testing a new way of work with a small group of clients. If it is successful or seems useful in meeting clients' needs, it may later be adopted for use on a larger scale. An example would be using a group approach to deliver a service.

2. *Changing an organization's goals*—One way this can be done is by changing the structure of influence in an agency by increasing the power of appropriate groups within the agency. For example, a client's advisory group could be developed. This would be a structure wherein client input into decision making affords a new source of information or influence.

3. *Fostering participation*—This is a means of encouraging broader participation in the functioning of an agency. For example, a staff group could be involved in the planning for a new program. One means of fostering participation is through providing some kind of benefit for the participation. This benefit could take the form of public recognition.

4. *Increasing the effectiveness of role performance*—This can be carried out by clarifying the role performance that is expected of those working in an agency. It can also be carried out by encouraging various kinds of staff development.[30]

In-service training for workers can be used to introduce new service delivery ideas. If the social worker is skillful in the use of group interaction, she can sometimes enable a staff group to examine a new idea and make plans for the adoption of that idea. Sometimes social workers are given the opportunity to lead an in-service session; in doing this, the use of knowledge from adult education and staff development literature can be most useful.[31]

Edward Pawlak has pointed out that an ideal time for bringing about change in an organization is at the point when leadership changes. He provides suggestions for workers who wish to engage in organizational change. Suggestions include influencing the selection of new leadership and tinkering with the manner in which rules are interpreted and enforced. Revising of roles or role interpretation is another means for change.[32]

It should now be apparent that a number of approaches and techniques are available to use in changing organizations. The choice of which to use is dependent on the change being sought and on the situation in which the change is sought. In making this choice two factors must always be considered: risk for the workers seeking the change and resistance of other persons within the organization.

Three kinds of risks may be involved when a social worker engages in changing from within: job loss, restricted upward mobility, and strained working relationships.[33] All three of these risks are not present in every situation, but a careful assessment should indicate which are present and the extent of the risk. Each social worker must then make the decision as to whether he is willing to take the risks involved before beginning to use this strategy.

Resistance is almost always present to some degree in change activity. Change upsets the system's functioning; it causes uncertainty. Thus, the social worker must be prepared to modify the plan to mitigate the resistance or to plan in other ways to modify the resistance. When dealing with resistance an attitude of compromise is often necessary. Individuals who are determined that their plan will be accepted regardless are most apt to encounter a negative response. Those who engage in joint consideration of a problem are most apt to find a solution acceptable to all concerned. Understanding the nature of the resistance and dealing with it are essential skills when using a change-from-within strategy.

Because social work is primarily practiced within organizations, particularly bureaucratic organizations, the change-from-within strategy is important to the social worker's repertoire. It is the social worker's ethical responsibility to work toward the humane delivery of social services in a manner that meets client needs. To do this, it is often necessary to bring about change in organizations. To help bring about change in the organization in which one is employed, the social worker can use the change-from-within strategy.

CASE EXAMPLE

A new social worker in a nursing home discovers that important information about family visits over the weekend and at night are not being transmitted to her. She first discusses the situation with the nursing supervisor. The supervisor is defensive about the staff in the nursing department. She says they do the best they can but are often short over the weekend, and besides, a lot of the information is not important anyway. The social worker then discusses the problem with the activity director, who has worked at the nursing home for some time. She finds that the nursing supervisor has harbored a long-time resentment of social workers. She believes that the nursing staff knows what is best for residents and that social work just adds time-consuming tasks to their work. The activity director states that one of the reasons the former social worker left was the problems in working with the nursing supervisor. The social worker inquires about where the administrator stands regarding the problem and is told that he tends to support the nursing supervisor.

The social worker and the activity director decide that if they work together perhaps they can bring about some change in the reporting of significant information from family visits. They discuss how the matter can be brought to a staff meeting. Between them they decide to keep track of incidents and the ramifications of lack of reporting. The social worker also decides to suggest to some families that they communicate their distress to the administrator. This plan results in several well-documented incidents and a couple of reports to the administrator. Several weeks after their initial discussion, the administrator brought the subject up at a staff meeting. The social worker was prepared with the documented situations, but rather than blaming the nursing supervisor, she suggested that perhaps the staff did not know the significance of such information or understand the need for charting the significant information. She suggested that perhaps an in-service training session might be one means of alleviating the problem. The nursing supervisor was most supportive of the plan and began to reinforce the importance of charting with her staff. She also began to develop a more cooperative relationship with the social worker.

CAUSE ADVOCACY

Social workers using a systemic approach to assessment should be sensitive to situations in which the block to need fulfillment lies in the functioning of societal institutions. Often these blocks affect not just one person or one family but groups of persons. In these situations a strategy that focuses on change in societal institutions needs to be considered. A cause advocacy strategy is one option.

Cause advocacy has been a concern of social work since its earliest days. The early twentieth-century social workers in settlement houses were concerned with social conditions as they affected the people with whom they worked. During the unsettled 1960s, cause advocacy was a major focus of some social workers. The cause-function debates of the profession relate to social work's concern with changing social institutions. (See Chapter 1 for a discussion of this issue.)

The literature on advocacy recognizes both *case advocacy* (advocacy in service of a client) and *cause advocacy* (advocacy in service of a class of persons who are victims of a social problem). George Brager has identified an advocate as the professional who identifies with the victims of social problems and who pursues modification in social conditions.[34] Robert Teare and Harold McPheeters identify the advocate role as helping clients obtain services in situations where they may be rejected or helping expand services to persons in a particular need.[35] (See also Chapter 12 for a discussion of the Teare-McPheeters role classification.)

There are a number of means to use in advocating for a class of persons. Robert MacRae identified the following:

1. Preparation of carefully worded statements of policy on lively social welfare issues,
2. Careful analysis of pending legislation,
3. Individual consultation with key legislators on the implications of pending measures,
4. Persuasion of influential organizations outside the welfare field to oppose or support pending legislation,
5. Creation of an ad hoc citizens committee composed of representative citizens of great influence and prestige, and
6. Continuous interpretation of social needs.[36]

J. Donald Cameron and Esther Talavera discuss an advocacy program where the emphasis was on participation in "important community planning and development groups, and other community organizations." The goal of this activity was "to keep the community needs of Spanish-speaking people visible and to effect the flow of resources to meet these needs."[37] Almost all the literature on social work with diverse racial groups calls for advocacy as an important component of any service provided to those groups.

Robert Sunley suggests the following as useful in a family advocacy program: 1) studies and surveys, 2) expert testimony, 3) case conferences with other agencies, 4) interagency committees, 5) educational methods, 6) position taking, 7) administrative redress, 8) demonstration projects, 9) direct contact with officials and legislators, 10) coalition groups, 11) client groups, 12) petitions, 13) persistent demands, and 14) demonstrations and protests.[38]

It would seem that there are two major approaches to cause advocacy. The first is influencing the political process; the second is organizing the people affected, or social action. Before discussing each of these major approaches, some issues pertinent to the use of advocacy will be considered. First is the position of an agency employee, particularly an employee of a public agency in advocacy activity. Constraints in public employment policy make it difficult if not impossible for public employees to engage in cause advocacy. This fact places an additional responsibility on social workers not so constrained to be cause advocates. Public employees can find some legal means to advocate. These include taking annual leave to testify at legislative hearings, providing factual data on the effects of policy on individuals, and giving clients information about organizations that can help them fight for their rights.

Advocacy activity may cause a backlash. Policy and procedure meant to assist one group of clients may cause additional difficulties for another group of clients. Money used to fund a needed program for one group of clients may be taken from an equally valuable program for another group. All workers who engage in advocacy need to carefully assess the possibility of backlash or the effect of the desired change on other parts of the service delivery system. They then must make interventive decisions in light of ethical considerations.

Another issue is related to the ethics of engaging in cause advocacy for persons who have not asked for or do not want that service or support. Some clients are very afraid of recriminations and feel they have more to lose than gain from advocacy activity on their own behalf. Others do not trust professionals. Does a social worker respond to her own sense of unfairness or outrage, or does the social worker respond to the wishes of clients?

Before engaging in cause advocacy a social worker should carefully assess and thoroughly understand the situation. The worker should also be certain that other means for alleviating the difficulty are not available. The risks involved should be thoroughly explored and seem worth taking for the outcomes anticipated. The outcomes expected should be realistically determined. Resources needed to complete the project should be available. Facts to be used should be verified and appropriate for the use to which they are to be put. Research techniques should be used where possible; they strengthen the case for change. With all the facts at hand, the social worker then decides whether to work to influence the political system or to organize the people affected by the problem.

Influencing the Political Process

Much of the service delivery system is heavily influenced by actions that take place in the political arena. Public social policy is an outcome of legislative action. Policy determines which programs will be supported and to what extent by governmental funds. Some social workers have always attempted to influence that political process, with varying degrees of success. The political process is heavily influenced by the climate of the times, so in times of a more liberal political climate, social workers tend to have more influence; in times of conservatism, less influence.

As with all social work strategies, influencing the political process takes understanding and skill. A thorough understanding of local, state, and national political processes is a must. Also, a thorough understanding of the issues involved is a necessity. An understanding of political decision makers as individuals and as they respond to others is another necessary understanding. Reliable data about how the problem under consideration is affecting people are very important. These data should include not only how the problem is affecting the client group but also how it is affecting other segments of the population. The costs of proposals under consideration is an important kind of knowledge. An assessment should be made of possible sources of resistance to any proposed change as well as of the nature of that resistance.

Gathering all the information needed to develop this understanding of the political process takes time and skill. Social workers should learn how to use governmental publications and documents as well as statistical material. These materials provide some of the needed information. Participation in political activities will also provide information. The establishment of working relationships with key political figures can be a means of gathering other needed information.

After the social worker has gained information and understanding about the political process and the particular issues involved, a decision should be made about the appropriate tactics to use in influencing that process with respect to a particular issue. This decision will depend in part on where that issue is in the political process. If it is still in the discussion stage, then suggestions for possible legislation might be the choice.

Some of the means social workers have used to influence the political process include:

1. Researching issues and providing facts to decision makers;
2. Testifying at hearings, again using facts whenever possible;
3. Lobbying or being present while the legislative process is taking place and influencing legislative votes when possible;
4. Working for the election of candidates who are sympathetic to social issues and to the needs of people; and
5. Letter-writing campaigns to inform decision makers about facts and attitudes.

Influencing the political process is a complex endeavor. Although most social workers are not in a position to be heavily involved in influencing this process, they can and should use the tactics that are available to them to influence the political process. They have an obligation to develop an understanding of the process and of the issues so they can participate in political advocacy in a responsible manner.[39]

Social Action Organizing

This approach has been a part of the social work response to human need from its earliest days. Jane Addams engaged in organizing for social action as she advocated for improved social conditions. More recently it has been used by Saul Alinsky and Richard Cloward[40] and was widely used during the period of social unrest in the 1960s. Since that time a theory base has been developing that supports the use of this approach to organizing oppressed peoples. It focuses on changing the societal power base or calls for basic institutional change. Alinsky's theory is sometimes referred to as a grassroots approach. It begins with people who see themselves as victims, not with professionals who decide what is needed.

The principal thrust is the organizing of groups of persons so that they can exert pressure on power structures, institutions, and political structures. Those who adhere to this approach believe that equity in society will come about only when existing power structures recognize the power of oppressed peoples; in other words, when the societal power base is broadened to include new groups of people. Tactics used are 1) crystallization of issues and taking action against an enemy target; 2) confrontation, conflict, or contest; negotiation where appropriate; and 3) manipulation of mass organizations and of political processes.

The social worker's first task is to organize the people, to get them involved in the action. In many ways, this is a self-help approach. The worker then enables the people to carry out the action.

Social workers need to develop advocacy skills if they are to help social institutions become more responsive to the needs of all persons. How the individual social worker uses these skills depends on three variables:

1. *The position of the worker in the social welfare system*—Some agencies place constraints on workers' involvement in cause advocacy. Also, workers who are working cooperatively with decision makers will probably not want to use conflict tactics.

2. *The client's desires regarding action*—If clients do not wish to take the risks involved in an advocacy action, these desires should be respected.

3. *The risks involved in the action*—If advocacy actions have the potential for bringing about backlash or negative influences on the client or on the social service system, advocacy should be used cautiously.

The worker serves as an expert in the process, an enabler, a negotiator, or whatever is needed by the people who direct the change activity.[41]

CASE EXAMPLE

About a year after Lucille (see Case Example on pages 351–352) had seen coordination mechanisms relative to services for senior citizens develop through a community-wide Senior Citizens Coalition, the housing issue seemed ripe for attention. During the elapsed year Lucille had been gathering information about the existence of a possible problem and its dimensions. She had asked the Coalition to provide information relative to the number of persons over age sixty-five known to have housing problems such as an inability to find appropriate, affordable housing; persons placed in a nursing home because of lack of appropriate housing choices; and numbers of housing units lost to other purposes such as razing for use of the land for commercial purposes or being converted to luxury units.

The issue came to a head when the City Council was asked for a zoning change that would allow a parking ramp to be built on property now containing an apartment that housed many senior citizens who had limited incomes.

Lucille carefully chose a small group, including Mr. Black, Mr. Jones (a member of the City Council who showed a concern about senior citizens), an affected senior citizen, and several other concerned persons. She asked the group to meet and discuss the situation. This group needed to move rather quickly because the zoning change was to come to the City Council in two weeks. The group refined the information that Lucille had gathered about affordable housing for seniors in the city. They were able to get the newspaper to run a feature article, which aroused some citizen concern. With the help of Mr. Jones, they contacted City Council members and city staff who were identified as involved in the planning for the parking ramp, and discussed the impact of the loss of housing on the seniors involved. They planned and carried out public testimony at public hearings regarding the zoning change. They were present with the involved seniors at the council meeting where the matter was considered.

The immediate outcome was that the City Council tabled the zoning change and appointed a committee made up of Council members and concerned citizens to study the situation further. Lucille and her committee planned to continue to monitor the work of this committee, to collect and provide them with needed information, and to testify as needed.

SUMMARY

Influence is an important component of the interventive repertoire of a social worker engaging in action with others on behalf of the client. The social worker should be able to use influence and to work with influentials.

Action relative to the coordination of services calls for a thorough understanding of the service delivery system. Communication is an important ingredient of coordination. The social worker enables coordination to come about by helping service deliverers to communicate. Case management and networking are strategies for developing coordination.

Program planning and development is the use of the planning process to develop new resources. Program planning may take place within an agency or by use of a community group. Self-help groups and volunteer programs are two means for enhancing the resources available to clients.

Environmental change is a strategy used to alter structural, cultural, and functional patterns in the client's environment. Patterns that are particularly important are those of relationships, space, and time. This strategy calls for creative action by the social worker.

Changing organizations from within may be the strategy of choice when agency functioning is the cause of the block to client need fulfillment. To use this strategy the worker first assesses the social system of the agency. Emphasis is placed on decision making and resistance to change. This strategy is important because of the social worker's ethical demand to work for humane delivery of social services.

Cause advocacy is concerned with changing societal institutions. Two main approaches are used: influencing the political process and organizing the victims.

The generalist social worker provides service to individuals, families, small groups, organizations, and communities. The focus is on transactions among systems, that is, on social functioning. This approach to social work calls for a wide variety of strategies, including those that do not focus on the client. Non-client-focused strategies call for action with other systems on behalf of clients. They focus on situations in the client's environment that are in some way affecting social functioning that should meet the client's needs. Ethically, a social worker must not only work with the client but also with systems that impinge on that client.

QUESTIONS

1. Discuss the strengths and limitations of the various kinds of coordination.

2. In a community with which you are familiar, identify a need you believe a self-help group can fill; a volunteer program can fill; and a grassroots group can fill. Using one of these resources, how would you go about working to provide a needed service?

3. Identify an environment that is nonsupportive of social functioning in some way. Discuss how you would change that environment to more adequately support social functioning.

4. What are the ethical considerations of working in an agency that is not meeting the needs of clients (needs for which it has responsibility)? How much risk would you be willing to take in bringing about needed change in an agency? At what point do you think it would be appropriate for you to use a change-from-within strategy?

5. When engaging in cause advocacy, should the response be to injustice or to client wishes? How can these two perspectives be reconciled?

SUGGESTED READINGS

Albert, Raymond. "Social Work Advocacy in the Regulatory Process." *Social Casework* 64 (October 1983): 473–481.

Amidei, Nancy. "How to Be an Advocate in Bad Times." *Public Welfare* 40 (Summer 1982): 37–42.

Auslander, Brian A., and Auslander, Gail K. "Self Help Groups and the Family Service Agency." *Social Casework* 69 (February 1988): 74–80.

Austin, Carol D. "Case Management: Myths and Realities." *Families in Society* 71 (September 1990): 398–405.

Austin, David. "I & R: The New Glue for the Social Services." *Public Welfare* 38 (Fall 1980): 38–43.

Berche, Anne Vandeberg, and Horejsi, Charles R. "Coordination of Client Service." *Social Work* 25 (March 1980): 94–98.

Connaway, Ronda S., and Gentry, Martha E. *Social Work Practice.* Englewood Cliffs, NJ: Prentice Hall, 1988 (Chapters 6 and 7).

Cox, Fred M., Erlich, John L., Rothman, Jack, and Tropman, John E., Eds. *Strategies of Community Organization,* 4th ed. Itasca, IL: F. E. Peacock, 1987 (Part Three, "Strategies").

Dean, Ronald B., and Patti, Rino J. "Legislative Advocacy: Seven Effective Tactics." *Social Work* 26 (July 1981): 289–296.

Figueira-McDonough, Josefina. "Policy Practice: The Neglected Side of Social Work Intervention." *Social Work* 38 (March 1993): 179–188.

Frey, Gerald A. "A Framework for Promoting Organizational Change." *Families in Society* 71 (March 1990): 143–147.

Froland, Charles. "Formal and Informal Care: Discontinuities in a Continuum." *Social Service Review* 54 (December 1980): 572–587.

Gulath, Padi, and Guert, Geoffrey. "The Community-Centered Model: A Garden-Variety Approach or a Radical Transformation of Community Practice?" *Social Work* 35 (January 1990): 63–68.

Gutheil, Irene A. "Considering the Physical Environment: An Essential Component of Good Practice." *Social Work* 37 (September 1992): 391–396.

Haeuser, Adrienne Ahlgren, and Schwartz, Florence S. "Developing Social Work Skills for Work with Volunteers." *Social Casework* 61 (December 1980): 595–601.

Halfon, Neal, Berkowitz, Gale, and Klee, Linnea. "Development of an Integrated Case Management Program for Vulnerable Children." *Child Welfare* 72 (July–August 1993): 379–396.

Harrison, W. David. "Reflective Practice in Social Care." *Social Service Review* 61 (September 1987): 393–404.

Hasenfeld, Yeheskel. "The Implementation of Change in Human Service Organizations: A Political Economy Perspective." *Social Service Review* 54 (December 1980): 508–520.

Hashimi, Joan Kay. "Environmental Modification: Teaching Social Coping Skills." *Social Work* 26 (July 1981): 323–332.

Herbert, Margot D., and Mould, John W. "The Advocacy Role in Public Child Welfare." *Child Welfare* 171 (March–April 1992): 114–130.

Hock, Charles, and Hemmes, George. "Linking Informal and Formal Help: Conflict Along the Continuum of Care." *Social Service Review* 61 (September 1987): 432–446.

Johnson, Louise C. "Networking: A Means of Maximizing Resources in Non-Metropolitan Settings." *Human Services in the Rural Environment* 8 (No. 2): 27–31.

Jorgensen, James D., and Klepinger, Brian W. "The Social Worker as Staff Trainer." *Public Welfare* 37 (Winter 1979): 41–49.

Kane, Rosalie A., Penrod, Joan D., Davidson, Gestur, Mascovice, Iru, and Rich, Eugene. "What Cost Case Management in Long Term Care?" *Social Service Review* 65 (June 1991): 281–303.

Kaplan, Karen Orloff. "Recent Trends in Case Management." In Leon Ginsberg, Ed., *Encyclopedia of Social Work, 18th ed. 1990 Supplement.* Silver Spring, MD: NASW Press (pp. 60–77).

Katz, A. H., and Bender, E. I., Eds. *The Strength in Us: Self Help Groups in the Modern World.* New York: New Viewpoints, 1976.

Kleinkauf, Cecilia. "A Guide to Giving Legislative Testimony." *Social Work* 26 (July 1981): 297–303.

Lauffer, Armoan, and Gorodezky, Sarah. *Volunteers.* Beverly Hills, CA: Sage Publications, 1977.

Lewis, Elizabeth. "Social Group Work in Community Life: Group Characteristics and Worker Role." *Social Work with Groups* 6 (Summer 1983): 18.

Loomis, James F. "Case Management in Health Care." *Health and Social Work* 13 (Summer 1988): 219–225.

Maguire, Lambert. *Understanding Social Networks.* Beverly Hills, CA: Sage Publications, 1983 (Chapter 5, "Self-Help Groups").

Maluccio, Anthony N. "Promoting Competence Through Life Experiences." In Carel B. Germain, Ed., *Social Work Practice: People and Environments: An Ecological Approach.* New York: Columbia University Press (pp. 282–302).

Meenaghan, Thomas M., Washington, Robert O., and Ryan, Robert M. *Macro Practice in Human Services.* New York: Free Press, 1982 (Chapters 6–9).

Moore, Stephen T. "A Social Work Practice Model of Case Management: The Case Management Grid." *Social Work* 35 (September 1990): 444–448.

Popple, Philip R. "Negotiation: A Critical Skill for Social Work Administrators." *Administration in Social Work* 8 (Summer 1984): 1–11.

Powell, Thomas J. *Working with Self-Help.* (Washington. D.C.: National Association of Social Workers, 1990.)

Rapp, Charles A., and Chamberlain, Ronna. "Case Management Services for the Chronically Mentally Ill." *Social Work* 30 (September–October 1985): 417–422.

Reid, William. "Interagency Coordination in Delinquency Prevention and Control." In Mayer N. Zald, Ed., *Social Welfare Institutions: A Sociological Reader.* New York: John Wiley & Sons, 1965.

Resnick, Herman, and Patti, Rino J., Eds. *Change from Within: Humanizing Social Welfare Organizations.* Philadelphia: Temple University Press, 1980.

Roberts-DeGennaro, Maria. "Developing Case Management as a Practice Model." *Social Casework* 68 (October 1987): 466–470.

Rothman Jack. "A Model of Case Management: Toward Empirically Based Practice." *Social Work* 36 (November 1991): 520–528.

Rothman, Jack, Elrich, John L., and Teresa, Joseph G. *Promoting Innovation and Change in Organizations and Communities: A Planning Manual.* New York: John Wiley & Sons, 1976.

Sarason, Seymour B., Carroll, Charles, Maton, Kenneth, Cohen, Saul, and Lorentz, Elizabeth. *Human Services and Resource Networks.* San Francisco: Jossey-Bass, 1977.

Scurfield, Raymond M. "An Integrated Approach to Case Services and Social Reform." *Social Casework* 61 (December 1980): 610–618.

Sheafor, Bradford W., Horejsi, Charles R., and Horejsi, Gloria A. *Techniques and Guidelines for Social Work Practice.* Boston: Allyn and Bacon, 1988 (Part IV).

Silverman, Phyllis R. *Mutual Help Groups: Organization and Development.* Beverly Hills, CA: Sage Publications, 1980.

Simons, Ronald L., and Aigner, Stephen M. *Practice Principles, A Problem-Solving Approach to Social Work.* New York: Macmillian, 1985 (Chapters 12 and 13).

Sonsel, George E., Paradise, Frank, and Stroup, Stephen. "Case-Management Practice in an AIDS Service Organization." *Social Casework* 69 (June 1988): 388–392.

Sosin, Michael, and Caulum, Sharon. "Advocacy: A Conceptualization for Social Work Practice." *Social Work* 28 (January–February 1983): 12–17.

Stevens, Ellen S. "Toward Satisfaction and Retention of Senior Volunteers." *Journal of Gerontological Social Work* 16 (3/4 1991): 33–41.

Weissman, Harold, Epstein, Irwin, and Savage, Andrea. *Agency-Based Social Work.* Philadelphia: Temple University Press, 1983.

Weissman, Harold H., Epstein, Irwin, E., and Savage, Andrea. "Expanding the Role Repertoire of Clinicians." *Social Casework* 68 (March 1987): 150–155.

Westly, Shirley, and Sanchez, Raymond. "Developing Self Help Groups: Integrating Group Work and Community Organization Strategies." *Social Development Issues* 5 (Summer–Fall 1981): 33–46.

Wilcox, Julie A., and Taber, Merlin A. "Informal Helpers of Elderly Home Care Clients." *Health and Social Work* 16 (November 1991): 258–265.

Wilson, Marlene. *The Effective Management of Volunteer Programs.* Boulder, CO: Volunteer Management Associates, 1976.

Zimmerman, Jerome H. "Negotiating the System: Clients Make a Case for Case Management." *Public Welfare* 45 (Spring 1987): 23–27.

NOTES

1. Eugene Litwak and Henry F. Meyer, "A Balance Theory of Coordination Between Bureaucratic Organizations and Community Primary Groups," *Administrative Science Quarterly* 11 (March 1966): 31–58, and *School, Family and Neighborhood: The Theory and Practice of School-Community Relations* (New York: Columbia University Press, 1974).

2. Karen Orloff Kaplan, "Recent Trends in Case Management," in *Encyclopedia of Social Work, 18 ed. Supplement,* Leon Ginsberg, Ed., (Silver Spring, MD: NASW Press, 1990), pp. 60–77.

3. Op. cit., p. 62.

4. Jack Rothman, "A Model of Case Management: Toward Empirically Based Practice," *Social Work* 36 (November 1991): 520–528.

5. Stephen T. Moore, "A Social Work Practice Model of Case Management: The Case Management Grid," *Social Work* 35 (September 1990): 444–448.

6. For further discussion of this concept, see Seymour B. Sarason, Charles Carroll, Kenneth Maton, Saul Cohen, and Elizabeth Lorentz, *Human Services and Resource Networks* (San Francisco: Jossey-Bass, 1977), and Louise C. Johnson, "Networking: A Means of Maximizing Resources in Non-Metropolitan Settings," *Human Services in the Rural Environment* 8 (No. 2): 27–31.

7. See Alice H. Collins and Diane Pancoast, *Natural Helping Networks: A Strategy for Prevention* (Washington, DC: National Association for Social Workers, 1976).

8. Jack Rothman, John L. Erlich, and Joseph G. Teresa, *Promoting Innovation and Change in Organizations and Communities: A Planning Manual* (New York: John Wiley & Sons, 1976), chap. 2.

9. For more information about each of the tasks identified, see Bradford W. Sheafor, Charles R. Horejsi, and Gloria A. Horejsi, *Techniques and Guidelines for Social Work Practice* (Boston: Allyn and Bacon, 1988), Part IV.

10. Marlene Wilson, *The Effective Management of Volunteer Programs* (Boulder, CO: Volunteer Management Association, 1976), is a good resource on developing volunteer programs.

11. Brian A. Auslander and Gail K. Auslander, "Self Help Groups and the Family Service Agency," *Social Casework* 69 (February 1988): 74–80.

12. For further discussion of self-help groups, see A. H. Katz and E. I. Bender, Eds., *The Strength in Us: Self Help Groups in a Modern World* (New York: New Viewpoints, 1976).

13. Florence Hollis, *Casework: A Psycho-Social Therapy*, 2nd ed. (New York: Random House, 1972), pp. 81–85 and chap. 9.

14. Max Siporin, *Introduction to Social Work Practice* (New York: Macmillan, 1975), p. 302.

15. Ibid., p. 305.

16. Richard M. Grinnel, Jr., and Nancy S. Kyte, "Environmental Modification: A Study," *Social Work* 20 (July 1975): 313–318.

17. See Robert Sommer, *Personal Space* (Englewood Cliffs, NJ: Prentice-Hall, 1969); Edward T. Hall, *The Hidden Dimension* (New York: Doubleday Anchor, 1969); and William H. Itlleson, Harold M. Proshansky, Leanne G. Rivlin, and Gary H. Winkel, *An Introduction to Environmental Psychology* (New York: Holt, Rinehart and Winston, 1974).

18. Carel B. Germain and Alex Gitterman, *The Life Model of Social Work Practice* (New York: Columbia University Press, 1980).

19. For further consideration of this topic, see Brett A. Seabury, "Arrangement of Physical Space in Social Work Settings," *Social Work* 16 (October 1971): 43–49; and Thomas Walz, Georgina Willenberg, and Lane deMoll, "Environmental Design," *Social Work* 19 (January 1974): 38–46.

20. See Richard E. Boettcher and Roger Vander Schie, "Milieu Therapy with Chronic Mental Patients," *Social Work* 20 (March 1975): 130–139.

21. For additional discussion, see Anthony N. Maluccio, "Promoting Competence Through Life Experience," in *Social Work Practice: People and Environments*, Carel B. Germain, Ed., (New York: Columbia University Press, 1979), pp. 282–302.

22. Irene A. Gutheil, "Considering the Physical Environment: An Essential Component of Good Practice," *Social Work* 37 (September 1992): 391–396.

23. See Carel B. Germain, "'Space': An Ecological Variable in Social Work Practice," *Social Casework* 59 (November 1978): 515–529.

24. Carel B. Germain, "Time: An Ecological Variable in Social Work Practice," *Social Casework* 57 (July 1976): 419–426.

25. Herman Resnick and Rino J. Patti, Eds., *Change from Within: Humanizing Social Welfare Organizations* (Philadelphia: Temple University Press, 1980), pp. 5–6.

26. This strategy is based on the work of Resnick and Patti, *Change from Within*, and the discussion that follows is heavily influenced by their work. For an early version, see Rino J. Patti and Herman Resnick, "Changing the Agency from Within," *Social Work* 17 (July 1972): 48–57.

27. See Rino J. Patti, "Organizational Resistance and Change: The View from Below," *Social Service Review* 48 (September 1974): 367–383.

28. Resnick and Patti, *Change from Within*, pp. 9–11.

29. Patti and Resnick, "Changing the Agency from Within."

30. Rothman, Erlich, and Teresa, *Promoting Innovation and Change in Organization and Community: A Planning Manual* (New York: John Wiley & Sons, 1976).

31. See James D. Jorgensen and Brian W. Klepinger, "The Social Worker as Staff Trainer," *Public Welfare* 37 (Winter 1979): 41–49.

32. Edward J. Pawlak, "Organization Tinkering," *Social Work* 21 (September 1976): 376–380.

33. Resnick and Patti, *Change from Within*, p. 12.

34. George A. Brager, "Advocacy and Political Behavior," *Social Work* 13 (April 1968): 15.

35. Robert J. Teare and Harold L. McPheeters, *Manpower Utilization in Social Welfare* (Atlanta, GA: Southern Regional Education Board, 1970), p. 30.

36. Robert H. MacRae, "Social Work and Social Action," *Social Service Review* 60 (March 1966): 1–7.

37. J. Donald Cameron and Esther Talavera, "Advocacy Program for Spanish-Speaking People," *Social Casework* 57 (July 1976): 427–431.

38. Robert Sunley, "Family Advocacy: From Case to Cause," *Social Casework* 51 (June 1970): 347–357.

39. It is expected that understandings to carry out these activities will come from political science courses and a course in social welfare policy. See also: Wilbur J. Cohen, "What Every Social Worker Should Know About Political Action," *Social Work* 11 (July 1966): 3–11; Greg Speeter, *Playing Their Game Our Way: Using the Political Process to Meet Community Needs* (Amherst, MA: Citizen Involvement Training Project, University of Massachusetts, 1978); Ronald B. Dean and Rino J. Patti, "Legislative Advocacy, Seven Effective Tactics," *Social Work* 26 (July 1981): 289–296; and Cecilia Kleinkauf, "A Guide to Legislative Testimony," *Social Work* 26 (July 1981): 297–303.

40. Saul D. Alinsky, *Reveille for Radicals* (Chicago: University of Chicago Press, 1946), and Richard Cloward and R. Elman, "Advocacy in the Ghetto," in *Strategies of Community Organization: A Book of Readings*, 1st ed., Fred M. Cox, John L. Erlich, Jack Rothman, and John E. Tropman, Eds. (Itasca, IL: F. E. Peacock, 1970), pp. 209–215.

41. Cox, Erlich, Rothman, and Tropman, *Strategies of Community Organization*, 4th ed., (1987), Part Three, IV, "Social Action," is an excellent source for this approach.

15

EVALUATION

Learning Expectations

1. Understanding the importance of and skill in the use of evaluation in the social work process.
2. Understanding of accountability as it relates to the client, the profession, the agency, and the community that supports the service.
3. Understanding of the various forms of evaluation and knowledge about when each form is appropriate.
4. Understanding of the various forms of recording and skill in the use of each.
5. Understanding of the use of research techniques in the evaluation process.
6. Appreciation of the computer to process evaluative data.
7. Understanding of ethical and legal issues relative to evaluation.

As an ongoing part of the social work process, evaluation is the means for determining if the goals and objectives of the social work endeavor are being reached. It also involves looking at the means being used to reach goals and objectives. Evaluation identifies spinoffs (unexpected outcomes), both negative and positive, from the helping activity. Evaluation should be continuous, but it becomes particularly important as each step is completed. Evaluation should occur after assessment to see that all needed information has been collected and that appropriate conclusions about the meaning of the information and about the client in the situation have been drawn. After planning, there should be evaluation to determine if the plan is complete and feasible. After action has been carried out, evaluation should be used to determine if the desired goals have been reached. Evaluation is also an important part of the termination process. Evaluation, then, is finding out if what is expected to happen is really happening. It looks at completed work and determines which methods and strategies worked and why. It is an opportunity to check with clients and significant others to see how it is going from their viewpoint. Evaluation of one's work is a professional obligation for every social worker, and should be a continuous process. Programs and agencies are obligated to carry out, on an ongoing basis, evaluation of the mission, purpose, and goals of the agency and its programs. Evaluation is necessary if social workers and the agencies for which they work are to be accountable to clients, support sources, and the general public.

This chapter will first consider this concern for accountability and how it relates to evaluation. It will then discuss various kinds of evaluation, techniques used in evaluation, and ethical issues related to evaluation.

ACCOUNTABILITY

In recent years, much emphasis has been placed on accountability in the social welfare field. In its simplest form, accountability is responsibility. However, the complexity of accountability begins to become apparent when one asks the question: Accountability to whom? The social worker is responsible to the client for upholding his part of any agreements or contracts and for providing the service agreed upon. The social worker is also responsible to the profession for upholding social work values and the *Code of Ethics* (see Chapter 3) in delivering services. The social worker is responsible to the agency that employs the worker for delivering the service within guidelines, programs, and policies developed by the agency. The agency, in turn, is responsible to the persons who provide support and sanction to the agency. This latter responsibility adds considerable complexity to accountability. Those who support the agency are a nebulous mass of individuals (e.g., taxpayers) who have no universally accepted goal for the service. The goals that do exist are often not congruent with the goals set by workers and clients.

Accountability is complex because of the multiple constituency of the social agency and because of the systemic nature of persons in situations. It is very difficult if not impossible to identify cause-and-effect relationships or all variables that may be operating in any situation. Thus, adequate hard data are elusive. The complexity of social service organizations further adds to the complexity of accountability. In all its complexity, accountability becomes an ambiguous concept.

Accountability has two components: efficiency and effectiveness. *Efficiency* refers to the cost of service. Because of the nature of human services, the counting of numbers of clients, time spent with clients, or cost of service in dollars and cents is not a sufficient way of accounting for work. Social costs also must be considered. This would include such things as how the service is impacting on the client's capacity to parent, or function in the work force. It would include how the service is affecting the functioning of systems in the client's immediate environment, or how the quality of life of the client, significant others, and the community in general is being affected. *Effectiveness* relates to whether the service leads to the goals for which it was intended. Because of the complexity of the human situation and the many individuals with differing goals concerned about agency programs, it is difficult to measure effectiveness. If goals that are measurable have been included in plans of action, however, it is possible to determine if those goals have been reached in a particular service situation. If agencies have well-defined purposes and goals, then evaluation and accountability have a sound base upon which to be carried out. The identification of goals and the evaluation of the service are key factors in accountability. Evaluation is not only important as a part of the social work process but necessary for agency functioning in the contemporary social and political scene.

Evaluation has been defined as "collection of data about outcomes of a program of action relative to goals and objectives set in advance of the implementation of that program."[1] The agency is most apt to be asked to be accountable in terms of its programs. The worker is accountable to the individual client and to the agency. In order for the agency to be accountable, it must develop ongoing means of evaluating both the efficiency and the effectiveness of programs. As a part of the agency, the worker must contribute data for the agency to use in its accountability responses and also become aware of evaluative mechanisms that may be useful for developing accountability responses. It is the social worker who has the best sense of the impact of programs on clients, who is aware of data that are available for use, and who is responsible for providing primary data. In order for a social worker to carry out this evaluation function, a knowledge of social research methods and techniques is necessary. Creativity in the use of information available can enhance the accountability capacity of an agency. Understanding the nature of program evaluation is also useful.

Bernie Jones has said that programs are evaluated for a number of specific reasons. Some of these are:

1. To find out how effectively a program is meeting its goals. (Is it making any difference? To whom?)
2. To obtain information that will help restructure a program or manage it more effectively. Perhaps the evaluator wants to see if a particular component should be eliminated or replaced.
3. To identify models for others to follow, or to test a theory or an approach to a problem. (What made the program work? Can any elements be used in other programs?)
4. To find out what staff members need in order to direct their program effectively.
5. To find out how well the program is working from the client's point of view, and how to make it more effective.
6. To improve public relations and fundraising efforts. (What will help sell a program to those whose funds or endorsements are needed?)
7. To meet the requirements of a funding source. (Is the program operating well enough to justify refunding?)[2]

Most of the concern for accountability comes from sources other than the client, but it is important for clients to be involved in developing accountability responses. Clients can provide useful information that cannot be obtained from other sources. Inclusion of the client's evaluation of service also increases the indexes of effectiveness available, but such inclusion is not without problems. Clients and organizations may differ in their view of what is important in determining accountability. The powerlessness of clients tends to cause their views and opinions to be overlooked. Clients also may not have the knowledge and the experience to evaluate a service in all its complexity. They can, however, be involved in the construction of questions to be considered in evaluation and in presenting a viewpoint as to the ideal service for the agency to engage in if it is to meet its goals.[3]

In order to fulfill professional responsibility in contemporary social work practice, all social workers must be concerned about issues of accountability. They must attempt to reconcile the different perspectives of the client, the agency, and the supporting public. They must cooperate with clients and other knowledgeable persons and develop means for evaluating services so that accurate assessments of the service being delivered are possible. They must attempt to insure that the right questions are being asked and that issues of both effectiveness and efficiency are addressed. As social workers carry out evaluative activities they should be ever mindful of the accountability requirements of contemporary social work practice. These requirements include those of the agency, funding sources, and community, as well as the worker's accountability to the client and the profession. They should collect adequate and accurate data to fulfill the accountability requirements related to both the worker-client relationship and to the agency as it justifies its existence and work to supporting bodies and to the general public.

CASE EXAMPLE

Ted is a social worker in the children and family division of a public social service agency. In his caseload are several families he really enjoys working with. These families have begun to make real progress in their capacity to parent their young children. Jim knows that their parenting standards are now meeting the expectations of the agency and society in general, and he believes they could achieve an even higher level of functioning with further work. Jim also knows that his caseload includes several families he does not like to work with. He wonders if it would not be better and quicker to just file petitions to remove the children and get it over with. On assessing his work with these families, he concludes that he really has not spent much time with them or given them sufficient opportunity to work on the needed changes. He concludes that the responsible way of dealing with his caseload is to taper off the contacts with the families who are doing well and no longer need intensive services and to begin to concentrate on those families who are having difficulty in making needed changes. He also concludes that it will be important for him to document carefully the work with these families in case at a later point he needs to file neglect petitions.

KINDS OF EVALUATION

Planning for evaluation when developing a plan of action is one way of assuring that the plan of action is carried out in a way that yields maximum information to the worker, the client, and the agency. If the information to be used in evaluation is identified before the action of the social work process begins, there is a better chance that such information will be available for use in evaluation.

In order to plan effectively and efficiently for evaluation, an understanding of the various kinds of evaluation and some of the means for carrying out the evaluative process is useful. Evaluation serves many purposes and takes a variety of forms. In its most simplified form, it is a worker thinking about what has happened and why it happened. During the termination phase of the social work process the worker and client together determine if the goals set out in the contract have been reached and then discuss what enabled the goal attainment. Evaluation involves discussing what has been helpful to the client and what could have been done differently. Program evaluation is more complex, involving statistical data or other research methodology. Evaluation is often referred to as summative or formative. *Summative evaluation* is concerned with outcomes and effectiveness. *Formative evaluation* is concerned with looking at the process of the work, at how the work during the various steps in the service influenced the final outcome of the work. It would look at such things as the nature of the relationship, the content of sessions, or the setting in which the work took place. Both types are important in social work practice, and so the evaluation process should have a balance of both types.[4] This section will point out a variety of other ways of looking at evaluation. The kind of evaluation is in part dependent on the stage of the work of the social work process or on the program or agency need for data to provide a base for accountability.

One way to develop an understanding of evaluation is to consider various classification schemes used relative to evaluation. The first classification to be considered is whether the evaluation is of a particular case, of a program within an agency, or of the agency itself. When considering a specific case, evaluation focuses on whether or not the goals set by the worker and client together were attained. Evaluation of the process of the work should focus on how the various components of the plan of action contributed to the reaching of the goal. Evaluation of the process of work is a joint endeavor of the worker and the client because the client is usually the best source of information about goal attainment and about the process of the work together. Workers often do some additional thinking about the client in a situation and how the client and his situation relate to other clients they have known. This is done so that the worker can develop understandings as to how to approach other clients who may be in similar situations in the future.

Program and agency evaluations determine effectiveness of agency ways of functioning. These kinds of evaluation are often concerned with efficiency of service provision. They are not apt to be personalized as a case evaluation is. Different kinds of evaluation call for different methods and techniques.

Different practice settings call for different kinds of information to be used in the evaluative process. For example, in a health care setting an evaluative plan can be developed using four elements: identification of the client's problems, the social work function, the time and resources involved, and the outcome of the intervention. Lists of the most common problems encountered in the setting can be developed, common functions of the social worker identified, a management system for staff developed, and a means for measuring outcomes established. In order to operationalize the evaluation system, the use of standard record forms is required. Each social worker then has responsibility for maintaining the required records related to her work and clients.[5]

Program evaluations serve four purposes. First, they are necessary to meet the requirements of outside funding and accreditation bodies. Second, they can provide indications of client satisfaction. Third, they can provide information that can be used in developing new practice knowledge and worker competence. Fourth, program evaluations can document the need for new services and/or service effectiveness to other service providers, funding sources, and the general public.

A second classification is qualitative versus quantitative evaluation. The contemporary service delivery system has been highly influenced by organizational management trends and the use of a quantitative base for evaluation. Clinical practice has also been influenced by behavioral psychology and its emphasis on measuring behaviors. The trend toward computerization of information and records also supports the push for quantitative data. However, most social workers believe that not all information can be dealt with in a quantitative manner. They believe there is a qualitative factor in human functioning. While behaviors can be measured, feelings and emotions cannot, and qualitative measures are a better mechanism for evaluating them.

A third classification is that of clinical evaluation versus management evaluation. While this classification might be closely related to the quantitative-qualitative classification (management generally using quantitative data; clinical generally using qualitative data), the use of these two types of evaluation is quite different. *Management evaluation* is used to make internal staffing and program decisions and to substantiate need for services and resources to support services. *Clinical evaluation* is limited to use by professional persons (worker and supervisor) and the client directly involved in the situation being evaluated. Because of the different usage, different information is sought for use in different types of evaluation, and different kinds of outcomes are expected. Sometimes data are used for both types of evaluation. This has the advantage of efficiency in collecting the needed information because it avoids the necessity of collecting two sets of data. It can be difficult, however, to use the same information for two different purposes. Management evaluation is apt to call for statistics. It may call for information about specific kinds of problems clients bring to an agency, but the information needs to be gathered in a manner that will yield categories of problems. Clinical evaluation is usually interested in the type of problems dealt with and specific information as to how the problem and its resolution is impacted by the client and her situation. This information loses some of its meaning when converted to categories or statistics.

Another classification is one developed by Michael Key, Peter Hudson, and John Armstrong.[6] They discuss evaluation approaches along a hard line–soft line continuum. *Hard line evaluation* focuses on aims and objectives set before the implementation of programs. Some degree of scientific objectivity is involved in this type of evaluation. *Soft line evaluation* is based on impressions and opinions. Each result yields quite different kinds of information. The worker needs to determine if hard line information will adequately provide for the evaluation needs and appropriately tell the necessary story. If not, then soft line information should be used either to tell the story or to supplement the hard line information.

Each type of classification points out a different dimension of evaluation. Each evaluative effort can be classified along a continuum related to each of the four classifications. When choosing evaluating methods and techniques, it is important to consider the requirements of the situation being evaluated, keeping the possibilities of all four of the above classifications in mind (case or program agency, quantitative or qualitative, clinical or management, hard or soft), and to choose methods that provide for the requirements of the particular situation.

CASE EXAMPLE

It is the last session of a treatment-oriented group. As part of the worker's preparation for that session, she considers how to help the group members evaluate the experience they have had in the twelve weeks they have been meeting. She decides to have each member first fill out an opinion survey of ten questions that ask about the individual's experience in the group. Some of the questions asked are: Were the goals you set for yourself at the beginning of the group experience met? If not met, why do you think they were not met? If met, how did the group experience facilitate the meeting of your goals? What would you have liked to be different about the group? The worker used this technique because she wanted to get individual input from each group member. She did it before a group discussion to evaluate the group so individuals would not be influenced by that discussion. The consideration of goal attainment would give her some material that could be quantified, thus meeting one of the agency's needs for documentation of outcomes of service provided.

She followed this up with a group discussion of what had happened in the work together. She did this knowing it was one means for helping group members review the experience, an important ingredient in the termination process. She hoped that the discussion would allow her to probe for additional material that would help her plan work with groups in the future.

TECHNIQUES FOR USE IN EVALUATING

The process of evaluation makes use of many of the same methods and techniques as does assessment, such as looking at information collected about the work and determining what has happened in the social work endeavor. The information may be gathered specifically for evaluative purposes or it may be information developed as part of the social work process. Much of this gathering of information is done using an interactive process (see Chapters 7 and 8). Processes, methods, and skills presented in earlier sections of this book can and should be adapted to the needs of the evaluation.

There are, however, some special techniques used to facilitate the evaluative process. These include various kinds of recording and a variety of research techniques. Related to recording and research is the use of the computer, a new and growing influence on evaluation. When planning for evaluation, social workers should look at various methods and techniques for collecting the information and choose those that can provide the information needed in the most reliable and efficient manner. This requires the same kind of creative planning used in developing the plan of action. This section will present some methods of keeping records and some ways of using research in evaluation.* It will also discuss implications for social work practice, and particularly for the evaluation process, and of the growth of information management using computers.

Recording

Social work has always placed considerable emphasis on recording. This recording has taken many forms. **Process recording**—a narrative report of all that happened during a client contact, including the worker's feelings and thinking about what has happened—is a form that at one time received great emphasis and was frequently used in the educational and supervisory processes. In recent years it has not been used as often, in part probably because it is extremely time consuming. Also, the intensive individual supervision of workers, which was once considered essential to social work and which made extensive use of recording, is no longer considered desirable in many settings. Recording, however, is still a technique that has value for students as they and their field supervisors evaluate their work. It is especially useful to the social worker striving to further develop understanding and skill in difficult situations or in situations in which the worker is developing new skills.

The usefulness of process recording depends to a considerable extent on the ability of the worker to recall exactly what happened and in what order and to look at the facts in an objective manner in order to get at underlying feelings and meanings. The worker must be willing to honestly record the actions and communications of both worker and client. When this technique is used in a supervisory process, the worker must have a trusting relationship with the supervisor. Because of its time-consuming qualities, process recording probably should not

---

*This section does not list all possible techniques, but does discuss some of the techniques in common use and considers how they are useful to the evaluative process. It is assumed students either have been or will be exposed to a research methods course that broadens the scope of the content in this chapter. Of particular relevance is evaluative research.

be used with every case or situation but with carefully selected ones particularly suited for the worker's own development and learning. Process recording is most often used when working with individuals but can also be used when working with larger systems. When process recording is used, confidentiality must be preserved. The written record must be kept in a secure place and only seen by those directly involved in the situation or supervising the worker. If a record is to be used for other purposes, such as teaching or as a case example, it must be completely disguised so that neither the person nor the situation can be identified.[7]

A technique used for purposes similar to the process recording is the taping, either in audio or video format, of interviews, group sessions, or other interactional occasions. This technique has value in that it allows the worker to see himself in action with the client. Sometimes it is also useful for the client to view what has happened as a means of evaluating behaviors and interactions. Unless the time is taken to evaluate the underlying elements of the situation (the feeling elements and the reasons behind behaviors), some of the learning potential of this technique is lost. When using the taping technique of recording, workers must obtain permission from the client to tape sessions. Sometimes taping may inhibit the client and have a negative effect on the work of the session. Again, confidentiality is an important consideration.

Another type of recording often used by social workers is the summary record. Though this type of record takes various forms depending on agency policy, it essentially includes entry data, often the social history, a plan of action, periodic summaries of significant information and actions taken by the worker, and a statement of what was accomplished as the case is closed. The periodic summaries may be made at specified periods of time (e.g., every three months) or they may be made when it is necessary to document some fact or action. The summary record is shorter and easier to use when considering the total service process. It is focused more on what happens with the client than on the worker's input and sifts out the important elements, discarding the superfluous.

Summary records are most important in situations in which long-term, ongoing contact with a client and a series of workers may be involved. These records provide a picture of what has happened in the past with a particular client. Agency policy often specifies the form and content of such records. This policy reflects the agency needs for information both to protect itself when questions about the handling of a particular case are raised and to provide the specific information needed for accountability purposes. As summary records may be subject to review by a number of people, questions of how to deal with confidentiality are important. It is usually good practice to include in summary recording only that which is required to be in the record and only verifiable information—not impressions, feelings, or information that can be misinterpreted.[8]

A contemporary kind of recording is the *problem-oriented record*, which is often found in health care settings where it is used not just by social workers but also by all health care professionals. This common recording system has advantages when working in an interdisciplinary setting. It is easily translated to computer data bases. It is succinct and focused.

Problem-oriented records contain four parts. First there is a data base that contains information pertinent to the client and work with the client. This would include such things as age, sex, marital status, functioning limitations, persons involved (family and other professionals), financial situation, or any test results. Second is a problem list that includes a statement of initial complaints and assessment of the concerned staff. Third are plans and goals related to each identified problem. Fourth are followup notes about what was done and the outcome of that activity.

Problem-oriented records take several forms. Usually they are developed so that they consist at least in part of checklists that can be converted into data to be used with a computer. One often-used form is *soaping* (*s*ubjective, *o*bjective, *a*ssessment, *p*lan). In this form, for each identified problem, subjective (the patient's report), objective (the facts as determined by clinical activity), assessment (a statement about the nature of the problem), and a plan for dealing with the problem are stated.[9]

Recent research carried out by Jill Doner Kagle indicates that workers have some difficulties in using what she terms as "new records." This type of record is narrowly focused on defining the need for service, service goals and plans, service activities, and the impact of service on the client situation. She found that many workers felt this kind of recording did not provide all the information they needed in providing service. Her work suggests that workers believe they need information on the dynamics of the situation and, perhaps, on the context of the client. Another difficulty workers encountered with the "new records" was that they did not provide for the "overdocumentation" which is called for in a world in which all professions are more often threatened with legal actions. The answer may lie in determining which cases need to have in-depth recording and which can have a "new record" approach.

Recordkeeping has always been an important part of the social worker's job. The type of recordkeeping has changed over time due to new practice demands and new technologies. Records have many different purposes that range from improving the worker's competence to obtaining data for accountability and research. It is important that social workers develop the capacity to accurately and efficiently maintain records required by any agency in which they are employed. They also need to discover what records are needed for their personal and professional growth.

CASE EXAMPLE

This example will illustrate three ways in which the same case material might be handled when recording and evaluating. The three techniques are process recording, summary recording, and problem-oriented recording.

Process Recording

On February 4, 1991, the nurse on surgery called to refer Mrs. Heart to me. She said that Mrs. Heart had been brought in for an emergency appendectomy two days ago. Yesterday afternoon she became very upset and showed much concern about how her children were being cared for. Nurses on the evening shift discussed the situation with Mr. Heart when he came to visit. The children, a boy age four and a girl age two, have been cared for by a neighbor during the day. Mr. Heart left them with a babysitter last night. He, too, showed some concern, saying that neither he nor his wife wanted the children with the neighbor as they questioned some of her childcare practices but he didn't know just what he could do right now. The request is for me to see Mrs. Heart to see if I can find suitable child care.

I immediately obtained the medical chart and found that she is medically doing well postsurgically. There is concern that her emotional state may affect her recovery rate. I then went to talk with Mrs. Heart in her room. I found an attractive, twenty-eight-year-old woman who was having some postoperative pain. I quietly introduced myself as the medical social worker. She began to say, "Please don't take my children away." She then began to cry and say, "I can't help it. Why did this have to happen? I love my children." I put my hand on hers and looked her in the eye and quietly said that I had not come to take her children away; that I could not do that as I am not a child welfare social worker. I explained that it was my job to help with problems that arose because people were sick and in the hospital. I told her that I was here because she seemed very concerned about her children and might need some help in finding care for the children while she was in the hospital and for a while when she got home. She again expressed concern that the children would be taken out of the home, although she was not as agitated as at first. I told her that usually children should remain in their familiar surroundings when parents are hospitalized as they are less apt to be upset about the situation if they stay in the home. Mrs. Heart then said, "I don't know what we can do. There are no relatives we can call on. Mr. Heart might lose his job if he stays home to take care of the children."

I then said I'd like to get to understand the situation better. I thought she could help me. Mrs. Heart by this time seemed quieter and more able to listen. I asked her to tell me about the children. [The recording would then continue to describe the interaction as the worker and client explore the situation and decide together what to do. The actual verbatim dialogue of the interview is recorded when possible. The record could end with a summary section that identifies the salient aspects of the situation, the plan developed, the next tasks for the worker and client, and the worker's evaluation of the interview.]

Summary Recording

February 4, 1991, social work services requested by Nurse Brown because Mrs. Heart is upset about childcare for her two children, a boy age four and a girl age two. Saw Mrs. Heart and developed with her a plan for the care of the children. We identified a friend who will care for children during the day until she is discharged. A babysitter will continue to be used in evenings when Mr. Heart visits. Worker will contact Homemaker's Service to set up plans for use of a homemaker when Mrs. Heart returns home until she is physically able to care for the children.

Problem-Oriented Recording

Name: Mrs. Linda Heart   *Age:* 28
Referral from: Nurse Brown   *Date:* February 4, 1991
Medical condition: Emergency appendectomy February 2, 1991

Subjective: Patient upset about care of her children while she is in hospital. Seems an appropriately concerned mother. Has good intelligence. Seems to have good relationship with husband.

Objective: Children are now being cared for by a neighbor during the day and father and babysitters at night. Parents do not feel comfortable with daytime arrangement. Mother will be in hospital three more days and needs some help with childcare for at least two weeks after she returns home.

Assessment: Alternative childcare arrangements should be explored with family to see if plans more in keeping with their desires can be found. The Hearts are unaware of community resources that might be of help to them. Mrs. Heart is verbal and able to discuss plans, but Mr. Heart should also be included in planning.

Plan: Obtain a list of community resources that may be of help to the Hearts. During visiting hours on February 4, 1991 discuss with both Mr. and Mrs. Heart possible solutions and set up a childcare plan for the next three weeks.

Research

Many research techniques are very useful in carrying out evaluations because evaluation and research share common considerations and concerns. The purpose of this discussion is to point out the relationship of practice and research when evaluating social work practice and to discuss a few research methods and techniques that are particularly suited for evaluation of practice. The research techniques chosen for discussion are: single-subject design, goal-attainment scaling, and the use of questionnaires, interviews, and observation.

Single-subject design is a research method used by many social workers in their work with individuals. To use this method a worker must have some competence in using either a behavioral model of social work or the task model of practice. A baseline is established for the client's behavior. Interventive methods aimed at bringing about a desired change in the behavior are identified. Goals that reflect the desired change are pinpointed. At varying points during the intervention, the target behavior is measured to determine the progress toward reaching the goal. After completion of the intervention, a final measurement is made to determine the extent to which the goal has been reached. The proponents of this method claim that not only can measurable results or outcomes of the intervention be obtained but its use develops what has come to be known as a casework-researcher. The *casework-researcher* is a worker who develops a capacity to be a highly skilled self-evaluator, whose accountability is enhanced. It is felt that *use of single-subject* design provides a reliable means of validating "scientific practice."[11] Critics of single-subject design believe that the range of applicability is very limited because the technique is only useful when using a behavioral framework for social work practice. They also believe that there are qualitative questions that must be answered and no provision is made in this methodology to do that. Questions also can be raised as to the lasting quality of the change when measurements are made during and directly after intervention. Is the planned intervention the cause of the desired change, or have other factors, either in the treatment situation or in the environment, contributed to the change?[12] The major contribution of single-subject design is its focus on goals and outcomes and the provision of a methodology for measuring outcomes, which moves evaluation toward the hard end of the soft-hard continuum.

A technique often used with the single-subject design is **goal-attainment scaling.** When using this technique, the goals are set so that the outcomes can be measured on a five-point scale. The five points on the scale are: most unfavorable outcome thought likely, less than expected outcome, expected outcome, more than expected outcome, most favorable outcome thought likely. Allowance for recording several goals is made by the development of a grid with goals on one axis and levels of predicted attainment on the other axis.[13]

Goal-attainment scaling has a major strength in that it allows for several measurements of success and failure to reach an outcome. By specifying a continuum of outcomes that can lead to maximal accomplishment by any client, the technique includes a growth factor. It also offers an evaluative mechanism (the five points on the scale) that can be converted to symbolic codes needed for computerization of data. The grid provides a quickly read summary of the outcomes of a specific episode of service.

The major limitations of goal-attainment scaling relate to the time needed to set up the scales for measurement. Some social workers believe the time spent in setting up the scales would better be used in working with the client. Also, some desired outcomes are very difficult to specify in the manner needed in this technique. Goal-attainment scaling also has some of the same limitations of the single-subject design, such as questions about the relationship of the change to the intervention, the emphasis on the outcome of goals, and the sustainment of the change over time. Goal-attainment scaling can be used if goals are set in the manner suggested in Chapter 12.

CASE EXAMPLE

Goal-Attainment Scaling

Goal: A plan for appropriate child care for the Heart children.

Least desirable outcome: No plan is developed.

Less than desirable outcome: Plan is developed that will adequately care for children but which leaves mother uncomfortable.

Expected outcome: Plan is developed that the Hearts feel comfortable with.

More than expected outcome: Plan is developed that not only is at expected level but which provides family with needed ongoing support.

More desirable outcome possible: Plan developed, Hearts begin to explore their desires regarding childcare and make modification to allow for needed flexibility and support.

Program Evaluation

When designing and carrying out a program evaluation,[14] the collection of data is a most important step (as it is in all research). In order to evaluate a program, it is necessary to first determine just what data are needed. Some of the data that might be useful include measures of client satisfaction; measures of success in meeting goals in a valid sample of clients served; cost effectiveness measures; determinations of the extent to which the need is being addressed by the program; worker effort and satisfaction; and community attitudes toward the program. It is usually necessary to collect data related to several indicators of program effectiveness and efficiency. Data may be already collected or collected specifically for purposes of the evaluation.

Important techniques used for collecting the data are research interviews, questionnaires, and observations. When used for research or evaluative purposes, the *interview* is usually more structured than the interventive interview used in the social work process. Usually there is a schedule, or questions in a specific order, which the interviewer is asked to follow. The interviewer is seeking specific information and should not engage in discussion that might change the interviewee's thinking about the situation being studied.

Social workers have knowledge and skill that can enhance the collection of information. They have knowledge of which information might be important for evaluative purposes. They have knowledge of how to seek and deal with particularly sensitive information. They have basic interviewing skills for engaging individuals in the work at hand, questioning techniques to use in reaching for needed information, and skill in observing and assessing the nonverbal communication of the interviewee. When a social worker is interviewing for evaluative purposes, the differences between an interventive interview and evaluative interview should be kept in mind. When those not involved in a program are doing the interviewing, social workers involved in the program can be of help in developing the schedule and giving insight about the information to be obtained.

Questionnaires are another valuable tool in program evaluation. A simple closed-question instrument, for example, to gather information about client satisfaction is used by some agencies. This instrument needs to be brief yet probe for the attitudes and feelings of clients about the service they receive. The questionnaire should be constructed so that the respondent will understand the questions in the way intended. Care should also be taken to insure an adequate response rate. When an agency is carrying out an evaluation of its programs, workers may be asked to help in the construction and administration of questionnaires.

Observing is another way of collecting needed data. Workers may be asked to contribute their observations to the data base. The worker should be clear about the information that is desired and the structure the evaluator has designed for the observation and the recording of the data. Often workers believe that, because of their knowledge of the situation, they may have a better way of structuring the observations and recording related to the observations. If this is the case, it is appropriate for them to discuss their concerns with the evaluator. However, if the evaluator decides not to incorporate the worker's suggestions, it is important for the worker to follow the evaluator's instructions and provide the information obtained in the desired form.

Understanding of research methods and technology is important to workers participating in agency and program evaluations.[15]

Use of Computers

The computer is becoming an important tool for use in the evaluative process. It can record and analyze information in new and more sophisticated ways that enhance the possibilities for data analysis and facilitate the storing and retrieval of data to document accountability.

Social workers, then, need to be aware of what computers can do and what their limitations are. They should know how to process information so it can be computerized, how to enter information, how to access existing data, and how to evaluate the usefulness of both hardware and software for social work purposes. They need to know enough about how computers operate in order to communicate with the computer expert or programmer about problems with a piece of equipment or a program. They need to be able to communicate about the tasks they want the computer to perform so that programs can be suggested to them, written for them, or modified to meet their needs.[16]

When preparing data for entry into a computer it is important to follow instructions very carefully. Categories identified by the computer program must be entered in the form called for. All of the information requested must be provided so that planned operations can be carried out. One very small error in making an entry can cause the computer to be unable to carry out the command as desired. The better the social worker understands how the computer processes data, the less likely the data will be entered incorrectly.

It is also important to understand who can be expected to have access to the information and the purposes for which the information will be used. This helps the worker evaluate whether the most pertinent information is being requested and whether client identification and confidentiality are being protected. If social workers have reason to question whether the information being sought will provide the answers or whether client identification or confidentiality are at risk, they have an ethical responsibility to inform those responsible for the operation of the programs and to insure that needed modifications are made.[17]

ISSUES RELATED TO EVALUATION

Accountability and evaluation techniques have raised several issues related to client rights, confidentiality, and protection of information, which this section will address more completely. The areas to be discussed are: client participation in the evaluation process, confidentiality of records, and the effect of privacy and open-access laws on the evaluation process.

Client Participation

When evaluating a particular episode of service there should be a strong element of client involvement. As the worker and client evaluate together what has happened and why it might have happened, plans can be adjusted when needed and contracts modified. If clients are to be involved in assessment, in planning, and in carrying out various tasks, then they are important sources for the information used in evaluation and must be a part of the evaluative endeavor so they can also be involved in making decisions to modify plans and contracts.

As the social work process with a particular client nears the end, or as goals have been met, evaluation becomes important for both worker and client. As a part of the termination process, evaluation provides opportunity for growth for both worker and client. Evaluation at termination will be discussed in the next chapter.

The involvement of the client in program and agency evaluation is seldom considered because the techniques used require training. The focus is primarily on accountability to funding sources or on administrative functioning. Clients who are already overburdened with their personal needs and problems usually have little energy to use in this evaluative process.

However, it would seem that clients should be important in this process as well. The basic reason for the existence of the service or the agency should be to meet client needs, to help clients to solve problems. Do they not have a perspective on the agency's functioning that is important to any evaluation of that agency or program? Also, if client-related information is being used, the guidelines for confidentiality which require client knowledge of its use and opportunity for input as to the validity of the information are important. It would seem, then, that social workers must see that the client perspective is one of the sets of information that is a part of any program or agency evaluation. Also it would seem that clients should have knowledge that such evaluation is taking place, of the information relative to them that is being used, and how that information is being used. In involving clients in this type of evaluation, the worker must make decisions as to how and when to involve the client.

The involvement of the client in the worker's evaluation of his or her own professional growth poses another set of considerations. Client input as to what was helpful and what was not useful is an important component of professional growth evaluation. However, for at least some clients, certain types of discussion might give that client a sense of insecurity in the worker's capacity to help. Some clients may need to feel the certainty that the worker knows what he or she is doing. The worker certainly should seek the client's input into the worker's professional evaluation process, but the worker also must place the client's interest ahead of her or his own. The worker must not use the evaluation time solely for his or her own purposes, but always see that the work also has value for the client and that when this ceases to be the case, the worker takes the information gathered and proceeds on his or her own or with colleagues or supervisors to evaluate professional growth.

Confidentiality

Responsible evaluation requires substantiating information. In order to be certain that information is available, it is essential that records of various kinds be kept. This use of records raises concerns about confidentiality of sensitive information about clients or identification of specific clients. Use of records intrudes on the confidential nature of the worker-client relationship, and it brings up the question of what is ethical disclosure of information about the client and the work with the client. The social worker has two responsibilities if the principle of confidentiality is to be maintained: first, to be sure the client is aware of the records that are to be kept and of the nature of information sharing that will be required of the worker, so client and worker can make an informed decision about the sharing of sensitive information; second, the worker must do all that is possible to insure that information and records are maintained and used only in ways that insure the protection of client identification and confidentiality.

Clients need to understand not only the confidential nature of their work with a social worker, but the limits of that confidentiality, that is, that information will be discussed with a supervisor or a professional team. Clients should be told what will be recorded, who will have access to their records, and how long these records will be kept. They need to know that records used in agency and program evaluation are depersonalized so identification of clients is protected. They need to know what information is shared with whom and why it is shared.

Workers also need to be sure that clients have given informed consent for the use of information in their records. A client should not be asked to give consent when he is desperate for service, a time when making an informed decision is difficult. It is wise for the worker to discuss the use of information at several points during the work together. If the client decides not to share information and knows the consequences of not sharing that information, then the worker should respect the client's right to withhold information to protect her privacy.

The sharing of information about clients often requires written consent of the client. This consent should be specific; that is, it should state the purpose for the sharing of the information and the persons with whom the information will be shared. Clients should be helped to understand their rights in signing or not signing such consents for release of information. Usually it is wise to have someone witness the client's signature. Because the release of information could become a part of a legal action, the advice of a legal expert should be obtained in developing a form for the release of information.[18]

Workers should monitor the use of client records in order for workers to see that information contained in records is not used improperly. When they detect improper or questionable use of records it is their responsibility to alert supervisors or other responsible persons to the situation. They can suggest ways in which the client's rights can be protected, such as depersonalizing information. If the improper use continues, a worker will need to decide what action needs to be taken to prevent unethical use.[19]

Effect of Privacy and Open-Access Laws

Recent federal and state legislation regulates the use of various kinds of records, including those used for evaluative purposes. This new legislation has generated a growing body of interpretation and judicial decisions regarding the application of these laws, which has further complicated issues of recordkeeping.

The Federal Privacy Act of 1974 (PL 93-579) in essence gives the client the right to see any record containing information about that client. It requires that no disclosure of information in any record be made with written consent from the client and that a record be kept indicating any disclosures of information to other persons.

Other laws have been enacted that call for open access to public records. In some cases these laws have been interpreted to mean that the records of public agencies and, in some cases, situations in which governmental funds have been involved are a matter of public record and can be disclosed in a variety of situations, including court proceedings. There seems to be a conflict between those two sets of laws—privacy and open-access—that has not been fully resolved.[20]

There is also another implication of these two sets of laws: it would seem that they discourage the keeping of confidentiality. It is essential for social workers and social work agencies to determine exactly what records must be kept and how to best manage those records so that client, agency, and the general public's best interests are met. Social workers should involve themselves in serious discussions to resolve these issues.

Three issues relating to evaluation—client participation, confidentiality, and the effect of privacy laws and open-access laws—have been raised. These issues need to be addressed by ongoing dialogue, creative thinking, and an ever-present sense of the ethics of the profession of social work. These are not the only issues that have or will arise regarding evaluation. Every social worker should be alert to identify other issues and to engage in discussions to resolve them.

SUMMARY

This chapter has considered evaluation as an ongoing part of the social work process. It has pointed out the growing demand for accountability to the client, agency, funding source, and general public. It has discussed various kinds of evaluation and their usefulness. Several tools used in the evaluative process were explained. It has also considered some important issues that exist for the social worker when engaging in the evaluation process. Evaluation is a skill that all social workers must possess and a process that all social workers must engage in if they are to adhere to the ethical principles of the social work profession.

QUESTIONS

1. What do you see as the positive outcomes of appropriate evaluation?

2. When a worker faces conflicting demands regarding accountability to clients (e.g., meeting client need) or agency accountability expectations, what thinking should go into resolving such conflicts?

3. What are the advantages of using a *summative* approach to evaluation? A *formative* approach?

4. What do you see as the similarities and the differences between case evaluation and program evaluation?

5. When should the various forms of recording be used? What are the strengths and limitations of each?

6. What research techniques, other than those discussed in this chapter, do you think might be helpful in the evaluation process?

7. What are advantages for using the computer to process evaluative information? The disadvantages?

8. What are the advantages and disadvantages of including client input into the worker's professional self-evaluation?

9. What can a social worker do when she finds that required recording is not being used within the guidelines for professional accountability?

10. How can a social worker address the open-access and right-to-privacy laws at the same time?

SUGGESTED READINGS

Brinkerhoff, Robert O., Brethower, Dale M., Hluchj, Terry, and Nowakowski, Jeri Ridings. *Program Evaluation.* Boston: Kluwer-Nijhoff, 1983.

Burch, Genevieve, and Mohr, Vicki. "Evaluating a Child Abuse Intervention Program." *Social Casework* 61 (February 1980): 90–99.

Cahill, Janet, and Feldman, Leonard H. "Computers in Child Welfare: Planning a More Serviceable Work Environment." *Child Welfare* 72 (January 1993): 3–12.

Caputo, Richard K. "The Role of Information Systems in Evaluation Research." *Administration in Social Work* 10 (Spring 1986): 67–77.

Compton, Beulah Roberts, and Galaway, Burt. *Social Work Processes*, 3rd ed. Homewood, IL: Dorsey Press, 1984 (Chapter 15, "Evaluation").

Finn, Jerry. "Security, Privacy, and Confidentiality in Agency Microcomputer Use." *Families in Society* 71 (May 1990): 283–295.

Geismar, Ludwig L., and Wood, Katherine M. "Evaluating Practice: Science as Faith." *Social Casework* 63 (May 1982): 266–272.

Gingerich, Wallace J. "Expert Systems and Their Potential Use in Social Work." *Family in Society* 71 (April 1990): 221–228.

Goodman, Catherine. "Evaluation of a Model Self-Help Telephone Program: Impact on Natural Networks." *Social Work* 35 (November 1990): 556–562.

Grinnell, Richard M., Jr. *Social Work Research and Evaluation.* Itasca, IL: F. E. Peacock, 1981.

Kagle, Jill Doner. "Record Keeping: Direction for the 1990's." *Social Work* 38 (March 1993): 190–196.

Kagle, Jill Doner. "Restoring the Clinical Record." *Social Work* 29 (January–February 1984): 46–50.

Kagle, Jill Doner. *Social Work Records.* Homewood, IL: Dorsey Press, 1984.

Key, Michael, Hudson, Peter, and Armstrong, John. "Evaluation Theory and Community Work." In *Strategies of Community Organization,* 3rd ed., Fred M. Cox, John L. Erlich, Jack Rothman, and John E. Tropman, Eds. Itasca, IL: F. E. Peacock, 1979 (pp. 159–175).

Kreuger, Larry W., and Ruckdeschel, Roy. "Microcomputers in Social Service Settings: Research Applications." *Social Work* 30 (May–June 1985): 219–224.

LeMendola, Walter, Glastonbury, Bryan, and Toble, Stuart, Eds. *A Casebook of Computer Applications in Social and Human Services.* New York: Haworth Press, 1989.

McCroskey, Jacquelyn, Nishimato, Robert, and Subramanian, Karen. "Assessment in Family Support Programs: Initial Reliability and Validity Testing of the Family Assessment Form." *Child Welfare* 70 (January–February 1990): 19–33.

Miller, Henry. "The Use of Computers in Social Work Practice: An Assessment." *Journal of Social Work Education* 22 (Fall 1986): 52–60.

Mutschler, Elizabeth. "Evaluating Practice: A Study of Research Utilization by Practitioners." *Social Work* 29 (July–August 1984): 332–337.

Nuehring, Elane, and Pascone, Anne B. "Single-Subject Evaluation: A Tool for Quality Assurance." *Social Work* 31 (September–October 1986): 359–365.

Nurius, Paula, and Cnaan, Ram A. "Classifying Software to Better Support Social Work Practice." *Social Work* 36 (November 1991): 536–541.

Nurius, Paula S., and Hudson, Walter W. "Computer Based Practice: Future Dream or Current Technology." *Social Work* 33 (July–August 1988): 357–362.

Rodwell, Mary K. "Naturalistic Inquiry: An Alternative Model for Social Work Assessment." *Social Service Review* 61 (June 1987): 231–246.

Ruckdeschel, Roy A., and Farris, Buford E. "Assessing Practice: A Critical Look at the Single-Case Design." *Social Casework* 62 (September 1981): 413–419.

Schrier, Carol J. "Guidelines for Record-Keeping under Privacy and Open-Access Laws." *Social Work* 25 (November 1980): 452–461.

Schwartz, Marc D., Ed. *Using Computers in Clinical Practice.* New York: Haworth Press, 1984.

Sheafor, Bradford W., Horejsi, Charles R., and Horejsi, Gloria A. *Techniques and Guidelines for Social Work Practice.* Boston: Allyn and Bacon, 1988 (pp. 137–145 and Chapter 13).

Simons, Ronald L., and Aigner, Stephen M. *Practice Principles: A Problem-Solving Approach to Social Work.* New York: Macmillan, 1985 (Chapter 9).

Streat, Yuri Yamada. "Case Recording in Children's Protective Services." *Social Casework* 65 (November 1987): 553–560.

Taylor, James B. *Using Microcomputers in Social Agencies.* Beverly Hills, CA: Sage Publications, 1981.

Tebb, Susan. "Client-Focused Recording: Linking Theory and Practice." *Families in Society* 72 (September 1991): 425–432.

Theobald, William F. *The Evaluation of Human Service Programs.* Champaign, IL: Management Learning Laboratories, 1985.

Tripodi, Tony. *Evaluative Research for Social Workers.* Englewood Cliffs, NJ: Prentice-Hall, 1983.

Weissman, Harold H. "Accountability and Pseudo-Accountability: A Nonlinear Approach." *Social Service Review* 57 (June 1983): 323–336.

Wilson, Suanna J. *Recording: Guidelines for Social Workers.* New York: Free Press, 1976.

Witkin, Belle Ruth. *Assessing Needs in Educational and Social Programs.* San Francisco: Jossey-Bass, 1984.

NOTES

1. Michael Key, Peter Hudson, and John Armstrong, "Evaluation Theory and Community Work," in *Strategies of Community Organization: A Book of Readings,* 3rd ed., Fred M. Cox, John L. Erlich, Jack Rothman, and John E. Tropman, Eds. (Itasca, IL: F. E. Peacock, 1979), pp. 159–175.

2. Bernie Jones, "Evaluating Social Service Programs," in *Grassroots Administration: A Handbook for Staff and Directors of Small Community Based Social Service Agencies,* Robert Clifton and Alan Dahms. (Monterey, CA: Brooks/Cole, 1980), p. 51.

3. For further discussion of client involvement in evaluation, see Peggy C. Giordano, "The Clients' Perspective in Agency Evaluation," *Social Work* 22 (January 1977): 34–38.

4. For further discussion of this balance, see Beulah Compton and Burt Galaway, *Social Work Processes,* 3rd ed. (Homewood, IL: Dorsey Press, 1984), chap. 15, "Evaluation."

5. Examples of this type of system are discussed in: Robert M. Spano, Thomas J. Kiresuk, and Sander H. Lund, "An Operational Model to Achieve Accountability for Social Work in Health Care," *Social Work in Health Care* 3 (Winter 1977): 123–141; and Patricia Volland, "Social Work Information and Accountability Systems in a Hospital Setting," *Social Work in Health Care* 1 (Spring 1976): 177–285.

6. Michael Key, Peter Hudson, and John Armstrong, "Evaluation Theory and Community Work," in *Strategies of Community Organization,* 3rd ed., Fred M. Cox, John L. Erlich, Jack Rothman, and John E. Tropman Eds. (Itasca, IL: F. E. Peacock, 1979), pp. 159–175.

7. For discussion and examples of this type of record, see Suanna J. Wilson, *Recording: Guidelines for Social Workers* (New York: Free Press, 1980). Also see Jill Doner Kagle, "Restoring the Clinical Record," *Social Work* 29 (January–February 1984): 46–56.

8. For discussion and examples, see Wilson, *Recording.*

9. For examples of problem-oriented records, see Spano, Kiresuk, and Lund, "An Operational Model," and Oystein Sakala LaBinca and Gerald E. Cubelli, "A New Approach to Building Social Work Knowledge," *Social Work in Health Care* 2 (Winter 1976–77): 139–152.

10. Jill Doner Kagel, "Record Keeping: Direction for the 1990's," *Social Work* 38 (March 1993): 190–196.

11. To expand understanding of what has been presented here in a very simplistic way, see Michael W. Howe, "Casework Self-Evaluation: A Single-Subject Approach," *Social Service Review* 48 (March 1974): 1–23 and Richard M. Grinnell, Jr., *Social Work Research and Evaluation* (Itasca, IL: F. E. Peacock, 1981), chap. 19, "Single-Subject Designs."

12. See Roy A. Ruckdeschel and Buford E. Farris, "Assessing Practice: A Critical Look at the Single-Case Design," *Social Casework* 62 (September 1981): 413–419.

13. Thomas J. Kiresuk and Geoffrey Garwick, "Basic Goal Attainment Scaling Procedures," in *Social Work Processes,* 2nd ed., Beulah Roberts Compton and Burt Galaway, Eds. (Homewood, IL: Dorsey Press, 1979), pp. 412–421.

14. For a more complete discussion of program evaluation, including sample instruments for use in this type of evaluation, see John S. Wodarski, *Rural Community Mental Health Practice* (Baltimore: University Park Press, 1983), chap. 6, "Rural Community Mental Health Program Evaluation," p. 135.

15. It is assumed that the social work student will develop the knowledge and skills needed to participate in agency and program evaluation in research courses. For further development of knowledge about these techniques, see William J. Reid and Audrey D. Smith, *Research in Social Work* (New York: Columbia University Press, 1981), particularly chap. 9, "Data Collection," and Norman A. Polansky, *Social Work Research,* rev. ed. (Chicago: University of Chicago Press, 1975), particularly chap. 6, "Collecting Data by Questionnaire and Interview," and chap. 7, "Observation of Social Interaction."

16. Social workers can use computers for tasks other than evaluation. See James B. Taylor, *Using Microcomputers in Social Agencies* (Beverly Hills, CA: Sage Publications, 1981); Lawrence H.

Boyd, Jr., John H. Hylton, and Steven V. Price, "Computers in Social Work Practice: A Review," *Social Work* 23 (September 1978): 368–371; and Dick Schoech and Tony Arangio, "Computers in the Human Services," *Social Work* 24 (March 1979): 96–102. The thrust of this discussion is limited to its use in evaluation since that is the subject of the chapter. However, much that is discussed about computer usage in evaluation is also relevant to other uses in social work.

17. See John H. Noble, Jr., "Protecting the Public's Privacy in Computerized Health and Welfare Information Systems," *Social Work* 16 (November 1971): 35–41, and Verne R. Kelley and Hanna B. Weston, "Computers, Costs, and Civil Liberties," *Social Work* 20 (January 1975): 15–19.

18. For further discussion of this issue and an example of a release of information, see Verne R. Kelley and Hanna B. Weston, "Civil Liberties in Mental Health Facilities," *Social Work* 19 (January 1964): 48–54.

19. See Mildred M. Reynolds, "Threats to Confidentiality," *Social Work* 21 (March 1976): 108–113.

20. For further discussion of this issue, see Carol J. Schrier, "Guidelines for Record-Keeping Under Privacy and Open-Access Laws," *Social Work* 25 (November 1980): 452–457.

16

TERMINATION

Learning Expectations

1. An understanding of the place of the termination process in the social work process.
2. An understanding of the kinds of termination.
3. An understanding of the worker's possible feelings about termination and of the need to recognize and deal with these feelings.
4. An understanding of the components of the termination process.
5. An understanding of the importance of ending and separation to clients and of possible reactions to termination.
6. An understanding of both the transfer and the referral processes.
7. An understanding of some techniques and skills used in the termination process.

The final stage of the social work process is termination, or the ending stage. Although ending the process is often slighted, it is nevertheless an important aspect of the social work endeavor. Termination is planned for from the beginning of the work together of worker and client. A social work relationship that focuses on meeting the needs of the client terminates when those needs are met. The time line that is a part of the plan of action specifies the anticipated time for termination.

The termination work can enhance the client's social functioning. It can also add to the understanding developed by both client and worker as they worked together. Any ending arouses feelings that may be strong. These feelings can be used as a means for growth, or they can be denied or suppressed, perhaps to arise and interfere with later social functioning. Handling a termination is an important skill for social workers to develop.

Evaluation is closely related to termination. Evaluation takes place during the entire social work process, but it is an important aspect of any planned termination.

In considering termination, two areas will be discussed: 1) the kinds of termination and the reasons for clients' and workers' terminating a helping relationship; and 2) the content of the termination process—dealing with feelings, stabilizing change, and evaluating with clients.

KINDS OF TERMINATION

Termination is an aspect of social work that is often given inadequate consideration. Endings are painful for workers as well as for clients. Workers sometimes make decisions about the desired goals of service that prolong the time of service beyond that which the client desires.[1] This has resulted in many unplanned terminations (those in which the client fails to keep appointments). According to William Reid, research has shown that:

1. Recipients of brief, time-limited treatment show at least as much durable improvement as recipients of long-term, open-ended treatment.
2. Most of the improvement associated with long-term treatment occurs relatively soon after treatment has begun.
3. Regardless of their intended length, most courses of treatment turn out to be relatively brief.[2]

In recent years an emphasis on short-term service has developed. This service considers the client's desires and expectations in the planning to a greater extent than in long-term service. Plans are much more specific, with specific goals and time frames for reaching those goals. Goals are also measurable so it is much easier to know when the purpose of the service has been fulfilled, the goals met, and the contract fulfilled. The ending is more apt to be planned by the worker and the client rather than the client deciding that the worker's help is no longer needed. These developments have brought about greater knowledge about termination and its importance.

Termination can take place at any point in the process: when the goals set by the worker and client have been reached and the client feels comfortable in carrying out those goals without help from the worker; when clients feel that sufficient help has been given so they can meet the need or deal with the problem on their own; when it becomes apparent that no progress is being made or that the potential for change is poor; or when a worker or an agency does not have the resources needed by the client or does not have the sanction of the agency to deliver the service needed. This last condition may result in a referral, which was discussed in Chapter 13. Sometimes clients terminate because the systems upon which they are dependent are threatened by the possibility of change in the client and influence the client to terminate. For example: a young person whose acting out is a symptom of family dysfunctioning may not be allowed to make changes needed to alleviate the need to act out because this would then expose the family system's dysfunctioning.

If a worker is leaving an agency, termination activity may result in transfer to another worker within an agency or referral to another agency for continued service. It may also result in a decision by the worker and the client to work on another goal or use another strategy in reaching an elusive goal and thus continue together with a new plan of action. However, termination usually results in separation of the client from both the worker and the agency.

Termination is an expectation discussed with clients from the beginning of the work together; it is planned for by the worker and the client together. When a worker senses that the client is not using the help being offered, or when the client is missing appointments or in other ways is indicating that termination may be advisable, it is time to discuss the possibility of termination. This is done to maximize the benefit that can come from a planned termination and to minimize feelings of anger and guilt that might interfere with seeking help in the future. Many times what a client has needed is someone to talk to about his need or problem. This discussion can lead to a better understanding of the need, to identification of the problem, to identification of some unknown resources, or to planning what can be done about the need or problem. The client does not always need or want any other interventive activity from a social worker or a social agency. Figure 16–1 shows the place of termination in the social work process.

When the worker-client relationship is being terminated because the worker is ending employment or is being transferred to a new position, special consideration should be given to the client's feelings. In some cases this is also a good time for the client to terminate with the agency as well. At other times, the decision is to transfer the client to a new worker. The client may be angry because the worker is breaking a contract. The client may be feeling deserted or may have a reawakening of old feelings about previous separations. The worker may be

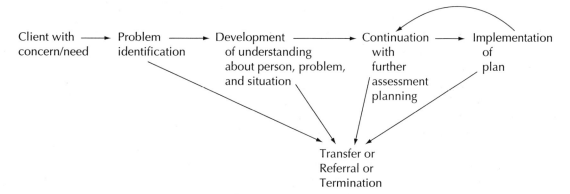

FIGURE 16–1   Termination and Its Place in the Social Work Process

experiencing feelings of guilt about leaving the client and breaking the contract. The worker also may be absorbed in plans for a new job or in the demands of a new situation. When transfer becomes necessary, it is important to recognize feelings that may impede the continuation of service to the client and deal with them when possible.

When a worker finds it necessary to engage in the termination process with a client because of his own plans to leave his current position, it is important to bring the client's feelings into the open, however painful. Sometimes clients can also deal with previous painful separations through this. The worker should be prepared to accept the client's anger and resentment and, whenever possible, should also help the client accept the new worker. Often a useful technique is for the worker to introduce the client to the new worker and for all three persons to discuss the work that has been done and the possibilities for future work. After this session, it is often important for the old worker and the client to have a last session alone so that they can say good-bye and terminate their relationship.

In order for a social worker to be effective in terminating with clients, she needs to be aware of some blocks to effective termination that arise because of her feelings and attitudes. There may be a tendency for the worker to hang on to clients. This may arise because of a reluctance to terminate a relationship in which the worker has been getting some of her own needs met. The hanging on may be because of a need to control others. Other reasons for hanging on may be that the worker expects more of the client or the situation than is warranted or that the worker is ambitious and is seeking "the perfect case." Sometimes a worker wants to compensate for what the client may have lost in relationships or otherwise. Awareness of these feelings and a focus on the client's needs and goals can prevent these blocks to effective termination.

Another factor of the termination phase is the nature of the worker-client relationship. Anytime a close working relationship develops, both the worker and the client are apt to have strong reactions to termination. Where this is the case, more time must be allowed for the termination process so that feelings of loss can be handled.

It should not, however, be assumed that all clients view termination as loss; some, especially those mandated to service, may view termination with relief. Other clients view the work together as a necessary interlude in their lives but are pleased they have gained understanding and coping skills so they can get on with the business of living without further help from the worker.

In fact, recent research done by Anne E. Fortune, Bill Pearlingi, and Cherie D. Rochell indicates clients do have positive feelings about termination. They feel pride and a sense of accomplishment in what they have been able to do. This study has limitations as it was carried out with a small group of voluntary practioneers in a limited geographic area. Case selection may have been limited to those for whom there was success.[3]

Howard Hess and Peg McCartt Hess have pointed out differences in termination, depending on context.[4] The nature of the relationship required in the work and the expected ongoing relationships with others who have been a part of the process affect the impact of termination. Hess and Hess discuss the difference between termination of the one-to-one relationship and the formed group where the loss is not only of the worker but of other group members. In the family and the friendship group, the only person terminating is the worker. They also note the differences in termination when the strategy has been counseling, education, or resource mobilization. The nature of attachment and the impact of termination are different in each of these situations. The content of the termination phase will be different in each situation.

If worker and client have developed the habit of consciously terminating *each session* together, they have developed a good base on which to develop the termination of work together. Summarizing each session—what has been done and what is to be done—should give the client a good sense of the process and how much time there is before the work is completed and termination takes place. Planning termination should avoid a surprise ending and the feelings of desertion that go with such endings. Evaluating at the end of each session should give the worker an understanding of the client's sense of the work together and allow for corrections so that unplanned or precipitous termination does not take place. What has been done in a small way at the end of each session can then be done in a more complete manner at the end of the work together.

COMPONENTS OF TERMINATION

Allen Pincus and Anne Minahan identify three major components of the termination process; disengagement, stabilization of change, and evaluation.[5] Like all other aspects of the social work endeavor, they are intermingled in practice and are separated only for purposes of discussion and study.

Disengagement

Endings bring about a cessation of relationships. If relationships have been meaningful, feelings are aroused and should be dealt with. An unplanned termination leaves the client to deal with these feelings on her own, which often results in a sense of unfinished business. It is assumed that the client is aware that termination will take place when goals have been reached. Nevertheless, when faced with actual termination, the client and the worker should face the reality of their feelings.

These feelings will vary from situation to situation; however, some common expectations about feelings at termination have been identified. The initial reaction is often one of denial, either of the reality of termination or of the feelings associated with it. Denial is one of the mechanisms of defense used to avoid painful feelings. An indication of this mechanism is the phenomenon of flight. This phenomenon is manifested by a client not keeping appointments after termination is discussed or by group members not being as involved in the group process as the time to terminate approaches. The temptation is for the worker to let the client go and to assume that he wants to deal with the termination feelings in this manner. It is important for the worker to reach for feelings at this point, so that client and worker can move through the termination process.

The next reaction to termination is usually a period of emotional reaction. Feelings or emotions may arise from fear of loss or fear of the unknown. There may be feelings of sadness or of grief over the impending loss; there may be anger. There may be an arousal of feelings associated with old wounds from previous disappointments and separations. There may be regression to old patterns of behavior. Regression may be a client's attempt to say that she is not ready for termination. At this stage it is important for the worker to accept the client's feelings and to help the client examine these feelings and the fears, anxieties, and past experiences that are the source of the feelings. Acceptance and help in the examination of feelings enables a working through of the feelings. In a sense, the client is helped to go through a process of mourning and is enabled to disengage from the relationship in a helpful manner.

Another means of dealing with disengagement is reminiscing about or reviewing what has been done in the work together. Doing this can help clients see the positive aspects of the work together as well as help them to develop the understanding that growth often has pain associated with it. At this time, workers also should try and minimize any guilt the client may have about the work together.

Clients sometimes regress when termination approaches; sometimes they also introduce new problems. The worker and client together need to examine why these new problems have been introduced and whether there is a valid reason for continuing the service with a focus on the new problems or whether the client can indeed work on these problems in other ways.

Clients' feelings vary as to intensity and nature about termination. If the intensity of the relationship or the period of time involved has been minimal, the feelings about termination will usually be less than if the relationship has been intense or of fairly long duration. Clients with feelings of success or satisfaction about the service will have different kinds of feelings about termination from those whose service experience has not been so positive. Clients who have had significant losses or separations in their lives—particularly if they have not had opportunities to deal with feelings about those losses—will have different feelings about separation from those clients for whom loss is not so significant. The client's capacity for independence or need for dependence will also influence feelings. A significant factor in the way a client deals with termination is what is happening in his life as a whole at that point in time. If a client is being called on to cope with many changes or other demands, termination may either be more difficult or may come as a relief. Another variable (already discussed) is whether or not the termination is the result of the worker's plans for a change of work position.

The social worker needs to develop skill in disengaging from relationships with clients. This needs to be done with consideration for, and sensitivity to, a client's feelings and needs. A useful technique for disengagement is to taper off involvement with the client as feelings are dealt with and other work of termination is completed. Appointments may be set further apart or more emphasis placed on what the client is to do for herself.

The worker needs to develop self-awareness about his own reactions to separation and loss. If the worker has difficulty with these tasks, he is going to be less able to help the client deal with the tasks of separation. The worker may wonder how to react to the intense feelings of the client that may arise in the process of termination. These feelings may be related not only to loss or grief over loss but to dissatisfaction about what the worker and client have been able to do together. Everyone tends to ignore or downplay that which is uncomfortable. If, because of their own discomfort, workers do not adequately reach for the client's feelings about termination and about their work together, they will fail to allow growth by the client in the management of feelings and in coping with life tasks.

The work of disengagement, then, is related not only to the particular social work situation but to past and future losses of the client and social worker. In helping the client disengage, the worker is sometimes helping the client deal with past losses and unresolved feelings about those losses. Also, the client is being provided with coping mechanisms for dealing with future loss, with understandings for dealing with grief and other experiences related to loss, which is, after all, a part of all human functioning. To bypass or minimize the disengagement process is to lose an opportunity for client growth.

Stabilization of Change

In helping a client deal with the feelings of termination and disengagement from the relationship, the client and the worker often review what has happened in the work together. This is also helpful in stabilizing the change that has taken place. It helps clients understand how they have grown and what has led to the growth. It also gives clients guidelines as to how future problems might be approached and dealt with. It gives clients the feeling that they have resources that can enable them to make it on their own and to know what those resources are.

One way to work on stabilization of change is for the worker and the client to review what has happened as they worked together. The time together should be considered a part of the ongoing social functioning of the client. It should be seen as one step, an important step, of the growth that results in better coping with life tasks and in more adequate social functioning. This view implies there are other steps to be taken, not with the worker but through new relationships or in ongoing coping with life situations. Continued growth is one way of stabilizing the change that has taken place. Worker and client can discuss the next steps and how the client can go about taking these steps. They plan ways of obtaining needed supports and resources for the client to use in taking these steps.

Together the worker and the client explore possible ways for dealing with situations similar to the one that brought the client to the agency for help. They consider how the learning that has taken place can be transferred to other situations.

The worker, together with the client, may also identify other resources in the client's environment that would be useful in coping with life situations. These may be natural helpers or other community systems, such as recreation programs, groups of people with similar concerns, and the like. These resources can be substitute or replacement support systems.

Usually the worker provides the client with the possibility of returning to the agency if future problems become overwhelming. It is important for the client to know that it is the agency that makes the service possible, and that even if the worker is no longer available, the agency will provide someone else to help. The client needs to be aware of the reality of workers coming and going, but that the agency is still there to provide the service. This awareness is particularly important for the client who may be terminating service against the advice of the worker.

Stabilization can also be encouraged by discussing possible goals for further growth and resources that can be used to enable growth. This discussion can examine how change took place as the worker and client worked together. The problem-solving process that was used can be examined and the worker can maximize the client's understanding of this process. The worker can also make certain the client understands the dysfunctional patterns that caused the problem they have been working on. This is done so the client can spot potential problems at an earlier stage and attempt to bring about change before serious problems develop.

Through the work of stabilizing the change, the worker gives the client realistic hope that the client can function without the worker's help. She attempts to establish within the client a sense of accomplishment and a sense of competence. The client's fears are recognized, examined, and suggestions are made about how to deal with them.

The stabilization of the change is an important stage in growth and change. Without conscious efforts to carry out the tasks involved in the stabilization, the client's capacity to sustain the desired change may be lessened.

Evaluation

The third component of termination is evaluation. Evaluation does not take place only at termination but is an ongoing part of the social work endeavor. It is, however, a particularly important component of the termination phase.

As the worker and client engage in evaluation during termination, the major focus is on the goal or goals set as a part of the plan of action and on the client's need or needs as identified in the assessment process. The major question to be answered is: Did we accomplish what we set out to do? If the goal was achieved and the need met, then what has been determined to be the purpose of the service has been accomplished. If the goal was met but the need remains troublesome, then the goal may not have been the right goal or other goals must be met as well.

When considering the outcome of service, it is useful to look at outcomes, not only from a behavioral point of view but also from the perspective of the attitudes involved or changed and the knowledge gained. It is also useful to look at the process of reaching the goal and to identify what has been useful and which parts of the process were not useful or might have been carried out differently. Any spinoffs or unexpected consequences of the work together should be noted. This aspect of evaluation is useful for both worker and client. It helps the client better understand how to cope with future problems and how to meet personal needs. It helps the worker gain greater understanding of the helping process and of means for working with clients.

The worker's openness to evaluating what has happened involves a certain amount of risk because the worker's mistakes and limitations may come to light. The client may be overly critical or display undue dissatisfaction, which may be one way the client expresses negative feelings related to termination. The worker needs to accept these feelings without becoming defensive and, with the client, carefully examine the negative feelings and sort out reality from feelings of abandonment or unrealistic dissatisfaction. Perhaps one of the reasons workers have not put sufficient emphasis on the termination process is that it is indeed a time for examining the performance of the worker. This is a threatening experience, but one that is essential for good social work practice.

Competence in guiding the termination process is one way of influencing client satisfaction over the work together. The client reviews what has happened, acknowledges improvement or progress, discovers his part in the process and how the experience may be transferred to other life experiences, and how he can continue his growth.

The social work endeavor is terminated through the intermingled activities aimed at disengagement, stabilization of change, and evaluation. Through these activities the client is helped to deal with feelings so that they will not inhibit future social functioning, and the client is readied to continue to grow and to cope with activities of living and with the environment and its expectations.

CASE EXAMPLE

A Student's Thinking on Terminating Field Experience

A dictionary defines *termination* as "to come to a limit in time; to end." I have known since the beginning of the semester that my time at the home was limited, but now that the time is actually coming to an end I feel a great loss. I have come to think of the residents as "my" people and am very protective of them. I care and worry about each and every one of them as if they were my own grandmothers and grandfathers, and feel they care about me also. Yet I have nevertheless worked toward this termination all semester by trying to get the residents to fend for themselves. One example of this is my card group. I have made great progress with this group of people as they have responded by becoming more and more independent to the point that they no longer need me there. They can now organize, keep score, and play together without a referee; and they do play. It gives me a great feeling of accomplishment knowing that this group of people can and will entertain themselves once I am gone.

However, I have learned that there is another aspect to termination—a selfish one on my part. As I said, I am no longer needed there. True, I feel great accomplishment in knowing that I created this independent group; but my price was the loss of authority and the sense of need and importance I felt as head of the group. I guess it is a little like what a parent must feel when sending a child out into the world. True, you feel proud and would want it no other way, but nevertheless there is a selfish feeling of loss that enters in also. I would expect that anytime a social worker has a success such as I have had and the resident has become more self-sufficient and less dependent, he or she will feel these pride/selfish loss feelings. It is something one must learn to deal with by realizing the importance of the success and the insignificance of the loss. In my case, I am extremely excited that my card group has progressed to the point that they can function without me. Many of the residents in the home have gotten to the point that they will not socialize, entertain themselves, or even consider doing something without supervision or leadership. They seem to refuse to think for themselves and will instead wait to be entertained by someone else. Obviously, this leads to decreased socialization due to their never mixing with others except when there is a planned activity. This also leads to reduced mental stimulation, which I feel is very closely related to confusion and forgetfulness often typical of the elderly. Therefore, my success at gaining some independence with these people has made me very proud.

I have discovered that talking about termination as being someday is very different from saying I will be leaving here in two weeks. Suddenly it is not only very real but it is also very close. I have had mixed reactions from the residents. Some have taken it quite nonchalantly. I suspect this is due to the fact that they have been through this before with other students and are getting used to people coming and going. However, some of the residents have taken it fairly hard, especially those who are forgetful and cannot remember my telling them I will be leaving; they act surprised every time I tell them. Some of the other residents are already asking me when I will be back and about who will they talk to when I am gone. I have tried to prevent this from happening as much as possible by encouraging residents to talk to Jane, too. However, once a relationship is established sometimes it is hard to get them to talk to someone else . . . that talking to me is often the basis for our good relationship in the first place. I guess all of these things are what make termination in a nursing home setting hard. This is not to imply that termination anywhere else is easy. I would imagine termination is hard no matter what. I can only judge what termination is like for me in my situation.

I have learned termination is a much more delicate situation than I first anticipated. I can see how a resident could easily get hurt and thus soured toward opening up and sharing with another person. They could easily become leery of developing a relationship for fear it will be stifled at the end of a semester. They could easily feel they were used and discarded by a student only out for personal gain and credit toward their graduation. I can recall one such resident when I first worked at the home. She obviously had had a bad experience with someone and had thus decided she would not be vulnerable again. She informed me during our first visit that she wanted to be left alone—besides, she did not think I cared anyway. She said she thought I was only doing my duty by being nice to her. Although I tried all semester to break through that barrier by always waving, smiling, or speaking to her, I never succeeded in breaking down those walls she had built around herself. Therefore, I am being very careful to tell residents early and as gently as possible that I am soon finished at the home. I am also being careful to avoid any promises about the future. Although I plan to visit as often as I can, many times those well-intentioned plans get smothered by other obligations. I do not want anyone sitting and waiting for my visits.

There is yet another aspect of termination that I have not yet discussed. That is termination with the staff. Jane and I have become very close and help each other with many complicated issues concerning residents. The old saying that two heads are better than one really applies with us. I feel we have truly become a team, even though I am a student. I realize Jane got along quite well without me and will again get along quite well after I am gone. However, we do work well together, and I know I will miss her. We have started new projects such as our new social history that I wish I could help her put into use. The new comprehensive care plans are almost finished and now will become most helpful for use with the residents. I regret having to miss being a part of their use.

As is obvious, I really enjoyed my semester at the nursing home and have let it become a part of me. I have learned much from those sometimes funny, sometimes ornery residents and will miss them. Termination is hard and not finished yet, but I can be happy that I will take a little from and give a little to each resident, and I can look forward to joyous reunions.

SUMMARY

The last stage of the social work process is termination. It is planned from the beginning of the process. Termination may lead to transfer to another worker.

There are three components of the termination work: disengagement, stabilization of change, and evaluation.

Social workers who engage the client in a well thought out termination process strengthen the client's capacity for social functioning in the future. They also enhance their own professional capacity through evaluating with the client what led to the desired outcome. Termination is an integral part of the total social work process.

QUESTIONS

1. What do you believe to be some reasons why "time-limited" social work has become popular?

2. Discuss your feeling about a termination with someone who has been important to you.

3. Discuss some of the reasons why clients may terminate prematurely.

4. When a social worker receives a client through transfer what should be kept in mind?

5. How does the nature of the client-worker relationship affect the termination process?

6. How can a worker appropriately deal with the threat of evaluation?

SUGGESTED READINGS

Compton, Beulah Roberts, and Galaway, Burt. *Social Work Processes,* 3rd ed. Homewood, IL: Dorsey Press, 1984 (Chapter 14, "The Endings in Social Work Practice").

Fortune, Anne, Pearlingi, Bill, and Rochell, Cherie D. "Reactions to Termination of Individual Treatment." *Social Work* 37 (March 1992): 171–178.

Hellenbrand, Shirley C. "Termination in Direct Practice." In Minahan, Anne, Ed., *Encyclopedia of Social Work,* 18th ed. Silver Spring, MD: National Association of Social Workers, 1987 (Vol. II, pp. 757–770).

Hepworth, Dean H., and Larsen, Jo Ann. *Direct Social Work Practice,* 2nd ed. Chicago: Dorsey Press, 1986 (Chapter 22, "The Final Phase: Termination and Evaluation").

Hess, Howard, and Hess, Peg McCartt. "Termination in Context." In Beulah Roberts Compton and Bert Galaway, Eds., *Social Work Processes,* 4th ed. Belmont, CA: Wadsworth, 1989 (pp. 46–657).

Shapiro, Constance Hoenk. "Termination: A Neglected Concept in the Social Work Curriculum." *Journal of Education for Social Work* 16 (Spring 1980): 13–19.

Shulman, Lawrence. *The Skills of Helping: Individual and Group,* 2nd ed. Itasca, IL: F. E. Peacock, 1984 (Chapter 5, "Endings and Transitions," and Chapter 14, "Endings and Transitions with Groups").

Siebold, Cathy. "Termination When the Therapist Leaves." *Clinical Social Work Journal* 19 (Summer 1991): 191–204.

Simons, Ronald L., and Aigner, Stephen M. *Practice Principles.* New York: Macmillan, 1985 (Chapter 10).

NOTES

1. See William J. Reid and Anne Shyne, *Brief and Extended Casework* (New York: Columbia University Press, 1969).

2. William J. Reid, *The Task Centered System* (New York: Columbia University Press, 1978), p. 5.

3. Anne E. Fortune, Bill Pearlingi, and Cherie D. Rochell, "Reactions to Termination of Individual Treatment," *Social Work* 37 (March 1992): 171–178.

4. Howard Hess and Peg McCartt Hess, "Termination in Context," in *Social Work Processes,* 3rd ed., Beulah Compton and Burt Galaway, Eds. (Homewood, IL: Dorsey Press, 1984), pp. 559–569.

5. See Allen Pincus and Anne Minahan, *Social Work Practice: Model and Method* (Itasca, IL: F. E. Peacock, 1973), chap. 13, "Terminating the Change Effort."

A P P E N D I X

MODELS OF SOCIAL WORK PRACTICE

Social work practice theory has been developed in a manner that gives a rich variety of approaches to practice. The various models or practice theories available have bean developed in different situations, based on various underlying assumptions, for use in many types of circumstances. Thorough study of each model is needed in order to use it with clients. The summaries presented here can be used to gain a preliminary understanding of the salient points of the various models of practice and to help the student decide on those models in which he or she desires to develop further understanding.

The original specification of models was primarily based on those appearing in:

Robert W. Roberts and Robert H. Nee, Eds., *Theories of Social Casework* (Chicago: University of Chicago Press, 1970).

Catherine P. Papell and Beulah Roberts Rothman, "Social Group Work Models: Possession and Heritage," *Journal of Education for Social Work* 2 (Fall 1966): 66–77.

Joan Stein, *The Family as a Unit of Study and Treatment,* Monograph One (Seattle: Regional Rehabilitation Institute, University of Washington, School of Social Work, 1969).

Jack Rothman, "Three Models of Community Organization," in Fred M. Cox, John L. Erlich, Jack Rothman, and John E. Tropman, Eds., *Strategies of Community Organization* (Itasca, IL: F. E. Peacock, 1970), pp. 20–36.

Other models have been added because of frequent references to them in social work literature.

The current update of this Appendix has considered models appearing in:

Francis J. Turner, Ed., *Social Work Treatment: Interlocking Theoretical Approaches,* 3rd ed. (New York: The Free Press, 1986).

Robert W. Roberts and Helen Northen, Eds., *Theories of Social Work with Groups* (New York: Columbia University Press, 1976).

Eleanor Reardon Tolson and William J. Reid, Eds., *Models of Family Treatment* (New York: Columbia University Press, 1981).

Jack Rothman with John E. Tropman, "Models of Community Organization and Macro Practice Perspectives: Their Mixing and Matching," in Fred M. Cox, John L., Erlich, Jack Rothman, and John E. Tropman, Eds., *Strategies of Community Organization*, 4th ed. (Itasca, IL: F. E. Peacock, 1987).

In some cases the update has resulted in a name change. Where this is true, the former name appears in parentheses. The name changes have been made in keeping with the usage of the literature cited above. One trend that was noted in the changes of model specification was that many now appear in individual, group, and family form. This is reflected in the updated source material. The number of models has been somewhat reduced from earlier editions of the book. This is due to omitting those models that are no longer heavily used in social work practice.

BEHAVIOR THERAPY (SOCIOBEHAVIORAL)

Source: Edwin Thomas, University of Michigan, School of Social Work, based on behavioral psychology. Developed as a reaction to the lack of specificity in traditional methods. Recent proponents of this model include Sheldon Rose (groups), John Wodarski (families), Richard Stuart (families), and Ray Thomison (families).

Underlying Theory: All behavior is learned. Behavior is sometimes controlled by consequences; at other times, it is controlled by stimuli (stimulus-response). Behavioral psychology.

Practice Theory: Assessment specifies behaviors; defines baselines; and specifies stimulus, antecedents, and consequences. Frequency, magnitude, and direction of problem behavior are monitored during and following intervention. Goals are very specific to behavioral change.

Practice Usage: In situations in which behavioral change is the goal.

References:

Edwin J. Thomas, "Behavioral Modification and Casework," in Robert W. Roberts and Robert H. Nee, Eds., *Theories of Social Casework* (Chicago: University of Chicago Press, 1970), pp. 181–218.

Joel Fischer and Harvey L. Gochros, *Planned Behavior Change* (New York: Free Press, 1975).

John Wodarski and Demmit A. Bagarozzi, *Behavioral Social Work* (New York: Human Sciences Press, 1979).

Ray J. Thomison, "Behavior Therapy," in Francis J. Turner, Ed., *Social Work Treatment: Interlocking Theroretical Approaches*, 3rd ed. (New York: The Free Press, 1986), pp. 131–154.

Bruce A. Thyer, "Behavioral Social Work: Is Not What You Think," *Arete* 16 (Winter 1991): 1–9.

COGNITIVE (RATIONAL, REALITY THERAPY)

Source: General category includes Adler's individual psychology, Ellis's rational-emotive psychotherapy, Glasser's reality therapy, and Werner's rational casework. An alternative to Freudian psychotherapy, which concerns itself with conscious thinking and behavior.

Underlying Theory: Behavior is mainly determined by a person's thinking and willing. Intensity of acts depends on strength of will. Cognitive theory important. Perceptions, goals, and patterns are principal concerns.

Practice Theory: Assessment focuses on present thinking, feeling, and behavior. The goal is to change the client's consciousness (the sum of thoughts, emotions, and behavior). The interaction focuses on problem solving and having client examine way he or she thinks and behaves in the living situation. Emphasis on "accurate thinking."

Practice Usage: Can be used with individuals, groups, families, and communities when resolution of problems is a focus. Should not be used to treat phobias, addictions, or psychoses.

References:

Harold D. Werner, *Rational Approach to Social Casework* (New York: Association Press, 1965).
Harold D. Werner, "Cognitive Theory," in Francis J. Turner, Ed., *Social Work Treatment: Interlocking Theoretical Approaches*, 3rd ed. (New York: The Free Press, 1986), pp. 91–130.
William Glasser, *Reality Therapy* (New York: Harper and Row, 1965).
Albert Ellis, *Reason and Emotion in Psychotherapy* (New York: Stuart, 1962).

COMMUNICATION (COMMUNICATIVE-INTERACTIVE)

Source: Work of Don Jackson and Jay Haley in the project on "Family Therapy in Schizophrenia" at the Palo Alto Research Foundation (initiated 1954). Virginia Satir exemplifies social work of this model. Recently Judith C. Nelson has expanded understanding of the use of communication theory in social work practice with particular emphasis on work with individuals and families.

Underlying Theory: Broad communication and transactional base. "Double-bind" communication, metacommunication, and family homeostasis are important concepts. Emphasis is on improved family functioning, particularly improved communication.

Practice Theory: Analysis of family functioning with emphasis on role functioning, rules, and communication modes. Often uses a "Family Life Chronology." Worker is seen as therapist and modeler of communication. Techniques include showing how a person looks to other family members, building self-esteem, making explicit roles and rules, and pointing out nonverbal communication.

Practice Usage: With family group with verbal orientation and willingness to make a time investment. Particularly useful when communication is problematic.

References:

Virginia Satir, *Con-Joint Family Therapy* (Palo Alto, CA: Science and Behavior Books, Inc., 1967).

Judith C. Nelson, "Communication Theory and Social Work Treatment," in Francis J. Turner, Ed., *Social Work Treatment: Interlocking Theoretical Approaches*, 3rd ed. (New York: The Free Press, 1986), pp. 219–244.

CRISIS INTERVENTION

Source: Study of a natural disaster and work of Erich Linderman and Gerald Caplan. Concepts of brief treatment. Work of Lydia Rapoport and Howard J. Parad, Smith College, School of Social Work (1962). Recently the leading proponent is Naomi Golan.

Underlying Theory: Eclectic theory base with emphasis on ego psychology and stress theory. Concerned with cognitive process. Uses public health model. Goal is the restoration of social functioning and enhancement of coping capacity.

Practice Theory: Assessment of client's personality structure, basic defenses, habitual adaptive patterns, the nature of the upset, potential for adaptive response, and resources available. Makes maximal use of the period of upset, reduces client tension and anxiety, gives hope, gives support, and helps with crisis situation. Teaches new patterns of problem solving and coping and corrects perceptions. Short-term service.

Practice Usage: In situations in which developmental or situational crisis is limiting adequate social functioning. Can be used with individuals, families, or groups of individuals in crisis.

References:

Lydia Rapoport, "Crisis Intervention as a Mode of Brief Treatment," in Robert W. Roberts and Robert H. Nee, Eds., *Theories of Social Casework* (Chicago: University of Chicago Press, 1970), pp. 267–311.

Samuel L. Dixson, *Working with People in Crisis: Theory and Practice* (St. Louis: C. V. Mosby, 1979).

Naomi Golan, "Crisis Theory," in Francis J. Turner, Ed., *Social Work Treatment: Interlocking Theoretical Approaches,* 3rd ed. (New York: The Free Press, 1986), pp. 296–340.

Howard J. Parad, Lola Selby, and James Quinlan, "Crisis Intervention with Families and Groups," in Robert W. Roberts and Helen Northen, Eds., *Theories of Social Work with Groups* (New York: Columbia University Press, 1976), pp. 304–330.

DEVELOPMENTAL

Source: Developed from work of Coyle (group self-direction), Wilson and Ryland (group autonomy and group decision making), and Phillips (member importance and here-and-now emphasis). Articulated by Emanual Tropp, Virginia Commonwealth University (1969), in part as a reaction to the infiltration of social work by group psychotherapy.

Underlying Theory: Uses an existential-humanistic philosophy. Human beings are seen as free, responsible, and capable of self-realization. Individuals should be treated with respect for their dignity and expected to be responsible. Purpose is to help individuals enhance social functioning through functioning in groups centered around common interests and concerns and to help groups function effectively and responsively.

Practice Theory: Assessment focused on the commonality of members. Uses release of feelings, support for individuals from the group, reality orientation, and self-reappraisal. Uses program content, member planning, group process, and worker use of self as means for achieving members' purposes.

Practical Usage: In voluntary situation with peer groups or formed groups.

References:

Emanual Tropp, *A Humanistic Foundation for Social Group Work Practice: A Collection of Writings by Emanual Tropp* (New York: Selected Academic Readings, 1969).

Emanual Tropp, "A Developmental Theory," in Robert W. Roberts and Helen Northen, Eds., *Theories of Social Work with Groups* (New York: Columbia University Press, 1976), pp. 198–237.

ECOLOGICAL (LIFE MODEL)

Source: Carel B. Germain, Columbia School of Social Work (1970).

Underlying Theory: Ecological approach. Concepts about transactions between people and their environment, adaptation, reciprocity, mutuality, stress, and coping. Also considers growth and development, identity, competence, autonomy, and relatedness. Uses Erikson. Concerned with environmental quality, organizations, and social networks.

Practice Theory: Assessment carried out by worker and client together seeking to understand meaning; focus on person and problem in order to set objectives and devise appropriate action. Engages positive forces in client and environment. Attempts to remove environmental obstacles and change negative transactions. Uses a process of engagement, exploration, contracting, ongoing, ending. Concerned with client need and vulnerability. Focus on life transitions, unresponsiveness of environments, crisis events, and communication-relationship difficulties. Action designed to increase self-esteem and problem-solving and coping skills. Also works to facilitate group functioning and influence organizational structure, social networks, and physical settings.

Practice Usage: For problem in social functioning.

References:

Carel B. Germain and Alex Gitterman, *The Life Model of Social Work Practice* (New York: Columbia University Press, 1980).

Carel B. Germain and Alex Gitterman, "The Life Model Approach to Social Work Practice Revisited," in Francis J. Turner, Ed., *Social Work Treatment: Interlocking Theoretical Approaches,* 3rd ed. (New York: The Free Press, 1986), pp. 618–644.

EXISTENTIAL

Source: Existential psychology and psychiatry. Krill, Denver University, developed use in social work (1969).

Underlying Theory: Basically philosophical. Protests the assumption that reality can be grasped by exclusively intellectual means. Distinguishes between subjective and objective truth. Gives priority to the subjective. Values human choice, self-determination, and individualization. Believes in the capacity for growth and change.

Practice Theory: Assesses only what is going on between people. Uses experience in which reality of how a person thinks of self and relates to others is gradually revealed. Teaches how to choose responses. Brings suffering into the open for understanding and acceptance. Develops a trusting relationship. Helps individuals to make commitments.

Practice Usage: Any situation in which the client is willing to develop self-awareness.

References:

Donald F. Krill, "Existential Social Work," in Francis J. Turner, Ed., *Social Work Treatment: Interlocking Theoretical Approaches,* 3rd ed. (New York: The Free Press, 1986), pp. 181–218.

Donald F. Krill, *Existential Social Work* (New York: The Free Press, 1978).

FEMINIST PRACTICE
(material provided by Mary Bricker-Jenkins)

Source: Developed by practitioners as an attempt to integrate feminist theory, commitments, and culture with conventional approaches to social work practice. Goes beyond a "nonsexist" and/or "women's issues" orientation.

Underlying Assumptions: The inherent purpose and goal of human existence is self-actualization, which is a collective endeavor involving the creation of material and ideological conditions that enable it. Systems and ideologies of domination/subordination, exploitation, and oppression and inimical to individual and collective self-actualization. Given the structural and ideological barriers to self-actualization, practice is explicitly political in intent. Women have unique and relatively unknown history, conditions, developmental patterns and strengths that must be discovered and engaged by practitioners.

Practice Theory: Assessment focuses on preferred and available patterns of strength in intellectual, emotional, social, cultural, physical and/or spiritual domains; special emphasis given to basic, concrete needs, safety, and perceptions of personal power. Underlying principle informing practice is that healing, health, and growth are functions of validation, consciousness, and transformative action, which are supported and sustained through resources to meet basic human needs, the creation of validating environments and relationships that preserve and nurture uniqueness and wholeness. Uses a range of conventional and nonconventional approaches. Frequent use of groups. Encourages and facilitates individual and collective action. Works for open, egalitarian, and collegial relationships with clients.

Practice Usage: In all kinds of settings, with all populations. Particular attention focused on women.

References:

Affilia: Journal of Women and Social Work.

Mary Bricker-Jenkins and Nancy Hooyman, *Not for Women Only: Social Work Practice for a Feminist Future* (Silver Spring, MD: National Association of Social Workers, 1986).

Nan Van Den Berg and Lynn Cooper, *Feminist Visions for Social Work* (Silver Spring, MD: National Association of Social Workers, 1986).

Mary Valentich, "Feminism and Social Work Practice," in Francis J. Turner, Ed., *Social Work Treatment: Interlocking Theoretical Approaches,* 3rd ed. (New York: The Free Press, 1986), pp. 564–589.

FUNCTIONAL

Source: Developed in 1930s at University of Pennsylvania School of Social Work by Jessie Taft and Virginia Robinson. Contemporary source work of Ruth Smalley and others.

Underlying Theory: Uses work of Otto Rank and, to some degree, of John Dewey and of Margaret Mead. Sees individual as defining self from himself or herself, from relationships, and from external conditions of life. Growth orientation. Respect for worth and dignity of persons. Concern that persons have opportunities to realize potential and that human power be released.

Practice Theory: Focus is on release of power for increased social functioning. Principles that guide service are: diagnosis (related to nature of service and participated in by client); use of time phases in process (beginnings, middles, endings); use of agency function; use of structure; and use of relationships.

Practice Usage: Can be used in most situations. Has been used with individuals, families, groups, and communities.

References:

Martha M. Dore, "Functional Theory: Its History and Influence on Contemporary Social Work Practice," *Social Service Review* 64 (September 1990): 358–374.

Ruth E. Smalley, *Theory for Social Work Practice* (New York: Columbia University Press, 1967).

Ruth E. Smalley, "The Functional Approach to Casework Practice," in Robert W. Roberts and Robert H. Nee, Eds., *Theories of Social Casework* (Chicago: University of Chicago Press, 1970), pp. 79–128.

Shankar A. Yelajc, "Functional Theory in Social Work Practice," in Francis J. Turner, Ed., *Social Work Treatment: Interlocking Theoretical Approaches,* 3rd ed. (New York: The Free Press, 1986), pp. 46–68.

Eleanor L. Ryder, "A Functional Approach," in Robert W. Roberts and Helen Northen, Eds., *Theories of Social Work with Groups* (New York: Columbia University Press, 1976).

GESTALT THERAPY

Source: Work of Fritz Perls, M.D., Ph.D., adopted by many social workers because of emphasis on "beginning where the client is."

Underlying Theory: Holistic, organismic, emphasis on hunger rather than sexuality, development of self through awareness and responsibility. One must take responsibility for one's own existence. Normal personality characterized by unity, integration, consistency, and coherence. Sovereign drive is self-actualization. Concern for paradoxes.

Practice Theory: Assess what the client is experiencing, what client wants. Process: lay groundwork, establish contact; negotiate consensus between client and therapist; grading, experiment within client's ability; surface client's awareness; locate client's energy; generate self-support; generate theme; choice of experiment; enact experiment; insight and completion.

Practice Usage: In situations in which worker and agency have time and inclination to allow client to develop self-knowledge and to engage in self-exploration. Most effective in oversocialized, restrained, constricted individuals.

Reference:

Michael Blugerman, "Contributions of Gestalt Theory to Social Work Treatment," in Francis J. Turner, Ed., *Social Work Treatment: Interlocking Theoretical Approaches*, 3rd ed. (New York: The Free Press, 1986), pp. 69–90.

INTEGRATIVE

Source: Ackerman was an early source of basic ideas. Family agencies an important source. Work of Pollak, Spiegal, Beatman, and Sherman also influential. Frances Scherz an important contributor (1966).

Underlying Theory: Based in a psychoanalytic frame of reference with particular emphasis on ego psychology and role theory. Eclectic in nature. Incorporates systems theory, small-group theory, family development tasks, and communication concepts. Assumes family is the link between the individual and the larger society.

Practice Theory: Assesses family structure, functioning, and history with emphasis on placement of current problems. Goal is to modify or change aspects of the family relationship system that are not functional. Worker enables and supports family members. Emphasis is on the here and now. Task-oriented. Uses advice, education, and guidance. Demonstrates techniques. Encourages appropriate role development, communication patterns, decision making, and family responsibility. Deals with resistance to change and fears of feelings and of destruction of the family. Helps family members expose hidden feelings and observe themselves.

Practice Usage: In situations in which there is a parent-child, family, or marital problem.

References:

Frances H. Scherz, "Theory and Practice of Family Therapy," in Robert W. Roberts and Robert H. Nee, Eds., *Theories of Social Casework* (Chicago: University of Chicago Press, 1970), pp. 219–264.

Laura Sue Dodson, *Family Counseling: A Systems Approach* (Muncie, IN: Accelerated Development, 1977).

Sonya L. Rhodes, "Family Treatment," in Frances J. Turner, Ed., *Social Work Treatment: Interlocking Theoretical Approaches,* 3rd ed. (New York: The Free Press, 1986), pp. 432–453.

Sanford N. Sherman, "A Social Work Frame for Family Therapy," in Eleanor Reardon Tolson and William J. Reid, Eds., *Models of Family Treatment* (New York: Columbia University Press, 1981), pp. 7–32.

LOCALITY DEVELOPMENT

Source: William W. Biddle, University of Missouri (1965). Contributing influences include work of United Nations in underdeveloped countries, experimental and demonstration projects of the Ford Foundation, Mobilization for Youth, Peace Corps, and work of settlement houses.

Underlying Theory: Eclectic. Draws from sociology, anthropology, and social psychology. Has an existential leaning. Sees community as eclipsed and lacking relationships. Uses problem-solving capacity of community persons.

Practice Theory: Assessment is problem solving with citizens. Process includes exploration, organization of community persons, discussion of problems, action, new projects, continuation. The goal is the development of community capacity and integration. The worker is an enabler, catalyst, coordinator, and teacher. Citizens participate in interactional problem solving. Involves a broad cross-section of people. Uses small task-oriented groups that seek consensus. Problem solving is primary.

Practice Usage: To involve a total community or neighborhood in discovering and solving problems.

References:

William J. Biddle, *The Community Development Process: The Rediscovery of Local Initiative* (New York: Holt, Rinehart and Winston, 1965).

Fred M. Cox, John L. Erlich, Jack Rothman, and John E. Tropman, Eds., *Strategies of Community Organization,* 4th ed. (Itasca, IL: F. E. Peacock, 1987), pp. 3–26 and Part Three, pp. 351–383.

MEDIATING

Source: William Schwartz, Columbia University, School of Social Work (1962). Lawrence Shulman also a major contributor. Work of Clara Kaiser and Helen Phillips also suggests this focus. Lawrence Shulman has continued to develop and expand usage with individuals, families, groups, and communities.

Underlying Theory: Social systems theory, symbolic interaction. Sociological understanding about: organizations, institutions, and communities as systems; game theory and small-group theory.

Practice Theory: Assessment is a systems assessment of the blocks to need fulfillment. Focus is on individual in interaction, group process, and impinging environment. Process includes: tuning in (worker readies self to move into process), beginning together, work, and transitions and endings. Goals related to mutual need for self-fulfillment as individuals and society reach out to each other. They are specified. Worker is a mediator and enabler, helps client reach out for what he or she needs, demands work, mobilizes healing powers of human association, and mutual aid. Clarifies communication and makes use of problem-solving process.

Practice Usage: Helping people negotiate difficult environments.

References:

> William Schwartz and Serapino R. Zalba, *The Practice of Social Group Work* (New York: Columbia University Press, 1971).
> Lawrence Shulman, *A Case Book of Social Work with Groups* (New York: Council on Social Work Education, 1968).
> Lawrence Shulman, *The Skills of Helping,* 2nd ed. (Itasca, IL: F. E. Peacock, 1984).
> William Schwartz, "Between Client and System: Mediating Function," in Robert W. Roberts and Helen Northen, Eds., *Theories of Social Work with Groups* (New York: Columbia University Press, 1976), pp. 171–197.

ORGANIZATIONAL (REMEDIAL-GROUP)

Source: A continuation of a group model known as remedial or preventive rehabilitive. Inception at University of Michigan in mid-1950s in the work of Robert Vinter and colleagues. Outgrowth of use of groups in clinical settings. More recently Paul H. Glasser and Charles D. Garwin have further developed this model, with particular emphasis on the organizational context of practice.

Underlying Theory: An eclectic base with contributions from social role theory, social-behavior theory, ego psychology, group dynamics, systems theory, and organizational theory.

Practice Theory: Assessment of relationship between client's problems, personality, and environment as well as individual's performance in the group and group process. Process includes intake, diagnostic treatment planning, group composition, treatment in the group, evaluation, and termination. Goal is individual change that is a remedy for social dysfunctioning. Focus on individual in the group. Uses direct and indirect influence, including program or activity. Concerned with the context for change, organizational prerequisites needed for change, and targets and strategies for change.

Practice Usage: To help malperforming individuals achieve a more desirable state of social functioning.

References:

Robert Vinter, *Readings in Group Work Practice* (Ann Arbor, MI: Campus Publishers, 1967).

Paul Glasser, Rosemary Sarri, and Robert Vinter, *Individual Change Through Small Groups* (New York: The Free Press, 1974).

Paul Glasser and Charles D. Garwin, "An Organizational Model," in Robert W. Roberts and Helen Northen, Eds., *Theories of Social Work with Groups* (New York: Columbia University Press, 1976), pp. 75–115.

PROBLEM SOLVING

Source: Helen H. Perlman, University of Chicago (1957). Blending of psychosocial and functioning models.

Underlying Theory: All human living is a problem-solving process. Eclectic, using ego psychology, Dewey's rational problem solving, role theory, and symbolic interaction.

Practice Theory: Assessment identifies and explains the nature of the problem, focuses on aspects of personality involved in the problem. Continuous appraisal of client's motivation, capacity, and opportunity. Goal is to help client cope as effectively as possible in carrying out social tasks and in relationships. Relationship with client of prime concern. Uses time in process. Conceptualized as a *person* with a *problem* comes to a *place* where he or she is offered help through a *process.*

Practice Usage: With individuals motivated to use help in a cognitive and interactive process.

References:

Helen H. Perlman, *Social Casework: A Problem-Solving Process* (Chicago: University of Chicago Press, 1957).

Helen H. Perlman, "The Problem-Solving Model," in Robert W. Roberts and Robert H. Nee, Eds., *Theories of Social Casework* (Chicago: University of Chicago Press, 1970), pp. 129–179.

Helen H. Perlman, "The Problem Solving Model," in Francis J. Turner, Ed., *Social Work Practice: Interlocking Theoretical Approaches,* 3rd ed. (New York: The Free Press, 1986), pp. 245–266.

PSYCHOSOCIAL

Source: Florence Hollis, Columbia School of Social Work (1964). Strongly influenced by work of Gordon Hamilton. Outgrowth of traditional diagnostic case work of 1930s.

Underlying Theory: Major source psychoanalytic theory, with emphasis on ego. Uses social science concepts of culture, role, communications theory, and social systems theory. Values acceptance of the client, self-determination, scientific objectivity, and insight.

Practice Theory: Assessment is a differential psychosocial diagnosis. Concerned with personality, etiology, and psychiatric classifications of disorders. Diagnosis very important. Goal is adjustment of the individual through change in perception, response, and communication. Relationship is of prime concern. Uses reflection, interpretation, ventilation, support, and environmental manipulation.

Practice Usage: With motivated verbal client willing to commit long-term involvement and with a desire for self-knowledge or insight.

References:

Florence Hollis and Mary E. Woods, *Casework: A Psychosocial Therapy,* 3rd ed. (New York: Random House, 1981).

Florence Hollis, "The Psychosocial Approach to Casework," in Robert W. Roberts and Robert H. Nee, Eds., *Theories of Social Casework* (Chicago: University of Chicago Press, 1970), pp. 33–75.

Francis J. Turner, "Psychosocial Theory," in Francis J. Turner, Ed., *Social Work Practice: Interlocking Theoretical Approaches,* 3rd ed. (New York: The Free Press, 1986), pp. 484–513.

Helen Northen, "Psychosocial Practice in Small Groups," in Robert W. Roberts and Helen Northen, Eds., *Theories of Social Work with Groups* (New York: Columbia University Press, 1976).

SOCIAL ACTION

Source: Saul Alinsky and Richard Cloward (1960s).

Underlying Theory: Eclectic and selective. Little theory development. Concepts used include: disadvantaged population, social injustice, deprivation, inequality. Concerned with power, conflict, confrontation. The community is seen as made up of conflicting interests that are not easily reconcilable and as having scarce resources.

Practice Theory: Goal is the shifting of power relationships and resources as well as basic institutional change that benefits "me and mine." The worker is an advocate, agitator, negotiator, and partisan. Client is seen as victim and employer of worker. Strategy is to crystallize issues and develop organization to take action against enemy target. Also uses conflict, confrontation, and negotiation. Manipulates mass organizations and political processes.

Practice Usage: When individuals are seen as victims of an unjust system.

References:

Saul Alinsky, *Rules for Radicals* (New York: Random House, 1967).

Fred M. Cox, John L. Erlich, Jack Rothman, and John E. Tropman, Eds., *Strategies of Community Organization*, 4th ed. (Itasca, IL: F. E. Peacock, 1987), pp. 3–26 and Part Three, pp. 384–422.

SOCIAL PLANNING

Source: Conventional community organization in planning and funding organizations and governmental planning agencies.

Underlying Theory: Sees the community as an entity with many interacting systems. Particular emphasis on decision making, power control, and the agency system. Political and economic considerations as important as is substantive knowledge about social problems. Emphasis is on rationality, objectivity, and professional purposefulness.

Practice Theory: Assessment identifies social problem, its cause, and its possible resolution. The process includes study and assessment of the problematic situation; determining preferences and influences relevant to the problem; examining alternative goals and strategies and their consequences; selection of goals, strategies, and programs; obtaining commitments to desired change, and designing and implementing a feedback-evaluative system. Worker is a fact gatherer and analyst, program designer, implementor, and facilitator. Consumers tend to be power structure of the community.

Practice Usage: Where rational planning toward the alleviation of social problems is desired.

References:

Robert Perlman and Arnold Gurin, *Community Organization and Social Change* (New York: John Wiley & Sons, 1972).

Fred M. Cox, John L. Erlich, Jack Rothman, and John E. Tropman, Eds., *Strategies of Community Organization*, 4th ed. (Itasca, IL: F. E. Peacock, 1987), pp. 3–26 and Part III, pp. 308–350.

SOCIALIZATION

Source: Developed by Elizabeth McBroom, School of Social Work, University of Southern California, to respond to poverty or "multiproblem" families.

Underlying Theory: Socialization as developed by anthropology, psychology, and sociology. Margaret Mead's use of meaning and selfhood in the "process of interaction." Erik Erikson's epigenetic model. John Dewey's cognitive process. Systems theory, connectiveness of human motivation with events, and feedback.

Practice Theory: Assessment locates client in milieu, looks for "islands of competence," and barriers to competent functioning. Considers external resources and lifestyle of client. Goal is increased competence in areas of work and parenting. Relationship is established by active response to client's request and by explicit communication of acceptance. Worker is an active provider and teacher. Uses contract. Supports client's motivation. Works on time orientation, verbal facility, functioning, and authority relationships. Creates success experiences. Models.

Practice Usage: With individuals and families who have not learned basic socialization skills and who need help of a concrete nature.

References:

Elizabeth McBroom, "Socialization and Social Casework," in Robert W. Roberts and Robert H. Nee, Eds., *Theories of Social Casework* (Chicago: University of Chicago Press, 1970), pp. 313–351.
Elizabeth McBroom, "Socialization Through Small Groups," in Robert W. Roberts and Helen Northen, Eds., *Theories of Social Work with Groups* (New York: Columbia University Press, 1976), pp. 268–303.

TASK

Source: William J. Reid and Laura Epstein, University of Chicago (1972). Influenced by Reid and Shyne's work, *Brief and Extended Casework.* Developed as an approach whose results (outcomes) can be empirically researched.

Underlying Theory: Eclectic. Selective. Use of general systems theory, communication theory, role theory, psychoanalytic theory, and certain parts of learning theory.

Practice Theory: Assessment is specification of target problem and desired outcome. Specifies tasks needed to resolve problems. Helps client carry out task as necessary. Goals are specific and limited and related to what the client wants. Uses communication to explore, structure, enhance awareness, and direct.

Practice Usage: For time-limited treatment of problems of living.

References:

William J. Reid and Laura Epstein, *Task-Centered Casework* (New York: Columbia University Press, 1972).

William J. Reid and Laura Epstein, *Task-Centered Practice* (New York: Columbia University Press, 1977).

William J. Reid, "Task-Centered Social Work," in Francis J. Turner, Ed., *Social Work Treatment: Interlocking Theoretical Approaches,* 3rd ed. (New York: The Free Press, 1986), pp. 267–295.

William J. Reid, "Family Treatment within a Task-Centered Framework," in Eleanor Reardon Tolson and William J. Reid, Eds., *Models of Family Treatment* (New York: Columbia University Press, 1981), pp. 306–331.

Charles D. Garwin, William Reid, and Laura Epstein, "A Task Centered Approach," in Robert W. Roberts and Helen Northen, Eds., *Theories of Social Work with Groups* (New York: Columbia University Press, 1976), pp. 238–267.

GLOSSARY

Accountability Evaluation of efficiency and effectiveness factors relating to the delivery of social services.

Action The process of carrying out a plan developed through the assessment and action phases of the social work process.

Action system System of people and resources involved in carrying out tasks related to goals and strategy of the helping endeavor.

Activity Doing something or performing tasks as opposed to talking about what to do or talking about feelings or ideas.

Agency The organization that employs the worker and manages resources used to help the client.

Assessment Ongoing process of the social work endeavor that develops an understanding of the person in the situation to use as the basis for action.

Blended family A family in which the parents have had previous marriages and have children from those marriages, as well as possibly having children from the present marriage.

Bond Emotional tie that determines the cohesiveness of a group; expressed in "we feelings" and commonly held values.

Boundary Point at which the interaction around a function no longer has the intensity that interaction of system members or units has. For example, when considering who is a member of a family system, the boundary is the point that divides those who are continually interacting around family concerns and issues and those who have little or no input into the family functioning.

Broker A social work role in which the worker provides the client with information about available resources and helps link the client with the resource.

Burnout A condition that some social workers develop. It is characterized by feelings of lack of appreciation, illness, tiredness, inability to laugh, dreading to go to work, and sleep disturbances.

Case advocate A social work role in which the worker pleads or lobbies for services for a client whom a service provider would otherwise reject.

Case conference Members of a team or a multiperson helping system in a formal meeting share information and plan for services to individuals and families they are all serving in some manner.

Case management A method for coordinating services in which a worker assesses with a client which services are needed and obtains and monitors the delivery of the services.

Cause advocacy Concern about and action on behalf of the victims of social problems that works toward the modification of social conditions.

Cause-function debate Debate between those who would place emphasis on removal of an evil in community life that impacts on individuals' social functioning and those who would place the emphasis on response to individual malfunctioning.

Client One who has either sought help from a social worker or is served by an agency employing a social worker.

Closedness A quality of social systems that describes the lack of ability of the system to allow information or individuals to permeate the system's boundary.

Collaboration The working together of several service providers with a common client toward a common goal.

Community Immediate environment of worker, client, and agency that is manifest as a social system.

Community benefits Organized efforts by the natural helping system to meet needs of a member of the system. Usually the effort is in response to a catastrophic situation.

Concern A feeling that something is not right. Interest in, regard for, and care about the well-being of self and other persons.

Conflict A struggle for something that is scarce or thought to be scarce.

Consultation A way of two or more people working together in which the consultant provides knowledge and expertise but has no power to require the consulted to accept the help or advice. The consulted examines the input from the consultant as to its usefulness in the situation under consideration.

Contract An agreement, verbal or written, between worker and client about the work to be done together. Goals, objectives, and tasks to be carried out by worker and client are specified.

Coordination The working together of two or more service providers in activity focused on a particular client or focused on persons in a particular category (e.g., the aged). Coordinative mechanisms include co-location of services, networking, linking, case management, collaboration, and a team approach.

Coping A person's efforts to deal with some new and often problematic situation or encounter or to deal in some new way with an old problem.

Crisis A state of disequilibrium or a loss of steady state due to stress and precipitating event in the life of a person who usually has a satisfactory level of functioning.

Diagnosis A term borrowed from the medical field. It relates to developing a statement as to the nature of the client's need and the situation related to that need. A more contemporary term is *assessment.*

Diagnostic approach A historic model of social work practice that places a primary emphasis on diagnosis. The contemporary model is usually referred to as the *psychosocial approach.*

Direct practice Action with individuals, families, and small groups focused on change in either the transactions within the family or small group, or in the manner in which individuals, families, and small groups function in relation to individuals and social systems in their environment.

Dual perspective Process of consciously perceiving, understanding, and comparing simultaneously the values, attitudes, and behaviors of the larger social system and those of the immediate family and community system.

Empowerment A process for increasing personal, interpersonal, or political power so that individuals can take action to improve their life situation.

Enabling Making it possible for an individual or system to carry out some activity they might not be able to engage in without support or help.

Entropy The quality of systems that describes the loss of energy and the capacity to carry out functions.

Environmental demands Expectations that people or social systems in an individual's or social system's environment place upon themselves relative to their social functioning.

Environmental manipulation A strategy to bring about change in a client's environment in order to enhance the client's social functioning.

Equifinality The capacity of two systems to achieve identical goals when starting from different conditions.

Equilibrium A fixed balance in a social system among the various subsystems and their functioning. Tends to represent a quality of stability and closedness.

Evaluation Collection and assessment of data about the outcomes of a plan of action relative to goals set in advance of implementing that plan.

Facilitation Enabling others to function effectively.

Feeling An intuitive sense of a situation or solution to a problem. Facts have not been sought. More of an emotional process than a cognitive one.

Felt need A need identified by a client.

Field of practice A system of policies, agencies, and services that focus on a social problem, a handicapping condition, a particular context, or a particular social system. A major organizing framework for the U.S. social welfare system.

Focal system The primary system upon which the social work process focuses in the change activity.

Formative evaluation Evaluation that looks at the process of the work.

Functional approach A historic model of social work practice that places emphasis on the role and tasks of the social worker in the helping situation rather than on a client's deviance or illness.

Gemeinshaft A characteristic of communities that demonstrates a sense of "we-ness" and informal functioning.

Generalist practice Practice in which the client and worker together assess the need in all of its complexity and develop a plan for responding to that need. A strategy is chosen from a repertoire of responses appropriate for work with individuals, families, groups, agencies, and communities. The unit of attention is chosen by considering the system needing to be changed. The plan is carried out and evaluated.

Genogram A pictorial assessment mechanism for showing intergenerational relationships and family characteristics.

Gesellschaft A characteristic of communities in which individuals tend to relate through institutions and other formal structures.

Goal The overall, long-range expected outcome of an endeavor.

Goal-attainment scaling An evaluation technique that not only specifies goals but also specifies outcomes at five levels: expected, more desirable, most desirable, less than desirable, and least desirable.

Group-building (group-maintenance) roles Those roles that focus on the maintenance of the group as a system. The roles may include encourager, harmonizer, or goal helper.

Group task roles Those roles related to the accomplishment of the functions or tasks of the group. The roles may include initiator, coordinator, or clarifier.

Holon A system that is part of a larger system and is made up of several smaller systems. Often the system of focus.

Homeostasis Fixed balance in a system that allows some permeation of the system's boundary by ideas and individuals, yet maintains the capacity of the system's structure to remain stable.

Human diversity A way of viewing persons in situations that considers culture, race, gender, and handicapping conditions as they affect human functioning. It views human behavior as highly relative to the social situation in which persons function.

Indirect practice Action taken with persons other than clients in order to help clients.

Individualization The process of looking at each person and each social system as unique, and planning the social work process keeping that quality in mind.

Influence General acts of producing an effect on another person, group, or organization through exercises of a personal or organizational capacity.

Influentials Persons within a community or an organization who have power and/or authority.

Interactional skill The capacity of social workers to relate to both clients and significant others, both individuals and social systems, in such a manner as to be helpful and to support the work at hand.

Intervention Specific action by a worker in relation to human systems or processes in order to induce change. The action is guided by knowledge and professional values as well as by the skillfulness of the worker.

Interventive action Activities carried out by the social worker and the client in order to bring about a planned change.

Interventive repertoire The package of actions, methods, techniques, and skills a particular social worker has developed for use in response to needs of individuals and social systems.

Knowledge Picture of world and the place of humans in it. Ideas and beliefs about reality based on confirmable or probable evidence.

Leadership (in groups) The filling of a number of roles in a group, particularly those needed for group functioning.

Life processes The biological, social, psychological, and spiritual courses of individuals and social systems as they develop and function through the life span.

Lifestyle Manner in which an individual or family functions in meeting needs, in interactions with others, and in patterns of work, play, and rest.

Locus of control The source of an individual's motivation or drive for action or change. The major concern is whether it lies within the individual or within the environment.

Mapping A pictorial assessment mechanism that shows the relationship of subsystems to each other or the relationship of a system to other systems in its environment.

Mediation A strategy in which a worker helps a client and a system in the immediate environment to reach out to each other and find a common concern or interest, and to do the work necessary to bring about a desired change.

Medical model Used in medical field and often appropriated by social workers. Characterized by a process of study, diagnosis, and treatment.

Moral code Specification of that which is considered to be right or wrong in terms of behavior.

Multifinality A situation when two systems start from identical conditions and reach different end states.

Multiperson helping system A situation in which more than two persons are involved, such as a social worker working with a small group of clients or several workers (a team) working with a single client.

Natural helpers People who possess helping skills and exercise them in the context of mutual relationships, as opposed to professionals trained in certain helping skills who are not part of a client's immediate community.

Natural helping systems A client's friends, family, and coworkers. Those in an individual's informal environment to whom one turns in time of need.

Need That which is necessary for either a person or a social system to function within reasonable expectations, given the situation that exists.

Needs assessment A process through which needs of a particular population or category of systems are determined.

Negative entropy The efficient use of energy by a system and the addition of energy to the system from the outside.

Network A loose association of systems. Not a social system but an entity that operates through mutual resource sharing.

Networking Development and maintenance of communication and ways of working together among people of diverse interests and orientations. One means of coordination.

Norming The process of setting norms, or expected ways of behaving.

Objectives Intermediate goals that must be reached in order to attain the ultimate goal.

Openness A quality of social systems that describes the capacity of the system to allow information and individuals to permeate the system boundaries easily.

Opportunity seizing A skill that involves use of a keen sense of when the time is right to develop a project or involve an individual or system in a change activity.

Paradigm A model used for thinking about phenomena being studied.

Patient An individual treated in a medical setting. Sometimes used in place of the term *client* in clinical social work.

Person in the situation The focus of the social work endeavor. The focus of the social worker is not just on the person or the social situation, but on the complex interaction of the two as that interaction affects both person and social situation.

Philosophy of life Beliefs about people and society and about human life, its purposes, and how it should be lived.

Plan of action The way or method for carrying out planned change in the social work endeavor. It is structured and specifies goals and objectives, units of attention, and strategy.

Private troubles Relates to the needs of individuals.

Problem (in social work) A social functioning situation in which need fulfillment of any of the persons or systems involved is blocked and in which the persons involved cannot by themselves remove the block to need fulfillment.

Problem-oriented record A four-point record containing a data base of pertinent information, a problem list, plans and goals, and followup notes (including outcomes).

Problem-solving process A tool used by social workers to solve problems in a rational manner. It proceeds through identifiable steps of interaction with clients. These steps include identification of the problem, statement of preliminary assumptions about the problem, selection and collection of information, analysis of information, development of a plan, implementation of the plan, and evaluation.

Process A recurrent patterning of a sequence of change over time in a particular direction.

Process recording Narrative report of all that happened during a client contact, including worker's thinking and feeling about what happened.

Profession A group of people who carry out some societal task. These trained and educated people work from systematic theory, carry authority and community sanction, and have a code of ethics and a culture.

Professional judgment The capacity to make practice decisions in a manner that is in keeping with the best knowledge available and with the values of the social work profession.

Professional relationship A relationship with an agreed upon purpose, a limited time frame, and in which the professional devotes self to the interest of the client.

Psychosocial approach See *Diagnostic approach.*

Public issues Relates to need from a societal perspective.

Referral The process by which a client is made aware of another service resource and helped to make contact with that resource to receive a needed service.

Reframing Stating a concern or a problem in a new way, from a different point of view.

Relationship Cohesive quality of the action system. Product of interaction between two persons.

Scientific philanthropy Systematic, careful investigation of evidence surrounding the need for service before acting on the need.

Self-help groups Voluntary groups in which members with common problems help each other.

Significant others Those persons in an individual's social network who have importance to, or impact on, the system being worked with.

Single-subject design A research method used when the *n* (number of subjects) is one. The comparisons are made from baseline data, with progress toward goals being measured.

Skill A complex organization of behavior directed toward a particular goal or activity.

Small group Three or more persons who have something in common and who use face-to-face interaction to share that commonality and work to fulfill needs and solve common problems—their own or others.

Social action A change strategy that organizes people (often oppressed people) so as to bring pressure on societal institutions for change in power distribution.

Social functioning People coping with environmental demands.

Social history A form of assessment of individuals or families. It includes information (historical and current) needed for understanding and working with clients.

Social impact assessment Interdisciplinary movement that focuses on environmental assessment of possible impacts of proposed change in social systems.

Social support network analysis Specification of the nature of an individual's or family's support network. Both pictorial and written depictions are used.

Social system A system composed of interrelated and interdependent parts (persons and subsystems).

Social work process A problem-solving process carried out with clients to solve problems in social functioning that clients cannot solve without help. It is conceptualized as study, assessment, planning, action, and termination.

Sociogram A pictorial assessment technique used with small groups to show the relationships between group members.

Special populations Refers to specific groups of people such as women, members of a particular minority group, those with a particular handicapping condition, and so on. These groups may need special consideration when providing services.

Steady state State of a system's functioning that provides a balance between stability and adaptive change.

Strategy An overall approach to change in a situation. Includes defining roles and tasks of both worker and client.

Summative evaluation Evaluation concerned with outcomes and effectiveness.

Support The use of techniques that help clients feel better, stronger, and more comfortable in some immediate way.

Team A group of persons, often representative of various professions, who work together toward common goals and plans of action to meet the needs of clients.

Termination The last phase of the social work process when the emphasis is on disengagement, stabilization of change, and evaluation.

Thinking Use of a cognitive process to sort out information or to engage in a problem-solving process.

Transactions Interactions influenced by other interactions within a situation. For example, the mother-child relationship is influenced by the father-mother relationship, and so on.

Treatment Term used for action segment of the social work process. Very often used in clinical social work.

Unit of attention The system or systems on which the change activity is focused; also called focal system.

Values What is held to be desirable and preferred. Guides for behavior.

SUBJECT INDEX

Figures and tables in the text are represented by *f* and *t* respectively.